# Evidence-Based Approaches and Conflict Studies

CW00470510

## Volume 5

This series aims to publish books on peace and conflict with evidence-based approaches, befitting an era best characterized by uncertainty and complexity. Even if occurrence of major wars among sovereign states has dramatically decreased, from 5 million soldiers killed between 1938 and 1945 per annum; through 100,000 soldiers killed between 1945 and 1989 per annum; to 10,000 soldiers killed between 1989 and 2019 per annum; many kinds of peace and conflict keep arising in the world, with extraordinary technological progress and unprecedented spatial coverage. All parts of the world now are so well connected and interdependent. At the same time, they easily and suddenly become sources of immense vulnerability and fragility, bringing one or another of them to the verge of collapse and destruction. The causes are diverse: climate change, migration, pandemic and epidemic disease, civil strife, religious dissonance, economic competition, arms races, terrorism, corruption—a virtual plethora of sources. Kofi Annan, former UN Secretary General, calls these and many others "problems without passports."

The basic methodological orientation sought in this series is broadly that of modern social and behavioral science. Of importance is that verifiable evidence (quantitative and qualitative, graphs and photos) be solidly attached to whatever arguments are advanced. Overseen by a panel of renowned scholars led by Editor-in-Chief Takashi Inoguchi, this book series employs a single-blind review process in which the Editor-in-Chief, the series editors, editorial board members, and specialized scholars designated by the Editor-in-Chief or series editors rigorously review each proposal and manuscript to ensure that every submission makes a valuable contribution that will appeal to a global scholarly readership.

More information about this series at http://www.springer.com/series/16598

Mai Kaneko-Iwase

# Nationality of Foundlings

Avoiding Statelessness Among Children
of Unknown Parents Under International
Nationality Law

 Springer

Mai Kaneko-Iwase
Maastricht University
Maastricht, The Netherlands

ISSN 2730-5651                    ISSN 2730-566X  (electronic)
Evidence-Based Approaches to Peace and Conflict Studies
ISBN 978-981-16-3007-1          ISBN 978-981-16-3005-7  (eBook)
https://doi.org/10.1007/978-981-16-3005-7

This Springer imprint is published by the registered company Springer Nature Singapore Pte Ltd.
The registered company address is: 152 Beach Road, #21-01/04 Gateway East, Singapore 189721,
Singapore

**Photograph of an ancient baby box, Florence, Italy**

「父母がともに知れない」子の国籍

Until 1875, the 'foundling wheel' at Ospedale degli Innocenti (Foundling Hospital) in Florence, Italy had taken in abandoned children. The hospital accepted the first child in 1445.
Photo © Mai Kaneko-Iwase, 2017.

*For Takeshi, Takeo and Mieko,*
*and in memory of my father,*
*Seiji Kaneko*

# Preface

This monograph is a fully revised and updated version of my dissertation to obtain the degree of Doctor at Faculty of Law, Maastricht University, which was successfully defended on 10 January 2020.

I have to thank so many people for having empowered me to accomplish this 'impossible' challenge—of completing my Ph.D. and this book, all while raising my little son, being a relatively supportive wife, writing during my leave, then returning to my job and working full(er) time and continuing to write, all of which pushed me to the edge. I found myself writing bits and pieces over years, during late nights and early mornings, most of my weekends and holidays.

Special thanks go first of all to my supervisor, Professor Emeritus Dr. Gerard-René de Groot. His decision to take me under his supervision was one of the luckiest things that have happened in my life. His meticulousness and wealth/depth of knowledge, combined with such a sweet personality, gave me a profound feeling of respect, honor, and gratitude. Thanks Dr. Olivier Vonk, my second supervisor, for his advice not only on the content but also on highly practical issues. I am indebted to Dr. Laura van Waas, whose fabulous training sessions I was lucky enough to participate in as part of my work, which intrigued me to get into the world of international statelessness law. Thanks Laura and other Assessment Committee members of mine for their valuable comments and advice, which definitely enhanced the quality of this book: Prof. Dr. Marta Pertegás Sender, Prof. Dr. Maarten P. Vink, and Prof. Dr. Patrick Wautelet. My heartfelt gratitude to Dr. Marieke Hopman and Dr. Mark Kawakami—such a great couple—for being my paranymphs. Having you two on board addressing my numerous worries was a real blessing.

Emeritus Professor Dr. Shōichi Kidana provided me with precious advice on the Japanese Nationality Act and beyond. Particular appreciation goes to Attorney Asahitarō Itō and Attorney Mitsuru Namba for advising me especially on the intricate details of Japanese evidence law.

Thanks to Attorney Paolo Farci, Enrico Guida, Katinka Huszar, and Gábor Gyulai for facilitating my field studies in Italy and Hungary and for guiding me through the Italian/Hungarian situations/laws. I appreciate the kindness of all those who responded to my interview requests and substantive or language-related inquiries, many of whose names are cited in my footnotes/bibliography.

In more general terms, I owe a lot to the core members of the Study Group on Statelessness in Japan, starting with Attorney Sōsuke Seki, Attorney Ayane Odagawa, Attorney Fumie Azukizawa, and Prof. Dr. Osamu Arakaki for providing the fora to discuss in depth different aspects of statelessness—including my own research—which has constantly inspired, motivated, and enlightened me. Senior/peer support from Dr. Yue Fū and Dr. Hajime Akiyama kept me motivated when I felt 'alone' in the world of Ph.D. candidates.

Thanks Jade Cooper, solicitor, and Ruth Haruna Borgwardt for their copyediting assistance. I should not forget to express my gratitude to Dr. Greg Rien for listening to—for almost 4 years—my worries and sharing with me his wisdom as somebody who also wrote his dissertation while working fulltime.

While I cannot emphasize more that the views expressed herein are my personal views and not those of the UN or UNHCR, I still wish to thank some from UNHCR. The guidance from Mark Manly, Radha Govil, and Jeanette Züfle that I received as part of my work at UNHCR in the field of statelessness definitely contributed to the building of my (though relative) meticulousness. The encouragement and understanding from Melanie Khanna, Dirk Hebecker, Dr. Naoko Obi, and Toshitsuki Kawauchi that my study should also help achieve the UNHCR's objective boosted my morale. At the end of the day, I decided to write this book in the hope that it will help, if even just a tiny bit, the granting of nationality to persons of unknown parents, who are among the most vulnerable.

Last but not least, thanks to Takeshi Iwase for being an outstandingly caring father and supportive husband—not only from the 'Japanese standard' but also from the global standard. Thanks, Takeo, now 6 years old, for being my reason for living and, on top of that, for being a particularly good son. I am grateful to my parents-in-law, Toshio and Sachiko Iwase, for being exceptionally understanding and supportive in-laws. Same goes for my feminist brothers Motomu and Tsuguru.

I owe a real debt of gratitude to Mieko Kaneko, my super-organized mother, for sacrificing so much throughout her life to enable my accomplishments (while achieving many herself, actually), and for being my role model as a strikingly strong and cultured woman.

Without all of you, none of this was possible.

And lastly, to my scientist father Seiji Kaneko, RIP, who passed away 23 years ago today while writing his unique doctoral dissertation on 'the biological clock of the cockroach'. You should know you are still remembered in the community for your intelligence and big heart. You are the one who gave me the idea of becoming a 'Dr.' when I was just a little girl. Your spirit was always there to encourage me when I wanted to give up—not just once, but almost *every day*.

This Ph.D./book is for you.

Majority of the content of this book was written based on the information available as of the end of January 2019 (and the web links were rechecked on 4 August 2019) unless the updates in 2020 are noted.

Tokyo, Japan                                                                        Mai Kaneko-Iwase
25 December 2020

# Executive Summary

The number of 'foundlings' around the world is possibly on the increase due to irregular migration, trafficking, armed conflicts, displacement, destruction of civil documentation systems, and disease pandemics among others.

Article 2 of the 1961 Convention on the Reduction of Statelessness (hereinafter the 1961 Convention) is a provision that leads to the acquisition of nationality by a 'foundling' 'found' in a member territory, to prevent her or his statelessness. Out of 193 UN member States, of which 75 (as of end December 2020) are parties to the 1961 Convention, at least 139 States or approximately 72 per cent have domestic provisions granting nationality to persons of unknown parents born or found in the territory. However, the wording of such 'foundling provisions' and their implementation differ significantly between States.

This book examines and proposes an appropriate definition for, and interpretation of, 'foundlings' 'found' in States' territories and 'proof to the contrary'—contained in article 2—as well as some key aspects of procedural standards such as the applicable burden and standard of proof in assessing unknown parentage—which have been largely unexplored in the scholarship to date. This is done mainly by: referring to the object and purpose of the 1961 Convention; the preparatory work and documents interpreting the Convention; complementary international human rights law standards including the best interests of the child under the 1989 Convention on the Rights of the Child (CRC); as well as by conducting a review of the text of relevant national legislation in all 193 UN member States and its actual implementation for a number of States including those that are not State parties to the 1961 Convention.

An examination of the preparatory work of the 1961 Convention and the 1930 Hague Convention on Certain Questions Relating to the Conflict of Nationality Law as well as, the wording of different UN language versions and of domestic foundling provisions, have confirmed that the term 'foundling' under article 2 of the 1961 Convention essentially refers to a child of unknown parents whose birthplace is either known or unknown.

The research has further found that in many States the most typical cases that benefit from foundling provisions are babies found abandoned in public places, or left in baby hatches or boxes operated by public or private organizations. In a number of countries, babies surrendered through a form of 'anonymous birth' where the biological mother is factually known but not legally known make up the majority of the cases who acquire nationality based on the foundling provision. In several States, the foundling provision is interpreted to cover many other categories of persons, including babies left behind at a hospital by the birth mother after delivery, children who are entrusted to/informally adopted by unrelated adults, orphans, lost children, and persons who have lost their memory. In many cases, fragments of information regarding their parent(s)' identities do exist, which however cannot be firmly established. In at least one of the countries, persons whose parent(s) go missing after registering their birth with invalid identity information have been confirmed nationality.

It was also found that being of 'unknown parentage' essentially means being of 'legally unknown parents', which means specifically that the person's legal parents do not exist, including where such existence of legal parents cannot be proven. This is because for one to acquire nationality under nationality law, legal parentage rather than factual parentage matters. Naturally, having 'legally unknown parents' includes instances where the parents are factually unknown.

The book also found that under some States' practice or legislation some children of unknown parentage who are otherwise stateless who are not necessarily recognized as 'foundlings' are granted nationality through other avenues including: by relaxing the requirements for late birth registration; on the basis of adoption by nationals; by being hosted at a child custody institution within the territory; or via recognition as stateless persons and facilitating their naturalization under the 1954 Convention relating to the Status of Stateless Persons. The existence of other avenues appears to reduce the need to interpret the foundling provision in the 1961 Convention in an 'inclusive' manner in such countries.

The book reveals that *being found* on the territory of a State is a *condition* (rather than being part of the definition of a 'foundling') that gives rise to the obligation of that State to grant nationality to the person found, and includes the situation where the person's birth within the territory is indeed established. One does not have to be literally 'abandoned' but she or he can be orphaned, lost, or informally adopted and later spontaneously approach or come into contact with the authorities.

Being 'found' should be broadly defined as 'having been seen in the territory by a person other than one's parents', or something to that effect. Notably, some States have previously applied their foundling provision in a full and inclusive manner, such as by confirming nationality for persons of unknown parents who have voluntarily approached the authorities at a much older age, in their 40–60s. In such cases, their presence in the territory in their childhood was established by evidence such as their own statements, school records, or testimony by non-State third persons such as neighbors.

The author reviewed the foundling provisions of 139 States (mainly read through English originals/translations except for those in Spanish and French). In relation to the 'age' of the person to be considered a 'foundling' and thereby granted nationality—which is not specified in the 1961 Convention—the review shows that the legislation of 17 States only grants nationality to persons of unknown parents who have been *born* in the territory, and at least 36 States limit the grant of nationality to persons who are 'new-born (or recently born)' when found. At the same time, ten States provide for the application of their foundling provisions to older children (3–15). A total of 15 States, or slightly more than 11 per cent of the 139 States with foundling provisions, either explicitly or by interpretation open up the target age to all 'minors'. Among such 15, ten States are explicitly open, either by using the term 'minor', or by using 'child' *and* defining 'child' as 'minor' (while the age of majority differs) within the same legislation. For the remaining five States among 15, relatively dependable information was available stating that the (undefined) term 'child' therein meant 'minor'. For the remaining 61 States (44 per cent) whose foundling provisions do not specify the age—using either the term 'child', 'foundling', or 'infant'—while no complementary information was readily located specifying the age of the person in question, there are indications that a number of the States (using 'child') might indeed cover all minors.

Based on these findings, and in light of the object and purpose of article 2 of the 1961 Convention and the right to nationality under article 7 of the CRC contracted by 192 UN member States, it is argued that an ideal foundling provision should cover all persons of unknown parentage found in the territory of a State before reaching the age of majority. This is because imposing various younger age limits is arbitrary under international law and goes against the best interests of the child. Many persons of unknown parentage are not able to account for the identity of their parents regardless of how old they become. The object and purpose of the foundling provision is essentially to prevent statelessness of persons of unknown parents (and often unknown birthplace) for whom there is no basis to determine (or acquire) nationality by *jus sanguinis* or *jus soli*.

The book further examines the term 'in the absence of proof to the contrary' in article 2 in the pre facto assessment for the purpose of (confirming) one's nationality acquisition based on the foundling provision. Further, it examines what constitutes the ground for the withdrawal post facto of such nationality.

As to pre facto assessment, while current State practice generally shows that evidence of birth outside the territory constitutes 'proof to the contrary' and disqualifies the person concerned from acquiring nationality based on the foundling provision, the travaux records of the 1961 Convention as well as limited statements from some administrative and judicial authorities indicate the room for an alternative interpretation. According to such an alternative interpretation, a child of unknown parentage found in the territory but born in another State could nevertheless acquire nationality of the State where found, as long as she or he is otherwise stateless. In other words, under such an alternative interpretation, having been born in another State does not constitute 'proof to the contrary' pre facto, but possession of another nationality does. This interpretation will be particularly relevant in today's climate of global migration, displacement, and human trafficking, where persons move between borders without necessarily securing evidence on their parentage.

With regard to the post facto withdrawal of nationality, the author stresses that it must not constitute arbitrary deprivation of nationality prohibited under international human rights law. For this purpose, the withdrawal of nationality must: have a clear basis in law; be the least intrusive means of achieving a legitimate purpose; and follow a due process. The nationality withdrawal upon the discovery or establishment of foreign parentage and/or birth may only be allowed if it is proven that the person concerned has indeed acquired foreign nationality as a result. Further, after the person has lived with the nationality for a certain number of years, it should be maintained even if non-withdrawal results in multiple nationality.

The book also examined the burden and standard of proof when a dispute occurs as to the 'unknown-ness' of one's parentage at the initial determination of a person's nationality. The author concludes that, as long as the person concerned asserts unknown parentage and duly cooperates and provides all the reasonably available evidence regarding the parents' unknown-ness, States should bear both the burden of producing evidence and the burden of persuasion regarding the *existence* of a legally recognized parent. If such a burden of proof is not fulfilled, the State should affirm the unknown-ness of the parents. In relation to the standard of proof or the 'degree' of unknown-ness of parentage, it is recommended that decision-makers recognize the 'unknown-ness' when they cannot be convinced within a pre-set deadline, that one of the child's legally recognized parents is *definitively* identified to the extent that it enables the confirmation of the child's nationality acquisition by *jus sanguinis*.

Drawn from the above including the best practice around the world, the book concludes by proposing a 'model provision' that can serve as an inspiration in reflecting article 2 of the 1961 Convention into domestic law or in drafting a new regional instrument:

> A person whose **legal parentage cannot be proven** who is **found** as a **child** in the territory shall **acquire the nationality** of X [the State where found], **unless her or his possession of a foreign nationality is proven**.

While not included in the above 'model provision' itself, it is essential that the assessment and confirmation of whether the person has acquired nationality under the above provision is done within a reasonable time. Reasonable time can be, for example, 6 months extendable to 1 year, after the declaration is made to the competent authority for the purpose of such nationality confirmation. Further, the withdrawal of nationality previously confirmed under a foundling provision, if envisaged, should be clearly regulated either within the same provision or by a separate provision, so as to avoid arbitrary nationality deprivation. As stated above, such provision should at least provide that, in case of discovery or establishment of foreign parentage and/or birth, nationality cannot be withdrawn unless the State concerned proves—within a limitation period—that the person possesses a foreign nationality. Further, the decision to withdraw, including when not resulting in statelessness, must be subject to individual proportionality assessment including best interests determination when involving children, as well as procedural safeguards such as the right to a fair hearing and effective remedy. This limitation period should be the maximum of 10 years from the date the State took an action to confirm her or his nationality, ideally with even a shorter deadline in light of the best interests of the child. The withdrawal should desirably have non-retroactive effect.

The model foundling provision and other interpretative guidance contained in this book should help ensure a full and inclusive application of article 2 of the 1961

Convention and equivalent national provisions in accordance with their object and purpose as well as the best interests of the child under the CRC. They should prove particularly useful in cases involving States under the effects of armed conflicts; or where documentation of civil and nationality status is not yet systematic; or where migration, displacement, and trafficking is widespread.

# Contents

# About the Author

**Dr. Mai Kaneko-Iwase** (1979), a researcher at Maastricht University, the Netherlands, studied international human rights law at the School of International and Public Affairs at Columbia University in New York where she obtained her Master's degree in 2004. She was awarded a Ph.D. (Law) from the Department of Private Law, Faculty of Law, Maastricht University in January 2020. Starting in 2004, she has worked for the United Nations High Commissioner for Refugees (UNHCR) primarily in Japan, but also in Pakistan, Lebanon, and Malaysia. As a UNHCR staff member, she has engaged in a wide range of operations such as refugee status determination, capacity building, advocacy, court advisory, resettlement, community services, and other interventions for the protection of refugees and stateless persons, as well as for the prevention/reduction of statelessness. She has also authored and reviewed studies and articles on statelessness inside and outside her work.

**Note:** This book was written by the author purely in her personal capacity. The views expressed herein are those of the author and do not reflect the views of the UN or UNHCR.

# Abbreviations

| | |
|---|---|
| 1930 Convention | Convention on Certain Questions relating to the Conflict of Nationality Law |
| 1951 Convention | Convention on the Status of Refugees |
| 1954 Convention | Convention on the Status of Stateless Persons |
| 1961 Convention | Convention on the Reduction of Statelessness |
| AAO | Administrative Appeals Office (US) |
| ACHPR | African Commission on Human and Peoples' Rights |
| ANUSCA | Associazione Nazionale Ufficiali di Stato Civile e d'Anagrafe [National Association of Civil Registrar Officials] (Italy) |
| ART | Assisted reproductive technology |
| AU | African Union |
| BIA | Board of Immigration Appeals (USA) |
| CEDAW | Convention on the Elimination of All Forms of Discrimination Against Women |
| CERD | Convention on the Elimination of All Forms of Racial Discrimination |
| CIS | Commonwealth of Independent States |
| CJEU | Court of Justice of the European Union (European Court of Justice) |
| CMW | UN Committee on the Protection of the Rights of All Migrant Workers and Members of Their Families |
| CRC | Convention on the Rights of the Child |
| CRPD | Convention on the Rights of Persons with Disabilities |
| DGRN | General Directorate of Registries and Notaries (Spain) |
| DHS | Department of Homeland Security (USA) |
| ECHR | European Convention for the Protection of Human Rights and Fundamental Freedoms (European Convention on Human Rights) |

| | |
|---|---|
| ECN | European Convention on Nationality |
| ECOSOC | United Nations Economic and Social Council |
| ECtHR | European Court of Human Rights |
| ENS | European Network on Statelessness |
| ETS | European Treaty Series |
| EUDO Citizenship | European Union Observatory on Democracy on Citizenship (now GLOBALCIT) |
| ExCom | UNHCR Executive Committee of the High Commissioner's Programme |
| FCA | Federal Court of Australia |
| GCM | Global Compact for Safe, Orderly and Regular Migration |
| GCR | Global Compact on Refugees |
| GLOBALCIT | Global Citizenship Observatory (formerly EUDO) |
| HCCH Study (March 2014) | HCCH, 'A Study of Legal Parentage and the Issues Arising from International Surrogacy Arrangement' (March 2014) |
| HCCH | Hague Conference on Private International Law |
| IACrtHR | Inter-American Court of Human Rights |
| IAO | Immigration and Asylum Office (Hungary) |
| ICCPR | International Covenant on Civil and Political Rights |
| ICJ | International Court of Justice |
| ICRMW | International Convention on the Protection of the Rights of All Migrant Workers and Members of Their Families |
| IJ | Immigration Judge (USA) |
| ILC | International Law Commission |
| ILEC Guidelines (2015) | ILEC Guidelines on Involuntary Loss of European Citizenship (2015) |
| ILEC | Involuntary Loss of European Citizenship Research Project |
| INA | Immigration and Nationality Act (US) |
| INS | Immigration and Naturalization Services (US) |
| IOM | International Organisation for Migration |
| IPU | Inter-Parliamentary Union |
| ISI | Institute on Statelessness and Inclusion |
| Kagetsu | Katei saiban geppō [Family court monthly report] (Japan) |
| LNTS | League of Nations Treaty Series |
| MENA | Middle East and North Africa |
| Minshū | Saikō saibansho minji hanrei shū [Supreme Court collection of civil cases, Japan] |
| NADRA | National Database and Registration Authority (Pakistan) |
| OAU | Organisation of African Unity |

| | |
|---|---|
| OFPRA | Office Français de Protection des Réfugiés et Apatrides (France) |
| RSD | Refugee Status Determination |
| SDG | Sustainable Development Goals |
| Tunis Conclusions (2014) | UNHCR, 'Summary Conclusions: Interpreting the 1961 Statelessness Convention and Avoiding Statelessness Resulting from Loss and Deprivation of Nationality' (March 2014) |
| UDHR | Universal Declaration of Human Rights |
| UN | United Nations |
| UNHCR Guidelines 4 (2012) | UNHCR, 'Guidelines on Statelessness No 4: Ensuring Every Child's Right to Acquire a Nationality through Articles 1–4 of the 1961 Convention on the Reduction of Statelessness' (21 December 2012) |
| UNHCR Guidelines 5 (2020) | UNHCR, 'Guidelines on Statelessness No 5: Loss and Deprivation of Nationality under Articles 5–9 of the 1961 Convention on the Reduction of Statelessness' (May 2020) |
| UNHCR Handbook (2014) | UNHCR Handbook on Protection of Stateless Persons (30 June 2014) |
| UNHCR | UN High Commissioner for Refugees |
| UNICEF | UN Children's Fund |
| UNTS | UN Treaty Series |
| USCIS | Citizenship and Immigration Services (USA) |
| VCLT | Vienna Convention on the Law of Treaties of 1969 |

# Chapter 1
# Introduction

**Abstract** Article 2 of the 1961 Convention on the Reduction of Statelessness (1961 Convention) provides for the acquisition of nationality by a 'foundling' 'found' in the territory. This chapter lays out the overall context including the fact that the number of 'foundlings' around the world is possibly increasing due to irregular migration, displacement, trafficking, armed conflicts, destruction of civil documentation systems and disease pandemics among others. After introducing the research questions and methodology, the chapter provides an overview of Annex 1 that compares the relevant parts of the nationality laws of 193 UN member States, including the definition of the term 'foundling provision' used throughout the book. It also provides the justification for the selection of the focus countries with in-depth analysis. The chapter also examines nationality grant to foundlings as a customary law norm, and the significance of the practice by some of the non-State parties to the 1961 Convention that provide inspiration for the 'model foundling provision' and its interpretative standards in Chap. 8.

## Introduction

> I do not know who my parents are. I do not remember who they are.

This is an account by Issa, approximately ten years old, who was entrusted to the imam of a mosque in eastern Côte d'Ivoire at the age of around three years old by his purported father, who never returned for him. Unlike the imam's other (legal) children, he cannot go to school. With no parent to protect him, he takes the family's sheep out to pasture and does errands for the house and for other people in the community. In 2015, the government of Côte d'Ivoire estimated that there were 300,000 persons of unknown parentage like Issa in the country, who have been abandoned as children and remained stateless with the lack of legal provision to grant nationality to foundlings.[1]

---

[1] Mirna Adjami, 'Statelessness and Nationality in Côte d'Ivoire—A Study for UNHCR' (December 2016) 57 <http://www.refworld.org/docid/58594d114.html> accessed 4 August 2019. See also UNHCR West Africa, 'The lost children of Côte d'Ivoire' (6 November 2015) <http://kora.unhcr.org/lost-children-cote-divoire/> accessed 4 August 2019. ISI and la Coalition de la société

> Life without documents is really hard. [...] I could not go abroad. And I was really afraid
> I was going to be deported. [...] Without them [foster parents] I would be nobody, I don't
> know where I would be, who I would be.[2]

This is an account of 19-year-old Agni Caldarar about how she felt growing up stateless, having been abandoned by her mother. Born in Poland to an apparently teenage Romanian mother, who then left her at the hospital, she was unable to confirm her acquisition of either Polish or Romanian nationality at or after birth. This was despite the fact that the Polish nationality law does contain a provision to grant nationality to persons of unknown parents born in the territory. It was not until she turned 18 that she had the opportunity to apply for Polish nationality through a special procedure. She thus spent her entire childhood stateless, while being raised by her foster parents.[3]

## 1.1  Why Foundlings?

The ordeal faced by the two children in Côte d'Ivoire and Poland described in the above quotes is unfortunately not a unique or rare story in the contemporary world. Migration, forced displacement and destruction due to armed conflicts aggravate the lack of documentation caused by under-developed birth and civil registration systems in less industrialized States. The number of orphans[4] worldwide is likely on increase[5] with the pandemic of diseases,[6] in addition to wars and generalized violence among

---

civile de lutte contre l'apatridie, 'Joint Submission to the Human Rights Council at the 33rd Session of the Universal Periodic Review (Third Cycle, April–May 2019), Côte d'Ivoire' (4 October 2018) <http://institutesi.org/UPR33_Cote_dIvoire.pdf> accessed 4 August 2019, in particular paras 7 and 27–31. The positive developments in recent years should nevertheless be highlighted. On 4 October 2019, the Minister of Justice and Human Rights of Côte d'Ivoire issued a circular authorizing judges across the country to grant nationality to stateless foundlings. UNHCR, '#IBelong Campaign Update, October-December 2019' (January 2020) 8 <https://www.refworld.org/docid/5e1c4b124.html> accessed 15 September 2020.

[2] ENS, 'Ending Childhood Statelessness: A Study on Poland, Working Paper 03/15' (June 2015) 1, 4 <https://www.statelessness.eu/sites/www.statelessness.eu/files/Poland.pdf> accessed 4 August 2019.

[3] Ibid 1, 4.

[4] See Sect. 1.4, as well as Chaps. 3 and 4 (including Sect. 4.3.7) on the relationship between orphans, foundlings and persons of unknown parents.

[5] Carole Batchelor is quoted to have stated: 'UNHCR has encountered thousands of stateless children in orphanages' in her presentation in 2002, in Laura van Waas, *Nationality Matters: Statelessness under International Law* (Intersentia 2008) 69. It is likely because many orphaned children are of unknown parentage.

[6] See, for example, Pius Tangwe Tanga, Princess Khumalo and Priscilla Gutura, 'Three Decades of HIV/AIDS Pandemic: Challenges Faced by Orphans in Tembisa, South Africa' in Nancy Dumais (ed), *HIV/AIDS—Contemporary Challenges* (IntechOpen 2017).

others. The widespread phenomenon of human trafficking,[7] especially of young children, can only make the issue more complex. Overall, it is possible that the number of foundlings in the world is on the rise. While the number of foundlings every year can be from tens to up to several hundreds in industrialized States (see Sects. 4.1 and 4.3), there might be thousands in particular in conflict-affected States, as mentioned in the context of Côte d'Ivoire (300,000) above.

'Foundlings' are one of the typical groups of persons historically recognized to be otherwise stateless in the absence of a special safeguard granting him/her nationality.[8] Foundlings also tend to be one of the most vulnerable categories of persons being not only otherwise stateless, but also for lacking those normally responsible for their protection and care, which makes it all the more difficult for them to access basic human rights.

National legislation granting nationality to 'persons of unknown parents born in the territory' and 'foundlings found in the territory' was already fairly common (see in particular Sects. 1.5.5.1 and 3.4) in national legislation when the 1961 Convention on the Reduction of Statelessness[9] (hereinafter the 1961 Convention) was being drafted, and even before that, when the 1930 Hague Convention on Certain Questions relating to the Conflicts of Nationality Laws (1930 Convention)[10] was being negotiated.

Article 2 of the 1961 Convention stipulates that:

A *foundling found* in the territory of a Contracting State shall, in the absence of proof to the contrary, be considered to have been born within that territory of parents possessing the nationality of that State. (emphasis added)

However, the term 'foundling' is highly abstract—what exactly does a 'foundling' mean? This is a basic, yet highly complex question—as I later discovered when reading the translation of the 1961 Convention in Spanish and Japanese—the languages the author happens to speak—more than ten years ago.

The Spanish version of the Convention said 'expósito' and the Japanese unofficial translation of the 1961 Convention literally said 'abandoned child' (棄児[kiji] or 遺棄された児童 [ikisareta jidō]),[11] neither of which seemed to be the same as

---

[7] See, for example, UN Office for Drugs and Crime (UNODC), *Global Report on Trafficking in Persons* (United Nations 2018).

[8] For example, in the words of Roberto Córdova, 'Without the presumption [of birth in the territory and consequently nationality grant *jus soli*] set up in the proposed article, the case of foundlings would constitute the typical case of statelessness. A foundling being, by definition, without known parents and without a known birthplace, happens to be the best example of a case in which neither of the two existing legal systems which confer nationality at birth, the jus sanguinis or jus soli, can be applied.' Roberto Córdova, 'Nationality, including Statelessness—Report on the Elimination or Reduction of Statelessness' (1953) 176 <http://legal.un.org/docs/?path=../ilc/documentation/english/a_cn4_64.pdf&lang=E> accessed 4 August 2019.

[9] *Convention on the Reduction of Statelessness*, New York, 30 August 1961, 989 UNTS 175 (entered into force 13 December 1975).

[10] *Convention on Certain Questions Relating to the Conflict of Nationality' Law*, 179 LNTS 89 (entered into force 1 July 1937).

[11] 'Mukokuseki no sakugen ni kansuru jōyaku' (unofficial translation of the 1961 Convention) included in Hiroshi Homma (ed), *Nanmin ni kansuru kokusai jōyakushu [Collection of International Treaties on Refugees]* (UNHCR Japan 1987).

the original term 'foundling' in English. However, at the same time, I could not immediately think of an alternative word in Spanish or Japanese for it. Indeed, I also failed to understand the precise meaning of the original term 'foundling' in English. Then I looked into Spanish and Japanese nationality law provisions which were similar[12] to article 2 of the 1961 Convention, along with the related case law and scholarly materials in the two languages—which offered relatively rich discussions around the concept. This also expanded my list of questions. This was indeed counterintuitive considering that Spain only became a State party to the 1961 Convention only during the last phase of my research—in September 2018—and Japan was not yet a State party (still so as of December 2020).

I was subsequently struck by the scarcity of detailed discussions—and particularly in relation to the practical aspects—of the *nationality* of 'foundlings'. This is in contrast to historical public interest in the lives of foundlings, demonstrated by novels and dramas—such as the world famous *Sans Famille*[13]—and in issues related to (prevention of) child abandonment and infanticide which has been vigorously examined in a variety of fields of study.[14]

While the scholarly body of knowledge on statelessness in general has expanded in recent years,[15] little has been written on foundlings in general. As will be discussed briefly in Sect. 1.4 and in more detail in Sect. 3.2, article 2 and the rest of the 1961 Convention as well as the United Nations High Commissioner for Refugees (UNHCR)'s relevant guidance, that is Guidelines on Statelessness No 4 (hereinafter the UNHCR Guidelines 4 [2012])[16] do not explicitly define a 'foundling' (or 'found'), and scholarly work and practical reports have fallen short of clearly or consistently delineating their meaning.

The 1997 European Convention on Nationality (hereinafter ECN)[17] also has a similar provision, article 6(1)(b), stipulating nationality grant to 'foundlings found in its territory who would otherwise be stateless'. The ECN, however, does not provide any definition either for the above terms, and the relevant part of the explanatory

---

[12] Article 2(iii), Japanese Nationality Act, Act No 147 of 4 May 1950, last amended by Act No. 88 of 2008.

[13] An 1878 French novel by Hector Malot. Hector Malot, *Sans famille* [Nobody's Boy] (E. Dentu 1878).

[14] See also Sect. 1.3.

[15] See for example Mark Manly and Laura van Waas, 'The state of statelessness research: a human rights imperative' (2014) 19 Tilburg Law Review 3, as well as Maria Jose Recalde-Vela, Sangita Jaghai-Bajulaiye and Caia Vlieks, 'The state of statelessness research: 5 years later' (2019) 24 Tilburg Law Review: Journal on international and comparative law 139.

[16] While no explicit 'definition' is provided, para 57 of the UNHCR's Guidelines 4 states 'children found abandoned in the territory of a contracting State (foundlings) acquire the nationality of that State'. UNHCR, 'Guidelines on Statelessness No 4: Ensuring Every Child's Right to Acquire a Nationality through articles 1–4 of the 1961 Convention on the Reduction of Statelessness' (21 December 2012) (hereinafter UNHCR Guidelines 4[2012]) <http://www.refworld.org/docid/50d 460c72.html> accessed 4 August 2019. However, this description is not complete, as touched upon in Sect. 1.4 and discussed in detail in Chap. 3.

[17] *European Convention on Nationality*, 6 November 1997, ETS 166 (entered into force 1 March 2000).

report providing the interpretive guidance is rather short and apparently contains some inadequacies, as discussed in detail throughout the book starting from Sect. 3.2.

Furthermore, the above materials also do not elaborate on the procedural aspects of how to identify a 'foundling' in the 1961 Convention, such as the burden and standard of proof when assessing whether or not the provision is applicable to a specific person. At the national level, the definition or interpretation of the terms such as 'foundling' 'found', as well as the evidentiary rules—if they are ever explicitly discussed at all— widely diverge and can be restrictive, which makes it difficult to fully achieve the object and purpose of preventing statelessness. It was then found that the guidance drawn from this book based on States' interpretation on how best to interpret the 'foundling provision'[18] is highly relevant to the situations involving States under-going, or recovering from, armed conflicts or with under-developed documentation systems, or where migration, displacement and trafficking is widespread.

With this in mind, and with the list of my research questions continuing to grow, I originally decided to endeavour to address the issues relating to nationality of foundlings as my PhD dissertation project which has now been updated and published as a book.

## 1.2  Objective

The objective of my book is to address the gaps in the existing literature mentioned above.

Specifically, it is to clarify the appropriate interpretation and application of article 2 of the 1961 Convention. In accordance with article 31 of the Vienna Convention on the Law of Treaties (VCLT), article 2 is to be interpreted in good faith and in accordance with the ordinary meaning of the terms used in the text, in their context and in light of the object and purpose of the 1961 Convention.[19] The 'object and purpose' of the 1961 Convention is to reduce statelessness by international agreement as in its preamble, thereby ensuring every individual's right to a nationality, including that of children.[20] As part of these efforts, the book will propose in its conclusion a model national provision reflecting article 2.

Article 2 of the 1961 Convention is indeed a codification of the principles common among legislation of many States at that time and as of today—including those currently not State parties to the Convention, and arguably a customary international norm, as elaborated in Sect. 1.5.5.1. The conclusions to be drawn from this book will also be useful in considering how domestic nationality law provisions aimed at preventing statelessness of foundlings should be interpreted and implemented *regardless* of whether the State is a party to the 1961 Convention. For States that

---

[18] See Sect. 1.5.2.3 for the definition of a 'foundling provision' in this book.

[19] *Convention on the Law of Treaties* (VCLT) 23 May 1969, Vienna, 1155 UNTS 331 (entered into force 27 January 1980).

[20] UNHCR Guidelines 4 (2012) para 1. See also Sect. 2.2.

have not adopted a nationality law provision addressing the nationality of foundlings, it is hoped that this book will be of use in formulating such a provision.

## 1.3  Research Questions

As indicated above, the fundamental research question is:

> How should article 2 of the 1961 Convention be interpreted and implemented to meet the object and purpose of the Convention?

This fundamental research question will be broken down into the following main questions:

(1)  What should be the definition of a 'foundling' 'found in the territory' and how should the definition be further interpreted?

(2)  What constitutes the 'proof to the contrary' pre facto in assessing whether to confirm acquisition of nationality, and what are the conditions for post facto withdrawal of nationality?

(3)  What should the procedure for confirming or granting nationality to foundlings (or in withdrawing such nationality) be like, especially the applicable burden and standard of proof?

The main questions above will be broken down further into sub-questions in each chapter, which would be too detailed to enumerate here.

This book is primarily a legal one, with focus on what happens to the nationality of foundlings, with its basis being on international human rights law, with the primary instrument being the 1961 Convention, backed up by the 1989 Convention on the Rights of the Child (CRC)[21] which is of paramount importance in determining the scope of the 1961 Convention obligations,[22] as well as other human rights instruments and international standards including UNHCR guidelines.

The plight of foundlings certainly cannot be resolved solely by granting her or him nationality. However, having a nationality, as briefly discussed in Sect. 2.6, gives a person a solid legal basis for claiming the protection of her or his rights vis-à-vis a State.

There are different reasons why children are orphaned and abandoned.[23] Abandoning a child in an unsafe place (one of the main causes of foundlinghood, as

---

[21] Convention on the Rights of the Child (CRC), New York, 20 November 1989, 1577 UNTS 3 (entered into force 2 September 1990).

[22] UNHCR Guidelines 4 (2012)'s paragraph 9 provides that articles 2 of the 1961 Convention must be interpreted in light of the provisions of the CRC including article 7 on the right to acquire a nationality and article 8 on the right to preserve identity including nationality, as well as article 3 setting out a general principle (which thus applies in conjunction with articles 7 and 8), requiring that all actions concerning children, including in the area of nationality, must be undertaken with the best interests of the child as a primary consideration.

[23] The typical reasons can include economic, social or cultural reasons, including poverty, preferences for male children, inability to raise children with disabilities and illness, stigmas against

discussed in Sect. 4.3.1, among others) is normally a criminal offence in any country. A number of States have safe and (normally) lawful ways of giving up a child such as leaving her or him in a 'baby box/hatch', through 'anonymous birth' or 'safe haven' laws, as also discussed in Sects. 4.3.2 (and part of 4.3.3) and 4.3.10. The legality of different forms of child abandonment, and whether these forms actually prevent abandonment, or how to better prevent abandonment (such as through the awareness raising on the above lawful measures or through counselling and assistance to women on the edge of abandoning children)[24] are all important issues but go beyond the scope of this book.

Other issues related to foundlings that are beyond the coverage of this book include the appropriate custody and care arrangements for foundlings in order to ensure their welfare and sound upbringing (generally family-based care, that is foster care or adoption is considered better than institutional care, for example).[25] There are also hotly debated issues about how the above lawful measures of abandonment and women's right to anonymity should be balanced with children's right to know their origin[26] and be cared for by her or his parents or father's parental rights, on which there is much more literature already available. Some of these issues will only be indirectly touched upon in the context of my analysis on how their statelessness can be prevented.

## 1.4  Working Hypothesis to Be Verified in Chaps. 3 and 6: Foundling is a Child of Unknown Parentage

As stated already in Sect. 1.1, the 1961 Convention and UNHCR Guidelines 4 (2012) laying out its interpretive guidance and the majority of practical and scholarly materials do not provide the definition of a foundling, which will be elaborated in Sect. 3.2.

---

children born out of wedlock, under-age and unexpected pregnancies including rape, and substance misuse/addiction, parental mental health problems/illness, parents' lack of (sex-) education and access to abortion. Sarah Aird, Helen Harnett and Punam Shah, *Stateless Children—Youth Who Are Without Citizenship, Booklet No 7 in A Series on International Youth Issues* (1st edn, Youth Advocate Program International 2002) 18.

[24] See, for example, The University of Nottingham, *Child Abandonment and its Prevention in Europe* (The University of Nottingham 2012) 34.

[25] See generally, ibid. UNICEF, 'Children in alternative care' (July 2017) <https://data.unicef.org/topic/child-protection/children-alternative-care/> accessed 4 August 2019.

[26] For example, this issue has been raised in relation to anonymous birth before the European Court of Human Rights (ECtHR). See *Odièvre v. France*, Application No 42326/98 [13 February 2013] (ECtHR), in which it was determined that article 8 of the 1950 European Convention on Human Rights (ECHR) was not violated partly because of the mother's right to privacy and also as the applicant was given non-identifying information about her mother and family. In a more recent case of *Godelli v. Italy*, Application No 33783/09 [25 September 2012] (ECtHR), ECtHR reached a different conclusion with regard to the Italian authorities, as following an anonymous birth, the applicant was not able 'to request either access to non-identifying information concerning […] her origins or the disclosure of the mother's identity' (para 58).

However, for practical purposes, mainly due to the difficulties in maintaining the flow of the discussions without mentioning what a foundling might mean at the outset, a hypothesis is hereby made—that the definition of being a 'foundling' contains two requirements—that her or his *parentage is unknown* and that she or he is a child (when found in the relevant country). This hypothesis was made based on a few existing materials which directly or indirectly define a foundling as a 'child of unknown parents', although these materials do not elaborate on the grounds for defining it as such.[27]

One of the two requirements, that is being of 'unknown parents', will be verified in Chap. 3. The other element, that is being a 'child' (when found), will be discussed in Chap. 6. While the issue of the 'age' of the child is also part of how a 'foundling' is defined, it is indeed closely related to the concept of being 'found'. While a person of unknown parents would normally *remain to be of unknown parents* regardless of her or his age—including after she or he reaches adulthood, and even after she or he is confirmed nationality by virtue of article 2—the application of article 2 is apparently limited to those found in the territory before reaching a certain age (the oldest of which can be the age of majority according to Chap. 6). Thus, mainly for the purpose of maintaining the flow of the discussions, it was decided that the issue of age is to be discussed in Chap. 6 where the definition of being 'found' is also examined.

## 1.5  Research Methodology and Limitation

These research questions were addressed mainly by literature review, field research and analysis of domestic foundling provisions equivalent to article 2 of the 1961 Convention and their practice including case law. Preliminary and follow-up research

---

[27] For example, as one of the older sources, UNHCR's 'Study on Statelessness' in 1949 suggests that foundlings are children of *unknown parentage* (and unknown birthplace. Whether the birthplace also needs to be unknown will be discussed in Chap. 3). Some of the recent UNHCR material indirectly provide a 'definition' of a foundling such as by explaining in bracket as 'foundlings (children whose parentage is unknown)' or by rewording it, generally as 'children of unknown parents (found on the territory)', while also qualifying it with the terms 'orphaned' or 'abandoned'. The latest material is UNHCR and IPU, *Good Practices in Nationality Laws for the Prevention and Reduction of Statelessness* (IPU November 2018) 9, 13–14 and 34. Also see UNHCR, 'Good Practices: Addressing Statelessness in South East Asia' (5 February 2011) 11 <http://www.refworld.org/docid/4d6e0a 792.html> accessed 4 August 2019; UNHCR, 'Good Practices Paper—Action 2: Ensuring that no child is born stateless, 20 March 2017' (20 March 2017) 5 <http://www.refworld.org/docid/58cfab 014.html> accessed 4 August 2019. While still a draft, the 2015 African Union (AU) Draft Protocol to the African Charter on Human and Peoples' Rights contains an article equivalent to article 2 of the 1961 Convention (article 5.2.a.), which refers to 'A child found in the territory of the State of unknown parents'. African Commission on Human and Peoples' Rights (ACHPR), 'Draft Protocol to the African Charter on Human and Peoples' Rights on the Specific Aspects of the Right to a Nationality and the Eradication of Statelessness in Africa' (2015) <https://www.achpr.org/public/ Document/file/English/draft_citizenship_protocol_en_sept2015_achpr.pdf> accessed 17 February 2020.

was carried out to ascertain what information is available, before determining the methodology. In particular, the actions laid out below were taken (some actions were taken simultaneously and the order is not necessarily chronological).

## 1.5.1  Languages

I conducted research mainly in English, Spanish and Japanese, in which I am fluent, and to a limited extent in French, of which I have basic knowledge. With regard to materials in other languages cited throughout this book, I read them through translation, as much as possible with assistance or confirmation from persons proficient in these languages with knowledge on legal matters.

## 1.5.2  Literature Review and Further Research

Review of the available academic and practical literature was first conducted, followed by further research on raw materials, inquiries and interviews.

### 1.5.2.1  Review of International and Regional Instruments and Standards

The *travaux préparatoires* (preparatory works, hereinafter 'travaux') and UNHCR guidelines especially the parts relating to article 2 of the 1961 Convention were examined. Materials related to the relevant provisions in other instruments such as the 1930 Convention and ECN were also referred to.

### 1.5.2.2  Review of Practical and Academic Materials

A further review of the available literature—starting with 'mapping' reports on statelessness and other studies on specific States commissioned/carried out by UNHCR,[28] European Network on Statelessness (ENS)[29] and Global Citizenship Observatory

---

[28] As summarized in the bibliography. UNHCR (-commissioned) country-specific studies are uploaded on the following page, under the section entitled 'Country and Region Specific Situations' <https://www.refworld.org/statelessness.html> accessed 4 August 2019.

[29] As summarized in the bibliography. All ENS country reports in the 'Ending childhood statelessness' series published up to December 2018 were referred to. Also referred to was ENS, 'No Child Should be Stateless' (2015) <https://www.statelessness.eu/resources/no-child-should-be-stateless-austria> accessed 4 August 2019, see in particular p 23. Other primary sources included ENS,

(GLOBALCIT, formally known as the European Union Observatory on Democracy on Citizenship—EUDO) on nationality and statelessness—was conducted. In relation to nationality of foundlings, the majority of those reports did *not* contain any analysis beyond the text of the relevant nationality law provisions. Only some reports additionally referred to birth registration related laws and bylaws, official commentaries[30] or information that came from administrative precedents[31] or personal interviews of the authorities.[32]

Other practical reports and academic articles on nationality and statelessness in different countries were also referred to, which yielded similar results, in the sense that most of them contained limited information on the actual practice beyond the text of nationality legislation.[33]

'Ending Childhood Statelessness: A comparative study of safeguards to ensure the right to a nationality for children born in Europe, Working Paper 01/16' (2016) <https://www.statelessness.eu/sites/www.statelessness.eu/files/file_attach/ENS_1961_Safeguards_Stateless_children.pdf> accessed 4 August 2019, and ENS 'Statelessness Index' country surveys also has a section on foundlings at <https://index.statelessness.eu/> accessed 4 August 2019.

[30] For example, UNHCR, 'Mapping Statelessness in The United Kingdom' (22 November 2011) <https://www.refworld.org/docid/4ecb6a192.html> accessed 4 August 2019 and ENS, 'Ending Childhood Statelessness: A Study on Italy, Working Paper 07/15' (2015) <http://www.refworld.org/docid/582327974.html> accessed 4 August 2019.

[31] For example, Gábor Gyulai, 'Statelessness in Hungary: The Protection of Stateless Persons and the Prevention and Reduction of Statelessness' (December 2010) <https://www.refworld.org/docid/4d6d26972.html> accessed 12 July 2019 and ENS, 'Ending Childhood Statelessness: A Study on Poland, Working Paper 03/15' (June 2015) <https://www.statelessness.eu/sites/www.statelessness.eu/files/Poland.pdf> accessed 4 August 2019.

[32] For example, UNHCR, 'Mapping Statelessness in Austria' (2015) <http://www.refworld.org/docid/58b6e5b14.html> accessed 4 August 2019 para 259, and ENS, 'Ending Childhood Statelessness: A Study on Italy, Working Paper 07/15' (2015) <http://www.refworld.org/docid/582327974.html> accessed 4 August 2019.

[33] As summarized in the bibliography, some of the main and limited articles referred to that address the issue of nationality of foundlings are: Yue Fū, 'Nihon de umareta kodomono kokuseki to mukokuseki nintei' ['Determination of statelessness for children born in Japan'] (PhD dissertation, University of Tsukuba 2016), a PhD dissertation dedicated to how statelessness and unknown parentage is assessed in applying article 2(iii) of the Japanese Nationality Act which mainly refers to Japanese scholarly articles, administrative instructions and court decisions; Ryūun Ō, 'Kiji no kokuseki' [Nationality of Abandoned Children] (1969) 4 Hōgaku Kenkyū [Hokkaigakuen daigaku hōgakkai] 169, which is one of the only few articles dedicated on the issue of the nationality of foundlings; Gerard-René de Groot, 'Children, their right to a nationality and child statelessness' in Alice Edwards and Laura van Waas (eds), *Nationality and Statelessness under International Law* (Cambridge University Press 2014) 144; Olivier Willem Vonk, Maarten Peter Vink and Gerard-René de Groot, 'Protection against Statelessness: Trends and Regulations in Europe' (May 2013) 47–48 <http://cadmus.eui.eu/bitstream/handle/1814/30201/eudocit_vink_degroot_statelessness_final.pdf?sequence=1> accessed 4 August 2019; Gerard-René de Groot, Katja Swider

### 1.5.2.3 Definition of 'foundling provision' and the Annex 1—Systematic Comparison of 193 States

With regard to domestic nationality law, it was considered relevant to have an overall view on how many States have enacted a domestic provision equivalent to article 2, how they formulate the provision and how the situation differs between State parties and non-State parties to the 1961 Convention as elaborated further in Sect. 1.5.5.2. A reference was made to the GLOBALCIT's database covering 173 States[34] on the mode of nationality acquisition as the starting point. It was noted, however, that the database did not cover all 193 UN member States and did not carry the exact wording of each legal provision. A whole new table was then created—attached to this book as Annex 1—by adding States to make a complete list of all 193 UN member States with full text of all the 'foundling provisions' accessible online.

To define at the outset, a 'foundling provision' in Annex 1 and throughout this book generally refers to a provision contained in a constitution (rare) or a nationality related law (common) including regulations, or in the nationality-related part of the Civil Code explicitly granting nationality to persons of unknown parents born or found in the territory, which can be considered equivalent to article 2 of the 1961 Convention. It should be noted that it was decided not to 'count' (as 'States with a foundling provision') States where there is no provision directly granting nationality to foundlings but whose birth registration related law allows the registration of birth of children found in the territory of unknown parents which results in the grant of that State's nationality. This is due to the inability to conduct a systematic and exhaustive research on the latest birth registration law, which was often only available in the original language.

It should also be noted that legal provisions granting nationality to persons born in the territory who are of unknown nationality or who are born of parents of unknown nationality are not counted as a 'foundling provisions' but rather classified as provisions 'complementary' in their absence and noted in Annex 1. For example, Greece's nationality law at article 1(2) provides a person born on Greek territory shall acquire the Greek nationality by birth, provided that such a person is of 'unknown nationality'.[35] Persons of unknown parents whose birth within the territory is established

---

and Olivier Vonk, 'Practices and approaches in EU member states to prevent and end statelessness' (2015) 29 <http://www.europarl.europa.eu/RegData/etudes/STUD/2015/536476/IPOL_S TU(2015)536476_EN.pdf> accessed 4 August 2019; Laura van Waas, *Nationality Matters: Statelessness under International Law* (Intersentia 2008) 68–71; Bronwen Manby, *Citizenship and Statelessness in Africa: The Law and Politics of Belonging* (Wolf Legal Publishers 2015) 127 and Table 2 on pp 128–129. An attorney and law professor Ralph A. Sarmiento has also published on his blog one of the few articles focusing on the nationality of foundlings. Ralph A. Sarmiento, 'The Right to Nationality of Foundlings in International Law' (3 December 2015) <https://attyralph.com/2015/12/03/foundlingsnationality/> accessed 4 August 2019.

[34] GLOBALCIT, 'Global Database on Modes of Acquisition of Citizenship, version 1.0' (2017) <http://globalcit.eu/acquisition-citizenship/> accessed 4 August 2019. Results of the search mode A03a 'foundlings' for 'all countries'.

[35] Greek Citizenship Code's article 1(2) has indeed been criticized in the context of nationality of foundlings for 'requiring the birth in the territory' and not covering those of unknown birthplace

can well benefit from article 1(2). However, due to the inability to conduct a systematic research on whether such provision for each State is intended to, or in practice, covering, persons of unknown parents, it was decided that States with only such a provision (granting nationality to a person of (parents of) 'unknown nationality') were counted as States without a 'foundling' provision.

Similarly, the existence of provisions granting nationality to persons born in the territory who are 'otherwise stateless' or more narrowly whose parents are stateless is noted as a 'complementary' provision.

'Unconditional'[36] *jus soli* provision that grants nationality at birth to all persons born in the territory is also covered in Annex 1 as a provision 'complementary' to a foundling provision.

Further, it was once contemplated whether the term 'unknown parentage (or parents) provision' should be used instead of 'foundling provision'. This is because one of the main purposes of this book is to redefine the term 'foundling' and propose an alternative, more legally accurate description of the persons who should benefit from article 2—and the conclusion of the book provides that a foundling is a person of unknown parents found when she or he is a child. However, for the sake of brevity, and given the fact that the term 'foundling' is the term currently used in the 1961 Convention, it was generally decided to use the term 'foundling provision' even when the relevant national law provision does not contain the term 'foundling' but contains the term '[a child of] unknown parents' or other terms.

Apart from the GLOBALCIT's database,[37] the databases of UNHCR-run refworld[38] and Citizenship Rights in Africa Initiative[39] were primarily referred to, to be cross-verified by Google searches in an effort to verify whether author was referring to the latest available documents.[40]

---

otherwise covered by article 2 of the 1961 Convention. For example, see ENS, 'Childhood Statelessness in Europe: Issues, Gaps and Good Practices' (2014) 20 <http://www.refworld.org/docid/5343a45f4.html> accessed 4 August 2019.

[36] 'Unconditional' *jus soli* provisions in Annex 1 in principle refer to provisions that grant nationality to all persons born in the territory based solely on such birth (with exceptions in many cases that, where the person's parent[s] is a diplomat[s] or enemy alien[s] the provision will not be applicable), without placing additional criteria such as the legal stay of the parent(s).

[37] GLOBALCIT, 'Global Nationality Laws Database' <http://globalcit.eu/national-citizenship-laws/> accessed 4 August 2019.

[38] UNHCR, 'Refworld nationality and statelessness/citizenship law/ nationality law database' <https://www.refworld.org/topic,50ffbce524d,50ffbce525c,0,LEGISLATION,.html> accessed 4 August 2019.

[39] Citizenship Rights in Africa Initiative, 'Database on nationality acquisition' <http://citizenshiprightsafrica.org/advanced-search/?fwp_themes=acquisition-of-nationality> accessed 4 August 2019.

[40] As noted in the Annex 1, while best efforts were made to access the versions carrying the latest amendments as of January 2019, especially for the countries whose translated versions of nationality laws were consulted, they might however not always be up to date. Further, for some of the countries, especially for which the English translations were consulted (such as those available on refworld), information such as the 'law number' or the 'year of enactment' was not readily available. For some countries, the description in the citation was unclear whether the date contained

In terms of the language, if the law is written in languages other than English and no English translation was already available, translation was newly made. Only when the relevant law was written in English, Spanish and French and Japanese was the original systematically verified.

Accession status to the 1961 Convention and ECN for each State is also indicated. Based on this table, comparisons and analysis were made in terms of the differences in the wording equivalent to a 'foundling' in each provision, whether there is a requirement of 'birth in the territory', the age limitation for a foundling when found to be granted nationality, as well as the structure of the foundling provisions. Annex 1 also provides the basis of considering significance of the practice by non-State parties, which will be presented in Sect. 1.5.5.

### 1.5.2.4 Analysis of Select Nationality and Birth Registration Related Legal Instruments, Case Law and Administrative Precedents

Among those included in Annex 1 which is a table of 193 States, the foundling provisions of some States was reviewed in more depth in accordance with the general criteria as laid out in Sect. 1.5.4. In addition to nationality legislation (or Civil Code or constitution as the case may be), birth registration related law (including where it is also regulated by the Civil Code) of a number of States was reviewed, which in many cases included at least one provision laying out the procedures on registering foundlings. However, the texts of birth registration related laws were in general short and quite similar among most States, which did not always help clarify the definitional and interpretational issues relating to the foundling provision as stated in the research questions. It was also found that some States have 'anonymous birth' related legislation or provision(s) incorporated in birth registration related law or Civil Code which were linked to the foundling provision (as discussed in detail in Sect. 4.3.10). Directly accessible bylaws of nationality law such as administrative instructions were referred to.

In addition, case law and administrative decisions were researched through existing literature, country-specific/international or publicly available/membership-based case law search engines. However, only a small number of directly or indirectly relevant and substantive case law or administrative decisions for a limited number of countries was found. These notable exceptions were Australia, Hungary, Japan, the Philippines, Spain and the US, to be discussed in Chaps. 4–7. Even then, especially for the Spanish and US decisions, the details of the facts of specific cases were often insufficient to make conclusive analysis. In some cases, however, even when some

---

therein referred to that of enactment or the last amendment. Nevertheless, as the foundling provision in much nationality legislation is an 'old' provision (already existent in its original version when enacted), the information on the last amendment was generally omitted from the column 'citation' of Annex 1.

information on unpublished individual cases was obtainable from the legal representatives, it was considered not suitable to be cited externally due to the sensitive
nature of the facts.[41]

### 1.5.2.5   Inquiry with Experts

A generic and detailed list of questions was developed with an initial intention to
systematically gather information—either verbally or in a written form on the implementation of the domestic foundling provision. Initial inquiries were subsequently
made (without necessarily attaching the list of questions) with persons with expertise
on statelessness—different UNHCR offices, the authors of the ENS/GLOBALCIT's
country-specific reports, some GLOBALCIT country experts and ENS's associate
members, inquiring whether they could provide information on the implementation
of the foundling provision including by answering the questionnaire.[42] In the majority
of cases, however, they responded that they had little information beyond the text
of the foundling-related legal provision to answer the definitional or interpretational
questions that I was intending to inquire, as there was no (detailed) publicly available
commentary, case law or administrative precedents. In the majority of the cases, the
experts contacted had never or rarely heard that the provision was being applied
beyond 'typical cases' (new-born babies abandoned in baby hatches or other places
or, at best, through anonymous birth), or that they were generally unaware of cases
where the interpretation of the provision was the issue. As such, for the majority of
the countries, it was concluded at the initial stage that many of the questions in the
list of questions mentioned above could not be filled out. Only partial answers to
parts of the most basic questions were gathered, mainly by referring to the texts of
the relevant legal provisions. The plan to utilize a standard list of questions was thus
suspended.

### 1.5.2.6   Field Visits and Interviews

Field visits and face-to-face interviews were carried out with key persons such as the
competent or relevant authorities, lawyers, academics and UNHCR staff members
in Italy, Hungary and, to a limited extent, Japan (rationale to be explained in more
detail in Sect. 1.5.4) to acquire any available information beyond what is available
on paper, especially on the interpretation of the relevant nationality law provision.
These visits were done as trial attempts to consider the subsequent need to conduct
similar visits. While valuable information was gained, which is reflected throughout
Chaps. 4–7, it appeared generally difficult for the counterparts in Italy and Hungary to

---

[41] For example, unpublished Japanese family court decisions of the cases represented by Attorney
Kensuke Ōnuki.

[42] As summarized in the bibliography—see especially the footnotes accompanying Sect. 1.5.4.

comment in detail/hypothetically on the interpretative issues of the foundling provision, when they have not implemented it so frequently beyond the 'typical cases' i.e. abandoned new-borns or children born of anonymous birth (in case of Italy). Based on this, no further field visits were conducted, and the focus was placed on written materials already available. Nevertheless, face-to-face interviews proved useful to gain a 'holistic' view on the above three States' situations including not only the application of the foundling provision but also the birth registration procedures, care arrangements and solutions other than the nationality grant based on the foundling provision.

A separate field interview conducted by the author with the French authority responsible for statelessness determination, while it was not focused on the nationality of foundlings, was also utilized for the purpose of this book: see Sect. 5.5.2.1.

### 1.5.3 Consideration Over the Possibility of Systematic Comparative Review and Ideal Focus Countries

Based on the above preliminary and follow-up research, consideration was made whether it was possible to conduct a systematic and detailed comparative review of some 'focus countries', based on the same set of information, on the interpretation and implementation of foundling provisions, and what the criteria would be for selecting such focus countries. The most ideal would have been to select the focus countries out of the 19 States[43] that are State party to *both* the 1961 Convention[44] and the 1997 ECN.[45] Second, consideration was made to put some focus on the States that actively participated in the drafting process of article 2 of the 1961 Convention and that are currently State parties to the 1961 Convention.[46]

Nevertheless, in the attempt to consider the feasibility of a comparative and systematic review of the focus countries, a significant challenge was encountered—as mentioned in the literature review (Sect. 1.5.2) above—with the general and fundamental lack of (detailed) publicly available information on how the domestic foundling provision is actually applied in most of the ideal focus countries and,

---

[43] Albania, Austria, Bosnia and Herzegovina, Bulgaria, Czech Republic, Denmark, Finland, Germany, Hungary, Luxembourg, Moldova, Montenegro, Netherlands, Norway, Portugal, Romania, Slovakia, Sweden and Ukraine.

[44] The number of State parties to the 1961 Convention stood at 75 as of the end of December 2020.

[45] State parties to the ECN was 21 as of the end of December 2020. In addition, eight States have signed but not ratified the Convention.

[46] Particular reference was made to the record of the meetings of the UN Conference on the Elimination or Reduction of Future Statelessness in Geneva, 1959, especially the Summary Record of the 5th Plenary Meeting on 31 March 1959, 5th Meeting of the Committee of the Whole on 3 April 1959, and 9th Plenary Meeting on 15 April 1959, where article 2 was extensively discussed and adopted.

indeed, most other States. The level of details of whatever information available differed significantly between States.

### 1.5.4  Adjusted Approach and Eventual Countries with Relative Details Included

In light of the preliminary findings above and due to the general lack of (information on) the actual practice by State parties and non-State parties, it was concluded that a systematic analysis comparing the same set of information between a fixed number of States was practically impossible. What was possible and more appropriate in order to achieve the research objectives was rather to make thematic analysis on definitional and interpretational issues, also fully utilizing whatever available information on practice in non-State parties.

Nevertheless, a certain degree of focus was still placed, as much as possible, on State parties to the both 1961 Convention and ECN as well as States that have participated in the drafting process of the 1961 Convention.

To lay out some details about the rationale for examining some States in more detail and not some others which would normally have been the focus countries:

Denmark, a State party to both the 1961 Convention and ECN and an active participant in the travaux that promoted and successfully had its own (stronger) formulation of article 2 than in the original ILC draft (see Chap. 3 for detail) adopted, was first considered as one of the States on which to focus. However, there was already available preliminary information that child abandonment in the country itself was relatively rare (along with Norway, which is also a State party to both Conventions),[47] and that its foundling provision appeared rather infrequently implemented,[48] which provided justification not to examine the country much beyond the travaux record and its nationality law.

With regard to Hungary, a State party to the 1961 Convention and ECN, there was already detailed available information as to its practice, namely administrative precedents and how it amended its birth registration related law to broaden the application of the foundling provision. This warranted a follow-up, starting with email inquiries with experts[49] followed by personal interviews during field visits (see Sect. 4.3.6,

---

[47] The University of Nottingham, *Child Abandonment and its Prevention in Europe* (The University of Nottingham 2012) 2.

[48] Email from Eva Ersbøll (Senior Researcher, the Danish Institute for Human Rights) to author (1 May 2017), in which she shared her preliminary impression with regard to Denmark.

[49] Such as Katalin Haraszti, 'Report by the Parliamentary Commissioner for Civil Rights in cases number AJB 2629/2010 and AJB 4196/2010' (September 2010) <https://www.ajbh.hu/documents/ 14315/131278/The+investigation+of+the+Ombudsman+on+the+repatriation+of+the+abadoned+ non-citizen+children+born+in+Hungary/122c30fb-8cf5-4192-9e95-f12a23d46436;version=1.1> accessed 4 August 2019.

along with 4.3.2).[50] Also with regard to Italy,[51] a State party to the 1961 Convention, which actively promoted the most liberal formulation and interpretation of article 2 during the travaux process as seen particularly in Sect. 7.3.1, there was already publicly available official commentary on the foundling provision and the legislation allowing for anonymous birth (see Sect. 4.3.10), which was used as a starting point for further follow-up with experts[52] followed by the subsequent interviews. The fact that these States were also party to the 1954 Convention and were two among the relatively small (but increasing) number of States[53] with a 'statelessness determination procedure' in place also enabled the analysis of how the mechanism to acquire nationality under the foundling provision and the system to protect stateless persons interact (see Sect. 4.6). Thus, Hungary and Italy were selected as pilot countries to conduct a field visit apart from Japan (however, see Sect. 1.5.2.6 on the limitations of field visits).

With regard to the Netherlands, State party to both Conventions that actively participated in the travaux process, while some literature was available on foundlings (*vondelingen*) in general mainly revolving around the issue of how to prevent child abandonment, the ethical issues surrounding baby hatches (*vondelingenkamer*) and the debate around 'birth under secrecy' (*bevallen onder geheimhouding*) in light of the children's right to know their origin,[54] no information was readily available on the actual application of its foundling provision including who normally benefits from it.[55]

---

[50] Such as email communications with Gábor Gyulai (Hungary) (starting on 25 April 2017) and email communications with Katinka Huszár (Protection Associate, UNHCR Hungary) (starting on 26 April 2017).

[51] Signed the ECN in 1997 but not ratified.

[52] Emails from Paolo Farci (attorney at law) to author (starting on 2 May 2017); email from Giulia Bittoni to author (7 May 2019); email from Giulia Perin (attorney at law) to author (1 May 2017); as well as emails from Enrico Guida (Statelessness Expert, UNHCR Italy) to author (starting on 28 April 2017).

[53] Approximately 20 States as of July 2020; about 12 as of July 2016. UNHCR, 'Good Practices Paper—Action 6: Establishing Statelessness Determination Procedures to Protect Stateless Persons' (July 2020) 5 <https://www.refworld.org/docid/5f203d0e4.html> accessed 20 August 2020 and UNHCR, 'Good Practices Paper—Action 6: Establishing Statelessness Determination Procedures to Protect Stateless Persons' (11 July 2016) <https://www.refworld.org/docid/57836c ff4.html> accessed 2 May 2019.

[54] There is information including comparison with other States on the specialized pages and related pages of two organizations, that is FIOM <https://fiom.nl/kenniscollectie/vondelingen> and NIDAA <https://www.nidaa.nl/vondeling-leggen>. NIDAA has a page listing many publications related to foundlings <https://www.nidaa.nl/onderzoek-nederland-en-belgie> such as Kerstin Van Tiggelen, 'Vondelingen in Nederland. Actoren en factoren in het naoorlogse debat' [Foundings in the Netherlands. Actors and factors in the post-war debate] (2016) 91 Mens en Maatschappij 211. They, however, do not discuss the issue of nationality grant under the foundling provision. Thanks goes to Nick Klein Douwel for his language support.

[55] UNHCR, 'Mapping Statelessness in the Netherlands' (November 2011) <http://www.refworld.org/docid/4eef65da2.html> accessed 4 August 2019 basically carried the text of the foundling provision.

With regard to Austria, a State party to the 1961 and ECN as well as Belgium, a State party to the 1961 Convention, both of which have actively participated in the drafting of article 2, there was available information that their foundling provision and its application were limited to new-borns or recently born babies.[56] With regard to Belgium, an expert consultant[57] suggested that there was no case law or administrative decisions directly relevant that can be cited. Thus, the discussion on those States in this book is mainly based on the travaux apart from the text of legislation and some practical reports.

With regard to Germany, a State party to both the 1961 Convention and ECN that took part in the travaux process, while information on the foundling provision including case law was not readily available, an administrative instruction by the competent authority and commentary on its foundling provision was referred to in Chaps. 6 and 7.[58]

With regard to Bosnia and Herzegovina, party to both the 1961 Convention and ECN, as well as Serbia, a State party to the 1961 Convention: based on the reports that there was a larger rate of undocumented persons as well as informal adoptions among the ethnic Roma communities residing in those States (and in other central and eastern European States), some research and inquiries[59] were made to experts. As discussed in Sect. 2.9, however, it was indicated that their situation generally tended to be addressed through the efforts to relax the (evidentiary and procedural) requirements for (late) *birth registration* and not by applying their foundling provisions. With regard to Albania, another State party to both the 1961 Convention and ECN, while some information was available on its administrative instructions, the contacts with

---

[56] UNHCR, 'Mapping Statelessness in Austria' (2015) <http://www.refworld.org/docid/58b6e5 b14.html> accessed 4 August 2019 para 259, and ENS, 'No Child Should be Stateless' (2015) 11 <https://www.statelessness.eu/resources/no-child-should-be-stateless-austria> accessed 4 August 2019; UNHCR, 'Mapping Statelessness in Belgium' (October 2012) <http://www.refworld.org/docid/5100f4b22.html> accessed 4 August 2019 para 577.

[57] Email from Wout Van Doren (Statelessness Consultant, Protection Unit for Belgium and Luxembourg, UNHCR Regional Representation for Western Europe) to author (3 August 2017).

[58] 'Vorläufige Anwendungshinweise des Bundesministeriums des Innern zum Staatsangehörigkeitsgesetz (StAG) in der Fassung des Zweiten Gesetzes zur Änderung des Staatsangehörigkeitsgesetzes vom 13 November 2014 [Federal Ministry of Interior, Preliminary instruction on implementation of the Nationality Law (StAG) as amended by the Second Act amending the Nationality Law of 13 November 2014] (BGBl. I S. 1714) (As of June 1, 2015) sec 4.2. (Germany)' <http://www.bmi.bund.de/cae/servlet/contentblob/463812/publicationFile/23664/ Anwendungshinweise_05_2009.pdf (last accessed 5 September 2017, inaccessible as of 1 July 2019); https://www.dortmund.de/media/p/ordnungsamt/pdf_ordnungsamt/Allgemeine_Verw altungsvorschrift_zum_Staatsangehoerigkeitsrecht.pdf> accessed 1 July 2019. Reinhard Marx, '§ 4 StAG' in Fritz/Vormeier (ed) *Gemeinschaftskommentar zum Staatsangehörigkeitsgesetz [Commentary on Nationality Law]* (Looseleaf edn, Walters Kluwer/Luchterhand July 2019) para 196 ff (pp 53–54.3). Author wishes to thank Henrike Janetzek Rauh and Gerard-René de Groot for referring to the source and translating the relevant parts.

[59] Emails from Ljiljana Kokotovic (Associate Protection Officer, UNHCR, Country Office for Bosnia and Herzegovina, Sarajevo) to author (9 and 21 August 2017), and Emails from Jelena Milonjic (Legal Associate, UNHCR Representation in Serbia) to author (5 and 7 July 2017).

an expert indicated that it was difficult to gather more information beyond what was already contained in the instructions.[60]

Among State parties to the 1961 Convention that are known to make readily available some types of court decisions (in English) in the public domain, a search through Westlaw Next—supplemented by refworld run by UNHCR and the case law database run by GLOBALCIT—were conducted. This research yielded two Australian cases (which are particularly discussed in Sect. 7.5). However, with regard to UK,[61] Canada and New Zealand, no directly relevant[62] case law was found through searches.

With regard to Spain, which became a State party to the 1961 Convention in September 2018 but not yet to ECN, the research in the Spanish language yielded relatively substantive precedents on the application of its foundling provision, as discussed in Chaps. 4, 6 and 7.

Given this scarcity of information on State parties, efforts were made to explore the practice of non-State parties. With regard to Japan, research in the Japanese language yielded significant case law as well as academic materials on the application of its foundling provision. The fact that Japan is an Asian country with historical focus on the *jus sanguinis* principle and being one of the 17 States today whose foundling provisions limit their scope to persons of unknown parents born in the territory also justified an extensive analysis.

Some references to France, another non-State party to the 1961 Convention, were included for its unique family law with regard to the establishment of maternal legal descent and application of the foundling provision to children born of anonymous birth.[63]

Consideration was also made on the possible differences between States that predominantly adopt the *jus sanguinis* principle and the *jus soli* principle in granting nationality. Specifically, it was assumed that in States that adopt the unconditional *jus soli* principle granting nationality to whoever is born in the territory, foundlings whose birth in the territory is established should normally acquire the nationality

---

[60] Email from Anisa Metalla (Senior Attorney at Law, Tirana Legal Aid Society) to author (25 July 2017), to author's inquiry.

[61] With regard to UK, a query response from an author of the indirectly relevant research article suggested that no further detailed information was readily available on UK's implementation of the foundling provision. Email on behalf of Solange Valdez-Symonds (Project for the Registration of Children as British Citizens (PRCBC)) to author (13 July 2017), in response to the author's inquiry relating to his article, that is Solange Valdez-Symonds, 'Barriers to citizenship facing stateless children born in the UK' (14 June 2017) <https://www.statelessness.eu/blog/barriers-citizenship-facing-stateless-children-born-uk> accessed 4 August 2019. The relevant mapping study by UNHCR, 'Mapping Statelessness in The United Kingdom' (22 November 2011) <https://www.refworld.org/docid/4ecb6a192.html> accessed 4 August 2019 was also consulted.

[62] Limited case law easily found were related to the adoption of foundlings or foundling hospital related litigation which did not address the nationality related issues.

[63] While no directly relevant and recent case law was readily located. A search through DALLOZ, <www.dalloz.fr> accessed 4 August 2019. Telephone conversation with UNHCR Paris (February 2018) following an email inquiry from the author to UNHCR Paris (27 June 2017).

of the country of birth regardless of whether their parentage is established or not.[64] This would already resolve the issue of nationality for cases whose birth in the territory is established but where there is partial information on the identity of the parent(s), where the 'unknown-ness' of the parentage is disputed, which would otherwise hinder nationality acquisition in *jus sanguinis* States (discussed in Sect. 5.6 in detail). Consequently, less focus was placed on pure *jus soli* States such as Canada and Latin American States, despite the fact that some of them are State party to the 1961 Convention.

Nevertheless, a relatively detailed analysis was made on the practice by the US (Chaps. 4–7) to clarify how one of the few unconditional *jus soli* States in advanced economies applies its foundling provision when the birth in the territory is not established for a person of unknown parentage found in the territory. The fact that the US also participated in the travaux process and—as mentioned above—published a number of administrative precedents and case law discussing the application of the national foundling provision also enabled the analysis.

Other than the States mentioned above, the practice of a number of other State parties and non-State parties in different regions including Africa, Asia, and MENA are referred to in different contexts for their unique formulation or implementation of their legislative provisions, or their case law or actual practice to grant nationality to foundlings (the Philippines and Pakistan, for example) in the absence of a clear domestic provision to do so, will be discussed.

### 1.5.5  Significance of Practice by Non-state Parties

As stated above, the book puts some focus on several States that are not State parties to the 1961 Convention and the ECN, which offer analysis and insights that are inspiring to the interpretation and implementation of the 1961 Convention. In particular, in formulating the recommendations at the end of this book, the author relied particularly heavily on the court decisions and administrative precedents from Spain, Australia, Japan and US only the first two of which are State parties. Japan—in addition to Spain—was eventually found to offer the most liberal interpretation of the foundling provision. The issue then arises as to how much value the practice by non-State parties have to inform the interpretation of a treaty.

According to article 31(b) (General rule of interpretation) of VCLT, subsequent practice in the application of the treaty can be used as a guide to interpreting the treaty so long as it establishes the agreement of the State parties regarding its interpretation. As such, the non-State parties' practice in implementing their national law provision equivalent to a treaty's provision may not be a direct source of interpretative guidance.

---

[64] See also the section on 'children found in a country or of unknown parentage (S02)' in Olivier Willem Vonk, Costica Dumbrava, Maarten Peter Vink and Gerard-René de Groot, '"Benchmarking" Legal Protection against Statelessness', in Laura van Waas and Melanie Khanna (eds), *Solving Statelessness* (Wolf Legal Publishers 2017) 163, 171–3.

However, the practice of non-State parties can be relevant and can surely be a source of inspiration for State parties for the reasons given below.

### 1.5.5.1  Customary International Norm? Codification of the Existing Nationality Legislation Principle into the 1930 and 1961 Convention

As Laura van Waas asserted in 2008, the grant of nationality to foundlings is arguably a matter of international customary law.[65] Such a position is essentially supported by, for example, the Supreme Court of the Philippines, a country that does not have an explicit foundling provision. The Court specifically stated that the principles found in article 14 of the 1930 Convention and article 2 of the 1961 Convention (to neither of which is the Philippines a State party) granting nationality to foundlings 'are generally accepted principles of international law' and that are binding on the Philippines.[66]

In order to substantiate this statement that nationality grant to foundlings is a rule of customary international law, *opinio juris sive necessitatis* needs to be established, that is that the States are legislating or practising in this way due to the conviction that they are legally compelled to do so, and there is systematic practice going into one direction.[67]

As to be mentioned also in Sect. 3.4.1, during the drafting process[68] of the 1930 Convention, there was already a predominant view that article 14 simply codified or reflected the existing nationality law provision or principle common in the majority of States. The Preparation Committee for the 1930 Hague Conference for the Codification of International Law indeed prepared the 'bases for discussion' for use during the Conference, which form 'a statement of the provisions upon which agreement appears to exist, or which do not give rise to divergencies of view [...]'.[69] In particular, it was observed that the attribution to the child of unknown parents the nationality of the country of birth was 'generally admitted' by States.[70]

---

[65] Laura van Waas, *Nationality Matters: Statelessness under International Law* (Intersentia 2008) 71.

[66] *G. R. No 221697 Mary Grace Natividad S. Poe-llamanzares v. Comelec and Estrella C. Elamparo, and G. R. No 221698–700 Mary Grace Natividad S. Poe-llamanzares v. Comelec, Francisco S. Tatad, Antonio P. Contreras and Amado D. Valdez* (Supreme Court of the Philippines).

[67] Article 38(1), 1945 Statute of the International Court of Justice, states 'The Court [...] shall apply: [...] international custom, as evidence of a general practice accepted as law [...]'.

[68] See Sect. 2.4.1 on the developments towards the adoption of the 1930 and the 1960 Convention.

[69] 'Bases of Discussion Drawn up for the Conference by the Preparatory Committee, First report of the preparatory committee', League of Nations, *Bases of Discussion Drawn up for the Conference by the Preparatory Committee, Volume I Nationality (Volume I-C.73.M.38.1929. V-BI-Geneva)* (Conference for the Codification of International Law, May 1929) p 5.

[70] Ibid. Bases of discussion drawn up by the preparatory committee: General Observations submitted by certain Governments, Point VII., 'Children born of parents who are unknown or have no nationality or are of unknown nationality', p 67.

The travaux of the 1930 Convention further shows that at least 22 of the 28 States which shared their substantive replies with the Preparatory Committee for the International Law Codification Conference had a domestic provision or norm equivalent to the principle eventually codified as article 14 of the 1930 Convention. Six remaining States referred to a *jus soli* provision granting nationality by birth in the territory.[71]

Further, in the words of Robert Córdova, the Special Rapporteur to ILC who played a crucial role in the travaux process of the 1961 Convention:

> [...] perhaps because in the case of a foundling the effect of statelessness on a person is more evident, *practically all national legislations* contain provisions which, by means of the presumption assimilate the foundlings to those persons which have been born in the territory of the State where they are found. This fact has actually placed *foundlings in a better situation* than other stateless persons, since practically all legislations extend to them the jus soli principle. [...](the provision to grant nationality to a person of unknown parentage and foundlings, author) may be considered as a *codification of national provisions* which refer to this question.[72]

---

[71] 28 States responded to the query (Australia, Austria, Belgium, Bulgaria, Chile, Czechoslovakia, Denmark, Egypt, Estonia, Finland, France, Germany, Great Britain, Hungary, India, Italy, Japan, Latvia, Netherlands, New Zealand, Norway, Poland, Romania, Siam, South Africa, Sweden, Switzerland, and US. The Irish Free State did not substantively respond to the query), and 22 States explicitly affirmed the grant of nationality to children of unknown parents. Five States (Great Britain, as well as Australia, India, New Zealand and South Africa under Great Britain's rule at the time) referred to the British nationality law rules where nationality was acquired by *jus soli*. Chile also referred to its *jus soli* rule granting nationality by birth in the territory. However, it is not clear whether children of unknown parents found, that is whose birth in the territory is not established, benefitted from such a *jus soli* rule. Ibid, 'Bases of discussion drawn up by the preparatory committee: General Observations submitted by certain Governments, Point VII', pp 62–7. See also 'Complete text of the replies made by the governments on the schedule of points submitted by the preparatory committee', pp 119–205 of the same document.

[72] Roberto Córdova, 'Nationality, including Statelessness—Report on the Elimination or Reduction of Statelessness' (1953) <http://legal.un.org/docs/?path=../ilc/documentation/english/a_cn4_64.pdf&lang=E> accessed 4 August 2019, p 176. The previous Special Rapporteur, Manly O. Hudson, also emphasized that 'A considerable number of States confer [...] their nationality on a child found in their territory [...]'. Manley O. Hudson, 'Report on Nationality, including Statelessness' in *Yearbook of the International Law Commission* (ILC 21 February 1952) 18 and 44. Brownlie also points this out. Ian Brownlie, *Principles of Public International Law* (Oxford University Press 2003) 383.

Annex 2 is a non-exhaustive table of at least[73] 26 States that reportedly had a foundling provisions during the travaux process of the 1961 Convention.

As shown, during the travaux of both the 1930 and the 1961 Convention, the foundling provision was already more common—including among States who were not part of the drafting process and/or who did not subsequently become State parties to the 1961 Convention—than the provision to grant nationality to children born in the territory whose parents are *known* and stateless (or unknown nationality) or cannot pass on nationality to their children.This trend still stands as of today (see Annex 1 and Sect. 1.5.5.2).

Due to this, as will be discussed further in Sect. 3.4, the drafting process of 1930 and 1961 Convention shows that the formulation of the foundling provision, that is article 14 of the 1930 and article 2 of the 1961 Conventions was much less controversial than that of article 15 and article 1 of the respective Conventions.

During the travaux of the 1930 Convention, it is noted with regard to Basis 11 (eventually adopted as article 14) that: 'This Basis did not lead to any difficulties as regards substance [...]',[74] and it is demonstrated that States had an easier time[75] voting for the provision to grant nationality to persons of unknown parentage and foundlings than to children of stateless persons, that is 'foreigners'. During the

---

[73] It should be noted that no verification of the original text of each national legislation, unlike Annex 1, was conducted for Annex 2. 'Section I. Existing legislation', 'Roberto Córdova, 'Nationality, including Statelessness—Report on the Elimination or Reduction of Statelessness' (1953) 175 <http://legal.un.org/docs/?path=../ilc/documentation/english/a_cn4_64.pdf&lang=E> accessed 4 August 2019. While Cordova on page 4 states that the list is based on Ivan S. Kerno, 'Nationality, including Statelessness—National Legislation Concerning Grounds for Deprivation of Nationality' (6 April 1953) <http://legal.un.org/docs/?path=../ilc/documentation/english/a_cn4_66.pdf&lang=EFS> accessed 4 August 2019, no information on the foundling provision is included in this document. Thus, it is unknown how many States were surveyed, and the 26 States is not exhaustive. Indeed, footnotes 157 and 158 of I(1)D, chapter 1, section I, Part Two, UNHCR, 'A Study of Statelessness' (August 1949) <https://www.unhcr.org/protection/statelessness/3ae68c2d0/study-statelessness-united-nations-august-1949-lake-success-new-york.html?query=A%20Study%20of%20Statelessness> accessed 4 August 2019, reedited by the Division of International Protection of UNHCR (1995) 135 also carry separate lists of countries with a provision granting nationality to children of unknown parents born in the territory and foundlings found respectively, but there are a number of States listed in these footnotes in the 1949 publication that are not included in Córdova's 1953 list. For example, article 2(iii) of the Japanese Nationality Act, Act No 147 of 4 May 1950 (replacing article 4 of the previous *Kokusekihō* [Nationality Act], Law No 66 of 1899 (*Meiji 32 nen*)) included in the 1949 Study is not included in the 1953 table.

[74] *Acts of the Conference for the Codification of International law held at the Hague from March 13th to April 12th, 1930. Volume I Plenary Meetings, Official No.: C. 351. M. 145. 1930. V.* (League of Nations 19 August 1930) 74.

[75] Ibid, p 74; *Acts of the Conference for the Codification of International law held at the Hague from March 13th to April 12th, 1930, Meetings of the Committees, Volume II Minutes of the 1st Committee Meetings: Nationality, Official No.: C. 351(a). M. 145(a). 1930. V.* (League of Nations 27 November 1930) 225–6; League of Nations, *Bases of Discussion Drawn up for the Conference by the Preparatory Committee, Volume I Nationality (Volume I-C.73.M.38.1929. V-BI-Geneva)* (Conference for the Codification of International Law, May 1929) 'Bases of discussion drawn up by the preparatory committee: General Observations submitted by certain Governments, Point VII., pp 62–7 as well as 'Complete text of the replies made by the governments on the schedule of points submitted by the preparatory committee, pp 119–205 of the same document.

travaux of the 1961 Convention, the major disputing point was mainly on the legal technique on how exactly to grant nationality and the difference between *jus soli* and *jus sanguinis* States, that is whether to presume birth in the territory or descent from a national.[76]

As a result, as also discussed in Sects. 3.4.2.3 and 3.4.5.2, both the 1930 and 1961 Conventions impose States a stronger obligation to grant nationality to foundlings as opposed to children born in the territory 'otherwise stateless'.[77]

While this was largely due to the common assumption that foundlings were highly likely to be children of nationals,[78] the travaux of the 1961 Convention also clearly shows that there was the recognition of the particular vulnerabilities of foundlings due to the lack of caretakers[79]—irrespective of the parents' nationality—which apparently made it easier for States to implement their general obligation to prevent statelessness.

Thus, within the 1961 Convention, the foundling provision is highly likely to be one of the 'more widely accepted of its articles'.[80]

### 1.5.5.2   Overview of Annex 1, a Comparative Table of 193 States—General Practice Accepted as Law?

It is now time to come back to provide some analysis of the comparative table of all 193 UN member States, included in this book as Annex 1. Out of 193 States researched, 75 States (as of the end of December 2020) are State parties to the 1961 Convention. Among 193, 139 States or approximately 72 per cent have a domestic provision granting nationality to foundlings or children of unknown parents. 58 States or approximately 77 per cent of the total number of 75 State parties to the 1961 Convention have a domestic foundling provision.

81 States out of 118 non-State parties, that is approximately 69 per cent, have a domestic foundling provision. Thus, the proportion of States with or without a

---

[76] Indirectly discussed in Sect. 7.4, in particular.

[77] In summary, while under article 14 of the 1930 Convention and article 2 of the 1961 Convention, foundlings are in principle to be automatically granted nationality, article 15 of the 1930 Convention providing for children of parents who are stateless or of unknown nationality is discretionary ('may obtain' the nationality) and article 1 of the 1961 Convention leaves a room for States to opt for non-automatic grant latest after children who would otherwise be stateless reach 18 years old.

[78] For example, see the comments by the Chairman speaking as the representative of Denmark, introducing his delegation's amendment to article 2, in United Nations, Summary Records, 5th Meeting of the Committee of the Whole held on 3 April 1959, A/CONF.9/C.1/SR.5, UN Conference on the Elimination or Reduction of Future Statelessness, Geneva, 1959 and New York, 1961 (3 April 1959) 7 <http://legal.un.org/docs/?path=../diplomaticconferences/1959_statelessness/docs/english/vol_2/a_conf9_c1_sr5.pdf&lang=E> accessed 4 August 2019. See more details in Sect. 3.4.5.2.

[79] As represented in the statement by the Danish representative recorded in ibid 8–9. See Sect. 3.4.5.2.

[80] Laura van Waas, *Nationality Matters: Statelessness under International Law* (Intersentia 2008), fn 100.

domestic foundling provision among State parties and non-State parties is quite similar.

Looking at Annex 1 for the regional tendency in each UNHCR-classified areas,[81] the region with the highest rate of inclusion of a foundling provision is the Middle East and North Africa (MENA), where 100 per cent, that is all 18 States, legislate specifically for it, despite the fact that only two, that is Libya and Tunisia, are State parties to the 1961 Convention.[82] Europe comes the second—out of 48 States, 96 per cent, that is 46 States, followed by Africa, where out of 48 States, 71 per cent or 34 States have a foundling provision.[83] For the Asia and Pacific region, out of 44 States, 55 per cent, that is 24 States[84] has a foundling provision. The region with the smallest ratio of States with a foundling provision is Americas, where, out of 35 States, 17 States, that is about 49 per cent, have a foundling provision, while there can be complementary provisions to be elaborated below.

Also complementing the information contained in Annex 1, an alternative source suggests that in 166 out of 189 countries surveyed (or 87.83 per cent) by the Supreme Court of the Philippines foundlings are recognized—assumingly including where there is no legal provision as such—as citizens, while the details and method of this research are unknown.[85]

---

[81] Classification was made according to the UNHCR Structure Worldwide, 'Geographical Regions and Sub-regions' (May 2009) <http://maps.unhcr.org/en/view?id=1522> accessed 4 February 2019.

[82] See Annex 1. Amit Sen and Zahra Albarazi, 'Efforts to prevent statelessness amongst children displaced by conflict in the Middle East and North Africa' in Laura van Waas and Melanie Khanna (eds), *Solving Statelessness* (Wolf Legal Publishers 2017) 405, 411. Footnote 21 states that 'in practice, challenges remain with respect to consistent implementation of the foundlings principle'. Zahra Albarazi in another report states that the foundling provision 'is understood to be implemented in all countries fully', except when a child is found in an area which is hosting a large refugee population, 'as there may be a belief that the child's parents are from the displaced population and not nationals'. Zahra Albarazi, 'Regional Report on Citizenship: The Middle East and North Africa (MENA), RSCAS/GLOBALCIT-Comp. 2017/3' (November 2017) 13 <http://cadmus.eui.eu/bitstream/handle/1814/50046/RSCAS_GLOBALCIT_Comp_2017_03.pdf?sequence=1&isAllowed=y> accessed 4 August 2019. See also Betsy Fisher, 'Why Non-Marital Children in the MENA Region Face a Risk of Statelessness' (January 2015) 4 and 7 <http://harvardhrj.com/wp-content/uploads/2015/01/Fisher_HRJ_01-05-15.pdf> accessed 4 August 2019.

[83] See Annex 1 of this book. See also Bronwen Manby, *Citizenship and Statelessness in Africa: The Law and Politics of Belonging* (Wolf Legal Publishers 2015) 127 and Table 2 on pp 128–9. (Note that Manby appears to refer to 'foundlings' to mean infants (of unknown parentage), and 'children of unknown parentage' to cover older children).

[84] See Annex 1 of this book. See also 'A good example is the explicit safeguard in the majority of nationality laws to ensure that foundlings [...] acquire a nationality.' UNHCR, 'Good Practices: Addressing Statelessness in South East Asia' (5 February 2011) 11 <http://www.refworld.org/docid/4d6e0a792.html> accessed 4 August 2019. See also Nicholas Oakeshott, 'Solutions to statelessness in Southeast Asia' in Laura van Waas and Melanie Khanna (eds), *Solving Statelessness* (Wolf Legal Publishers 2017) 345, 359 mentioning the usefulness of strengthening the foundling related safeguard in Thailand.

[85] Supreme Court of the Philippines citing the statement by the Chief Justice, at the 2 February 2016 Oral Arguments, *G. R. No 221697 Mary Grace Natividad S. Poe-llamanzares v. Comelec and Estrella C. Elamparo, and G. R. No 221698-700 Mary Grace Natividad S. Poe-llamanzares v.*

It should also be noted, however, that while 17 State parties to the 1961 Convention are without a specific domestic foundling provision, reflecting article 2 of the 1961 Convention, in some States, article 2, as a 'self-executable' provision can be applied directly, depending on the status of international treaties vis-à-vis national laws, as provided usually in the countries' constitution.[86]

Further, out of the 54 States without a domestic foundling provision, 20 States—in particular the Latin American States, with the lowest ratio of States with a foundling provision—unconditionally grant nationality by *jus soli*, thus already addressing the nationality issue for children of unknown parents whose birth in the territory is established (or in some cases presumed).

Further, as mentioned in Sect. 1.5.2.3 and as seen in Annex 1, 13 States (among 54) without a foundling provision nevertheless have a separate provision for nationality grant to persons (of known parentage) born in the territory who are either otherwise stateless or of unknown nationality or born of stateless parents or parents of unknown nationality. Thus, persons of unknown parents whose birth in the territory is established (or presumed) might benefit from this provision in the absence of a foundling provision.

Even with regard to 37 non-State parties where there is no explicit legal provision granting nationality to a foundling, it is often the case that many foundlings are in practice recognized as nationals due to case law such as in the Philippines (see Sect. 5.6.2) and judicial and administrative instructions such as Pakistan (see Sect. 4.3.2). A number of States are currently considering to introduce provisions to grant nationality to foundlings.[87]

Annex 1 shows that the number of States with a domestic foundling provision, that is 139, and 72 per cent out of 193 States is significantly more than the number of States that have a provision to grant nationality to persons born in the territory who would 'otherwise be stateless' or, more narrowly, children of parents who are stateless or unknown nationality, which is 86 States out of 193, that is 62 per cent at the time of writing.[88] It should be also noted that, while the majority of the 'foundling'

*Comelec, Francisco S. Tatad, Antonio P. Contreras and Amado D. Valdez* (Supreme Court of the Philippines).

[86] For example, in the email from Juan Ignacio Mondelli (Senior Regional Protection Officer (Statelessness), UNHCR Americas Bureau) to the author (28 June 2017), six States were referred to, that is Argentina, Bahamas, Brazil, Ecuador, Guatemala and Uruguay—all State parties to the 1961 Convention without a foundling provision—as countries where article 2 can be directly applied (at least theoretically).

[87] For example, during the UNHCR event entitled High-Level Segment on Statelessness in October 2019, some of the States currently without foundling provisions made pledges involving safeguarding foundlings against statelessness (at least Côte d'Ivoire, Gambia, Lesotho, Malawi, Namibia and Nigeria). UNHCR, 'High-Level Segment on Statelessness: Results and Highlights' (2020) <https://www.refworld.org/docid/5ec3e91b4.html> accessed 15 September 2020.

[88] To identify the States with a provision granting nationality to persons born in the territory who would 'otherwise be stateless', the GLOBALCIT's Global Database on Modes of Acquisition of Citizenship was consulted as the starting point. As the database contains the data for 173 States, additional research was conducted for the remaining States to make a complete list of 193 States. GLOBALCIT, 'Global Database on Modes of Acquisition of Citizenship, version 1.0. ' (2017)

provisions apparently provide for an 'automatic grant' (see Sect. 5.8.2), that is where nationality is acquired as soon as the legal criteria is fulfilled, the 'otherwise stateless' provision for a number of States provides for 'non-automatic' grant including through discretionary naturalization, with some States requiring (legal) residency for some years.

In terms of the actual practice of foundling provisions, as observed in Sect. 4.3, few reports were encountered where 'typical' cases of foundlings (especially those under Sects. 4.3.1, 4.3.2 and 4.3.10—including babies of unknown parents abandoned in baby hatches or other places) face issues acquiring nationality.

The principle laid out in article 2 of the 1961 Convention is also reproduced in subsequent international and regional instruments, that is article 6(1)(b) of the ECN, and article 7 paragraph 3 of the Covenant on the Rights of the Child in Islam[89] (while the latter does not specify which State is required to fulfil the obligation) and article 5.2.a of the Draft Protocol to the African Charter on Human and Peoples' Rights on the Specific Aspects of the Right to a Nationality and the Eradication of Statelessness in Africa.[90]

It can now be said that there is evidence of a widespread State practice, carried out over a significant period of time, where foundlings are provided nationality of the state on which they are found with or without a special legal provision in both *jus soli* and *jus sanguinis* States.

The above assertion is further strengthened by the fact that the avoidance of statelessness in general is in recent years increasingly referred to as a 'fundamental principle of international law'[91] and customary international law,[92] with the number

---

<http://globalcit.eu/acquisition-citizenship/> accessed 4 August 2019 (Searched by 'A03b [born stateless]' '2016' 'all countries'). Bronwen Manby also comments there are more States that have a specific safeguard for foundlings/children of unknown parentage than the States that have the same for otherwise stateless persons born in the territory in Africa. Bronwen Manby, *Citizenship and Statelessness in Africa: The law and politics of belonging* (Wolf Legal Publishers 2015) 127 and Table 2 on p 128–129.

[89] Organization of the Islamic Conference, Covenant on the Rights of the Child in Islam (June 2005) <http://www.unhcr.org/refworld/docid/44eaf0e4a.html> accessed 4 August 2019.

[90] ACHPR, 'Draft Protocol to the African Charter on human and peoples' rights on the specific aspects of the right to a nationality and the eradication of statelessness in Africa' (2015) <https://www.achpr.org/public/Document/file/English/draft_citizenship_protocol_en_sept2015_achpr.pdf> accessed 17 February 2020.

[91] That statelessness should be avoided is now recognized by the UN Human Rights Council as 'fundamental principle of international law', which has in several occasions urged 'all states to adopt and implement nationality legislation with a view to avoiding statelessness, consistent with fundamental principles of international law'. For example in the UN Human Rights Council, 'Human rights and arbitrary deprivation of nationality: resolution/adopted by the Human Rights Council' (16 July 2012) para 4 <https://www.refworld.org/docid/5016631b2.html> accessed 4 August 2019.

[92] In addition to Laura van Waas, *Nationality Matters: Statelessness under International Law* (Intersentia 2008), some scholars assert that the principle that statelessness is to be prevented has crystallized into a norm of customary international law; para 2, UNHCR, 'Interpreting the 1961 Statelessness Convention and Avoiding Statelessness Resulting from Loss and Deprivation of Nationality' (March 2014) (hereinafter 'Tunis Conclusions [2014]') <http://www.refworld.org/docid/533a754b4.html> accessed 4 August 2019.

of State parties to the 1961 Convention drastically increased, for example from 33 to 75 States between 2010 (when UNHCR resumed its accession campaign) to the end of December 2020.

Given that the grant of nationality to foundlings is arguably a customary international norm, analysis of the implementation of the equivalent provision by non-State parties to the 1961 Convention is all the more relevant.

## 1.6   Qualitative Rather than Quantitative Research

While Chap. 4 contains limited available statistical information possibly related to the number of foundlings, as explained in Sect. 4.1, it was not feasible to accurately identify the number of persons who (are qualified to) acquire nationality based on the foundling provision. More importantly, identifying the number of foundlings itself would not have contributed to address the research questions of this book. Thus, this book uses qualitative, rather than quantitative, analysis methods.

## 1.7   Structure

This book is split into eight chapters. Chapters 3–7 have a 'Summary and conclusions' section at the end where the essence of the findings can be found.

Chapter 2 will introduce the fundamental concepts and principles that lay the foundation for the chapters to follow, such as nationality and statelessness, the international legal framework to address statelessness, the relationship between documentation and nationality, and how legal parentage under family law is established, which is essential to determine nationality acquisition by *jus sanguinis*.

In Chap. 3, the hypothesis made in Sect. 1.4 that one of the requirements for qualifying as a 'foundling' is to be of 'unknown parents' will be verified.

In Chap. 4, the definition of 'unknown-ness' of the parentage, which Chap. 3 confirms to be one of the requirements to qualify as a foundling, will be further examined.

Chapter 5 will examine the burden of proof in establishing unknown parentage, as well as the 'standard of proof' or the required 'extent' of unknown-ness of the parentage.

Chapter 6 will examine the term 'found' in the territory in article 2 of the 1961 Convention, and the closely related issue of the 'maximum age'—as being a 'child' when found is the other one of the two requirements to qualify as a foundling in the hypothesis in Sect. 1.4.

Chapter 7 will examine the term 'absence of proof to the contrary' in article 2 pre facto before the confirmation of nationality under the foundling provision, and the conditions for the post facto withdrawal of the nationality.

Chapter 8 makes recommendations, based on the findings of the previous chapters, as to how article 2 of the 1961 Convention can be incorporated into national legislation, or what the relevant interpretative guidelines should include, and how future regional human rights or nationality related instruments should stipulate regarding the nationality of foundlings, by offering a model provision and its interpretive guidance.

# Chapter 2
# Nationality, Statelessness, Family Relationships, Documentation and Foundlings

**Abstract** This chapter reviews the basic concepts relevant to the book to contextualize and facilitate the understanding of the remaining chapters. It starts with the definition of being stateless vis-a-vis being a national, and reviews the international legal framework to address statelessness. The chapter also reviews the relationship between documentation and nationality, including how undocumented parentage (and birthplace) might lead to some persons falling within the definition of a foundling and thus becoming (otherwise) stateless. This Chapter also reviews the linkage between family law and nationality law, with the determination of parentage being the preliminary question for identifying one's nationality. It reviews the basics of how maternal and paternal legal parentage is established, including the rules of private international law. It also contains the definition of a 'factual parent' and a 'legal parent, and provides general indications as to when some persons might end up without any legal parentage while biological parents may be known.

Before going into the central issue, that is the nationality of foundlings, some contextualization is necessary. This chapter will—though rather cursorily—review the basic concepts and discussions relating to nationality and statelessness and contextualize where foundlings fall within this discourse.

## 2.1 Statelessness Around the World and Efforts to Address Statelessness

UNHCR reported on a global number of 4.2 million 'stateless persons' including those of undetermined nationality in 76 countries at the end of 2019, but the true extent of statelessness is estimated to be much higher.[1] This includes large groups of people and isolated individual cases around the world. The well-known groups of people who have been affected by statelessness include Bidoons and Kurds in the

---

[1] UNHCR, 'Global Trends Forced Displacement in 2019' (18 June 2020) <https://www.unhcr.org/5ee200e37.pdf> accessed 21 September 2020.

Middle East, Black Mauritanians in Mauritania/Senegal, Rohingyas in Myanmar, hill tribes in Thailand, Roma in Europe, some persons from the former Yugoslav Federation or USSR in Europe who have fallen through the cracks of the laws when their countries disintegrated, those of Haitian descent in the Dominican Republic and Nubians in Kenya.

During the first several decades after the adoption of the 1954 and 1961 Conventions, statelessness did not receive sufficient attention. However, following the dissolution of the former Soviet Union and the break-up of the former Yugoslavia in the 1990s, international concerns over statelessness gradually started to be revitalized.[2]

In recent years, many States have taken significant steps towards preventing and reducing statelessness.[3] According to UNHCR, between 2003 and 2013, actions by States led to more than four million stateless people acquiring a nationality or having their nationality confirmed.[4] In Nepal, 2.6 million persons, who had never possessed any documents to prove their nationality, were able to receive citizenship certificates in 2007 due to the revised nationality law.[5] In Sri Lanka, the so-called Hill Tamils, descendants of immigrants from India, were able to acquire or confirm Sri Lankan nationality after the nationality law was amended in 2003 and a citizenship campaign was carried out with the support of the UNHCR.[6] In Bangladesh, an estimated 250,000 Urdu-speaking Biharis were recognized as Bangladeshi citizens following a 2008 landmark decision by the Supreme Court.[7]

The UNHCR furthered its endeavours in addressing statelessness towards the fiftieth anniversary of the 1961 Convention in 2011. In November 2014, the UNHCR launched the #IBelong Campaign to End Statelessness within ten years by 2024,[8] which was welcomed by the UN General Assembly Resolution in December 2014. The campaign established a Global Action Plan to End Statelessness,[9] which provides a guiding framework of ten actions to be undertaken by States in order to resolve existing major situations of statelessness, to prevent new cases of statelessness from

---

[2] Chapter 6, UNHCR, 'The State of the World's Refugees: A Humanitarian Agenda' (1997) <http://www.unhcr.org/3eb7ba7d4.pdf> accessed 4 August 2019.

[3] See in general UNHCR, 'Good Practices Paper—Action 1: Resolving Existing Major Situations of Statelessness' (23 February 2015) <http://www.refworld.org/docid/54e75a244.html> accessed 4 August 2019.

[4] UNHCR, 'How UNHCR Helps Stateless People' <http://www.unhcr.org/how-unhcr-helps-stateless-people.html> accessed 4 August 2019.

[5] UNHCR, 'The Excluded' (2007) 147.

[6] UNHCR, 'Good Practices Paper—Action 1: Resolving Existing Major Situations of Statelessness' (23 February 2015) <http://www.refworld.org/docid/54e75a244.html> accessed 4 August 2019.

[7] UNHCR, 'Note on the Nationality Status of the Urdu-Speaking Community in Bangladesh' (17 December 2009) <http://www.unhcr.org/refworld/docid/4b2b90c32.html> accessed 4 August 2019 para 3; see also UNHCR, 'Good Practices Paper—Action 1: Resolving Existing Major Situations of Statelessness' (23 February 2015) <http://www.refworld.org/docid/54e75a244.html> accessed 4 August 2019.

[8] The Campaign has its own website with updates on its achievements regularly published: UNHCR, 'Every person has the right to say #IBELONG' <http://ibelong.unhcr.org> accessed 4 August 2019; please also see UNHCR, 'A Special Report: Ending Statelessness within 10 Years' (November 2010) <http://www.unhcr.org/546217229.html> accessed 4 August 2019.

[9] UNHCR, 'Global Action Plan to End Statelessness' (4 November 2014) <http://www.refworld.org/docid/545b47d64.html> accessed 4 August 2019.

emerging, and to better identify and protect stateless populations. Many States, including non-State parties to the above Conventions, have revised their nationality laws such as by removing gender discrimination from their nationality laws[10] or by establishing statelessness determination procedures in recent years.[11] As of end of 2019, 341,000 formerly stateless persons are known to have acquired nationality since the start of the #IBelong Campaign in 2014.[12] The number of state parties to the 1954 and 1961 Conventions, which used to be small compared to other treaties such as the 1951 Convention relating to the Status of Refugees (hereinafter the 1951 Convention),[13] went up significantly. Since 2010 when renewed accession campaign started till February 2020, the number of State parties to the 1954 Convention has increased from 65 to 94, and that of the 1961 Convention from 33 to 75; and these numbers are expected to increase further.

Further, the UNHCR organized a series of expert meetings on statelessness during 2010–14 on the interpretation and implementation of the 1954 and 1961 Conventions, and the discussions were captured in four summary conclusions.[14] Building on these conclusions, the UNHCR issued three guidelines relating to the interpretation of the 1954 Convention, during 2012 on the interpretation of the statelessness definition, statelessness determination procedures and the status of stateless persons, which have been combined into the *Handbook on Protection of Stateless Persons* in 2014 (hereinafter the UNHCR Handbook [2014]).[15] In relation to the interpretation of the 1961 Convention, the UNHCR issued the guidelines on interpreting its article 1 to 4 on ensuring children's right to a nationality in 2012 (UNHCR Guidelines 4[2012]), and articles 5–9 on loss and deprivation of nationality in 2020 (hereinafter UNHCR

---

[10] See for example, UNHCR, 'Good Practices Paper—Action 3: Removing Gender Discrimination from Nationality Laws' (6 March 2015) <http://www.refworld.org/docid/54f8377d4.html> accessed 4 August 2019 and UNHCR, 'Background Note on Gender Equality, Nationality Laws and Statelessness 2018' (8 March 2018) <http://www.refworld.org/docid/5aa10fd94.html> accessed 4 August 2019.

[11] For example, see UNHCR, 'Good Practices Paper—Action 6: Establishing Statelessness Determination Procedures to Protect Stateless Persons' (11 July 2016) <https://www.refworld.org/docid/57836cff4.html> accessed 2 May 2019.

[12] UNHCR, 'Global Trends Forced Displacement in 2019' (18 June 2020) 58 <https://www.unhcr.org/5ee200e37.pdf> accessed 21 September 2020.

[13] *Convention relating to the Status of Refugees*, Geneva, 28 July 1951, 189 UNTS 137 (entered into force 22 April 1954).

[14] These are: UNHCR, 'Expert Meeting—The Concept of Stateless Persons under International Law ("Prato Conclusions")' (May 2010) <http://www.refworld.org/docid/4ca1ae002.html> accessed 4 August 2019; UNHCR, 'Statelessness Determination Procedures and the Status of Stateless Persons ("Geneva Conclusions")' (December 2010) <http://www.refworld.org/docid/4d9022762.html> accessed 4 August 2019; UNHCR, 'Interpreting the 1961 Statelessness Convention and Preventing Statelessness among Children ("Dakar Conclusions")' (September 2011) <http://www.refworld.org/docid/4e8423a72.html> accessed 4 August 2019; Tunis Conclusions (2014).

[15] UNHCR, *UNHCR Handbook on Protection of Stateless Persons* (30 June 2014) <http://www.refworld.org/docid/53b676aa4.html> accessed 4 August 2019. See in general, Mai Kaneko, 'Mukokuseki ni kansuru UNHCR shin handobukku/gaidorain tō no kaisetsu' [Commentary on the newly published UNHCR Handbook and Guidelines on Statelessness] (December 2014) 4 Refugee Studies Journal 45.

Guidelines 5[2020]),[16] which are the most relevant to this book. The UNHCR's guidelines on the interpretation of articles 5–9 of the 1961 Convention on avoiding statelessness resulting from loss and deprivation of nationality is expected to be published in the future. All these efforts have been crucial in clarifying international standards in relation to statelessness and reinvigorating the international legal framework and activities in addressing statelessness.

The international human rights mechanisms have also started to more actively engage in statelessness and nationality by issuing resolutions, recommendations and comments and other documents.[17] New regional instruments, resolutions or declarations on statelessness are being drafted and adopted.[18] The prevention and resolution of statelessness is being promoted in relation to the Sustainable Development Goals (SDG), especially in the context of Target 16.9, 'provide legal identity for all, including birth registration'.[19] The historic 2016 New York Declaration for Refugees and Migrants[20] and the Global Compact on Refugees[21] adopted by the UN General Assembly in December 2018 encourage support for the #IBelong Campaign to end statelessness and accession to the 1954 and the 1961 Convention. The Global Compact for Safe, Orderly and Regular Migration (GCM)[22] adopted by the majority of UN member States and formally endorsed by the UN General Assembly on 19 December 2018 calls for strengthening of measures to reduce statelessness including by registering migrants' births.[23]

---

[16] UNHCR, 'Guidelines on Statelessness No 5: Loss and Deprivation of Nationality under Articles 5–9 of the 1961 Convention on the Reduction of Statelessness' (May 2020) HCR/GS/20/05 (hereinafter UNHCR Guidelines 5 [2020]) <https://www.refworld.org/docid/5ec5640c4.html> accessed 25 August 2020.

[17] See in general Melanie J. Khanna and Peggy Brett, 'Making Effective Use of UN Human Rights Mechanisms to Solve Statelessness' in Laura van Waas and Melanie Khanna (eds), *Solving Statelessness* (Wolf Legal Publishers 2017).

[18] For example, see Juan Ignacio Mondelli, 'Eradicating Statelessness in the Americas: The Brazil Declaration and Plan of Action' in Laura van Waas and Melanie Khanna (eds), *Solving Statelessness* (Wolf Legal Publishers 2017) 285, and Bronwen Manby, Ayalew Getachew and Julia Sloth-Nielsen, 'The Right to a Nationality in Africa: New Norms and New Commitments' in Laura van Waas and Melanie Khanna (eds), *Solving Statelessness* (Wolf Legal Publishers 2017) 261.

[19] Radha Govil, 'The Sustainable Development Goals and Solutions to Statelessness' in Laura van Waas and Melanie Khanna (eds), *Solving Statelessness* (Wolf Legal Publishers 2017) 47.

[20] UN General Assembly, 'New York Declaration for Refugees and Migrants: resolution/adopted by the General Assembly' (3 October 2016,) <http://www.refworld.org/docid/57ceb74a4.html> accessed 4 August 2019 para 72.

[21] United Nations, 'Report of the United Nations High Commissioner for Refugees. Part II Global compact on refugees' (17 December 2018) <https://www.unhcr.org/gcr/GCR_English.pdf> accessed 4 August 2019, see in particular Sect. 2.9 and also Sect. 2.8.

[22] United Nations, 'The Global Compact for Safe, Orderly and Regular Migration (GCM)' (19 December 2018) <https://www.iom.int/global-compact-migration> accessed 4 August 2019 para 20(e).

[23] Tendayi Bloom, 'Statelessness and the Second Revision of the Global Compact for Migration: What Still Needs to Be Addressed?' (5 June 2018) <https://www.statelessness.eu/blog/statelessness-and-second-revision-global-compact-migration-what-still-needs-be-addressed> accessed 4 August 2019.

## 2.2 Right to Nationality Under International Law

Nationality or citizenship[24] provides the link, which associates an individual with a political entity and reflects the legal bond[25] between a State and an individual. This bond gives an individual membership and distinct identity in the world and forms the solid legal basis to claim the protection of rights that are typically reserved for nationals. The key rights as nationals include the right to reside within the territory of the State, to return to that country in case of travel and the right to take part in the administration of the state, referred to as political rights. The corresponding duties of nationals in many States may include their allegiance to the State encompassing, for example, the obligation to pay certain tax such as income tax or to perform military or equivalent services. States, on the other hand, are expected to guarantee various rights to their nationals and are supposed to exercise jurisdiction over their nationals including those residing abroad.[26]

Nationality used to be even described as a 'right to have rights'.[27] However, the development of human rights standards have made it undisputable at least in theory that enjoyment of certain human rights are regardless of the possession of a nationality, as provided for in various international human rights instruments and national legislation—which is termed as 'denationalization' of protection.[28] Nonetheless, stateless persons often find themselves in a situation where they cannot exercise basic civil, social and economic rights. Being without a nationality, they often lack identity documents that are required to access certain rights or services, and are unable to depart from their country of residence and legally enter another country and stay there with a valid legal status. They can be subject to long years of detention for illegal entry or stay in the country where they moved to or even in the country where they were born.[29] Against this background, the right to a nationality has itself been

---

[24] In some contexts, 'citizenship' and 'nationality' can be two different legal concepts. In the former Soviet Union for example, while the former reflected a political status, the term 'nationality' referred to members of the same ethnic or linguistic group. Despite these differences in certain contexts, the terms nationality and citizenship are commonly used to denote a legal bond between a state and an individual and are therefore used interchangeably, as will be done in this book.

[25] Article 2(a) *European Convention on Nationality*, 6 November 1997, ETS 166 (entered into force 1 March 2000). *Nottebohm Case (Liechtenstein v. Guatemala); Second Phase [6 April 1955]* (International Court of Justice (ICJ)) 4.

[26] See further discussion on what it means to be 'considered a national' in Sect. 2.6.

[27] Hannah Arendt, *The Origins of Totalitarianism* (Harvest Book, Hb244, 1st edn, Harcourt, Brace, Jovanovich 1973). Echoed for example in *Trop v. Dulles*, 356 US 86 [1958] (US Supreme Court).

[28] Separate Opinion of Judge A.A. Cancado Trindade, Inter-American Court on Human Rights, *Case of the Yean and Bosico Children v. The Dominican Republic* [8 September 2005] (Inter-American Court of Human Rights (IACrtHR)), Series C, Case 130, paras 7 and 11, also cited in Laura van Waas, *Nationality Matters: Statelessness under International Law* (Intersentia 2008), fn 24, p 221.

[29] See for example Michelle Foster and Hélène Lambert, 'Statelessness as a human rights issue: a concept whose time has come' (2016) 28 International Journal of Refugee Law 564.

recognized as a human right. In particular, article 15 of the Universal Declaration of Human Rights (UDHR)[30] stipulates that 'everyone has the right to a nationality'.

Article 7 of the CRC provides that 'the child shall be registered immediately after birth and shall have the right from birth to a name, the right to acquire a nationality [...]'.[31] Article 8 of the CRC requires a State party 'to respect the right of the child to preserve his or her identity, including nationality' without unlawful interference. Article 24 of the International Covenant on Civil and Political Rights (ICCPR)[32] also provides for the child's right to be registered at birth and to acquire a nationality. Other instruments also support this right to nationality—for example, article 18 of the Convention on the Rights of Persons with Disabilities (CRPD),[33] article 5 of the International Convention on the Elimination of All Forms of Racial Discrimination (CERD),[34] article 9 of the Convention on the Elimination of All Forms of Discrimination Against Women (CEDAW)[35] and article 29 of the International Convention on the Protection of the Rights of All Migrant Workers and Members of Their Families (ICRMW).[36]

The development of regional human rights frameworks also works to complement those international instruments. The American Convention on Human Rights (article 20), the African Charter on the Rights and Welfare of the Child (article 6), the Arab Charter on Human Rights (article 29) and the Convention on Human Rights and Fundamental Freedoms of the Commonwealth of Independent States (CIS Convention on Human Rights, article 24) all confirm the right to a nationality as a human right. The American Convention and the African Charter specifically guarantee the right of every child to acquire the nationality of the State in which they are born if they would otherwise be stateless. The Covenant on the Rights of the Child in Islam (article 7) guarantees the right to nationality determination and the right to a

---

[30] Universal Declaration of Human Rights (hereinafter UDHR), UNGA res 217A (III), 10 Dec 1948.

[31] Article 7 of the CRC for children's right to nationality without specifying which State is obliged to grant nationality to children. Nevertheless, the CRC Committee's interpretation of article 7 is that it requires States to grant nationality to all otherwise stateless children born on the territory. See for example the Institute of Statelessness and Inclusion (ISI), 'An analysis of the work of the Committee on the Rights of the Child' (September 2015) <www.institutesi.org/CRC_nationality_paper.pdf> accessed 4 August 2019; ISI, 'Addressing the right to a nationality through the Convention on the Rights of the Child: A Toolkit for Civil Society' (June 2016) 16 <www.institutesi.org/CRC_Too lkit_Final.pdf> accessed 4 August 2019.

[32] *International Covenant on Civil and Political Rights* (ICCPR), New York, 16 December 1966, 999 UNTS 171 (entered into force 23 March 1976).

[33] *Convention on the Rights of Persons with Disabilities* (CRPD), New York, 13 December 2006, 2515 UNTS 3 (entered into force 3 May 2008).

[34] *International Convention on the Elimination of All Forms of Racial Discrimination* (ICERD), New York, 7 March 1966, 660 UNTS 195 (entered into force 4 January 1969).

[35] *Convention on the Elimination of All Forms of Discrimination Against Women* (CEDAW), New York, 18 December 1979, 1249 UNTS 13 (entered into force 3 September 1981).

[36] *International Convention on the Protection of the Rights of All Migrant Workers and Members of Their Families* (ICRMW), New York, 18 December 1990, 2220, UNTS 3 (entered into force 1 July 2003).

nationality for children of unknown descent. Although the European Convention on Human Rights (hereinafter ECHR) does not directly address questions of nationality, the European Court of Human Rights (hereinafter ECtHR) came to the conclusion in 2011 that denial of citizenship had a negative impact on the applicant's 'social identity' encompassed in the right to respect for private life protected under article 8 of the ECHR.[37] Further, the ECN at article 4 provides for the principles for the rules on nationality of each State party recognizing that (a) everyone has the right to a nationality; (b) statelessness shall be avoided; and (c) no one shall be arbitrarily deprived of her or his nationality; and further establishes detailed standards for the attribution of nationality to ensure these principles. However, it is apparent that ensuring this right to all human beings has turned out to be a challenge in many countries.

## 2.3  Domestic Rules for Acquisition and Loss of Nationality

Most States' nationality laws adopt similar criteria for the acquisition of nationality by birth, that is based either on by birth on the State's soil (*jus soli*) or by descent (*jus sanguinis*), or the mixture of the two. Nationality can be acquired later in life such as by residence within the state (such as through naturalization), marriage with a national or by adoption by a national. The majority of States have a mixture of automatic and non-automatic modes of nationality acquisition. Automatic modes are those where a change in nationality status takes place by operation of law (*ex lege*). According to automatic modes, nationality is acquired as soon as the criteria set forth by law are met, such as birth on a territory or birth to nationals of a State. By contrast, in non-automatic modes of acquisition, an act of the individual or a State authority is required before the change in nationality status takes place.[38]

Once acquired, nationality can be lost during the course of one's life, either automatically or non-automatically. This can happen through renunciation, where a person voluntarily gives up nationality, loss of citizenship where a person ceases to be a national automatically when certain legal conditions are met, or deprivation when a person's nationality is withdrawn by a decision of the authorities.

## 2.4  International Legal Framework to Address Statelessness

As stated above, nationality is conferred and withdrawn by States based on their domestic law. While in principle every State has the sovereignty to draw up its own nationality legislation and policies, developments in international law over the course of the last century have set notable limits to State discretion in this regard. As the

---

[37] *Genovese v. Malta,* Application No 53124/09 [11 October 2011] (ECtHR).

[38] UNHCR Handbook (2014), paras 25 and 26.

Permanent Court of International Justice highlighted in its Advisory Opinion on the Tunis Nationality Decrees of 1923[39]: 'the question of whether or not a certain matter is or is not solely within the domestic jurisdiction of a state is essentially a relative question; it depends on the development of international relations'. It then held that even in respect of matters which, in principle, were not regulated by international law, the right of a state to use its discretion might be restricted by obligations that it might have undertaken towards other States, so that its jurisdiction became limited by rules of international law.[40] This principle was later reflected in article 1 of the 1930 Convention,[41] which was the first international attempt to ensure that all persons have a nationality. It states that:

> it is for each state to determine under its own law who are its nationals. This law shall be recognized by other states *in so far as it is consistent with international conventions, international custom*, and the principles of law generally recognized with regard to nationality. (italics added)

This essentially means that the manner in which a State exercises its right to determine its citizens needs to conform to the relevant provisions in international law. Article 14 of the Hague Convention provides safeguards for foundlings and persons of unknown parentage (which is the main focus of this book), and article 15 for children born of parents without nationality or of unknown nationality.

Throughout the twentieth century, international instruments have gradually developed to place more importance on human rights over claims of state sovereignty as also acknowledged by ILC.[42]

Today, the 1961 Convention and the 1954 Convention are the two international instruments dedicated to addressing statelessness. Among the substantive articles, articles 1–4 of the 1961 Convention address the acquisition of nationality at or by birth. In particular, article 1 of the 1961 Convention provides for acquisition of nationality by persons born in the territory who would otherwise be stateless,[43] while article 2 provides for the grant of nationality to foundlings—which is the very focus

---

[39] *Nationality Decrees Issued in Tunis and Morocco*, Advisory Opinion No 4 [7 February 1923] (Permanent Court of International Justice).

[40] The advisory opinion is often cited as one of the evidence that determination of nationality (in principle) 'belongs to domestic jurisdiction'. However, scholars including Yasuhiro Okuda, for example, provide critical analysis on such reading of the advisory opinion: 'The conception that nationality belongs to the domestic jurisdiction of the state only rephrases a given—that assigning a particular nationality is done through domestic law and not international law'. Yasuhiro Okuda, *Kosekihō to kokusai oyakohō* [Nationality Act and International Family Law] (Yūhikaku 2004) 53–6, commenting on the views on the same advisory opinion by Ian Brownlie, 'The relations of nationality in public international law' (1963) 39 British Year Book of International Law 284.

[41] See Sect. 2.4.1 on the developments leading to its adoption.

[42] UNHCR, 'Nationality and Statelessness: Handbook for Parliamentarians No. 22' (July 2014) 6 <https://www.refworld.org/docid/53d0a0974.html> accessed 4 August 2019. Paragraphs 20 and 57 of the UN Human Rights Council, Human rights and arbitrary deprivation of nationality: report of the Secretary-General, A/HRC/13/34 (14 December 2009) <https://www.refworld.org/docid/4b8 3a9cb2.html> accessed 4 August 2019.

[43] On a side note, the term 'would otherwise be stateless' in articles 1 and 4 of the 1961 Convention is actually misleading, as it is written as if the articles do not cover persons who are already stateless.

of this book. Article 5–9 cover the loss of deprivation of nationality, with article 10 on avoiding statelessness in case of transfer of territory.

The 1954 Convention includes the universal definition of a stateless person (see Sect. 2.5) and sets forth the criteria State parties should adopt to regulate and improve the legal status of stateless persons residing on their territory and to ensure the protection of their fundamental rights and freedoms.

However, these Conventions are only one part of the overall international legal framework to address statelessness, which developed both prior and subsequent to their adoption at the international and regional level. The full spectrum of 'international statelessness law' comprises a multitude of treaties, soft law standards and customary law norms that are intended to ensure the right to a nationality and the rights of stateless people, including the international human rights instruments mentioned above providing for or supporting the right to nationality.

These treaty obligations are further supplemented by the general principle of international law that statelessness should be avoided. As also mentioned in Sect. 1.5.5.2, this principle has been endorsed by the UN Human Rights Council, which has urged 'all states to adopt and implement nationality legislation with a view to avoiding statelessness, consistent with fundamental principles of international law'[44] with the result that they are applicable to all States, irrespective of a State's precise treaty commitments. Further, there is also a view that, as a result of State practice such as the ratification of the treaties mentioned above and adoption by consensus of many international resolutions on nationality, the principle that statelessness is to be prevented has crystallized into a norm of customary international law.[45] Spiro adeptly pointed out the emergence of international citizenship law in late 2000s, following which, among others, de Groot and Vonk asserted that 'international standards on nationality law'[46] have now been established and need to be respected, including the principle that statelessness must be avoided.

---

The current expression is only correct if the State automatically grants nationality to a child at birth— as it refers to the moment when the baby is born, and he or she consequently never experiences statelessness. However, when the State party opts for non-automatic grant upon application, the child will remain stateless until the application procedure is completed, the duration of which could range from several days up to, theoretically, 18 years of age or even more. Thus, precisely speaking, article 1 of the 1961 Convention should have read: 'who would otherwise be stateless if nationality of the contracting State is not granted, or is stateless until such nationality is granted' or something to that effect. In this book, the author will strive to use this or another wording that clearly includes both of these categories of persons when necessary, but for simplicity of the language, will also use '(otherwise-) stateless persons'.

[44] For example, in the UN Human Rights Council, 'Human rights and arbitrary deprivation of nationality: Resolution/adopted by the Human Rights Council' (16 July 2012) para 4 <https://www.refworld.org/docid/5016631b2.html> accessed 4 August 2019.

[45] Council of Europe, 'Explanatory Report to the European Convention on Nationality, 6.XI.1997' (1997) para 33 <https://rm.coe.int/16800ccde7> accessed 4 August 2019. Tunis Conclusions (2014) para 2.

[46] See his most widely cited article, Peter J. Spiro, 'A new international law of citizenship' (2011) 105 American Journal of International Law 694. Gerard-René de Groot and Olivier Willem Vonk, *International Standards on Nationality Law: Texts, Cases and Materials* (Wolf Legal Publishers 2016).

### 2.4.1 Developments Towards Adoption of the 1961 Convention

The overview of the timeline of the developments towards the adoption of the 1961 Convention will be introduced here, just to contextualize the detailed discussions in Chapt. 3 on the drafting process of the 1961 Convention and the evolution of article 2 and its relationship with article 1.[47]

The League of Nations since World War I had an interest in avoiding statelessness, so as to prevent the 'abnormalities' going against the State sovereignty and international order.[48] The Assembly of the League of Nations of 22 September 1924 adopted a resolution envisaging the creation of a standing organ called the Committee of Experts for the Progressive Codification of International Law. This Committee was to prepare a list of subjects the regulation of which by international agreement was most 'desirable and realizable'. After certain consultations with governments and the League Council, the Assembly decided in 1927 to convene a diplomatic conference to codify three topics that had been considered to be 'ripe for international agreement' by the Committee of Experts, among which was the issue of nationality. The preparation of the conference was entrusted to a Preparatory Committee, which was to draw up reports showing points of agreement or divergence that might serve as 'bases of discussion'. Delegates from 47 governments participated in the First Conference for the Codification of International Law which met at The Hague from 13 March to 12 April 1930, as a result of which the 1930 Hague Convention was adopted.[49]

Nevertheless, the 1930 Convention was not comprehensive enough[50] to prevent statelessness and did not attract many State parties. As Manley O. Hudson later stated

---

[47] This section is mainly based on the United Nations, 'History of the two draft conventions, one dealing with the elimination of future statelessness and the other with the reduction of future statelessness, prepared by the International Law Commission' [A/CONF.9/6] (Conference on the Elimination or Reduction of Future Statelessness, Geneva) <http://legal.un.org/docs/?path=../diplomati cconferences/1959_statelessness/docs/english/vol_1/a_conf9_6.pdf&lang=E> accessed 4 August 2019; ILC, 'Summaries of the Work of the International Law Commission: Nationality including statelessness' (15 July 2015) <http://legal.un.org/ilc/summaries/6_1.shtml> accessed 4 August 2019; Paul Weis, 'The United Nations Convention on the reduction of statelessness, 1961' (1962) 11 International & Comparative Law Quarterly 1073. For the handy summary of historical developments leading up to statelessness specific international framework (and its relationship with the international refugee protection regime), see Osamu Arakaki, 'Mukokusekichiijōyaku to mukokuseki sakugen jōyaku' [1954 Convention relating to the Status of Stateless Persons and 1961 Convention on the Reduction of Stateless Persons: The developments leading up to their adoption and the overview of the Conventions] (October 2014) 86 Hōritsu Jihō No 1,078 35 [author translation].

[48] Osamu Arakaki, 'Mukokusekichiijōyaku to mukokuseki sakugen jōyaku' [1954 Convention relating to the Status of Stateless Persons and 1961 Convention on the Reduction of Stateless Persons: The developments leading up to their adoption and the overview of the Conventions] (October 2014) 37, 86 Hōritsu Jihō No 1078.

[49] See in general, ILC, 'League of Nations Codification Conference' <http://legal.un.org/ilc/league. shtml> accessed 4 August 2019.

[50] The 1930 Convention, for example, has been criticized for lacking provisions dealing with prevention of statelessness due to loss or deprivation of nationality by States. Kōki Abe attributes this to

in asserting the need for international legislation to reduce future statelessness, 'The (1930) Hague Convention […] have done little to reduce statelessness […]'.[51]

After World War II, the need for the United Nations to explore the appropriate responses to the issues of statelessness was acknowledged. In 1948 UN Economic and Social Council (hereinafter ECOSOC) made a request to the then (first) Secretary General Trygve Lie to conduct a study including for the purpose of considering the necessity of drafting and concluding a statelessness-specific international instrument. The United Nations' 'Study of Statelessness' was then conducted and published in 1949. After the 1949 Study, ECOSOC established an ad hoc committee in August 1949, mandated to draft Conventions for refugees and stateless persons. Following the 11 August 1950 ECOSOC Resolution 319BIII(XI), which urged ILC to draft international instruments necessary to eliminate statelessness, ILC carried out a study on nationality including statelessness between 1951 and 1954. It appointed Manley O. Hudson in 1951 and Roberto Córdova in 1952 as the successive special rapporteurs, and Ivan S. Kerno as an individual expert. Paul Weis, a scholar and practitioner on statelessness issues later also joined the process.[52] In 1953, on the basis of a report containing draft articles submitted by Córdova, ILC adopted two draft Conventions for governments' comments—one on the elimination of future statelessness imposing stricter obligations on the contracting parties than the other one with the more modest aim of merely reducing statelessness, making it more easily acceptable for States. Discussions revolved around the differences between *jus sanguinis* and *jus soli*, and the gaps between internal law and international law. In 1954, ILC redrafted some of the articles in light of the comments made by governments and adopted the final drafts of both Conventions that were submitted to the UN General Assembly. General Assembly on 4 December 1954 as resolution 896 (IX) requested an international conference of plenipotentiaries be convened. In accordance with this resolution, the United Nations Conference on the Elimination or Reduction of Future Statelessness met at Geneva from 24 March to 18 April 1959, with representatives of 35 States participating. The Conference decided to use as the basis for its discussion the draft Convention on the reduction of future statelessness and adopted provisions aimed at reducing statelessness at birth. The second part of the Conference, in which representatives of 30 States participated, met in New York from 15 to 28 August 1961. The Conference adopted the Convention on the Reduction of Statelessness on 30 August 1961 which entered into force on 13 December 1975 in accordance with its article 18.

---

the fact that the focus of attention in international law in the early twentieth century was on the legal technicalities of how to eliminate the conflict in nationality laws. Kōki Abe, 'Overview of Statelessness: International and Japanese Context' (April 2010) 18 <https://www.refworld.org/docid/4c344c252.html> accessed 4 May 2019.

[51] Manley O. Hudson, 'Report on Nationality, including Statelessness' in *Yearbook of the International Law Commission* (ILC 21 February 1952).

[52] ILC, 'Summaries of the Work of the International Law Commission: Nationality including statelessness' (15 July 2015) <http://legal.un.org/ilc/summaries/6_1.shtml> accessed 4 August 2019.

## 2.4.2   Relevance of UNHCR Guidance

Article 11 of the 1961 Convention envisages the establishment within the framework of the United Nations a body to which a person claiming the benefit of the 1961 Convention may apply for the examination of his claim and for assistance in presenting it to the appropriate authority. The UN General Assembly assigned the mandate to the UNHCR to assist stateless persons under article 11 of the 1961 Convention by Resolutions 3274 (XXIV) of 1974 and 31/36 of 1976. The UNHCR's mandate to address statelessness has since then been expanded through subsequent GA Resolutions 49/169 of 1994 and 50/152 of 1995, and now covers not only state parties to the two statelessness Conventions but the entire world.[53] Furthermore, Conclusion No 106 of the UNHCR Executive Committee of the High Commissioner's Programme (hereinafter ExCom) adopted in 2006 (and endorsed by GA Resolution 61/137 of 2006) organizes UNHCR's statelessness activities into four categories, that is identification, prevention and reduction of statelessness, and protection of stateless persons. UNHCR has been requested by its ExCom to take a comprehensive approach in cooperation with governments, other UN organizations and civil society. Proactive responses by the UNHCR have been called upon, such as supporting governments in closing gaps in laws/implementation of the laws that may cause statelessness, or promoting systematic birth registration.[54]

Based on the mandate given by the General Assembly, the UNHCR is considered to have the authority to interpret existing international law provisions relating to statelessness as well as to formulate guidance and policies to guide state practice, for example by issuing guidelines and providing direct technical advice to states. For example, a decision by the Hungarian Constitutional Court on 23 February 2015 commented on the authoritative nature of UNHCR's guidelines on statelessness, stating that: '[W]hile the [UNHCR] Guidelines belong to the so-called non-binding international instruments, it is nevertheless indisputable that UNHCR is the most authentic entity to interpret international legal questions and practice related to the Statelessness Convention.'[55] While the UNHCR's interpretive guidance itself

---

[53] See in general Mark Manly, 'UNHCR's Mandate and Activities to Address Statelessness' in Alice Edwards and Laura van Waas (eds), *Nationality and Statelessness under International Law* (Cambridge University Press 2014) 88. For analysis of pre-1995 UNHCR engagement on statelessness, see Matthew Seet, 'The origins of UNHCR's global mandate on statelessness' (1 March 2016) 28 International Journal of Refugee Law 7. See also Mai Kaneko, 'Statelessness and UNHCR's work: from a forced displacement perspective' (May 2014) 75, 9 Tokyo University CDR Quarterly 46, and its Japanese version: Mai Kaneko, 'Dai 3 shō: Mukokuseki sha no mondai to UNHCR ni yoru taiō' [Chapter 3: Statelessness and UNHCR's Work] in Kei Hakata and others (eds), *Nanmin/kyōsei idō kenkyū no furontia* [New Frontiers in Refugee/Forced Migration Studies] (Gendai jinbunsha 2014) 75.

[54] For more details regarding UNHCR's role in addressing statelessness, see UNHCR, 'UNHCR Action to Address Statelessness: A Strategy Note' (March 2010) 4, <http://www.unhcr.org/refworld/docid/4b9e0c3d2.html> accessed 4 August 2019.

[55] The Hungarian Court then concluded that the requirement in Hungarian law, under which only lawfully staying persons could apply for stateless status was a breach of international law. 'Resolution 6/2015 (II.25.) of the Constitutional Court on the determination whether the term 'lawfully'

certainly is not legally 'binding', they must not be dismissed as irrelevant but regarded as authoritative statements whose disregard requires justification.[56]

## 2.5  Stateless Person Definition and Interpretation

The notion of statelessness is a mirror of the concept of nationality and describes a situation where an individual is 'not considered as a national by any state *under the operation of its law*', as stipulated in article 1 of the 1954 Convention relating to the Status of Stateless Persons. The 1961 Convention is silent on the definition of statelessness and it is generally understood that it refers to the one in the 1954 Convention.[57] This definition is recognized by the International Law Commission (ILC) as customary international law.[58] Thus, non-State parties to the 1954 Convention are also to adopt this definition. The UNHCR Handbook advises that this definition should be interpreted in a full and inclusive manner, bearing in mind the object and purpose of the 1954 Convention.[59] As the 1954 Convention definition is that a person is not considered as a national 'under the operation' of law, a careful analysis is necessary on how a State implements or 'applies its nationality laws in an individual's case in practice' and not just on the text of the relevant country's nationality law.[60] The Handbook stresses that the term 'law' in the definition should be interpreted broadly to cover not just legislation passed by parliaments, but also ministerial decrees, regulations, orders, judicial case law, and, in appropriate cases, customary practice.[61] If the written law is substantially modified by its implementation, the

---

in section 76(1) of Act II of 2007 on the Conditions of Entry and Stay of Third-Country Nationals is contrary to the Fundamental Act and the annulment thereof' (25 February 2015) <http://www.refworld.org/docid/5542301a4.html> accessed 4 August 2019.

[56] While said in the context of discussing UNHCR's supervisory role under article 35 of the 1951 Convention relating to the Status of Refugees, Walter Kälin's view can be considered relevant by analogy in statelessness law. Walter Kälin, 'Supervising the 1951 Convention Relating to the Status of Refugees: Article 35 and Beyond' in Erika Feller, Volker Türk and Frances Nicholson (eds), *Refugee Protection in International Law: UNHCR's Global Consultations on International Protection* (Cambridge University Press 2003) 627. Also, see in general James C Simeon, *The UNHCR and the Supervision of International Refugee Law* (Cambridge University Press 2013).

[57] Carol A. Batchelor, 'Stateless persons: some gaps in international protection' (1995) 7 International Journal of Refugee Law 232, 250.

[58] ILC, 'Draft Article on Diplomatic Protection with Commentaries' (2006) 49 <http://legal.un.org/ilc/texts/instruments/english/commentaries/9_8_2006.pdf> accessed 4 August 2019.

[59] Para 14 read together with the general guidance in later paragraphs (especially paras 22–56), UNHCR Handbook (2014). Also refer to article 31(1) of VCLT, which sets out this primary rule of interpretation of a treaty.

[60] UNHCR Handbook (2014) para 23.

[61] UNHCR Handbook (2014) para 22. For an analysis of State practice in light of these Handbook's positions, see for example Betsy L. Fisher, 'The operation of law in statelessness determinations under the 1954 Statelessness Convention' (2015) 33 Wisconsin International Law Journal 254;

determination of statelessness should be made in light of the modified version.[62] In conducting a statelessness assessment the current view of the competent authority responsible for conferring, withdrawing or for clarifying nationality status of the State concerned is crucial.[63] Where the competent authorities treat an individual as a non-national even though she or he would appear to meet the criteria for automatic acquisition of nationality, it is such authorities' position rather than the letter of the law that is determinative.[64] States thus 'must accept that a person is not a national of a particular State if the authorities of that State refuse to recognize that person as a national' and 'cannot avoid its obligations based on its own interpretation of another State's nationality laws which conflicts with the interpretation applied by the other State concerned'.[65] Where a State asserts that an individual holds another nationality, such assessment 'should be informed by consultations with and written confirmation from the State in question'.[66]

## 2.6   The Definition of Being 'considered a national'

In order to have further understanding of this definition of a 'stateless person', it is important to examine what it means to be 'considered a national'. UNHCR Handbook 2014 paragraph 53 discusses this briefly. In short, according to the Handbook, being a national means that a person is granted legal status for being considered by the relevant State to be under its jurisdiction on the basis of nationality. This is generally accompanied by the right of (re-)entry and residence in the State's territory.[67] The Handbook states, however, that the fact that in some countries the rights associated with nationality are fewer than those enjoyed by nationals of other States

---

Katia Bianchini, *Protecting Stateless Persons: The Implementation of the Convention Relating to the Status of Stateless Persons across EU States* (Brill | Nijhoff 2018), especially pp 223–32.

[62] UNHCR Handbook (2014) para 24.

[63] UNHCR Handbook (2014) paras 27–44.

[64] UNHCR Handbook (2014) para 37. While not citing UNHCR's guidance, in Japan for example, a family court adjudication took the same approach as part of deciding on the adoption arrangement. In this case, a child born out of wedlock of a Chinese woman in Japan was considered to be stateless. The Chinese embassy had stated that the child 'would not be given Chinese nationality or a passport' and that the child's 'birth registration form would not be accepted'. The family court noted that while according to the 1980 Chinese nationality law article 5 the child should have normally acquired Chinese nationality *jus sanguinis*, the 'possession or non-possession of nationality is a matter ultimately decided by China'. This is a positive adjudication reflecting the international standard that the view of the competent authorities, and not the determining authority's own reading of the text of the law, is decisive. Sendai Family Court, Adjudication, 24 June 2016 (*Heisei 28 nen*), unpublished. The author is grateful for Tazuru Ogawa of Across Japan for providing the information on this case.

[65] Tunis Conclusions (2014) para 6.

[66] UNHCR Guidelines 5 (2020) para 81.

[67] UNHCR Handbook (2014) para 53. *Hanrei Jihō No* 286, p 25 [13 December 1961 (*Shōwa 36 nen*)] (Tōkyō District Court).

or indeed fall short of those required in terms of international human rights obligations does not render nationals of that State stateless. According to the Handbook,
while diminished rights may raise issues regarding the effectiveness of the nationality
and violations of international human rights obligations, this is not relevant to the
application of the stateless person definition in the 1954 Convention. The Handbook
(2014) asserts that: 'Historically, there does not appear to have been any requirement
under international law for nationality to have a specific content in terms of rights of
individuals.'[68] However, there are continued discussions as to whether there is such
thing as the 'minimum substantive content of nationality', and whether mere possession of nationality without such minimum content already amounts to statelessness.
For example, Alice Edwards briefly mentions that the lack of (re-)admission prospect
may amount to statelessness 'depending on the circumstances'.[69]

Researchers such as Gábor Gyulai[70] and Hajime Akiyama[71] look at this issue from
a different and practical perspective—they have cast a rather provocative question,
which is, whether not being registered with the authorities could amount to 'not
being considered a national', from a definitional point of view. Gyulai, highlighting
the term 'consider' in the 1954 Convention statelessness definition, states:

> 'Consider' is a transitive verb, referring to an action through which a state attributes a certain
> quality to a person. [...] Can a State 'consider' a person in a certain manner, can it apply
> its law in practice in a way that is adapted to the individual circumstances of the person, if
> it is not aware of this person's existence? This indicates a significant discrepancy between
> the traditional approach towards nationality and the more 'practice and protection' oriented
> interpretation of the 1954 Statelessness Convention and UNHCR guidance.[72]

---

[68] UNHCR Handbook (2014) fn 37.

[69] Alice Edwards and Laura Van Waas, 'The Meaning of Nationality in International Law in an Era of
Human Rights—Procedural and Substantive Aspects' in Alice Edwards and Laura van Waas (eds),
*Nationality and Statelessness Under International Law* (Cambridge University Press 2014) 11, 41.
As cited by Edwards in this article, there historically exists a comparatively larger accumulation of
case law and academic literatures on the definition, nature and function of nationality. To give some of
the well-cited ones: Paul Weis, *Nationality and Statelessness in International Law* (2nd edn, Kluwer
Academic Publishers Group 1979); Ian Brownlie, 'The relations of nationality in public international
law' (1963) 39 British Year Book of International Law 284; Peter J Spiro, 'A new international law
of citizenship' (2011) 105 American Journal of International Law 694; Ivan Shearer and Brian
Opeskin, 'Nationality and Statelessness', in Brian Opeskin, Richard Perruchoud and Jillyanne
Redpath Cross (eds), *Foundations of International Migration Law* (Cambridge University Press
2012) 93–122; Eric Fripp, *Nationality and Statelessness in the International Law of Refugee Status*
(Hart Publishing 2016) 51–2, in particular section A8.

[70] Gábor Gyulai for European Council on Refugees and Exiles, 'The right to a nationality of refugee
children born in the EU and the Relevance of the EU Charter of Fundamental Rights' (February
2017) 12 <https://www.ecre.org/wp-content/uploads/2016/12/refugee-children-nationality-LEAP-
leaflet.pdf> accessed 4 August 2019.

[71] See Hajime Akiyama, 'Mukokusekisha towa dareka: Kokusaihōniokeru mukokusekisha no teigi
to mitōrokusha no kanrensei kara' ['Who is a Stateless Person? Definition of a Stateless Person
in International Law and Unregistered Persons'] (2015) 67, 22 Kankyō sozō [Social-Human
Environmentology].

[72] Gábor Gyulai, 'The right to a nationality of refugee children born in the EU' (Hungarian Helsinki
Committee December 2010) 12.

While the lack of registration, documentation, and prolonged inability of establishing possession of nationality has been described in recent years as one of the causes of statelessness (see Sect. 2.9), the predominant discourse has explained this phenomenon as a matter of proof or evidence. Akiyama and Gyulai's discussions are unique in a sense that they look at this phenomenon as a matter of the content of what it means 'to be considered as a national under the operation of laws', and suggest how being undocumented could possibly fulfil the definition of being stateless. Nevertheless, as Gyulai also points out,[73] further development in discussions, doctrine, jurisprudence and literature seems necessary to properly clarify this issue, which goes well beyond the scope of this book.

## 2.7  Notes on Other Related Concepts

It will be useful to review some of the terminology that is used in statelessness discourse as well as in this book. More specifically, the terms 'de facto stateless persons', 'persons of undetermined nationality' and 'persons at risk of statelessness' could be used for example by some authors to refer to cases of foundlings (persons of unknown parents) for whom the acquisition of nationality has not been confirmed because their legal parents have not definitively been identified. However, for the reasons detailed below, I choose not to use the first and the third terms for precision purposes except when citing other authors, while 'persons of undetermined nationality' is used to a limited extent in Sect. 5.7.

### 2.7.1  De Facto Stateless Persons

This term, that the author chooses *not* to use, and which is no longer reported on[74] in UNHCR statistical reports, is still frequently used in discourse on statelessness by practitioners and academics in different fields, including in some documents cited in this book. It thus needs clarification. The Final Act of the Conference that drew up the 1961 Convention, which is non-binding in nature, contains a reference to 'de facto' stateless persons. Resolution No I recommends: 'persons who are stateless de facto should as far as possible be treated as stateless de jure to enable them to acquire

---

[73] Ibid 12.

[74] This was mid-2019, 'based on an assessment that de facto statelessness was often incorrectly used to refer to people who meet the statelessness definition in the 1954 Convention and who should therefore be reported as such'. UNHCR, 'Global Trends Forced Displacement in 2019' (18 June 2020) 70 <https://www.unhcr.org/5ee200e37.pdf> accessed 21 September 2020. See also the technical paper stating 'Distinctions between stateless and de facto stateless populations and what comprises undetermined populations are especially ambiguous'. UNHCR Statistical Reporting on Statelessness (October 2019) 9 and 11. <https://www.unhcr.org/statistics/unhcrstats/5d9e182e7/unhcr-statistical-reporting-statelessness.html> accessed 21 September 2020.

an effective nationality'.[75] The definition of de facto statelessness has evolved and even expanded over years as detailed by Hugh Massey in 2010, where it was at times defined as 'persons lacking an effective nationality', 'persons who do not enjoy the rights attached to their nationality', and 'persons who are unable to establish their nationality (or who are of undetermined nationality)'.[76] In recent years, the concept of de facto statelessness has been considered by the UNHCR as well as a number of scholars and practitioners to be *counter-productive*, not least as it has often led to a narrow interpretation of the concept of statelessness due to the concept's broad and ambiguous definition or interpretation.[77] At the same time, in contrast with 'de facto stateless persons', persons who fall within the scope of article 1(1) of the 1954 Convention have been sometimes referred to as 'de jure stateless persons' even though the qualification 'de jure' is not used in the Convention itself. The UNHCR Handbook thus emphasizes that: '[C]are must be taken that those who qualify as 'stateless persons' under article 1(1) of the 1954 Convention are recognized as such and *not* mistakenly referred to as 'de facto stateless persons.'[78] This is important not to exclude those who meet the article 1(1) definition from protection guaranteed under the 1954 Convention, and to have their children's statelessness avoided under the 1961 Convention.

That being said, the 'definition' of a 'de facto stateless person' broadly agreed upon during the UNHCR-convened Expert Meeting on the concept of stateless persons under international law in 2010 is: '[P]ersons outside the country of *their nationality* who are unable or, for valid reasons, unwilling to avail themselves of the protection of that country' (emphasis added).[79] Protection, in this sense, refers to the right of diplomatic protection exercised by a State of nationality in order to remedy an internationally wrongful act against one of its nationals, as well as diplomatic and

---

[75] There is also an implicit reference in the Final Act of the 1954 Convention. See UNHCR Handbook (2014) para 7, as well as fn 3.

[76] Hugh Massey, 'UNHCR and De Facto Statelessness, LPPR/2010/01' (April 2010) <https://www. refworld.org/docid/4bbf387d2.html> accessed 4 August 2019, especially pp 27–52. See also Mai Kaneko, 'Mukokuseki ni kansuru UNHCR shin handobukku/gaidorain tō no kaisetsu' ['Commentary on the newly published UNHCR Handbook and Guidelines on Statelessness'] (December 2014) 45, 47–8, 4 Refugee Studies Journal 45.

[77] See for example, Laura van Waas, *Nationality Matters: Statelessness under International Law* (Intersentia 2008); Laura van Waas, 'The UN Statelessness Conventions' in Alice Edwards and Laura van Waas (eds), *Nationality and Statelessness under International Law* (Cambridge University Press 2014) 64 and 81; and Jason Tucker, 'Questioning de facto statelessness: by looking at de facto citizenship' (2014) 19 Tilburg Law Review 276; Stephanie Gordon, 'Defining Statelessness: a Chinese Case Study' (5 February 2015) <https://www.ein.org.uk/blog/defining-stateless ness-chinese-case-study> accessed 4 August 2019; Katia Bianchini, *Protecting Stateless Persons: The Implementation of the Convention Relating to the Status of Stateless Persons across EU States* (Brill | Nijhoff 2018), pp 233–4.

[78] UNHCR Handbook (2014) para 7.

[79] UNHCR, 'Expert Meeting – The Concept of Stateless Persons under International Law ("Prato Conclusions")' (May 2010) <http://www.refworld.org/docid/4ca1ae002.html> accessed 4 August 2019, II.A.2., UNHCR Handbook (2014) fn 4.

consular protection and assistance generally, including in relation to the right to return to the State of nationality.[80]

While this issue in general is relatively of peripheral importance to the central theme of this book itself, the author wishes to provide some views on this to contribute to the ongoing discussion over the concept of de facto statelessness. First, it is crucial to note within the above definition within the Tunis Conclusion (2014) that a de facto stateless person *does* have a 'country of nationality'. The same document further indicates that for an individual to fall within this definition, she or he must *'formally possess a nationality'*.[81] While there is no definition of the word 'formally recognized as a national', the term needs to be understood in light of the 1954 Convention and the UNHCR's relevant guidance in the Handbook (2014). In particular as per paragraphs 22–56 of the Handbook, it should be recalled that a person needs to be currently considered a national under the operation of law by the competent authorities of the country of origin, rather than that she or he 'appears to', or 'should', be a national based on the letter of the relevant nationality law. Apparently as a reflection of the 'low' standard of proof that the Handbook (2014) advocates for statelessness recognition, which is 'to a reasonable degree',[82] paragraph 92 of the Handbook also states: '[S]tatelessness *will not be established* to a reasonable degree where the determination authority is able to point to *clear evidence* that the individual is *a national*' (emphasis added).

A flip side of the same coin may be that there needs to be 'clear evidence' that an individual is a national, to be considered to 'formally possess' a nationality. However, this 'clear evidence' appears difficult to secure, in some of the persons who might be referred to as de facto stateless persons.

One of the examples of such persons are (the majority of) refugees—particularly their children born abroad,[83] who have been generally considered 'typical examples' of de facto stateless persons. It is true that only a relatively small number of refugees are born stateless prior to crossing the border from their country of origin, or have their nationality withdrawn before or after their flight to another country. At the same time, it might become difficult—depending on individual circumstances—for some refugees to prove that they are 'formally' or 'clearly' considered nationals. This is not least because some refugees lack or lose identity or nationality documents, and are by definition unable or unwilling (except for those fleeing a non-State agent of persecution, or generalized violence) to approach the authorities of the country of nationality to acquire proof of being considered a national. This is exacerbated with the lapse of time, and across the generations—becoming more evident for children and descendants of refugees born in the countries of asylum. While most refugee children are supposed to have automatically acquired their parents' nationality by *jus sanguinis* at birth under the law of their country(ies) of nationality, there is often no way for them to directly confirm such a fact. Many States simply do not respond

---

[80] Ibid II.A.2., UNHCR Handbook (2014) fn 4.

[81] Ibid II.A.3.

[82] UNHCR Handbook (2014) para 91.

[83] See for example UNHCR Guidelines 4 (2012) para 28.

to individual inquiries.[84] Some asylum-seekers or refugees do indeed approach the authorities for a passport issuance or birth registration, and some of them are indeed denied a passport (re-)issuance or birth registration of their children.[85] But in many of these cases the consular authorities do not 'articulate' the reasons for denying such consular assistance—whether it is because due to their status as asylum-seekers or refugees, or because of their lack of (parents') proof as to nationality, or that they do not consider the individuals as nationals.[86] While refusal of consular assistance or refusal to (re-)admit the person into the territory does *not* always mean that the person is stateless, it could also constitute indirect evidence of statelessness, depending again on individual circumstances.

Importantly, under the UNHCR's guidance, when assessing nationality in the absence of evidence of the position of competent authorities, such as when an individual has never come into contact with a State's competent authorities: '[I]t is important to assess the State's general attitude in terms of nationality status of *persons who are similarly situated*.'[87] Having said this, it might often become difficult to define 'persons similarly situated', and gather sufficient evidence such as publicly available reports on the 'general attitude' of the competent authorities towards such persons (including any possibility of loss or deprivation of nationality)—in order to conclude there is 'clear evidence' that the refugees concerned are currently considered nationals, 'within a reasonable time'.[88]

While often not the case, paragraph 12 of the Prato Expert Meeting Conclusions also notes that, 'unresolved situations of de facto statelessness, in particular over two or more generations, may lead to de jure statelessness'. Reference should also be made to the analysis by Gyulai in Sect. 2.6 on the nationality status of children of refugees, as well as the Sect. 2.7.2 on the relationship between documentation and nationality.

---

[84] UNHCR Handbook (2014) para 97.

[85] Ayane Odagawa and others, 'Typology of Stateless Persons in Japan' (2017) 62–6 and 70–3 <https://www.unhcr.org/jp/wp-content/uploads/sites/34/2018/01/TYPOLOGY-OF-STATEL ESS-PERSONS-IN-JAPAN_webEnglish.pdf> accessed 4 August 2019, See for an example of an episode of a child of Vietnamese refugees born abroad being issued a letter by the Vietnamese embassy in the Hague that her 'claim to be recognized as a Vietnamese national was not evidenced sufficiently by documentary proof' (despite the fact that she had shown the embassy officials her parent's Vietnamese passports and her own birth certificate). This case has clearer evidence of statelessness due to the issuance of such a letter, but in many cases verbal statements by the consulates can be the only indirect evidence. Sangita Jaghai, 'Statelessness at home: the story of a stateless student at Tilburg Law School' (2014) 110, 19 Tilburg Law Review 108.

[86] See the preceding footnote. According to the Study Group on Statelessness in Japan, 'The expression of the views by the consulates […] is significant when one assesses the nationality […]. However, one cannot always get a clear expression of the view that "the person concerned is not a national" along with the reasons for such a view from the authorities'. Ayane Odagawa and others, 'Typology of Stateless Persons in Japan' (2017) 160 <https://www.unhcr.org/jp/wp-content/uploads/sites/34/2018/01/TYPOLOGY-OF-STATELESS-PERSONS-IN-JAPAN_webEnglish.pdf> accessed 4 August 2019.

[87] UNHCR Handbook (2014) para 38.

[88] UNHCR Handbook (2014) paras 71, 74 and 75.

More discussions are thus necessary to define what it means to have 'clear evidence' of nationality, or what it means to recognize statelessness at a standard of proof of 'to a reasonable degree' in practice, which goes beyond the scope of this book. Thus, all the more careful assessment must be made when classifying certain persons to be de facto stateless rather than de jure stateless.

Considering the foregoing, the author avoids using the term 'de facto statelessness' and also eschew qualifying persons as defined in article 1(1) of the 1954 Convention as 'de jure' stateless persons in this book.

## 2.7.2  Persons of Undetermined Nationality

UNHCR's ExCom Conclusion[89] No 106 (LVII) refers to the concept of 'undetermined nationality' and requests States and the UNHCR to make efforts to identify persons whose nationality is undetermined. In general, a person is referred to be of undetermined nationality when they 'lack proof of possession of any nationality and at the same time have or are regarded as having important links to more than one State',[90] where a preliminary review has shown that it is not yet known whether she or he possesses a nationality or is stateless. Some States use 'unknown nationality', 'unclear nationality', or 'nationality under investigation' instead. As to be discussed especially in Sect. 5.7, finding that somebody is of undetermined nationality should only be taken as an interim measure and the determination needs to be made as soon as possible so as not to prolong one's status of undetermined nationality.[91]

---

[89] See UNHCR ExCom, 'Conclusion on Identification, Prevention and Reduction of Statelessness and Protection of Stateless Persons No 106 (LVII)—2006' (6 October 2006) <https://www.refworld.org/docid/453497302.html> accessed 4 August 2019.

[90] UNHCR, 'Global Trends Forced Displacement in 2019' (18 June 2020) 66 <https://www.unhcr.org/5ee200e37.pdf> accessed 21 September 2020. More precisely, persons with undetermined nationality for UNHCR statistical purposes are defined as those are persons who 'Lack proof of possession of any nationality, [a]nd fulfill at least one of the following two criteria: (a) Have links to more than one State on the basis of birth, descent, marriage or habitual residence or (b) Are perceived and treated by authorities in the State of residence as possessing links which give rise to a claim of nationality of another State on the basis of such elements as historic ties, race, ethnicity, language or religion (replaced c) and (d) with (a) and (b) as the original appeared to be typos, author)'. See UNHCR, 'Annual Statistical Report Guidelines' (January 2020) 15–16 <https://pop data.unhcr.org/ASR_instructions.pdf> accessed 15 September 2020.

[91] Para 22, Council of Europe: Committee of Ministers, *Recommendation CM/Rec(2009)13 and explanatory memorandum of the Committee of Ministers to member states on the nationality of children* (Council of Europe Publishing 9 May 2009). UNHCR Guidelines 4 (2012) para 22. See also the UNHCR paper on statistics stating: 'The definition of undetermined populations also raises questions regarding the threshold for when populations should be recorded as stateless and when as undetermined nationality'. UNHCR Statistical Reporting on Statelessness (October 2019) 11–12. <https://www.unhcr.org/statistics/unhcrstats/5d9e182e7/unhcr-statistical-reporting-statelessness.html> accessed 21 September 2020.

### 2.7.3  Persons at Risk of Statelessness

Another common term in the statelessness literature is a person 'at risk of state-lessness'. There is no universal or established definition for this term either, but it is generally used to describe persons who are (in possession of nationality but) at relatively heightened risk (and not just a mere possibility) of becoming stateless. Identifying such persons is helpful for the purpose of preventing statelessness from arising. However, the term 'persons at risk of statelessness' is also often used to refer to persons without proof of possession of nationality and at risk of not being recognized as nationals—in such a case, such a person's possession of nationality is often not firmly established (while statelessness cannot be declared yet either). In such a context, the term 'undetermined nationality' and a 'at risk of statelessness' overlap and become synonymous. At any rate, 'risk' is a question of a degree and not everybody lacking birth registration, for example, should be referred to as a person at risk of statelessness. See, for example, Sect. 2.9.

## 2.8  Causes of Statelessness Including Foundlinghood

An individual can either be born to be stateless or lose her/his nationality and become stateless at a later stage in life. The main causes of statelessness can be summarized into several direct causes, such as conflict of nationality laws, gaps in or lack of neces-sary safeguards in nationality laws, administrative barriers in accessing nationality and arbitrary deprivation of nationality. In addition, lack of documentation could lead to risk of statelessness, as discussed in detail in Sect. 2.9. Discrimination (for example against women or ethnic or religious minorities), migration and displacement often increase the risk of statelessness.[92]

Conflict of laws or gaps and nationality laws are major causes for statelessness to occur at birth. For example, when a child is born in a country that grants nationality solely based on the *jus sanguinis* principle, to parents whose country of nationality adopts a strict *jus soli* principle, the child will be left stateless. In countries which only apply the *jus sanguinis* principle, stateless persons have no choice but to pass on their statelessness to their children. Laws limiting women's ability to pass on nationality to their children produce statelessness if the children are unable to acquire their father's citizenship.

Based on the hypothesis made in Sect. 1.4 that a foundling refers to a person of unknown parentage found when a child whose birthplace may or may not be known (discussed in detail after Chap. 3 and on), foundlings would be stateless in the absence of a specific safeguard, as the facts forming the basis for acquiring nationality by *jus sanguinis* and (in some cases) by *jus soli* are unknown.

---

[92] For a useful summary of the causes of statelessness, see UNHCR, 'Self-Study Module on State-lessness' (1 October 2012) <https://www.refworld.org/docid/50b899602.html> accessed 4 August 2019.

Some may lose nationality and become stateless later in life upon change of civil status such as marriage, divorce or adoption due to conflict of or gaps in nationality laws. Statelessness can also occur upon a person's attempt to change her or his nationality, such as when renouncing the current nationality but failing to naturalize. Some states provide for the automatic or non-automatic loss of citizenship if a person has taken up residence abroad for a prolonged period of time. States might deprive of nationality individuals or groups of persons.[93] State succession or redrawing of international borders has been known as another cause of statelessness throughout history.[94]

## 2.9   Documentation of Birth, Parentage and Nationality

While it used to be understood that statelessness is typically—if not mainly—caused by the 'conflict of laws' situations as described above, the lack of documentation (civil or nationality registration) as a 'new' (while not actually new) or major cause[95] of statelessness has increasingly been recognized in recent years. How the lack of documentation relating to parentage and birthplace is interlinked with foundlinghood will now be examined.

---

[93] Note that, as discussed in Sect. 7.6.1, deprivation and loss of nationality resulting in statelessness is generally considered to be 'arbitrary' if it is not prescribed by law; is not the least intrusive means proportionate to achieving a legitimate aim; and/or takes place without due process.

[94] State succession refers to any transfer of territory or sovereignty between states, that is where an existing State is replaced by two or more States; when part of a State separates to form a new State; when territory is transferred from one State to another; or when two or more States unite to form a new State.

[95] Laura van Waas, *Nationality Matters: Statelessness under International Law* (Intersentia 2008) 151–2. See also UNHCR, 'Birth Registration: A Topic Proposed for an Executive Committee Conclusion on International Protection' (9 February 2010) <http://www.unhcr.org/refworld/docid/4b97a3242.html> accessed 4 August 2019. See in general Benjamin N. Lawrance and Jacqueline Stevens, *Citizenship in Question: Evidentiary Birthright and Statelessness* (Duke University Press 2017). See also Inge Sturkenboom, 'Under the Radar and Under Protected: The Urgent Need to Address Stateless Children's Rights' (8 November 2012) <https://www.statelessness.eu/blog/under-radar-and-under-protected-urgent-need-address-stateless-children%E2%80%99s-rights> accessed 4 August 2019. Michelle Foster, Jane McAdam and Davina Wadley, 'Part two: the prevention and reduction of statelessness in Australia – an ongoing challenge' (2017) 40 Melb UL Rev 456, 481–2 in particular. See also Mai Kaneko, 'Statelessness and UNHCR's work: from a forced displacement perspective' (May 2014) 9 Tokyo University CDR Quarterly 46, 49.

### 2.9.1 Lack of Documentation is Not Equivalent to Statelessness

To be very clear at the outset, under many nationality laws, nationality is acquired automatically as soon as the substantive legal criteria are met, independent of registration and documentation of the person as a national.[96] Nevertheless, as Bronwen Manby states: 'The question of identification is conceptually distinct from the question of legal status in a country, but increasingly inseparable in practice'.[97] As UNHCR Guidelines 4 (2012) acknowledges, 'registration of the birth provides proof of descent and of place of birth and, therefore, underpins implementation of the 1961 Convention and related human rights norms'.[98] It has been pointed out that individuals who have no birth registration certificate to prove their parentage and birthplace can be denied proof of nationality, and may be at risk of not being recognized by the relevant competent authorities as their national.[99] Lack of registration of marriages, divorces and deaths can also render a child stateless where the mother cannot transmit her own nationality in the given situation.[100]

Theoretical entitlement to a nationality is 'increasingly not meaningful if a state does not recognize the person as a national' through the issuance of the relevant documents that enable them to function as proof of nationality including birth certificates, national identity cards, and passports.[101]

It has also been emphasized that migrants, trafficked persons, refugees and other displaced persons can be particularly vulnerable, depending on their individual circumstances, to lack of documentation and consequent statelessness.[102]

---

[96] UNHCR Guidelines 4 (2012) para 55.

[97] Bronwen Manby, 'Identification in the Context of Forced Displacement: Identification for Development' (2016) 4 <http://documents.worldbank.org/curated/en/375811469772770030/pdf/107276-WP-P156810-PUBLIC.pdf> accessed 4 August 2019.

[98] UNHCR Guidelines 4 (2012) para 55. Indeed, Goal 7, one of the ten 'UNHCR Global Actions to End Statelessness by 2024' as part of #IBelong campaign is to 'ensure birth registration for the prevention of statelessness'. UNHCR, 'Global Action Plan to End Statelessness' (4 November 2014) <http://www.refworld.org/docid/545b47d64.html> accessed 4 August 2019.

[99] See for example UNHCR, 'Good Practices Paper – Action 7: Ensuring birth registration for the prevention of statelessness' (November 2017) <http://www.refworld.org/docid/5a0ac8f94.html> accessed 4 August 2019, in particular Sect. 1.3.

[100] UNHCR, 'In Search of Solutions: Addressing Statelessness in the Middle East and North Africa' (2016) 4 <http://www.refworld.org/docid/5829c32a4.html> accessed 4 August 2019. See also Sect. 2.10 on the relationship between parentage and nationality acquisition.

[101] Bronwen Manby, 'Identification in the Context of Forced Displacement: Identification for Development' (2016) 5 <http://documents.worldbank.org/curated/en/375811469772770030/pdf/107276-WP-P156810-PUBLIC.pdf> accessed 4 August 2019.

[102] See among others, ibid; Sophie Nonnenmacher and Ryszard Cholewinski, 'The Nexus between Statelessness and Migration' in Alice Edwards and Laura van Waas (eds), *Nationality and Statelessness Under International Law* (Cambridge University Press 2014) 247; Catherine Blanchard and Sarah Joy, 'Can't Stay. Can't Go. – Refused Asylum Seekers Who Cannot Be Returned' (2017) 8–9 <https://www.refworld.org/docid/591965984.html> accessed 4 August 2019, in particular Sect. 1.3 (The Risk of Statelessness); Zahra Albarazi and Laura van Waas, 'Statelessness and Displacement:

In addition to having their documents that they initially possessed lost or destroyed, some proportion of the world has never been registered at birth or later sometimes for over generations. Lack of registration may be due to discrimination, poverty or lack of awareness. The situation of 'risk of statelessness' arising out of lack of birth and citizenship registration for the Roma population as 'legally invisible persons' in the western Balkans and elsewhere has been highlighted and efforts are being strengthened in recent years.[103] Lack of birth registration might simply be because of the absence of a systematic mechanism of documenting civil or nationality status in one's country of origin in general. As Polly Price and others point out, even the system of the unconditional grant of nationality by *jus soli*, as is common in the Americas, and otherwise considered highly effective in preventing statelessness, might not function properly where it is not accompanied by meticulous and generally recognized documentation.[104]

True, according to the United Nations Children's Fund (UNICEF), the births of around one fourth of the global population of children under five have never been registered,[105] and most of them are not at risk of statelessness. Many unregistered or undocumented people—especially those who remain in their countries of origin—do not necessarily face the situation where their nationality itself is doubted, such as in the sense of being threatened to be expelled from the territory[106]—while they might have difficulties accessing some of the rights that those with proof of nationality can. Whether the lack of registration could amount to statelessness (and not just 'risk of statelessness') can also depend on individual circumstances including the reasons for

Scoping Paper' (2015) <http://www.institutesi.org/stateless_displacement.pdf> accessed 4 August 2019; Zahra Albarazi and Laura van Waas, 'Understanding Statelessness in the Syria Refugee Context' (2016) <http://www.refworld.org/docid/584021494.html> accessed 4 August 2019; Lucy Hovil, 'Ensuring that Today's Refugees are not Tomorrow's stateless Persons: Solutions in a Refugee Context' in Alice Edwards and Laura van Waas (eds), *Nationality and Statelessness under International Law* (Cambridge University Press 2014). Mai Kaneko, 'Statelessness and UNHCR's work: from a forced displacement perspective' (May 2014), 9 Tokyo University CDR Quarterly 46.

[103] Among others, see European Roma Rights Centre (ERRC), ENS and ISI, 'Statelessness, Discrimination and Marginalisation of Roma in the Western Balkans and Ukraine' (October 2017) <https://www.statelessness.eu/sites/www.statelessness.eu/files/attachments/resources/roma-belong.pdf> accessed 4 August 2019.

[104] According to Polly Price, for example in Mexico, up to 30 per cent of the children born in Mexico might remain unregistered since birth, and when they migrate in an irregular manner to the US, their nationality can be questioned. Polly J. Price, 'Jus Soli and Statelessness: A Comparative Perspective from the Americas' in Benjamin N. Lawrance and Jacqueline Stevens (eds), *Citizenship in Question: Evidentiary Birthright and Statelessness* (Duke University Press 2017) 2, 7–42, 27, 496; Polly J Price, 'Stateless in the United States: current reality and a future prediction' (2013) 46 Vand J Transnat'l L 443.

[105] UNICEF Data, 'Birth Registration' (January 2018) <https://data.unicef.org/topic/child-protection/birth-registration/#> accessed 4 August 2019.

[106] See the definition of being considered a 'national' under Sect. 2.6.

such lack of registration and whether the lack of registration has not been resolved—within a reasonable timeframe—after 'actions reasonably expected to be taken by persons similarly situated have been taken' by the individuals or others concerned.[107]

Even where undocumented people migrate or become displaced, there can be ways to establish their identity and nationality in the absence of any documentary proof. This can be done for example by assessing the statements of the persons themselves, their family members, neighbours or community leaders and thus evaluating the credibility of their possession of nationality as done by some governments.[108]

### 2.9.2   When Establishing Nationality Without Documents Becomes Difficult

Having said the above, establishing ones' identity and nationality without documents can be difficult, for example for those who left the country of nationality early in their life or the second generation and so on, born outside their (grand)parents' countries of origin. The system of registration of birth of children of nationals born abroad (especially while irregularly staying in a foreign country) itself might be complicated with regard to some States.[109] Worse, if they and their ancestors have lived without documentation over generations and/or have moved between a number of countries—as often observed in this era of migration and forced displacement—compounded by the lack of awareness on the importance of documentation, the situation can become really complicated. In such a case, not only the person's but the (grand) parents' identity including the key facts such as their own parentage, date and place of birth, marriage, and duration of residence in the country(ies) of (previous) habitual residence can go undocumented. It may be that the persons involved themselves do not know these facts either.

To make matters more complicated, persons born out of wedlock of parents who are nationals of States where the restriction in the civil registration law, criminal

---

[107] See especially 'Category L (Unregistered Persons)' in Ayane Odagawa and others, 'Typology of Stateless Persons in Japan' (2017) 124–129 <https://www.unhcr.org/jp/wp-content/uploads/sites/34/2018/01/TYPOLOGY-OF-STATELESS-PERSONS-IN-JAPAN_webEnglish.pdf> accessed 4 August 2019.

[108] See for example, Jana M. Seng, 'Cambodian nationality law and the repatriation of convicted aliens under the Illegal Immigration Reform and Immigrant Responsibility Act' (March 2000) 443, 467, 10 Pac Rim L & Pol'y J 443, citing a political consular of the embassy of Cambodia in the US. As per Cambodia, if a (former) resettled refugee being subjected to deportation has no citizenship documentation, officials often conduct an interview to decide whether to readmit him, asking about the fluency in Khmer, familiarity with Cambodian culture and former long-term residence in Cambodia—which can, however, be difficult to prove and be subject to abuse of power by officials according to Seng.

[109] Tirana Legal Aid Society (TLAS) and others, 'Statelessness, Discrimination and Marginalisation of Roma in Albania' (February 2018) 29 <https://www.statelessness.eu/sites/www.statelessness.eu/files/attachments/resources/roma-belong-albania-english-language.pdf> accessed 4 August 2019.

penalties for adultery, and social stigma prevent or deter unwed parents from registering their children's births—such as many countries in MENA region—may end up facing difficulties establishing the existence of legally recognized parents.[110] This includes cases where the father does not acknowledge paternity and the mother is not allowed to register the birth of a non-marital child under the civil registration law.[111] Even where the mother–child relationship under the letter of family law *ex lege* has been established for the fact of parturition,[112] if there is practically no way of registering the parenthood, it becomes tantamount to the non-existence of the mother–child relationship. A number of States that adopt the paternal *jus sanguinis* principle do exceptionally allow women to pass on nationality to their children born out of wedlock or of unknown father. Even so, without being able to officially register the birth and the mother–child relationship, it becomes difficult to confirm the possession of such nationality.[113]

Undocumented persons (on the move) can face even more problems when they are separated from or lose contact with their parents (and other relatives), or when their parents are deceased—as it will then become logistically impossible to prove not only their nationality but also parentage (and date or place of birth which the parents could have been able to testify even verbally).

---

[110] With regard to how the combination of gender discriminatory nationality laws, civil registration requirements, criminal penalties for adultery, and societal attitudes prevent or deter unwed parents from registering their children's births and creates statelessness, see Betsy Fisher, 'Why Non-Marital Children in the MENA Region Face a Risk of Statelessness' (January 2015) <http://harvardhrj. com/wp-content/uploads/2015/01/Fisher_HRJ_01-05-15.pdf> accessed 4 August 2019, and Betsy Fisher, 'Statelessness in the GCC: Gender Discrimination beyond Nationality Law, ISI Statelessness Working Paper Series No 2015/01' (December 2015) 3 <http://www.institutesi.org/WP2015_01. pdf> accessed 4 August 2019.

[111] According to Betsy Fisher, 'Why Non-Marital Children in the MENA Region Face a Risk of Statelessness' (January 2015) <http://harvardhrj.com/wp-content/uploads/2015/01/Fisher_HRJ_01-05-15.pdf> accessed 4 August 2019, any form of birth registration in Bahrain, Qatar, and Saudi Arabia, requires the parents to show documentation of their marriage.

[112] Email from Betsy Fisher to author (24 February 2017). The author thanks Betsy Fisher for pointing to the Bahraini Family Law (No. 19/2009) article 71 as an example of legislation that appears to suggest that maternity even for an extramarital child is established by the mere fact of delivery under family law regardless of whether the birth can be registered: 'Filiation of the mother is established and its effects ensue whether it was the result of a legal relationship or an illegal relationship resulting in birth, or the admission of the mother'.

[113] Betsy Fisher indeed suggests that the persons born out of wedlock in such countries may only be able to have their birth registered as 'foundlings' to acquire nationality even though the parent(s) have not 'abandoned' them (and are indeed caring for them). (Former) foundling citizens, however, face a severe social stigma in the region. Betsy Fisher, 'Statelessness in the GCC: Gender Discrimination beyond Nationality Law, Statelessness Working Paper Series No 2015/01' (December 2015) 3 <http://www.institutesi.org/WP2015_01.pdf> accessed 4 August 2019.

### 2.9.3   Late Birth Registration as a Measure to Prevent Statelessness Arising from Lack of Documentation

To prevent the statelessness arising from lack of documentation, allowing 'late/subsequent birth registration' (and consequent recognition of nationality), free of charge without rigorous conditions and evidentiary requirements, has been considered an effective measure.[114] Such measures have apparently been allowed even in situations where the person's birth within the territory cannot be (firmly) established. Moreover, some reports seem to suggest that a person's legal parentage can be registered via late registration when such parent–child relationship might not be—at least firmly—established, where the person was born at home, or with parents having already deceased or gone missing leaving limited information, and when DNA testing or other measures to establish descent are not possible.[115] When such birth registration actually leads to certification of citizenship acquired by *jus sanguinis* with the registered parent(s) being a national, then that is quite positive.

Indeed, it is normally more desirable that a person's legal parentage and birthplace—even though not documented initially—can be documented with evidentiary requirements being lowered. However, in some states, such late documentation might not be allowed in some situations, or might not necessarily lead to nationality confirmation.

### 2.9.4   Lack of Documentation of Parentage and Having Unknown Parents

There is indeed only a fine line between not having one's parentage registered, and having (legally) unknown parents. Nevertheless, such a linkage is not always recognized, partly due to the lack of clarity as to the definition of 'unknown-ness' of the parentage and the applicable standard of proof.

For example, with regard to Serbia, in a survey report that is focused on birth and citizenship registration of Roma, Ashkali, and Egyptians, there is a reference that one of the reasons for a proportion of respondents in 2010 and 2015 not being registered on vital records of citizens was that some of their parents are 'unknown': 'In this situation, the most common reason is the fact that they are not registered in birth registries, but *there are other reasons, such as unknown* or indifferent *parents (sic)*

---

[114] See for instance the good practice providing for late birth registration from Serbia and Kosovo in UNHCR, 'Handbook on Statelessness in the OSCE Area: International Standards and Good Practices' (28 February 2017) 54–5 <http://www.refworld.org/docid/58b81c404.html> accessed 4 August 2019. See also UNHCR, 'Good Practices Paper—Action 7: Ensuring birth registration for the prevention of statelessness' (November 2017) <http://www.refworld.org/docid/5a0ac8f94.html> accessed 4 August 2019.

[115] See Case E. O. on pp 35–7 of Vaša prava BiH, *Legal Analysis of Legislation of Bosnia and Herzegovina Regulating the Area of Birth Registration* (2018).

*Kosovo* descent, etc.' (emphasis added).[116] In such a case of 'unknown parents', however, rather than late birth registration, the applicability of article 13 of the Citizenship Act which automatically grants nationality to a child of unknown parents found in Serbia[117] could have been explored, which was apparently not the case and not mentioned in the report.[118]

Another report which is dedicated to examining the issues related to lack of birth registration and risk of statelessness in Bosnia and Herzegovina also mentions persons of unknown parents, again without discussing the applicability of article 7 of the country's nationality law granting nationality to children of unknown parents born or found in the territory.

> A special category are persons who were born at home twenty or more years ago, whose parents died or are *unknown*, and who do not know the date and place of their birth, which makes the process of their registration in civil records very difficult. In such cases, the procedure is more complicated; they must find witnesses who would be heard before the competent authority in relation to circumstances of their birth. However, those witnesses often cannot recall all the relevant facts essential to the process, such as the correct date and place of the birth, and other circumstances relating to the birth, due to the lapse of time. Very often, these persons do not have any physical evidence of their identity as they have been 'legally invisible' their whole life. (emphasis added)[119]

It is evident from this that lack of birth registration indeed results in unknown parentage. However, the report does not mention anywhere the applicability of article 7 of the Law on Citizenship providing that[120] 'BiH citizenship is acquired by a child born or found on the BiH territory [...] whose both parents are unknown [...].' Moreover, the same report goes on to state that the authoring agency is not aware of any actual cases so far where a special procedure especially designed to register children of unknown parentage was undertaken.[121]

---

[116] UNHCR, 'Persons at Risk of Statelessness in Serbia: Progress Report 2010–2015' (June 2016) 27 <http://www.refworld.org/docid/57bd436b4.html> accessed 4 August 2019.

[117] Article 13 'A child born or found in the territory of the Republic of Serbia (foundling) acquires citizenship of the Republic of Serbia by birth if both his parents are unknown or of unknown citizenship or without citizenship of if the child is without citizenship [...]'. Law on Citizenship of the Republic of Serbia [Serbia] (2014) <https://www.refworld.org/docid/4b56d0542.html> accessed 4 August 2019.

[118] See also Praxis, 'Analysis of the Procedures for Determining the Date and Place of Birth and for the Exercise of Rights to Citizenship and Registration of Permanent Residence in Serbia' (December 2016) <http://praxis.org.rs/images/praxis_downloads/Report_UNHCR_2016_-_28.11. pdf> accessed 4 August 2019, which refers, in the section entitled 'Children without Recognised Paternity and Acquisition of Citizenship by Birth' pp 18–19, to the applicability of article 13, while it is not clear whether it is asserting citizenship on the basis of parents being unknown, stateless or of unknown nationality.

[119] See Vaša prava BiH, *Legal Analysis of Legislation of Bosnia and Herzegovina Regulating the Area of Birth Registration* (2018) 22.

[120] Law on Citizenship of Bosnia and Herzegovina Unofficial Consolidated Text (as amended up to 2013) <https://data.globalcit.eu/NationalDB/docs/BIH%20Law%20on%20Citizenship%20(con solidated)%20EN.pdf> accessed 25 December 2020.

[121] See Vaša prava BiH, *Legal Analysis of Legislation of Bosnia and Herzegovina Regulating the Area of Birth Registration* (2018) 26.

Certainly, not having one's parentage registered does not always amount to 'unknown parentage', especially if such registration is feasible and the person(s) concerned have simply not taken the actions reasonably expected to be taken to register such facts. Nevertheless, in some cases, for example where the parents decease without documents establishing their own identity and/or the parent–child relationship with the person concerned, the (late) registration of parentage can become impossible, leaving the person in a legal limbo as a person 'at risk of state-lessness' or 'undetermined nationality'. As mentioned in Sect. 2.7.2 and in Sect. 5.7, a person should not be classified to be of 'undetermined nationality' (or 'at risk of nationality') indefinitely, and the determination whether she or he is a national of a particular country or stateless needs to be taken within a reasonable timeframe. The standard of proof in establishing (otherwise) statelessness should be low, that is 'to a reasonable degree'.[122]

### 2.9.5  Where Foundling Provisions Are Correct Solutions

For persons whose parentage and birthplace are not documented who are found in the territory after reaching their adulthood (see Chap. 6 on the maximum age to be considered a 'foundling'), having their status as 'stateless persons' recognized can be one of the ways to resolve their situation. For example, a family court in Japan in December 2016 issued a noteworthy adjudication[123] that recognized as a 'stateless person' a migrant woman of undocumented parentage and date/place of birth. She had claimed to have been born in China and migrated to a remote village in Thailand when a small child. She had entered Japan with a forged passport in early 1990 and, by the time of the family court adjudication, her parents and relatives could not be traced, and she could not prove either Thai or Chinese nationality.[124]

However, at least for persons who are found in the territory when still a child, if their parents cannot eventually be legally established, article 2 of the 1961 Convention or the equivalent domestic foundling provision should be the legally correct solution. This is possible by interpreting the definition of 'unknown parents' or ('found in the

---

[122] UNHCR Handbook (2014) para 91, UNHCR Guidelines 4 (2012) para 21.

[123] On the nature of a Japanese family court adjudication on registering unregistered persons into a family register, refer to fn 48, Chap. 4 of this book entitled 'Nature of Japanese family court adjudications permitting registration into family register'.

[124] Based on the copy of the adjudication provided by Fumie Azukizawa, Ayane Odagawa and Sōsuke Seki who were the legal representatives of the case. Tōkyō Family Court Tachikawa Branch, Adjudication, 5 December 2016 (*Heisei 28 nen*), unpublished. Briefing by Attorney Fumie Azuk-izawa, Ayane Odagawa and Sōsuke Seki, legal representatives, on ibid at a session of the Study Group on Statelessness in Japan, 20 January 2017. More information on the case can be found in English in Ayane Odagawa and Sōsuke Seki (eds), Study Group on Stateless in Japan, 'Typology of Stateless Persons in Japan' (2017) 95–96 <https://www.unhcr.org/jp/wp-content/uploads/sites/34/2018/01/TYPOLOGY-OF-STATELESS-PERSONS-IN-JAPAN_webEnglish.pdf> accessed 4 August 2019.

territory') 'inclusively', setting the standard of proof low or by reversing the burden of proof to establish 'unknown parentage', as discussed further in Sects. 4.3.9 and 5.9.

## 2.10   Family Law and Nationality

As this book focuses on the nationality of foundlings who are provisionally defined as children of *unknown parents* (to be confirmed in Chaps. 3 and 6), it is essential to, although cursorily, review the basics of the law of parentage, including the basis, evidence and procedures for establishing legal parentage. In particular, when the concerned person's 'factual parent(s)' (explained in Sect. 2.10.1) has(have) been definitively identified, it is essential to assess whether legal parentage is established with such parent(s) in accordance with the rules laid out in this section in order to determine whether or not she or he is of unknown parents.

With this book's focus being on the prevention of statelessness at the time of birth, the establishment of the initial legal parentage automatically at the time of birth or non-automatically shortly after birth (such as by acknowledgement and registration of parentage) will be mainly discussed below. Establishment of legal parentage by adoption and the consequent nationality acquisition, and annulment of legal parentage in general, will only be mentioned when relevant in Chap. 4 and on.

### 2.10.1   Distinction Between 'factual parent' and 'legal parent'

This book will use the concepts of 'factual parent' and 'legal parent' from time to time. Section 2.10.2 will talk about the relationship between legal parentage and the acquisition of nationality. In Sect. 4.4 whether a foundling under article 2 of the 1961 Convention essentially means a child whose parents are 'factually' or 'legally' unknown will be discussed. Before such discussion, though, what 'factual' parent(s) means—normally used as an opposite term of a 'legal' parent—needs to be explained. This term has often been used without clear definition in previous literature related to foundlings in family law and nationality law.

The author hereby decides that in this book, a 'factual parent' when used in contrast to a 'legal parent' means a person who has not been recognized as a parent under the relevant *law*. The relationship between the factual parent and the child concerned does not entail legal effects and is not protected by law. Such 'factual parent' is either:

(1)   a biological (genetic) parent; or
(2)   a person with no biological (genetic) relationship with the child concerned, but is nevertheless acting as a parent,

   and:

(a)   she or he does not fulfil the legal requirements to be recognized as a legal parent; or

(b)   while it is asserted that she or he fulfils the legal requirements to be a legal parent, she or he has not been recognized as such because;

    (i)   she or he has not undergone the required procedure to establish such legal parenthood; or

    (ii)  based on the available evidence, the decision-maker's level of conviction has not reached the established standard of proof as to the person's fulfilment of the legal requirements.

As seen above, also to be reconfirmed particularly in Sect. 4.4, when it comes to nationality or statelessness it is ultimately the legal parentage, and not biological or factual parentage that matters as the former is the basis for nationality grant under the law.

Needless to say, for any human being, biological parents, that is the mother (or mothers—in case of surrogacy, the one who provides ovum and the one who deliver the baby) and the father (who provides sperm) definitely exist. Legal parents may or may not exist. For example, in a number of States, even if it is clearly established (with a DNA testing result strongly supporting the parent–child relationship) in the eyes of the civil registration authority that a specific male is the biological father of a child born out of wedlock, the legal paternity can only be established through the completion of the relevant legal procedure such as registration or litigation.[125] In such States, even if the biological father has been taking good care of the child for years, his nationality cannot be passed on to his 'child' based on such biological and factual relationship.

As will be seen in Sect. 2.10.5 (and Sects. 2.10.6 and 2.10.7), while it is usually a biological parent that is recognized as a legal parent, in some cases a biological parent cannot be recognized as a legal parent, at least without tedious procedures. Likewise, somebody other than the biological parent of a person can be recognized as a legal parent. As will be seen below, apart from 'traditional' cases, such as when a married woman in some States gets pregnant with a baby of a man other than the husband, in recent years surrogacy arrangements are often recognized as giving rise to such situations. Non-biological parents can also establish legal parentage in some States, on the basis of the apparent status (*possession d'état*). Biological and non-biological parents can also become legal parents by adopting children. It might however happen that nobody, including the child's biological parents can be recognized as a legal parent, depending on the circumstances and the relevant law of the parents and the country of birth. Even when those who can legally be recognized as parents do exist, such legal parentage might not have yet been established, recognized and registered as such by a State.

When the concerned person's factual parent(s) has(have) been definitively identified, establishment of legal parentage needs to be assessed in order to determine

---

[125] The rules for establishing legal parentage are to be discussed in Sect. 2.10 (especially Sect. 2.10.5.2) below.

whether she or he is of unknown parents. On the other hand, if a factual parent has not been (definitively) identified, it might not be necessarily useful to examine the existence of a legal parent–child relationship between the child and the potential factual parent.

### 2.10.2  Legal Descent Under Family Law to Be Determined Before Nationality by Jus Sanguinis

Family relationship is often a preliminary question that must be pre-determined[126] before a child's nationality, or lack thereof, is finally determined. This is because nationality acquisition by *jus sanguinis* under nationality law normally requires that there exists, as a prerequisite, (1) parent–child relationship(s) under family law (see, however, Sect. 2.10.3). The exception is when a child is born in a country that adopts pure or 'unconditional' *jus soli* principle where anybody born in the territory automatically acquires the nationality of that country regardless of his/her parentage or the parents' residency status. In that case, at least the possession of one nationality is confirmed as long as her or his birth in the territory is established. Even when a person acquires nationality for merely having been born in the territory, however, whether the person acquires any other nationality needs to be determined based on that person's legal descent. Thus, when examining a person's nationality status, it is normally necessary to first examine the parent–child relationship, which is a matter of private law independent from nationality acquisition.[127]

### 2.10.3  Legal Parentage Under Family Law Vis-à-Vis Under Nationality Law

'Legal parentage' most commonly refers to the parent–child relationship recognized under family law,[128] contained in the Civil Code in a number of States. The parentage

---

[126] Shōichi Kidana, *Chikujōchūkai kokusekihō* [*Article-by-Article Commentary to Nationality Law*] (Nihon kajo shuppan, 2003) 110–11. Yue Fū, 'Nihon de umareta kodomono kokuseki to mukokuseki nintei' ['Determination of statelessness for children born in Japan'] (PhD dissertation, University of Tsukuba 2016) 79.

[127] Yue Fū, 'Nihon de umareta kodomono kokuseki to mukokuseki nintei' ['Determination of statelessness for children born in Japan'] (PhD dissertation, University of Tsukuba 2016) 79. Hidefumi Egawa, Yoshirō Hayata and Ryōichi Yamada, *Kokusekihō* [*Nationality Law*] (Yūhikaku 1997) 63–4.

[128] On this point, the author noted that a study paper by HCCH in March 2014 contains a paragraph entitled 'Nationality by descent: from the genetic or legal parents?' which reads at para 40: 'in 31 States, it was reported that a child may acquire the nationality of the State by descent if one or both of the child's legal parents is / are a national of the State. In contrast, in seven States, nationality by descent is acquired if one or both of the genetic parents are nationals of the State'. While the basis for the distinction between 'legal parents' and 'genetic parents' in this context is unclear (with no

for the purpose of acquisition of nationality under nationality law has traditionally referred to the parentage established under family law. However, in some cases nationality law provides its own definition of who is considered to be a 'parent' for nationality acquisition purposes, and this may not always coincide with the rules concerning the establishment of legal parentage in family law,[129] giving rise to the issue of 'conflict' between nationality law and family law. In some cases, while nationality law refers to family law for the criteria and the procedure to establish the parent–child relationship, the effect of such establishment of parentage might have different temporal scope in nationality law than in family law.[130]

Further, in recent years it has been observed, including by the Hague Conference on Private International Law (hereinafter HCCH), that nationality laws in some States have not yet 'caught up' with developments in science such as reproduction through assisted reproductive technology (ART) and surrogacy and the consequent evolution of family laws concerning the establishment and contestation of legal parentage.[131] In summary, family law and nationality law might recognize a different person as a legal parent (while in some cases they might not recognize anybody as a legal parent).

To categorize, while hypothetically, this could result in the situations where:

(1)    a child has a legal parent according to the family law of the State, but that legal parent cannot pass her or his nationality to the child under the nationality law;

(2)    a child can acquire the nationality of her or his parent under the nationality law, but that parent cannot be recognized as a legal parent under the family law, and;

(3)    a child does not have a parent neither under family nor nationality law and thus does not acquire any nationality by *jus sanguinis*.

---

clarification on the relevant questionnaire and responses by the seven States), it is arguable that, if 'genetic parents' in this context are allowed to pass on nationality to their child, it means they are indeed 'legal parents' at least under nationality law (even if they are not recognized as legal parents under the relevant family law). HCCH, 'A Study of Legal Parentage and the Issues Arising From International Surrogacy Arrangement' (March 2014) 24 para 45 <https://assets.hcch.net/docs/bb90cfd2-a66a-4fe4-a05b-55f33b009cfc.pdf> accessed 4 August 2019 (hereinafter 'HCCH Study (March 2014)').

[129] Ibid.

[130] For example, in Japan, the effect of post-natal recognition of paternity for children born out of wedlock, stipulated under Civil Code, goes back to the time of birth in terms of inheritance rights and so on. However, such a retroactive effect is not recognized under the Nationality Act as per a Supreme Court ruling. Judgement, *Shūmin* vol 208, p 495 [22 November 2002 (*Heisei 14 nen*)] (The Supreme Court (Petty Bench II)). A person may acquire nationality at the time of registration of paternity recognition if done under the age of 20 under article 3(2) of the Japanese Nationality Act, Act No 147 of 4 May 1950. Scholars and lawyers advocate for the retroactive effect for nationality purposes. See Ayane Odagawa and Sōsuke Seki (eds), Study Group on Stateless in Japan, 'Typology of Stateless Persons in Japan' (2017) 79–81 and 88 <https://www.unhcr.org/jp/wp-content/uploads/sites/34/2018/01/TYPOLOGY-OF-STATELESS-PERSONS-IN-JAPAN_webEnglish.pdf> accessed 4 August 2019. Another example is article 4(1) of the Dutch Nationality Act, which regulates in detail the different timings after the judgment when the child acquires the Netherlands nationality depending on the circumstances of the case. Netherlands Nationality Act, 19 December 1984.

[131] HCCH Study (March 2014) 24 para 45.

Persons under category (1) would be otherwise stateless (unless known to have been born in a country granting nationality through the unconditional *jus soli* provision). As Gerard-René de Groot points out, the Council of Europe Recommendation CM/Rec(2009)13 principle 12 requests member States to apply to children their provisions on nationality acquisition by *jus sanguinis* if, as a result of a birth conceived through ART, a child–parent family relationship is established by law— which depends on private international law and domestic law of the country of the commissioning parents.[132] Nevertheless, if this principle was to fail, then those under category (1) can fall within the scope of article 1 (rather than article 2) of the 1961 Convention or an equivalent domestic nationality law provision granting nationality to persons born in the territory who would otherwise be stateless in the country of birth. In this case, the children have parent(s) legally responsible for their custody.

Persons under category (2) will not be stateless but will have difficulties in securing parental care and protection among other implications arising from the lack of parent– child relationship under family law unless a separate procedure such as adoption is undertaken. They, however, fall outside article 2 of the 1961 Convention and thus this book's scope.

Persons under category (3), that is without legally recognized parents both under family law and nationality law will be otherwise stateless (again, unless known to be born in an unconditional *jus soli* country), and fall within article 2 of the 1961 Convention and thus within the scope of this book.

For the purpose of this book, 'a person of unknown legal parentage' will thus refer to a person without a legal parent–child relationship recognized neither under family law nor nationality law, unless otherwise specified.

## *2.10.4   Relevance of the Law of Parentage*

The objective of the law on parentage is to determine who the child's parents are for the purpose of the effects that the law attaches to the parent–child relationship. In terms of the criteria or the basis for legal parentage, it tends to be generally assumed—as discussed above—that the biological parents are legal parents of the child. However, different issues have been debated in the law of parentage especially in recent decades as a result of a combination of changing family patterns and advances in medical science. The question of whether the biological father and mother should be recognized as the legal parent of the child—or someone else should

---

[132] Council of Europe: Committee of Ministers, *Recommendation CM/Rec(2009)13 and explanatory memorandum of the Committee of Ministers to member states on the nationality of children* (Council of Europe Publishing 9 May 2009) 25; Gerard-René de Groot, 'Children, Their Right to a Nationality and Child Statelessness' in Edwards and van Waas (eds), *Nationality and Statelessness under International Law* (Cambridge University Press 2014) 144 and 166.

be—is becoming more and more relevant in the contemporary world.[133] This question is often asked when, for example, protection of the mother and her child is involved (such as cases of rape or potential child abandonment), or the protection of existing family life (such as extramarital versus marital relationship), or where ART, in particular surrogacy, is involved, including where the intended parents are of the same sex.[134]

Determination of the legal parents becomes more complicated in an international case when the situation has foreign elements, that is where the persons involved have connections with more than one country and legal system, where private international law rules become relevant.

There are different methods to establish legal parentage, automatically and non-automatically, by means of, mainly, an administrative action, by apparent status and by judicial establishment.[135] A closely related but separate issue is that of evidence—how establishment of legal parentage can be proven, which varies from state to state.[136] Explaining those issues in detail, however, goes beyond the scope of this book.

## 2.10.5 Establishment of Legal Parentage in Cases of Natural Reproduction

Below, the rules on legal parentage common in many national legislation in terms of the criteria and the procedure in cases of natural production as well as in surrogacy cases will be reviewed. The basic rules of private international law will subsequently be reviewed rather cursorily. The summary below heavily relies on the work of the Permanent Bureau of the HCCH, which has been studying the private international law issues in relation to the legal parentage of children, in particular in relation to international surrogacy arrangements.[137]

---

[133] Kees Jan Saarloos, 'European private international law on legal parentage? Thoughts on a European instrument implementing the principle of mutual recognition in legal parentage' (Ph.D. dissertation, Maastricht University 2010) 1.

[134] Ibid 1.

[135] Ibid 88.

[136] For detailed discussion on evidence of legal parentage in some European States, including on the meaning and the evidential value of information that appears on the child's birth record as well as the procedure that leads to the stating of the information on the birth record, refer to ibid, section 4 'Evidence of legal parentage' 91–111.

[137] See for general information HCCH's web page on its Parentage/Surrogacy Project, <https://www.hcch.net/en/projects/legislative-projects/parentage-surrogacy> . In addition, the author relied on the work of Kees Jan Saarloos and Michael Wells-Greco as precious materials dedicated to discuss the law of parentage and private international law including that arising out of inter-country surrogacy arrangements.

### 2.10.5.1   Maternal Legal Descent

In the vast majority of States, the woman who gives birth to a child is the legal mother of the child 'by operation of law' that is, automatically, by virtue of the *mater semper certa est* principle.[138] For example, in some States, legal maternity arises automatically based on the Civil Codes themselves,[139] which state that the woman who gives birth to the child shall be the child's legal mother. Some States have established such a principle through jurisprudence.[140]

In a minority of States, such as France, a birth mother's legal maternity does not technically arise 'by operation of law'. These States provide for the non-automatic establishment of legal maternity, and has required acknowledgement of maternity or administrative action.[141] For example, the relevant legislation in some States provide that an 'act (registration) of birth', based on the attestation and declaration of birth by the physician and mother respectively, must be made in order for the legal maternity to be established.[142] In such cases, the woman, who might not be limited to the birth mother,[143] who is mentioned on the birth record as the mother of the child, shall be considered the legal mother of the child.[144] Whether to enter the mother's particulars

---

[138] HCCH Study (March 2014) 8; Kees Jan Saarloos, 'European private international law on legal parentage? Thoughts on a European instrument implementing the principle of mutual recognition in legal parentage' (Ph.D. dissertation, Maastricht University 2010) 16–17. Some States do not have specific provisions on legal maternity in case of natural reproduction. It is considered self-evident that the woman who gives birth to the child is the child's mother. Ibid 16–17.

[139] Dutch and German law for example. Kees Jan Saarloos, 'European private international law on legal parentage? Thoughts on a European instrument implementing the principle of mutual recognition in legal parentage' (PhD dissertation, Maastricht University 2010) 16–17.

[140] Ibid 16–17. The text of Japanese Civil Code, which is influenced not only by the German Civil Code but also by the French Civil Code for historical reasons, provides the possibility of voluntary recognition of both paternity and maternity for persons born out of wedlock, but due to the case law, the maternal parentage is understood to arise automatically upon delivery. For example, see Teiko Kiyosue, 'Dairishussan ni okeru boshikankei: bunbenshugi no genkai' ['Mother–child relationship in surrogacy cases: limitations of the principle that the woman who gives birth is the legal mother'] (2012) 18 Hokudai Hōsei Jānaru 1. Section 4.5 also touches on the legal maternity under Japanese law. See also ECtHR jurisprudence such as the case of *Marckx v. Belgium* (1979) in the ECtHR. Before the ECtHR's judgement in this case, under Belgian law, no legal bond between an unmarried mother and her child resulted from the mere fact of birth, even though the birth mother was duly recorded on the birth certificate. To create the bond, the mother either had to recognize maternity in specific proceedings or to adopt the child. In both cases, the child's inheritance rights remained less than a child born in wedlock received automatically. The ECtHR held that there had been breaches of ECHR article 8 (private and family life) and article 14 (non-discrimination) among others. *Marckx v. Belgium*, Application No 6833/74, 13 June 1979 (ECtHR).

[141] For example, France and Canada (Quebec). HCCH Study (March 2014) 8 <https://assets.hcch.net/docs/bb90cfd2-a66a-4fe4-a05b-55f33b009cfc.pdf> accessed 4 August 2019.

[142] Ibid 8.

[143] It is noted, however, that the birth mother is normally envisaged to be the legal mother even in France. Kees Jan Saarloos, 'European private international law on legal parentage? Thoughts on a European instrument implementing the principle of mutual recognition in legal parentage' (PhD dissertation, Maastricht University 2010) 17.

[144] Ibid 42.

on the birth record would be voluntary, so the mother can avoid the establishment of her legal maternity by deciding not to enter her personal details.[145] In other words, in these States, the declaration of birth to the registration authorities is seen as a form of 'acknowledgement of maternity'.[146] Thus, even if the birth mother is known, if both the mother and father refuse to recognize the child, the child is without legal parentage.

It should also be noted that in many States the criteria or the procedure for the establishment of legal maternity have traditionally been different depending on whether the child is born in or out of wedlock, the former being automatic, and the latter being non-automatic. However, some States have moved away from this and no longer differentiates between those born in and out of wedlock.[147]

Further, a form of 'anonymous birth', where the birth mother can choose to give birth without revealing her identity on the child's birth record or certificate or vis-à-vis the civil registration authorities, is possible in a small number of States. Such States include France, Italy, Germany (as of 1 May 2014),[148] Slovakia[149] and Czech

---

[145] Ibid. Article 326 of the French Civil Code allows the mother to go one step further by requesting the protection of her anonymity. See Sect. 4.3.10.

[146] HCCH Study (March 2014) 8 <https://assets.hcch.net/docs/bb90cfd2-a66a-4fe4-a05b-55f33b 009cfc.pdf> accessed 4 August 2019. According to Saarloos, the function of acknowledgment of maternity under French law has thereby become 'obsolete' since the recording of the mother's name on the child's birth record is enough to establish her legal maternity. Kees Jan Saarloos, 'European private international law on legal parentage? Thoughts on a European instrument implementing the principle of mutual recognition in legal parentage' (PhD dissertation, Maastricht University 2010) 43.

[147] For example, under French law, prior to 1 July 2006 when the Ordonnance 2005/759 entered into force, the establishment of legal maternity was dependent upon the marital status of the mother. If the mother was married, legal maternity was established by the recording of the mother's name on the birth record. For children born out of wedlock, the birth record was not enough evidence for the establishment of legal maternity, requiring an express acknowledgment of maternity (repealed article 334-8 of the Civil Code). However, article 311-25 of the current Civil Code provides that legal maternity is established by recording the mother's name on the child's birth record, and this applies both to married and unmarried women. This amendment was made to correct the different treatment between children born in and out of wedlock. Kees Jan Saarloos, 'European private international law on legal parentage? Thoughts on a European instrument implementing the principle of mutual recognition in legal parentage' (PhD dissertation, Maastricht University 2010) 42.

[148] Answer to Question 7 at p 7. HCCH, 'Questionnaire on the Private International Law Issues Surrounding the Status of Children, including issues Arising from International Surrogacy Arrangements' (April 2013) <https://assets.hcch.net/upload/wop/gap2014pd3in.pdf> accessed 4 August 2019.

[149] Slovakia's answer to the ibid, at Question 7 states that 'A woman can ask for delivery under the cover of anonymity. The personal data of the mother are not indicated on the medical documentation. The birth certificate only includes: the date and place of birth and the sex of the child'.

Republic[150]—some of which explicitly state that they otherwise provide for automatic establishment of legal maternity upon parturition[151]—allow for a form of anonymous birth. The exact method, such as who gets to know the mother's identity, and whether it is linked to nationality grant, varies. The details of how anonymous or secret birth work in some States and how it might produce a person of unknown parentage is discussed in Sect. 4.3.10.

#### 2.10.5.2 Paternal Legal Descent

Three primary methods exist in many States as the means by which a man may establish his legal paternity, that is legal presumption, voluntary acknowledgement and by judicial or administrative decision. In some States, legal parentage can be established on the basis of apparent status, as will be discussed below.

(1) *By legal presumption*: In most States, a man will be presumed to be the legal father of a child (and registered as such) if that child is born during his marriage to the woman who gave birth to the child, or within a defined period[152] following its termination, whether by death, dissolution or annulment. This means the principle to presume *pater is est quem nuptiae demonstrant* ('the father is he who is married to the mother') is applied.[153] The main rationale cited for this long-standing legal presumption is that it is considered more likely than not that the husband of the birth mother is the genetic father of the child and, from a child welfare perspective, it is better for the child to have a registered father at birth. It is possible in many States to rebut this legal presumption by, for example, proving that the husband is not the biological father of the child either at the time of the initial registration of the child or later after a court decision.[154] In other States, it is not possible to register a man other than the husband where the *pater est* presumption applies unless the husband's paternity

---

[150] For Czech Republic only for women with permanent residence in the Czech Republic (with the exception of women whose husband is presumed to be the legal father because of the existence of marriage with her) has the right to confidentiality' of her personal identity. Czech Republic's answer to ibid, Question 7 at p 7.

[151] See the responses to Question 8a of ibid for Germany, Slovakia and Czech Republic. In these States, the anonymous or secret birth regime generally appears to be a practical measure taken through the birth registration regulations rather than the substantive rule of family law. In contrast, France (and Italy) explicitly indicates in the questionnaire that the woman who gives birth to the child is not always the legal mother by operation of law upon the birth of a child. See France (and Italy')'s answer to Question 8.

[152] Timeframes vary.

[153] In many States, if the child is born within a defined period following the termination of a marriage and during this period the birth mother has remarried, the child will be presumed to be the child of the new marriage.

[154] HCCH Study (March 2014) 9 <https://assets.hcch.net/docs/bb90cfd2-a66a-4fe4-a05b-55f33b 009cfc.pdf> accessed 4 August 2019.

has been successfully challenged in court.[155] Where a court application is made to contest legal paternity, States' approaches vary as to whether, for example, conditions are placed on who can challenge legal paternity, whether DNA evidence may be relied upon, and whether a limitation period applies.[156]

(2)  *By voluntary acknowledgement, or recognition of paternity either at the time of birth registration or subsequently*: In many States, it is possible for a putative legal father to voluntarily 'acknowledge' his legal paternity over a child born out of wedlock where the paternity has not arisen by operation of law through legal presumption.[157] However, the conditions and procedures for acknowledgement differ between States. The mother's and/or the child's consent may or may not be required, while it could be replaced by the consent of a court, also depending on the timing of the acknowledgement.[158] While in a majority of States, proof of a genetic connection with a child is not a necessary precondition for a man to undertake an acknowledgement, its absence is a ground for subsequently challenging legal paternity if discovered.[159] In some States, it is possible to acknowledge paternity before the birth of the child, while in many States this is not permitted.[160] There can be special rules applying in cases of acknowledgement of adulterous (as above) or incestuous children.

(3)  By judicial or administrative decision: In many States, it is possible for a non-contentious (which is not being challenged) application to be made to the relevant State authorities for a decision establishing or confirming the legal parentage of a child.[161] In many States, legal paternity may also be established by the court where there is a dispute as to the child's legal paternity.[162]

In addition to these three main methods, in a small number of States, such as France[163] and Canada (Quebec State),[164] legal parentage (in theory, for both paternity and maternity) can be established on the basis of the apparent status of a child where she or he de facto enjoys the rights (and duties) that are attached to the possession of the status (*possession d'état*) of being the child of a particular person. For example, article 311-1 of the French Civil Code provides that the apparent status of parentage

---

[155] Ibid 9.

[156] Ibid 9.

[157] Ibid 10.

[158] Ibid 10.

[159] Ibid 10.

[160] Ibid 10.

[161] Ibid 10.

[162] Ibid 10.

[163] Kees Jan Saarloos, 'European private international law on legal parentage? Thoughts on a European instrument implementing the principle of mutual recognition in legal parentage' (PhD dissertation, Maastricht University 2010) 52–56.

[164] HCCH Study (March 2014), fn 40 and Canada's response to the HCCH questionnaire, HCCH, 'Questionnaire on the Private International Law Issues Surrounding the Status of Children, including issues Arising from International Surrogacy Arrangements' (April 2013) <https://assets.hcch.net/upload/wop/gap2014pd3in.pdf> accessed 4 August 2019.

is established by a sufficient collection of facts that indicates the descent of a person from a family to whom he is said to belong. The article also contains a non-exhaustive list of facts that together constitute an apparent status of parentage.[165]

## 2.10.6 Establishment of Legal Parentage for Surrogacy Cases

Among different forms of ART, surrogacy—especially international surrogacy arrangements—can give rise to a situation where a person ends up with no legal parents, as will be seen in Sect. 4.5. Thus, this section will review the general trends in the establishment of legal parentage following a surrogacy arrangement.

'Surrogacy' is defined as 'the agreement-based practice whereby one woman[166] carries a child for another[167] with the intention that the child should be handed over after birth'.[168] International surrogacy arrangements involving a foreign country are growing phenomena. The surrogate mother normally carries a child that has been created with the ovum of the commissioning mother or of an egg donor, but sometimes of her own egg. The sperm is normally of the commissioning mother's husband or a partner, but could be of a donor. In surrogacy cases, up to three women can be the potential mother of the child, namely the one that provides ovum, the surrogate mother who delivers the child, and the one who commissions the surrogacy. The commissioning couple may both be the genetic parents, or just one, or neither of them may be genetically related to the child.

The regulation of surrogacy in internal law varies significantly.[169] In some States, there is an express prohibition of all forms of surrogacy arrangements within their jurisdiction, often with criminal sanctions for third parties involved in facilitating such arrangements, especially where payments have been made.[170] In other States,

---

[165] Kees Jan Saarloos, 'European private international law on legal parentage? Thoughts on a European instrument implementing the principle of mutual recognition in legal parentage' (PhD dissertation, Maastricht University 2010), p 54. According to Saarloos, these facts are that the child has been treated by the alleged parent as his or her child, that the alleged parent took care of the education and the maintenance of the child, that the family, society and the public authorities considered the alleged parent the parent of the child and that the child bears the name of the alleged parent. A harmonious collection of these facts indicates that the child is the child of the person involved. As to the quality of the relationship, the apparent status needs to be continuous, peaceful, public and univocal.

[166] Hereinafter 'surrogate mother'.

[167] Hereinafter 'commissioning parent(s)'.

[168] Veronique Boillet and Hajime Akiyama, 'Statelessness and international surrogacy from the international and European legal perspectives' (2017) 27 Swiss Review of International and European Law 513, 513, 522.

[169] HCCH Study (March 2014) paras 22–25. Michael Wells-Greco, *The Status of Children Arising from Inter-Country Surrogacy Arrangements* (Eleven International Publishing 2016); see generally Chap. 3, part I.

[170] HCCH Study (March 2014) para 22–5. Michael Wells-Greco, *The Status of Children Arising from Inter-Country Surrogacy Arrangements* (Eleven International Publishing 2016), 1.3, 3.3–3.5.

surrogacy arrangements remain unregulated in internal law although, in most of these States, general provisions of law might be considered to have been breached in the case of a for-profit arrangement.[171] In some States, surrogacy arrangements made solely between the parties are not prohibited.[172] In some States, even for-profit surrogacy is permitted, but this position more often results from either an absence of any regulation, or from permissive legislation or judicial precedent.[173]

For the States in which surrogacy is either prohibited or unregulated, the child's legal parentage will normally be established according to the generally applicable legal parentage rules, irrespective of the surrogacy arrangement. Normally the surrogate birth mother would be the legal mother in the first instance, except for the States in which anonymous birth is possible or it is possible for the birth mother to choose not to register her name.[174] In many jurisdictions, intending or commissioning parents often have no or limited options of establishing legal parenthood. Legal paternity may be established by legal presumption (most commonly if the surrogate, that is the birth mother, is married), but also by voluntary acknowledgement or by court order, leaving room for the intending or commissioning father to establish his paternity. In some States, it may be possible for the intending parent(s) to subsequently adopt a child born to a surrogate mother while there have been cases in which adoption has been refused, for example where the surrogacy arrangement was for-profit.[175]

In States in which there are some regulations over surrogacy, the most common position is that the birth mother will still be the legal mother at birth and the legal parentage will be transferred to the intending mother after the birth of the child (provided the legislative criteria have been met), either by a specific procedure to transfer legal parentage or by adoption.[176] In relation to legal paternity, again it is most common that the general provisions on legal parentage will apply at birth and hence the husband of the birth mother will be the legal father, or the intending father may, in some circumstances, be able to voluntarily acknowledge his paternity in accordance

---

[171] HCCH Study (March 2014) <https://assets.hcch.net/docs/bb90cfd2-a66a-4fe4-a05b-55f33b009 cfc.pdf> accessed 4 August 2019 paras 22–25. Michael Wells-Greco, *The Status of Children Arising from Inter-Country Surrogacy Arrangements* (Eleven International Publishing 2016) 1.3, and 3.6 and 3.7.

[172] HCCH Study (March 2014) paras 22–25 <https://assets.hcch.net/docs/bb90cfd2-a66a-4fe4-a05b-55f33b009cfc.pdf> accessed 4 August 2019.

[173] For example, India. Ibid 15. Michael Wells-Greco, *The Status of Children Arising from Inter-Country Surrogacy Arrangements* (Eleven International Publishing 2016), 1.3, and 3–8 and 3–10, See Sect. 4.5, which discusses the Baby Manji Case of 2008.

[174] HCCH Study (March 2014) 17 <https://assets.hcch.net/docs/bb90cfd2-a66a-4fe4-a05b-55f33b 009cfc.pdf> accessed 4 August 2019.

[175] Ibid 17 para 26.

[176] Ibid 17 para 27; Kees Jan Saarloos, 'European private international law on legal parentage? Thoughts on a European instrument implementing the principle of mutual recognition in legal parentage' (PhD dissertation, Maastricht University 2010) 16; Michael Wells-Greco, *The Status of Children Arising from Inter-Country Surrogacy Arrangements* (Eleven International Publishing 2016) 3.2.1.

with the general rules of the State.[177] In some States, the intending parents may be registered as the legal parents of the child directly through some procedures by virtue of the surrogacy contractual arrangement.[178] In other jurisdictions, it is possible to obtain a court decision prior to the birth stating that the intending parents will be the legal parents of the child immediately upon birth.[179]

### 2.10.7 Private International Law on Parentage and Conflict of Laws in Surrogacy Cases

In an international case, for example where the persons involved have connections with more than one country,[180] issues of private international law, such as whether to apply the law of the country of birth or of the parent's nationality, can arise. In some cases where the legal parentage is determinative for the acquisition of nationality by descent, it may not be clear which law should apply to determine who is or are the child's legal parent(s).[181] States' private international law rules concerning the establishment and contestation of legal parentage vary significantly, with regard to questions such as jurisdiction, applicable law or the recognition of legal parentage already established abroad.[182]

In terms of the international 'jurisdiction' to determine the legal parentage of a child, it is directly related to the obligation to register a birth.[183] The registration of the birth at the place of birth is generally mandatory under local law, and many international and regional organs such as the Council of Europe recommend that States register the birth of all children born in the territory even if the parents are irregular migrants or unknown to safeguard the right to a nationality.[184] Further,

---

[177] HCCH Study (March 2014) 17, para 27.

[178] Ibid 17 para 27.

[179] Ibid 17 para 27.

[180] Needless to say, if there is no foreign parent or State involved in the case, that is the parents are both nationals of the same country and the child is born in the country of the parents' nationality, then the family relationship is to be determined based on the family law of that country. Hidefumi Egawa, Yoshirō Hayata and Ryōichi Yamada, *Kokusekihō* [Nationality law] (Yūhikaku 1997) 63–4; Yue Fū, 'Nihon de umareta kodomono kokuseki to mukokuseki nintei' ['Determination of statelessness for children born in Japan'] (PhD dissertation, University of Tsukuba 2016) 79.

[181] HCCH Study (March 2014) 24 para 45 <https://assets.hcch.net/docs/bb90cfd2-a66a-4fe4-a05b-55f33b009cfc.pdf> accessed 4 August 2019.

[182] HCCH, 'Background Note for the Meeting of the Experts' Group on the Parentage / Surrogacy Project' (January 2016) 11 <https://assets.hcch.net/docs/8767f910-ae25-4564-a67c-7f2a002fb5c0.pdf> accessed 4 August 2019.

[183] Kees Jan Saarloos, 'European private international law on legal parentage? Thoughts on a European instrument implementing the principle of mutual recognition in legal parentage' (PhD dissertation, Maastricht University 2010) 126–7. HCCH Study (March 2014) 34–5.

[184] Appendix to the Council of Europe: Committee of Ministers, 'Recommendation CM/Rec(2009)13 of the Committee of Ministers to member states on the nationality of children'

States have different policy towards registration of birth abroad—mainly of a child of a national.[185]

Where the putative or biological parent(s) of a child born in the territory is (are) foreign, different legal systems may address such a case in applying different laws. If the father or the mother is a foreign national, the existence of the parent–child relationship is basically determined based on the applicable (governing) law designated in accordance with the private international law of the State that is examining such family relationship.[186] Which law is applicable to resolve the issue of the parent–child relationship thus depends on the domestic private international law legislation of the country concerned.[187]

In terms of the automatic establishment of legal parentage by operation of law, according to the HCCH Study (March 2014), in some States, regardless of any foreign elements in the case, the competent authorities in registering a child's birth will always apply the State's *lex fori* ('internal law') to the question of who is or are the legal parent(s) of the child by operation of law.[188] In some States, the applicable law rules are only established in relation to legal paternity since legal maternity is always established according to the '*mater est*' maxim, that is the *lex fori* always applies to the question of legal maternity.[189] According to HCCH, in many other States, if the situation has foreign elements, the applicable law rules of the State will apply to determine which law governs the question of the child's legal parentage arising by operation of law, with the 'child's nationality at the time of her or his birth being a common connecting factor'.[190] However, the child's nationality to be acquired by *jus sanguinis* cannot be determined without first establishing the child's parentage. This is a bit of a chicken or egg situation. Nevertheless, for children born in a country granting nationality by *jus soli* unconditionally, (one of) their nationality can be

---

(9 December 2009) para 23 <https://www.refworld.org/docid/4b83a76d2.html> accessed 4 August 2019.

[185] Kees Jan Saarloos, 'European private international law on legal parentage? Thoughts on a European instrument implementing the principle of mutual recognition in legal parentage' (PhD dissertation, Maastricht University 2010) 126–7. HCCH Study (March 2014) 34–5.

[186] Shōichi Kidana, *Chikujōchūkai kokusekihō* [Article-by-article commentary to nationality law] (Nihon kajo shuppan 2003) 111. Yue Fū, 'Nihon de umareta kodomono kokuseki to mukokuseki nintei' ['Determination of statelessness for children born in Japan'] (PhD dissertation, University of Tsukuba 2016) 79.

[187] Needless to say, private international law on parentage becomes relevant to the extent that national legal systems on parentage are different. If the legal systems involved in a particular case all adopt the same solution there is no need to make a choice of law.

[188] It is not fully clear from the report, as acknowledged in the report, whether the States responded as such were referring to their internal or private international law. HCCH Study (March 2014) 23 para 43, and footnote 194 <https://assets.hcch.net/docs/bb90cfd2-a66a-4fe4-a05b-55f33b009cfc.pdf> accessed 4 August 2019.

[189] For example, Finland and Sweden reported this is the case, as of the time of the HCCH Study (March 2014). Ibid 38 para 78.

[190] Ibid 37 para 75.

determined without considering their parentage and so can be used as a connecting factor.[191]

However, in most States, other connecting factors may also be relied upon and the choice of law is often based on the child's best interests. The nationality of the person seeking to establish her or his legal parentage is also a commonly used connecting factor.[192] In some States, the applicable law rules depend upon whether the putative parents are married or not.[193] In some States, legal parentage is determined in accordance with the law of the person's domicile.[194]

In terms of the law applicable when legal parentage is voluntarily acknowledged, in a number of States the local legislation applies to determine the substantive and/or formal validity of the acknowledgement.[195] In some States the applicable law rules have been established that may lead to the application of foreign law, while additional rules may exist.[196]

In the context of children born by ART, including surrogacy, in a background note the HCCH in 2016 stated, in analyzing the connecting factors under the relevant applicable law rules that 'it is sometimes not possible to use the terms "mother" or "father" as connecting persons for the purposes of the applicable law rules because it may not be clear who those persons are'.[197] Even if the applicable law rules appoint the same legal system, it is still possible, for example, that the foreign law is not applied if the result of its application is considered unacceptable because the foreign law violates the public policy of the State involved.[198]

States' private international law approaches on recognition of legal parentage already established abroad—when the birth concerned occurs in another State— also vary. In relation to foreign public documents (for example birth certificates or documents on voluntary acknowledgement), States have adopted a variety of approaches from recognition (subject to varying conditions) to methods that simply determines legal parentage de novo based on applicable law rules. In relation to foreign judicial decisions (such as on establishment, contestation or annulment of legal parentage), the 'recognition' approach is more common, often subject to indirect

---

[191] Shōichi Kidana, *Chikujō kaisetsu kokusai kazokuhō* [Article-by-Article commentary on international family law] (Nihon kajo shuppan 2017) 312.

[192] HCCH Study (March 2014) para 75, p 37. In many States exceptional rules apply for stateless persons and refugees where their personal status shall be governed by the law of the country of their domicile or their residence in the absence thereof. This is codified in not only article 12 of the 1951 Convention and article 12 of the 1954 Convention but also in private international legislation including in that of some of the non-State parties to the two Conventions.

[193] Ibid 37 para 76.

[194] Ibid 37 para 77.

[195] Ibid 38 para 82.

[196] Ibid 39 para 82.

[197] HCCH, 'Background Note for the Meeting of the Experts' Group on the Parentage / Surrogacy Project' (January 2016) <https://assets.hcch.net/docs/8767f910-ae25-4564-a67c-7f2a002fb5c0.pdf> accessed 4 August 2019.

[198] Ibid 13 para 46.

rules of jurisdiction and certain procedural safeguards (various grounds for non-recognition).[199] Non-recognition of a foreign decision happens, for example, if the jurisdiction of the foreign court was assumed contrary to the requirements of the recognizing State, or contradicts an earlier final decision of the recognizing State, or, again, is manifestly contrary to the public policy of the recognizing State.

There are conflict of laws situations, especially in the context of international surrogacy arrangements, where a person recognized as a legal father or mother by a particular State is not recognized by another State, which could recognize another person as such.[200] In the worst-case scenario, there might be cases where a person ends up without any legally recognized mother or father, while their intended or commissioning parent(s) and genetic or biological parent(s) is (are) definitively known. Statelessness may then be the consequence—which might fall within the central concern of this book. This will be further discussed in Sect. 4.5.

---

[199] Ibid, in particular pp 13–15.

[200] Just as one example, Saarloos refers to a case where a child is conceived with donor sperm, German law provides that the legal paternity of the sperm donor can be established while this is not possible under Dutch law. Kees Jan Saarloos, 'European private international law on legal parentage? Thoughts on a European instrument implementing the principle of mutual recognition in legal parentage' (PhD dissertation, Maastricht University 2010) 2.

# Chapter 3
# Defining a 'Foundling'

**Abstract**  This chapter provides the definition of 'foundling', except for the issue of 'age' when 'found', which is explained in Chap. 6. This chapter reveals that being 'found' on the territory is a condition that gives rise to the obligation of that State to grant nationality, and includes the situation where the person's birth within the territory is indeed established. An examination is made on the travaux préparatoires of article 14 of the 1930 Hague Convention on Certain Questions Relating to the Conflict of Nationality Law and article 2 of the 1961 Convention to examine the relationship between 'foundling (found in the territory)', 'child of unknown parents (born in the territory)', and 'person (born in the territory) who would otherwise be stateless'. The comparison of the wordings of article 2 of the 1961 Convention in the five UN language versions and domestic foundling provisions leads to the conclusion that the term 'foundling' essentially refers to a child of unknown parents.

This chapter sets out to define, in general terms, who a 'foundling' is, apart from the element of the age when found, which will be separately addressed in Chap. 6. A working hypothesis was presented in Sect. 1.4, that the essential requirement for being a foundling is that a person's parentage is unknown, based on several key pieces of literature. This chapter sets out to verify this hypothesis. Particularly, it will examine the questions:

(1)  Are 'foundlings' and 'children of unknown parentage', different, or are they the same?
(2)  Are foundlings persons whose parentage and birthplace are both unknown?
(3)  Is it a requirement that the person is 'abandoned' ('or deserted') or 'orphaned' to qualify as a foundling?

For the purpose of addressing question (1) above, the positioning of 'children of unknown parents born in the terrritory' within the structure of the 1961 Convention ie where it fits between article 1 and 2 will be examined. Leaving more detailed discussions on the nature and the content of being 'found' to Chap. 6, the relationship between the concept of 'having been born' and 'having been found' in the territory will be explored, for the purpose of determining whether unknown birthplace is part of the definition of a foundling, in order to examine question (2) above.

M. Kaneko-Iwase, *Nationality of Foundlings*, Evidence-Based Approaches to Peace and Conflict Studies 5, https://doi.org/10.1007/978-981-16-3005-7_3

This will be done based on the analysis of the evolution of the international legal framework to prevent statelessness of foundlings starting with the 1930 Convention, the travaux of the key instruments, the wording of the different UN language versions of the 1961 Convention, as well as the wording and definition of the equivalent term in domestic legislation in different languages.

## 3.1 'Found' in the territory': The Condition for Granting Nationality—Not Part of Who a Foundling Is

Before starting a detailed examination on the definition of a 'foundling', the nature of the term 'found' must be examined. The English version of the 1961 Convention in article 2 and article 6(1)(b) qualifies the term 'foundling' with an adjective 'found', that is 'a foundling found in the territory of a Contracting State shall [...]'. Reading the foregoing text, one may realize that, strictly speaking, being 'found in the territory' is not part of the definition of who a 'foundling' is. An alternative reading will make the sentence redundant. Rather, being 'found in the territory' is a condition that needs to be fulfilled in order for a particular contracting State's obligation—essentially to provide its nationality to a foundling—arises.[1] Naturally, a contracting State's obligation does not normally get triggered towards a foundling found on the territory of another State (see Sect. 7.3.1 however). Nevertheless, it will be seen in Sect. 3.3 and elsewhere that some materials (such as the French version of the 1961 Convention, and some national legislation and practical or academic materials) use the term 'a child found (in the territory)' to replace the term 'foundling'—confusing or combining the condition of nationality grant with the definition of a foundling.

## 3.2 Lack of an Established Definition of a 'Foundling'—Available 'Definitions'

As mentioned in Sects. 1.1 and 1.4, article 2 of the 1961 Convention as well as article 6(1)(b) of the ECN do not contain the definition of the term 'foundling'. UNHCR Guidelines 4 (2012) and the ECN's Explanatory Report, each providing the Conventions' interpretive guidelines, have limited and differing statements on the definition of who a 'foundling' is.

UNHCR Guidelines 4 (2012) paragraph 57 rephrases the term 'foundlings' as 'children found abandoned in the territory of a Contracting State'. On the other

---

[1] Ryūun Ō takes the same position that being found is a 'condition' rather than part of the foundling definition. Ō Ryūun, 'Kiji no kokuseki' ['Nationality of abandoned children'] (1969) 4 Hōgaku Kenkyū [Hokkaigakuen daigaku hōgakkai] 169.

hand, 'foundlings' under article 6(1)(b) of the ECN are explained in its Explanatory Report,[2] which specifically states that:

> The term 'foundlings' here refers to new-born infants[3] found[4] abandoned[5] in the territory of a State with *no known parentage* or nationality[6] who would be stateless if this principle were not applied. It is taken from article 2 of the 1961 Convention on the Reduction of Statelessness. (emphasis added)

As briefly mentioned in Sects. 1.1 and 1.4, traditionally, since before the issuance of the UNHCR Guidelines 4 in 2012, the majority of the UNHCR documents[7] and scholarly and practical materials[8] on childhood statelessness also did not clearly define the term 'foundling' and/or equated the terms 'abandoned or orphaned children' with the term 'foundling', which is not precise as will be examined in Sect. 3.6.

---

[2] Council of Europe, 'Explanatory Report to the European Convention on Nationality, 6.XI.1997' (1997) para 48 <https://rm.coe.int/16800ccde7> accessed 4 August 2019.

[3] On the discussion of the appropriateness of restricting a foundling to a 'new-born infant', see in general Chap. 6, and in particular Sect. 6.7.

[4] It should be pointed out that the word 'found' here is unnecessary as article 6(1)(b) states 'foundling found' (in the territory) and the Explanatory Note para 48 here is trying to define the term 'foundling' and not 'foundling found'.

[5] On the discussion of the appropriateness of restricting the term foundling to cover those who are 'abandoned', see Sect. 3.6.

[6] The conjunction 'or' in this phrase 'with no known parentage *or* nationality' in the Explanatory Note para 48 appears to be an error. It should have, more precisely, read 'and'—'with no known parentage *and* nationality'. As it is written now, it appears as if article 6(1)(b) covers persons of unknown nationality whose parentage is known. However, this interpretation is not likely to stand as this would favour a person of known parentage of unknown nationality found in the territory over a person of known parentage who would otherwise be stateless born in the territory (for whom ECN separately provides in article 6(2) basically stating that nationality can be granted either *ex lege* or non-automatically).

[7] Just to give two among numerous examples, UNHCR's well-cited 2004 Questionnaire on state-lessness uses 'abandoned children' and 'orphans' interchangeably to mean 'foundlings', which is not accurate, as will be discussed in Sect. 3.6. The same tendency is observed in academic literature including the most well-cited ones. UNHCR, 'Final Report concerning the questionnaire on state-lessness pursuant to the Agenda for Protection Geneva' (March 2004) <http://www.unhcr.org/pro tect/PROTECTION/4047002e4.pdf> accessed 4 August 2019, p 23. UNHCR's 'Self-Study Module on Statelessness' (1 October 2012) does not contain the word 'foundling' at all and only 'orphaned or abandoned children'. UNHCR, 'Self-Study Module on Statelessness' (1 October 2012) <https://www.refworld.org/docid/50b899602.html> accessed 4 August 2019.

[8] For example, Maureen Lynch, 'Lives on Hold: The Human Cost of Statelessness' (February 2005) 5 <https://www.refworld.org/docid/47a6eba00.html> accessed 4 August 2019; Laura van Waas, *Nationality Matters: Statelessness under International Law* (Intersentia 2008) 68–71 (with the title of the section being 'Abandoned or orphaned children'). Laura van Waas (2008), however, at fn 94 defines a 'foundling' 'to refer to any child who has been abandoned and whose parents are unknown'. Gerard-René de Groot, 'Children, Their Right to a Nationality and Child State-lessness' in Edwards and van Waas (eds), *Nationality and Statelessness under International*

Only several recent UNHCR materials indirectly provide a 'definition' of a foundling such as by rewording it as 'children of unknown parents'[9] or explaining in bracket as 'foundlings (children whose parentage is unknown)'[10] or 'children who have been abandoned or orphaned and whose parents are unknown ("foundlings")'[11] and 'abandoned children whose parents cannot be identified ("foundlings")'.[12] The latest and clearest example is the UNHCR and Inter-Parliamentary Union (hereinafter IPU)'s Handbook in 2018 on good practices in nationality laws, which indeed carries 'model legal provisions'[13] providing 'safeguards for foundlings' reflecting article 2 of the 1961 Convention. The Handbook provides two options as model provisions, the first one of which reads 'A child […] found on the territory and his/her parents are unknown', while the second option reads 'A foundling found on the territory […]'.

GLOBALCIT's Glossary on Citizenship and Nationality, compiled by leading scholars and practitioners of nationality matters, defines a 'foundling' as a 'child of *unknown parentage found abandoned* on the territory of a state' (emphasis added).[14]

In terms of the ordinary meaning of the term 'foundling', *Oxford Living Dictionaries* define it as: 'An infant that has been abandoned by its parents and is discovered and cared for by others.'[15] *Merriam Webster's Dictionary* defines it as: '[A]n infant

---

*Law* (Cambridge University Press 2014) 144; Olivier Willem Vonk, Maarten Peter Vink and Gerard-René de Groot, 'Protection against Statelessness: Trends and Regulations in Europe' (May 2013) 47–8 <http://cadmus.eui.eu/bitstream/handle/1814/30201/eudocit_vink_degroot_statelessn ess_final.pdf?sequence=1> accessed 4 August 2019. The title of the section is 'Foundlings of unknown parentage found in a country', which indeed indirectly defines a foundling. However, p 47 states 'Article 2 of the 1961 Convention establishes that "children found *abandoned* in the territory of a contracting State (foundlings)" acquire the nationality of that State' (emphasis added). Gerard-René de Groot, Katja Swider and Olivier Vonk, 'Practices and Approaches in EU Member States to Prevent and End Statelessness' (2015) 29 <http://www.europarl.europa.eu/RegData/etudes/STUD/ 2015/536476/IPOL_STU(2015)536476_EN.pdf> accessed 4 August 2019, has clearer and more accurate description of who a foundling is. The title of the relevant section states 'Foundlings of unknown parentage found in a country (S02)' which starts with the sentence 'As regards the position of children found in a country of unknown parentage', thus containing the most accurate definition of a foundling.

[9] UNHCR, 'Good Practices Paper—Action 2: Ensuring that no child is born stateless, 20 March 2017' (20 March 2017) 5 <http://www.refworld.org/docid/58cfab014.html> accessed 4 August 2019.

[10] UNHCR, 'Good Practices: Addressing Statelessness in South East Asia' (5 February 2011) 11 <http://www.refworld.org/docid/4d6e0a792.html> accessed 4 August 2019.

[11] UNHCR and IPU, *Good Practices in Nationality Laws for the Prevention and Reduction of Statelessness* (IPU November 2018) 9.

[12] Ibid 13.

[13] Ibid 34.

[14] The GLOBALCIT, 'Glossary on Citizenship and Nationality' <http://globalcit.eu/glossary_cit izenship_nationality/> accessed 4 August 2019. This definition is adopted by an attorney and law professor Ralph A. Sarmiento, 'The Right to Nationality of Foundlings in International Law' (3 December 2015) <https://attyralph.com/2015/12/03/foundlingsnationality/> accessed 4 August 2019.

[15] Oxford Living Dictionaries, 'Meaning of foundling in English' (2019) <https://en.oxforddictio naries.com/definition/foundling> accessed 4 August 2019.

found after its unknown parents have abandoned it.'[16] The *Black's Law Dictionary* defines it to mean: 'A deserted or exposed infant; a child found without a parent or guardian, its relatives being unknown. It has a settlement in the district where found.'[17] Thus, there is no consistent definition of a foundling, within ordinary non-law and law dictionaries.

It is notable that the English text of article 7(3) of the Covenant on the Rights of the Child in Islam does not use the term 'foundling' but rather stipulates a right to nationality of a 'child of unknown descent or who is legally assimilated to this status'.[18] While still a draft pending adoption by the African Union, the Draft Protocol to the African Charter on Human and Peoples' Rights on the Specific Aspects of the Right to a Nationality and the Eradication of Statelessness in Africa[19] also provides, in article 5.2.a, automatic nationality grant retroactively at birth to 'A child found in the territory of the State of unknown parents'. It also apparently replaces the term 'foundling'.

The non-existence of an established definition or inconsistency of the commonly used definition of the term 'foundling' makes the relevant discussion confusing and slows down the development of the scholarly theory and international standards.

Below, a step-by-step analysis will be made on the wording of national legislation, the 1961 Convention, and the travaux process leading up to the adoption of the 1961 Convention, to verify the hypothesis that the essential requirement or the core definition for being a foundling is that a person's parentage is unknown.


## 3.3  Language Analysis

A quick review of domestic foundling provisions in English, the wordings of article 2 of the 1961 Convention and equivalent national provisions in five other UN official languages as well as those in several non-UN official languages will be presented below. It is worth reminding ourselves that the issue of the person's age when found is yet another issue which will be discussed in conjunction with the efforts to define the term 'found' in Chap. 6.

---

[16] Merriam Webster's On-line Dictionary, 'Definition of foundling' (2019) <https://www.merriam-webster.com/dictionary/foundling> accessed 4 August 2019.

[17] 'Black's Law Dictionary Online' <https://thelawdictionary.org/foundling/> accessed 4 August 2019.

[18] The Covenant's implementation and interpretation is widely unknown. Some analysis of how this provision of the Covenant combines the principles enshrined in CRC and Islamic Law is contained in Azizah Mohd, 'Abandoned child's right to identity protection in Malaysia' (2011) 8 US-China Law Review 389–400.

[19] ACHPR, 'Draft Protocol to the African Charter on human and peoples' rights on the specific aspects of the right to a nationality and the eradication of statelessness in Africa' (2015) <https://www.achpr.org/public/Document/file/English/draft_citizenship_protocol_en_sept2015_achpr.pdf> accessed 17 February 2020.

### 3.3.1   The Term 'foundling'—Is It Used in Domestic Nationality Legislation in English?

The English term 'foundling' originates from the past participle 'found'.[20] The English version of the 1961 Convention in article 2 further qualifies the term 'foundling' with an adjective 'found', that is 'a foundling found in the territory of a Contracting State shall […]'.

The British Nationality Act of 1948 valid as of 1953[21] did not contain any provision relating to foundlings. The US Immigration and Nationality Act of 1952 already had a provision granting nationality to 'a person of unknown parentage found in the United States'.[22]

Then, is the term 'foundling' used in domestic nationality legislation currently in force? Indeed, as seen in annex 1, only two[23] out of at least 27 States[24] whose relevant law is assumingly originally written in English and contains a provision equivalent to article 2 of the 1961 Convention (regardless of whether they are State parties or not) actually use the term 'foundling' within the main text of the relevant provision.[25] All other States adopt instead another term in their relevant provision rephrasing the term 'foundling'.

---

[20] Oxford University Press, 'Oxford Living Dictionaries' (2019) <https://en.oxforddictionaries. com/definition/foundling> accessed 4 August 2019.

[21] British Nationality Act 1948 (1948) <http://www.legislation.gov.uk/ukpga/Geo6/11-12/56/ena cted> accessed 4 August 2019. It is noted, however, that section 4 of the Act provides for nationality acquisition by *jus soli* stating that 'Any person born in the United Kingdom and Colonies is a citizen at birth […]' thus preventing statelessness in case the birth in the territory is established. Also see 4th session of ILC: ECOSOC, 'The Problem of Statelessness—Consolidated Report by the Secretary-General, A/CN.4/56 and Add.1' (26 May 1952) 103–5 <http://legal.un.org/ilc/documentation/eng lish/a_cn4_56.pdf> accessed 4 August 2019.

[22] USCIS, Immigration and Nationality Act of 1952 [USA] (2 August 2019) <https://www.uscis. gov/ilink/docView/SLB/HTML/SLB/act.html> accessed 4 August 2019, in its original version as of its enactment in 1952, section 301(a).

[23] Papua New Guinea (section 22) and Tuvalu (article 43). See annex 1.

[24] Antigua and Barbuda, Australia, Barbados, Belize, Canada, Eswatini (formerly Swaziland), Fiji, Ghana, Guyana, Ireland, Kenya, Malta, Mauritius, New Zealand, Papua New Guinea, Rwanda, Saint Kitts and Nevis, Saint Lucia, Singapore, South Sudan, Sri Lanka, Tuvalu, Uganda, United Kingdom of Great Britain and Northern Ireland, US, Zambia, Zimbabwe. Thanks goes to Menique Amarasinghe for advising on the languages in which Sri Lankan laws are written.

[25] Interestingly, several of those States which do not use the term 'foundling' within the main text of the relevant nationality provision indeed use the term 'foundling' in the title of the provision (such as section 47 of Eswatini nationality law and article 140(13) of the Constitution of the Republic of Singapore—see annex 1). However, as there was insufficient information as to how much weight can be placed on the wordings of titles of legal provisions in each State, no analysis in this regard was made. Some States use the term 'foundling' within separate birth registration related laws. For example, Australia: Births, Deaths and Marriages Registration Act 1997, 2019 section 8(2) (Responsibility to have birth registered) 'If a child is a foundling, the person who has custody of the child is responsible for having the child's birth registered under this Act.' New Zealand: Births, Deaths, Marriages, and Relationships Registration Act 1995, section 7 (Foundlings) '(1) A person who— (a) believes that a child in the person's charge is recently born and was found abandoned in

Twelve States out of these 27 States use the term '(newborn) infant/child/minor' whose parents are 'unknown/not known' (who is found or born in the territory).[26] Ten States out of 27 use the term 'abandoned[27](newborn) infant/child'. Six States adopt the term 'deserted[28] (newborn) infant/child/minor'. Three States use both the term a child (of) 'unknown parents' and 'deserted'[29] in the same provision.

As to be seen by Sect. 3.6, and further confirmed through Sect. 4.3, being 'abandoned' or 'deserted' does not necessarily mean that the person is of unknown parents nor is otherwise stateless. Adopting the term 'abandoned child' and 'deserted child' instead of 'foundling' does not accurately reflect the object and purpose of the relevant provision. Having said this, the fact that the parents of the 'abandoned child' found in the territory are unknown appear to be simply assumed in many States. For example, in *SZRTN v. Minister for Immigration and Border Protection*, the Federal Court of Australia stated that 'found abandoned' included the connotation that the person's parents are unknown. It stated: 'The language of 'found abandoned' may be directed, particularly if the section's concern is, indeed, with statelessness, at the situation of a person who is literally found and about whose parentage nothing is known.'[30]

In summary, very few nationality law provisions written in English currently in force use the term 'foundling', and more States use the term a 'child of unknown parents' than 'abandoned child' or 'deserted child'.[31]

---

New Zealand; and (b) is not satisfied that a Registrar has been notified of the child's birth— shall as soon as is practicable tell a Police employee, who shall notify the Registrar-General. [...]'.

[26] Belize (section 7), Ghana (section 8), Kenya (section 8) Rwanda (article 9), Saint Lucia (7(2)), Singapore (article 140(3)), South Sudan (section 8(4)), Sri Lanka (section 7), Uganda (section 11(1)), United States (section 301(f)), Zambia (article 32(2)), Zimbabwe (article 36(3)).

[27] Antigua and Barbuda, Australia, Barbados, Fiji, Guyana, Malta, Mauritius, New Zealand, Saint Kitts and Nevis, United Kingdom of Great Britain and Northern Ireland.

[28] Belize, Canada, Eswatini (formerly Swaziland), Ireland, South Sudan, Sri Lanka.

[29] Belize, South Sudan and Sri Lanka. It should be noted that these three States are double-counted in this paragraph, thus bringing the total number of the countries to 30 and not 27, the total number of English-written nationality laws with foundling provisions.

[30] *SZRTN v. Minister for Immigration and Border Protection* [2015] FCA 305 (Federal Court of Australia).

[31] The English translation of several States' nationality laws do not even use the term 'abandoned' or 'deserted' to qualify the term 'child' (instead of 'of unknown parents') but use unique terms. Indonesian nationality law at article 4(11) states 'Children born in Indonesian territory whom at the time of birth both parents [...]' *whereabouts* are undetermined' [emphasis added]. Nevertheless, its actual interpretation/application is apparently not widely known. Law of the Republic of Indonesia No. 12 on Citizenship of the Republic of Indonesia, 1 August 2006 <http://www.refworld.org/docid/4538aae64.html> accessed 4 August 2019. Email inquiry with Isa Soemawidjaja, Assistant Protection Officer, UNHCR Indonesia (25 October 2018). The Nepalese Citizenship Act section 3(3) states 'Every child found in the territory of Nepal, whose *paternal and maternal addresses are undetermined*, shall be considered a citizen of Nepal by descent until his/her father or mother are found' [emphasis added]. But the information on its application could not readily be located. Nepal Citizenship Act 2063 (2006), Act No. 25 of the year 2063 (2006), 26 November 2006 http://www.refworld.org/docid/4bbca97e2.htmlaccessed 4 August 2019.

### 3.3.2 *'Foundling' in Five Other UN Official Language Versions of the 1961 Convention and Domestic Nationality Laws*

The text of the 1961 Convention in four of the five UN official languages other than English, carried in the certified true copy[32] of the Convention—all of which are considered equally authentic—have different connotations: The French version states 'L'enfant trouvé (sur le territoire'd'un Etat contractant)' meaning 'the child found (on the territory of a contracting State)', the Spanish version uses the term 'un expósito' the term equivalent to a foundling deriving from the term 'exposed', to be followed by 'que ha sido hallado en el territorio de un Estado contratante' ('found on the territory of a contracting state').[33] The Russian version uses 'найденыш'—the term equivalent to a foundling which derives from the Russian word 'found' -followed by '[,] обнаруженный' ('found on the territory of a contracting state').[34] The French and Russian versions focus more on the fact that the person is found. The French version, interestingly, unlike other versions, does not even carry the qualification 'found' separate from the word 'enfant trouvé' ('found child'), the word equivalent to a foundling. The Chinese version states '(在缔约国领土内发现之)'弃儿'—which can be translated as 'an abandoned child' (found on the territory of a contracting State)'.[35]

It is of particular interest that the Chinese version is quite different from the English word by saying 'an abandoned child', but its appropriateness will be discussed in Sect. 3.6 and further examined in Sect. 4.3.

To make the matter more complicated, while some States whose nationality law is written in the above five UN languages adopt the term used in article 2 of the 1961 Convention to express the concept equivalent to a 'foundling', many States use another term.

---

[32] All the five language versions of the 1961 Convention are available at <https://treaties.un.org/doc/Treaties/1975/12/19751213%2003-00%20AM/Ch_V_4p.pdf>.

[33] 'Diccionario de la lengua española, La Asociación de Academias de la Lengua Española defines 'expósito' as 'Dicho de un recién nacido: Abandonado o expuesto, o confiado a un establecimiento benéfico' <http://dle.rae.es/?id=HKnPEfD> accessed 4 August 2019.

[34] Translated by Inna Gladkova, former Protection Officer (Statelessness) of UNHCR. Email to the author (13 November 2019).

[35] Translated by Yue Fū, whose PhD dissertation (2016) is cited throughout this book. While not included in the certified true copy of the 1961 Convention, the version in Arabic, another UN official language, uses the words which can be literally translated as 'a picked-up child (allaqit) found (in the territory of a contracting State)'. Arabic version of the 1961 Convention <http://www.refworld.org/cgi-bin/texis/vtx/rwmain/opendocpdf.pdf?reldoc=y&docid=5b3e1fde4> accessed 4 August 2019.Translated by Ala'a Zaitoun.

For example, in French, Belgium's nationality law article 10(3) refers to: 'L'enfant nouveau-né trouvé (en Belgique)' which can be translated as 'a newborn child found (in Belgium)' (author translation).[36] However, while not a State party, article 3(1) of the Federal Act on Swiss Citizenship states that 'L'enfant mineur de filiation inconnue (trouvé en Suisse)' ('A minor child of unknown parentage (found in Switzerland)') acquires Swiss citizenship.[37]

In Spanish, the Spanish Civil Code article 17.1.d) uses the term '(los nacidos en España) cuya filiación *no resulte determinada*' ('(those born in Spain) whose parentage is *not determined*') (author translation). It should be noted that the same article goes on to state that minors whose first known place of stay is the Spanish territory are presumed to have been born in the Spanish territory; thus there is no requirement for the persons of undetermined parentage to have been born in Spain to acquire nationality under this provision.[38] Article 13(4) of Costa Rica's Constitution says 'El infante, de padres ignorados' ('a young child of unknown parents').[39] While not a State party, Mexico's nationality law article 7 refers to 'el niño expósito (hallado en...)'.[40]

The translation of the 1961 Convention as well as domestic nationality legislation in the languages other than the five official UN languages use various terms to express the target person. For example, the Italian government's official translation of the term 'foundling (found in the territory)' under article 2 of the 1961 Convention is 'Il figlio d'ignoti (trovato abbandonato nel territorio di uno Stato)', which can be translated[41] as ' a son or daughter of the unknown (persons) (found abandoned in the

---

[36] 'Code de la nationalité belge 28 Juin 1984 [Belgium Nationality Code, 28 June 1984]' <https://www.ejustice.just.fgov.be/cgi_loi/change_lg.pl?language=fr&la=F&table_name= loi&cn=198406283> accessed 2 August 2019; (Translation in UNHCR, 'Mapping Statelessness in Belgium' was relied upon) (October 2012) <http://www.refworld.org/docid/5100f4b22.html> accessed 4 August 2019.

[37] Federal Act on Swiss Citizenship, 20 June 2014 <https://www.admin.ch/opc/en/classified-com pilation/20092990/index.html> accessed 28 February 2020. The original French version is Loi sur la nationalité suisse du 20 juin 2014 <https://www.admin.ch/opc/fr/classified-compilation/20092990/ index.html>.

[38] Translation by author from Spanish original: 'Extractos del Código Civil (Título primero: de los españoles y extranjeros) Vigencia desde 01 de Mayo de 1889. Revisión vigente desde 05 de Agosto de 2018 hasta 29 de Junio de 2020 [Spain, Extract of Civil Code ('Title 1: Spanish nationals and foreigners') In force since 1 May 1889. Revision effective from August 5, 2018 to June 29, 2020]' <http://noticias.juridicas.com/base_datos/Privado/cc.l1t1.html#l1t1> accessed 2 August 2019.

[39] Constitución Política de 7 de Noviembre de 1949 y sus Reformas (Título II Los Costarricenses) [Costa Rica, Political Constitution of 7 November 1949 and its Reforms (Title II Costa Rican nationals)] <http://www.tse.go.cr/pdf/normativa/constitucion.pdf> accessed 2 August 2019.

[40] Ley de Nacionalidad, Nueva Ley publicada en el Diario Oficial de la Federación el 23 de enero de 1998 [Mexico, nationality law, new law published in the official report of the federation on 23 January 1998] <http://www.diputados.gob.mx/LeyesBiblio/pdf/53.pdf> accessed 2 August 2019 (reflecting the changes up to 23 April 2012).

[41] Author thanks Paolo Farci, Attorney at Law for his advice on this translation. Interview with Paolo Farci, Attorney at Law (Florence, Italy, 22 May 2017). See fn 44, Chap. 3 of this book on the translation of the term 'il figlio'.

territory)'.[42] The Hungarian government's official translation of the 1961 Convention refers to: '(területén) talált gyermeket' ('child found (in the territory)').[43]

In terms of domestic nationality legislation, the Italian nationality law article 1(2) states 'il figlio di ignoti (trovato nel territorio)' which can be translated as 'a son or daughter of unknown (persons) (found in the territory)'.[44] The Hungarian Citizenship Act section 3(3)(b) refers to: 'az ismeretlen szülőktől származó (Magyarországon talált) gyermeket' ('children born to unknown parents (found in Hungary)').[45]

### 3.3.3  Observations Based on the Text of the 1961 Convention and Legislation in Different Languages

To preliminarily summarize the previous two sections, the term 'foundling' used in article 2 of the 1961 Convention is rarely used in contemporary domestic legislation in English to describe the person who would acquire nationality under the provision equivalent to article 2, which is more commonly replaced by the term a child of 'unknown parents' or to a lesser extent an 'abandoned' or 'deserted' child (while the latter two might not be a legally precise description of the target person either). The review of the text of article 2 in five other UN official languages found that the term 'foundling' is replaced by various equivalent terms which—while quite difficult to translate into English—more or less refer to a 'found (French and Russian)/exposed (Spanish)/abandoned (Chinese) child'.

The examination of the domestic legislation in these non-English UN and other languages suggest that the term 'foundling' is, again, very often replaced by the

---

[42] Legge 29 settembre 2015, No 162 Adesione della Repubblica italiana alla Convenzione delle Nazioni Unite sulla riduzione dei casi di apolidia, fatta a New York il 30 agosto 1961. (15G00176) (GU Serie Generale n.237 del 12–10-2015) [Law of 29 September 2015, No 162 Accession of the Italian Republic to the UN Convention on the Reduction of Statelessness, concluded at New York on 30 August 1961] (Italy) <https://www.gazzettaufficiale.it/eli/id/2015/10/12/15G00176/sg> accessed 2 August 2019.

[43] Act XV of 2009 promulgating the 1961 Convention in Hungary [tr Gábor Gyulai] <http://njt.hu/cgi_bin/njt_doc.cgi?docid=123906.177515> accessed 2 August 2019.

[44] Note on the translation of 'il figlio': A slight modification of the translation was made by the author from the translation on refworld that is 'Act No 91 of 5 February 1992, Citizenship' <https://www.refworld.org/docid/3ae6b4edc.html> accessed 4 August 2019. This version translates 'il figlio' as 'a person'. Further, ENS, 'Ending Childhood Statelessness: A Study on Italy, Working Paper 07/15' (2015) <http://www.refworld.org/docid/582327974.html> accessed 4 August 2019 translates it as a 'child'. The author translated 'il figlio' as 'a son or daughter' to convey the meaning more accurately upon the advice from Paolo Farci, Attorney at Law. According to Farci, 'il figlio' refers to the family relationship between a parent and his or her son or daughter and its meaning is not limited to a (small) child or a minor. The original of article 1(2) states: 'è considerato cittadino per nascita il figlio di ignoti trovato nel territorio della Repubblica, se non venga provato il possesso di altra cittadinanza'. See, however, Sect. 6.7.1, on Italy's position on the age of a foundling. Interview with Paolo Farci, Attorney at Law (Florence, Italy, 22 May 2017).

[45] Hungary: Act LV of 1993 on Hungarian Citizenship [Hungary] (1 October 1993) <http://www.refworld.org/docid/3ae6b4e630.html> accessed 2 August 2019.

term 'a child (person) of unknown parents (found in the country concerned)' or something to that effect. These observations seem to support this book's assertion later on (including in the final conclusions) that there is no need to 'stick to' the term 'foundling', which is ambiguous in itself, in reflecting article 2 of the 1961 Convention into domestic legislation or in formulating the relevant provision in future regional instruments.

## 3.4  Evolution of the Foundling Provision within International and Regional Instruments

To further examine the hypothesis laid out in Sect. 1.4 that one of the two requirements for being a foundling is the person's unknown parentage, an analysis will be made first on the development of the international legal framework relating to foundlings, starting with the 1930 Convention. This will be followed by further analysis of the text of some of the domestic laws in force during the drafting process of the 1930 and the 1961 Convention and further complemented by the actual practice today in some States.

### 3.4.1  Codification of Nationality Legislation Principle into the 1930 and 1961 Conventions: 'Foundling provision' More Common than 'Otherwise stateless' Persons Provision

As already detailed in Sects. 1.5.5.1 and 2.4.1, the codification process of the 1930 and 1961 Conventions[46] was carried out while making references to the national legislation around the world in place at that time. The nationality law provision granting nationality to a foundling found in the territory (or a person of unknown parentage born in the territory) was—and still is—even more common than the provision to grant nationality to children born in the territory whose parent(s) is (are) known who would otherwise be stateless when the 1931 and 1961 Convention were drafted.

As already discussed in Sect. 1.5.5.1 and to be discussed in Sects. 3.4.2.3 and 3.4.5.2, many States during the drafting process of the 1930 and 1961 Conventions had an easier time voting for the former—the foundling provision—than the provision to grant nationality to otherwise stateless children.

---

[46] See also Sect. 2.4.1 on the developments towards the adoption of the 1930 and the 1960 Convention in general.

## 3.4.2 The 1930 Hague Convention

The 1930 Convention was the first international instrument that addressed the prevention of statelessness, including of foundlings, as mentioned in Sect. 2.4.1.

### 3.4.2.1  Two-Fold Structure of Article 14: (1) a Child of Unknown Parents and (2) a Foundling

Article 14 of the 1930 Convention provides:

> A child *whose parents are both unknown shall have the nationality of the country of birth*. If the child's parentage is established, its nationality shall be determined by the rules applicable in cases where the parentage is known.
>
> A *foundling* is, until the contrary is proved, *presumed to have been born on the territory* of the State in which it was found. (emphasis added)

Thus, article 14 provides for two categories of children separately.

(1)   a child of unknown parentage (born in the territory); and
(2)   a *foundling* (found in the territory).

The 1930 Convention itself does not contain the definition of these two separate categories of persons.

From the context within the article, however, it could already be inferred that under article 14 of the 1930 Convention the term 'foundling' is to be construed as a child of unknown parents whose place of birth is unknown, which is distinguished from a child whose parents are unknown but whose place of birth is known to be in the territory of a specific country. By presuming that a foundling has been born in the territory where she or he is found, both categories of persons (1) and (2) above equally acquire a nationality.

### 3.4.2.2  Who Can Be a Child of Unknown Parents Born in the Territory?

From a simple reading of article 14 of the 1930 Convention, a question might arise: who was supposed to fall within the category (1) above, that is a person of unknown parents born in the territory? If a persons' parentage is not known, is her or his birthplace not normally unknown too?

The accessible record of the drafting process of the 1930 Convention does not carry detailed discussions in relation to article 14,[47] especially the type of persons who would qualify as (1) a child of unknown parents or (2) a foundling.

---

[47] The author consulted, among others, *Acts of the Conference for the Codification of International law held at the Hague from March 13th to April 12th, 1930. Volume I Plenary Meetings, Official No.: C. 351. M. 145. 1930. V.* (League of Nations 19 August 1930); *Acts of the Conference for the Codification of International law held at the Hague from March 13th to April 12th, 1930, Meetings*

However, the evolution of the articles (or the 'basis of discussions') leading up to the final adoption of article 14, as well as the review of national legislation and observations made in preparation of the 1930 Conference for the Codification of International Law in the Hague, as well as materials written afterwards, provide clarifications.

The relevant article (article 3) in the preliminary Draft Convention initially drafted in 1926 by M. Rundstein (hereinafter Rundstein Draft Convention), the Rapporteur for the Committee of Experts for the Progressive Codification of International Law, stated:

> (Article 3) A child born of *parents who are unknown* or whose nationality cannot be ascertained acquires the nationality of the State in which it was *born or found* when it cannot claim another nationality in right of birth, proof of such other nationality being admissible under the law in force at the place where it was found or born. (emphasis added)[48]

Thus, the English version of article 3 of the Rundstein Draft Convention did not even contain the term 'foundling', but rather a person of unknown parents, born or found in the territory.

As mentioned in Sect. 1.5.5.1, the Preparatory Committee of the Conference for the Codification of International Law subsequently drew up the 'Bases of Discussions' to be later adopted as articles of the 1930 Convention. In this context, the Preparatory Committee requested the information from governments to provide their existing nationality legislation as well as their feedback on the draft articles of the Rundstein Draft Convention. The preparatory committee specifically requested the information on 'nationality of a child of unknown parents' (as well as of parents having no nationality, or of parents of unknown nationality).[49] Twenty-two out of the 28 governments whose substantive responses are on record stated that their nationality related law contained provisions granting their nationality to 'foundlings' or 'children of unknown parents' born or found in the territory (while the exact wordings used in the relevant laws (in English) to describe the persons who benefit from such provisions sometimes differed). The rest of the States that responded had a *jus soli* provision granting nationality by birth in the territory.[50]

While the majority of the responding States did not clarify what it meant to have 'unknown parents', the responses from two States, that is of Belgium and the Netherlands, offer some clarification.

---

*of the Committees, Volume II Minutes of the 1st Committee Meetings: Nationality, Official No.: C. 351(a). M. 145(a). 1930. V.* (League of Nations 27 November 1930). League of Nations, *Bases of Discussion Drawn up for the Conference by the Preparatory Committee, Volume I Nationality (Volume I-C.73.M.38.1929. V-BI-Geneva)* (Conference for the Codification of International Law, May 1929).

[48] 'Draft Convention Drawn up by M. Rundstein, Rapporteur of the Committee of Experts for the Progressive Codification of International Law', Text modified by M. Rundstein in consequence of the Discussion in the Committee of Experts. League of Nations, *Bases of Discussion Drawn up for the Conference by the Preparatory Committee, Volume I Nationality (Volume I-C.73.M.38.1929. V-BI-Geneva)* (Conference for the Codification of International Law, May 1929) 210.

[49] Ibid 118–19.

[50] See fn 71, Chap. 1 of this book on the responses from the 28 governments.

The Netherlands's response to the preparatory committee first stated that it would seem desirable for the Convention in the making to limit nationality grant to children of unknown parents born in the territory or found in the territory, and not to children whose parents are stateless or of unknown nationality, which was initially proposed by the Preparatory Committee:

> As regards these questions, it would seem desirable to keep within the limits laid down in the Netherlands Law of 1892, which attributes nationality only to the *children of unknown parents born in the Kingdom of the Netherlands* in Europe or in the oversea territories or *found in the Netherlands.* (emphasis added)[51]

The Netherlands's 1892 law on nationality prevailing at the time provided, while in principle stipulating nationality grant by *jus sanguinis*, that the following were of Dutch nationality by virtue of *jus soli*:

> Illegitimate *children not recognized* either by the father or by the mother, *born in* the Kingdom of the Netherlands in Europe;
>
> [...]
>
> *Children found or abandoned* in the Kingdom of the Netherlands in Europe, as long as there is no evidence to show their origin as legitimate, legitimised or recognized children. (emphasis added)[52]

It is thus clear that the Netherlands envisaged—as cases of 'children of unknown parents born in the Netherlands'—children (born out of wedlock) who were without legally recognized parents.

Belgium's reply to the Preparatory Committee on this issue only carries its prevailing nationality law provision, ie the Law of May 15th, 1922:

> Article E.—The following are of Belgian nationality:
>
> [...]2. Children born in Belgium of parents who are *legally unknown.* Until proof to the contrary is established, abandoned children found in Belgium are deemed to have been born on Belgian soil. (emphasis added)[53]

While legislated later than the adoption of the 1930 Convention, Belgium's article 1(2) of the 1932 law[54] also carries the same phrase—that 'Children born in Belgium

---

[51] League of Nations, *Bases of Discussion Drawn up for the Conference by the Preparatory Committee, Volume I Nationality (Volume I-C.73.M.38.1929. V-BI-Geneva)* (Conference for the Codification of International Law, May 1929) 65. Bases of Discussion Drawn up for the Conference by the Preparatory Committee, Point VII. Text of Point VII, Responses of governments, Observations, Basis of discussion No 11.

[52] Ibid 65. Bases of Discussion Drawn up for the Conference by the Preparatory Committee, Point VII. Text of Point VII, Responses of governments, Observations, Base de discussion No 11.

[53] Cited in ibid 65. Bases of Discussion Drawn up for the Conference by the Preparatory Committee, Point VII. Text of Point VII, Responses of governments, Observations, Base de discussion No 11.

[54] Article 1(2) stated: 'Children born in Belgium of legally unknown [parents]. A foundling discovered in Belgium is présumée, pending proof to the contrary, to have been born in Belgian territory' and are Belgian nationals. Article 1(2) of the consolidated Nationality Act of 14 December 1932 (les lois coordonnées sur l'acquisition, la perte et le recouvrement de la nationalité (A.R. du 14 Décembre 1932) cited in 4th session of ILC: ECOSOC, 'The Problem of Statelessness—Consolidated Report by the Secretary-General, A/CN.4/56 and Add.1' (26 May 1952) 106 <http://legal.un.org/ilc/documentation/english/a_cn4_56.pdf> accessed 4 August 2019.

of parents who are *legally unknown*' (emphasis added) was a Belgian national, while foundlings discovered in the territory were presumed to have been born in Belgium.[55] Indeed, the ILC's travaux documents[56] leading up to the 1961 Convention shows that the typical cases envisioned by 'children born in Belgium of legally unknown parents' were persons (born out of wedlock) who are not recognized by their mothers or fathers.[57]

Thus, at least for the Netherlands and Belgium, children of 'unknown parents' meant children (whose parent(s]) might be factually known but) who do not have any parent with whom they have a legal parent–child relationship.

Having reviewed the responses from the governments, the Preparatory Committee noted in their 'observations' that: 'In the case of a *foundling* or of a *child whose parents are juridically not known*, the attribution to the child of the nationality of the country of birth is generally admitted' (emphasis added).[58] It is thus apparent that for the Preparatory Committee a person of 'unknown parents' born in the territory meant a person whose birth in the territory was established and whose parents might be factually known but legally unknown, that is a person who has no legally recognized parents.

The 1930 Hague Conference was subsequently held. Here again the French representative is also recorded to have stated that 'the sole purpose of the article [14] is to determine the nationality of an *illegitimate child* if the parents are unknown' (emphasis added).[59] This again confirms that, for many States, a person of unknown parents were typically children born out of wedlock.

Here, it would be useful to recall the historical background. Given the stigma associated with giving birth out of wedlock, it is reasonable to assume that more unmarried than married couples (women) tended to abandon their children on the

---

[55] See Sect. 4.4 for contemporary examples of nationality laws which use the term 'legally unknown parents'.

[56] 4th session of ILC Ibid 113.

[57] Belgium's reply to ILC related to the drafting of the 1961 Convention also include a statement that: 'The provisions on the effect of the *recognition of illegitimate children* may mean that a child born in Belgium of *legally unknown* parents, which has been considered as Belgian, would lose its nationality [...] If recognized the first place by an alien, such a child would lose the status of a Belgian national even if it did not acquire the nationality of the alien [...] Certain provisions of Belgian law may [...] lead to statelessness. Such would be the case for the following: [...] an illegitimate child recognized first by its mother whose country's law does not ertend [sic. 'extend'] her nationality to the child; an illegitimate child recognized by its father either before or after recognition by its mother; if the law of the father's country does not extend the father's nationality to the child' (emphasis added). 4th session of ILC ibid 113.

[58] League of Nations, *Bases of Discussion Drawn up for the Conference by the Preparatory Committee, Volume I Nationality (Volume I-C.73.M.38.I929. V-BI-Geneva)* (Conference for the Codification of International Law, May 1929) 67. Bases of Discussion Drawn up for the Conference by the Preparatory Committee, Point VII. Text of Point VII, Responses of governments, Observations, Basis of discussion No 11.

[59] Statement by M. de Navailles (France). *Acts of the Conference for the Codification of International law held at the Hague from March 13th to April 12th, 1930, Meetings of the Committees, Volume II Minutes of the 1st Committee Meetings: Nationality, Official No.: C. 351(a). M. 145(a). 1930. V.* (League of Nations 27 November 1930) 225 and 293.

street, a baby hatch or other places to be found during this period.[60] Further, it is
also likely that the French delegation was referring to children born 'anonymously',
whose place of birth was indeed known but whose mother did not reveal her identity,
resulting in parents being legally 'unknown'. As explained in Sect. 2.10.5.1, and as
discussed further in Sect. 4.3.10, some States require the mother's 'recognition' of her
maternity over the child to establish the maternal legal descent, or allow mothers to
give birth anonymously in the presence of medical professionals but without having
their identity revealed and to leave the child under institutional care. The typical
example is France, where, at least since the French Revolution in the 1780s, women
have long had the right to give birth secretly or anonymously.[61] By 1930, two out of
three public hospitals freely admitted pregnant women who ask for secrecy in giving
birth.[62]

The following proposal by Portugal during the 1930 Hague Conference to amend
the Basis No 11 also suggests that Portugal considered that 'unknown parents' meant
'legally unknown parents' rather than factually unknown parents: 'A child whose
parents are unknown at law has the nationality of the country of birth.'[63]

It can thus be assumed that the typical cases foreseen as a 'a child of unknown
parentage born in the territory' at the time of drafting 1930 Convention was: A person
who is known to have been born in the territory of parents who might be factually
known but legally unknown such as a child born out of wedlock not recognized by
either mother or father, and born under the system of anonymous birth.

### 3.4.2.3  The 'supremacy' of the Obligation for Children of Unknown Parents and Foundlings (Article 14) Over That for Children of Stateless Parents (Article 15)

Basis No 11 was subsequently discussed at the 1930 Conference for the Codification
of International Law held in the Hague, and was finally adopted as article 14 of the
1930 Convention with a minor modification, which states:

A *child whose parents are both unknown* shall have the nationality of the *country of birth*. If
the child's parentage is established, its nationality shall be determined by the rules applicable
in cases where the parentage is known.

A *foundling is*, until the contrary is proved, presumed to have been born on the territory of
the State in which it was found. (emphasis added)

---

[60] Nadine Lefaucheur, 'The French "tradition" of anonymous birth: the lines of argument' (2004)
18 International Journal of Law, Policy and the Family 319, 320.

[61] Ibid.

[62] Ibid 321.

[63] Annex II. Observations and proposals submitted to the plenary committee relating to the bases
of discussion drawn up by the Preparatory Committee, *Acts of the Conference for the Codification
of International law held at the Hague from March 13th to April 12th, 1930, Meetings of the
Committees, Volume II Minutes of the 1st Committee Meetings: Nationality, Official No.: C. 351(a).
M. 145(a). 1930. V.* (League of Nations 27 November 1930) 293.

Thus, article 14 included references to both a child of unknown parents and a foundling, unlike the Rundstein Draft Convention. On the other hand, article 15 of the 1930 Convention as finally adopted states:

> Where the nationality of a State is not acquired automatically by reason of birth on its territory, *a child born on the territory of that State of parents having no nationality, or of unknown nationality,*[64] *may* obtain the nationality of the said State. The law of that State shall determine the conditions governing the acquisition of its nationality in such cases. (emphasis added)

It is noted that, unlike article 14 providing for mandatory ('shall') grant of nationality to children born of unknown parents born in the territory (and foundlings whose birth in the territory is presumed), article 15 leaves the nationality grant up to each State ('may').

Indeed, the draft 'basis of discussion 12' (eventually adopted as article 15) prepared by the Drafting Committee of Experts was subject to extensive discussions during the drafting process, where a number of countries expressed reservations against the obligation to grant nationality to children of parents who are stateless or of unknown nationality due to economic and other reasons.[65] The final text of article 15 reflects the compromises among States. This was in contrast with the draft 'basis 11' which was adopted as article 14 with little discussion, apart from on the addition of a provision regarding the case in which the filiation of a child of unknown parents is established later.[66]

---

[64] While not within the scope of this book, it is noted that, unlike the 1961 Convention, the 1930 Convention does not cover all persons who would otherwise be stateless. Notably, it excludes persons whose parent(s) is (are) not stateless but nonetheless cannot pass on their nationality to them.

[65] *Acts of the Conference for the Codification of International law held at the Hague from March 13th to April 12th, 1930. Volume I Plenary Meetings, Official No.: C. 351. M. 145. 1930. V.* (League of Nations 19 August 1930) 74.

[66] The 'Basis of Discussion No 11' drawn up by the Preparatory Committee read as follows: 'A child whose parents are unknown has the nationality of the country of birth. A foundling is, until the contrary is proved, presumed to have been born on the territory of the State in which it was found.' Ibid 74; *Acts of the Conference for the Codification of International law held at the Hague from March 13th to April 12th, 1930, Meetings of the Committees, Volume II Minutes of the 1st Committee Meetings: Nationality, Official No.: C. 351(a). M. 145(a). 1930. V.* (League of Nations 27 November 1930) 225–6; League of Nations, *Bases of Discussion Drawn up for the Conference by the Preparatory Committee, Volume I Nationality (Volume I-C.73.M.38.1929. V-BI-Geneva)* (Conference for the Codification of International Law, May 1929). Specifically, see 'Bases of discussion drawn up by the preparatory committee: General Observations submitted by certain Governments, Point VII.' at pp 62–7 as well as 'Complete text of the replies made by the governments on the schedule of points submitted by the preparatory committee' at pp 119–205.

### 3.4.3   1949 UN Study of Statelessness

In principle, the 1949 UN Study of Statelessness basically confirmed the 'two-category approach' as in article 14 of the 1930 Convention, and dedicates separate paragraphs for 'children born of unknown parents' and 'foundlings'.

The 1949 Study refers to 'children of unknown parents' to mean 'Children whose birth in the country is established but the identity and consequently the nationality of whose parents is unknown'.[67] The Study further explains that this category refers to 'children whose mother's identity has not been revealed, but who are known to have been born in the country concerned'.[68] The Study asserts that in consideration of the fact that the 'unknown parents' of a child likely possess the nationality of the country of birth:

> it is normal for the country of birth to grant its nationality to such children. It should be added that a child born of unknown parents will be brought up in the country of birth and no distinction will be made between it and other nationals. (emphasis added)[69]

On the other hand, the 1949 Study describes 'foundlings' as children whose:

> parents are quite unknown, and it is not even certain that the children were born in the country where they were found. But in the majority of cases this is so. It is thus usual for the law to presume that foundlings were born in the country concerned. It is desirable that the rule that a foundling is presumed to have been born in the country where he was found, which has not yet been adopted in all legislations, should be adopted everywhere. (emphasis added)[70]

Thus, the 1949 Study still distinguished between 'children of unknown parents' and 'foundlings' by the fact that the former's birthplace is known to be in the territory, and the latter's, unknown.

An interesting feature of the 1949 Study was, however, that the Study in its recommendation at the end grouped 'children of unknown parents born in the territory' with all other children born in the territory who would otherwise be stateless, that is children born of parents who are stateless or of undetermined nationality or who cannot pass on their nationality to their children. The Study separately recommended grant of nationality to foundlings where they were found.[71] This is distinct from the categorization in the 1930 Convention, where the persons of unknown parents born in the territory and foundlings were grouped together and fell within article 14, while

---

[67] UNHCR, 'A Study of Statelessness' (August 1949) 135–6, paras D and E <https://www.unhcr.org/protection/statelessness/3ae68c2d0/study-statelessness-united-nations-august-1949-lake-success-new-york.html?query=A%20Study%20of%20Statelessness> accessed 4 August 2019, reedited by the Division of international Protection of UNHCR, 1995.

[68] It is likely that persons born under the anonymous birth scheme are envisaged here as typical examples. See also Sect. 3.4.2.2.

[69] UNHCR, 'A Study of Statelessness' (August 1949) 116–17 <https://www.unhcr.org/protection/statelessness/3ae68c2d0/study-statelessness-united-nations-august-1949-lake-success-new-york.html?query=A%20Study%20of%20Statelessness> accessed 4 August 2019.

[70] Ibid 116–17.

[71] Ibid paras D and E and 148.

persons born in the territory of stateless or unknown-nationality parents fell within another category under article 15.

### 3.4.4 ILC Study on Nationality Including Statelessness and Draft Conventions

The codification process of the 1961 Convention was also carried out by making references to the national legislation around the world in place at that time. During this drafting process by the ILC, a foundling was described as a person.

[B]y definition, *without known parents and without a known birthplace*, happens to be the best example of a case in which neither of the two existing legal systems which confer nationality at birth, the jus sanguinis or jus soli, can be applied. (emphasis added)[72]

In terms of the formulation of recommendations, the subsequent documents produced through ILC's Study on Nationality including Statelessness tended to maintain the 'renewed' two-tiered categorization done in the recommendations of the 1949 UN Study (and not the one under the 1930 Convention), that is 'persons of unknown parents born in the territory' grouped together with all 'other persons born in the territory who would otherwise be stateless', on one hand, and 'foundlings found in the territory' on the other hand.

### 3.4.5 ILC Draft Conventions on Reduction of Future Statelessness and Denmark's Proposal

The travaux process of the 1961 Convention based on the ILC Draft Conventions carries records of a series of discussions from which some inferences can be made about the 'definition' of a foundling. During the drafting process, the fact that a foundling's parents are 'unknown' was mentioned several times and appeared to be presupposed throughout.[73] However, it also appeared to be presupposed that foundlings' birthplace was normally unknown, and no specific reference was made

---

[72] Roberto Córdova, 'Nationality, including Statelessness—Report on the Elimination or Reduction of Statelessness' (1953) 176 <http://legal.un.org/docs/?path=../ilc/documentation/english/a_cn4_64.pdf&lang=E> accessed 4 August 2019.

[73] See for example the statement by United Arab Republic '(article 2) presupposed that the parents of the foundling were unknown'. United Nations, Summary Records, 5th Meeting of the Committee of the Whole held on 3 April 1959, A/CONF.9/C.1/SR.5, UN Conference on the Elimination or Reduction of Future Statelessness, Geneva, 1959 and New York, 1961 (3 April 1959) 8 <http://legal.un.org/docs/?path=../diplomaticconferences/1959_statelessness/docs/english/vol_2/a_conf9_c1_sr5.pdf&lang=E> accessed 4 August 2019. Also see the statement by the Netherlands: 'a foundling, although of unknown parents [...]' at the United Nations, Summary Records, 5th Plenary Meeting held on 31 March 1959, A/CONF.9/SR.5, UN Conference on the Elimination or Reduction of Future Statelessness, Geneva, 1959 and New York, 1961 (31 March

to persons of unknown parents born in the territory. No clear answer can be found as to whether a person of unknown parents born in the territory was included in the concept of a 'foundling'. Nonetheless, the discussions relating to the distinction between article 1 and article 2 are of particular importance in considering this question.

### 3.4.5.1   Original Dependency of Article 2 on Article 1

Article 2 of the ILC Draft Convention on the Reduction of Future Statelessness[74] (which was the same as the Draft Convention on the Elimination of Future Statelessness) adopted by ILC in 1954 at its sixth session stated: '*For the purpose of article 1,*[75] a foundling, so long as his place of birth is unknown, shall be presumed to have been born in the territory of the Party in which he is found' (emphasis added).

The original article 2 in the ILC Draft Statelessness Reduction Convention thus provided that article 2 was dependent on article 1—in the sense that the *jus soli* rule of article 1 (nationality grant for an otherwise stateless child born in the territory) was to be extended to foundlings.[76] On the other hand, article 1 evolved significantly, based on the draft 'Reduction' (and 'Elimination') Convention during the UN Conference on the Elimination or Reduction of Future Statelessness in 1959 and 1961 due to the reservations expressed by a number of States towards mandatory automatic nationality grant as well as their efforts to make the provision relevant to both *jus soli* and *jus sanguinis* systems. As examined more closely in Sect. 3.4.5.2, the final version of article 1 that was eventually included in the 1961 Convention provided that member States can make the nationality acquisition either automatic upon birth, or non-automatic upon application becoming available latest at the age of 18 years. Thus, if article 2 of the Draft Convention was to be kept as it was, a

---

1959) 3 <http://legal.un.org/docs/?path=../diplomaticconferences/1959_statelessness/docs/english/vol_2/a_conf9_sr5.pdf&lang=E> accessed 4 August 2019.

[74] ILC Draft Convention on the Reduction of Future Statelessness, adopted by ILC at its sixth session, in 1954, and submitted to the General Assembly as part of the Commission's report covering the work of that session (at para 25). *Yearbook of the International Law Commission, vol II* (United Nations 1954).

[75] Article 1 of the Draft Convention on the Reduction of Future Statelessness stated: 'A person who would otherwise be stateless shall acquire at birth the nationality of the Party in whose territory he is born, (sic)'. On the other hand, article 1 of the Draft Convention on the Elimination of Future Statelessness stated '(1.) A person who would otherwise be stateless shall acquire at birth the nationality of the Party in whose territory he is born. (2.) The national law of the Party may make preservation of such nationality dependent on the person being normally resident in its territory until the age of eighteen years and on the condition that on attaining that age he does not opt for and acquire another nationality. [...]' Text adopted by ILC at its sixth session, in 1954, and submitted to the General Assembly as a part of the Commission's report covering the work of that session (at para 25). The report appears in ibid.

[76] This is also pointed out by Laura van Waas, *Nationality Matters: Statelessness under International Law* (Intersentia 2008) 69–70.

foundling found in the territory may have had to remain stateless and wait for the maximum of 18 years to acquire the nationality of the country where found.

### 3.4.5.2 Subsequent 'independence' of Article 2 from Article 1 for Strengthening of the States' Obligation for Foundlings Over that for Persons Otherwise Stateless

Against the initial dependency of the draft article 2 on article 1, a number of States expressed their reservations—in particular, the Danish representative submitted its own version of the draft Convention, which made article 2 independent from article 1, while imposing a stronger obligation on States vis-à-vis foundlings falling within article 2.

The Danish representative, in recommending the amendment to the ILC draft, stated that the goal of formulating article 2 that way was to ensure that foundlings are on a stronger footing than children born on the territory otherwise stateless, whose parents are, according to him, in most cases, non-nationals. He stated that: 'Statistics tended to show that *most foundlings were* not in fact children of stateless persons, but *of parents who were nationals* of the country in whose territory they were found […]' (emphasis added).[77]

The Danish representative also stated in a different 1959 session:

> [T]he great majority of *foundlings were born in the territory* of the State in which they were found *and were children of nationals of that State* and not of stateless persons; hence it would be wrong to apply to all foundlings rules applicable to the children of stateless persons. (emphasis added)[78]

Nevertheless it should be duly noted that the Danish representative also added that the above does not mean that article 2 is not to be applied when the unidentified parent(s) of the person is(are) highly likely to be a foreign national. The Danish representative stated.

---

[77] The comments by the Chairman speaking as the representative of Denmark, introducing his delegation's amendment to article 2, United Nations, Summary Records, 5th Meeting of the Committee of the Whole held on 3 April 1959, A/CONF.9/C.1/SR.5, UN Conference on the Elimination or Reduction of Future Statelessness, Geneva, 1959 and New York, 1961 (3 April 1959) 7 <http://legal.un.org/docs/?path=../diplomaticconferences/1959_statelessness/docs/english/vol_2/a_conf9_c1_sr5.pdf&lang=E> accessed 4 August 2019. The author, however, complements his statement by adding that 'otherwise stateless children' who are not foundlings are not limited to children of stateless parents, but also others such as children of parent(s) who are unable to pass on nationality to the child.

[78] United Nations, Summary Records, 5th Plenary Meeting held on 31 March 1959, A/CONF.9/SR.5, UN Conference on the Elimination or Reduction of Future Statelessness, Geneva, 1959 and New York, 1961 (31 March 1959) 2 <http://legal.un.org/docs/?path=../diplomaticconferences/1959_statelessness/docs/english/vol_2/a_conf9_sr5.pdf&lang=E> accessed 4 August 2019.

*even if a foundling were the child of foreign parents,* those parents would not be present to undertake the child's education. [...] and it was surely better that the child should acquire at birth the nationality of that country than that he should have to wait until the age of eighteen [...]. (emphasis added)[79]

In support of the Danish government, the United Arab Republic, for example, stated that 'for humanitarian reasons', foundlings should be granted nationality of the country where found.[80] The United Arab Republic representative also stated that article 2 was autonomous from article 1 providing for otherwise stateless persons born in the territory, as article 2 'presupposed that the parents of the foundling were unknown. If the nationality of the father or mother of the foundling were known, *then other provisions would apply*' (emphasis added).[81]

True, the assumption that foundlings are likely to be children of nationals was indeed behind many States' support to nationality grant to foundlings, and such assumption is still often invoked today.[82] However, from the above, the bottom line for those promoting the 'independence' of article 2 from article 1 rather appears to be their conviction that, basically, persons of unknown parentage were in need of stronger protection in the absence of caretakers than other children who would otherwise be stateless, ultimately regardless of who their parents actually are.

Here, it became rather clear that, at least in the mind of many drafters of the 1961 Convention, the most significant distinction between article 1 and article 2 was whether the children's parents are known (article 1) or unknown (article 2).

The Danish government's assertion generally gained support and its proposal to make article 2 independent from article 1 was agreed upon. Foundlings found in the territory were thus supposed to automatically acquire nationality in any State under article 2, unlike their counterparts who fell within article 1.

---

[79] United Nations, Summary Records, 5th Meeting of the Committee of the Whole held on 3 April 1959, A/CONF.9/C.1/SR.5, UN Conference on the Elimination or Reduction of Future Statelessness, Geneva, 1959 and New York, 1961 (3 April 1959) 8 <http://legal.un.org/docs/?path=../diplom aticconferences/1959_statelessness/docs/english/vol_2/a_conf9_c1_sr5.pdf&lang=E> accessed 4 August 2019.

[80] United Nations, Summary Records, 5th Plenary Meeting held on 31 March 1959, A/CONF.9/SR.5, UN Conference on the Elimination or Reduction of Future Statelessness, Geneva, 1959 and New York, 1961 (31 March 1959) 3 <http://legal.un.org/docs/?path=../diplomaticconfe rences/1959_statelessness/docs/english/vol_2/a_conf9_sr5.pdf&lang=E> accessed 4 August 2019.

[81] It is assumed from the context that the representative meant to say 'the identity of the father or mother' when he said 'the nationality of the father or mother of the foundling'. United Nations, Summary Records, 5th Meeting of the Committee of the Whole held on 3 April 1959, A/CONF.9/C.1/SR.5, UN Conference on the Elimination or Reduction of Future Statelessness, Geneva, 1959 and New York, 1961 (3 April 1959) 8 <http://legal.un.org/docs/?path=../diplom aticconferences/1959_statelessness/docs/english/vol_2/a_conf9_c1_sr5.pdf&lang=E> accessed 4 August 2019.

[82] This is even so in non-State parties such as the Philippines. See Sects. 1.5.5.1 and 5.6.2, for more discussions on the Philippines' Supreme Court case law in 2016. *G. R. No 221697 Mary Grace Natividad S. Poe-llamanzares v. Comelec and Estrella C. Elamparo, and G. R. No 221698–700 Mary Grace Natividad S. Poe-llamanzares v. Comelec, Francisco S. Tatad, Antonio P. Contreras and Amado D. Valdez* (Supreme Court of the Philippines); *G.R. 221,538 Rizalino David v. Senate Electoral Tribunal & Mary Grace Poe Llamanzares* (Supreme Court of the Philippines).

However, simply deleting the reference to 'For the purpose of article 1' in the ILC draft would have led to the result that in a *jus sanguinis* State a foundling found would not have acquired the nationality of that State. The Danish government thus subsequently made an amended proposal as follows: 'A foundling found in the territory of a Contracting State shall, in the absence of proof to the contrary, *be considered as a national of that State*' (emphasis added).[83] However, the Danish government's amended proposal above was not adopted, seemingly because of the disagreements over what constituted proof to the contrary, especially over whether birth outside the territory disqualifies the person from the application of article 2 (see Sect. 7.3.1.1).

### *3.4.6  The 1961 Convention*

As already mentioned in Chap. 1, article 2 of the 1961 Convention, as finally adopted, stipulates that: 'A *foundling found* in the territory of a Contracting State shall, in the absence of proof to the contrary, be considered to have been born within that territory of parents possessing the nationality of that State' (emphasis added).

As a foundling found is considered to have been born within the territory of the State to citizen parents, it was intended that in a *jus soli* State she or he acquires the nationality of the presumed country of birth, and in a *jus sanguinis* State the child will acquire the nationality of the presumed parents.[84]

The issue of how exactly States formulate their own provision, which are supposed to reflect this article, in their own domestic legislation, especially in terms of how, technically, they enable foundlings to acquire their nationality, is a different question that will be discussed in Sects. 7.4–7.5.

---

[83] Article 4 of the Danish Proposal. United Nations Conference on the Elimination or Reduction of Future Statelessness Geneva, 1959 and New York, 1961, A/CONF.9/4 (15 January 1959) 15, Denmark: Memorandum with Draft Convention on the Reduction of Statelessness' <http://legal.un.org/docs/?path=../diplomaticconferences/1959_statelessness/docs/english/vol_1/a_conf9_4.pdf&lang=E> accessed 4 August 2019.

[84] Inferred from, for example, the Danish representative's statement during the 5th Plenary Meeting. United Nations, Summary Records, 5th Plenary Meeting held on 31 March 1959, A/CONF.9/SR.5, UN Conference on the Elimination or Reduction of Future Statelessness, Geneva, 1959 and New York, 1961 (31 March 1959) 2 <http://legal.un.org/docs/?path=../diplomaticconferences/1959_statelessness/docs/english/vol_2/a_conf9_sr5.pdf&lang=E> accessed 4 August 2019.

### 3.4.7  A Child of Unknown Parents Born in the Territory: Left Between Article 1 and Article 2?—'merger' with 'a foundling found in the territory'

It should now be highlighted that, unlike the 1930 Convention, article 2 of the 1961 Convention only refers to a 'foundling found in the territory'. Indeed, article 2 and the rest of the 1961 Convention do not carry any reference to a 'child (person) of unknown parents (born in the territory)'. Likewise, no definition is separately provided for 'a foundling' 'found' anywhere in the 1961 Convention. As discussed in detail in Sect. 3.2, the UNHCR Guidelines 4 (2012) do not explicitly define a foundling, and only mention children without legally recognized parents (born in the territory) as those who should also be considered foundlings.[85]

It is again time to ask the question: where does a 'child (person) of unknown parents' fits in, within the 1961 Convention? Do 'foundlings' under article 2 of the 1961 Convention only refer to persons of unknown parents whose birthplace is also unknown? Or, do persons of unknown parents whose birth in the territory is established qualify as foundlings under article 2?

In considering this question, it is relevant to refer to the final version of article 1 of the 1961 Convention. Paragraph 1 states.

> A Contracting State shall grant its nationality to a *person born in its territory who would otherwise be stateless*. Such nationality shall be granted:
>
> (a) at birth, by operation of law, or
>
> (b) upon an application being lodged with the appropriate authority [...]. (emphasis added)

Article 1 paragraph 2(a) then makes such a non-automatic procedure as allowed under article 1 paragraph 1(b) available at the latest when the person turns 18. It is noted that, unlike article 15 of the 1930 Convention, which had limited coverage, article 1 of the 1961 Convention is formulated to cover all persons born in the territory who would otherwise be stateless including persons whose parent(s) cannot transmit their nationality to them.[86] Then, another question would arise—are persons of unknown parents born in the territory covered by article 1 rather than article 2, as they are indeed 'otherwise stateless', without known parents to inherit any nationality from?

---

[85] UNHCR Guidelines 4 (2012) para 61.

[86] The comments by the Chairman, speaking as the representative of Denmark, stated that 'otherwise stateless children' are not limited to children of stateless parents, but also others such as children of parent(s) who are unable to pass on nationality to the child. United Nations, Summary Records, 5th Meeting of the Committee of the Whole held on 3 April 1959, A/CONF.9/C.1/SR.5, UN Conference on the Elimination or Reduction of Future Statelessness, Geneva, 1959 and New York, 1961 (3 April 1959) 7 <http://legal.un.org/docs/?path=../diplomaticconferences/1959_statelessness/docs/english/vol_2/a_conf9_c1_sr5.pdf&lang=E> accessed 4 August 2019.

To consider this question, it is again worth reminding ourselves that, just like the 1930 Convention effectively favour children of unknown parents and foundlings under article 14 over children of parents who are stateless or of unknown nationality under article 15, article 2 of the 1961 Convention also was meant to 'favour' foundlings over otherwise stateless persons under article 1. This was due mainly to the fact that the former did not have parents legally responsible for protection and care (see Sect. 3.4.5.2). It is logical to infer that the State representatives when pushing for a stronger obligation to grant nationality to foundlings (than to otherwise stateless persons) presupposed that persons of unknown parentage known to have been born in the territory were to fall within article 2. This comes naturally as the two categories of persons share the common feature—that they do not have legal parents responsible to protect and care for them. It would be absurd and illogical if a person of unknown parents whose birth is known to have taken place in the territory of the State concerned is excluded from the scope of article 2 and be put at a more disadvantageous position than those of unknown parents whose birthplace is not known. The proof of birth in the territory (which fulfils one of the 'presumed' facts[87]) should only strengthen the person's claim to the nationality, and not weaken it. The fact that the birthplace is known to be in the territory of a certain contracting State should only put the latter category of persons at a stronger footing.

Thus, in light of the fact that the 1961 Convention was drafted subsequent to the 1930 Convention, and that the two Conventions shared a similar objective, it can be inferred that the two originally separate categories of persons, that is children of unknown parentage born in the territory on one hand and foundlings found in the territory on the other hand, in the 1930 Convention were merged in the 1961 Convention.

It can then be concluded that a 'foundling' in the 1961 Convention refers simply to a child[88] of 'unknown parents', regardless of whether the person's birthplace is known to be in the territory or not. In other words, a foundling's parents are always unknown, but his/her birthplace can either be known or unknown.

However, as mentioned in the preceding section, this was not articulated at least as far as the available travaux record can be verified. As a result, it risks differing interpretation by States on whether persons of unknown parentage born in the territory were to be treated in the same vein as other persons of known parentage born in the territory otherwise stateless (article 1), or as foundlings (article 2) under the 1961 Convention. Having said that, the majority of the State parties adopted the same interpretation as adopted by the author when reflecting article 2 in their domestic laws (see Sect. 3.7).

---

[87] See Sect. 7.2 around the point that 'birth in the territory' is a 'presumed' fact within the structure of article 2 of the 1961 Convention.

[88] As stated elsewhere, the issue of up to what age the relevant person can be considered a foundling when found in the territory will be discussed in Chap. 6.

## 3.4.8   ECN and Its Explanatory Report

Article 6, paragraph 1 of the ECN provides:

> Each State party shall provide in its internal law for its nationality to be acquired ex lege by the following persons:
>
> (a) *children one of whose parents possesses*, at the time of the birth of these children, the nationality of that State party [...],
>
> (b) *foundlings found* in its territory who would otherwise be stateless.[89] (emphasis added)

The ECN's Explanatory Report[90] providing its interpretive guidance states:

> The term 'foundlings' here refers to new-born infants[91] found[92] abandoned[93] in the territory of a State with *no known parentage* or[94] nationality who would be stateless if this principle were not applied. It is taken from Article 2 of the 1961 Convention on the Reduction of Statelessness. (emphasis added)

Thus, the Explanatory Report confirms that a foundling is of unknown parentage: Article 6(1)(b) provides foundlings found in the territory with the same automatic *ex lege* acquisition guaranteed for a child of a national.[95]

On the other hand, paragraph 2, article 6 of the ECN provides:

> Each State party shall provide in its internal law for its nationality to be acquired by *children born on its territory who do not acquire at birth another nationality*. Such nationality shall be granted:
>
> a. at birth ex lege; *or*
>
> b. subsequently, to children who remained stateless, upon an application being lodged with the appropriate authority, by or on behalf of the child concerned, in the manner prescribed by the internal law of the State party. Such an application may be made subject to the lawful and habitual residence on its territory for a period not exceeding five years immediately preceding the lodging of the application. (emphasis added)

---

[89] On the difference between article 2 of the 1961 Convention and article 6(1)(b) of the ECN with the former containing 'in the absence of proof to the contrary' and the latter using 'who would otherwise be stateless', see Sect. 7.3.1.2.

[90] Council of Europe, 'Explanatory Report to the European Convention on Nationality, 6.XI.1997' (1997) para 48 <https://rm.coe.int/16800ccde7> accessed 4 August 2019.

[91] On the discussion of whether restricting it a foundling to 'new-born infant' is appropriate, please see in general Chap. 6 and, in particular, Sect. 6.7.

[92] It should be pointed out that the word 'found' here is unnecessary as article 6(1)(b) states 'foundling found' (in the territory) and the Explanatory Report para 48 here is trying to define the term 'foundling' and not 'foundling found'.

[93] On the discussion of whether including in the definition of a foundling 'abandoned' is appropriate, please see Sect. 3.6.

[94] See fn 6 of this chapter on this word 'or' in the Explanatory Report, which appears to be an error.

[95] While this will be discussed in Sect. 7.3.1.2, it is noted already here that ECN's article 6(1)(b) provides no reference to 'presumption' (of birth from citizen parents in the territory) or 'in the absence of the proof to the contrary' as in the 1961 Convention, but simply provides the nationality acquisition criteria.

Just as the 1961 Convention, the 1997 ECN clearly distinguishes the two categories of persons, that is foundlings found in the territory and persons otherwise stateless born in the territory, in terms of the mode of nationality acquisition. Article 6(2) of the ECN, like article 1 of the 1961 Convention, gives States an option to either grant their nationality automatically *ex lege* at birth or non-automatically upon application. Thus, under ECN, the provision for a 'foundling found' in the territory under article 6(1)(b) is clearly stronger than the States' obligation towards 'otherwise stateless children' born in the territory under article 6(2) of the ECN. The difference is that ECN obliges States to open up such an application procedure much earlier than under the 1961 Convention (which allows for a waiting period of a maximum of 18 years of age), that is after the maximum of five years of lawful and habitual residence in the territory.

The same question might arise here: where does a person of unknown parentage born in the territory fit in, between article 6(a)(b) and article 6(2)? While the ECN and Explanatory Report are not explicit, it is logical to interpret that the concept of 'having been born' is included in that of 'being found'. The term 'foundling' is already defined in the Explanatory Report as referring to a person of unknown parentage, and an alternative interpretation might give a person of unknown parentage born in the territory lesser right (such as only being able to apply for nationality after five years of lawful and habitual residence) compared to her or his counterpart whose place of birth is unknown who is granted nationality automatically. Again, the fact that the birthplace is known to be in the territory of a contracting State should only put the former category of persons on a stronger footing.

Thus, it can once again be concluded that a 'foundling' under article 6(1)(b) of the ECN basically refers to a child of unknown parentage, regardless of whether the birthplace is known or unknown.[96]

## 3.5 The Overall Difference Between 'persons of unknown parentage' and Other 'persons otherwise stateless'

Now that it has been established that foundlings essentially mean 'persons of unknown parentage', what are, then, the differences between 'persons of unknown parentage' and other children who would 'otherwise be stateless born in the territory' in the absence of the relevant safeguards? As stated earlier, the most significant difference noted by those involved in the travaux is that otherwise stateless children normally have at least one parent who is legally responsible for her or his protection and care (unless such parent becomes unavailable for one reason or another such as parental death, illness or neglect).

---

[96] From this, a related question arises—can a child of unknown parents who are found in the territory who nevertheless is known to have been born abroad acquire nationality where found? This will be addressed in Sect. 7.3.1.

In terms of procedures and assessments, otherwise stateless children are supposed to have both their descent and birthplace (in or outside the territory) known,[97] based on which their (otherwise) *statelessness* can be determined, in accordance with *jus soli* and *jus sanguinis* principles. However, for children both of whose parents (and birthplace) are unknown, there is no way of determining the concerned persons' nationality status in the absence of any special provision addressing such a special circumstance. The exception is that if the children of unknown parents are known to have been born in the territory of States that grant nationality by *jus soli* regardless of the parentage of the persons concerned, they are to acquire that nationality without a special provision.

In other words, on one hand, children whose parentage is known need to have the nationality status of their parent(s), and the parent(s)'s ability to transmit nationality assessed in order to see whether they are 'otherwise stateless'. On the other hand, foundlings need to first have their foundlinghood, that is unknown parentage, established, from which their (otherwise) statelessness in the absence of the relevant safeguards, will consequently be established.

## 3.6 Does a 'foundling' Need to Have Been Intentionally 'abandoned' and Passively 'found' on the Territory?

Before discussing what 'unknown parents' actually mean in detail, it is worth discussing whether the word 'foundling' can be replaced by the words '(orphaned or) abandoned children'—which has been mentioned in Sects. 3.2, 3.3.1 and 3.3.2 in particular.

'Abandoned children' are indeed the most typical cases of foundlings also envisaged by the drafters of the 1961 Convention.[98] Further, along with an 'abandoned child', 'orphaned child'—many of whom can also be stateless[99]—is also used in some academic and UNHCR literature as an interchangeable word for a foundling. 'Abandonment' in combination with the word 'found' can be commonly construed as situations where the children are left behind by parents with the intention of not

---

[97] See, however, Sect. 3.8 on the fact that persons of known parentage of unknown birthplace who are otherwise stateless also exist, and fall through the crack of the 1961 Convention.

[98] For example, see discussions between the representatives of Denmark, Belgium and Israel, who, without defining the word 'foundling' repeatedly referred to situations where 'an abandoned child were found in the territory'. United Nations, Summary Records, 5th Meeting of the Committee of the Whole held on 3 April 1959, A/CONF.9/C.1/SR.5, UN Conference on the Elimination or Reduction of Future Statelessness, Geneva, 1959 and New York, 1961 (3 April 1959) 6–11 <http://legal.un.org/docs/?path=../diplomaticconferences/1959_statelessness/docs/english/vol_2/a_conf9_c1_sr5.pdf&lang=E> accessed 4 August 2019.

[99] Carol Batchelor, 'The International Legal Framework Concerning Statelessness and Access for Stateless Persons. Contribution to the European Union Seminar on the Content and Scope of International Protection: Panel 1—Legal basis of international protection, Madrid, 8–9 January 2002' (8 January 2002) 4 <https://www.refworld.org/docid/415c3be44.html> accessed 4 August 2019; Laura van Waas, *Nationality Matters: Statelessness under International Law* (Intersentia 2008) 69.

fulfilling their obligation to care for them—for example, in a baby hatch or on the street—then passively discovered by a third party. Having said this, as mentioned in Sect. 3.3.1, the term 'found abandoned' tends to be interpreted by States to include the connotation that the person's parents are unknown.[100]

However, being abandoned or orphaned is only a 'cause' of making a person's parents 'unknown' which the author confirmed as the core definition of a foundling through Sects. 3.2–3.4. Needless to say, not all abandoned or orphaned children are of unknown parentage. A person can be abandoned or orphaned after being registered with the authorities and acquiring nationality through her or his known parent(s).

Nevertheless, as was noted in Sects. 3.3.1 and 3.3.2, even the Chinese version of article 2 of the 1961 Convention uses the term an 'abandoned child' instead of a 'foundling', along with nationality laws of a number of mainly (former) common-wealth countries. In this context, the rule set out in article 33 of VCLT is relevant: When a comparison of the authentic texts discloses a difference of meaning, and the application of articles 31 (General Rule of Interpretation) and 32 (Supplementary Means of Interpretation) does not resolve such a dispute, the meaning that best reconciles the texts, having regard to the object and purpose of the treaty, is to be adopted.[101] As discussed above, given the historical evolution of the foundling concept including the travaux of the 1961 Convention demonstrating that the term 'foundling' essentially means a 'child of unknown parentage' as well as the fact that the English and four other language versions of article 2 of the 1961 do not use the term 'abandoned', it can be concluded that the element of being intentionally 'abandoned' is not required to fall within article 2 of the 1961 Convention.

In any case, as seen in Sect. 3.3.1 and annex 1, a relatively small number of countries use the term 'abandoned' in its nationality legislation. If 'abandoned child' is used to replace the word 'foundling' and is understood in the most common way as mentioned above, this could work against the object and purpose of the relevant provision in the 1961 Convention and ECN, which is to prevent statelessness. There are many other persons who are not intentionally 'abandoned' (or orphaned), who nonetheless are of unknown parentage and will remain stateless unless the nationality of the territory where she or he is identified, is granted. As will be discussed in Sect. 4.3, a person can be lost, born anonymously in the presence of medical personnel and left behind, or even have biological parents taking care of her or him who cannot be recognized as a legal parent (and 'voluntarily approach' the authorities to be 'found').

---

[100] *SZRTN v. Minister for Immigration and Border Protection* [2015] FCA 305 (Federal Court of Australia).

[101] Interview with Gerard-René de Groot, Professor Emeritus at Maastricht University School of Law (5 October 2017) based on the relevant paragraph in his 'Background Paper' for UNHCR—convened Expert Meeting on Preventing Statelessness among Children in Dakar, Senegal (23–24 May 2011) on the differences between the five UN language versions of the 1961 Convention.

## 3.7 The Distinction Between 'children of unknown parents', 'foundlings' and 'otherwise stateless persons' Within Domestic Nationality Laws

Having said the above, as seen in annex 1 and Sect. 3.3, there was, and still is, a wide range of how States legislate in this regard. The following provides a classification of foundling provisions[102] focusing on whether or not, and how, national legislation distinguishes (1) 'children (or persons) of unknown parents born in the territory' (abbreviated to 'children of unknown parents' in this section for the sake of simplicity), (2) 'foundlings found in the territory' (abbreviated to 'foundlings') and (3) 'persons who would be otherwise stateless born in the territory' (abbreviated to 'otherwise stateless persons').

### 3.7.1 (1) Children of Unknown Parents, (2) Foundlings and (3) Otherwise Stateless Persons Distinguished

Some States have a similar formulation as the 1930 Convention, where children (persons) of unknown parents are by law presumed or recognized to have been born in the territory in which they are found, thereby acquiring nationality provided for children of unknown parentage born in the territory. Those laws normally provide for nationality grant for persons born in the territory otherwise stateless separately from the above two categories.

#### Spain

For example, article 17.1.c) of the Spanish Civil Code states:

The following persons are Spanish nationals by birth (*de origen*):

(c) Those born in Spain to foreign parents, *if both lack a nationality or if the legislation of the State of either of the parents does not give the child a nationality.* (emphasis added)

Then article 17.1.d) goes on to state:

(d) Those *born in Spain* whose parentage is not determined (*los nacidos en España cuya filiación no resulte determinada*). To these effects, minors (*los menores de edad*) whose first known place of stay is the Spanish territory *are presumed to have been born in* the Spanish territory. (author translation)[103]

---

[102] See also Sect. 1.5.2.3 for the definition of a 'foundling provision'.

[103] While not a State party, other examples include Republic of Korea. Article 2 para 1, sub-para 3 of the Republic of Korea's Nationality Act provides for acquisition of Korean nationality by a child born in Korea of unknown parentage and article 2 para 2 provides that 'an abandoned child found in the Republic of Korea shall be recognized as born in the Republic of Korea'. Republic of Korea: Law No 16 of 1948, Nationality Act [(20 December 1948).
<https://data.globalcit.eu/NationalDB/docs/01_South%20Korea_Nationality%20Act%20u pdated%20up%20to%20amendment%20on%2019%20June%202014%20%5bENGLISH%5d_1. pdf> accessed 3 August 2019.

*France*

While not a State party, article 19–1 of the French Civil Code states the following persons are French nationals.

1. A child born in France of *stateless parents*;

2. A child born in France of *alien parents and to whom the transmission of the nationality* of either parent is *not* by any means *allowed* by foreign Nationality Acts. […]. (emphasis added)

Preceding the above, article 19 stipulates: 'A child *born in* France of unknown parents (*l'enfant né en France de parents inconnus*) is French […]' (emphasis added). Article 19–2 then goes on to say: '[A] child whose record of birth was drawn up in accordance with *Article 58* of this Code Shall be presumed born in France' (emphasis added).

Article 58 of the French Civil Code in turn stipulates the obligation of a person who has '*found* a new-born child' ('*aura trouvé un enfant nouveau-né*') to make a declaration about it to the civil status officer of the place where she or he discovered the child, and the subsequent duties by the civil status officer.[104]

## 3.7.2  (1) Children of Unknown Parents 'born or found' Distinguished From (3) Otherwise Stateless Persons

Some legislations provide for nationality grant to children of unknown parentage who are 'born or found' in the territory, making their interpretation clear that having been 'born' in the territory is included in the term 'found' under article 2 of the 1961 Convention. For example, article 8(1) of Law No 8389, dated 5 August 1998 'On Albanian Nationality', as amended provides that: 'A child *born or found* within the territory of the Republic of Albania acquires the Albanian nationality if he is born to unknown parents, and as a result the child would otherwise remain stateless' (emphasis added).[105]

---

[104] French Civil Code (tr Georges Rouhette with the assistance of Anne Rouhette-Berton) <http://www.fd.ulisboa.pt/wp-content/uploads/2014/12/Codigo-Civil-Frances-French-Civil-Code-english-version.pdf> accessed 4 August 2019. Checked against the original French version of Code Civil (France) <https://www.legifrance.gouv.fr/affichCode.do?cidTexte=LEGITEXT000006070721> accessed 4 August 2019.

[105] Law on Albanian Citizenship, Law No 8389 (6 September 1998) <http://www.refworld.org/docid/3ae6b5c10.html> accessed 3 August 2019. While not a State party, article 9 of the Slovenian Citizenship Act takes the same approach: '1. A child born or found on the territory of the Republic of Slovenia of unknown parentage or whose parents are of unknown citizenship or have no citizenship at all shall acquire citizenship of Republic of Slovenia.' Citizenship of the Republic of Slovenia Act [Slovenia], ZDRS-UPB2 (7 December 2006) <https://www.refworld.org/docid/50bdfabf2.html> accessed 3 August 2019.

### 3.7.3  (1) Children of Unknown Parents Included in (2) Foundling Concept

In some other States, 'children of unknown parents *born* in the territory' are, as a matter of interpretation, included in the concept of 'children of unknown parents *found* in the territory', both of which are distinguished from other persons born in the territory granted nationality on statelessness related ground.

#### Hungary

Hungarian Citizenship Act section 3 states: 'Until proven to the contrary, the following persons shall be recognized as Hungarian citizens: (a) children born in Hungary of stateless persons residing in Hungary; (b) children born of unknown parents and *found* in Hungary' (emphasis added).[106]

As will be seen in Sect. 4.3.6, Hungary clearly interprets that having been 'born' in the territory is included in the term 'found' in the territory above.

### 3.7.4  (1) Children of Unknown Parents Grouped Together with (3) Otherwise Stateless Persons

Under some States' legislation, 'children of unknown parents born in the territory' are explicitly grouped together with other persons born in the territory 'otherwise stateless', while the nationality grant to foundlings or 'persons of unknown parents found in the territory' is stipulated under a separate provision.

#### Italy

For example, article 1(1)(b) and 1(2) of the Italian nationality legislation states.

> 1. The following shall be *citizens by birth*:
>
> [...]
>
> (b) A son or daughter *born in the territory of the Republic both of whose parents are unknown* or *stateless*, or who *do not follow the citizenship of their parents* under the law of the State to which the latter belong.
>
> 2. A *son or daughter found in the territory of the Republic whose parents are unknown* shall be considered citizens by birth [...] (emphasis added)[107]

---

[106] Hungary: Act LV of 1993 on Hungarian Citizenship [Hungary] (1 October 1993) <http://www.refworld.org/docid/3ae6b4e630.html> accessed 2 August 2019.

[107] Article 1(1)b and 1(2) of Legge No 91, 5 febbraio 1992, Nuove norme sulla cittadinanza [Italy, Law 5 February 1992 No 91, New provisions on citizenship] (5 February 1992) <http://www.refworld.org/docid/46b84a862.html> accessed 3 August 2019.

*Belgium*

The Belgian nationality legislation article 10(1) reads: '[A] child born in Belgium is Belgian if she or he would otherwise be stateless at any moment before she or he reaches the age of 18 or is "emancipated"'. Then article 10(3) states: 'A new-born child found in Belgium is presumed, until the contrary is proved, to be born in Belgium.'[108] Thus, by presuming the person's birth in Belgium, article 10(3) makes the *jus soli* grant of Belgian nationality, which is provided to 'otherwise stateless' persons born in the territory under article 10(1) of the same article applicable to a 'new-born infant[109] found in Belgium' (*'l'enfant nouveau-né trouvé en Belgique'*). Logically, a person of unknown parents born in the territory, while not specifically referred to in article 10(1), should be covered by article 10(1) as they fulfil the requirements under the section ('birth in the territory' plus being otherwise stateless without Belgian nationality), and there is no need to 'presume' their birth in Belgium.

Grouping together persons of unknown parents with other persons born in the territory otherwise stateless is acceptable as long as the automatic grant of nationality at the time of birth is guaranteed to the former, in light of the object and purpose of article 2 of the 1961 Convention.

### 3.7.5   No Nationality Grant (in Principle) to (2) Foundlings Whose Birth in the Territory is **Not** Established

As in annex 1, out of 193 States researched, and out of 139 States that have a foundling provision, the legislation of 17 States' (four of which are State parties to the 1961 Convention) provides nationality only to children of unknown parentage *born* in the territory. Foundlings whose birth in the territory is not established would not be able to benefit from such legislation unless such in-country birth is somehow presumed.

Article 11(2) of the Chadian Nationality Code states 'Children born in Chad of unknown parents (are Chadians...)'.[110] While not a State party to the 1961 Convention, Japanese Nationality Act [*Kokusekihō*] article 2(iii) states that a child is a Japanese national 'When both parents are *unknown* or have no nationality in a case where the child is born in Japan'. That being said, as will be discussed in detail in Sect. 6.4, the Japanese Family Register Act [*Kosekihō*] along with court adjudications have indeed allowed the confirmation of Japanese nationality under the above article 2(iii) for persons found on the territory whose place of birth is unknown.

---

[108] Belgium Nationality Code, 28 June 1984. Translation in UNHCR, 'Mapping Statelessness in Belgium' (October 2012) <http://www.refworld.org/docid/5100f4b22.html> accessed 4 August 2019.

[109] See Sect. 6.4 on the issue of age limitation by Belgium.

[110] Ordonnance 33/PG.-INT. du 14 août 1962 portant code de la nationalité tchadienne, 14 August 1962 [Ordinance 33 / PG.-INT. of 14 August 1962 on the Chadian Nationality Code](Chad) <https://www.refworld.org/docid/492e931b2.html> accessed 7 August 2019.

On a separate note, as seen in Sect. 1.5.5.2 and annex 1, 13 out of 54 States without 'foundling provisions' have separate provisions for nationality grant to persons born in the territory who are either otherwise stateless or of unknown nationality or born of parents who are stateless or of unknown nationality, which could cover persons of unknown parents whose birth in the territory is established.

## 3.8  Persons Who Fall Through the Crack of the 1961 Convention and ECN: Persons of Known Parentage of Unknown Birthplace, Otherwise Stateless

Having reviewed the above, the existence of one category of persons—who is not able to invoke any of the provisions within the 1961 Convention and ECN—was revealed. That is, persons whose parent(s) is (are) known, whose birthplace is nonetheless unknown, who would otherwise be stateless. These persons cannot invoke article 1 of the 1961 Convention or article 6(2) of the ECN because their place of birth has not been proven to be in the territory of the State where they are found or identified. They cannot invoke, for the same reason, article 4 of the 1961 Convention and article 6(4)(b) of the ECN because it is not clear whether they were born outside the territory of the country of nationality of one of the parents. Yet, these persons cannot invoke article 2 of the 1961 Convention or article 6(1)(b) of the ECN because their parents are not unknown.

Such cases must be rather rare—normally, if one of the parents is known, that person should have information on the birthplace of the child. However, there could be cases where the birth in a certain territory cannot be proven due to the lack of documentary proof (while no contrary proof exists) or, for example, the parent(s) is (are) incapable—for various reasons—of knowing or remembering the birthplace.[111] Such persons would have to remain stateless at least for years until they could access naturalization as a stateless person. In the absence of any applicable provision, it would surely be desirable that the birth in the territory is presumed where the child concerned is identified, as long as there is no proof to the contrary.

---

[111] Upon consultation, Gerard-René de Groot indeed confirmed he was aware of an actual case where a Roma mother, where she was stateless and the small child was (otherwise) stateless, could not exactly recall which of the several European countries where she had been moving around that the child was born, largely due to lack of awareness on the importance of birthplace. No documentary proof was found either. They could not invoke with any State the nationality acquisition for an otherwise stateless child born in the territory. Interview with Gerard-René de Groot, Professor Emeritus at Maastricht University School of Law (5 October 2017).

In this context, reference to some of the cases introduced in Chaps. 4 and 6 might prove useful, in terms of different indirect evidence relied upon—in the absence of direct evidence establishing birth in the territory—supporting the fact that the person was 'born' in the territory[112] (or even that the person was 'found' at an early age which could be used to assert presumption of birth[113]) and how it was (positively) assessed by States.

Further, it will be pertinent that domestic legislation or any future regional instrument addresses this gap so that statelessness of persons otherwise stateless of known parentage but unknown birthplace can be prevented.

## 3.9  Summary and Conclusions: A Foundling is of 'unknown parentage'

The aim of this chapter was to define who a 'foundling' is. A working hypothesis presented in Sect. 1.4, was that one of the two legal requirements for being a foundling (in addition to being a child when found in the territory discussed in Chap. 6) under article 2 of the 1961 Convention was that a person's parentage is unknown. This chapter aimed to examine this hypothesis by reviewing the relevant international instruments, their travaux, national legislation and related materials. Further, an examination was made of whether a foundling's birthplace—that is not only parentage—needs to be unknown to qualify as a foundling.

Before going into detailed examination, the nature of the term 'found' in article 2 was clarified—that it is a condition for a State to grant its nationality to a foundling, rather than forming part of the foundling definition. The alternative reading would make article 2 redundant.

National legislation around the world was reviewed, where it was found that there are only very few domestic nationality law provisions which use the word 'foundling' as used in the English version of article 2 of the 1961 Convention, or the equivalent term in five other official language versions of the Convention. In many States, the nationality law provision equivalent to article 2 refers to a child (whose age when found will be discussed in Chap. 6) of 'unknown parents'. In a minority of States, the provision simply refers to a 'child found' or an 'abandoned (or 'deserted') child found' in the territory without reference to such child's parents being 'unknown', which, however, is implicit in the provision.

Two categories of persons, that is a 'child of unknown parentage born in the territory' and 'a foundling found in the territory', were historically and typically distinguished in domestic legislation and in the 1930 Convention, until at least during the ILC Study on Nationality including Statelessness that ended in 1954. Under article 14 of the 1930 Convention, a foundling—a child of unknown parentage and unknown

---

[112] For example, the Japanese family court adjudication—Sects. 4.3.8 and 6.4.

[113] For example, Spanish administrative decision in Sect. 4.3.9, and US decision in Sect. 4.3.5, which are also discussed in Sects. 5.6.1, and 6.4–6.7.

birthplace in this context—was presumed to have been born in the territory and whereby was granted the same treatment (automatic grant of nationality where born) as a child of unknown parentage born in the territory. This treatment was distinctively better than a child born in the territory of known parents who are stateless or unknown nationality whose nationality acquisition was at States' discretion under article 15.

However, from a literal reading of the 1961 Convention, the position of a person *of unknown parents 'born in the territory'* is rather ambiguous—it is no longer clear whether a person of unknown parentage *born in the territory* falls within article 1, or article 2. Nevertheless, this doubt was resolved by examining the travaux.

The ILC's draft article 2 was originally dependent on the nationality grant by jus soli under article 1 (allowing for non-automatic grant after 18 years of age or even later), by presuming a foundling's birth in the territory, but was separated from it. There were a number of country representatives who asserted that article 2 should be independent from article 1, with the intention to make the State obligation under article 2 'stronger', to ensure automatic grant of nationality to them at birth.

This was because, as expressed by a number of country representatives during the negotiations in adopting the 1961 Convention, children of unknown parentage were considered to have a stronger claim for nationality where born or found than children born on the territory who would otherwise be stateless because (1) they are likely to have been born in the territory from parents who are nationals of the concerned State and, more importantly, (2) they are in the most vulnerable situation without those legally responsible for protection and care, regardless of the likelihood of having been born in the territory of citizen parents.

Another major difference between the persons covered by article 1 (and 4) as opposed to article 2 of the 1961 Convention is that, unlike for the former, for the latter category of persons there is no basis to determine their possession of nationality based on the *jus sanguinis* principle, and often on the *jus soli* principle.

As discussed in Sect. 3.4.7, it can be understood that the two originally separate categories of persons, that ie 'persons of unknown parentage born in the territory' and 'foundlings found in the territory' in the 1930 Convention were merged together in the 1961 Convention, in light of the fact that the 1961 Convention was drafted subsequent to the 1930 Convention, and the two Conventions shared a similar objective.

It is thus concluded that children of unknown parentage, regardless of whether their place of birth is known or unknown, are meant to be covered by article 2 and not article 1. It was also confirmed that having been literally 'abandoned' is not a requirement to qualify as a foundling or to acquire a nationality as a foundling (while having been 'found' is a requirement for article 2 to apply).

This 'favour' of persons of unknown parentage over persons whose parent(s) is (are) known but are otherwise stateless was replicated in ECN. Article 6(1)(b) apparently covers persons of unknown parents whose birth in the territory is known, as it provides for nationality grant *ex lege*, which is distinct from article 6(2) (for otherwise stateless persons born in the territory) under which the State may indeed opt for non-automatic grant.

Based on the above, it was determined that the term 'found' in the territory in article 2 of the 1961 Convention and article 6(1)(b) of the ECN covers 'birth' in the territory.

As already stated at the outset in Chap. 1, the other element of the foundling definition, that is the age at which a person of unknown parents can be considered a 'foundling' will be discussed in Chap. 6.

Hereafter, the terms 'child of unknown parentage' or alike are used interchangeably with a 'foundling' regardless of whether the person's place of birth is known or unknown. However, as the official term used in the 1961 Convention is a 'foundling', the term would need to be used in order to avoid confusion in a number of contexts. Further, as already detailed in Sect. 1.5.2.3, the term 'foundling provision' has been and will continue to be used throughout this book generally referring to a legal provision explicitly granting nationality to persons of unknown parents born or found in the territory. While it was once contemplated whether the term 'unknown parentage (parents) provision' should rather be used in light of the above conclusion, it was eventually decided to, in principle, adopt the term 'foundling provision' even when the relevant national law provision does not contain the term 'foundling'. Chapter 4 will take this forward by examining how the term 'unknown parents' should then be interpreted.

# Chapter 4
# Defining 'Unknown-ness' of Parentage

**Abstract** This chapter further clarifies the meaning of 'unknown parents'. Whether 'unknown' means so in a factual sense, or in a legal sense, is also clarified. This will be done through analysing the implementation of domestic foundling provisions based on legal precedents and other materials. Examination is made on more than 10 categories of persons (including orphaned or informally adopted children, children abandoned including in baby boxes or those born under anonymous birth systems), who have actually been considered to fall within foundling provisions in States such as Spain, Italy, Hungary, USA and Japan. This chapter concludes that 'unknown parentage' essentially means being of 'legally unknown parents', which means specifically that the person's legal parents do not exist, including cases where such existence of legal parents cannot be proven. In this context, the applicability of article 2 to persons without legal parents born out of surrogacy arrangement is also considered.

In Chap. 3, it was determined a foundling under article 2 of the 1961 Convention is a person of 'unknown parents' whose birthplace may or may not be known. It was also concluded that having been 'found in the territory' is not part of who a foundling is, but is a condition to grant nationality.

The next step is to examine what it means that parents are 'unknown'. For this purpose, an examination will be made on what sorts of situations or categories of persons are considered to fall within the foundling provision. Whether 'unknown' means so in a factual sense, or in a legal sense, will also be examined. This will be done mainly through analyzing the information gathered through interviews, available judicial or administrative precedents, administrative rules or other information on the actual implementation of the foundling provisions in State parties as well as non-State parties to the 1961 Convention and ECN.

Reference will be made to some procedural aspects of how some categories of person of unknown parents get registered with the government and have nationality confirmed, in order to facilitate a holistic understanding of the issues.

In the course of reviewing State practice, the practice of several non-State parties without a foundling provision will also be mentioned, which might not be helpful in interpreting the term 'unknown' per se, but may be useful in showing the customary nature of nationality grant to persons of unknown parentage.

Further, the alternative measures taken by some States to grant nationality to persons of unknown parentage who are nonetheless not recognized as such will also be referred to.

## 4.1  Note on the Statistical Information

In order to show the magnitude of the issues, some numerical information about some category of persons of unknown parents will be referred to, whenever available. However, it should be noted that, at the outset, the exact number of persons who acquire nationality under the foundling provision in any country per year is generally unavailable. A number of States have a decentralized system where the competent authority in each municipality has an authority to (de facto) make decisions on birth registration, and even on nationality issues, while they might consult the central authority on complicated cases. Many States do *not* maintain or readily make available the central statistics and/or do not provide breakdown of the reasons for nationality grant or confirmation.[1]

For countries that have safe haven laws and anonymous birth systems (see Sects. 2.10.5.1 and 4.3.10), the numbers (if kept) of children surrendered under these schemes often reflect a significant portion of the persons who acquire nationality under the foundling provision. For many countries that have baby hatches that are indeed operated or tolerated by States, most of the children dropped in these cradles could be understood to have acquired nationality either under the applicable foundling provision (or under a wider interpretation of another nationality law provision). It is, however, noted that in some cases such numbers might include the cases where the parent(s) changed their mind after the surrender and took the children back, for whom, thus, the foundling provision was not invoked in the end.

While many States often have statistics available for 'abandoned children' in general, they often do not distinguish between so-called 'open abandonment' or

---

[1] For example, Italy has a decentralized governance system. Each municipality in general has an authority to determine whether a person is of unknown parentage born or found in Italy and thus falls under article 1(1)(b) or article 1(2) of Law 91/92 granting Italian nationality. In large cities such as Rome, Milan, Turin, Florence, usually this function is performed by the citizenship department (can also be called citizenship office) of the Population Register Office, acting on behalf of the government. However, for complicated cases, municipalities are to consult with the central competent authority on nationality matters, which is the Central Direction for Civil Rights, Citizenship and Minorities of the Department for Civil Liberties and Immigration of the Ministry of Interior. Interview with Central Direction for Civil Rights, Citizenship and Minorities of the Department for Civil Liberties and Immigration of the Ministry of Interior Italy (Rome, Italy, 23 May 2017). The author wishes to thank Helena Behr and Enrico Guida for facilitating her communications with the office. Also confirmed by the ENS, 'Ending Childhood Statelessness: A Study on Italy, Working Paper 07/15' (2015) 11 <http://www.refworld.org/docid/582327974.html> accessed 4 August 2019.

'secret abandonment'.[2] In the former, that is 'open abandonment', parents relinquish their parental rights for institutional or family-based care such as foster care or adoption, after the children concerned have already been duly registered with the authorities as their own children. In the latter, 'secret abandonment', the parents (at least intend to) remain anonymous. Further, even if the given statistics specifically focus on secret abandonment, they normally do not carry details as to whether the parent(s) was eventually identified as a result of an investigation or other means. Statistics related to the number of 'orphans' normally include many children whose have already been duly registered at birth whose parentage is also firmly established. Thus they can only give remote indications.

So, overall, very few statistics, if any, exists on the number of foundlings or persons of unknown parentage including those who acquire nationality on the basis of foundling provisions around the world.

## 4.2  One Parent or Both Parents Unknown?

The first basic question that might arise is whether failure to identify one of the parents suffices to qualify as a person of unknown parentage.

In an American administrative decision by the Administrative Appeals Office (AAO) in 2013, the applicant had pursued his request for a certificate of citizenship based on the foundling provision, that is article 301(f) of the Immigration and Nationality Act (INA) asserting that the identity of his father was unknown. It was determined that the applicant was ineligible as his mother and the mother's identity – shown on his school records—was known (which the applicant did not dispute), and therefore, he was not of 'unknown parentage'. AAO concluded that section 301(f) of the Act confers citizenship upon those individuals both of whose parents' identities are unknown, not just one parent. AAO also cited the US Department of State's Foreign Affairs Manual, chapter 7 § 1118(a), explaining that section 301(f) of the Act applies to 'a child of unknown *parents*'.[3]

This is reasonable as the identification of one legal parent normally allows the determination of whether the child is in possession of or is entitled to a nationality by *jus sanguinis* or by *jus soli*.

Needless to say, a person whose parent(s) is (are) legally known, who has her or his parent–child relationship(s) legally established, but who does not 'know' such parent(s) personally and substantively in the sense of having had a close relationship with her/him/them cannot be considered a 'person of unknown parentage'. This is

---

[2] The University of Nottingham, *Child Abandonment and its Prevention in Europe* (The University of Nottingham 2012) 2.

[3] AAO, *Re Applicant 2013* WL 5,504,816 (DHS) [19 February 2013]. At any rate, even if the applicant could establish that he is of unknown parents, his birth outside the territory was also established (before the age of 21) thus he was not eligible for confirmation of American nationality.

pointed out by a US Court of Appeals in *Orea-Hernandez v. Attorney Gen. of US* (2011), often cited in foundling-related cases in the US.[4]

## 4.3   Categories of Persons Considered to Be of 'unknown parents' Under National Foundling Provisions

Below lays out main categories of persons who have been considered to fulfil the requirements under the foundling provision in a number of State parties and non-State parties to the 1961 Convention, focusing mainly on how the term 'unknown parents' has been applied. It should be noted that the categorization of some of the case examples is a non-exclusive one, based on the most prominent feature of the case, and a case categorized into one category might also fit into another category.

### 4.3.1   Babies Abandoned on Streets and Other Places

Many States—which include States without a 'foundling provision' in their law as described in Sect. 1.5.2.3—grant nationality to babies who are found abandoned in unsafe places like on the street, in front of a hospital or a church, where their parents do not turn up or are untraceable. Many States without a 'foundling provision' have a provision on registration of abandoned children in their birth registration related legislation and grant nationality to such children.

In terms of States with a foundling provision in its nationality law, for example, in Hungary, when a child is abandoned on the street, within a few hours the municipality where the child is found registers the concerned child, and fictitious Hungarian parents' names will be assigned. Then the child immediately is confirmed to have Hungarian nationality under article 3(3)b granting nationality to a child of unknown parents found in Hungary.[5]

---

[4] See *Orea-Hernandez v. Attorney General of US*, 449 Fed. Appx. 143 [2011] (United States Court of Appeals, Third Circuit). The Court of Appeals ruled that the America's foundling provision, that is section 301(f) of the INA 1952, did not apply to an individual who claimed he never 'knew' his father who died before he was born and who was also estranged from his mother. However, the author finds the court's reasoning rather incomplete. While it is correct that how close the person was to his or her parent(s) is not relevant to nationality acquisition, the judgement does not articulate whether Orea-Hernandez's parent (mother in this case) is legally known, that is whether the parent–child relationship has been proven. At any rate, it was obvious that Orea-Hernandez did not meet the requirements under section 301(f) INA as his birth outside the US (in Mexico) was established, and he was apparently not stateless, evidenced by his possession of a Mexican passport.

[5] Interview with Benko Zsuzsanna, Attorney at law, Child Protection Services of Budapest, and former (till 2009) Deputy Head of Division, Social and Guardianship Division, Guardianship Department at the Municipal Government Office, Fifth District Guardianship Office (Budapest, Hungary, 25 May 2017).

In Italy, five children were either abandoned on the street, in garbage bins or public baths in the first half of 2013.[6] These children, if their parents are unknown, acquire Italian nationality based on article 1(2) of its nationality law granting nationality to persons of unknown parents found in the territory.[7]

Japan, a non-State party to the 1961 Convention, whose Nationality Act at article 2(iii), if literally taken, grants persons of unknown parents born in the territory, is one of the 18 such States (see annex 1). However, as also discussed in section 6.4, article 57 of the Family Registration Act[8] provides that a '*kiji*' (which is literally an 'abandoned child'[9]) found in the territory will speedily have her/his family registry (*koseki*—which can be used as conclusive proof of Japanese nationality)[10] created. It is an established scholarly theory, judicial and administrative practice in Japan that a *kiji* found in the territory of Japan is de facto presumed to have been born in Japan in the absence of evidence to the contrary.[11] A *kiji* thus fulfils the 'birth in Japan' requirement under article 2(iii), and thus is confirmed a Japanese national. A *kiji*

---

[6] Fondazione Francesca Rava, 'Società Italiana di Neonatologia (SIN) e ninna ho insieme a tutela dell'infanzia abbandonata. Al via un'indagine conoscitiva sulla realtà dell'abbandono neonatale in Italia per impostare programmi preventivi efficaci di aiuto alle madri in difficoltà' ['SIN and Ninna ho Working Together to Protect Abandoned Children. Launch of a survey on infant abandonment reality in Italy to set up effective preventive programs to help mothers in need'] (13 June 2013) <https://www.nph-italia.org/notizie/174/sin-e-ninna-ho-insieme-a-tutela-dell-infanzia-abba/> accessed 3 August 2019.

[7] Interview with Central Direction for Civil Rights, Citizenship and Minorities of the Department for Civil Liberties and Immigration of the Ministry of Interior, Italy (Rome, Italy, 23 May 2017).

[8] Japanese Family Register Act article 57(1): 'A police official who has found an abandoned child [kiji] or has received a report that an abandoned child was found shall inform the mayor of the municipality [...]'. Article 57(2) states: 'When having received information as set forth in the preceding paragraph, the mayor of a municipality shall give a name to the child and designate his/her registered domicile [*honseki*] [...]'. Japanese Family Register Act, Act No 224 of 22 December 1947. Ryūun Ō, 'Kiji no kokuseki' ['Nationality of abandoned children'] (1969) 4 Hōgaku Kenkyū [Hokkaigakuen daigaku hōgakkai] 169.

[9] The government's (yet unofficial) translation 'kiji' under article 57 of the Family Register Act is an 'abandoned child'. However, there is no definition of the term 'abandoned child' including the person's age in the Family Register Act. The Nationality Act itself does not provide for nationality of a *kiji* or an abandoned child, but only of a person of unknown parents born in the territory. Ibid.

[10] 'Koseki [family register] registers and authenticate family relationship from a person's birth to death, is created for Japanese nationals, and is one and only system to authenticate even one's Japanese nationality' (author translation). *koseki* thus functions as a centralized registry to document nationals. Civil Affairs Bureau and Ministry of Justice, 'Koseki' ['Family Register', author translation] <http://www.moj.go.jp/MINJI/koseki.html> accessed 15 July 2019.

[11] Shōichi Kidana, *Chikujōchūkai kokusekihō* [*Article-by-Article Commentary to Nationality Law*] (Nihon kajo shuppan, 2003) 202; Hidefumi Egawa, Yoshirō Hayata and Ryōichi Yamada, *Kokusekihō* [*Nationality Law*] (Yūhikaku 1997) p 78; Ryūun Ō, 'Kiji no kokuseki' ['Nationality of abandoned children'] (1969) 4 Hōgaku Kenkyū [Hokkaigakuen daigaku hōgakkai] 169, 186. Yue Fū, 'Nihon de umareta kodomono kokuseki to mukokuseki nintei' ['Determination of statelessness for children born in Japan'] (PhD dissertation, University of Tsukuba 2016) 125.

whose place of birth and parents are unknown is even considered 'a typical case' granted nationality under the first criteria[12] of article 2(iii).[13]


### 4.3.2  Baby Boxes or Baby Hatches

Another typical category of persons throughout the world who acquire nationality based on a 'foundling provision' is those who are left in baby hatches. For many of these facilities, parent(s) will not normally be seen by the institution receiving the child and remain unknown both factually and legally, unless they leave their identification information or turn up at a later stage. Baby hatches have existed for centuries, while their exact forms or shapes have evolved. State-funded or State-regulated baby hatches or foundling wheels were already quite common in medieval times in Europe. An actual foundling wheel[14](no longer in use)can still be seen today, for example, in front of the Institute of Innocents in Florence, Italy, which was founded in 1419 to accommodate abandoned children.[15]

While there are many other States where baby hatches are operated,[16] only those States for which some information was accessible indicating that children left therein acquire nationality based on the applicable foundling provisions or under other arrangements were included below.

In present days, in terms of States with a foundling provision, for example, in Germany, numerous baby hatches (*Babyklappe*) have long existed, although they are

---

[12] The second criteria under article 2(iii) of Nationality Act is that parents are stateless.

[13] Ryūun Ō, 'Kiji no kokuseki' ['Nationality of abandoned children'] (1969) 4 Hōgaku Kenkyū [Hokkaigakuen daigaku hōgakkai] 169, p 186. Yue Fū, 'Nihon de umareta kodomono kokuseki to mukokuseki nintei' ['Determination of statelessness for children born in Japan'] (Ph.D. dissertation, University of Tsukuba 2016) 125.

[14] A foundling wheel was typically a cylinder set upright in the outside wall of the building, like a revolving door. Parents placed the child in the cylinder and turned it around so that the baby was inside a child welfare institution, a hospital or a church, subsequently ringing a bell to alert caretakers. Interview with Maria Grazia Giuffrida, President, Istituto degli Innocenti (Rome, Italy, 22 May 2017).

[15] Ibid. Formerly called a Foundling Hospital or Spedale degli Innocenti, Institute of Innocents is one of the oldest institutes which are still in operation. The Institute of Innocents today accommodates children who cannot live with parents (not necessarily children of unknown parents) and destitute mothers.

[16] For example, see the University of Nottingham, *Child Abandonment and its Prevention in Europe* (University of Nottingham 2012) 18.

not legally regulated.[17] There were 93 baby hatches around Germany as of 2017.[18] According to the German Youth Institute (Deutschen Jugendinstituts), in a ten-year survey period preceding 2011, 278 new-borns were placed in baby hatches operated by some of the baby hatch operators who participated in the survey.[19] Out of 278, 152 remained to be of unknown parentage as they were not reclaimed and were released for adoption. In the remaining cases, the identity of the parents could be determined, including where the mothers took the children back to themselves. This happened in some cases immediately, but in others, some months after delivery. The children left in baby hatches and remain of unknown parentage are reported to have no problem in confirming their nationality under the foundling provision (article 4(2) of the German Nationality Act).[20]

In Italy, ten or more every year are left in baby hatches around the country. These children acquire Italian nationality based on article 1(2) of its nationality law granting nationality to persons of unknown parents found in the territory.[21]

In Hungary, the main instances where section 3(3)b of its nationality law granting nationality to foundlings are babies who are left on baby hatches. At least three baby hatches reportedly exist in Budapest, and around 25 hatches exist throughout Hungary, but three to four children a year are left there.[22]

---

[17] See Christiane Henze, 'Babyklappe und anonyme Geburt' ['Baby Hatches and Anonymous Birth'] (2014) 14–16 <www.hwr-berlin.de/fileadmin/downloads_internet/publikationen/beitraege_ FB4/Heft_2_2014_Fachbereich_Rechtspflege.pdf> accessed 4 August 2019. Also see Joelle Coutinho and Claudia Krell, *Anonyme Geburt und Babyklappen in Deutschland. Fallzahlen, Angebote, Kontexte* [*Anonymous Birth and Baby Hatches in Germany*] (Deutsches Jugendinstitut 2011) 214–15, in particular '5.4.2 Staatsangehörigkeit' ['Nationality'].

[18] Süsse Anna Kein Einzelfall, 'Wie viele Kinder kommen in die Babyklappe?' ['How Many Children Come in the Baby Flap?'] *Bild News* <https://www.bild.de/news/inland/babyklappe/ wie-viele-kinder-kommen-in-die-babyklappe-51658362.bild.html> accessed 4 August 2019. The overview of the number of baby hatches can be found on this chart posted on the Findel-baby project's website, <http://www.sternipark.de/fileadmin/content/PDF_Upload/Findelbaby/Bab yklappenliste__Stand_Juni_2016_.pdf> , accessed 22 July 2017, inaccessible as of 4 August 2019. On file with author.

[19] According to the news article referred to, the Institute published in 2011, 'the first and the only comprehensive study so far' on baby flaps in Germany. Süsse Anna Kein Einzelfall, 'Wie viele Kinder kommen in die Babyklappe?' ['How Many Children Come in the Baby Flap?'] *Bild News* <https://www.bild.de/news/inland/babyklappe/wie-viele-kinder-kommen-in-die-babykl appe-51658362.bild.html> accessed 4 August 2019.

[20] Joelle Coutinho and Claudia Krell, *Anonyme Geburt und Babyklappen in Deutschland. Fallzahlen, Angebote, Kontexte* [*Anonymous Birth and Baby Hatches in Germany*] (Deutsches Jugendinstitut 2011), in particular '5.4.2 Staatsangehörigkeit' ['Nationality'] 214–15. Also, see Christiane Henze, 'Babyklappe und anonyme Geburt' ['Baby Hatches and Anonymous Birth'] (2014) 14–16 <www.hwr-berlin.de/fileadmin/downloads_internet/publikationen/beitraege_ FB4/Heft_2_2014_Fachbereich_Rechtspflege.pdf> accessed 4 August 2019. The author wishes to thank Ruth Breitenstein in assisting in translation of German text into English.

[21] Interview with Central Direction for Civil Rights, Citizenship and Minorities of the Department for Civil Liberties and Immigration of the Ministry of Interior, Italy (Rome, Italy, 23 May 2017).

[22] In 2015, three babies were left in baby hatches in Budapest, and one baby in another area in Hungary. One baby was left in Budapest in 2016. Interview with Gábor Kuslits, Director of Child Protection Services of Budapest (25 May 2017).

In Poland, children left in baby hatches (*Okno życia*, literally 'window of life' in Polish), are considered typical cases that benefit from the country's foundling provision.[23]

In Japan, the one and only baby hatch in the country, operated by Jikei hospital in Kumamoto city, took in 137 babies over ten years since its establishment in May 2007.[24] In a number of cases, the parent(s) was (were) subsequently identified. However, as for the children whose parents were not identified, they were considered to be *kiji* (abandoned children). As explained in Sect. 4.3.1, *kiji* are typical cases to whom article 2(iii) of Japanese Nationality Act (granting nationality to persons of unknown parents born in Japan) is applied. Those considered *kiji* would then have their Japanese family register created by the Kumamoto city office.[25]

As mentioned in Sect. 1.5.5.2, some States without a foundling provision in their law have confirmed the nationality acquisition by children abandoned in baby hatches.

In Pakistan, while there is no explicit nationality provision granting nationality to foundlings, that is children of unknown parents, some children of unknown parentage staying in 'orphanages' have de facto been confirmed nationality by being issued a computerized national identity card (CNIC), a document issued only to Pakistani citizens that is usually perceived as conclusive proof of citizenship. According to the Edhi Foundation, a social welfare institute running centres for orphans and other persons around the country, some 15,000 babies had been dropped in their baby hatches placed in front of their facilities during the two decades preceding 2012.[26] Until 2013, children of unknown parentage were not allowed to register with the National Database and Registration Authority (NADRA), the competent authority in registering nationals, and were not allowed to vote.[27] In 2011, the Supreme Court of Pakistan took notice of the refusal by NADRA of applications for registration of children of unknown parentage, which was originally raised by the founder of the Edhi Foundation seeking registration of 'orphans'.[28] While this case was pending, NADRA developed and implemented an 'Orphanage Registration Policy', based on

---

[23] Interpretation provided by the Ministry of the Interior, cited in the ENS report. According to article 15 a child of unknown parents shall acquire Polish citizenship when found within the territory of the Republic of Poland. ENS, 'Ending Childhood Statelessness: A Study on Poland, Working Paper 03/15' (June 2015) 9–10 <https://www.statelessness.eu/sites/www.statelessness.eu/files/Pol and.pdf> accessed 4 August 2019.

[24] Asahi Shimbun News, 'Nananin chū go nin wa jitaku de umu' ['Five Out of Seven Gave Birth 'Isolated' at Home'] (29 May 2018) <https://www.asahi.com/articles/ASL5X77P8L5XUBQU00Y. html> accessed 25 May 2018, inaccessible as of 4 August 2019, on file with author.

[25] Kumamotoshi yōhogojidō taisaku chiiki kyōgikai, 'kōnotori no yurikago' daisanki kenshōhōkokusho' (September 2014) <https://www.city.kumamoto.jp/common/UploadFileDsp. aspx?c_id=5&id=6463&sub_id=1&flid=43570> accessed 4 August 2019.

[26] Tariq Malik, 'Children of Registered Orphanages to get Smart ID Cards Free of Cost' (24 August 2013) <http://www.nadra.gov.pk> accessed 23 May 2016, inaccessible as of 4 August, on file with author.

[27] Ibid, inaccessible as of 4 August, on file with author.

[28] An orphan's parents might not necessarily be unknown but an 'orphan' here appears to refer to a child of unknown parents. See Sect. 3.6 and Chap. 6.

which certain orphanages and children registered therein—many of them apparently of unknown parentage, having been dropped into baby hatches (or also abandoned in unsafe places)—are registered with NADRA and issued with a child registration certificate (also referred to as CRC) and subsequently a CNIC (when the child turns 18 years of age). According to a news source, by September 2013, NADRA had issued around 1,000 child registration certificate free of cost to the 'orphans' residing in registered orphanages.[29] A former Chairman of NADRA stated in a media announcement in 2013 that 'children without known parentage will have the fundamental right to be a citizen of Pakistan and get an identity under section 9 of NADRA Ordinance 2000'.[30] Based on this action by NADRA, the Supreme Court directed in May 2014 to the provincial governments to facilitate the process.[31]

Many other States are known to operate baby hatches some of which are established by the government, but the information relating to whether and how their nationality is confirmed was limited in the public domain.[32]

---

[29] It is assumed that not all 1,000 children were those left in baby hatches – they might have become of unknown parentage or otherwise remained without proof of Pakistani nationality due to other reasons such as that they were orphaned, informally adopted or trafficked and subsequently fell under the care of the childcare agencies. However, as the Edhi Foundation has referred to 'children left in baby hatches' in the context of their request for issuance of child registration certificates, this example from Pakistan is provided in this particular section. Pakistan Observer, 'NADRA Issues 1000 Smart Cards to Orphans' (4 September 2013) <http://pakobserver.net/detailnews.asp?id= 217151> accessed 4 August 2019; The Newspaper's Staff Reporter, 'Nadra Told to Identify, Register Unclaimed Children' (10 December 2014) <http://www.dawn.com/news/1149899/nadra-told-to-identify-register-unclaimed-children> accessed 4 August 2019; and Nasir Iqbal, 'Nadra Unveils Landmark Policy for Registration of Orphans' (30 May 2014) <http://www.dawn.com/news/110 9455/nadra-unveils-landmark-policy-for-registration-of-orphans> accessed 4 August 2019.

[30] Statement by Tariq Malik, former Chairman of NADRA, cited in an article on the NADRA's website. Tariq Malik, 'Children of Registered Orphanages to get Smart ID Cards Free of Cost' (24 August 2013) <http://www.nadra.gov.pk> accessed 23 May 2016, inaccessible as of 4 August, on file with author. Section 9 of the NADRA Ordinance provides for registration of citizens as follows: 'Every citizen in or out of Pakistan who has attained the age of eighteen years shall get himself, and a parent or guardian of every citizen who has not attained the age shall [...] get such citizen registered [...].' 'The National Database and Registration Authority Ordinance' (2000) <http://nas irlawsite.com/laws/nadra.htm> accessed 23 May 2016, inaccessible as of 4 August, on file with author.

[31] See also the European Asylum Support Office (EASO), *Country of Origin Information Report: Pakistan Country Overview* (EASO April 2015) 42–3 <https://www.easo.europa.eu/sites/default/ files/public/EASO_COI_Report_Pakistan-Country-Overview_final.pdf> accessed 7 August 2019.

[32] For example, China's first baby hatch opened by in 2011 in Hebei province, and over the next three years another 32 baby hatches opened in 16 provinces with the initiative of the government. Guangzhou's baby hatch, for example, received 262 babies in the first 50 days after opening in January 2014. In China, roughly 100,000 children are reportedly abandoned every year, which is understood to include those openly given up for institutional care or adoption, those secretly abandoned in unsafe places in addition to babies abandoned in baby hatches. Jiayi Diao, 'Child Abandonment China's Growing Challenge' (13 September 2015) <https://beijingtoday.com.cn/2015/09/ child-abandonment-chinas-growing-challenge/> accessed 4 August 2019. See also Connie Young for CNN, 'China "Baby Hatch" Inundated with Abandoned, Disabled Children' (30 June 2014)

### 4.3.3  Babies Entrusted or Surrendered to a Third Person

#### Spain

Before going into the examples of cases who were considered to fall within this category where the Spanish foundling provision was applied, it will be useful to first explain the nature of Spain's administrative decisions to be discussed below.

#### Introduction to DGRN Resolutions

In Spain, the Dirección General de los Registros y del Notariado, referred to as DGRN[33] (General Directorate of Registries and Notaries), an administrative body within the Ministry of Justice is competent in deciding on the acquisition and loss of nationality under the relevant provisions within the Spanish Civil Code. The DGRN has issued a series of resolutions[34] and confirmed nationality under its foundling provision, that is article 17.1.d) of Civil Code. In all the six cases available to the

---

<http://edition.cnn.com/2014/06/30/world/asia/china-baby-hatches-jinan/index.html> accessed 4 August 2019. The Chinese nationality law does not have a clear 'foundling provision' but only article 6, which provides: 'Any person born in China whose parents are stateless or of uncertain nationality and have settled in China shall have Chinese nationality'. Nationality Law of the People's Republic of China (issued 10 September 1980) <http://en.pkulaw.cn/display.aspx?id=b2c ecafdd3bc71cabdfb&lib=law> accessed 7 August 2019. The fact that the baby hatches are set up on the government's initiative gives rise to an assumption that these children abandoned therein should be recognized as Chinese nationals, but there was no information available whether and how this is done.

[33] The DGRN deals with civil status and nationality, and has largely been in charge of producing administrative guidelines, which have proven essential for interpreting nationality related legal provisions. This body implements the Spanish nationality legal provisions and its decisions can be appealed before contentious-administrative courts (the National Court (Audiencia Nacional), and the Supreme Court (Tribunal Supremo)). 'Both the administrative decisions by the DGRN, and the judicial decisions, especially those by the Supreme Court, have also become a rich, yet dispersed and not always consistent, source of interpretation of citizenship law in Spain.' Ruth Rubio Marín and others, 'Country Report on Citizenship Law: Spain, RSCAS/EUDO-CIT-CR 2015/4' (2015) <http://cadmus.eui.eu/bitstream/handle/1814/34480/EUDO_CIT_2015_04-Spain. pdf;sequence=1> accessed 4 August 2019.

[34] The author obtained and read in Spanish six out of seven of the original resolutions mentioned in the compilation made by the Permanent Observatory on Immigration under the Ministry of Employment and Social Issues (now the Ministry of Labour and Social Security). Aurelia Álvarez Rodríguez y, *Nacionalidad de los hijos de extranjeros nacidos en España Regulación legal e interpretación jurisprudencial sobre un análisis de datos estadísticos de los nacidos en territorio español durante el período 1996–2002* [*Nationality of the Children of Foreigners Born in Spain: Legal Regulation and Jurisprudential Interpretation on an Analysis of Statistical Data of Those born in Spanish Territory During the Period 1996–2002*] (Observatorio Permanente de la Inmigración (for Ministerio de Trabajo y Asuntos Sociales (now the Ministerio de Empleo y Seguridad Social) 2006), pp 83–5. For the remaining one, the Ministry of Justice official contacted via email stated it was unavailable. Email from Biblioteca Central Ministerio de Justiciato (Central Library of the Ministry of Justice), Spain to author (14 September 2017). i) Res. DGRN de 10 de junio de 2005 (BOE, 1-VIII-2005, pp 27,158–9 (Anexo III.3.25)), ii) Res. DGRN 3.a de 9 de octubre de 1996 (191) (BIMJ, núm. 1795, 1997, pp 1018–20; RAJ, 1997, núm. 2550; Actualidad Civil (Registros), 1997-3, núm. 287,

author (discussed below), the civil registry authorities of the relevant city had originally refused to carry out (late) birth registration despite the petition by the persons
concerned or their guardians, stating among others that their birth in the territory
was not established. In most of the six cases, responding to the appeals filed by the
persons concerned, DGRN generally applied article 17.1.d) in a full and inclusive
manner, including to highly 'atypical' cases and those found after reaching a certain
older age, which will be classified and introduced separately under several categories
of persons below (some of which will also be discussed in Chaps. 6 and 7).

Article 17.1.d) of Civil Code states that a person is a Spanish national by birth if
'born in Spain *whose filiation is not determined*. For this purpose, minors whose first
known place of sojourn is Spanish territory are presumed to be born on the Spanish
territory' (emphasis added; author translation).

In two of the DGRN resolutions known to the author, babies was entrusted to the
local city Child Protection Board in Spain, which requested their late birth registration, where DGRN affirmed the Spanish nationality under article 17.1.d) of the
Civil Code having determined that their filiation is unknown and that their first known
place of stay is a city in Spain. As detailed in Sect. 7.5, in the DGRN resolution dated
10 January 1995,[35] the baby was entrusted to the Board by a purported midwife who
lived in Morocco, who stated she has attended the birth of the baby, which occurred
in her house. In the DGRN resolution dated 9 October 1996,[36] the baby was entrusted
to the Board by the purported mother herself. While the mother regularly went to one
of the health centres in a Spanish city before delivery, and was assisted in the centre
after the delivery, the childbirth itself was supposed to have occurred in Morocco.
In both of these cases, there were doubts that the babies' birth occurred in Morocco,
which was, nevertheless, not established. As this point relates more to the term 'in
the absence of contrary proof', how DGRN assessed the possibility of birth outside
the territory will be discussed in Sect. 7.5.

pp 251–2), iii) Res. DGRN 4.a de 7 de octubre de 1996 (BIMJ, núm. 1794, 1997, pp 905–8), iv)
Res. DGRN 3.a de 21 de junio de 1996 (BIMJ, núms. 1782–3, 1996, pp 3606–8), v) Res. DGRN de
10 de enero de 1995 (190) (BIMJ, núm. 1737, 1995, pp 1390–2; RAJ, 1995, núm. 1453; Actualidad
Civil (Registros), 1995-3, núm. 286, p 218), vi) Res. DGRN de 9 de agosto de 1993 (188) (BIMJ,
núm. 1685, 1993, pp 4645–8; RAJ, 1993, núm. 6899).Thanks go to Josué Jiménez for facilitating
author's inquiry with the Ministry of Justice.

[35] Res. DGRN de 10 de enero de 1995 (190) (BIMJ, núm. 1737, 1995, pp 1390–2; RAJ, 1995, núm.
1453; Actualidad Civil (Registros), 1995-3, núm. 286, p 218).

[36] Res. DGRN 3.a de 9 de octubre de 1996 (191) (BIMJ, núm. 1795, 1997, pp 1018–20; RAJ, 1997,
núm. 2550; Actualidad Civil (Registros), 1997-3, núm. 287, pp 251–2).

### *United States*

*Babies anonymously surrendered under 'safe haven law'.*

In the US, beginning in Texas in 1999, 'Baby Moses[37] laws' or infant safe haven laws have been enacted in all 50 States, the District of Columbia, and Puerto Rico as an incentive for mothers in crisis to safely relinquish their babies to designated locations where the babies are protected and provided with medical care until an alternative care arrangement is found. Safe haven laws generally allow the parent, or an agent of the parent, to remain anonymous and to be shielded from criminal liability and prosecution for child endangerment, abandonment, or neglect in exchange for surrendering the baby to a safe haven.[38] The age limitation[39] for the babies in question vary. For example, in approximately 11 States and Puerto Rico, only infants who are 72 h old or younger may be relinquished to a designated safe haven. Approximately 19 States accept infants up to one month old. Other States specify varying age limits in their statutes, with New Mexico setting it at 90 days and North Dakota setting the age at one year from birth.[40]

Many babies are born at home or non-medical facilities, but some States' safe haven laws can function in a similar manner as 'anonymous birth' or 'confidential birth' scheme available in France, Italy and some other countries, whereby the mother can give birth to the baby and surrender her or him without having her identity information recorded on the baby's birth certificate.[41]

Safe haven arrangements are regulated by State laws rather than by federal laws. No information was—at least readily—located as to under which provision of the US Immigration and Nationality Act the children surrendered under safe haven law

---

[37] This comes from the fact that Moses began his life as an abandoned baby—a baby boy was born from the house of Levi of the Hebrews, and was hidden for three months to avoid being killed by the Egyptians, as per Pharoah's order. When the baby could not be hidden any longer, his mother put him in a basket made of bulrushes and placed it among the reeds by the river bank. The daughter of Pharoah came down to bathe at the river and saw the basket with the baby inside. She took pity on the baby and arranged him to be nursed and spared for Pharoah's order. Exodus 2:1–10, Old Testament.

[38] US Department of Health and Human Services Administration for Children and Families Administration on Children and Youth and Families Children's Bureau (Child Welfare Information Gateway), 'Infant Safe Haven Laws' (current through (December 2016) <https://www.childwelfare.gov/topics/systemwide/laws-policies/statutes/safehaven/> accessed 4 August 2019.

[39] The issue of age is otherwise discussed separately in Chap. 6 for other categories of persons discussed in this section. However, as this sub-section is the only part in this book where safe haven laws are (cursorily) discussed due to the lack of information on the relevant nationality acquisition mechanism, comments on the ages are hereby made.

[40] US Department of Health and Human Services Administration for Children and Families Administration on Children and Youth and Families Children's Bureau (Child Welfare Information Gateway), 'Infant Safe Haven Laws' (current through (December 2016) <https://www.childwelfare.gov/topics/systemwide/laws-policies/statutes/safehaven/> accessed 4 August 2019.

[41] For example, see the Inter-Agency Council on Child Abuse and Neglect (ICAN), 'Safely Surrendered and Abandoned Infants in Los Angeles County—2002–2017' (2018) 33 <http://ican4kids.org/Reports/Safely%20Surrended/SSBL%20Report%202018.pdf> accessed 4 August 2019.

acquire US citizenship[42] while it could be speculated that article 301(f) of the Immigration and Nationality Act granting nationality to persons of unknown parents found in the territory is the basis. At any rate, the normal arrangements are that the children surrendered under safe haven law are registered to have been born in the US even in the absence of direct evidence for such in-land birth, thereby acquiring US nationality. For example, Louisiana (which provides that infants up to one month of birth can be accepted) provides in its article 1153 C of the Children's Code:

> The hospital shall forward the infant's birth information to the Bureau of Vital Statistics, for issuance of a birth certificate, unless it is determined that one has already been issued. Unless otherwise known, the infant shall be presumed to have been born in Louisiana.[43]

The infant thus acquires US nationality on the basis of (presumed) birth in the territory.

### 4.3.4 Persons Who Suffer Memory Loss or Are Mentally Disabled Whose Parents Thus Cannot Be Identified

In Albania, children with unknown parents who suffer memory loss or are mentally disabled can acquire Albanian nationality.

According to article 49(4) of Law No 10129, dated 5 November 2009 'On Civil Status', as amended, the registration rules applicable to children of unknown parents found in the territory apply to:

> children with unknown parents who suffer memory loss or are mentally disabled and cannot be identified. (The situation can be changed for a found child, when the memory returns, he/she recovers from the mental disease or he/she is identified in any other way.)

Such children acquire Albanian nationality under article 8(1) of the Law on Albanian Nationality providing nationality grant to a child of unknown parents born or found in the territory.[44]

Further, the Albanian registration rules for children of unknown parentage also apply to 'an adult person who has lost his/her memory, are [sic] mentally disabled, is

---

[42] Author's inquiry to several States' government agencies in charge of implementing safe haven law was not responded to. In one case, the in-house attorney at law essentially stated, while confirming that anonymously surrendered children acquire US nationality, that he was not aware of the legal basis within the Immigration and Nationality Act for such nationality acquisition. Email from Assistant General Counsel, Child and Family Service Agency Washington, DC to author (29 August 2017), in response to the author's inquiry on 22 August 2017 on DC Code §4-1451. A similar statement was shared in the email from Dorian Needham (Attorney at law, who has worked in the US immigration law field) to author, 27 September 2017.

[43] Article 1153 (Medical evaluation of the infant) C, 'Louisiana Children's Code, chapter 13 (Safe Haven Relinquishments)' <http://www.dcfs.la.gov/assets/docs/searchable/OCS/SafeHaven/SafeHavenLawCHCArticle13.pdf> accessed 4 August 2019.

[44] Cited in ENS, 'Ending Childhood Statelessness: A Study on Albania, Working Paper 06/15' (June 2015) 8 <https://www.statelessness.eu/sites/www.statelessness.eu/files/Albania.pdf> accessed 4 August 2019.

found with a deceased parent or unidentified parent, except when the person speaks only foreign language. In this case, he is registered as a stateless person'.[45] While problems had existed for years concerning civil registration of persons of unknown parents in Albania, this provision was used to resolve the situation. While details remain unclear, reportedly many children of various circumstances[46] were registered and automatically have acquired the Albanian nationality.[47]

These civil registration law provisions of Albania are quite liberal and practical—in some States children or adults with memory loss or mental disability can remain stateless (while it is noted the law requires adults to speak the local Albanian language).

In Japan also, there has been at least one family court adjudication[48] in 1988 (by Mito family court)[49] where an adult male who was found at a coastal location in 1984 was considered to suffer memory loss as to his own identity and was confirmed Japanese nationality based on the foundling provision. For the person concerned, a family register was created as a Japanese national under article 4 of the old Nationality Act (article 2(iii) of the current Act) providing nationality to a person of unknown parents born in Japan. The claimant could not remember anything about his parents, siblings, where he grew up and the names of the schools he attended. However, he spoke the Japanese language without much of an accent, was able to make accounts about historical incidents of Japan, and was very familiar with Japanese geography. While the exact year or date of birth could not be ascertained, he was registered to have been born on 3 November 1941, that is he was 46 years of age at the time of the family court adjudication. As this case is significant as to how the court found that

---

[45] According to article 49 paragraph 6 of Law No 10129, dated 5 November 2009 'On Civil Status', as amended, cited also in ibid 8.

[46] As far as Tirana Legal Aid Society—the author of the ENS Report on Ending Childhood State-lessness (Albania)—is aware, 'the practice was used in numerous cases' but the civil status office does not keep segregated data, but rather general data counting the number of registered children (not specifically foundlings). Email from Anisa Metalla (Senior Attorney at Law, Tirana Legal Aid Society) to author (25 July 2017), to author's inquiry.

[47] ENS, 'Ending Childhood Statelessness: A Study on Albania, Working Paper 06/15' (June 2015) 8 <https://www.statelessness.eu/sites/www.statelessness.eu/files/Albania.pdf> accessed 4 August 2019.

[48] *Nature of Japanese family court adjudications permitting registration into family register*: A *shūseki kyoka shinpan* (an adjudication for the permission for the registration of an unregistered person (into a family register)) refers to an adjudication issued by a family court to register persons who are not registered on family register, based on article 110 of the Family Register Act of Japan. Upon the petition by the person concerned and a consequent positive adjudication by a family court to permit the person to be registered, the person concerned would then submit a notification to be registered on a family register, which is an effective way of proving the person's Japanese nationality. However, a family court adjudication does not have the same effect as a *kokuseki kakunin hanketsu* (a positive judgement upon a litigation filed against a district court, which can be appealed to a high court and the Supreme Court). The family register created based on a family court adjudication will be deleted if a finalized judgement by such a court confirms that the person concerned does not have Japanese nationality. See Yasuhiro Okuda, *Kosekihō to kokusai oyakohō* [*Nationality Act and International Family Law*] (Yūhikaku 2004) 140–1.

[49] *Adjudication, Kagetsu* Vol 41, No 4 p 82 [7 October 1988 (*Shōwa 63 nen*)] (Mito Family Court).

the claimant had been 'born in Japan' in the absence of any direct evidence, it will be discussed in more detail in Sect. 6.4.

### 4.3.5  Children Informally Adopted and Raised by Unrelated Adults

Especially in developing or less-industrialized States but even in some fully industrialized States, children of unknown parents can be 'informally' or 'unofficially' adopted or raised within communities, rather than being formally adopted in accordance with civil law procedures.[50] In some States, children who have been informally—outside the legal framework—adopted and raised by unrelated persons have been confirmed their nationality under the relevant foundling provision when their parents could not be identified. In some States, however, informally adopted children remain stateless (see the example of Issa in Côte d'Ivoire at the very beginning of Chap. 1).

*Spain*

*DGRN Resolution 4.a of 7 October 1996*[51]

Summary of facts

In this case, on 12 June, 1994, Mr ATB, a Spanish national and a resident of city S, filed a request at the Civil Registry for late birth registration of the female minor—around six years old at the time—known as MJTC, so that he and his wife JCL of Spanish nationality can formally adopt the minor, who de facto had lived with them as their daughter. Mr ATB stated that he and his wife, after several efforts made before the competent organizations of the location C on the issues of adoption, contacted people they do not know (note: the original text of the resolution is unclear but probably an illicit organization), with whom they signed various documents; and that, always in strict good faith, they agreed with those people what they thought constituted the adoption of the minor; that they do not know the minor's exact place and date of birth, although she had lived with them as their daughter for six years since several days after her birth, and that they have taken care of and provided for all her needs. Mr ATB also stated that those people gave them the minor, stating that the minor had been born on 22 February of 1988, without specifying either her origin or the identity of her parents, or the place of her birth.

The documents submitted were the couple's marriage certificate, a certified baptism note administered to MJTC where she is described as the couple's daughter,

---

[50] Mirna Adjami, 'Statelessness and Nationality in Côte d'Ivoire—A Study for UNHCR' (December 2016) 49 <http://www.refworld.org/docid/58594d114.html> accessed 4 August 2019. See also Laura Parker, 'Foundlings in Côte d'Ivoire' in Institute on Statelessness and Inclusion (ISI) (ed), *The World's Stateless Children* (Wolf Legal Publishers 2017) 369–70.

[51] Res. DGRN 4.a de 7 de octubre de 1996 (BIMJ, núm. 1794, 1997, pp. 905–8).

as well as the certificate of registration of the couple, which also includes the minor, issued by the mayor of their residence; certificate of an accredited school where the minor is enrolled and a medical certificate. The chief brigade of the Civil Guard—judicial police section—certified the faultless conduct of the couple and their attitude of absolute cooperation in order to clarify the facts described. Witness information was provided with the intervention of two witnesses, who were neighbours of the couple and stating that they knew the minor since she was a few days old and that she always lived in their home, and the forensic doctor also determined the age and sex of the minor.

### Summary of decision

DGRN determined that legal presumption is applicable to the present case where a girl was abandoned by her mother, whose filiation is unknown (*se desconoce*) and of which there is no certainty over the place of birth, but only that the actions of abandonment took place in another city in Spain. MJTC was confirmed Spanish nationality under article 17.1.d) of the Civil Code.

### Caselaw and the title of a sub-section

*DGRN resolution on 10 June 2005 (informally adopted child whose alleged birth outside the territory was not proven).*[52]

### Summary of facts

This involves a case of an undocumented minor girl known as SH claiming to be of 11 years of age found engaged in begging on streets in Barcelona along with an adult male known as OH who was also not carrying any documents, claiming himself to be her father. The minor was found by the police force of Catalonia and was handed over to the Directorate General of Child and Adolescent Care (hereinafter the Child Care Directorate) on 18 July 2002. The Child Care Directorate by its resolution of 14 October 2002 declared the minor to be in a situation of abandonment and arranged the girl to be hosted in a public reception centre. The self-claimed parents who were domiciled in Rubí, Barcelona and originally from Bosnia and Herzegovina, 'who appeared to be nationals of Romania' (details unknown from the DGRN decision) did not prove their identity either. On 26 May 2003, the reception centre produced a multidisciplinary report showing that the alleged parents did not prove their parentage over the girl. By resolution of 22 July 2003, the Child Care Directorate adopted the protective measure of fostering in a different family along with her brother while the alleged parents opposed to the measure. The minor was forensically examined, as a result of which her approximate age was assessed to be ten years. Although the alleged parents claimed that the child was born in Rome, the result of the investigation was negative, after having requested the Civil Registry of Rome for a copy of the birth certificate. On 19 July 2004, the Child Care Directorate made a petition that the maternity and paternity of the alleged parents of the minor be determined through biological tests.

---

[52] Res. DGRN de 10 de junio de 2005 (BOE, 1-VIII-2005, pp 27,158–9 (Anexo III.3.25)).

Summary of decision

DGRN's reasonings on how the element of 'undetermined filiation' under article 17.1.d) of the Spanish Civil Code was fulfilled is notable:

> As for the indeterminacy of the child's filiation, there is not much room for doubt either. [...] it continues to be well established in this case what is legally and strictly presupposed, that the minor's proven affiliation does not appear to have been proven or determined in any way. [...] we observe that the affiliation does not appear proven nor inscribed in any Civil Registry, neither by document or judicial sentence, nor by presumption of matrimonial paternity (not only for not indicating the marriage, but for missing also the previous determination of the maternal filiation), nor, finally, by the strictly supplementary possession of status'. [...] 'sine qua non [essential, author])' requirement for possession of status is the 'tractatus [treatment, author]', of material and affective behaviour characteristic of the relationship of filiation given to the child by the parents, [and, author] in the present case, admitting such a thing would amount to accepting its derogation [...] the official declaration of abandonment of the child [...] was declared precisely because the child has lacked that material and affective behaviour that is proper of parents towards their children. Finally, it is not pointless to remember that this conclusion is supported and confirmed by other superior principles of our legal system relevant in the case, such as the primacy of the child's interest [...] as more worthy of protection, and the right of every child to registration of their birth and a nationality resulting from Article 7 of the Convention on the Rights of the Child of 20 November 1989.

DGRN thus recognized the minor SH as a Spanish national under article 17.1.d) of the Civil Code and ordered late birth registration to be carried out in the Civil Registry of Barcelona. DGRN then noted, quite significantly:

> The eventual determination of the filiation of the minor must not lead to the loss of the Spanish nationality now declared, which is definitive and not provisional because it is a nationality by birth (nacionalidad de origen). Finally, it is not appropriate at this time to decide on the request for the practice of biological test submitted untimely after lodging the appeal, as it is a new issue outside the requested qualification [...]. (emphasis added)

In the same decision, DGRN also discussed the other element in article 17.1.d), that is whether the claimant's first known place of stay was within the Spanish territory. DGRN specifically addressed how the self-claimed parents' allegation of a minor's birth outside the territory should be assessed. On a separate note, it is also noteworthy that claimant's age at the time of decision was approximately 13 years old. As these relate more to the issue of 'proof to the contrary', and indirectly the issue of being 'found', this part of this DGRN decision will be discussed in Sects. 6.4 and 6.5, as well as Sect. 7.5.

Analysis

The DGRN decision of 10 June 2005 is especially notable considering that the child was accompanied by her self-claimed parents. The decision only carries limited facts, and a number of uncertainties persist, including how the report produced by the public reception centre concluded that the self-claimed parents did not prove their parentage over the child.

What is clear, however, is that DGRN interpreted article 17.1.d) of Civil Code in light of the object and purpose of the provision, supporting it with the primacy of the child's best interests and right to nationality under article 7 of the CRC.

It was also notable that DGRN denied the need to carry out a DNA test to establish the parentage despite the Child Protection Directorate's request, ruling that it was untimely and is 'a new issue outside the requested qualification'. DGRN immediately before that even notes that the subsequent establishment of parentage will not result in her loss of Spanish nationality, which appears to be an established principle[53] in Spain but which appears somewhat out of context in this decision. No information is included in the decision whether the self-claimed parents themselves were willing, or unwilling, to have their DNA tested. If the self-claimed parents were opposed to the DNA test, it can be considered strong evidence of the lack of their paternal and maternal relationship with the child, and it flows naturally that DGRN denies such parental relationship. However, it is also possible that the self-claimed parents did not oppose to the DNA test to be carried out. In that case what becomes clear is DGRN's intention to place the well-being of the child before anything else, which even appears to go beyond the discussion of unknown parentage strictly for the purpose of determining one's nationality.

For DGRN, determining that the claimed parents did not establish their legal parentage over the claimant served the child's best interests, considering that the child lacked the care that was normally expected of parents. If the minor's legal parentage was to be determined simply based on the result of DNA test, the child could have been, in the worst-case scenario, simply deported out of Spain along with her parents.

*USA*

In the US, at least one person who had been informally adopted is known to have been confirmed American nationality by USCIS in 2006, as below. It should be noted that section 301 (f) of INA[54] states that 'The following shall be nationals and citizens of the United States at birth: [...] (f) a person of *unknown parentage found* in the United States while *under the age of five years* [...]' (emphasis added).

*USCIS decision on 29 November 2006: the Newark Case[55]*

In this case (the 2006 Newark Case), four children[56] were 'found' by the police going through dumpsters for food. They were not accompanied by parents, and the police

[53] Paloma Abarca Junco, 'La Reforma Del Derecho De La Nacionalidad De 1990, Boletín De La Facultad De Derecho, núm. i' (1992) 73–4 <http://e-spacio.uned.es/fez/eserv/bibliuned:BFD-1992-1-E9B3BB01/PDF> accessed 4 August 2019.

[54] USCIS, Immigration and Nationality Act of 1952 (US) (2 August 2019) <https://www.uscis.gov/ilink/docView/SLB/HTML/SLB/act.html> accessed 4 August 2019.

[55] USCIS's administrative decision where USCIS confirmed nationality of a person in Newark on 29 November 2006 (referred to as the '2006 Newark Case' in this book), which is reported in Chris Nugent and Doug Burnett of the Holland & Knight Community Services Team, 'The Foundling Statute' (23 January 2007) <https://www.ilw.com/articles/2007,0123-nugent.shtm> accessed 4 August 2019. Author thanks Colleen Cowgill and Lindsay Jenkins for informing her of this precedent. Email from UNHCR Washington to author (18 July 2017).

[56] The published article on this case is not clear about the children's age when they were 'found' by the authorities, but they were above high school age when their cases were being determined, and they had been found 'years' before that time but certainly well after the age of five years. Chris Nugent

brought them to social services and the State court of New Jersey. The court was suspicious of the alleged mother. The judge ordered DNA testing, which determined that 'the women [sic] whom the children considered their mother, was a biological stranger'.[57] It was also found that the four children were not biologically related. In the case of two of the children, their Newark birth certificates were determined not to be authentic. The same occurred with the other two children with their certificates of birth abroad, supposedly issued by the US embassy in Haiti.

The court ruled that the children were victims of abuse and neglect and recommended that the woman who raised them be investigated by the Attorney General for welfare fraud. However, the woman died of cancer before any steps were taken. With the self-claimed mother's death, the circumstances of how the children came to be in the US were 'buried as well'. 'The net result was four young teenagers, who only knew the United States, with no documents or relatives to say how or where their lives began'.[58]

The children were in high school at the time when their cases were being determined, but, without citizenship or a green card, they could not get a social security card which made obtaining a job, a driver's licence and even admission to a college impossible.

The attorney who had taken up the case and other advocates made efforts to prove that the children were found in the US under the age of five. With regard to one of the children, they successfully tracked down a doctor in Newark who saw her when she was about two years old and obtained a copy of her medical record. Finally, on 29 November 2006, the child was 'given a certificate of citizenship which declared her US citizenship since the date of her birth over 18 years ago' based on the foundling statute.[59]

However, for the three other children, pursuing nationality under the foundling provision was not possible as 'there was a total absence of documentation or other evidence which could show that the children were present in the United States prior to the age of five years old', and they were granted green cards. As this case raises the issue of the definition of being 'found' as well as 'proof to the contrary', it will be discussed in Sects. 6.4–6.7 and Sect. 7.5 respectively.

Moreover, in a number of other US cases, persons in seemingly similar situations were not recognized as a person of unknown parentage. As these US cases mainly raise the issue of the extent of unknown-ness or the 'standard of proof', they will be discussed in Chap. 5.

### *Japan*

Japan has a series of family court adjudications where informally adopted persons of unknown parents have acquired nationality under its foundling provision. In one High

---

and Doug Burnett of the Holland & Knight Community Services Team, 'The Foundling Statute' (23 January 2007) <https://www.ilw.com/articles/2007,0123-nugent.shtm> accessed 4 August 2019.

[57] Ibid.

[58] Ibid.

[59] Ibid.

Court decision and two family court adjudications in the 1970s and 1980s reviewed below, the courts confirmed the Japanese nationality of persons who approached the authorities after reaching adulthood whose parentage could not be determined having been informally adopted by unrelated adults. Two of them even had a history of migration to neighbouring States. In all three cases, the claimants were in their 50s or 70s at the time of the court decision to confirm their Japanese Nationality Act under article 4 of the old Japanese Nationality Act[60] (equivalent to article 2(iii) of the current Nationality Act). Cases of informal adoption might still occur today as indicated by an unpublished family court adjudication in 2013 confirming Japanese nationality, referred to at the end of this sub-section.

*Takamatsu High Court decision on 26 August 1976*[61]

### Summary of facts

The claimant, ever since she can remember, called herself by the pseudonym Kinuyo Sugiyama and was living in Taiwan, which was being colonized by Japan at the time. She vaguely remembers that she was brought along with her parents from inland Japan to Taiwan when she was around three years old. She also remembers to have been told by the parents that she was born in prefecture X in Japan. The claimant was told by her neighbour that her parents did not legally marry because the father was the eldest son and the mother was the eldest daughter of the respective family. When she was about seven years old, her father went missing, and when she was around eight years old her mother died of illness. The claimant subsequently sustained her life by doing odd jobs such as an errand runner and a babysitter for other families. The claimant returned to inland Japan after turning 18 years old, and de facto married a Japanese national when she was around 20. After her common-law husband passed away from illness, and she became elderly and needed to receive a welfare allowance, she filed a petition to be registered in the family register.

### Summary of decision

The court accepted the above facts and ruled that,

> as the claimant has not received any formal education, and in light of her profile and age, insufficient awareness on certain things or lapse of memory is a normal occurrence, and even not remembering the parents' exact first name and family name correctly may well occur [...] It is appropriate to recognize the assertion that the claimant was born in Japan and grew up in an environment where Japanese language was used since from early childhood, based on the previously stated facts, the claimant's appearance, attitude and all other facts in the case.

The court confirmed the claimant's Japanese nationality and granted permission to be registered in a family registry, because 'it is clear that there is no legal father–child relationship between the father and the claimant' and the mother's name or place of

---

[60] *Kokusekihō* [Nationality Act], Law No 66 of 1899 [*Meiji 32 nen*].

[61] *Judgement, Kagetsu* Vol 26, No 2, p 104 [26 August 1976 (*Shōwa 51 nen*)] (Takamatsu High Court).

birth are not clear. The claimant's (approximate) age at the time of the adjudication was 74 years old.

*Ōsaka Family Court Adjudication on 27 January 1979*[62]

Summary of facts

The claimant, when he was eight months old, was de facto adopted by a couple of Chinese nationality. The claimant had been told by his adoptive father that he was born on 9 May 1925 in town X in Kyōto city, and his biological father's name was unknown, and his mother was a *geisha* (a professional entertainer) from Hyogo prefecture named Kane Taguchi, and had a brother named Kiyoharu Taguchi. The claimant graduated in 1938 from the Ōsaka city-run public elementary school named Y. The claimant left Japan from Kōbe port on 27 February 1938 and migrated to China. The claimant's parents subsequently died. The applicant wished to return to Japan, but could not have his family registry located and thus filed a request for registration.

Summary of decision

The court ruled that the only thing known about the claimant's mother was her name, and her family registry could not be located, let alone his father, whose name was not known. The court thus confirmed the claimant's Japanese nationality. The claimant's approximate age at the time of the adjudication was 54 years old.

*Tōkyō High Court judgement (29 June 1983)*[63]

Summary of facts

The claimant was informally adopted by a Taiwanese husband and wife residing in Kōbe City, Kōbe Prefecture, Japan when he was probably around one month after birth, in around 1928. The couple had the claimant registered as their own biological child under the Taiwanese family register in September 1928. He had, however, been told by the de facto adoptive parents that his parents were Japanese nationals (called by Japanese names—while their identity and possession of Japanese nationality was uncertain) and requested the confirmation of his Japanese nationality.

Summary of judgement

The State (Minister of Justice) appealed against the Tōkyō District Court decision affirming the claimant's nationality. The State argued that the provision on Japanese nationality acquisition based on one's unknown parentage and birth in Japan only applies to abandoned children (*kiji*), which essentially meant babies and infants abandoned by parents and discovered by a third party.

Against this assertion, the court ruled that 'when both parents are unknown' in the Nationality Act meant 'when both father and mother, with whom the child has

---

[62] *Adjudication, Kagetsu* Vol 32, No 2, p 89 [27 January 1979 (*Shōwa 54 nen*)] (Osaka Family Court).

[63] *Judgement, Kagetsu* Vol 36, No 7, p 82 [29 June 1983 (*Shōwa 58 nen*)] (Tōkyō High Court).

legal parent–child relationship, are unknown'. The court then noted that while most cases of unknown parentage are indeed abandoned children, however,

> if we were to limit the application of the provision to such abandoned children as claimed (by the Minister of Justice, author), it will *go against the object and purpose* of the provision which is to prevent statelessness as much as possible. There is no justification for interpreting the provision that way. (emphasis added)

The approximate age of the claimant at the time of judgement confirming his Japanese nationality was 55 years old.

*Unpublished Family Court Adjudication May 2013*

Some might think that this case law from the 1970s and 1980s might be irrelevant to the situation in Japan today or in any other fully industrialized States. However, 'informal adoptions', as stated at the beginning of this section, can happen even in fully developed States. While the details of the adjudication could not be disclosed,[64] according to an immigration attorney, a family court in May 2013 confirmed Japanese nationality of a person falsely registered under an unrelated persons' family registry, whose actual parentage could not be tracked down.

Summary of facts

The claimant X was originally registered under the family register of a Japanese male A as a child between him and his wife (B of foreign nationality). However, from the circumstances surrounding the child-care arrangement, it was apparent that she had actually been born of a couple of foreign nationality, both of whose true names and addresses, however, were unknown. Upon a lawsuit, the family court in July 2009 ruled that no parent–child relationship existed between A, B and X. X's original Japanese family registry as A's child was consequently deleted; thus X lost her Japanese nationality. After being temporarily registered as a foreigner with the Immigration Bureau, X filed a petition with a family court to have her family register created in September 2012. As her parents were determined unknown, X gained an adjudication confirming her Japanese nationality under article 2(iii) of Japanese Nationality Act.[65]

---

[64] Ōnuki in the interview stated that it was difficult to obtain the permission from the claimants— who were generally out of reach—to share the adjudications with the author. Interview with Kensuke Ōnuki, Attorney at Law (Tokyo, Japan, 4 March 2017).

[65] 'Cases admitted into family registry: Represented by Kensuke Ōnuki, Attorney at Law, Satsuki Law Firm, Tōkyō' <http://www.satsukilaw.com/archives/category/exam/%e5%9b%bd%e7%b1%8d/%e5%b0%b1%e7%b1%8d%e8%a8%b1%e5%8f%af> accessed 4 August 2019.

### 4.3.6 New-Born Babies Left Behind at a Hospital by Biological Mothers (of Foreign Appearance)

There are situations where birth mothers do not necessarily 'abandon' their children on the street or a baby hatch, but who abscond soon after delivering their children medical institutions in the territory making it impossible to ascertain their identity (let alone the children's fathers' identity).[66]

In most States, a mother, when delivering a child, has to provide her identity information to the medical institution and her name will be recorded on a certificate of delivery issued by the attending medical personnel. The delivery certificate (which can also be called a 'birth certificate') will in turn be used to register the child with the civil registration authorities, as a consequence of which the acquisition or lack thereof of the nationality of the country of birth or that of parent(s)' nationality will be confirmed.

In a minority of States where 'anonymous birth' is legal and nationality is granted under the foundling provision (see Sect. 4.3.10) to children born under such scheme, it is assumed that this sort of cases will eventually be processed under such framework even if the mother does not invoke the right to anonymous birth.

However, in States without the 'anonymous birth' option, a definitional or evidential issue arises with regard to the application of the foundling provision. The medical institution might have some knowledge of who the mother might be, and there may be some indications that she or he is a foreigner, but her identity may not be officially or legally established. Some States have established administrative or judicial guidance specifically to address this situation.

#### Hungary

Section 3(3)b of Hungarian Citizenship Act states: 'Until proven to the contrary, the following persons shall be recognized as Hungarian citizens: [...] b) children of unknown parents found in Hungary.'[67]

In Hungary, until 2011, children in these circumstances were unable to invoke section 3(3)b, and remained classified by the Hungarian authorities as being of 'unknown nationality'.[68] In 2010, the Parliamentary Commissioner for Civil Rights

---

[66] Yue Fū, 'Nihon de umareta kodomono kokuseki to mukokuseki nintei' ['Determination of Statelessness for Children Born in Japan'] (PhD dissertation, University of Tsukuba 2016) 137; Hidefumi Egawa, Yoshirō Hayata and Ryōichi Yamada, *Kokusekihō [Nationality law]* (Yūhikaku 1997) 72.

[67] Hungary: Act LV of 1993 on Hungarian Citizenship (Hungary) (1 October 1993) <http://www.refworld.org/docid/3ae6b4e630.html> accessed 2 August 2019.

[68] Gábor Gyulai, 'Nationality Unknown? An Overview of the Safeguards and Gaps Related to the Prevention of Statelessness at Birth in Hungary' (2014) 9 <http://helsinki.hu/wp-content/uploads/Nationality-Unknown-HHC-2014.pdf> accessed 4 August 2019.

(the Ombudsperson),[69] the Hungarian Helsinki Committee[70] and SOS Children's Village Foundation[71] raised the nationality issues faced by the children born in a hospital to an unknown father and (apparently foreign) mother who is 'known', but whose identity and nationality is not officially established.

The mother's identity and nationality were often registered in the hospital registry based on verbally communicated data (if no identity documents are shown), without any guarantee of the data being genuine. The problems faced by these children ranged from inability to receive childcare services and to be adopted, to an undesirable 'repatriation' to the (alleged) mother's country of nationality, when it was finally established, sometimes only years later.

Following these advocacy efforts, a new provision was introduced into the relevant pieces of legislation in order to remedy the situation in 2011.

Specifically, section 9(7) of Law-Decree on Civil Registration, Marriage and Names as well as section 61(5) of the Act on Civil Registration Procedures have been inserted to state: 'If the mother did not prove her identity upon giving birth, nor within 30 days following the birth, and abandons the child in the institution (where the birth took place, author), the child shall be considered a found child of unknown parents'.[72]

Thus, the child left behind at a hospital in Hungary can now invoke article 3(3)b of the Citizenship Act and can confirm automatic[73] acquisition of Hungarian nationality.

These amendments were significant, legislatively providing for an inclusive definition of a foundling (rephrased as a 'child of unknown parents found in the territory' in Hungarian, as also mentioned in Sect. 3.3.2).

---

[69] Katalin Haraszti, 'Report by the Parliamentary Commissioner for Civil Rights in cases number AJB 2629/2010 and AJB 4196/2010' (September 2010) 16 <https://www.ajbh.hu/documents/14315/131278/The+investigation+of+the+Ombudsman+on+the+repatriation+of+the+abadoned+non-citizen+children+born+in+Hungary/122c30fb-8cf5-4192-9e95-f12a23d46436;version=1.1> accessed 4 August 2019.

[70] Gábor Gyulai, 'Statelessness in Hungary: The Protection of Stateless Persons and the Prevention and Reduction of Statelessness' (December 2010) 43–46 <https://www.refworld.org/docid/4d6d26972.html> accessed 12 July 2019.

[71] Katalin Haraszti, 'Report by the Parliamentary Commissioner for Civil Rights in cases number AJB 2629/2010 and AJB 4196/2010' (September 2010) 16 <https://www.ajbh.hu/documents/14315/131278/The+investigation+of+the+Ombudsman+on+the+repatriation+of+the+abadoned+non-citizen+children+born+in+Hungary/122c30fb-8cf5-4192-9e95-f12a23d46436;version=1.1> accessed 4 August 2019.

[72] Law-Decree 17 of 1982 on Civil Registration, Marriage and Names (Hungary), section 9(7), as inserted by section 1(4) of Act XLIX of 2011 and amended by section 78(3) of Act XCII of 2011, as well as section 61(5) of Act I of 2010 on Civil Registration Procedures (Hungary) (entering into force on 1 July 2014) which contain an identical provision.

[73] Gyulai notes that nationality acquisition under article 3(3)b is 'automatic,' while it is not clear from the text whether it is automatic acquisition at birth or at the time when the person is found on the Hungarian territory. Gábor Gyulai, 'Nationality Unknown? An Overview of the Safeguards and Gaps Related to the Prevention of Statelessness at Birth in Hungary' (2014) 2, 9, and 21 <http://helsinki.hu/wp-content/uploads/Nationality-Unknown-HHC-2014.pdf> accessed 4 August 2019.

Considering that this legislative change can be seen as a positive model for other States where the definition of a 'children of unknown parents' is restrictively interpreted, a field visit was made to Hungary in May 2017 to find out about its actual implementation.

The responses from the central competent authorities on nationality matters were that they had just taken over the mandate of nationality determination from another authority, and there were very few cases born in Hungary of missing parents in any case, which made it difficult to respond to the author's inquiry.[74] Further, the information gathered from interviews with other relevant agencies and experts[75] indicated that the newly inserted sections in the civil registration laws cited above might not be utilized so often. It appeared that the instances where section 3(3)b of Citizenship Act granting nationality to foundlings might still be limited to the 'straightforward' cases where babies are left in baby hatches[76] or abandoned on the street.

According to the Guardianship Department at the Municipal Government Office, Fifth District Guardianship Office with authority over non-Hungarian citizen minors in need of State guardianship staying in the territory of Hungary:

> Babies left behind at the hospital are registered to be of 'unknown nationality' and they would have to naturalize. Same applies to situations of children who are once registered at birth (with a Hungarian municipality) under an apparently valid document(s) of the mothers, where the mothers abscond and the embassies of the mothers' purported nationality do not confirm the nationality of the children. If a new-born child is found on a hatch or street, then yes, article 3(3)b is applied. But if the mother left the child in that way (leaving at hospital after delivery), the identity of the mother is *known*, and *not unknown*. In this case, the child protection authorities get involved and the guardians would have to apply for (facilitated) naturalization (after adoption).[77]

It appeared that instead of benefiting from the sections expanding the interpretation of section 3(3)b, children for whom foreign mothers go missing (after delivering the baby at a Hungarian hospital) and whose nationality cannot be confirmed with the supposed country of mothers' nationality tended to access nationality through subsequent adoption, which may be only possible after three years (see Sect. 4.6 (alternative ways of acquiring nationality)) of adoption. At any rate, according to the Guardianship Department, the number of cases left behind at a hospital in recent years is only 10–20 a year.[78] According to the Department, until the 2000s, persons

[74] The author contacted the central authority competent to determine who is a Hungarian national under the nationality law, that is the Citizenship and Registry Department, Budapest Metropolitan Government Office, for an interview which could not be entertained at the time for this reason. Emails and telephone communications from Citizenship and Registry Department, Budapest Metropolitan Government Office (Budapest, Hungary) to author (May to August 2017).

[75] See the bibliography for the list of experts interviewed.

[76] On babies left in baby hatches in Hungary, see Sect. 4.3.2.

[77] Interview with Róbert Kunszt, Head of Guardianship Department at the Municipal Government Office, Fifth District Guardianship Office (Budapest, Hungary, 25 May 2017).

[78] Ibid.

from neighbouring countries such as Romania, Slovakia, and Serbia came to Hungary and gave birth and left the children in hope of better future for their children.[79]

Thus, these instances where foreign women go missing from hospitals used to be 'hundreds' a year up to the mid-2000s. However, there are now only a few cases, with the socio-economic situations in neighbouring States such as Romania and Slovakia improving,[80] and as 'they know that the authorities of Hungary will track down the mother and the child will be returned to the mother's country of origin'.[81]

This might explain the possible underutilization of the new legislation broadening the interpretation of the unknown parentage nationality law provision.

Through the author's interview with the Immigration and Asylum Office (IAO), the agency in charge of statelessness determination in Hungary, it also became clear that some children born in Hungary whose foreign mothers go missing, end up in statelessness determination procedures (who might apply for naturalization later on). IAO was indeed aware of two cases born in the early 2000s at a hospital in Hungary whose mother went missing. IAO recognized them as stateless in 2015 and 2016 when they were 12 and 13 years old respectively.[82] They had presumably been living in childcare institution since birth. According to the IAO, in the first case, the mother was a self-claimed Vietnamese national, and no information was available of the father, including on the birth certificate of the child. The guardian of the child asked for statelessness status for the child. The IAO contacted the Vietnamese authority to inquire whether the child was a Vietnamese national, but no response was received. The IAO decided to recognize the child as a stateless person.

In the other case, the birth mother of the female child left at a hospital had claimed to be a Mongolian citizen. She had produced a Mongolian passport, and her name and the nationality of the mother was recorded as per the passport on the birth certificate issued by the municipality. No information about the father was found. When the IAO asked whether the child was a Mongolian national or not, the Mongolian embassy did not respond affirmatively. The girl was not found on the Hungarian registry. The girl got a humanitarian residence permit based on her 'statelessness'.[83]

It could not be ascertained whether section 9(7) of Law-Decree on Civil Registration, Marriage and Names as well as section 61(5) of Act on Civil Registration Procedures, which entered into force in 2014, could retroactively apply to these cases who were born in early 2000.

At any rate, these cases might indicate the potential usefulness of further raising the awareness among the relevant authorities and actors—not only the ones responsible

---

[79] Ibid.

[80] Ibid.

[81] Interview with Benko Zsuzsanna, Attorney at law and a legal guardian, Child Protection Services of Budapest former (till 2009) Deputy Head of Division, Social and Guardianship Division, Guardianship Department at the Municipal Government Office, Fifth District Guardianship Office (Budapest, Hungary, 25 May 2017).

[82] Interview with Zsófia Huszka, Legal Officer/Statelessness focal point at the Immigration and Asylum Office (IAO), Prime Minister Office, Division for Migration, Ministry of Interior, Hungary (Budapest, Hungary, 26 May 2017).

[83] Ibid.

for implementing the nationality law or registering births—but also the statelessness determination authorities, childcare institutions and even adoptive or foster families, on the available foundling provision and its interpretative guidance. Further enhancing the coordination among these actors might also help to ensure the full utilization of the above legislative revisions (however limited such cases might be today in Hungary). This is true not only in Hungary but also in all States.

### Romania

In Romania, laws relating to registration of birth of children of unknown parents and consequently the nationality law granting nationality to 'children who are found in Romania […] if none of their parents is known'[84] are applied 'to children who are abandoned by the mothers in hospitals or other healthcare institutions, if the identity of the mother in unknown'.[85]

### Japan

*Baby left behind by the mother of foreign appearance at a hospital: Supreme Court Judgement (27 January 1995) (the Baby Andrew Case).*[86]
Japan has relatively well-known case law in this regard. In this case, the claimant, Andrew, was born in a Japanese hospital. The mother who gave birth to him, who did not speak Japanese, appeared to be Filipino according to the hospital staff. She absconded without leaving any documents to prove her identity. The Minister of Justice located a certain level of information regarding the identity of a woman who is highly probably to be the same person as Andrew's mother (such as her immigration entry record in Japan and birth registration with the Filipino authorities). However, these pieces of evidence were slightly inconsistent with the identity-related facts verbally claimed by Andrew's mother to the hospital staff. The embassy of the Philippines denied Andrew the confirmation of his Filipino nationality. The Supreme Court considered that Andrew's parents were 'unknown' in according with article 2(iii) and confirmed his Japanese nationality.

---

[84] Article 5. (A. By birth)—'(3) Children who are found in Romanian territory are regarded as Romanian citizens until proven otherwise, if none of their parents is known.' Law on Romanian Citizenship no. 21/1991 (as amended by L. nr.112/2010, 17 June 2010) <https://data.globalcit.eu/NationalDB/docs/ROM%20Citizenship%20Law%201991%20(English_consolidated%20version%2017%20June%202010).pdf> accessed 4 August 2019.

[85] ENS, 'Ending Childhood Statelessness: A Study on Romania, Working Paper 01/15' (2015) 12 <http://www.statelessness.eu/sites/www.statelessness.eu/files/Romania.pdf> accessed 10 February 2017.

[86] *Minshū* Vol 49, No 1, p 56 [27 January 1995 (*Heisei 7 nen*)] (Supreme Court); (1997) Japanese Annual of International Law (JAIL) 129. While the commentaries on this case are mostly in Japanese language (to be cited extensively in Sect. 5.6.3) some analysis in English exists: Yasuhiro Okuda, 'The United Nations Convention on the Rights of the Child and Japan's international family law including Nationality Law' (2003) Zeitschrift für Japanisches Recht [Journal of Japanese Law] 92. See also Stacey Steele, 'Comments on OKUDA, statelessness and Nationality Act of Japan: Baby Andrew becomes a teenager and other changes?' (2004) Zeitschrift für Japanisches Recht [Journal of Japanese Law].

As this ruling contains valuable discussions on how 'unknown-ness' of parents should be assessed when there is evidence supporting that a particular person is 'highly probable' to be one's parent, the detailed facts and the reasoning of this judgement will be discussed in Sect. 5.6.3, which is dedicated to the issue of burden and standard of proof.

However, these sorts of case—left behind by birth mothers at hospitals—do not benefit from the foundling provision in some States. For example, while a non-State party to the 1961 Convention and ECN, in Macedonia, if the birth of a child has been witnessed by a doctor but a false identity information was provided by her or his birth mother, the mother will be considered 'known'.[87]

With regard to Poland, another non-State party (which signed but not ratified ECN), one example of such children is quoted in the opening of this book. Agni was abandoned at the hospital by a (self-claimed) Romanian Roma teenage mother. Before abandoning her, Agni's birth mother did give her name and nationality to the hospital personnel. Agni was not able to acquire Polish citizenship because her mother was not considered 'unknown' by the authorities. She was also unable to confirm the acquisition of Romanian nationality at the Romanian embassy, with the officials saying that Agni was not present in Romanian registers and they determined that it was impossible to identify where her birth mother was currently living. In another similar and reported case, Maria Jakab and her foster parents had to go through legal struggles until she turned 17 for her to receive citizenship.[88] There are reportedly at least 30 similar cases of abandoned children each year known to the embassy of Romania in Poland.[89] This is because, according to the interpretation adopted by the authorities responsible for implementing the foundling provision, those who benefit from that provision are abandoned children left in baby hatches,[90] whose parents' identities are thus completely unknown.

---

[87] ENS, 'Ending Childhood Statelessness: A Study on Macedonia, Working Paper 02/15' (June 2015) 8–9 <http://www.statelessness.eu/resources/ending-childhood-statelessness-study-macedonia> accessed 10 February 2017.

[88] 'Born stateless: Maria's story (Maria Jakab, 17, Poland)' *Stateless Voices* <http://www.stateless voices.com/born-stateless/> accessed 1 August 2017 (undated but assumed to have been released in 2014), inaccessible as of 4 August 2019, on file with author.

[89] ENS, 'Ending Childhood Statelessness: A Study on Poland, Working Paper 03/15' (June 2015) 4–5, 9–10 <https://www.statelessness.eu/sites/www.statelessness.eu/files/Poland.pdf> accessed 4 August 2019. Article 14 of the Polish law on citizenship, a child shall acquire Polish citizenship at birth when the child is born within the territory of the Republic of Poland of parents who are unknown, stateless or whose citizenship cannot be determined. According to article 15 a child of unknown parents shall acquire Polish citizenship when found within the territory of the Republic of Poland.

[90] Ibid 9.

## *4.3.7 Orphans*

As mentioned in Chap. 1, the term 'orphans' is commonly used—along with the term 'abandoned children'—interchangeably with the term 'foundlings'. This is not correct as parents can pass away after duly registering their children and legally establishing their parentage. However, it is true that particularly in non-industrialized States where birth registration is not systematic, or where there have been armed conflicts, many orphans indeed remain to be of unknown parentage.

Even in Japan, the term 'orphaned children' is included among typical cases who can benefit from its foundling provision. The official position subscribed by the Japanese competent authority, the Civil Affairs Bureau, Ministry of Justice, is that those who can have their family registry created under article 57 of Family Register Act who can thus confirm their nationality under article 2(iii) Nationality Act include those 'orphaned', as long as their parentage cannot be identified.[91]

While more recent case law or administrative decisions confirming nationality of orphans could not be located in the public domain, an old Japanese family court case involving a World War II orphan might be a good inspiration for States currently affected by armed conflict.

*Tōkyō Family Court Adjudication on 9 September, 1966*[92]

Summary of facts

The claimant's house was destroyed and his father killed, and his mother and elder brother went missing, during World War II. He thus became orphaned at around the age of 10, the year the war ended. Because of his vague but unverified memory, such as that he used to live in a Korean community, and his father was called by Korean names, the claimant used to believe that he was Korean and even registered himself with the Japanese authorities as a foreigner, but could not prove the fact that he was of Korean origin when he attempted to marry a Japanese national. The record retained at the Japanese primary school which he attended carried the claimant's date of birth

---

[91] The same policy document refers to abandoned children, runaway children (see Sect. 4.3.8) and 'lost' children as other typical cases who could have their family register created under article 57 of the Family Register Act and have their nationality confirmed under article 2(iii) of Nationality Act. Taishō 4.6.23 minji 361 gō hōmukyokuchō kaitō [Official inquiry response from the Director of the Legal Affairs Bureau, 23 June 1915, No.361], and Shōwa 25.11.9 minji kō dai 2910 gō kaitō [Official inquiry response, 9 November 1950, civil affairs No.2910], as referred to in '75 Kiji hakken chōsho no sakusei oyobi koseki no kisai—Shōwa 27.6.7 minji kō dai 804 gō tsūtatsu [Drafting of the report of finding an abandoned child and the entry into the family register—in relation to the Civil Affairs Circular, 7 June 1952, No 804]' in Mitsuo Kimura and Masajirō Takezawa (eds), *Shori kijun to shiteno koseki kihon senrei kaisetsu* [*Commentary on the Basic Precedents Relating to Family Register Administration for Reference as Processing Criteria*] (Nihon kajo shuppan 2008) 473. Ryūun Ō, 'Kiji no kokuseki [Nationality of Abandoned Children]' (1969) 4 Hōgaku Kenkyū [Hokkaigakuen daigaku hōgakkai] 169, p 287. Yue Fū, 'Nihon de umareta kodomono kokuseki to mukokuseki nintei' ['Determination of Statelessness for Children Born in Japan'] (PhD dissertation, University of Tsukuba 2016) 145.

[92] *Kagetsu* Vol 19, No.3, p 73 [9 September 1966 (*Shōwa 41 nen*)] (Tōkyō Family Court).

(in Japan) and the domicile in a particular city in Ōsaka prefecture. Nonetheless, no family registry (which is strong proof of Japanese nationality) was indeed located including in the claimed area of domicile.

Summary of adjudication

The court stated that it was clear that the claimant was born in Japan, though it is unclear from the decision how the claimant's birth in Japan was established. There were indeed doubts that the claimant's father was from Korea based on the names that the claimant and his family were called, and even the actual name of the claimant's father and mother could be confirmed. The court concluded that the claimant was of unknown parentage born in Japan, thereby confirming his Japanese nationality based on the foundling provision.

Due to Japan's colonization of Korea, there were ethnic Korean communities throughout Japan. The fact that unknown parentage was recognized despite the claimant's previous registration as Korean demonstrates the court's view that mere likelihood of foreign parentage is irrelevant as long as the person's parent is not firmly identified. On a separate note, the claimant was 31 years old at the time of this court decision.

### 4.3.8  Runaway Child

In another old Japanese family court adjudication, a person who was not 'abandoned' by parents but who voluntarily, or was compelled to, run away from his mother, was recognized to be of unknown parentage and confirmed Japanese nationality. Again, this sort of situation would be very rare in today's industrialized world, but this adjudication can serve as an inspiration for States where, for example, birth registration is not systematic.

*Adjudication by the Ōita Family Court Bungotakada Branch 31 January 1975*[93]

Summary of facts

The claimant, ever since he can remember, was working as a residential worker with a woman identifying herself to be his mother A in a farm run by B. He was told by A that he was born on 22 June 1913 in the far south in Kagoshima, but was never told anything about his father. With the workload being unbearable, the claimant left the farm without permission of his mother when he was about 13 years old. He subsequently worked at different places, then in 1944 de facto married a woman, C, with whom he had one daughter, D, in 1946. Not having had any school education and being almost illiterate, the claimant had not been aware of anything about his family registry until his daughter D was to be enrolled in a junior high school. In this process A realized that D was an illegitimate child (as the marriage had not been registered

---

[93] *Kagetsu* Vol 28, No.1, p 84 [31 January 1975 (*Shōwa 50 nen*)] (Ōita Family Court Bungotakada Branch).

under the claimant's family register, which in the end could not be located). In order to legitimize her he needed to legally marry C. The claimant subsequently traced back and visited B around 1958, then inquired about his mother, A. However, B, while acknowledging that the claimant was working at B's farm, adamantly claimed that he did not know anything about A, and even started to allege that the claimant was Korean. The claimant could not confirm whether his mother, A, was dead or alive, let alone her whereabouts, and exhausted all the means of obtaining any information about his family registry. Repeated investigations to find the claimant/his mother A's family registry were carried out with cooperation from the local administration officials in charge of family registry, with the name of the place where he was told he was born, as well as the family name of his mother A as the key information. The investigation did not yield any result, and upon the advice from a local administration official, the claimant even once registered himself as a foreigner (stateless) in 1972. The claimant subsequently requested this family court's adjudication to permit him to be registered in a family registry as a Japanese national.

Summary of adjudication

The court in its reasoning emphasized that the object and purpose of the then article 2(iv) of the Nationality Act (article 2(iii) under the current Nationality Act), was to:

> [P]revent as much as possible the increase of statelessness which is the possible negative effect caused by adopting a strict *jus sanguinis* principle, and to actively include into the body of nationals, the persons who are born in the territory of Japan – while taking into consideration the nature of the nation as a community of persons who are linked by territorial connections, and who habitually reside in the territory and become socially and economically part of the human component of the nation, and who are also culturally assimilated with the society – which meets the national interest. (emphasis added; author translation)

The Court in this case also presented a notable argumentation with regard to whether the claimant fulfilled the other requirement under article 2(iv) (sic)[94] that is birth in Japan, and this part of the adjudication will be discussed in Sect. 6.4. As a side note, the claimant's age at the time of adjudication was 61 years old.

## 4.3.9   A Person of Undocumented Parentage

As examined in Sect. 2.9, there is indeed a fine line between persons lacking documentation on parentage (and birthplace) and persons of unknown parentage.

In Spain, there has been a DGRN decision in 1993 that confirmed Spanish nationality—under its foundling provision, that is article 17.1.d) of the Civil Code—of a man of undocumented parentage and birthplace, who had previously been registered with a city hall as a stateless foreigner. He was 38 years old at the time he

---

[94] As written in the adjudication. The claimant was supposedly born on 22 June 1913, it should be the Nationality Act of 1899 that is applicable to him, which provides for nationality grant to persons of unknown parents born in Japan in article 4, and not in article 2(iv) of the 1950 Nationality Act (now article 2(iii)).

approached the city hall for late birth registration, and 41 years old at the time of the DGRN decision.

## DGRN Resolution of 9 of August 1993[95]

### Summary of facts

On 3 October 1990, AML, a single male and a resident of city M, filed a petition with the civil registry of city C for his late registration of birth, stating that he was born in city C on 25 April 1952. While he was unable to prove his parentage, he submitted his foreign registration card issued by the Superior Police Headquarters of city M, on 3 April 1990, where he is recorded to have been born in city C on the above date with nationality status as 'stateless'. AML stated regarding his family circumstances that his mother, LS, had died in Ceuta[96] in 1983 or 1984. His father, MH, died on Street C, number 40 of area C approximately in 1977. While the basis is not clear from the text of the decision, the claimant's parents were speculated (but not proven) to be Moroccan (which is mentioned only at the end of the DGRN decision). AML stated that he also has a sibling who lived in area B del P of city C.

### Summary of decision

The DGRN ruled that AML was a Spanish national for fulfilling the criteria of article 17.1.d) of the Civil Code. In doing so, the DGRN stated that:

> [E]ven if one's filiation is not registered, this does not mean that the born one necessarily has Spanish nationality by 'jus soli', which will only happen when such filiation is not determined or legally established (*acreditada legalmente*) with respect to the presumed Moroccan progenitors born outside of Spain, according to the legislation of such parents [...].

This DGRN decision is remarkable, as AML, the person concerned, had never been 'abandoned' or 'left' by, or 'separated' from his parents. Rather, they simply died, when AML was an adult, that is around 25 years old (in the case of his father) and 31 or 32 years old (in the case of the mother). The only reason—as it appears from the decision—why AML was considered to be of 'undetermined parentage' under article 17.1.d) of the Civil Code was that there was no or insufficient evidence available to establish the identity of AML's parents and his legal parent–child relationship with the parents. Meanwhile, as will be discussed in Sect. 6.4, AML's fulfilment of the other elements required under article 17.1.d) (to benefit from the legal presumption of having been born in the territory)—that he was a 'minor' whose 'first known place of stay' was Spain—was established by his own statements corroborated by AML's neighbours, acquaintances and friends testifying that they have known AML living in the specific neighbourhood in Spain since he was a baby or a child.

---

[95] Res. DGRN de 9 de agosto de 1993 (188) (BIMJ, núm. 1685, 1993, pp 4645–8; RAJ, 1993, núm. 6899).

[96] The decision carries—probably by error—the city name Ceuta once and it could be assumed that the area 'C' stands for Ceuta, which is a Spanish city on the north coast of Africa, separated by 14 km from Cadiz province on the Spanish mainland by the Strait of Gibraltar and sharing a 6.4 km land border with Morocco.

### 4.3.10 Children Born Through Anonymous Birth Scheme

By reviewing the actual State practice around the world, it was found that one of the typical cases who benefit from the foundling provision in some States are persons whose mothers opt for a form of 'anonymous' birth with whom the maternal legal descent is not established. What the system is called and how exactly the anonymity works depends on the State.[97] However, the common feature for the anonymous birth schemes that are relevant to this book is that while the mother gives birth in a medical facility, the identity of the mother is not registered with the competent authorities on civil status or nationality matters as the child's legal mother. In those cases, the biological mother is factually known to the medical professionals, but are not legally known for family law and nationality law purposes.

***France***

As mentioned in Sect. 2.10.5.1, in addition to Chap. 2 and in Chaps. 1 and 3, in France, at least since the French Revolution in the 1780s, women have long had the right to give birth secretly (referred to as *'accouchement sous X'*).[98] In today's France, approximately 600 women a year give birth anonymously, with the figure in 2014 being 625.[99]

As of today, any pregnant woman, including married women and non-French nationals, who wishes to give birth anonymously is to notify the medical team of the health facility (public or private) of her choice. 'No identification information can be requested and no investigation can be conducted.'[100] The establishment of both legal maternity and legal paternity is put in the hands of the mother by granting her the right to give birth anonymously and by making it possible not to register her husband as the father of the child.[101]

---

[97] See for example the useful comparison chart created by FIOM, an organization based in the Netherlands, although they do not analyze the nationality acquisition aspect of the anonymous birth schemes. 'Bevallen onder geheimhouding' ['Giving Birth Under Confidentiality'] <https://fiom.nl/sites/default/files/files/factsheet_bevallen_onder_geheimhouding.pdf> accessed 4 August 2019.

[98] Nadine Lefaucheur, 'The French "tradition" of anonymous birth: the lines of argument' (2004) 18 International Journal of Law, Policy and the Family 319.

[99] According to the latest report of the National Observatory on Endangered Children, these 625 births represent a rate of 76.5 births under secrecy per 100,000 live births, which is less than one birth per thousand. Quoted by Solène Cordier for le Monde, 'L'accouchement sous le secret, une spécificité française' ['Childbirth under Secrecy, a French Specificity'] (3 July 2016) <http://www.lemonde.fr/famille-vie-privee/article/2016/07/03/l-accouchement-sous-le-secret-une-specificite-francaise_4962761_1654468.html#GBQ2XcFDusARUD6B.99> accessed 1 August 2017, inaccessible as of 4 August 2019, on file with author.

[100] French government's official website has a specialized page on anonymous birth. 'Accouchement sous X (Verified July 12, 2016)' <https://www.service-public.fr/particuliers/vosdroits/F3136> accessed 4 August 2019.

[101] Kees Jan Saarloos, 'European Private International Law on Legal Parentage? Thoughts on a European Instrument Implementing the Principle of Mutual Recognition in Legal Parentage' (PhD dissertation, Maastricht University 2010) 89.

Article 326 of the French Civil Code[102] provides for anonymous birth. After a child's birth, his mother may request that the secrecy as to her admittance and identity be preserved (*Lors de l'accouchement, la mère peut demander que le secret de son admission et de son identité soit préservé*).[103]

Children whose mother gives birth anonymously acquire French nationality under the combination of articles 19, 19-2[104] and 58[105] of the Civil Code.

Article 19 stipulates: 'A child born in France of unknown parents (l'enfant né en France de parents inconnus) is French. [...].' Article 19-2 then provides for presumption of birth in France for those whose record of birth was drawn up under article 58. Article 58 of the Civil Code is a special provision providing for how the record of birth should be drawn up when a new-born child is 'found' in the French territory. Article 58 also provides for children whose birth in France is known but whose mother's identity is unknown, stating that: 'Similar records shall be drawn up, on declaration of the Children's aid services, for children placed under their guardianship and deprived of a known record of birth or *for whom the secret as to birth has been claimed*.'[106]

## *Italy*

Out of about 550,000 children born each year throughout Italy, about 400 are 'rejected' or not recognized by parents,[107] who are considered to have been born

---

[102] Article 326 is contained under section 2 on the 'Des actions aux fins d'établissement de la filiation' ['Actions for the Establishment of Parentage'], Chapitre III on actions relating to filiation (Des actions relatives à la filiation), Title VII on filiation (De la filiation), of Book 1 on persons (Des personnes) of the French Civil Code.

[103] See also article L. 222-6 of Code de l'action sociale et des familles [Code of social care and families, tr Anne-Cecile Duputel] (2 November 2018) <https://www.legifrance.gouv.fr/affichCode. do;jsessionid=9D46C017566F085FB91968FAC07348E0.tplgfr24s_3?idSectionTA=LEGISCTA0 00006157583&cidTexte=LEGITEXT000006074069&dateTexte=20181107> accessed 4 August 2019.

[104] Article 19 and 19-2 are contained in section 2 on French by birth in France (Des Français par la naissance en France), chapter II on French nationality by origin, Title 1 bis on French Nationality, Book 1 of the French Civil Code.

[105] Article 58 is under section 1 on declarations of births (Des déclarations de naissance), chapter II on acts of birth (Des actes de naissance), Title II on acts on civil status (Des actes de l'état civil), Book I of the French Civil Code.

[106] Article 58, French Civil Code.

[107] According to the figures released by the Juvenile Court, cited in research conducted by the Italian Society of Neonatology (data as of 2013). Cited in Fondazione Francesca Rava, 'Società Italiana di Neonatologia (SIN) e ninna ho insieme a tutela dell'infanzia abbandonata. Al via un'indagine conoscitiva sulla realtà dell'abbandono neonatale in Italia per impostare programmi preventivi efficaci di aiuto alle madri in difficoltà' ['SIN and Ninna ho Working Together to Protect Abandoned Children. Launch of a Survey on Infant Abandonment Reality in Italy to Set Up Effective Preventive Programs to Help Mothers in Need'] (13 June 2013) <https://www.nph-italia.org/notizie/174/ sin-e-ninna-ho-insieme-a-tutela-dell-infanzia-abba/> accessed 3 August 2019. Referred to in the Email from Tessa Onida (General Area Director, Research and Monitoring Services, Istituto degli Innocenti, Florence, Italy) to author (31 May 2017).

of the 'anonymous birth scheme', who compose the majority[108] of the persons who acquire nationality under the country's 'unknown parentage' provision.

The Decree of the President of the Republic No 396/2000 foresees the possibility for a mother to give birth in anonymity: article 30 (Birth Declaration (*Dichiarazione di nascita*)) paragraph 1 states 'The declaration of birth is made by one of the parents, by a special attorney, or by a physician or midwife or other person who has assisted the childbirth, respecting the mother's will not to be named.'[109] The mother can then leave the child in institutional care. In these cases, the child is considered to be born of unknown parents; thus, the Italian nationality law should apply and nationality should be granted at birth by operation of law under article 1(1)(b) of Law No 91/1992.

It is noted that the anonymous birth option is available to any woman regardless of her marital status, nationality or legal status. Figures[110] from a survey conducted by the 'Ninna ho project'[111] between 2013 and 2014[112] showed that 48.2% of women surveyed who gave birth anonymously were single, while 25% were 'either married (including widows and those divorced) or cohabiting with a partner'.[113] 62.5% of women were foreign women and 37.5% were women of Italian citizenship,[114] often with serious economic difficulties. Most foreign women came from eastern Europe (58.8%), followed by Africa (14.7%), Asia (11.8%), central Europe and South America (5.9%) and North America (2.9%).[115]

---

[108] According to an interview with the Citizenship Office of Florence, the annual number of persons granted nationality due to their unknown parentage within Florence is no more than ten persons a year, 'the vast majority of whom—if any—are born of women who do not wish to recognize the child and exercise their right to give birth anonymously'. Interview with Ms. Gandolfo, Director, Citizenship Office of the Municipality of Florence (Florence, Italy, 22 May 2017). Author thanks Attorney Paolo Farci as well as Lara Zunelli for facilitating her communication with the Office.

[109] Article 30 (Birth Declaration / Dichiarazione di nascita), Decree of the President of the Republic No 396/2000. Thanks goes to Marcello Bertocchi for his language support.

[110] Interview with Central Direction for Civil Rights, Citizenship and Minorities of the Department for Civil Liberties and Immigration of the Ministry of Interior, Italy (Rome, Italy, 23 May 2017). Also confirmed by the Citizenship Office of Florence and UNHCR Italy. Confirmed through Interview with Enrico Guida, Statelessness Expert, UNHCR Rome (23 May 2017). See also ENS, 'Ending Childhood Statelessness: A Study on Italy, Working Paper 07/15' (2015) 23 <http://www.refworld.org/docid/582327974.html> accessed 4 August 2019. Direzione Centrale Per I Diritti Civili and others, 'La Cittadinanza Italiana—La Normativa, Le Procedure, Le Circolari [Italian Citizenship—Legislation, Procedures, Circulars]' (31 March 2003) 18 <https://www.asgi.it/banca-dati/cittadinanza-italiana-normativa-procedure-circolari/> accessed 4 August 2019.

[111] Project of Fondazione Francesca Rava, N.P.H. Italia Onlus e dal Network KPMG in Italia, supported by Ministry of Health and the Italian Society of Neonatology.

[112] Survey conducted between July 2013 to June 2014. Ninna ho project, 'Dati sul fenomeno dei bambini non riconosciuti alla nascita' ['Data on the Phenomenon of Children Unrecognized at Birth'] <https://www.ninnaho.org/wp-content/uploads/2017/05/Osservatorio.pdf> accessed 4 August 2019.

[113] The percentage of those currently married is not provided in the survey. Ibid.

[114] It is unknown whether it is statistically significant. Ibid.

[115] It is unknown whether it is statistically significant. Ibid.

So how exactly does the 'anonymity' work in Italy? While it is called 'anony-mous', according to the author's interviews with the competent authorities on nation-ality matters, the mother normally provides information on her identity at the hospital where she is to give birth. It is 'anonymous' in a sense that the name of the mother will be withheld by the attending medical personnel away from the third party including the child who she gave birth.[116] It is normally when the mother expresses her wish not to recognize the child that the mother is informed of the choice of 'anonymous birth'.

When the biological mother opts for birth in anonymity, the child is to be assigned a name and issued with a birth record (*atto di nascita*) within the time limit of ten days after birth, where it will be written: 'born of a woman who does not want to be identified'.[117]

In the case of anonymous birth, the declaration of birth is done by a doctor or midwife or another person who assisted the childbirth. The medical institution where the anonymous birth occurred must immediately report the fact of an unrecognized infant to a public prosecutor at a Juvenile Court, which allows the opening of a procedure for adoption.[118] In its report, and in any subsequent communication to the judicial authority, identifying details of the mother must be omitted.[119]

### Germany (Confidential birth or birth under pseudonym)

Germany has generally subscribed to the principle of *mater semper certa est* (the mother is always certain) and has not legalized completely anonymous birth, which is considered to contradict the German legal tradition that focuses on biological descent as evidence, especially in case of children born out of wedlock.[120] However, the law regarding confidential birth (*vertraulichen geburt*)[121] was passed in June 2013, and entered into force in May 2014. In Germany, between May 2014 to 2017, there were '335 confidential births', that is more than 100 a year'.[122]

---

[116] Interview with Central Direction for Civil Rights, Citizenship and Minorities of the Department for Civil Liberties and Immigration of the Ministry of Interior, Italy (Rome, Italy, 23 May 2017). Also confirmed by the Citizenship Office of Florence and UNHCR Italy.

[117] Ministry of Health, 'Parto in anonimato' [Birth in Anonymity'] (Updated 11 April 2017, first edn 15 April 2008) <http://www.salute.gov.it/portale/donna/dettaglioContenutiDonna.jsp?lingua= italiano&id=1011&area=Salute%20donna&menu=nascita> accessed 4 August 2019.

[118] Ibid.

[119] Ibid.

[120] Barbara Willenbacher, 'Legal transfer of French traditions? German and Austrian initiatives to introduce anonymous birth' (2004) 18 International Journal of Law, Policy and the Family 343, 350–1.

[121] *Gesetz zum Ausbau der Hilfen für Schwangere und zur Regelung der vertraulichen Geburt [SchwHiAusbauG]* [Act on the Extension of Assistance for Pregnant Women and on the Regulation of Confidential Birth].

[122] It is unknown up to which date this number 335 covers, but assumed to be sometime in 2017. Carla Bleiker, 'Germany: Confidential Birth: a Safe, Private Way Out for Pregnant Women' (2017) <www.dw.com/en/confidential-birth-a-safe-private-way-out-for-pregnant-women/a-39662482> accessed 4 August 2019.

Under this system, a woman can call a free-of-charge, 24/7 hotline anonymously. Professionals will refer her to a nearby counsellor, who will provide emotional support and medical care. The woman can give birth at a hospital under a pseudonym.[123] The woman has to use her own ID to register with her counsellor. However, that counsellor would be the only person who knows the mother's real identity, and her identity will not be revealed to anyone else during her pregnancy or after giving birth, until the child turns 16. When the woman gives birth, the child is put up for adoption. The personal information of the mother is recorded and kept in a sealed envelope by federal authorities until the child's 16th birthday. When the child turns 16 years old, she or he is given contact information for the mother, in case she or he wishes to meet the mother.[124]

The Nationality Act was then amended to make it clear that children born under confidential birth acquire German nationality under section 4 of the Nationality Act providing nationality to foundlings found in the territory.[125] The amended Nationality Act section 4(2) reads:

'Section 4 […] (2) A child which is found on German territory [foundling (*Findelkind*)] shall be deemed to be the child of a German until otherwise proven. The first sentence shall apply mutatis mutandis to a child born to a mother under condition of anonymity in accordance with Section 25 (1) of the Act to Prevent and Resolve Conflicts in Pregnancy [Schwangerschaftskonfliktgesetzes (SchKG)].[126]

Even before the law was passed, completely 'anonymous birth' (*anonyme geburt*) as practised in France was available in practice, but not regulated by law. Further, even today, some clinics are known to allow for completely anonymous birth.[127]

---

[123] Federal Government of Germany, 'Bericht der Bundesregierung zu den Auswirkungen aller Maßnahmen und Hilfsangebote, die auf Grund des Gesetzes zum Ausbau der Hilfen für Schwangere und zur Regelung der vertraulichen Geburt ergriffen wurden' ['Report by the Federal Government on the effects of all measures and offers of assistance, which were taken under the law for the extension of the assistance for pregnant women and for the regulation of confidential birth'] (12 July 2017) <https://www.bmfsfj.de/blob/117448/74c7e8b3ef0960d03b66ade5f0958df6/bericht-vertrauliche-geburt-2017-data.pdf> .

[124] Carla Bleiker, 'Germany: Confidential Birth: a Safe, Private Way Out for Pregnant Women' (2017) <www.dw.com/en/confidential-birth-a-safe-private-way-out-for-pregnant-women/a-39662482> accessed 4 August 2019; Stephanie Höppner, 'New Law to Give Orphans Right to Know Mother's Identity' (10 June 2013) <www.dw.com/en/confidential-birth-a-safe-private-way-out-for-pregnant-women/a-39662482> accessed 4 August 2019.

[125] Federal Government of Germany, 'Bericht der Bundesregierung zu den Auswirkungen aller Maßnahmen und Hilfsangebote, die auf Grund des Gesetzes zum Ausbau der Hilfen für Schwangere und zur Regelung der vertraulichen Geburt ergriffen wurden' ['Report by the Federal Government on the effects of all measures and offers of assistance, which were taken under the law for the extension of the assistance for pregnant women and for the regulation of confidential birth'] (12 July 2017) <https://www.bmfsfj.de/blob/117448/74c7e8b3ef0960d03b66ade5f0958df6/bericht-vertrauliche-geburt-2017-data.pdf> .

[126] Staatsangehörigkeitsgesetz (StAG) [The Nationality Act of Germany] (1913) <https://www.gesetze-im-internet.de/stag/BJNR005830913.html> accessed 5 September 2019.

[127] Carla Bleiker, 'Germany: Confidential Birth: a Safe, Private Way Out for Pregnant Women' (2017) <https://www.dw.com/en/confidential-birth-a-safe-private-way-out-for-pregnant-women/a-39662482> accessed 4 August 2019.

Despite the recommendations by different authors that the children born anonymously should be considered to have acquired German nationality under article 4(2) of the Nationality Act,[128] there have been reports that, unlike children left in a baby hatch, they have sometimes remained stateless until the adoption process was completed. This is reportedly due to the fact that their place and time of birth is 'known' to the medical personnel reporting on the anonymous birth.[129] This might have depended on the specific municipality where the birth was reported,[130] and it is unknown whether the issue of nationality for children born anonymously has been resolved today. It is essential that States where anonymous birth is tolerated ensure that automatic acquisition of nationality at birth is confirmed for those who are born through such scheme.

*Japan*

While it has not been implemented yet, Jikei hospital of Kumamoto city, which operates Japan's only baby hatch, is currently considering to start allowing women to give birth in confidence (modelling the confidential birth mechanism adopted by Germany). A recent news article reported that the competent authorities on nationality matters confirmed that it is possible to create Japanese family registry (obviously based on article 2(iii) of Nationality Act on children born of unknown parents) for children born under such scheme.[131]

### 4.3.11  Persons Whose Mothers Go Missing After Registering Their Birth with Invalid or Incomplete Identity Information

Section 4.3.6 discussed babies who are left behind by the mother at the hospital before registering the babies' birth. In contrast, this category is about children born in the territory (specifically Japan) whose (foreign) biological mothers go missing and/or deported (often having cared for the children for several years) after having

---

[128] Nils Dellert, 'Die anonyme Kindesabgabe: anonyme Geburt und Babyklappe' (2009) Peter Lang 35.

[129] Joelle Coutinho and Claudia Krell, *Anonyme Geburt und Babyklappen in Deutschland. Fallzahlen, Angebote, Kontexte* [*Anonymous Birth and Baby Hatches in Germany*] (Deutsches Jugendinstitut 2011). Also, see Christiane Henze, 'Babyklappe und anonyme Geburt [Baby hatches and anonymous birth]' (2014) 14–16 <www.hwr-berlin.de/fileadmin/downloads_internet/publikati onen/beitraege_FB4/Heft_2_2014_Fachbereich_Rechtspflege.pdf> accessed 4 August 2019.

[130] Joelle Coutinho and Claudia Krell, *Anonyme Geburt und Babyklappen in Deutschland. Fallzahlen, Angebote, Kontexte* [*Anonymous Birth and Baby Hatches in Germany*] (Deutsches Jugendinstitut 2011) 214–15 (5.4.2 Staatsangehörigkeit).

[131] Asahi Shimbun News, 'Naimitsu shussan demo koseki sakusei 'kanō' hōmushō ga kenkai' ['It Is "Possible" to Create Japanese Family Register for Those Born Through 'Confidential Birth-Ministry of Justice's view-'] (19 May 2018) <https://www.asahi.com/articles/ASL57760LL57UBQU00D. html> accessed 15 July 2019.

their children registered at birth with authorities, yet with false or incomplete identity information about herself, whose legal maternity then cannot be verified and established with the authorities of the purported country of origin of such mother.

The biological father, in such cases, was either unknown, went missing, was deported, and/or was denied acknowledgment of paternity. The claimants had generally been under the care of a friend or acquaintance upon the request from the apparent biological parent(s) before going under the care of a government-run/-commissioned child custody facility and/or the issuance of the family court adjudication to admit the person into the family registry.[132]

In Japan, persons in this situation have been confirmed Japanese nationality under article 2(iii) of the Nationality Act for having been born in Japan of 'unknown parentage'.

The one publicly known case is the Yokohama family court adjudication in 2003[133] (while there are other similar though unpublished cases as below). In this case, the claimant's mother, calling herself Viviana Cantoria,[134] gave birth to the claimant in Japan. The claimant's birth was notified to the relevant city office, and the claimant was registered under the Japanese family register of a Japanese male, to whom Viviana Cantoria at the time was legally married, who thus was considered the claimant's 'father'. Separately, Viviana Cantoria supposedly held a Filipino passport and was assumed to have been registered as a foreign resident with the relevant city by producing such a passport. However, the city could not issue a certificate of such registration as it could not locate the relevant record.[135] Viviana is quoted to have later stated to her attorney representing her for the purpose of the divorce procedure from her husband that the Filipino passport she had produced was fraudulent. Viviana went through the procedure to leave Japan when the claimant was about one year and eight months old after the divorce from his Japanese 'father', under whose family register the claimant was registered. The 'father' subsequently and successfully denied his paternity over the claimant and the claimant was deleted from the initial father's family registry.

The Yokohama family court later confirmed the claimants' Japanese nationality under article 2(iii) of the Nationality Act, for having been born in Japan of unknown parents. The family court stated that (as the identity of the claimant's real or biological father could not be confirmed) and 'as it cannot be confirmed that his real or biological mother is a Filipino national, he cannot acquire Filipino nationality'. The claimant was nine years old when the adjudication was issued.

As this case—while indirectly—offers some hints on the 'extent of unknown-ness' in assessing 'unknown parentage', it will be discussed in more detail in Sect. 5.6.3.3.1, along with the Baby Andrew case of 1995 mentioned in Sect. 4.3.6.

---

[132] Interview with Kensuke Ōnuki, Attorney at Law (Tokyo, Japan, 4 March 2017). *Decision, Kagetsu* Vol 56, No 3, p 68 (Yokohama Family Court).

[133] *Decision, Kagetsu* Vol 56, No 3, p 68 (Yokohama Family Court).

[134] Pseudonym assigned by the Yokahama Family Court.

[135] Interview with Kensuke Ōnuki, Attorney at Law (Tokyo, Japan, 4 March 2017). *Decision, Kagetsu* Vol 56, No 3, p 68 (Yokohama Family Court)70.

Further, while the original adjudications could not be accessed or disclosed,[136] Kensuke Ōnuki,[137] one of the several known attorneys at law who has continuously represented persons of unknown parentage, states he has successfully secured the creation of family registry for all—approximately ten-persons he represented from around 2002–2006 asserting nationality under article 2(iii).

The summary of the two family court adjudications among the ten, based on the limited facts published, are as follows.[138]

*7 June 2004 adjudication*: The child's birth notification (registration) form submitted to the Japanese municipality office carried the name of the mother, whose nationality was 'Thai'. However, the mother disappeared around when the child turned one-year-old. A woman of foreign nationality resident in Japan had been caring for the child before the adjudication.

*August 2004 adjudication*: The child's birth notification form submitted to the Japanese municipality carried the name of the mother, who was recorded as a Thai national, with an attachment of her official address registration form (presumably what was issued in Thailand).

Based on this, as well as a personal interview with Ōnuki and several other information sources such as a manual developed by a network of government-commissioned child foster care facilities or orphanages (jidōyōgoshisetsu),[139] the general trends of recent family court adjudications can be discerned.

In cases where the birth registration with a Japanese municipality has been validly completed by the mother with the mother's name and nationality, normally a photocopy of her passport or some sort of an official document (issued by the authorities of supposed country of nationality) to establish her identity is attached. However, such an 'official' document cannot necessarily prove who the mother is. This is, for example, because the document may have been forged, may be genuine but belong to another person, or there may be discrepancies in the personal details between what the biological mother has said elsewhere or written on other documents.

---

[136] Family court adjudication hearings are not open to public as in civil, administrative or criminal litigations. Only selected adjudications are published through the family court bulletin. Ōnuki in the interview stated that it was difficult to obtain the permission from the claimants—who were generally out of reach—to share the adjudications with the author. Interview with Kensuke Ōnuki, Attorney at Law (Tokyo, Japan, 4 March 2017).

[137] Ibid.

[138] 'Cases admitted into family registry: Represented by Kensuke Ōnuki, Attorney at Law, Satsuki Law Firm, Tōkyō' <http://www.satsukilaw.com/archives/category/exam/%e5%9b%bd%e7%b1% 8d/%e5%b0%b1%e7%b1%8d%e8%a8%b1%e5%8f%af> accessed 4 August 2019.

[139] Manual developed by a network of government-commissioned child custody facilities in Chiba prefecture which contains guidance for child welfare professionals on how to secure nationality for children admitted into those facilities whose parents are unknown or missing. Chiba ken wakōdo jiritsu shien kikō jimukyoku (ed), *Jidō yōgoshisetsu no nyūsho jidō no kokuseki/zairyūshikaku mondai no tebiki (shian)'* [*Manual to Resolve Nationality and Residency Status Issues for Children Admitted to Child Custody Facilities (Provisional Version)*] (2014) <http://www.wakoudo.org/rep ort/kokuseki/kokusekimondai_tebiki.pdf> accessed 7 August 2019.

In these sorts of case, the claimants' legal representatives, child custody facilities or legal guardians—either upon request by the family court or spontaneously—contact (though not always—see below) the embassies of the supposed countries of nationality of parent(s).[140] This is to verify whether the claimant has acquired nationality of the parent(s) and can have her or his own passport issued. This is in turn expected to confirm whether the mother (father)–child relationship is recognized by the authorities of the countries of parent(s)' nationality under the family law of these countries (supposedly with the exception of cases where the nationality cannot be passed on despite the fact that the parent–child relationship is established).

It appears thus that Japanese family courts today tend to recognize a person to be a child of 'unknown' parents where the authorities of the country of nationality of the purported parent(s) do not recognize such parent–child relationship. However, it is also noted that if, from the general circumstances, the non-recognition of legal parentage by the relevant authorities is already apparent, such confirmation might not even be necessary.[141]

The implications of this practice on the standard of 'unknown-ness' of parentage will be discussed in Sects. 5.6.3.3.1 and 5.6.3.3.2.

### 4.3.12 A Person Whose Biological Father is Definitively Known But Has Not Legally Recognized His Paternity Thus is Unknown (Not a Foundling as Mother is Known But Stateless)

In Japan, it has been an established scholarly theory,[142] solidified by case law, that children whose parent(s) is (are) factually known but is (are) not recognized as legal parents are covered by its foundling provision. As stated earlier, article 2(iii) of the Japanese Nationality Act (article 4 of the 1899 Act) *ex lege* grants nationality at birth to a person born in Japan 'When both parents are unknown or are without nationality'.

One example is that a child born out of wedlock in 1948 in Japan from a mother of French nationality, who did not recognize her maternity over the child, had acquired Japanese nationality under article 4 of the 1899 Act. The child's Japanese nationality

[140] Ibid.

[141] Ōnuki states there were some cases in which the court acknowledged the parents' unknown-ness without verification with the embassy. Interview with Kensuke Ōnuki, Attorney at Law (Tokyo, Japan, 4 March 2017).

[142] Hidefumi Egawa, Yoshirō Hayata and Ryōichi Yamada, *Kokusekihō* [Nationality Law] (Yūhikaku 1997) 79; Shōichi Kidana, *Chikujōchūkai kokusekihō* [*Article-by-Article Commentary to Nationality Law*] (Nihon kajo shuppan, 2003) 204; Yue Fū, 'Nihon de umareta kodomono kokuseki to mukokuseki nintei' ['Determination of Statelessness for Children Born in Japan'] (PhD dissertation, University of Tsukuba 2016) 137.

was lost after the mother submitted a notification of recognition of maternity in 1967 (see also Sects. 4.4 and 7.6.2.1).[143]

Further, in relation to the Tōkyō High Court judgement (29 June 1983) discussed in Sect. 4.3.5,[144] the State had originally asserted that the term 'when both parents are unknown' under article 4 of the then Nationality Act only covered abandoned small children for whom nothing is (factually) known about their parents (that is, *kiji* under article 72 of the previous Family Register Act). In response, the Tōkyō High Court ruled that: '[I]t is appropriate to interpret that "when both parents are unknown" [...] meant that for the child concerned, both the father and mother with whom there exists legal parent–child relationship, are unknown.[...]' While this Tōkyō High Court judgement specifically was about a person informally adopted by unrelated adults whose 'real' parents were both factually and legally unknown, this interpretation that 'unknown parent' means *legally* unknown has been confirmed by recent case law.

*Tōkyō Family Court Tachikawa Branch's Adjudication on 5 December 2016*[145]

In this case, discussed in Sect. 2.9, the court determined that the claimant, born in Japan but without birth registration, was of unknown father under the meaning of article 2(iii), as his biological father had not recognized paternity[146] over the claimant. The factual and biological father had been living with and providing for the claimant for more than 20 years, and the father's identity was clearly known to the adjudicating family court.

It is interesting to note that in this case, the claimant's mother, who was not legally married to the claimant' father (with him being married to another woman at the time of the claimant's birth), was not unknown but rather had difficulties proving

---

[143] Minji kō dai 2888 gō minjikyokuchō kaitō, 1 October 1967 (*Shōwa 42 nen*) *Koseki* Vol 247, 58 cited in Shōichi Kidana, Chikujō kokusekihō—kadai no kaimei to jōbun no kaisetsu- [Nationality law—Clarification of Issues and Article-by-Article Commentary] (Nihon kajo shuppan, forthcoming 2021) 324.

[144] *Judgement, Kagetsu* Vol 36, No 7, p 82 [29 June 1983 (*Shōwa 58 nen*)] (Tōkyō High Court).

[145] *Tōkyō Family Court Tachikawa Branch, Adjudication*, 5 December 2016 (*Heisei 28 nen*), unpublished. More details of the case are available in Ayane Odagawa and Sōsuke Seki (eds), Study Group on Stateless in Japan, 'Typology of Stateless Persons in Japan' (2017) 95–6 <https://www.unhcr.org/jp/wp-content/uploads/sites/34/2018/01/TYPOLOGY-OF-STATEL ESS-PERSONS-IN-JAPAN_webEnglish.pdf> accessed 4 August 2019.

[146] Strictly speaking, one might wonder whether simply making the biological father—married with another woman at the time of the claimant's birth—recognize his paternity over the claimant (if not voluntarily, by arbitration or lawsuit) was an option. However, according to the claimant's legal representative, Attorney Ayene Odagwa, as the claimant was already over 20 at the time of this present family court adjudication, such paternity recognition would not have led to the claimant's acquisition of Japanese nationality under article 3(1) of the Nationality Act allowing for children under 20 for whom paternity is acknowledged post-birth to acquire nationality by notification. This would still have left the claimant stateless. The intention by the family court to resolve the claimant's unstable status clearly comes through in this quoted paragraph. Briefing by Attorney Fumie Azukizawa, Ayane Odagawa and Sōsuke Seki, legal representatives, on the *Tōkyō Family Court Tachikawa Branch, Adjudication*, 5 December 2016 (*Heisei 28 nen*) at a session of the Study Group on Statelessness in Japan, 20 January 2017.

her nationality. The mother was essentially considered 'stateless' by the family court. The mother's legal parentage over the claimant was established by the mere fact of delivery, presumably with the Japanese family law being considered by the court to be the applicable law with the mother being stateless in accordance with Japanese private international law. The case nevertheless was considered to fall within article 2(iii) of the Japanese Nationality Act providing for nationality to persons born in Japan of unknown or stateless parents—with the case being a 'mixed case' where the father fulfilled the first criterion ('unknown') and the mother the second criterion ('stateless'). This interpretation was in accordance with the relevant administrative instruction by the Civil Affairs Bureau and a common scholarly theory.

The court, confirming the claimant's Japanese nationality acquired under article 2(iii), stated:

> [W]hen the father is *unknown* for the purpose of article 2(iii) is understood to mean when there is no legal father-child relationship *at the time of the child's birth*, and the [claimant's, author] *father is his biological father*, but as the father has not recognized his paternity over the claimant, there is no legal father-child relationship […]. (emphasis added)[147]

The court went on to refer, in the same sentence, to the object and purpose of the provision (article 2(iii)), that is to prevent statelessness, as the contrary interpretation would have left the claimant without nationality.

In this particular precedent, the claimant's (stateless) mother was known; thus the claimant was not a foundling. Nevertheless, it is significant that this precedent confirms that according to the logic of the court, the claimant would have been recognized as a full-fledged foundling, that is a person of unknown parents, if her or his mother was also unknown. For example, suppose hypothetically that (1) the mother was factually known but had not legally established her maternity over the claimant according to the family law of her country of nationality (where the mother were from a country where she could choose not to establish her maternity even when her parturition of the child is established), or more typically (2) the mother were factually unknown, for example having gone soon after giving birth to the claimant without leaving firm evidence of her own identity. According to the reasoning of the court, and also given the previous precedents, the claimant would have been confirmed nationality under article 2(iii) of the Japanese Nationality Act.[148]

---

[147] Ibid.

[148] In this particular family court adjudication of 5 December 2016, the factual and biological father concerned was a Japanese national. Some might speculate that the family court's conclusion could have been different if the factual father were a foreign national, that is that the court might have found it difficult to consider him 'unknown'. Nevertheless, Attorney Kensuke Ōnuki, an immigration and nationality lawyer who has obtained family court adjudications confirming Japanese nationality of persons of unknown parentage for approximately ten cases from around 2002 to 2006 under article 2(iii), confirmed that there was at least one among such cases where the factual father of the claimant (minor at the time of adjudication)—who had taken care of the child concerned for some time—was fairly clearly 'known' to the relevant family court to be a foreign national. The court determined that there nonetheless existed no proof of legal father–child relationship between the child and biological father including in light of the applicable family law of the country of father's nationality. Interview with Kensuke Ōnuki, Attorney at Law (Tokyo, Japan, 4 March 2017).

On a separate note, the claimant's mother gave birth to him in a hospital in Japan, but this fact was not firmly established as the mother had used a fake name. The claimant's birth in Japan was nevertheless presumed, which is also mentioned in Sect. 6.4.

## 4.4  Legally Unknown v. Factually Unknown Parents—The Former Matters

It is now time to re-examine the frequently asked question raised in the introduction to this chapter. Does 'unknown' parentage mean that the parents are unknown in a legal sense or in a factual sense? The UNHCR Guidelines 4 (2012) paragraph 61 states:

> A child born in the territory of a Contracting State without having a parent, who is legally recognized as such (eg because the child is born out of wedlock and the woman who gave birth to the child is legally not recognized as the mother), is *also* to be treated as a foundling and immediately to acquire the nationality of the State of birth. (emphasis added)

Footnote 41 accompanying paragraph 61 of the UNHCR Guidelines 4 (2012) states: 'The same applies for legal systems which have retained requirements that mothers must recognize children born out of wedlock in order to establish a family relationship.'

From the term 'also to be treated as a foundling' under paragraph 61, the UNHCR Guidelines 4 (2012) appears to define 'unknown-ness' of parentage as covering both factually and legally unknown parents. The Explanatory Report on ECN is silent on this issue.

However, is the expression correct, that the 'concept of a foundling covers not only a child of factually unknown parents and legally unknown parents'?

*Legally unknown parents include factually unknown parents.*

As discussed in Sect. 2.10.1 entitled 'Distinction between "factual parent" and "legal parent"', when it comes to nationality matters, it is ultimately the latter—legally recognized parentage, and not biological or factual parentage that essentially matters as the former is the basis for nationality grant under nationality law.

Nevertheless, the concepts of factually unknown parents and legally unknown parents are not mutually exclusive. Indeed, if a parent is factually unknown, then she or he cannot be legally known anyways (while legally unknown parent might be factually known). In other words, the concept of 'legally unknown parents' includes factually unknown parents. For example, for babies born at home and abandoned on a street or left in a baby hatch (Sects. 4.3.1 and 4.3.2), their parents are normally factually unknown, and there is no way for their existence to be legally established either.

Indeed, some old[149] and current foundling provisions explicitly use the term (children born in the territory of) 'legally unknown parents' in providing nationality to them. Currently, at least two States do so. Article 5(3) of Luxembourgish law grants nationality to a minor born in Luxembourg 'of legally unknown parents'.[150] Article 3(a) of the Burundian law provides nationality to 'a child born in Burundi of legally unknown parents'.[151]

As mentioned in Sect. 4.3, the fact that legal parentage is what eventually matters has been indeed disputed, and eventually acknowledged, in some jurisdictions.

In Hungary (Sect. 4.3.6), a child whose birth mother went missing without leaving accurate information about her identity after delivering a baby in a hospital in Hungary was previously not recognized as a 'child of unknown parents' under section 3(3)b of the Hungarian Citizenship Act. According to the relevant Hungarian authorities, this was not least because:

> [T]he staff of the healthcare institution where the birth took place *actually met the foreign woman*, that is, the biological mother, thus *the mother's identity is not unknown*. [...] for legal purposes, it is irrelevant that the mother cannot be identified later on the basis of the data she has given or even evidenced by documents. (emphasis added)[152]

This interpretation was rectified following the Ombudsperson report (September 2010), which led to legislative changes that entered into force in 2014 to recognize that the mother was 'unknown' under its foundling provision if she 'did not prove her identity upon giving birth, nor within 30 days following the birth [...]' as discussed in Sect. 4.3.6.

With regard to Italy, the Ministry of Interior has explicitly confirmed that 'unknown parents' include all cases where the parents are unknown from a legal point of view even if the parent(s) is (are), strictly speaking, not unknown from a factual or biological point of view.[153] Italy indeed systematically grants nationality under its foundling provision to persons born under the anonymous birth scheme as seen in Sect. 4.3.10.

In Japan, as seen in Sect. 4.3.12 (and to a lesser extent Sects. 4.3.6 and 4.3.11) it has been an established scholarly theory, solidified by case law, that children whose parents are (at least to some extent) factually known but are not recognized as legal

---

[149] See the example in Sect. 3.4.2.2 on Belgium's article E (2) of the 1922 nationality law and article 1(2) of the 1932 law.

[150] Luxembourg Nationality Law, 8 March 2017 <http://legilux.public.lu/eli/etat/leg/loi/2017/03/08/a289/jo> accessed 4 August 2019.

[151] Loi 1/013 du 18 juillet 2000 portant reforme du code de la nationalité, 1/013, 18 July 2000 (author translation) <http://www.refworld.org/docid/452d01c94.html> accessed 4 August 2019.

[152] Katalin Haraszti, 'Report by the Parliamentary Commissioner for Civil Rights in cases number AJB 2629/2010 and AJB 4196/2010' (September 2010) <https://www.ajbh.hu/documents/14315/131278/The+investigation+of+the+Ombudsman+on+the+repatriation+of+the+abadoned+non-citizen+children+born+in+Hungary/122c30fb-8cf5-4192-9e95-f12a23d46436;version=1.1> accessed 4 August 2019.

[153] ENS, 'Ending Childhood Statelessness: A Study on Italy, Working Paper 07/15' (2015) 23 <http://www.refworld.org/docid/582327974.html> accessed 4 August 2019.

parents are covered by its foundling provision, that is article 2(iii) of the Nationality Act.

### 4.4.1 Need to Consider International Private Law

Further, as reviewed in Sect. 2.10.7, when examining whether legal parentage is established or not and when foreign elements exist, the decision-maker needs to refer to international private law to determine the applicable law that may be the domestic family law (and nationality law) of the factual parent(s). This has been emphasized for example by Japanese nationality law and private international law scholars.[154] In practice also, a child born out of wedlock in 1948 in Japan from a mother of French nationality who did not recognize her maternity over the child, acquired Japanese nationality under article 4, the foundling provision of the then Japanese Nationality Act of 1899 (see also Sects. 4.3.12 and 7.6.2.1). It is obvious that the family court that examined the case applied the French family law requiring recognition of maternity (see Sect. 2.10.5.1) when assessing whether the child's legal parentage was established.[155] The Tōkyō High Court in the 1994 Baby Andrew case[156] also looked into, though hypothetically, Filipino family law provisions when examining whether there was a legal mother–child relationship between the alleged Filipino birth mother and the child born in a hospital in Japan (Sect. 4.3.6). This was however a purely hypothetical consideration because, in the Baby Andrew case, the birth mother was factually known to some extent, but her identity was not definitively (discussed in Sect. 5.6.3) known, until which time legal parentage could not meaningfully be examined.

Thus it can be concluded that a foundling is of 'legally unknown' parents, which means that her or his legally recognized parents do not exist, or such existence cannot be proven under any of the applicable laws. Chapter 5 will take this further to discuss the issue of burden and standard of proof (or the required extent of 'unknown-ness').

---

[154] For example Yasuhiro Okuda, 'Nihon de umareta fubo fumei no ko no kokuseki' ['The nationality of children born in Japan of unknown parents'] (1995) 133 Bessatsu Juristo (Yūhikaku, May 1995) 247. Yasuhiro Okuda, 'Kokusekihō nijō sangō ni tsuite (Jō) ['On article 2(iii) of Nationality Act-Part 1'] (1994) Kosekijihō 11, 15, 17; 432.

[155] Minji kō dai 2888 gō minjikyokuchō kaitō, 1 October 1967 (Shōwa 42 nen) Koseki Vol 247, 58 cited in Shōichi Kidana, Chikujō kokusekihō—kadai no kaimei to jōbun no kaisetsu [Nationality Law—Clarification of Issues and Article-by-Article Commentary] (Nihon kajo shuppan, forthcoming 2021) 324.

[156] Tōkyō High Court 26 January 1994 (Heisei 6 nen), Minshū Vol 49, No.1 (Baby Andrew Case) 193.

## 4.5 Persons Without Legal Parents as a Result of Surrogacy Arrangements: Applicability of Foundling (Unknown Parentage) Provisions?

The law of parentage and general issues and rules relating to the establishment of legal parentage in cases of international surrogacy arrangements were cursorily reviewed in Sect. 2.10.7. In recent years, there have been a growing recognition and literature[157] on how statelessness can arise from surrogacy arrangements. Statelessness issues can most typically arise out of international surrogacy arrangements when the commissioning parents from a country where commercial surrogacy is either prohibited or not regulated by law commission surrogacy in another country. The laws relating to parentage and citizenship in countries where surrogacy is not formally legalized normally do not contain provisions for the commissioning parents to become the legal parents of the child born in a foreign country via surrogacy. As a result, the authorities of the commissioning parents' country of nationality may, for example, end up applying its family law rules applicable to normal reproduction and conclude that the birth mother, that is the surrogate mother, is the legal mother. States may do so even if the normal applicable law rules designate the law of the mother's nationality to establish the legal maternity, because the surrogacy arrangement goes against public policy under its private international law rules.[158] If the surrogate mother's country of nationality also excludes the surrogate mother as the parent, for example, because of the law that legalizes surrogacy and designates the commissioning parents to be the legal parents, the child can end up stateless. Worse, the country of birth of the child might not have any applicable regulations in place, so might not recognize any legal parentage for the child.[159] The exception is where the child is born in a country with unconditional *jus soli* provision to grant nationality to all those born in the territory.[160]

---

[157] For example, Claire Achmad, 'Securing Every Child's Right to a Nationality in a Changing World: The Nationality Implications of International Surrogacy' in Laura van Waas and Melanie Khanna (eds), *Solving Statelessness* (Wolf Legal Publishers 2017)191. Michael Wells-Greco, *The Status of Children Arising from Inter-Country Surrogacy Arrangements* (Eleven International Publishing 2016) chapter 5. Gerard-René de Groot, 'Children, Their Right to a Nationality and Child Statelessness' in Edwards and van Waas (eds), *Nationality and Statelessness under International Law* (Cambridge University Press 2014) 144 and 165–7. One of the most detailed discussion on various reasons leading to statelessness among surrogate children is available in Sanoj Rajan, 'International surrogacy arrangements and Statelessness' in *The World's Stateless Children* (Wolf Legal Publishers 2017) 374 and 377. Brianne Richards, '"Can I take the normal one?" Unrelated commercial surrogacy and child abandonment' (2015) 44 Hofstra Law Review 7. Many other pieces of literature will be cited in this section below.

[158] See, for example, the detailed description of the Japanese courts and authorities' approach to surrogacy cases in the next sub-section on the Baby Manji Case.

[159] As to be seen in the Baby Manji case analysis in the next sub-section.

[160] Such as children born in the US of a surrogate mother who acquire American citizenship at birth as in a number of known surrogacy cases.

Some existing literature articulates that the primary cause of statelessness arising out of international surrogacy is the disagreement or differing understanding between States over who the legal parent(s) is (are).[161]

Some have pointed out that the international law regime to address statelessness is inadequate to offer an effective remedy to stateless children born from surrogacy arrangements.[162] Boillet and Akiyama in particular validly point out that article 1 of the 1961 Convention might not be applicable when, for example, the State where the child is born considers the commissioning parent(s) to be legal parent(s), and assert that the child should have acquired the nationality of the parent(s).[163] From the doctrinal or 'international standards' point of view, however, article 1 should still be applied considering that, if the competent authorities of the country of nationality of the commissioning parents do not recognize their parentage, then the child does not acquire nationality *jus sanguinis*, and it is the competent authorities' view that is decisive[164] in determining statelessness.

Having said this, as seen in the Baby Manji case below, there are situations where nobody is recognized as a legal parent, at least by the country of birth. The existing literature reviewed by the author did not link the surrogacy related 'statelessness' with the concept of a 'foundling' and have not examined the applicability of article 2 of the 1961 Convention or article 6(1)(b) of the ECN.[165] This can be partly because the term 'foundling'—as discussed in Chap. 3—is ambiguous and equivocal, and the fact that it essentially means 'a person of unknown parents'—which this book has clarified—is not recognized.

---

[161] Veronique Boillet and Hajime Akiyama, 'Statelessness and international surrogacy from the international and European legal perspectives' (2017) 27 Swiss Review of International and European Law 513, and 523; Jyothi Kanics, 'Preventing and addressing statelessness: in the context of international surrogacy arrangements' (2014) 19 Tilburg Law Review 117, 125–6; Patrick Balazo, 'Cross-border Gestational Surrogacy in Japan and the Spectre of Statelessness, Statelessness Working Paper Series No 2017/5' (May 2017) <http://www.institutesi.org/WP2017_05.pdf> accessed 4 August 2019; Michael Wells-Greco, *The Status of Children Arising from Inter-Country Surrogacy Arrangements* (Eleven International Publishing 2016), chapter 5.

[162] Tina Lin, 'Born lost: stateless children in international surrogacy arrangements' (2013) 21 Cardozo Journal of International and Comparative Law 545, 560.

[163] Veronique Boillet and Hajime Akiyama, 'Statelessness and international surrogacy from the international and European legal perspectives' (2017) 27 Swiss Review of International and European Law 513.

[164] UNHCR Handbook (2014) para 37.

[165] None of the articles mentioned in fn 157 (and 161) of this chapter for example discusses the applicability of article 2 of the 1961 Convention or a domestic foundling provision. Sanoj Rajan refers to article 1 of the 1961 Convention as a relevant international legal provision which is, however, not attuned to prevent statelessness arising out of surrogacy. Sanoj Rajan, 'International Surrogacy Arrangements and Statelessness' in *The World's Stateless Children* (Wolf Legal Publishers 2017) 381–2. Jyothi Kanics, 'Preventing and addressing statelessness: in the context of international surrogacy arrangements' (2014) 19 Tilburg Law Review 117, suggests the usefulness of considering whether statelessness determination procedures could also provide solutions for stateless children born from international surrogacy arrangements or 'whether there is a need to create other new measures to assist such children to acquire the nationality of their intending parents'.

The author wishes to point out that if there are stateless child without legally recognized parents resulting from a surrogacy arrangement, the 'foundling provision' (of the country of birth) could apply. These children can well be described as 'foundlings' under article 2 of the 1961 Convention, under the definition of this book established in Chap. 3. Of course, this should only be a 'complementary' measure for the international efforts to regulate surrogacy, to harmonize private international law rules and domestic family and nationality legislation in order to prevent lack of legal parentage from occurring in the first place, as discussed below.

It would be first useful to review, rather than continuing these theoretical discussions, an actual case where the lack of legal parentage led to statelessness. Below is an analysis of the Baby Manji case, an internationally well-known case of statelessness arising out of international surrogacy. As most of the previous literature on this case does not closely examine the family law and private international law rules to clarify whether Manji really lacked legal parentage, we will also review this aspect.

**The Baby Manji Case (2008)**

One of the famous cases of statelessness arising out of surrogacy involves Japanese intended parent(s) entering into an international surrogacy contract in India, which went wrong, known as the Baby Manji Case of 2008.[166] The case involves a baby born in Anand, Gujarat, India in July 2008 to Japanese intended parents through an Indian surrogate mother. Manji's intended parents, Ikufumi and Yuki Yamada, entered into a gestational surrogacy contract through an Indian clinic with a married Indian woman named Pritiben Mehta. The couple used Mr Yamada's sperm but used a third party donated ovum of an anonymous Indian woman (that is, not that of Ms Yamada or Ms Mehta's).[167] The Yamadas divorced one month before Manji was born. Mr Yamada, the intended father, still wanted to raise Manji while his former wife did not.

Legal paternity and Japanese nationality

After Manji's birth, when Mr Yamada tried to bring Manji to Japan, the Japanese embassy did not issue a passport, that is Manji was not recognized as a Japanese national. Mr Yamada was not able to recognize his paternity vis-à-vis the Japanese government over Manji prior to and after her birth, and was advised by the government

---

[166] The author read more than 20 articles relating to the Baby Manji case but each case contained slightly different facts (and sometimes legally inaccurate descriptions) as also pointed out in Kari Points, 'Commercial Surrogacy and fertility Tourism in India: The Case of Baby Manji' (2009) <http://www.duke.edu/web/kenanethics/CaseStudies/BabyManji.pdf> at its fn 1. As the article carrying the most comprehensive facts, the author in the end primarily referred to ibid while complementing it with others. The information source for factual part of this section is thus from the Kari Points's (whose page number the author still cited when considered useful) unless otherwise indicated.

[167] On this point, there is contradicting information between the Indian Supreme Court ruling (that is *Baby Manji Yamada v. Union of India & ANR.* [2008] and all other information sources consulted by author—while the Supreme Court states that Yuki Yamada, the (former) wife of Mr Yamada is baby Manji's 'biological mother', all other information sources state that the ovum is not of Yuki Yamada but of another woman (a third party person other than the surrogate birth mother).

to adopt her. There is no available source that clarifies the rationale for this advice. The following is a preliminary analysis of the accessible and existing Japanese law and jurisprudence.

As far as Japanese family law is concerned, Japanese private international law, that is the Act on General Rules for Application of Laws, provides, in article 29(1):

> In the case of a child born out of wedlock, the formation of a parent-child relationship with regard to the father and the child shall be governed by the father's national law at the time of the child's birth, and with regard to the mother and the child by the mother's national law at said time. [...][168]

Thus, for Japan, it was Japanese law that governed the establishment of the father–child relationship between Mr Yamada and Manji, and the Indian law, between the Indian surrogate mother and Manji. Under Japanese family law, that is article 779 of the Civil Code, a father may affiliate his child out of wedlock to establish his legal paternity.

The reason for Yamada's inability to recognize the child likely had to do with the status of the woman that the government of Japan apparently recognized as a 'mother'. Indeed, the government of Japan, when consulted about Manji's passport, reportedly said that it would use the 'birth mother's nationality' as the basis to determine the nationality of the child.[169] The basis and conclusion of this statement is not available, and only speculations based on precedents on some previous surrogacy cases are possible.

If article 29(1) of the Act on General Rules for Application of Lawswas applied, the government of Japan would have reached the conclusion that the Indian surrogate mother cannot be Manji's legal mother under Indian law (as will be seen below). However, it is apparent that the government of Japan exceptionally applied Japanese family law against its applicable law rules in order to recognize the Indian surrogate birth mother as the legal mother. Japanese family law, based on the Supreme Court case law,[170] recognizes as the mother the woman who delivers a baby.

This method had been taken by previous court decisions dealing with cases involving children born of a foreign surrogate mother in a foreign country. For example, there was a case where a Japanese husband and wife entered into a surrogacy

---

[168] Japanese private international law. Act on General Rules for Application of Laws, Act No 78 of 21 June 2006. Article 29(2) further states: 'Acknowledgement of parentage of a child shall be governed by the law designated in the first sentence of the preceding paragraph, or by the national law of the acknowledging person or of the child at the time of the acknowledgement.[...]' In this case, the child's 'national law' cannot be determined to be either Japanese law or Indian law as the legal parentage could not be established, as pointed out by Kidana as the general rules. Shōichi Kidana, *Chikujō kaisetsu kokusai kazokuhō* [*Article-by-Article Commentary on International Family Law*] (Nihon kajo shuppan, 2017) 312.

[169] Sarah Mortazavi, 'it takes a village to make a child: creating guidelines for international surrogacy' (2012) 100 The Georgetown Law Journal 2249, 2274–5.

[170] *Judgement, Minshū* Vol 16, No 7, p 1247 [27 April 1962 (*Shōwa 37 nen*)]) (Supreme Court). This is despite article 779 of Civil Code, which indeed indicates that for a child born out of wedlock, the woman has to recognize the child to establish legal maternity. See Sect. 2.10.5.1 and fn 140, chapter 2.

contract with an American woman living in California (married to an American man) using the husband's sperm and the ovum of yet another American woman (married to an American man). The Ōsaka High Court in its decision on 20 May 2005 initially assessed, following the applicable law rules designated by previous Japanese private international legislation in effect at the time, the 'illegitimate' parent–child relationship between the commissioning wife under the Japanese law, and the ovum donor as well as the surrogate mother, under California State law (which provided that the commissioning parents were the child's legal parents). The High Court then preliminarily denied the existence of legal maternity over the child with respect to all three women.[171] Nevertheless, the court in the end decided to apply Japanese law to recognize the legal mother–child relationship out of wedlock between an American surrogate mother and the child, considering that the surrogacy contract went 'against the public order'.[172]

In a subsequent case, the Japanese Supreme court on 23 March 2007 also had affirmed the principle that the surrogate birth mother is the legal mother in the case involving an actress, Aki Mukai, where Mukai and her husband entered into a surrogacy contract with an American woman residing in Nevada. This time, the Supreme Court denied the validity of the foreign court judgement, that is the ruling of the Nevada Second Judicial District Court, declaring Mukai and her husband to be the legal parents of the child, asserting that such content of the judgement was contrary to public policy in Japan as stipulated under article 118(iii) of the Code of Civil Procedure.[173] The Supreme Court then stated that 'under the interpretation of the current Civil Code, the Court has no choice but considering the woman a mother who became impregnated with and delivered the child [...]'.[174]

It now becomes apparent that Mr Yamada was considered not eligible to recognize his paternity over Manji because the Indian surrogate 'mother' was married, and the paternity presumption of another man, that is the birth mother's husband, was in effect, which prevented the paternity recognition under Japanese law.[175]

---

[171] Article 18(1) of the then amended Act on the Application of Laws (Hōrei) Law No 10 of 1898, equivalent to article 29(1) of the current Act on General Rules for Application of Laws). See the analysis of Yasuhiro Okuda, *Kokusaikazokuhō* [*International Family Law*] (Akashi Shoten 2015) 255.

[172] Osaka High Court decision, 20 May 2005 <http://sokonisonnzaisuru.blog23.fc2.com/?mode=m&no=166> accessed 4 August 2019.

[173] It is unknown why Osaka High Court decision on 20 May 2005 did not discuss this point. Article 118 'A final and binding judgment rendered by a foreign court is valid only if it meets all of the following requirements: [...] (iii) the content of the judgment and the litigation proceedings are not contrary to public policy in Japan': Code of Civil Procedure, Act No 109 of 26 June 1996.

[174] *Minshū* Vol 61, No 2, p 619 [23 March 2007 (*Heisei 19 nen*)] (Supreme Court (Petty Bench II)) (Japanese) (at p 10). Kidana, for example, is critical of this case law, as, among others, it results in a situation where the woman (surrogate mother)—who neither has genetic connection or the will to care for the child—is recognized as the child's mother, which goes against the child's best interests. See Shōichi Kidana, *Chikujō kaisetsu kokusai kazokuhō* [*Article-by-Article Commentary on International Family Law*] (Nihon kajo shuppan, 2017) 310–16.

[175] Article 772(1) Civil Code, 'A child conceived by a wife during marriage shall be presumed to be a child of her husband'. Civil Code, Act No 89 of 27 April 1896 (Japan). Administrative

India's view on Manji's legal father

Commercial surrogacy is legal[176] in India but there was (and still there is) no binding laws and regulations on this matter as of 2008.[177] From India's point of view, Mr Yamada was, at least in the beginning, not recognized as Manji's legal father, but Yamada 'had to resort to adopting Manji in India to gain her custody', as 'The Indian legal system does not recognize or regulate surrogacy, and contracting parents will usually adopt children born to surrogates'.[178] However, Mr Yamada could not adopt Manji under the India's Guardians and Wards Act of 1890, which did not allow a single man to adopt a female child.

Meanwhile, a non-binding 2005 National Guidelines for Accreditation, Supervision & Regulation of ART Clinics in India, issued by the Indian Council of Medical Research under the auspices of the Indian Ministry of Health, stated that the surrogate child's 'birth certificate shall be in the name of the genetic parents'[179] and '[a] child born through ART shall be *presumed to be the legitimate child of the couple,*

---

precedents also confirm that when the mother is married, recognition of paternity by another man cannot be done. Even if a father were to submit a prenatal paternity recognition notification in such a case, it will not be accepted. Ministry of Justice's response on 24 March 1899 (*Meiji 32 nen*) cited in Yasuhiro Okuda, *Kosekihō to kokusai oyakohō* [*Nationality Act and International Family Law*] (Yūhikaku 2004) 206–8. Theoretically, it was possible to recognize paternity over a child delivered by a woman married to another man, after the non-existence of parent–child relationship is confirmed as a result of mediation or litigation with a family court post-birth. At any rate, post-birth recognition of paternity, even if it were possible by Mr Yamada, would not have led to Manji's acquisition of Japanese nationality under the Japanese Nationality Act at the time, unless he married the birth mother. The law was amended on 12 December 2008 allowing Japanese nationality to be granted to children born out of wedlock of foreign mothers recognized post-birth by Japanese fathers.

[176] *Baby Manji Yamada v. Union of India & ANR.* [2008].

[177] The latest in the government's effort to legislate on this issue is the Surrogacy (Regulation) Bill 2016, which totally prohibits commercial surrogacy in India. However, as of today, 'surrogacy arrangements in India are regulated by ART Guidelines and the decision of the Supreme Court in Baby Manji's case', because the Bill mentioned above has not yet been passed by the Parliament. Sanoj Rajan, 'Ending Statelessness arising out of Surrogacy in India: The Latest Developments' (2017) <https://www.statelessness.eu/blog/ending-statelessness-arising-out-surrog acy-india-latest-developments> . See also the Indian government's response to HCCH, 'Questionnaire on the Private International Law Issues Surrounding the Status of Children, including issues Arising from International Surrogacy Arrangements' (April 2013) <https://assets.hcch.net/upload/ wop/gap2014pd3in.pdf> accessed 4 August 2019.

[178] Kari Points, 'Commercial Surrogacy and Fertility Tourism in India: The Case of Baby Manji' (2009) 5 <http://www.duke.edu/web/kenanethics/CaseStudies/BabyManji.pdf> . Vera Mackie, 'Birth Registration and the Right to Have Rights: the Changing Family and Unchanging Koseki' in David Chapman and Karl Jakob Krogness (eds), *Japan's Household Registration System and Citizenship: Koseki, Identification and Documentation* (Routledge Studies in the Modern History of Asia 2014) 203, 215.

[179] See Indian Council of Medical Research and National Council of Medical Sciences, 'Code of Practice, Ethical Considerations and Legal Issues' in Radhey S. Sharma and others (eds), *National Guidelines for Accreditation, Supervision & Regulation of Art Clinics in India* (Indian Council of

born within wedlock, with consent of both the spouses, and with all the attendant rights of parentage […]'.[180]

Probably because Yamada's divorce contributed to the complication, the Municipal Council of Anand in the beginning refused to issue Manji a birth certificate and referred the case to national level for advice. Yamada hired an Indian attorney, who filed an appeal with the Indian government to issue documents for Manji. The Municipality on 8 August issued a 'provisional'[181] birth certificate for Manji indicating the name of Mr Yamada, the genetic father, leaving the line for 'mother's name' blank.[182]

While the Supreme Court of India later acknowledged that Manji's birth certificate indicated Mr Yamada as Manji's 'genetic father',[183] the court somehow avoided to explicitly recognize Mr Yamada as her 'legal father'.

Lack of legal mother and non-acquisition of Indian nationality

Meanwhile, Mr Yamada tried to apply for an Indian passport for Manji. India does not grant nationality by *jus soli*. A child of an Indian mother acquires Indian nationality by *jus sanguinis*. However, the municipality was uncertain which mother should appear on the birth certificate. The anonymous egg donor had no rights and responsibilities to Manji, and the surrogate birth mother's responsibilities were terminated when Manji was born in accordance with her prior agreement under the Indian law. Japanese law, based on the Supreme Court case law, recognizes as the mother only the woman who delivers a baby.

This shows that while Manji had initially three arguable and potential mothers— the intended mother who had contracted for the surrogacy, the egg donor and the gestational surrogate—it turned out that none of them was recognized as Manji's legal mother under Indian law.

Not having any legally recognized Indian parent, the government of India refused to issue Manji an Indian passport.

---

Medical Research 2005) 3.5.4. These parts are also cited in Usha Rengachary Smerdon, 'Birth registration and citizenship rights of surrogate babies born in India' (2012) 20 Contemporary South Asia 341. Also cited in Tina Lin, 'Born Lost: Stateless Children in International Surrogacy Arrangements' (2013) 21 Cardozo Journal of International and Comparative Law 545, 560.

[180] Ibid Chap. 3, Sect. 3.12. Furthermore, '[i]n the case of a *divorce* during the gestation period, if the offspring is of a donor programme—be it sperm or ova—the law of the land as pertaining to a normal conception would apply'. Ibid Chap. 3, Sect. .3.12.4. The term 'land' in the last sentence is assumed to be India. However, in the end, as discussed later in this section, the Indian surrogate birth mother was not recognized as Manji's mother, and at least at first Yamada was not legally recognized as Manji's father by the Indian government.

[181] Trisha A. Wolf, 'Why Japan should legalize surrogacy' (2014) 23 Pacific Rim Law & Policy Journal 461.

[182] Seema Mohapatra, 'Stateless babies & adoption scams: a bioethical analysis of international commercial surrogacy' (2012) 30 Berkeley Journal of International Law 412.

[183] *Baby Manji Yamada v. Union of India & ANR* [2008].

Statelessness and admission to Japan

As Mr Yamada had to return to Japan with his visa expiring, his mother travelled to India and petitioned the Supreme Court of India for temporary custody to take Manji out of India. Two months after Manji was born, the Supreme Court granted the grandmother temporary custody.[184]

The Indian Supreme Court nonetheless requested India's Solicitor General to clarify India's stance on Manji's 'parentage and citizenship'.[185] The Solicitor General on 15 September 2008 stated that the decision about Manji's passport was up to the Union Government.[186] In mid-October, Rajasthan regional passport office granted Manji an 'identity certificate' issued to persons who are stateless or unable to get a passport from their country of nationality. The certificate did not mention Manji's nationality, mother's name or religion, and it was valid only for Japan. On 27 October 2008, the Japanese embassy issued Manji a one-year visa on humanitarian grounds, with which Manji Yamada entered Japan on 2 November 2008. Mr Yamada reportedly adopted Manji after arrival in Japan,[187] as advised by the government of Japan.[188] While no publicly available report to confirm Manji' subsequent acquisition of Japanese nationality was located, the Japanese Nationality Act article 8(ii) allows facilitated naturalization for a child adopted by a Japanese person who has continuously lived in Japan for one year or more. Further, utilizing the transitional measure of the amendment to article 3 of the Japanese Nationality Act on 12 December 2008 (allowing Japanese nationality to be granted to children born out of wedlock of foreign mothers recognized post-birth by Japanese fathers), Manji could also have acquired nationality upon Mr Yamada acknowledging his paternity post-birth.

Statelessness due to lack of legal parentage

Thus, from Japan's perspective, Manji had a legal mother (Indian surrogate mother) but no legal father. From the perspective of India, Manji's country of birth, Manji had, at least in the beginning, no legal mother and a father. While the Supreme Court of India later acknowledged that Manji's birth certificate indicated Mr Yamada as Manji's 'genetic father', the court somehow avoided to explicitly recognize him as her 'legal father'. Despite the fact that India later issued an identity certificate carrying

---

[184] Ibid.

[185] Kari Points, 'Commercial Surrogacy and fertility Tourism in India: The Case of Baby Manji' (2009) 6 <http://www.duke.edu/web/kenanethics/CaseStudies/BabyManji.pdf> .

[186] Ibid 5.

[187] The following article states that Manji was adopted by Mr. Yamada in a few days after having arrived in Japan, citing p 6 of ibid. However, the latter article on the contrary states 'However, nearly a year after her birth, no evidence had surfaced that Baby Manji's still-precarious legal status in Japan had changed.' Maki Fujita, 'Iryō tsūrizumu ni okeru hōteki shakaiteki mondai [legal and social issues surrounding medical tourism]' (2019) 20 Shiga daigau keizai gakubu kenkyūnenpō [Shiga University Department of Economics Annual Report] 63.

[188] Hindustan Times, 'Surrogate Baby Born in India Arrives in Japan' (3 November 2008) <http://www.hindustantimes.com/world/surrogate-baby-born-in-india-arrives-in-japan/story-clfjpEmKM 0wORsHNmwG7CP.htm> accessed 1 March 2018, inaccessible as of 4 August 2019, on file with author.

Yamada's name as Manji's father, it is unclear whether India formally recognized Yamada as Manji's legal father. At any rate, Manji was, at least initially, a person of unknown parentage born in India who was stateless.

**Foundling (unknown parentage) provision as a 'fall-back' measure?**

It appears it was the best solution at the time that Manji got admitted to Japan and (probably) acquired Japanese nationality via adoption. As a number of authors critiqued, however, Manji's citizenship issues could have been avoided if surrogacy was regulated in Japan. If formally legalized, legislative changes would be made to the Civil Code of Japan for establishing parentage and, therefore, citizenship for babies born under surrogacy agreements.[189]

With regard to India, a non-State party to the 1961 Convention, there is no specific provision under its nationality law granting Indian nationality to persons of unknown parents born or found in India.[190] However, even then, it appears that practice exists to register an orphans without a birth certificate as a national and issue an Indian passport.[191] Such practical response could have arguably been extended to Manji, as a back-up measure, based on Manji's unknown parentage, if, hypothetically, Yamada refused taking Manji back, or Manji's travel to Japan and subsequent adoption was somehow not possible, in order to avoid statelessness.

Once again, before even discussing the applicability of article 2 of the 1961 Convention or the equivalent nationality law provision, there is no doubt that surrogacy should be appropriately regulated by each country so as to prevent any case without legal parentage and thus statelessness arising out of it. In cases where the

---

[189] For example, Kari Points, 'Commercial Surrogacy and fertility Tourism in India: The Case of Baby Manji' (2009) 7 <http://www.duke.edu/web/kenanethics/CaseStudies/BabyManji.pdf> . It is argued that if surrogacy is legalised by Japan, couples would first of all would not have to travel abroad and babies would be born in Japan to a Japanese intended mother, surrogate, and egg donor. Richard F Storrow, 'The phantom children of the republic: international surrogacy and the new illegitimacy' (2012) 20 American University Journal of Gender Social Policy and Law 561.

[190] Indian Citizenship Act 1955. Sitharamam Kakarala, Deepika Prakash and Maanvi Tiku, *India and the Challenge of Statelessness: A Review of the Legal Framework relating to Nationality*, vol 2019 (National Law University, Delhi 2015) 32–3. While it does not contain a discussion on persons of unknown parentage, p 9 of the article by Asha Bangar also states it is unlikely that Citizenship Act would grant nationality via jus soli to children born in the territory of India who are vulnerable to statelessness. Asha Bangar, 'Statelessness in India, Statelessness Working Paper Series No 2017/02' (June 2017) <http://www.institutesi.org/WP2017_02.pdf> accessed 4 August 2019.

[191] Vishal Joshi and Hindustan Times, 'Orphans can get passport without birth certificate' (29 May 2015) <https://www.hindustantimes.com/chandigarh/orphans-can-get-passport-without-birth-certificate/story-crq9mnNqb6AyhuXybvxjEK.html> accessed 4 August 2019. The article explains about an order of the Ministry of External Affairs which says a birth certificate is not mandatory to process passport applications of 'orphans or abandoned children'. According to the MEA circular cited in the article, documents issued by the educational institution, by the head of the orphanage/childcare home (in case of minor) or by applicant himself (in case of major) before the first class judicial magistrate categorically stating his/her date of birth/place of birth can be admitted in lieu of a birth certificate. It can be assumed that at least some of the 'orphans or abandoned children' without birth certificates described here are without recorded legal parentage.

commissioning parent(s) maintain their will to care for the child born out of surrogacy, and where there is no other party (such as the birth mother or donor of sperm or ovum) fighting to establish maternity or paternity over the child, it would normally be better for the children to acquire the same nationality(ies) as their parent(s), which would make it easier for the family to live in the same country and maintain their unity.[192] Thus, in order to prevent the unknown parentage and the consequent statelessness arising out of (failed) surrogacy, the countries of nationality of the intending parent needs to make efforts to enable the child's acquisition of nationality by speedily allowing for establishment of parentage, at least through adoption if not automatic acquisition.

Apart from the relevant efforts in different countries, the Permanent Bureau of the HCCH has been studying the private international law issues arising from the legal parentage or 'filiation' of children, as well as more specific issues in connection with international surrogacy arrangements through its Parentage/Surrogacy Project, initiated in 2015.[193] The project is still ongoing and is expected to take more time to publish materials providing concrete proposals to prevent or resolve surrogacy-induced statelessness.[194]

Meanwhile, if the country of birth sees that the child lacks legal parents, and if there is no prospect for nationality acquisition in the reasonable timeframe, then the 'foundling' provision to provide nationality to persons of unknown parents born or found in the territory can be applicable as the 'back-up' measure. The author, however, is not aware of any cases so far where the government of the country of birth of the child born of a surrogate mother provided nationality on the basis of her or his lack of legal parentage.

---

[192] In the context of arguing that applying 1 of the 1961 Convention is not the best solution, Boillet and Akiyama validly point out that it can be against the best interests of the child if he child's nationality and intended parents' nationality are different. 'Also, if the child will not live in the State in which he or she was born, the child will be a "foreigner" in the country of domicile'. Véronique Boillet and Hajime Akiyama, 'Statelessness and international surrogacy from the international and European legal perspectives' (2017) 27(4) Swiss Review of International and European Law 513, 530.

[193] See HCCH, 'Questionnaire on the Private International Law Issues Surrounding the Status of Children, including issues Arising from International Surrogacy Arrangements' (April 2013) <https://assets.hcch.net/upload/wop/gap2014pd3in.pdf> accessed 4 August 2019.

[194] Sanoj Rajan, 'International Surrogacy Arrangements and Statelessness' in *The World's Stateless Children* (Wolf Legal Publishers 2017). Interview with Gerard-René de Groot, Professor Emeritus at Maastricht University School of Law (5 October 2017).

## 4.6  Alternative Avenues of Nationality Grant via Adoption, Institutional Care, Facilitated Naturalization or Late Birth Registration

In the course of the above research including during the filed interviews in Italy and Hungary, it became clear that some States address the otherwise statelessness of persons of unknown parents not necessarily by 'inclusively interpreting' the definition of 'unknown parents' or 'foundlings' but through alternative avenues, such as nationality grant through adoption or institutional care.

### Italy

In Italy, as soon as a report of an anonymous birth or a child abandonment is filed with a juvenile court, a swift identification of suitable adoptive parents will start.[195] Article 3(1) of law 91/1992 on nationality provides that a 'foreign minor adopted by an Italian citizen shall acquire citizenship'. The minor concerned acquires Italian nationality from the moment of registration of the adoption act in the Population Registry.[196] Adoption by Italian nationals is readily available. 1,397 minors were declared adoptable by 29 juvenile courts in Italy 2014, of which 278 had been 'abandoned' at birth.[197] There were 657 families who had expressed their willingness to adopt a child as of 2014[198] and thus there are only limited cases where an abandoned child faces difficulties finding a family to adopt her or him.[199] Article 3(3) of law 91/1992 stipulates that 'If the adoption of an adopted person is revoked, she or he shall lose Italian citizenship,' however, this is on the condition that the person 'possesses or has reacquired another citizenship.'[200] Therefore, the law provides for an additional measure to prevent statelessness of persons of unknown parents. However, as mentioned by the Children's Ombudsman's Office, some children unrecognized at birth or abandoned in baby hatches or other places can be sick or handicapped, which

---

[195] Interview with Ms Gandolfo, Director, Citizenship Office of the Municipality of Florence (Florence, Italy, 22 May 2017). Confirmed through Interview with Enrico Guida, Statelessness Expert, UNHCR Rome (23 May 2017). 'Parto in anonimato' (11 April 2017) <http://www.salute.gov.it/portale/donna/dettaglioContenutiDonna.jsp?lingua=italiano&id=1011&area=Salute%20donna&menu=nascita> accessed 4 August 2019.

[196] Article 34 para 3 of the Law No 184 of 4 May 1983 related to the right of the child to have a family (Italy), as amended by Law n. 476 of 31 December 1998, as cited in footnote 115 of ENS, 'Ending Childhood Statelessness: A Study on Italy, Working Paper 07/15' (2015) 24 <http://www.refworld.org/docid/582327974.html> accessed 4 August 2019.

[197] Latest available data according to #Truenumbers, an Italian data journalism website. '#Truenumbers' (5 September 2017) <http://www.truenumbers.it/adozioni-in-italia/> accessed 4 August 2019.

[198] Ibid.

[199] Interview with Ester Di Napoli, PhD and Fellow, Autorità garante per l'infanzia e l'adolescenza (guardianship authority for infants and adolescents) (23 May 2017).

[200] See also article 51 para 1 of the Law 184 of 4 May 1983 as cited in ENS, 'Ending Childhood Statelessness: A Study on Italy, Working Paper 07/15' (2015) 24 fn 116 <http://www.refworld.org/docid/582327974.html> accessed 4 August 2019.

makes it difficult to secure adoption.[201] In such cases, the person would have to resort to acquiring nationality under article 4(2) upon turning 18 years old (if birth in Italy is established), resort to the statelessness determination procedure and/or apply for (facilitated) naturalization under article 9 of the 91/1992 law.

### Hungary

In Hungary, according to the relevant law,[202] six weeks after the birth (or presumably after the 'finding') of the child, the guardianship is confirmed to be with the guardianship authorities and adoption starts to be arranged. For example, when the mother places the child into a baby hatch, it is provisionally construed that she legally agrees to the adoption of the child. The parent(s) can claim the child back within this period. On 43th day after the authorities found the abandoned child, the adoption normally happens.

Thus, the counterparts in Hungary emphasized that even if the child does not acquire nationality under section 3(3)b of the Citizenship Act, the child can acquire Hungarian nationality through naturalization with facilitated conditions on the basis of adoption by a Hungarian national after three years.[203] Reportedly, adoption is readily available; within Budapest alone, 400 families are registered for adopting children and it is rarely difficult to arrange an adoption.

### Russia

While the worldwide trend is to move from institutional to family-based care such as adoption and foster family arrangements for children who cannot be cared for by their parents, in some States institutional care is more common due to social, cultural

---

[201] Interview with Ester Di Napoli, PhD and Fellow, Autorità garante per l'infanzia e l'adolescenza (guardianship authority for infants and adolescents) (23 May 2017).

[202] Civil Code article 120, chapter 4 as cited in the interview with Benko Zsuzsanna, Attorney at law and a legal guardian, Child Protection Services of Budapest former (until 2009) Deputy Head of Division, Social and Guardianship Division, Guardianship Department at the Municipal Government Office, Fifth District Guardianship Office (Budapest, Hungary, 25 May 2017). According to Benko Zsuzsanna, the following Act on child protection is relevant: 15/1998 Decree of the Ministry of Welfare, which regulates the activities of the authorities re adoption. It sets the deadline for adoption arrangement as six weeks.

[203] Hungary: Act LV of 1993 on Hungarian Citizenship (1 October 1993) <http://www.refworld.org/docid/3ae6b4e630.html> accessed 2 August 2019, section 4 (Naturalization): '(1) A non-Hungarian citizen may be naturalised upon his or her application if [...](2) *A non-Hungarian citizen who resided in Hungary continuously over at least a period of three years prior to the submission of the application and in whose case the conditions defined in Subsection (1) paras b) to e) are satisfied may be naturalised on preferential terms* provided that (..)c) the person was adopted by a Hungarian citizen [...][...] (6) Children of minor age *adopted by a Hungarian citizen can be naturalized irrespective of their domicile*' (emphasis added). Gábor Gyulai argues that nationality acquisition upon adoption, however, should be automatic as, under Hungarian family law, adoption accords the legal status of the biological child to the adopted child vis-à-vis the adoptive parent(s) and their relatives. Section 4:132(1) of Act V of 2013 on the Civil Code, as cited by Gábor Gyulai, 'Nationality Unknown? An overview of the safeguards and gaps related to the prevention of statelessness at birth in Hungary' (2014) 19 <http://helsinki.hu/wp-content/uploads/Nationality-Unknown-HHC-2014.pdf> accessed 4 August 2019.

and other factors.[204] In some cases, due to the illness and disabilities that abandoned children often suffer, they cannot be matched with foster or adoptive families. As a result, persons of unknown parentage sometimes remain stateless while under institutional care for extended years.[205]

Some States like Russia appears capable of addressing such situations with the provision to grant nationality to children who are hosted at a child custody institution.[206] Article 27 (Citizenship of children and incapable persons under guardianship or trusteeship), paragraph 2 of the Federal Law on the Citizenship of the Russian Federation states:

> A child placed under supervision in a Russian organization for orphans and children whose parents lost guardianship shall acquire the citizenship of the Russian Federation under the simplified procedure in accordance with Item 'd' of Part 6 of Article 14 of this Federal Law [...].[207]

### Latvia

Not only children found in the territory of unknown parents but also other children left without parental care, and who are under extra-familial care, are Latvian citizens. Section 2(1) 5) and 6) provides as follows:

> A Latvian citizen is: [...] 5) (a child who has been found in the territory of Latvia and whose parents are unknown, or) other child *left without parental care who is under extra-familial care in Latvia*, except a child for whose parents the custody rights have been suspended; 6) an *orphan who is under extra-familial care in Latvia.* (emphasis added)[208]

Provisions of this sort, which provide nationality for children hosted in facilities for children without parents, can be found in several former USSR States.

Further, as already discussed in Sect. 2.9, some States relax (late) birth registration requirements—in terms of the procedure and evidence—to register persons who

---

[204] See generally, the University of Nottingham, *Child Abandonment and its Prevention in Europe* (The University of Nottingham 2012). UNICEF also publishes various materials such as: UNICEF, 'Children in Alternative Care' (July 2017) <https://data.unicef.org/topic/child-protection/children-alternative-care/> accessed 4 August 2019.

[205] See, for example, Ayane Odagawa and Sōsuke Seki (eds), Study Group on Stateless in Japan, 'Typology of Stateless Persons in Japan' (2017) 95–102 <https://www.unhcr.org/jp/wp-content/uploads/sites/34/2018/01/TYPOLOGY-OF-STATELESS-PERSONS-IN-JAPAN_webEnglish.pdf> accessed 4 August 2019.

[206] Also suggested by Email from UNHCR Russia to author (30 June 2017).

[207] Russian Federal Law on the Citizenship of the Russian Federation (as Amended in 2017) (29 July 2017) <https://www.refworld.org/docid/50768e422.html> accessed 4 August 2019. It is also noted that article 27 para 1 provides for nationality acquisition of children under guardianship or trusteeship of a citizen of the Russian Federation under the simplified procedure. Further, under article 26 para 2 of the same law, a child adopted by a citizen of the Russian Federation acquires Russian citizenship from the day of his or her adoption.

[208] Latvian Law on Citizenship 1994 (as amended up to 2013). <https://likumi.lv/ta/en/en/id/57512-citizenship-law> accessed 4 August 2019. See also 'Ending Childhood Statelessness: A Study on Latvia' (2015) 14–15 <http://www.statelessness.eu/sites/www.statelessness.eu/files/Latvia_0.pdf> accessed 4 August 2019.

would normally encounter difficulties in producing documents substantiating their descent from a national(s) (and birth in-country), where parents are dead or missing.

The availability of these 'alternative' ways of granting nationality automatically or at least speedily to children of unknown parents in general minimizes the need to interpret the foundling provision in a 'generous' manner. These alternative measures, as well the availability of anonymous birth and baby hatch avenues, where nationality is granted under the foundling provision, might be one of the major reasons why the statelessness of persons of unknown parents does not necessarily surface as a major issue in some countries.

## 4.7 Summary and Conclusions: 'unknown parents' Mean They Do Not Legally Exist or Their Existence is Not Proven

Chapter 3 defined a foundling to be a person of unknown parents. It was clarified that the birthplace of a foundling may or may not be known. The aim of this chapter was then to clarify what 'unknown parents' means.

Section 4.3 found that in many States around the world, the most 'conventional' cases who are confirmed nationality based on the foundling provision are new-borns found literally abandoned on the street or other places, or those left in baby hatches where available. In some States, the most typical cases granted nationality based on the foundling provision are children surrendered through a form of 'anonymous birth' where the biological mother gives birth at a medical facility but her identity does not get registered with the authorities to establish her as the legal mother of the child. It was also found that in some States, like Spain, Japan, and the US, the application of the foundling provision has covered many other categories of persons who are not physically 'abandoned', but whose parents' identity cannot be proven. These include not only orphans, but also those who are lost or separated from their parents who, having been informally adopted or have lived under the care of unrelated persons, are found or voluntarily approach the authorities to be found including those who have reached adulthood (see Chap. 6 on the issue of age). In States like Hungary and Japan, children who are left behind at a hospital by the mother after delivery, who goes missing and whose identity cannot be proven, are confirmed nationality under the foundling provision.

Based on Sects. 4.3, Sect. 4.4 considered whether a person whose (biological) parent is factually known but not legally recognized as such can fall within the foundling provision (see also Sect. 2.10.1). It was recalled that historically, even at the time when the 1930 Convention was being drafted, some States provided in their legislation for nationality grant to persons born in the territory of factually known but legally unknown parents. The review of the current State practice also found that in a number of countries, the fact that there is (are) factually known parent(s) does not matter in the end, and that 'a person of unknown parents' essentially means that she or he does not have legally recognized parents, or the existence of a person's legal parent is not proven. Considering the object and purpose of article 2 of the 1961 Convention and equivalent nationality law provisions, that is to prevent statelessness, what should ultimately matter in the context of recognizing somebody to be of 'unknown parentage' is whether she or he would otherwise remain stateless due to the lack of legally recognized parentage, based on which a nationality is granted by *jus sanguinis*.

It was, however, noted that those 'atypical' cases are not always treated as foundlings in some other States. In such States narrow interpretation of the unknownness of parents and excessive requirement of proof tends to hinder the resolution of the statelessness of persons of unknown parentage. However, it was also found that some States grant nationality to children of unknown parentage who they do not recognize to fall within their foundling provisions but who are otherwise stateless through other measures. Such alternative avenues can include nationality grant on the basis of adoption by nationals or of being hosted at child custody institutions within the territory, through late birth registration, or through recognition as stateless persons and facilitating their naturalization under the 1954 Convention or equivalent domestic provisions. *The* availability of these 'alternative' ways of granting nationality automatically or at least speedily to children of unknown parents in general minimizes the need to interpret the foundling provision in a 'generous' manner. These alternative measures as well the availability of anonymous birth and baby hatches might be one of the major reasons why the statelessness of persons of unknown parents does not necessarily surface as a major issue in some countries.

While it is rather theoretical, it was also asserted in this chapter that persons born out of a surrogacy arrangement who do not have legal parents due to the conflict of laws should also be recognized to be of unknown parentage. As a 'back-up measure' in case the children concerned cannot acquire nationality in any other way, they could possibly be granted nationality of the country of birth based on the foundling provision.

It was noted that it was all the more important—before examining a person's nationality or statelessness—to first ascertain whether one's parentage is established based on the relevant family law, duly considering the rules of private international law, as also discussed in Sect. 2.10.

# Chapter 5
# Burden and Standard of Proof in Determining Unknown-ness of Parentage

**Abstract** In this chapter addresses the issues of burden and standard of proof to establish 'unknown parentage' under article 2 of the 1961 Convention and equivalent domestic foundling provisions. Case law from several States including that of Japan offering the most detailed and inclusive guidance on this will be reviewed. In order to make the UNHCR's guidance on burden and standard of proof in statelessness (and refugee) determination more usable in different jurisdictions, some of the conceptual differences in evidential standards, in particular between common law and continental law systems, will be reviewed. Among others, in terms of the standard of proof or the 'degree' of unknown-ness of parentage, the author concludes that decision-makers should recognize the 'unknown-ness' when they cannot be convinced within a pre-set deadline, that one of the child's legally recognized parents is *definitively* identified to the extent that it enables the confirmation of the child's nationality acquisition by *jus sanguinis*.

Chapter 3 defined that one of the (two) essential requirements to qualify as a 'foundling' is to be of 'unknown parents'. Chapter 4 examined what 'unknown parents' exactly meant, by reviewing various scenarios that have been considered to fall within the definition, and concluded that 'unknown' should be interpreted to mean legally unknown (which encompasses being factually unknown), that is legally recognized parents do not exist or their existence has not been proven.

Apart from the issue of definition and its interpretation, however, who bears the 'burden of proof' and where the 'standard of proof' is set—when a dispute occurs—greatly affects the outcome of a case in any field of law. Many cases are won or lost depending upon which party is better able to convince the court or decision-maker of the existence of facts favourable to them.

As a general rule, in most legal systems, a claimant bears the initial responsibility of substantiating her or his claim. However, as will be discussed, especially in Sect. 5.2, proving a negative fact—especially for a child to prove one's own unknown parentage—can be extremely difficult. Thus, this chapter will be dedicated to addressing who should bear the burden of proving unknown parentage under article 2 of the 1961 Convention and equivalent nationality legislation, and to what degree it needs to be proven, when a dispute occurs at the initial determination of a person's nationality. These are complicated and disputed issues in some States.

Apart from being of 'unknown parentage', there is yet another 'prerequisite fact' that needs to be fulfilled in order for article 2 of the 1961 Convention to apply to the person concerned, which is to have been 'found in the territory' as a child. The burden and standard of proof in establishing this element will be briefly discussed in Sect. 6.9, which will discuss the definition of being found and the issue of a foundling's age when found. This is because proving having been 'found (when a child)' being an affirmative fact is distinctive in nature from proving 'unknown parentage'. Further, the burden and standard of proof in establishing 'the contrary' in article 2 will be cursorily discussed in Sect. 7.7, where the definition of proof to the 'contrary' and its consequences will be discussed.

Along with some other judicial decisions, a special focus will be placed on Japanese case law, specifically the Baby Andrew Case of 1995 (along with some subsequent family court adjudications), which provide one of the most detailed and inclusive guidance on the burden of proof and the extent of parents' 'unknown-ness'. It is noted that the UNHCR's standards on evidentiary rules related to statelessness laid out in its Handbook (2014) and the Guidelines 4 appear to be predominantly derive from those of common law systems. Such standards, if literally taken, might not easily fit into the legal contexts of some States—for example those of Japan, whose civil litigation law is primarily based on that of German law, belonging to the continental law systems. In order to make the UNHCR's evidentiary standards more usable regardless of jurisdictions, some of the differences in such standards, in particular between common law and continental law, will be discussed.

## 5.1   Lack of International Standards on the Burden and Standard of Proof in Establishing the Applicability of the Foundling Provision

The 1961 Convention and ECN are silent on the issues of burden and standard of proof. In terms of international legal instruments, as an indirectly relevant standard, article 8 of the Council of Europe Convention on the Avoidance of Statelessness in relation to State Succession calls for the standard of proof to be 'lowered' in order to facilitate the granting of nationality with a view to preventing statelessness. However, the Convention does not detail what is considered an appropriate standard of proof.[1]

Little has been written on the burden and standard of proof in the field of statelessness law in general. The limited literature available is mostly about those (to be) adopted in the 'stateless determination procedure' for the purpose of protecting

---

[1] Pointed out also by Laura van Waas, *Nationality Matters: Statelessness under International Law* (Intersentia 2008) 207.

stateless persons by granting statelessness status[2] in a 'migratory' context.[3] Little is available on the assessment of whether a child born in the territory would be 'otherwise stateless', and even less on whether a child born or found in the territory is of 'unknown parents'.

Having said this, some limited literature exists on the evidentiary standards to determine whether one is of unknown parentage and can invoke the foundling provision, which will be discussed in more detail in Sect. 5.6.

As stated in the introduction, as a general rule, in most legal systems, a claimant bears the initial responsibility of substantiating her or his claim. However, in terms of how to establish 'statelessness' for the purpose of protecting stateless persons under the 1954 Convention, the UNHCR in its Handbook (2014)[4] in short advocates that the burden of proof should be 'shared', and the standard of proof should be 'to a reasonable degree', which is lower than the standard of proof applied in normal criminal, civil or administrative standards (see Sect. 5.5.2.1). These standards[5] take into consideration the fact that proving the negative is inherently difficult, including due to the difficulties in gathering evidence, and that the consequences of incorrect decisions are serious. Further, UNHCR Guidelines 4 (2012), which concern the

---

[2] For example, Katia Bianchini, *Protecting Stateless Persons: The Implementation of the Convention Relating to the Status Of Stateless Persons across EU States* (Brill | Nijhoff 2018) 129–30, 141–5, 165–6, 189–92. Laura van Waas, *Nationality Matters: Statelessness under International Law* (Intersentia 2008) chapter III, section 3 and Gábor Gyulai, 'The Determination of Statelessness and the Establishment of a Statelessness-Specific Protection Regime' in Alice Edwards and Laura van Waas (eds), *Nationality and Statelessness under International Law* (Cambridge University Press 2014) 116, 137–41 rather briefly discusses the evidentiary issues including the burden and standard of proof.

[3] In UNHCR guidelines and scholarly and practical literature, a notable distinction has been drawn between statelessness in the 'migratory context' and statelessness in situ ('in place'). Stateless persons in situ live in their 'own country' such as the country of birth or habitual residence, which may necessitate different legal responses to address statelessness. In the context of this discourse, the term 'statelessness status determination' has been considered useful mainly for the former population rather than the latter due to the latter's long-established ties to their countries of residence. However, the distinction between stateless persons in the 'migratory' and 'in situ' contexts is often difficult to draw. Further, it is not clear how the distinction between the legal responses appropriate for stateless persons in the 'migratory' and 'in situ' contexts relates to the two different regimes under the 1954 and 1961 Conventions. Paragraph 58 of the UNHCR Handbook (2014), which is specifically on the implementation of the 1954 Convention, advises that for the in situ population, it may be more appropriate to undertake 'targeted nationality campaigns' or 'nationality verification efforts' for 'acquisition, reacquisition or confirmation of nationality of the country where they reside' (which could well be implemented as part of the States' 1961 Convention obligation). In contrast, UNHCR Guidelines 4 (2012) on the implementation of the 1961 Convention articles 1–4 do not—interestingl—contain any reference to the distinction between these two contexts. Due to these uncertainties, this section only made an analysis of the distinction between the assessments for two different purposes under the 1954 and 1961 Conventions. For detailed analysis on the distinction of these two contexts, see generally Caia Vlieks, 'Contexts of Statelessness: The Concepts 'Statelessness in Situ' and 'Statelessness in the Migratory Context' (11 August 2014) <http://arno. uvt.nl/show.cgi?fid=136498> accessed 4 August 2019.

[4] UNHCR Handbook (2014) paras 89 and 91.

[5] UNHCR Handbook (2014) para 88. These standards also replicate those applicable in RSD due to the similarity of the nature of the assessments involved.

interpretation of articles 1–4 of the 1961 Conventions, essentially provide the same standards for determining when a child born in the territory is 'otherwise stateless'. In terms of the burden of proof, the Guidelines 4 paragraph 20 states:

'Because of the difficulties that often arise when determining whether an individual has acquired a nationality, *the burden of proof must be shared* between the claimant and the authorities of the Contracting State to obtain evidence and to establish the facts as to whether an individual would otherwise be stateless. (emphasis added)

In terms of the standard of proof, the Guidelines 4 paragraph 21 states:

The consequence of an incorrect finding that a child possesses a nationality would be to leave her or him stateless. Therefore, decision makers need to take into account Articles 3 and 7 of the CRC and adopt an appropriate standard of proof, for example that it is established to a 'reasonable degree' that an individual would be stateless unless she or he acquires the nationality of the State concerned. Requiring a higher standard of proof would undermine the object and purpose of the 1961 Convention.

The Guidelines 4 (2012) further refer the readers to the UNHCR Handbook (2014) dealing with stateless person status determination for details on evidence assessment and procedural safeguards, which are obviously considered applicable by analogy to the 'otherwise statelessness' assessment. [6]However, the Guidelines 4 (2012) does not discuss the evidentiary standard to be adopted in examining the applicability of article 2, that is to decide whether one is of unknown parents. The travaux offers only some hints. The ECN's Explanatory Note does not address the issue of burden and standard of proof in general, including on article 6(1)(b).

## 5.2 Applicability of the UNHCR Evidentiary Standards for 'otherwise-statelessness asessment' to the Foundling Related Assessment

The question arises whether the burden and standard of proof rules in determining 'otherwise-statelessness' under articles 1 and 4 of the 1961 Convention be applied in determining whether the person is of unknown parentage under article 2?

It would be relevant first—at least theoretically—to examine the similarities and differences in the nature of assessing 'unknown parentage' and 'otherwise statelessness', including which is more difficult to prove.

First of all, the determination of unknown parentage is closely related, but is one step before, that of 'otherwise statelessness'. If a child is found in a territory and determined to be of legally unknown parents, then she or he is normally[7] automatically considered 'otherwise stateless'.

---

[6] See fnn 12 and 13 of UNHCR Guidelines 4 (2012).

[7] This is with the exception where the child's birth in another State and his or her acquisition of such State's nationality has already been established. See Sect. 7.3.1 on the issue of foundlings born in another State.

The concept of a 'person of *un*known parents' has many similarities with the concept of state*less*ness. Just like 'statelessness', they require 'proof of a negative',which, as stated above, is in general difficult to attain. The consequences of an incorrect decision denying recognition of unknown parentage are serious. The person might end up remaining stateless, being wrongly attributed a nationality of the purported parent(s) whose existence cannot be firmly proven. In some cases, the person might be erroneously considered to be 'of known parents' but 'otherwise stateless', which could result in slower access to nationality than if properly determined to be of unknown parentage.[8]

So, what are the differences between the two categories of persons? The first obvious difference, which was also emphasized during the travaux of the 1961 by States and discussed in Sects. 3.4 and 3.5, is that children of unknown parentage are not accompanied by his legal parents[9] who are supposed to legally represent them for any legal acts or procedures, unlike most of the 'otherwise stateless' children of known parents when they come to the attention of the authorities. For 'typical cases' of foundlings such as babies abandoned on streets and discovered by a third person, there is no way for the children themselves to bear any sort of burden of proof. The situation is not much different for children entrusted by parents to, or informally adopted by, an unrelated person when they were small children. It would be essentially the responsibilities of that third person to approach the civil registration authorities to register the child and explain the details of whatever the person knows, such as where, when and how she or he found the child. Such children will most often be first hosted by a child protection facility, which would act as the child's guardian and/or a legal representative until foster care or adoption arrangement can be made. The children of unknown parents by definition normally do not have persons who truly feel responsible to secure them a nationality, who can explain in detail when, where and how they came to the world.

In this context, it is relevant to remember that the UNHCR Guidelines 4 (2012) emphasize the need to respect the 'special procedural considerations to address the acute challenge faced by children, especially unaccompanied children, in communicating basic facts with respect to their nationality'.[10] The UNHCR Handbook (5.1) at paragraph 66 also advises that: '[A]dditional procedural and evidentiary safeguards for child [statelessness] claimants include […] provision of appropriately trained

---

[8] As discussed in Sects. 1.5.5.2, 3.4.2.3 and 3.4.6, among others, there are significantly more States with a foundling provision (at least 139 States out of 193 UN member States) than those with a provision granting nationality to children born in the territory of known parents otherwise stateless (at least 86 States). Some States among them also provide faster or easier access (automatically by birth) to nationality for children found in the territory of unknown parents, as compared to persons of known parents born in the territory who are otherwise stateless (who might have to wait for years, sometimes up to 18 years of age). Thus, not being able to be recognized as 'unknown parentage' but are nevertheless stateless might mean delayed access to nationality.

[9] In a small number of cases, they are accompanied by parent(s) not legally recognize—such as biological parent(s) under some circumstances or commissioning parent(s) in the case of a child born of surrogacy.

[10] UNHCR Guidelines 4 (2012) para 21.

legal representatives, interviewers and interpreters, *as well as the assumption of a greater share of the burden of proof* by the State'.[11] This guidance indicates that for persons of unknown parents, there might even be more need to relax the evidentiary requirements.

The issue of uneven access (between the child concerned and the State) to evidence can be even clearer in cases of persons of unknown parents as compared to those of otherwise stateless children, whose known parents can at least endeavour to gather evidence to support their statelessness or inability to pass on their nationality to the children—although it can be difficult with the State being in a better position to do so in relation to certain evidence.[12] In the cases of children of unknown parents, it is often the case that the State where the child is found has to investigate evidence such as the immigration records or information from the relevant State with regard to the purported parent(s), or any match on the (transnational) DNA database.[13] Such evidence most likely cannot be accessed by the children concerned or even their legal representatives.

It is also relevant to note that in terms of recognizing statelessness, 'the view of the competent authorities' of the relevant country regarding the nationality status of the individual is decisive—with the key element of 'statelessness' being that the person is 'not considered a national *by any State*', as discussed in Sect. 2.5. Statelessness could in some circumstances thus be ultimately proven directly by a piece of documentary evidence—with written statements from the competent authorities of the country or countries with which the applicant has a relevant link saying that she or he is not a national. In contrast, when one's legal parents are factually unknown, such unknown-ness normally cannot be directly proven by a piece of documentary evidence.[14]

In terms of the types of the evidence being assessed, they are similar to some extent, but are also different in that for persons of unknown parents, the information relied upon can be less, as there is typically no testimony by or documents relating

---

[11] UNHCR Handbook (2014).

[12] With regard to the State being better placed to access certain evidence to determine statelessness in general, see for example UNHCR Handbook (2014) para 97.

[13] Transnational exchanges between governments of DNA profiles has at times resolved the situation of a foundling. In June 2013 a new-born boy was found in Roermond, the Netherlands. A DNA profile obtained from the towel in which the child was wrapped turned up a match with a profile in the German database of a baby girl found in 2011 in Cologne, Germany. Shortly afterwards, a 25-year-old woman came to the attention of the police, who confessed to having abandoned two children. Additional DNA tests confirmed that she was indeed the mother. Netherlands Forensic Institute, *Annual Report 2013*, p 15 cited at p 2, ch 5 in University of Leiden, 'The Light's at the End of the Funnel! Evaluating the Effectiveness of the Transnational Exchange of DNA Profiles Between the Netherlands and other Prüm Countries' (November 2015) <https://dnadatabank.forens ischinstituut.nl/binaries/Report%20PIES%20T5%20Taverne%20Broeders%20Opmaak%20UL% 2026112015%20ISBN%20DEF%20met%20omslag_tcm37-225619.pdf> accessed 1 February 2018 (link unavailable as of 1 July 2019, on file with author).

[14] However, for persons whose parent(s) is(are) *factually* known who is (are) nevertheless not recognized as legal parents, a piece of documentation issued by the country of nationality(ies) of the parent(s) indicating that the parent–child relationship between the parent(s) and the child is not recognized by the competent authorities can directly prove the unknown parentage.

to their parents. Also, while assessment of otherwise statelessness needs assessment of nationality law provisions of the parents, for persons of unknown parents, family law and its actual application of the State(s) of the nationality of the parents might be necessary.

While the assessment of statelessness is a 'mixed question of fact and law',[15] the nature of assessment of unknown parentage can be considered to be even closer to legal assessment than finding of facts—in the sense that it is about assessing whether the 'base facts' can be considered to form the situation described as the parents are 'unknown'. When referring to the degree of the parents' 'unknown-ness' for the 'unknown-ness' to be considered proven, depending on the jurisdiction, it may not be even appropriate to refer to it as a 'standard of proof' but instead the 'definition', 'interpretation' or the 'content' of what 'unknown' means.[16] Even in jurisdictions where the concept of the 'standard of proof' applies in this regard, it is possible to argue that the standard of proof in establishing the unknown-ness of the parentage and birthplace should be set even lower than that for proving statelessness, given that it is impossible to directly prove it by documentary evidence.

That being said, paradoxically, for the most 'typical cases' of foundlings such as babies abandoned (or left in a baby hatch) on the street and then discovered, it could indeed be much 'easier', in a sense, to prove that their parents are 'unknown' than it is for some of the children to prove their 'otherwise statelessness'.

The difficulty in proving unknown parentage typically arises when there is a certain amount of evidence with regard to the identity of the parents, including in some of the cases introduced in Sect. 4.3, including cases where a baby is left by the birth mother at the hospital or is entrusted to a third person.

However, the fact that the child herself or himself who has been left behind is normally not in a position to explain about her or his parentage though remains the same for both 'typical' and 'atypical' cases. Even for the most 'atypical' cases where a person of unknown parents becomes known to the authorities after reaching an older age or even adulthood, the situation might not be too different from where the person comes to the attention of the authorities as babies or young children. This is because, as discussed in Sect. 6.7.2 and elsewhere, a person who does not know about her or his parentage (and birthplace) does not know such fact(s) regardless of how old she or he becomes. That being said, as an older child or adult, what she or he can be reasonably expected to provide would be all the details she or he can remember such as about how, where, with whom, doing what when, she or he has lived so far.

Based on this, it can be theoretically concluded that these standards promoted by the UNHCR with regard to the 'otherwise statelessness' assessment, that is the 'shared burden of proof' and 'to a reasonable degree' standard, might not necessarily be directly applicable to the determination of 'unknown parentage'. In most of the foundling cases, it would not be possible to place any burden on the person concerned

---

[15] UNHCR Handbook (2014) para 23.

[16] Please refer, for example, to Sect. 5.6.3.2.3 and fn 87 of this chapter on Parents' 'unknown-ness' as *'kihanteki yōken'* in Japanese law.

to prove her or his own, unknown, parentage. The standard of proof might need to be lowered even more or, indeed, depending on some jurisdiction, it might not be even appropriate to talk about the standard of proof as an assessment of unknown parentage is more about legal assessment.

Whether this theoretical conclusion is indeed true will be reviewed below, including by examining State practice, including case law.

Further, on a separate note, there are also concerns that the UNHCR's above evidentiary standards can be quite difficult to implement in some States, as the conception and flexibility of burden and standard of proof diverge, in particular between common law and continental law[17] jurisdictions. Sections 5.5 and 5.6 also address these intricate issues.

## 5.3  Burden and Standard of Proof—Irrelevant in Administrative Procedures?

Determination of whether one has acquired nationality based on the foundling provision is normally first carried out by an administrative body, and often involves authorities such as the police and civil registration authorities—apart from the competent authorities on nationality matters. They would interview the witnesses, such as those who found the foundling, or the foundling herself or himself if she or he can talk, or her or his legal representative. Upon the competent administrative body deciding that the applicant is not of unknown parentage found on the territory, depending on the countries, the applicant might be able to appeal to an administrative review body. Subsequently or alternatively, the foundling may also be able to appeal to or apply directly to an administrative tribunal or a judicial court that adjudicates on her or his nationality in an inquisitorial process, or that hears the applicant and the State authority that has made the negative decision in an adversarial process.

The burden and standard of proof are concepts originally developed in the judicial context. In some jurisdictions, these concepts tend to be considered non-existent or less relevant in an administrative procedure that is non-adversarial. However when it comes to international statelessness law standards, in particular those in the UNHCR's Handbook (2014) or the Guidelines 4 (2012), the concepts of burden and standard of proof are still relevant when an administrative body is considering whether to affirm or deny an application. It would come down to which party— the administrative body or the applicant—is obliged to produce evidence and who bears the burden of facing the 'consequence' (which is, for the administrative body, to recognize the unknown parentage and eventually and consequentially nationality,

---

[17] Continental law jurisdictions make up the majority of States currently operating a statelessness-specific determination and protection mechanism. Gábor Gyulai, 'The Determination of Statelessness and the Establishment of a Statelessness-Specific Protection Regime' in Edwards and van Waas (eds), *Nationality and Statelessness under International Law* (Cambridge University Press 2014) 116, fn 79.

and for the applicant, to be denied the same) in situations of uncertainty ('*non liquet*'), which will be discussed in detail below.


## 5.4  The Applicant's Duty to Cooperate and the Non-adversarial Nature of the Procedure

Despite the inherent difficulties of gathering evidence, the claimant, the person who found the claimant, the claimant's guardian and legal representative all have a duty to be truthful and provide as full an account of the circumstances of the claimant's birth or discovery as possible. They are required to provide all evidence reasonably available to themselves.[18] Authorities, in particular those in charge of determining who are their nationals, are required to obtain and present all relevant evidence reasonably available to them.[19] Just like the procedure to determine statelessness, the procedure to confirm nationality based on foundlinghood needs to be protection-oriented, non-adversarial and collaborative, whereby the applicant and the decision-maker (and the State if litigation) cooperate to clarify whether the applicant comes within the definition of a foundling.


## 5.5  Need for Clarification of Evidentiary Terms and Concepts

The definition of the terms 'burden of proof' and 'standard of proof', the legal terms expressing evidentiary rules, as well as their functions and the standards adopted, may differ between jurisdictions, and particularly between common law and continental law countries.[20] Although in the context of refugee status determination (RSD), experts convened by the UNHCR have raised as issues the difficulties in applying the UNHCR-promoted burden and standard of proof, stating that: '[E]videntiary standards in refugee law that have emerged from *common law jurisdictions* are *often*

---

[18] UNHCR Guidelines 4 (2012) para 20, while it only talks about otherwise stateless children. UNHCR Handbook (2014) para 89. Paragraphs 91–93 also points out, where an applicant does not cooperate in establishing the facts, including by deliberately withholding information, then he or she may not be recognized as stateless—which, by analogy, can also apply in foundling cases.

[19] UNHCR Guidelines 4 (2012) para 20.

[20] Juliane Kokott, *The Burden of Proof in Comparative and International Human Rights Law: Civil and Common Law Approaches with Special Reference to the American and German Legal Systems* (Kluwer Law International 1998) 2. See also Mojtaba Kazazi, *Burden of Proof and Related Issues: A Study on Evidence Before International Tribunals* (Kluwer Law International 1996) 22–3. Also, see UNHCR, 'Note on Burden and Standard of Proof in Refugee Claims' (16 December 1998) para 3 [4] <www.refworld.org/docid/3ae6b3338.html> accessed 12 July 2019. (Note: The original English version of this document contains two paragraphs numbered '2'. Thus, the paragraph numbered '3' that is cited here should have been numbered '4'.).

*difficult or impossible to use or interpret in civil law systems*, due to a fundamentally different approach to evidentiary matters' (emphasis added),[21] the other way around is also probably true. Some Japanese case law will be reviewed in Sect. 5.6.1 based on whose guidance some of the conclusions and recommendations of this chapter will be drawn—and the readers from common law jurisdictions might have difficulties understanding some of the Japanese courts' guidance.

Clarification of the differences in the conception or (in)flexibility of the burden and standard of proof between jurisdictions at the outset is thus necessary for discussing more precisely and consistently the evidentiary issues in determining the 'unknown parentage'. That way, this book will have relevance to the widest range of jurisdictions.

## 5.5.1  Burden of Proof

The meaning of the term 'burden of proof' differs particularly between common law and continental law systems, influenced by the predominantly adversarial or inquisitorial nature of the system.[22]

### 5.5.1.1  Two Kinds of 'burden of proof': Burden of Production Versus Burden of Persuasion

In some predominantly adversarial common law systems—for example, the US system—'burden of proof' includes two distinct responsibilities: The 'burden of production' (referred to as the subjective burden of proof) and the 'burden of persuasion' (the objective burden of proof). The burden of production constitutes the obligation of coming forward with sufficient evidence to support a particular proposition

---

[21] UNHCR, 'Summary of Deliberations on Credibility Assessment in Asylum Procedures, Expert Roundtable, 14–15 January 2015, Budapest, Hungary' (5 May 2015) para 56 <http://www.refworld.org/docid/554c9aba4.html> accessed 12 July 2019.

[22] According to Kokott, the difference mainly comes from the fact that, in (strictly) adversarial proceedings, the burden of producing evidence is imposed on the parties, while the court is limited to considering the evidence submitted by them. Therefore, the non-production of evidence by a party may lead to a rejection of that party's assertions. In inquisitorial proceedings, judges may, or may even be required to, investigate and find the evidence on their own. However, after considering all the evidence, the judge may still be unable to find the necessary degree of persuasion. In predominantly inquisitorial proceedings, the term burden of proof thus normally means the 'burden of persuasion'. The distinction between the burden of production and persuasion in the common law systems also serves to delineate the functions of the judge and jury, which traditionally does not exist in continental law system. Juliane Kokott, *The Burden of Proof in Comparative and International Human Rights Law: Civil and Common Law Approaches with Special Reference to the American and German Legal Systems* (Kluwer Law International 1998) 2. See also Mojtaba Kazazi, *Burden of Proof and Related Issues: A Study on Evidence Before International Tribunals* (Kluwer Law International 1996) 24–6.

of fact. This is distinct from the burden of persuasion or risk of non-persuasion of the adjudicator, which is about how courts should decide in situations of *non liquet* after hearing the two parties. The burden of persuasion, therefore, is about which of the two parties benefits from and which party bears the burden of facing the adverse consequence caused by the (non-)accrual of a legal effect on the basis of the existence/absence of a certain fact(s).[23] In contrast, in continental law systems— for example under the German[24] (especially in the constitutional or administrative law field), French[25] and Japanese[26] systems[27]—the two types of burden are often not clearly distinguished, and the term 'burden of proof' used in isolation normally refers to the burden of persuasion.

However, in the context of statelessness determination, the UNHCR has referred to 'burden of proof' as 'the question of which party bears the responsibility of proving a claim or allegation'.[28] Based on these descriptions, it is clear that the UNHCR does not use the words 'burden of proof' to mean the burden of persuasion. Its use can be considered to be generally equivalent to the concept of burden of production in a

---

[23] The concept of burden of proof is most prominently defined and developed by a German scholar Leo Rosenberg. Leo Rosenberg, *Die Beweislast auf der Grundlage des BGB. und der ZPO (1965)* [*Shōmeisekinin ron [Theories on Burden of Proof]*] (Takuji Kurata (tr), Hanrei Taimuzusha 1987) 21.

[24] Juliane Kokott, *The Burden of Proof in Comparative and International Human Rights Law: Civil and Common Law Approaches with Special Reference to the American and German Legal Systems* (Kluwer Law International 1998) 2. According to Kokott, in the German system, the concept of burden of production does exist, but the distinction between the burden of producing evidence and the burden of persuasion is of no major significance. This is mainly because there is no jury system and the burden of production (or 'subjective burden of proof') 'goes no further than the burden of persuasion' (objective burden of proof). Thus, the two types of burden are often used interchangeably, but it is the burden of persuasion that is the key component of burden of proof. Ibid 9 and 49.

[25] Mojtaba Kazazi, *Burden of Proof and Related Issues: A Study on Evidence Before International Tribunals* (Kluwer Law International 1996) 26.

[26] In general, the Japanese legal system was most largely influenced by German law starting in 1868 (along with French law) thus in general considered to belong to the continental law system. *Hōritsu yōgo jiten [Dictionary of Legal Terminologies]* (Jiyūkokuminsha 2011) 4. However, it is also described as a 'hybrid' between continental law and common law. Its civil litigation law was drafted primarily based on German law but subsequently American law elements were incorporated.

[27] In the Japanese civil litigation law (which applies to administrative litigation) the term *shōmei-sekinin* (or *kyoshō-sekinin* (a criminal law term) or *risshō-sekinin*—synonyms that can all be translated as 'burden of proof') normally refers to the burden of persuasion, which is referred to as *kyakkanteki shōmeisekinin* meaning 'objective burden of proof'. The concept equivalent to 'burden of production' (referred to as *shukanteki shōmeisekinin* meaning 'subjective burden of proof') does exist, but the party that bears the burden of production is normally the same as the party that bears the burden of persuasion. Author's summary from several materials including Shiro Kawashima, *Minjisoshōhō [Civil Procedure and Evidence]* (Nihon Hyōronsha 2013) 576 and Makoto Itō, *Minjisoshōhō [Civil Procedure]* (Kōbundō 1989) 356–8. There are thus even disputes about whether the concept of subjective burden of proof has any added value in Japanese law. Yoko Tamura, 'America Minji sosshō ni okeru shōmei ron' ['Rules of evidence in American civil litigations'] (2011) 5–6 Ritsumeikan Hōgaku 197.

[28] UNHCR Handbook (2014) para 89.

sense that it is the obligation to investigate, gather and produce evidence to enable the decision-making.

### 5.5.1.2 'Shared' Burden of Proof: Impossible?

For those from jurisdictions where the term 'burden of proof' normally means 'burden of persuasion', the 'shared burden of proof' principle advocated by UNHCR and international statelessness or refugee scholars may very well be incomprehensible. As already quoted in Sect. 5.1, paragraph 20 of the UNHCR Guidelines 4 (2012) states:

> Because of the difficulties that often arise when determining whether an individual has acquired a nationality, the burden of proof must be *shared* between the claimant and the authorities of the Contracting State to obtain evidence and to establish the facts as to whether an individual would otherwise be stateless. (emphasis added)

If one interprets 'burden of proof' in paragraph 20 to mean 'burden of persuasion', the paragraph becomes logically impossible.[29] This is because the consequence of a *non-liquet* cannot be 'shared'. However, through sharing the burden of production between the claimant and the decision-maker/respondent, it becomes easier for the evidence in support of the applicant's claim to reach the standard of proof, thereby increasing the chance that the decision-maker decides in favour of the applicant. The sharing of the burden of production thus has a close relationship with the burden of persuasion.

In order to eschew confusion, whenever possible the author will use 'burden of production' to mean the burden of gathering and producing evidence, which is referred to as 'burden of proof' in international statelessness law and refugee law. This will distinguish it from 'burden of persuasion', which will also be used below in the context of my proposal of promoting the reversal of the burden. However, in analyzing jurisprudence in Sect. 5.6, it was sometimes difficult to tell—when the original court decisions are saying 'burden of proof'—which one of the two types of burden of proof the judge was referring to, especially with regard to the US and Filipino decisions. In such cases, the original term 'burden of proof' was simply used.

### 5.5.1.3 Reversal of Burden of Persuasion

While the burden of persuasion cannot be 'shared', it is entirely possible that it is 'reversed'. The basic principle in distributing the burden of persuasion ('he who claims must prove') mentioned in Sect. 5.1 has been adjusted or reversed[30] in many jurisdictions in fields of law including human rights law. This has been done generally

---

[29] For example, Hideyuki Kobayashi, *Shōkohō* [*Law of Evidence*] (Kōbundō 1989) 356.

[30] The typical examples include cases involving discrimination or sexual and gender-based violence, in which for the claimant to prove his or her victimization may be very difficult. Juliane Kokott,

taking into consideration factors such as the nature of the matter, difficulties in proving certain facts including lack of witnesses and documentary evidence, unequal power relationship or resources between the claimant and the respondent, uneven access to evidence and the principle of justice with the aim of achieving the equality of arms between the parties in accordance with the principle of justice. The author believes that given the foregoing, this reversal of the burden of persuasion is also appropriate in the context of the determination of unknown parentage, which will be elaborated further below.

## 5.5.2   Standard of Proof

The UNHCR has referred to the standard of proof in statelessness determination as the 'threshold of evidence' to be met by the applicant in persuading the adjudicator as to the truth of her or his factual assertions.[31] This definition of 'standard of proof' appears to be generally in line with what is adopted in substantiation of statelessness (and refugee-related) claims across jurisdictions, which can sometimes be referred to as the 'level of conviction'.

### 5.5.2.1   Standard of Proof in Different Jurisdictions and Fields of Law

In continental law countries, for a court to hold against the defendant, the judge typically must be convinced that the facts brought forward by the plaintiff in support of the claim are indeed true. In principle, continental law does not distinguish between civil law and criminal law: the standard of proof is 'intime conviction' throughout,[32]

---

*The Burden of Proof in Comparative and International Human Rights Law: Civil and Common Law Approaches with Special Reference to the American and German Legal Systems* (Kluwer Law International 1998) at p 12 summarizes the situation in Germany where the principle of distribution of burden of proof in civil litigation does not always apply in constitutional or human rights law. See in general the development of the principle of reversal of burden of persuasion in discrimination cases in Europe, European Commission, 'Reversing the Burden of Proof: Practical Dilemmas at the European and National Level' (December 2014) <http://ec.europa.eu/justice/discrimination/files/burden_of_proof_en.pdf> accessed 4 August 2019. For Japanese practice see, for example, Masatoshi Kasai and Kazuhiro Koshiyama (eds), *Shin Comentāru minjisoshōhō [New commentary on civil litigation law]* (2nd edn, Nihon hyōronsha 2013) 759–62.

[31] UNHCR, 'Note on Burden and Standard of Proof in Refugee Claims' (16 December 1998) para 7 (actually para 8) <www.refworld.org/docid/3ae6b3338.html> accessed 12 July 2019: UNHCR Handbook (2014) para 91. For example, 'shōmei-do' (which can be translated as 'standard of proof') in Japanese civil litigation generally has the same meaning, where it is defined as 'the concept to determine, at what level of conviction the court can treat a specific disputed fact as it actually existing', *Hōritsugaku shōjiten [Concise Law Dictionary]* (4th edn, Yūhikaku 2008). However, it is a term that is not normally used in administrative procedure.

[32] Christoph Engel, 'The Preponderance of the Evidence versus Intime Conviction—A Behavioural Perspective on a Conflict between American and Continental European Law' (August 2008) 2 < https://www.coll.mpg.de/pdf_dat/2008_33online.pdf > accessed 4 August 2019.

which is often equated with 'beyond reasonable doubt'.[33] In general, courts or administrative decisions in continental law countries do not describe or debate in detail the applicable standard of proof. Numerically expressing the standard of proof—such as equating 'intime conviction' with '80 or 90 per cent level of probability that a certain fact exists'—is often criticized as inaccurate. This was also clear when the author interviewed the Office Français de Protection des Réfugiés et Apatrides (OFPRA), the French statelessness determination authority, about what standard of proof they used. When asked by author to express 'sufficiently precise and serious' evidence (said to be necessary for statelessness recognition in France)[34] in percentage or ratio, and whether it was equivalent to 'balance of probabilities' or 'reasonable likelihood', OFPRA essentially responded that it was neither possible to express it numerically nor to equate it with these standards. It was asserted that whether evidence is 'sufficiently serious' 'depends on the case'—and the assessment is done holistically, taking into consideration the circumstances unique to each case.[35] Gábor Gyulai, writing in the context of statelessness determination in Hungary, stated that with Hungary being a continental law jurisdiction, its administrative and judicial decisions typically do not describe the standard of proof in detail.[36]

In contrast, in common law systems—for example in US law—the standard of proof is much more clearly articulated. There are mainly three different standards of proof.[37] In criminal law, the charge must be established 'beyond a reasonable doubt'. In civil law, normally the plaintiff wins only if 'the preponderance of the evidence' is in her or his favour (that is 'more likely than not' or 51 per cent probability that a fact exists). Only in a limited number of 'civil law matters', of particular gravity for the defendant, such as removal proceedings of foreigners, the intermediate standard of 'clear and convincing evidence' must be met.[38]

---

[33] There are criticisms that intime conviction is not the same as 'beyond a reasonable doubt'. Some scholars assert it is higher than that, while others argue it is actually lower, with some stating that the intime conviction cannot be expressed in numerical terms and equating the two is problematic in light of the different legal systems behind the two. Ibid 4. Karim A. A. Khan, Caroline Buisman and Christopher Gosnell, *Principles of Evidence in International Criminal Justice* (Oxford University Press 2010) 37.

[34] UNHCR, 'Good Practices Paper—Action 6: Establishing Statelessness Determination Procedures to Protect Stateless Persons' (11 July 2016) 10 <https://www.refworld.org/docid/57836cff4. html> accessed 2 May 2019.

[35] Interview with Mourad Derbak, Chief of the Europe Division and officials of the Statelessness, Department of the OFPRA (Paris, France, 14 December 2016). Author wishes to thank Dia Jacques Gondo and Kavita Brahmbhatt for facilitating her communications with the office.

[36] Gábor Gyulai, 'Statelessness in Hungary: The Protection of Stateless Persons and the Prevention and Reduction of Statelessness' (December 2010) 25 <https://www.refworld.org/docid/4d6d26972. html> accessed 12 July 2019.

[37] *Addington v. Texas* [1979] (US Supreme Court), cited in Christoph Engel, 'The Preponderance of the Evidence versus Intime Conviction—A Behavioural Perspective on a Conflict between American and Continental European Law' (August 2008) 2 < https://www.coll.mpg.de/pdf_dat/2008_33on line.pdf> accessed 4 August 2019.

[38] Christoph Engel, 'The Preponderance of the Evidence versus Intime Conviction—A Behavioural Perspective on a Conflict between American and Continental European Law' (August 2008) 2 < https://www.coll.mpg.de/pdf_dat/2008_33online.pdf > accessed 4 August 2019.

#### 5.5.2.2 Standard of Proof Relating to Statelessness in General: International Standards, State Practice and the Challenges in Adopting a Low Standard

As mentioned in Sect. 5.2, the UNHCR advocates to adopt 'to a reasonable degree' standard to determine whether somebody is stateless under the 1954 Convention, and appears to promote the same standard in the context of assessing the 'otherwise statelessness' of children born in a contracting State under the 1961 Convention.

Nevertheless, as mentioned in Sect. 5.1, little has been written on the latter, that is the standard of proof adopted by States in determining 'otherwise-statelessness', let alone 'foundlinghood' or 'unknown parentage' under the 1961 Convention. The nationality legislation, the majority of currently accessible administrative documents and judicial and administrative decisions are silent on these issues, except for some of those introduced in Sect. 5.6.

Given the scarcity of the information relating to the evidentiary standards in determining unknown parentage, it is useful to at least summarize the State practice on this with regard to determination of statelessness.

With regard to countries that have already established a statelessness determination procedure, Gyulai states that the growing body of legislation and jurisprudence indicates the States' recognition that the concept of 'proving' in the context of statelessness determination should be 'flexible', and that the standard of proof should not be high.[39]

For example, the regulation of the Philippines explicitly adopts a 'to a reasonable degree' standard to prove statelessness.[40] In Hungary, the relevant legislation sets a lower standard of proof by stipulating that the applicant for statelessness determination shall 'prove or substantiate'[41] her/his claim. In France, a claim of statelessness will be established on the basis of all available evidence that is 'sufficiently precise and serious'.[42] While it is not possible to numerically express this standard as stated

---

[39] Gábor Gyulai, 'Statelessness in Hungary: The Protection of Stateless Persons and the Prevention and Reduction of Statelessness' (December 2010) 138 <https://www.refworld.org/docid/4d6d26 972.html> accessed 12 July 2019. For example, in Italy, the Italian Supreme Court stated that the loss of former nationality does not have to be proven by an official State declaration, but can be shown through the demonstration of acts by which the State denies protection to the individual concerned. Judgement No 14918 of 20 March 2007 of the Supreme Court of Appeal, Italy, cited in Gyulai in this article. See also other examples on p 139 and fn 81 of the same article by Gyulai.

[40] 'Department Circular No 058—Establishing the Refugees and Stateless Status Determination Procedure [Philippines]' (18 October 2012) <https://www.refworld.org/docid/5086932e2.htmls > accessed 4 August 2019.

[41] *Hungary, Act II of 2007 on the Admission and Right of Residence of Third Country Nationals*, section 79(1). Gyulai states the term 'substantiate' was copied from the similar Hungarian provision referring to asylum procedures that reflects the UNHCR standard. Gábor Gyulai, 'Statelessness in Hungary: The Protection of Stateless Persons and the Prevention and Reduction of Statelessness' (December 2010) 25 < https://www.refworld.org/docid/4d6d26972.html > accessed 12 July 2019.

[42] UNHCR, 'Good Practices Paper—Action 6: Establishing Statelessness Determination Procedures to Protect Stateless Persons' (11 July 2016) 10 <https://www.refworld.org/docid/57836cff4.html> accessed 2 May 2019.

earlier, the description of anecdotal examples given during the interview with the author shows that this threshold of evidence can be fairly low. For example, OFPRA referred to two cases where children born abroad out of wedlock of a woman of Tunisian and Moroccan nationality respectively were recognized as stateless. In both cases, while the child's father obviously did not recognize paternity, the child must have acquired the nationality of the mother automatically at birth under the text of the applicable nationality law, both of which had adopted acquisition of nationality through maternal descent. However, basically due to the discrimination against a child born of an extramarital relationship, the children could not have their birth registered with the respective authorities (where obviously there was no clearly articulated statement by the authorities that the children were 'not nationals'). OFPRA did not directly contact the relevant State authorities but only relied on the applicants' (mothers') statement, submissions as well as general country of origin information.[43] While these two cases were born outside France and thus were examined by statelessness determination authorities, as they involve children whose birth registration was denied by the authorities of the purported countries of origin, they can be good examples as to the standard of proof in recognizing the otherwise statelessness of children born in the territory.

That being said, a high standard of proof in recognizing statelessness has been pointed out as one of the most problematic issues, especially where there is no dedicated statelessness determination procedure. For example, in Finland, '[b]ecause of the high standard of proof and heavy burden of proof regarding statelessness, a person's nationality is sometimes determined as unknown or not known rather than stateless, even though there are very strong indications of statelessness'. The situation is similar in the Netherlands and Norway.[44]

Even in Hungary, where there is a statelessness determination procedure adopting the 'significantly lowered' standard of proof ('substantiate'), Gábor Gyulai states recognition has been denied in some instances due to excessive requirements to prove statelessness, sometimes accompanied by the explicit omission of the term 'substantiate' in the text of the decision.[45]

The UK's administrative guidance on the leave to remain on statelessness grounds explicitly adopts a standard higher than what is recommended by UNHCR, that is

---

[43] Interview with Mourad Derbak, Chief of the Europe Division and officials of the Statelessness, Department of the OFPRA (Paris, France, 14 December 2016).

[44] UNHCR, 'Mapping Statelessness in Finland' (November 2014) 43 <http://www.refworld.org/docid/546da8744.html> accessed 4 August 2019. UNHCR, 'Mapping Statelessness in the Netherlands' (November 2011) para 66 <http://www.refworld.org/docid/4eef65da2.html> accessed 4 August 2019. In Norway, the relevant authority applies the preponderance of evidence (more likely than not) standard of proof. UNHCR, 'Mapping Statelessness in Norway' (October 2015) 32 <http://www.refworld.org/docid/5653140d4.html> accessed 4 August 2019.

[45] Gábor Gyulai cites, for example, a case where a former Soviet citizen was rejected statelessness status, where the government argued that he did not fulfil his obligation to 'prove' his statelessness. According to Gyulai, '[...] This constitutes an apparent disregard of the lowered standard of proof (the word "substantiate" was not even used [...]'. Gábor Gyulai, 'Statelessness in Hungary: The Protection of Stateless Persons and the Prevention and Reduction of Statelessness' (December 2010) 29 <https://www.refworld.org/docid/4d6d26972.html> accessed 12 July 2019.

the 'balance of probabilities' (ie 'more likely than not'),[46]which has been pointed out.[47] In other words, the applicant must establish that she or he is more likely to be stateless than to be a national of a country to be recognized as such.

Regarding the 'to a reasonable degree' standard advocated by the UNHCR in establishing statelessness, it can thus be concluded that, while it appears accepted in some States, some States appear to be facing difficulties adopting it. This may be partly due to the fact that this guidance is not easy to implement or has not yet 'sunk in' among decision-makers around the world. The author believes that this might partly be caused by the peculiar formulation of the UNHCR's guidance, which recommends that a negative fact be recognized at a low standard of proof. This is complicated, almost like a 'double negative' construction. It is noted that while the 'to a reasonable degree' standard is the same threshold as advocated by the UNHCR in the context of RSD, the latter is a little more straightforward. This is because in RSD, positive facts (the well-founded fear of being persecuted and so on) need to be recognized at such a low standard of proof.

Indeed, it is time to think about the basic question: what exactly does it mean, to prove that a person is otherwise stateless or of unknown parents, at a low standard of proof?

From the point of view of a decision-maker or assessor on the ground, it might be confusing to start the statelessness assessment by considering whether she or he is convinced at a low standard of proof, that is 'to a reasonable degree' that the person concerned is not considered a national. In terms of a natural thought process, it is much more straightforward to first examine whether there is sufficient evidence to determine that the person is otherwise considered a national, or that the person's parent is known—which is the reverse of being stateless or unknown parents– the opposite side of the same coin.

My proposal, which will be laid out in Sect. 5.9, would be thus to look at the low standard of proof from its flip side: to require a high standard of proof for establishing the opposite fact that is possession of another nationality or known-ness of a parent. It would then have to be the decision-maker who bears the burden of proving the opposite fact of what has been asserted by the claimant herself or himself.This is called the reversal of burden of persuasion.

---

[46] Section 4.2, UK Home Office, 'Asylum Policy Instruction: Statelessness and applications for leave to remain Version 2.0' (18 February 2016) <https://www.gov.uk/government/uploads/system/upl oads/attachment_data/file/501509/Statelessness_AI_v2.0__EXT_.pdf> accessed 4 August 2019.

[47] See for example, Sarah Woodhouse and Judith Carte, 'Statelessness and Applications for Leave to Remain: a Best Practice Guide' (3 November 2016) 23 <https://www.refworld.org/docid/58d cfad24.html> accessed 4 August 2019; Katia Bianchini, 'A comparative analysis of statelessness determination procedures in 10 EU States' (2017) 52 International Journal of Refugee Law 29, 42.

## 5.6   State Practice on the Burden and the Standard of Proof in Determining Unknown Parentage

Only limited information is available as to the State practice on the burden and standard of proof in determining the applicability of the foundling provision in general. Among those currently accessible, only three States' judicial decisions specifically addressed the issues, namely Japan, the Philippines, and the US.

The US case law discussed in Sect. 5.6.1 addressed the burden and standard of proof in relation to its foundling provision, which was, however, largely based on the existing jurisprudence on the burden of proof in proving the claim to be a 'native-born citizen' in general under the Immigration and Nationality Act (INA).

The Philippine's Supreme Court decisions in March and September 2016, discussed in Sect. 5.6.2, addressed the issue of who bears the burden of proving a foundling's parentage (and birthplace) in the absence of a foundling provision in domestic law.

With regard to Japan, Sect. 5.6.3 carries in-depth analysis with regard to its case law on the burden of proof and the required 'extent of unknown-ness' of parentage—which could be described as the 'standard of proof' by readers from common law systems—to benefit from its foundling provision. As this Japanese case law (supported by subsequent family court adjudications) offered among the most inclusive guidance in this regard, recommendations in this chapter were predominantly drawn from it.

### 5.6.1   US

A review of cases accessible through the Westlaw database (eight in total), which are decisions by administrative bodies and courts,[48] was carried out. In seven of those cases, the petitioners invoked the US foundling provision but were rejected. In one case, the petitioner was confirmed US nationality, while the reasons are not available on the accessible record.[49] Separately, in one another case, that is the

---

[48] Search in Westlaw Next yields the following cases: (1) Hernandez v. Ashcroft, 114 Fed. Appx. 183 [2004] (United States Court of Appeals, Sixth Circuit); (2) *Johnson v. Attorney General of US*, 235 Fed. Appx. 24 [2007] (United States Court of Appeals, Third Circuit); (3) *AAO, Re Applicant* 2007 WL 5,338,559 (DHS) [10 August 2007]; (4) AAO, *Re Applicant* 2010 WL 6,527,657 (DHS) [24 May 2010]; (5) *Orea-Hernandez v. Attorney General of the US* (United States Court of Appeals for the Third Circuit); (6) AAO, *Re Applicant* 2011 WL 10,845,097 (DHS) [15 September 2011]; (7) AAO, *Re Applicant* 2013 WL 5,504,816 (DHS) [19 February 2013]; and (8) AAO, *Re Applicant* 2016 WL 8,315,993 (DHS) [30 November 2016]. The author wishes to thank UNHCR Washington for informing her of those decisions.

[49] AAO, *Re Applicant* 2010 WL 6,527,657 (DHS) [24 May 2010]. Claimant's lawsuit is *Lumbard v. DHS,* et al., 09-CV-0107 (CD. Cal 2009), which is also unavailable in Westlaw Next.

2006 Newark Case (discussed in Sect. 4.3.5)[50] unavailable on Westlaw, the case was confirmed nationality via an administrative decision by the Citizenship and Immigration Services (USCIS). According to the attorney at law who represented the 2006 Newark Case, there were 'no reported cases where this statute [the foundling provision, INA § 301(f)] has been successfully used in the past 65 years [until the decision in November 2006]'.

The review of the above seven negative decisions indicated that the burden and standard of proof was at the heart of the issue in rejecting many of the claims.

As mentioned in earlier chapters, section 301(f) of the INA, which is section 1401(f), Title 8 of US Code, provides that the following is an American national at birth: 'A person of *unknown parentage found* in the United States *while under the age of five years*, until shown, prior to his attaining the age of twenty-one years, not to have been born in the United States' (emphasis added). In almost all cases reviewed, it was essentially ruled that the burden of proof (both burden or production and persuasion) lay with the claimant, at least with regard to the first two elements,[51] that is that the person is of unknown parents and was found in the US under the age of five. The applicable standard of proof was cited as a preponderance of the evidence.

The decision-makers mostly and simply applied the general principle enshrined in the Code of Federal Regulations, Title 8. (Aliens and Nationality), section 341.2 (Examination upon application) applicable to all applications for certificate of nationality (regardless of the ground for such claim), which provides:

> Proof. *The burden of proof shall be upon the claimant*, or his parent or guardian if one is acting in his behalf, *to establish the claimed citizenship* by a *preponderance of the evidence*'. Under the preponderance of evidence standard, it was generally sufficient that the proof establish that something is probably true. (emphasis added)

The majority of the cases reviewed were almost all rejected on the basis that the claimant did not fulfil her or his burden of proof. Among them, some clearly did not meet one or more of the two prerequisite facts, or there was proof to the contrary (that the person concerned was born abroad which is the disqualification ground under section 301(f) of the INA (such as that one of the parents was clearly known, or birth outside the territory was established)). Most of those nine cases contained insufficient facts—especially the facts relating to whether the claimant's legal parentage was established and to what degree, in order to examine whether the

---

[50] Chris Nugent and Doug Burnett of the Holland & Knight Community Services Team, 'The Foundling Statute' (23 January 2007) <https://www.ilw.com/articles/2007,0123-nugent.shtm> accessed 4 August 2019. In this 29 November 2006 Newark Case, only limited information is available on this web-based article, and it is unknown how exactly the 'unknown parentage' assessment was done including the burden and standard of proof applied.

[51] For example, see AAO, *Re Applicant* 2016 WL 8,315,993 (DHS) [30 November 2016] (30 November 2016), which specifically mentions 'The Director concluded that the Applicant provided insufficient evidence to establish that he was born of unknown parentage or that he was found in the United States, as required under section 301(f) of the Act.' It also mentions 'The Applicant is presently under the age of 21. The issue in this case is whether he has demonstrated that he is a person of unknown parentage found in the United States while under the age of 5'.

decision-maker's findings that the applicant did not satisfy the 'preponderance of evidence' standard was justified—to make meaningful comments.

One of the cases, however, merits analysis in detail. The Court of Appeals case of *Johnson v. Attorney General of the US* contains more detailed facts and reasonings on the burden and standard of proof, and so is examined below.[52]

### *Johnson v. Attorney General of the US*[53]

In this 2007 case, the claimant was left under the care of a neighbour at around the age of four by his purported brother who was subsequently murdered, with no conclusive evidence regarding the claimant's place of birth or parentage remaining. A birth certificate issued in Jamaica was found in the house of the deceased (purported) brother, but it was unclear whether it belonged to the claimant.

### Summary of facts[54]

In the spring of 1987, the claimant's purported brother, 'Robert Cross', left the claimant in the care of a neighbour, Ethel White in Brooklyn. The claimant was at that time known as 'Troy Jenkins'. Not long after Cross left Johnson with White, she learned that Cross had been murdered. A month after Cross was killed, police gave White a birth certificate that they found in the home of Robert Cross during the investigation. The birth certificate was for 'David Lloyd Johnson' who was born to a female named Hazel Francis on 8 October 1982 in Kingston, Jamaica. This surprised White because, if it belonged to the claimant, it meant that Johnson was five, a year older than she had always thought. The claimant had a Jamaican accent when White first met him. White made inquiries in an attempt to find someone else to care for the claimant, but her efforts were fruitless. Accordingly, the claimant continued to live with White, who acted as his guardian as he grew up. Since White had no official records to establish Johnson's age or identity, she used the birth certificate police found to enrol him in school. Thus, all of his school records bore the name, 'David Johnson' and that was how he was known throughout his years in school. Although the claimant stayed with White for several years, he was a troubled teen and left home when he was about 15 years old. Johnson's juvenile arrests brought him to the attention of the immigration authorities. In June 1999 Immigration and Naturalization Services (INS) initiated removal proceedings against Johnson, and the first immigration hearing followed.

---

[52] *Johnson v. Attorney General of US*, 235 Fed. Appx. 24 [2007] (United States Court of Appeals, Third Circuit)—case of United States Court of Appeals, Third Circuit (17 May 2007).

[53] Ibid.

[54] Ibid. The facts are as summarized in the Court of Appeals' judgement in its 'Background' section with appropriate modifications. It was unclear whether all the facts cited here were those found credible by the Court of Appeals as the decision does not distinguish between accepted facts and rejected facts. As this book focuses on the specific aspect of his case, that is his nationality claim, the term 'claimant' was used to replace the term 'appellant' as used in the judgement.

Decision by the first immigration judge and subsequent facts

After the claimant's initial removal hearing, on 12 March 2001, Immigration Judge (IJ) Van Wyke held that the INS, the immigration authorities at the time, did not fulfil its burden of proof that the claimant was an alien by 'clear and convincing evidence', the standard required in deportation proceedings.[55] While the original copy of IJ Van Wyke's decision is unavailable,[56] below is a summary of what is cited in the Court of Appeals decision in 2007.

In summary, IJ Van Wyke held that the claimant's country of citizenship was 'unknown', and that he was not removable. Before such a decision, in asserting that the claimant was an alien, the INS invoked the birth certificate that had been found in Cross's apartment and was given to the appellant's guardian. IJ Van Wyke, however, ruled that the birth certificate was not sufficiently probative of the claimant's alienage for several reasons. The last name on that certificate was not the same as Johnson's brother's last name ('Cross'), and the name of the mother recorded on the birth certificate did not correlate with either Johnson or his brother. The certificate had a different name than how the claimant was known by ('Troy Jenkins') and it was 'simply part of the possessions in the apartment that he lived in with his brother before his brother was killed'.

IJ Van Wyke also dismissed the significance of the claimant's Jamaican accent because, although it was consistent with the government's contention that the claimant had been born in Jamaica, he could have acquired the accent growing up in an environment with many Jamaican people in New York. IJ Van Wyke rather considered White's testimony that she thought the claimant was older than on the birth certificate was significant and probative because White had raised children and grandchildren and would be able to determine age.

IJ Van Wyke specifically stated:

[I]t is not clear and convincing that the birth certificate that ended up being used for him to go to school by a person who did not know either his mother or his father and barely knew his purported brother, and knew him by a different name than is on that certificate, is the only link that we have between the respondent's possible birth in Jamaica and the person who is before me today…*[T]hat may not even come to a preponderance of the evidence and if* it does, it certainly *does not rise to the level of being clear and convincing.* (emphasis added)[57]

Accordingly, IJ Van Wyke concluded that the INS had not tied the birth certificate to Johnson by 'clear and convincing' evidence. The Board of Immigration Appeals

[55] For example, *Woodby v. INS* [1966] (US Supreme Court) (US 1966); *Ramon-Sepulveda v. INS* [1984] (INS) n. 2 (9th Cir.1984).

[56] Inaccessible. Summarized as 'The First Removal Hearing' in *Johnson v. Attorney General of US,* 235 Fed. Appx. 24 [2007] (United States Court of Appeals, Third Circuit). The attorney who represented the claimant was not in possession of a copy of IJ Van Wyke's decision. Telephone conversation with Joseph C. Hohenstein (Attorney at Law, Orlow & Orlow, Philadelphia, US) (2 March 2018) following the email from author to Joseph C. Hohenstein (26 August and 14 September 2017).

[57] Ibid.

(BIA) affirmed the decision by IJ Van Wyke. Subsequently, on 12 March 2001, IJ Van Wyke ordered the removal proceedings terminated, and the claimant was released.

Despite IJ Van Wyke's ruling, which determined the claimant's nationality to be 'unknown', the INS subsequently twice issued him an 'arrival record' form (I-94) carrying the details taken from the birth certificate, stating Jamaica as his 'country of citizenship'. In order to obtain the employment, the claimant needed a social security card, for which he was obliged to fill the application with personal details consistent with his I-94.

Subsequently, the INS filed a motion to reopen based on new evidence of the claimant's social security application, where he stated Jamaica as his country and Hazel Francis as his mother. The second IJ this time held that the INS met the burden of proof by clear and convincing evidence. The BIA affirmed.

Meanwhile, the claimant filed a declaratory judgement action for the judiciary to conclude that he was actually a US citizen based on the foundling provision, that is section 301(f) of INA, and, therefore, not subject to removal, which was examined by the US District Court for the Eastern District of Pennsylvania.[58]

District Court ruling on the nationality claim

In the District Court, the claimant's attorney argued that the claimant '*can meet his burden* of proof on the requirement(s) under section 301(f) (including that he was of unknown parents) '*by virtue of the Government's failure to demonstrate alienage*' (emphasis added). The attorney argued that a foundling could not be required to prove his own unknown parentage because she or he does not have first-hand knowledge of this information, asserting that a person who is requesting recognition of citizenship under section 301(f) 'by definition [...] does not know the circumstances of her or his birth because of "unknown parentage"'.[59]

The District Court acknowledged the potential evidentiary problems created for a foundling who is required to prove the elements in section 301(f). However, the court determined that the claimant nonetheless bore the initial burden of establishing his nationality claim by preponderance of the evidence, and that the claimant did not fulfil it (the reason for this assessment is unclear from the Court of Appeals decision). With regard to the burden of proof, the District Court largely relied upon the language of section 301(f) of the INA, along with the previous jurisprudence, with *Delmore v. Brownell*[60] as an example, which placed the burden on the party

---

[58] *David Johnson v. Attorney General of the United States Department of Homeland Security* (United States District Court for the Eastern District of Pennsylvania) (12 September 2005). It is not found through Westlaw, and the claimant's attorney was not in possession of the copy. Telephone conversation with Joseph C. Hohenstein (Attorney at Law, Orlow & Orlow, Philadelphia, US) (2 March 2018).

[59] Joseph C. Hohenstein et al., 'Brief on Burden of Proof' submitted to the US District Court for the Eastern District of Pennsylvania, Philadelphia, Pennsylvania (undated), provided to author by the claimant's then legal representative. Email from Joseph C Hohenstein to author (2 March 2018), on file with author.

[60] *Delmore v. Brownell* [1956] (United States Court of Appeals Third Circuit) (3d Cir.1956).

seeking an affirmation of a status of a citizen by birth in the US territory under the INA in general.

The claimant appealed the second IJ's grant of INS's motion to reopen and also appealed the District Court's denial of his nationality claim to the Court of Appeals.

Court of Appeals' ruling

Significantly, with regard to the BIA's decision to reopen the case, the Court of Appeals ruled that the BIA had 'abused its discretion' (noting that such reversal of a BIA decision can only be made if it is 'arbitrary, irrational, or contrary to law').[61] This was because of 'newly discovered evidence', that is the claimant's social security application was not considered 'material evidence' to suffice reopening, as it was based on the birth certificate, which IJ Van Wyke had found could not be relied upon. The Court of Appeals stated:

> IJ Van Wyke terminated removal hearings because all of the government's proof could be traced to a very suspect birth certificate. That IJ painstakingly analysed the evidence admitted at the first removal hearing and concluded that, although the government's proof was not limited to that birth certificate, the government's evidence was nevertheless only as strong as the reliability of that document.

> Given the circumstances surrounding White's possession of that document, the discrepancies between the document and Johnson's [that is the claimant's] probable age and name, as well as other circumstances that undermined the reliability of the birth certificate, IJ Van Wyke concluded that any claim of Johnson's alienage that rested upon that document was not established by the clear and convincing proof the law required for removal. Indeed, as noted above, the IJ was skeptical that the proof even satisfied the preponderance standard.[62]

With regard to the claimant's social security card application, the Court of Appeals stated:

> [A]n additional instance of Johnson using information from the birth certificate and the erroneously issued I-94 could hardly transform the quality or reliability of the information on the birth certificate. [...] in order to obtain employment, it was necessary for Johnson to use the only documents he had-the birth certificate and the I-94. [...] Given the Catch 22 Johnson was caught in, and the questions surrounding the birth certificate, nothing indicates that the Social Security application would have altered IJ Van Wyke's decision.[63]

With regard to the claimant's nationality claim, the Court of Appeals agreed with the claimant's attorney, that: 'it is *exceedingly difficult for an alien to prove his/her citizenship under the foundling statute*' (emphasis added).[64] Nevertheless, the Court of Appeals still affirmed the order by the District Court that the claimant had the burden of establishing the requirements under the section 301(f) by a preponderance of the evidence, again referring to *Delmore v. Brownell*.[65] The Court of Appeals thus denied the claimant's US nationality under the foundling statute.

---

[61] *Johnson v. Attorney General of US*, 235 Fed. Appx. 24 [2007] (United States Court of Appeals, Third Circuit) (17 May 2007) para [5.3] **9 and para [4].

[62] Ibid para [4].

[63] Ibid para [5] **12.

[64] Ibid para [6] **13.

[65] *Delmore v. Brownell* [1956] (United States Court of Appeals Third Circuit) (3d Cir.1956).

Analysis

The first IJ Van Wyke's ruling, which became valid again with the Court of Appeals'
decision to nullify the BIA's reopening decision, did indeed conclude that INS could
not prove the claimant's (foreign) parentage and thus alienage, and that the claimant
was of 'unknown nationality'.

However, the holding of the US Court of Appeals left the claimant in a legal
limbo (as admitted by the Court of Appeals itself in the decision). The claimant was
considered unable to prove that he is a citizen of the US, while the government could
not establish that he is a foreigner, either.

Even if the claimant's unknown parentage could not be acknowledged, it should
have been at least clear that he was stateless, as one cannot remain to be of 'unknown
nationality' forever.[66]

While there was no publicly available record of what eventually happened in the
claimant's case, the information received from the claimant's attorney was that, to
his knowledge, the claimant's nationality status was never resolved afterwards, while
he has not been deported either.[67] According to the attorney, due in large part to the
fact that he was unable to secure an appropriate identification and the confirmation
of his nationality status, he was thereafter not able to secure employment and was far
from leading a stable life (details withheld by author for privacy purposes). This case
truly shows that instability on nationality status can lead to marginalization, which
goes against the interest of the State.

It is not clear from the judgement how the Court of Appeals arrived at the above
conclusion to affirm the District Court's decision, thereby denying the claimant's
nationality claim. While the Court of Appeals—being a trier of facts—was not in a
position to directly assess the facts, the Court of Appeals appears to have indirectly
affirmed the District Court's assessment that the claimant did not fulfil his burden of
proving his unknown-ness of his parentage (and having been found in the US under
the age of five) at the preponderance of evidence. This is somewhat puzzling as the
Court of Appeals, in ruling that the newly discovered evidence was not material to
suffice reopening, gives the impression that it is indirectly and de facto supporting IJ
Van Wyke's finding that INS did not fulfil its burden of proving Johnson's alienage,
as the evidence produced '*may not even come to a preponderance of the evidence
and if it does, it certainly does not rise to the level of being clear and convincing*'

---

[66] As a side note, even if the claimant cannot be recognized as an American national under the
foundling statute, it would be appropriate for the government to at least consider recognizing him
stateless, as the first IJ back in March 2001 already recognized him to be of 'unknown' nationality. It
is noted, however, that the US is not a State party to the 1954 Convention and there is no established
statelessness determination procedure for the purpose of protecting stateless persons at the time of
writing. See UNHCR, 'Representing Stateless Persons Before US Immigration Authorities' (August
2017) <http://www.refworld.org/docid/59a5898c4.html> accessed 4 August 2019 and UNHCR,
'Citizens of Nowhere: Solutions for the Stateless in the US' (December 2012) <http://www.ref
world.org/docid/50c620f62.html> accessed 4 August 2019.

[67] Telephone conversation with Joseph C. Hohenstein (Attorney at Law, Orlow & Orlow, Philadelphia, US) (2 March 2018) following the email from author to Joseph C. Hohenstein (26 August and
14 September 2017).

(emphasis added). The flip side of the same coin—of the State's inability of prove alienage on a preponderance of evidence—should logically be the claimant's ability to prove US citizenship at the same standard of proof, based on the US's foundling provision, that is section 301(f) of INA.

At any rate, it should be pointed out that *Delmore v. Brownell*, which the Court of Appeals (and before that the District Court) referred to in determining the burden and standard of proof in this case, is not a case of a foundling or a person of unknown parents. It was a normal case of a person of known parentage whose birth in the US was disputed, but eventually confirmed.[68] The nature of the claim is very different—in *Delmore* the claimant had to prove the affirmative—that he was born in the US. However, in a foundling case, the claimant has to prove the negative—that her or his parents are not known (in addition to the fact that she or he was found under the age of five). It is arguable that the burden and standard of proof applied to claims for nationality in general *cannot*, blindly, be applied to foundling claims as they are without legal parents to help them explain how their existence in the world came about, and are not in a position to prove their own unknown parentage.

Indeed, administrative instructions from other States also appear to blindly apply the general burden and standard of proof applied to nationality claims invoking the foundling provision. For example, the UK Home Office's Nationality Guidance on automatic Acquisition of UK Nationality states:

> The burden of proof to establish a claim to citizenship: The Immigration Act 1971 puts the burden of proving a status on the applicant or person making a claim. Section 3(8) of the 1971 act, as amended, provides that: 'When any question arises under this Act whether or not a person is a British citizen [...] ... it shall lie on the person asserting it to prove that he is.' [...] Standard of proof: [...] 'the standard of proof applicable to the right of abode, whether that right be dependent on citizenship or relationship, is that of the normal balance of probabilities'. This means that a right of abode or claim to citizenship is established if the evidence that it exists outweighs, however slightly, the evidence that it does not. [...].[69]

While not explicitly stated, from the context this guidance can also be assumed to apply to the foundling provision included in the same document on page 8, in the absence of the foundling-specific burden and standard of proof laid out separately.

Decision-makers should, however, realize that, nationality claims based on one's unknown parentage or otherwise statelessness fundamentally differ from other nationality claims based on affirmative facts such as birth in the territory or descent from a national. Considering the object and purpose of legislating such nationality law provisions, that is to prevent statelessness, it is appropriate that States develop the burden and standard of proof rules that are tailor-made to the specific circumstances of foundlings. Some States have done this. Below are examples from the Philippines and Japan.

---

[68] *Delmore v. Brownell* [1956] (United States Court of Appeals Third Circuit) (3d Cir.1956).

[69] UK Home Office, 'British citizenship: Automatic Acquisition (part of Nationality Guidance)' (27 July 2017) 5 <https://www.gov.uk/government/publications/automatic-acquisition-nationality-policy-guidance> accessed 4 August 2019.

## 5.6.2  The Philippines

The Philippines is not a State party to the 1961 Convention and does not have a legal provision to grant nationality to a foundling ie a person of unknown parents found on the territory. However, reportedly, such persons have, in general, been confirmed Filipino nationality in practice.

*Supreme Court decisions on 8 March and 20 September 2016 (the Grace Poe Case)*

This practice was formalized through the Supreme Court rulings in 2016[70] on the case of Ms Grace Poe, a presidential candidate alleged to be non-Filipino and non-eligible as she was a child of unknown parentage found abandoned in a church in the Philippines. One of the central issues that the 2016 decisions of the Supreme Court addressed was the issue of burden and standard of proof. The party denying Poe's Filipino nationality claimed that being foundlings are not mentioned in the citizenship criteria under the 1935 Constitution, they cannot be citizens, and Poe had the burden to present evidence to prove her natural filiation with a Filipino parent. However, the Supreme Court rejected this assertion, and instead ruled, basically, that it is the party disputing a foundling's Filipino nationality who bears the burden to prove that both her or his parents are alien.

Limitations of the Grace Poe Case judgements

Before going into detailed analysis on the standard and burden of proof, possible limitations of these decisions need to be noted. First, these decisions were delivered essentially in response to political allegations that Senator Poe was not a Filipino citizen by birth, after Poe had already been found as a foundling as a newborn and had been living as a Filipino citizen most of her 48 years of life, carrying a Filipino passport. It could thus be argued that some of the guidance might not be directly applicable when it comes to the situation where an individual, who has just been found on the territory and not yet been recognized as a foundling, wishes to assert Filipino nationality. Second, the fact that the case is about the most 'typical' scenario—of an abandoned new-born with no clue on their parents—definitely made it easier to affirm the concerned person's nationality. The Supreme Court also stated:

> This case certainly does not decide with finality the citizenship of *every single foundling* as natural-born. The circumstances of each case are unique, and *substantial proof may exist to show that a foundling is not natural-born*. The nature of the Senate Electoral Tribunal and its place in the scheme of political powers, as devised by the Constitution, are likewise different from the other ways to raise questions of citizenship. (emphasis added)[71]

---

[70] G.R. No 221697 *Mary Grace Natividad S. Poe-llamanzares v. Comelec and Estrella C. Elamparo, and G.R. No 221698–700 Mary Grace Natividad S. Poe-llamanzares v. Comelec, Francisco S. Tatad, Antonio P. Contreras and Amado D. Valdez* (Supreme Court of the Philippines), *G.R. 221,538 Rizalino David v. Senate Electoral Tribunal & Mary Grace Poe Llamanzares* (Supreme Court of the Philippines).

[71] G.R. No 221538 *Rizalino David v. Senate Electoral Tribunal & Mary Grace Poe Llamanzares* (Supreme Court of the Philippines) 2.

Last but not least, the 1935 Constitution did not explicitly provide nationality grant to foundlings, the Supreme Court had to argue that, based on the travaux of the Constitution and the customary international law binding the Philippines, the *jus sanguinis* constitutional provision granting nationality to children of a Filipino father implicitly covered foundlings. The Supreme Court stated:

> Adopting these legal principles from the 1930 Hague Convention and the 1961 Convention on Statelessness is rational and reasonable and consistent with the jus sanguinis regime in our Constitution. The presumption of natural-born citizenship of foundlings stems from the presumption that their parents are nationals of the Philippines.[72]

The Supreme Court supported the argument that there was a 99.8 per cent possibility that Poe is a Filipino national by birth, invoking the statistics with Filipino-foreigner breakdown of all births within the Philippines during 1968 when Poe was born. In the Supreme Court's mind, this was supported by circumstantial evidence, such as that there was no international airport in the area where Poe was found, and that Poe had typical Filipino physical features, and the fact that Poe was a newborn abandoned in a church, which showed how an ordinary Filipino would have behaved.[73]

Thus, the focus of the Supreme Court in Poe's case—that is what the party disputing Poe's Filipino nationality was eventually required to prove—was whether one of Poe's parents is Filipino, rather than whether they are 'unknown'. This means that if the foundling found appears foreign, or the circumstances show that her or his parent(s) are likely non-Filipino, the guidance in the Poe decisions might not apply. As reviewed in chapter 5, the intention of at least the majority of the drafters of the 1961 Convention was to grant nationality to persons of unknown parents even if it is likely that she or he was a child of a foreigner. This puts great limitation to the applicability of the court's guidance to other foundling cases.

Guidance on the burden and standard of proof

Nevertheless, the decisions still contain some universally applicable guidance. Specifically, the Supreme Court placed the burden of proof on the party disputing a foundling's nationality considering that a foundling, who is of unknown parentage, should not be expected to prove who their parents are.

In affirming the Senate Electoral Tribunal's decision affirming Poe's Filipino nationality, the Supreme Court's decision in September 2016 stated:

> The Senate Electoral Tribunal knew the limits of human capacity. *It did not insist on burdening private respondent with conclusively proving*, within the course of the few short months, *the one thing that she has never been in a position to know throughout her lifetime.* Instead, it conscientiously appreciated the implications of all other facts known about her finding. […] (emphasis added)[74]

---

[72] *G.R. No 221697 Mary Grace Natividad S. Poe-llamanzares v. Comelec and Estrella C. Elamparo, and G.R. No 221698–700 Mary Grace Natividad S. Poe-llamanzares v. Comelec, Francisco S. Tatad, Antonio P. Contreras and Amado D. Valdez* (Supreme Court of the Philippines) 33.

[73] See in ibid 33.

[74] *G.R. No 221538 Rizalino David v. Senate Electoral Tribunal & Mary Grace Poe Llamanzares* (Supreme Court of the Philippines) 18.

The Supreme Court also noted that:

In the process, it [Senate Electoral Tribunal, author] avoided setting a damning precedent for all children with the misfortune of having been abandoned by their biological parents. Far from reducing them to inferior, second-class citizens, the Senate Electoral Tribunal did justice to the Constitution's aims of promoting and defending the well-being of children, advancing human rights, and guaranteeing equal protection of the laws [...].[75]

The Supreme Court then considered the disputing party's allegations that the burden of evidence shifted to Poe upon a mere showing that she is a foundling was a 'serious error'. The Supreme Court stated:

His emphasis on private respondent's supposed burden to prove the circumstances of her birth places upon her an impossible condition. To require proof from private respondent [referring to Poe, author.] borders on the absurd when there is no dispute that the crux of the controversy – the identity of her biological parents – is simply not known.[76]

The Supreme Court also made an important remark on the nature of the procedure to confirm a foundling's nationality. The court specifically rejected the assertion by the party disputing Poe's nationality that the process to determine foundlinghood leading to the issuance of a 'foundling certificate' are acts to 'acquire or perfect' Philippine citizenship, which made a foundling a naturalized Filipino at best. The court asserted that, unlike the naturalization process, a foundling was a natural-born citizen who did not have to perform any act to acquire nationality, as the determination of foundling status is done 'not by the child but by the authorities'.[77] The Supreme Court's finding that a foundling did not have to perform any act himself apparently contributed to its conclusion that there was a presumption that all foundlings found in the Philippines are Filipino nationals by birth, unless there is substantial proof otherwise.

The Supreme Court cited in this context footnote 121 of section 5 of the Republic Act (RA) No 8552 entitled an Act Establishing the Rules and Policies on the Adoption of Filipino Children and For Other Purposes (otherwise known as the Domestic Adoption Act of 1998), which provided:

Location of Unknown Parent(s). – It shall be the duty of the Department or the child-caring agency which has custody of the child to exert all efforts to locate his/her unknown biological parent(s). If such efforts fail, the child shall be registered as a *foundling* and subsequently be the subject of legal proceedings where he/she shall be declared abandoned. (emphasis modified from the original)[78]

---

[75] Ibid 19.

[76] Ibid 40.

[77] *G.R. No 221697 Mary Grace Natividad S. Poe-llamanzares v. Comelec and Estrella C. Elamparo, and G.R. No 221698–700 Mary Grace Natividad S. Poe-llamanzares v. Comelec, Francisco S. Tatad, Antonio P. Contreras and Amado D. Valdez* (Supreme Court of the Philippines) 29.

[78] *G.R. 221,538 Rizalino David v. Senate Electoral Tribunal & Mary Grace Poe Llamanzares* (Supreme Court of the Philippines) 55.

## 5.6.3  Japan

Article 2(iii) ofthe Japanese Nationality Act provides for automatic nationality grant upon birth to children born in Japan of parents who are unknown, and there have been a number of cases on this, which have already been discussed in Sect. 4.3, which examined the interpretation of 'unknown-ness' by reviewing different categories of persons whose parentage can be considered 'unknown'. Among them, there is one binding Supreme Court judgment, namely the Baby Andrew Case of 1995, which for the first time and at length addressed the 'extent of unknown-ness' requirement and the issue of the burden of proof in substantiating 'unknown parentage'. The analysis below will start with the Baby Andrew Case and go on to subsequent family court adjudications, this time in view of analyzing the extent of unknown-ness and the burden of proof.

### 5.6.3.1  High Standard of Proof in Japanese Civil/Administrative Litigations and Procedures

Before going into the details of the court adjudications, introducing the specific context of Japanese litigation law would be useful. In Japan, the standard of proof for civil/administrative litigation, which in practice can also be applied in administrative procedures, is generally considered to be set at 'high probability' (*kōdo no gaizensei*),[79] which may be slightly below, but could as well be equivalent to, the criminal standard of 'beyond reasonable doubt'. This is significantly higher than the 'balance of probabilities' standard of proof generally applied in civil litigation in common law countries. In Japanese judicial practice, courts rarely 'lower'—at least officially—the standard of proof per se. Lowering the standard of proof is normally reserved for certain exceptional cases, where there is specific legislation stipulating a lowered standard of proof or a policy decision by the government.[80]

Largely due to this standard of proof that is 'fixed' at the high level, it has been a challenge to promote the adoption of the UNHCR-advocated 'low' standard of proof ('to a reasonable degree') in the field of statelessness and refugee law in Japanese judicial and administrative proceedings.

Likely due to this, in the context of Japanese jurisprudence, administrative instructions and scholarly theories, what is normally expressed as the need to 'lower the standard of proof' in other jurisdictions or in UNHCR literature has tended to be

---

[79] *Todai byōin lumbar jiken,* The Supreme Court, 24 October 1975 (*Shōwa 54 nen*) [1975] (Supreme Court).

[80] In practice, in absence of these official grounds, several court decisions in recent years have lowered the standard of proof (as low as something equivalent to the 'balance of probabilities' standard) in cases where it was considered difficult to prove the relevant facts due to their nature. These include a case involving sexual assault in a closed room. *Judgement, Hanrei Jihō No 1681, p* 112 [10 December 2004 (*Heisei 16 nen*)] (Sendai High Court Akita Branch). Cited with commentary in Yoko Tamura, 'Minji soshō ni okeru shōmeido ron saikō', Ritsumeikan Hōgaku' (2009) 327/328 Ritsumeikan Hōgaku 517.

discussed as the need to 'widen the interpretation' of the relevant legal definition, which essentially has the same effect, as discussed below.

The guidance below can be particularly useful for jurisdictions where the standard of proof tends to be high and inflexible, like Japan.

### 5.6.3.2   Baby Andrew Case (1995)[81]—Case Law on De Facto Reversed Burden of Persuasion and Broad Interpretation (Lowered Extent) of 'unknown-ness' of Parentage

*Summary of facts*

Andrew was born on 18 January 1991 at a hospital in Nagano Prefecture, Japan. The mother who delivered Andrew disappeared five days after Andrew's birth, without registering him with a Japanese city office. No information was found on his father's identity. When the mother was admitted to the hospital for delivery, she did not have any documents that proved her identity. Andrew's mother only communicated with the hospital staff through broken English and gestures. There were discrepancies in the spelling of Andrew's mother's name, between the medical record made by the hospital staff, the hospital admission certificate (unknown who filled this out), and the document giving consent for the adoption by an American pastor (written on behalf of Andrew's mother by a friend of accompanying her at the time). None of these records carried Andrew's mother's nationality. The hospital staff, as well as the pastor who later adopted Andrew, had the impression that his mother was from the Philippines. The doctor who attended to Andrew's birth submitted a birth registration form to the relevant municipality with no nationality indicated for Andrew and the mother. The city office in consultation with the local legal affairs bureau registered Andrew, stating that both Andrew and his mother were Filipino nationals. This initial nationality determination was based on the above accounts of the hospital staff and the pastor. However, when the pastor and his wife later approached the Filipino embassy for the issuance of a passport to Andrew, the embassy rejected the request, stating that as long as the mother's Filipino nationality cannot be proven, the child's Philippine nationality cannot be recognized.[82] Andrew was then reregistered under the alien registration database to be 'stateless'.

Thus, despite these facts, Andrew's automatic acquisition of Japanese nationality under article 2(iii) was apparently not recognized by the Ministry of Justice. Asserting the fact that Andrew was born in Japan to 'unknown' parents, the case was

---

[81] This section is the summary of accepted facts by the Supreme Court and Tōkyō High Court, as indicated in the respective decisions, unless otherwise indicated. *Minshū* Vol 49, No 1, p 56 [27 January 1995 (*Heisei 7 nen*)] (Supreme Court); *Baby Andrew Case, Minshū* Vol 49, No 1, p 193 [26 January 1994 (*Heisei 6 nen*)] (Tōkyō High Court). See also *Minshū* Vol 49, No 1, p 182, 190 [26 February 1993 (*Heisei 5 nen*)] (Tōkyō District Court).

[82] This sentence carries the fact as claimed by Andrew's advocates. This response from the Filipino embassy was not explicitly included in the accepted facts but was obviously not disputed and is thus included. *Minshū* Vol 49, No 1, pp 182, 190 [26 February 1993 (*Heisei 5 nen*)] (Tōkyō District Court), 188.

taken to court to confirm his Japanese nationality. In its effort to defend its rejection of Andrew's Japanese nationality, the Ministry of Justice produced evidence relating to an individual with a very similar name and date of birth ('Rosete, Cecilia, M' (hereinafter Rosete)) who it considered to be Andrew's mother. This included the immigration entry record into Japan of an individual identifying herself as a Philippine national, the record of issuance of a Filipino passport to an individual provided by the Philippines' authorities, and the birth certificate registered in the Philippines based on which this passport was issued. However, there were discrepancies between the records produced by the Ministry of Justice relating to Rosete and the records relating to Andrew's mother mentioned above, including the divergent spelling of the first and middle names, as well as a five-year-difference of the years of birth, and the absence of a year of birth in the Filipino authority's passport issuance record.[83]

*The distribution of burden of persuasion affecting the three courts' decisions*

The District Court concluded that the evidence submitted by the Ministry of Justice was not sufficient to conclude that Ms X and Andrew's mother were the same person. The court then confirmed that Andrew had acquired Japanese nationality upon birth, basically stating that the evidence offered by the Ministry was not sufficient to prove that the mother was 'known', thereby de facto placing the burden of persuasion on the Ministry to prove that the mother was known. The appellate Tōkyō High Court reversed the judgement and denied Andrew's possession of Japanese nationality, largely because the court interpreted the 'unknown parentage' requirement narrowly and placed on Andrew a heavy burden of proving that both 'parents are unknown'.[84] Unlike the District Court, the High Court determined that, based on the evidence provided by the Ministry of Justice, there is a high probability Ms X from the Philippines was Andrew's mother, and, therefore, the fact that Andrew's parents are 'unknown' has not been proven.

On appeal, the Supreme Court confirmed Andrew's Japanese nationality, largely following the reasoning of the District Court, with slight modifications. In short, the Supreme Court recognized Andrew's Japanese nationality by (1) broadly defining the requirement that 'both parents are unknown' and (2) de facto shifting the burden to prove that the parents are 'known' to the Ministry, in their efforts to achieve the object and purpose of article 2(iii), that is prevention of statelessness. Below, I will

---

[83] Apart from numerous articles to be cited below, some analysis in English have been published on this case. Yasuhiro Okuda, 'The United Nations Convention on the Rights of the Child and Japan's international family law including nationality law' (2003) Zeitschrift für Japanisches Recht [Journal of Japanese Law] 92. See also Stacey Steele, 'Comments on OKUDA, statelessness and Nationality Act of Japan: Baby Andrew becomes a teenager and other changes?' (2004) Zeitschrift für Japanisches Recht [Journal of Japanese Law] 18.

[84] *Baby Andrew Case, Minshū* Vol 49, No 1, p 193 [26 January 1994 (*Heisei 6 nen*)] (Tōkyō High Court).

translate[85] and comment on the relevant part of the decision to show how exactly this was done.

*Broad interpretation or 'lowered extent' of the 'unknown parentage' requirement.*

First, the Supreme Court provided a broad interpretation of unknown parentage as follows:

> [...] 'when both father and mother are unknown' in Article 2(iii) means when both father and mother are *not definitively identified* [*tokutei-sarenai*].[86] This requirement should be considered to be satisfied where *it* [the evidence available] *is not sufficient to definitively identify the father or mother in spite of a high possibility* [*kanōsei ga taka(ku)*] *that a certain individual is the child's father or mother.* This is because, even if there is a high possibility that a person is the child's father or mother, the nationality of the child cannot be determined on the basis of such a person's nationality, and it is not until that person is *definitively identified* that the *child's nationality can be determined* on the basis of her or his nationality. (emphasis added)

The fact that the concept of 'parents are unknown' was broadly interpreted to mean that parents are unknown from a reasonable person's point of view (rather than that parents are 'unknown' in abstract terms, which is very difficult to prove) covering the situation where a specific person has been identified as highly likely (but not definitively) to be an individual's parent had an important logical consequence on the burden of proof. That is, once the individual concerned establishes facts suggesting that both their mother and father are 'unknown' as defined above, the State becomes unable to rebut the court's finding unless they definitively identify a parent.[87] This will now be explained in more detail.

---

[85] The author newly translated the relevant parts of the Supreme Court decision on the Baby Andrew Case for the purpose of this book. It was decided not to adopt the translation of the decision included in the (1997) *Japanese Annual of International Law* (JAIL) 129, cited for example by Stacey Steele, 'Comments on OKUDA, statelessness and Nationality Act of Japan: Baby Andrew becomes a teenager and other changes?' (2004) Zeitschrift für Japanisches Recht [Journal of Japanese Law] 187–9. This is because there was some room for improvement in the translation, including that it is not a word-for-word translation where the details that have been missed are crucial in understanding the significance of the judgement, and that its translation of *tokutei sareru*, which is one of the most important phrases in the judgement, is rather inconsistent (see fn 86 of this chapter on the translation of *tokutei sareru*).

[86] The original Japanese words *tokutei sareru* in isolation or on their own would in most cases be simply translated as 'identified', but in order to properly reflect the intended meaning, it was translated as 'definitively identified'. When there is 'high possibility' (*kanōsei ga takai*) that somebody is one of the parents of the child concerned in the Supreme Court's view is 'insufficient' to say that the parents are known. Thus, *tokutei sareru* in the context of this judgement meant being identified at a higher certainty level than being identified at a high possibility. This is the reason *tokutei sareru* is translated as 'definitively identified'. *Minshū* Vol 49, No 1, p 56 [27 January 1995 (*Heisei 7 nen*)] (Supreme Court).

[87] *Parents' 'unknown-ness' as 'kihanteki yōken' in Japanese law:* The commentary on the judgement by Mariko Watahiki, a Supreme Court secretariat officer at the time, essentially supports this analysis. While she does not express it as a 'broad interpretation' of a legal requirement, she frames it as the court construing the term 'parents are unknown' as a *'kihanteki yōken'* (or *'hyōkateki yōken'*), which can be translated as a 'legal requirement that entails legal assessment'. Mariko

*De facto reversed burden of persuasion*

The typical approach in Japanese civil or administrative litigation and procedures is that the person who is asserting a specific right generally has the burden of proof with respect to the legal requirement that needs to be fulfilled in order for the right to be accrued, in accordance with the general principle in civil litigation common throughout the world.[88]

The burden of persuasion was the key issue that the Supreme Court had to decide upon, because it was on this point that the two lower courts as well as the two opposing parties disagreed most significantly. Andrew's legal representatives had been arguing throughout that proving that something is 'unknown' is extremely difficult and thus the burden of proving whether Andrew's parents are 'unknown' was on the Ministry of Justice and, unless the State proves that either Andrew's 'mother or father is known', Andrew's Japanese nationality should be confirmed.[89]

Further, Andrew's attorneys is said to have argued that, in addition to the difficulties in establishing the requirement that 'both parents are unknown', there was an issue of uneven access to evidence, that is that the State was the party in the best position to make inquiries and gather evidence as to the parents' identity as they had financial and administrative resources.[90]

The State had argued that the burden of proof in relation to the fact that Andrew's parents are unknown lay with Andrew himself. The State asserted that they should thus only be required to 'rebut' (*hanshō*) the evidence produced by Andrew that his

---

Watahiki, 'Tokino hanrei' ['Caselaw in the limelight'] (1–15 May 1995) Juristo 225. *Kihanteki yōken* is Japanese civil litigation law's technical terminology meaning that unlike normal legal requirements that are factual and can be directly proven by evidence, this legal requirement requires legal assessment for which only the 'base facts' need to be proven. See for example, Wataru Murata, 'Dai rokkō: Kihanteki yōken' ['Lesson 6: Legal Requirements That Entail Legal Assessments'] in Wataru Murata and Yamanome Akio (eds), *Yōken jijitsuron sanjukkō* [*30 Lessons on the Theory of Proof in relation to Application of Law to Required Facts*] (3rd edn, Kōbundō 2012 [*Heisei* 24]) 88–91 (the author wishes to thank Shigeo Miyagawa for his translation assistance); Shigeo Itō (ed), *Yōkenjijitsu shōjiten* [*Concise Dictionary of Proof in relation to Application of Law to Required Facts*] (Seirin Shoin 2011) 41, 205, 208. The analysis by Watahiki that unknown parentage is a *'kihanteki yōken'* is significant in a sense that it impacts on the consideration of what facts need to be directly proven by evidence, based on which a legal assessment of whether the requirement of 'unknown-ness' can be conducted. On a separate note, it would be interesting to consider whether 'statelessness' can be also considered as *'kihanteki yōken'*, which would have a significant impact on the statelessness assessment in the context of Japanese law. However, as it is not directly relevant to this book and too specific to the Japanese jurisdiction, the author wishes to save the analysis for another opportunity.

[88] For example, Toshihiko Tsuruoka, 'Gyōsei soshō ni okeru shōmei sekinin' ['Burden of Proof in Administrative Litigations'] in Hiromasa Minami and others (eds), *Jōkai gyōsei jiken soshōhō* [*Article-by-Article Commentary on Administrative Case Litigation Act*] (4th edn, Kōbundō 2014).

[89] Tōkyō High Court, 26 January 1994 (*Heisei 6 nen*), *Minshū* Vol 49, No.1, pp 193, 196.

[90] Yoshirō Hayata, 'Kokusekihō nijō sangō no "Fubo ga tomo ni shirenai toki" no igi' ['The meaning of "when both parents are unknown" under article 2(iii) of Nationality Act'] (1995) 1068 Juristo 269.

parents are unknown rather than to fully prove (*honshō*) the opposite fact that 'either (Andrew's) father or mother is known'.[91]

After considering these arguments, the Supreme Court held:

> [...] It is reasonable to understand that the burden of proof in relation to the fact that both 'parents are unknown' under article 2(iii) *lies with the claimant*. However, *when the claimant proves that s/he is in a situation based on which it can be considered from a reasonable person's viewpoint (shakai-tsūnen jō) that her/his father and mother cannot be definitively identified*, considering the various circumstances regarding the father and mother including the situation at the time of birth,[92] it should be understood that *it can be provisionally (ichiō) determined [nintei]*[93] *that s/he has satisfied the requirement that her/his parents are unknown*. (emphasis added)

The Supreme Court first followed the traditional approach in administrative litigation by affirming that the burden of proving the unknown parentage lay with Andrew who was claiming to possess Japanese nationality on the basis of article 2(iii). However, in order to prevent the negative consequence of this traditional approach, that is that Andrew would remain stateless, the court de facto reversed the burden of proof by imposing a heavy responsibility on the Ministry to rebut the evidence that the parents are unknown, which was only possible by definitively proving that 'parents are known'. This was the reflection of the broad definition adopted by the court in relation to 'unknown parentage'.[94]

---

[91] *Minshū* Vol 49, No 1, p 56 [27 January 1995 (*Heisei 7 nen*)] (Supreme Court).

[92] This is the wording based on which Mariko Watahiki considers that the court construed the 'unknown-ness' of parents as a *'kihanteki yōken'*, that is a legal requirement that entails legal assessment, as explained in fn 87 of this chapter on *Parents' 'unknown-ness' as 'kihanteki yōken' in Japanese law*. Mariko Watahiki, 'Tokino hanrei' ['Caselaw in the limelight'] (1–15 May 1995) Juristo 225.

[93] The *Japanese Annual of International Law* translates the judgement's wording *ichiō no nintei* using legal terminology such as 'prima facie determined' and 'presumption'. However, such translation has a legal implication and is incorrect in the author's view. De facto presumption of facts (*jijitsujō no suitei*) is a legal technique that is utilized to lower the standard of proof and lighten the burden of persuasion of the claimant, when the facts that the claimant is supposed to prove is very difficult to prove. It is not apparent from the Japanese original that the court resorted to this de facto presumption of facts, which the respondent or the State was supposed to rebut. The Supreme Court did not mention anything about the difficulties in proving the unknown-ness of the parents. As explained by Watahiki, a Supreme Court officer in her commentary to the decision, the Supreme Court rather appears to have construed the term both 'parents are unknown' under article 2(iii) of Nationality Act as a legal requirement that entails legal assessment (*kihanteki yōken*), which can be considered fulfilled when the base facts—indicating that the definitive identification of the parents' identity is difficult—are established. See above fn 87 of this chapter on *Parents' 'unknown-ness' as 'kihanteki yōken' in Japanese law*. Ibid.

[94] Yoshirō Hayata, 'Kokusekihō nijō sangō no "Fubo ga tomo ni shirenai toki" no igi' ['The meaning of "when both parents are unknown" under article 2(iii) of Nationality Act'] (1995) 1068 Juristo 269. Yoshirō Hayata notes that there is room for the argument that an administrative litigation case seeking to confirm nationality does not fall within the usual parameters of a civil case and thus the civil law burden of proof should not be applied. He notes that proving that 'both parents are unknown' is an extremely difficult thing to do. Further, the party in the 'best position' to 'collect evidence and make inquiries' in such cases, is the State. Indeed, in recent years, the academic discourse has developed further in relation to how the burden of persuasion should be distributed

As stated above, legal requirements under article 2 (iii) should be considered satisfied *where there is a high possibility that* a certain individual is the child's father or mother [*chichi matawa haha de aru kanōsei wa takai*], *which is nevertheless not sufficiently high to definitively identify* the father or mother [*nao kore wo tokutei suruniwa itaranai*]. From this it follows that *the above* provisional *determination cannot be considered to have been refuted even if the Party disputing the child's acquisition of a Japanese nationality by rebuttal proves* [*hanshō ni yotte risshō*] *the existence of circumstances indicating the high possibility that a specific person is the claimant's father or mother*, as long as it [the evidence, author] is *not sufficient to definitively identify* [*tokuteisuruni itaranai*] that the person is indeed the father or the mother of the claimant. (emphasis added. The original Japanese text carries an emphasis in a form of an underline, under different sentences.)

The court thus de facto[95] imposed the burden of persuasion on the State to prove that the claimant's father or mother has been 'definitively identified', in order to rebut the provisional determination that Andrew has satisfied the 'unknown parentage' requirement. This means, if the State cannot prove that the father or mother has been definitively identified, the claimant's possession of Japanese nationality will be conclusively confirmed. It appears that, by making it difficult for the State to rebut the claimant's rather fragile proof that his 'parents are unknown', the Supreme Court aimed to rescue the claimant in light of the object and purpose of article 2(iii).

The court explains its rationale of de facto shifting the burden of persuasion to the State as follows:

The Nationality Act... provides that a child who was born in Japan shall be a Japanese national when both father and mother are unknown or have no nationality (Article 2(iii)). If

---

taking into consideration a variety of factors, including the aim of achieving equality between the parties, the nature of the case in question, and the difficulty of proving the necessary requirements. Juliane Kokott, *The Burden of Proof in Comparative and International Human Rights Law: Civil and Common Law Approaches with Special Reference to the American and German Legal Systems* (Kluwer Law International 1998) at 12 also summarizes the situation in Germany where the principle of distribution of burden of proof in civil litigation may not apply in constitutional or human rights law.

[95] Read with an understanding of Japanese civil litigation law theory and practice, the judgement demonstrates that there is no formal reversal of burden of persuasion, as described by some authors such as Stacey Steele, 'Comments on OKUDA, statelessness and Nationality Act of Japan: Baby Andrew becomes a teenager and other changes?' (2004) Zeitschrift für Japanisches Recht [Journal of Japanese Law] 18. The respondent or the State is not formally imposed the burden to provide a full proof (*honshō*) of the opposite fact that Andrew's father or mother is 'known'. This is because the court clearly recognizes that the burden of proof in relation to the fact that Andrew's parents are unknown lies with Andrew himself. In such a case, the State should only be required to 'rebut' (*hanshō*—which is indeed mentioned in the above judgement) to have judges lose confidence about his prior provisional determination that Andrew's parents being unknown, by producing counterevidence, in order for the Court to deny Andrew's Japanese nationality. However, because the court had skilfully defined 'unknown parentage' very broadly—to mean all situations where both parents cannot be 'definitively identified' (even if there is evidence of an individual being 'highly likely' to be father or mother), it became essentially impossible for the State to 'rebut', unless they manage to fully convince the judges that Andrew's parents are definitively identified—which is actually the fact opposite to the fact asserted by Andrew. Thus, it can be said that the Supreme Court de facto (and not formally) reversed the burden of persuasion. This is the very point criticized by Okuda and other nationality law scholars, asserting that the court should have simply assigned the full burden of persuasion on the respondent or the State.

the principle that the nationality of a child shall depend on the parents' nationality is to be maintained, a child whose father and mother are unknown will be stateless. Therefore, in order to prevent the occurrence of stateless persons as much as possible, the Act is intended to recognize the acquisition of Japanese nationality by a child born in Japan in such a situation.

The judges thus emphasized the purpose of the legislation, pointing out that article 2(iii) had been included in the Nationality Act to avoid the instances of stateless children that arose out of Japan's *jus sanguinis* system. The Supreme Court obviously recognized that the child's right to a nationality was of paramount importance.

Academics, including Okuda and Hayata,[96] renowned scholars of nationality law, while largely commending the Supreme Court's de facto reversal of the burden of persuasion enabling the confirmation of Andrew's Japanese nationality, argued that the Supreme Court could have gone further to explicitly place the entire burden of persuasion on the State. Okuda argued that once the claimant asserts that her or his parents are unknown and produces evidence just sufficient for the court to recognize the need to examine the matter (which apparently refers to the applicant's fulfilment of the burden of production), the full burden of persuasion should be placed on the respondent (State) to prove that the claimant's parent is known, failure of which will lead to the court affirming the claimant's acquisition of Japanese nationality at birth.[97]

*Was the standard of proof 'lowered'?*

Having said this, to the eyes of the readers from jurisdictions where the standard of proof can be set flexibly reflecting the nature of the case, what does the Supreme Court's argument cited earlier—especially the assertion that 'one is of unknown parents until a parent is "definitively identified"'—indicate? The first look at the above excerpts would give such readers an impression that the court set a low standard of proof for Andrew (who was unable to provide sufficient proof that both of his parents are 'unknown'), in its efforts to prevent statelessness. The court considers that parents need to be 'definitively identified' to the extent that the child's nationality can be determined based on the identified parent's nationality. If converted into the language of standard of proof, this wording 'definitively identify' may suggest that the judge's level of conviction needs to be something like the level of 'beyond a reasonable doubt'.

---

[96] Yoshirō Hayata, 'Kokusekihō nijō sangō no "Fubo ga tomo ni shirenai toki" no igi' ['The meaning of "when both parents are unknown" under article 2(iii) of Nationality Act'] (1995) 1068 Juristo 269. Yoshirō Hiroshi Sano, in his commentary on the District Court decision on Baby Andrew had already pointed this possibility out. Hiroshi Sano, 'Kakyūshin toki no hanrei' ['Decisions of lower courts in the limelight'] (1993) Juristo 126.

[97] For Okuda's detailed commentary on the discussion over the burden of proof in relation to article 2(iii), see Yasuhiro Okuda, 'Saikōsai hanrei hihyō' ['Critique on Supreme Court case law'] (1995) Hanrei Jihō 174; Yasuhiro Okuda, 'Nihon de umareta fubo fumei no ko no kokuseki' ['The nationality of children born in Japan of unknown parents'] (1995) 133 Bessatsu Juristo 246–7. Yasuhiro Okuda, *Kosekihō to kokusai oyakohō* [*Nationality Act and International Family Law*] (Yūhikaku 2004) 128–32; Yasuhiro Okuda, *Kazoku to kokuseki* [*Family and Nationality*] (Akashi Shoten 2017) 169–91.

On close inspection, one realizes that the court did not specifically refer to an applicable 'standard of proof' anywhere within the decision. This normally means the court adopted the same standard of proof as other civil or administrative litigation (requiring the proof of 'high probability' of the existence of a fact) for all the relevant facts.

Nonetheless, in practice, the court's adoption of the 'broad interpretation' of the unknown parentage requirement had the same effect as adopting a lower standard of proof in proving the same requirement. Further, de facto requiring the State to prove 'one of the parent is known', which was very narrowly construed, mirroring the broad definition of 'both parents are unknown', had the same result as requiring a high standard of proof to be satisfied by the State for the court to be convinced that one of the parent is known.

*Low standard of proof (and reversed burden of persuasion) can be substituted by a broad interpretation of the 'unknown parents' definition*[98]

Needless to say, the issue of how to interpret the definition of 'unknown-ness' of parents is a substantive issue, and where to set the standard of proof is primarily a procedural issue. However, there is a fine line between whether a certain matter is an issue of the standard of proof that needs to be satisfied to prove the fulfilment of a legal requirement, or an issue of the interpretation (or the substantial content) of the same legal requirement. The distinction between the two ultimately is a matter of expression and is of a technical nature rather than a substantive one. As demonstrated above, interpreting the legal requirement of 'unknown parentage' 'widely' had the same effect as 'lowering' the standard of proof to prove the fulfilment of such requirement (and/or to reverse the burden of persuasion), meeting the object and purpose of the Japanese foundling provision to prevent statelessness.

Thus, the guidance above from Japanese caselaw can be useful not only for fellow continental law jurisdictions, but also for common law States. It is useful for countries where the standard of proof is generally high and inflexible, as those legally representing foundlings can—instead of promoting the lowering of the 'standard of proof' for establishing the parents' 'unknown-ness'—promote the widening of the definition or the interpretation of 'unknown-ness' which could have more success prospect.

---

[98] This analysis was drawn from the author's discussions over years with several Japanese attorneys, in particular Hiroshi Miyauchi, as well as Allan Mackey, former President of International Association of Refugee and Migration Judges (IARMJ) primarily in the context of refugee law, specifically RSD—relating to how the nature of the term 'well-founded fear of being persecuted' in article 1A (2) of the 1951 Convention is best described in the Japanese context. The conclusion of our discussions was that expressing the term 'well-foundedness of fear' (which is a *'kihanteki yōken'* or a 'legal requirement that entails legal assessment as described in fn 87 of this chapter) as a 'standard of proof'—as has traditionally and generically been done by UNHCR—was technically inacurate and confusing in the Japanese legal context. Instead it can be more accurately described as the 'threshold of well-foundedness of the fear' or the degree of the future risk of persecution for the fear to be considered 'well-founded', as a matter of interpretation, of the content of the 'well-founded fear' legal requirement. The author takes this opportunity to thank them.

As a reflection of the wide definition or interpretation of the 'unknown-ness' of the parentage, advocates can also promote the principle that if the decision-maker cannot prove the 'known-ness' of parents—which is interpreted narrowly—she or he should be recognized as a foundling. Countries that already adopt the lower standard of proof for substantiating 'unknown-ness' can adopt the principle that if the decision-maker cannot prove an individual's 'parents' known-ness' at a high standard of proof, she or he should be recognized to be of unknown parents.

### 5.6.3.3   Subsequent Family Court Adjudications: Even Broader Interpretation of 'parents are unknown'?

The Baby Andrew Case was expected to influence administrative practice to ensure the implementation of article 2(iii) to confirm the acquisition of Japanese nationality by children whose parents are unknown. Indeed, the Ministry of Justice has explicitly confirmed in a Parliamentary session that the administrative authorities in charge of the maintenance of family registry are carrying out their work in accordance with the guidelines laid out in the Baby Andrew Case.[99] The current implementation of article 2(iii) has been studied, including by Yasuhiro Okuda, but is largely unclear.[100] No statistics are available of persons who acquire Japanese nationality under article 2(iii).[101]

Since the Supreme Court judgement on Baby Andrew, there has been at least one known High Court decision (which does not significantly go beyond the case law

---

[99] Response by Itsurō Terada, the then Director General of the Civil Affairs Bureau to the question by Nobuo Matsuno, Parliamentarian of Democratic Party. *Dai 162 kai kokkai shūgiin hōmuiinkai gijiroku dai 24 gō [Legal Affairs Committee of the House of Representatives, Official Record of the Proceedings of the 162nd Session of the Diet]* (15 June 2005 [*Heisei 17 nen*]) (author translation).

[100] Yasuhiro Okuda previously conducted a series of research on the nationality of children under institutional care around Japan. He has reported that there might be some children hosted in child foster homes around Japan who likely possess Japanese nationality based on article 2(iii) following the guidance from the Baby Andrew Case, but who are registered as foreigners or stateless. See Yasuhiro Okuda, *Sūji de miru kodomo no kokuseki to zairyū shikaku [Nationality and Visa of Children: Statistical Analysis]* (Akashi Shoten 2002). See also Yasuhiro Okuda, *Kazoku to kokuseki [Family and Nationality]* (Akashi Shoten 2017), pp 191–6; chapter 4 part II of Yasuhiro Okuda and others, *Yōshi engumi assen—Rippō shian no kaisetsu to shiryō [Proposal for Adoption Service Law, Comments and Materials]* (Nihon kajo shuppan 2012). It is reported that depending on the facility, if some sort of information is available on one of the parents, the child is considered '*okizari-ji*' (a child left behind), not necessarily a person of unknown parents, which is not a legal concept with any implication towards Japanese nationality. The Japanese Statelessness Study Group (Mukokuseki kenkyūkai) members' hearing with Shinagawa Child Protection Centre on 12 August 2014. Sari K. Ishii also echoes similar findings. Sari K. Ishii, 'Access to citizenship for abandoned children: how migrants' children become "stateless" in Japanese orphanages' (2020) Journal of Ethnic and Migration Studies 1. Also see Kayoko Ishii and Fumie Azukizawa, *Gaikoku ni tsunagaru kodomo to mukokuseki—jidōyōgoshisetsu eno chōsa kekka to gutaiteki taiō rei [children with links with foreign countries and statelessness—the results of the survey with child foster care facilities and examples of actual responses]* (Akashi Shoten 2019).

[101] Kōki Abe, 'Overview of Statelessness: International and Japanese Context' (April 2010) 37 <https://www.refworld.org/docid/4c344c252.html> accessed 4 May 2019.

prior to Baby Andrew)[102] and an unknown number of positive family court adjudications in relation to persons of unknown parents under article 2(iii). Available ones have already been summarized in Sect. 4.3.11. While only some of the family court adjudications are currently accessible, they generally seem to reflect the guidance laid out in the Baby Andrew case, and even develop it further.

Among them, the Yokohama Family Court's adjudication, which is publicly available, offers some hints on the issue of the extent *of* 'unknown-ness' of parentage, and so is reintroduced, with more detailed facts and reasoning than in Sect. 4.3.11.

*Yokohama Family Court's Adjudication in 2003*[103]

As also discussed in Sect. 4.3.11, in this case, a woman calling herself Viviana Cantoria,[104] considered to have been in possession of a Filipino passport, gave birth to Z on 29 March 1994, while married to Y, a Japanese national. Z was registered in Y's Japanese family registry upon birth as a child between Viviana and Y. Viviana and Y divorced on 4 October 1995. Y gained a court ruling on 1 November 1995 confirming that Z was not actually his biological child. Based on this ruling, Y filed a request to have Z deleted from his family registry on 9 January 1996, and Z was deleted on 13 January 1996. This meant Z's Japanese nationality, which Z was once considered to have acquired by *jus sanguinis* from Y, was nullified. Z thus 'lost' his Japanese nationality.[105] Viviana left Japan on 15 November 1995, that is when Z was about one year and eight months old, and her subsequent whereabouts are unknown.

---

[102] The Tōkyō High Court decision on 12 May 1999 basically confirmed the Japanese nationality of a person born in Japan on 1 May 1950 under article 2(iii) of the Nationality Act where the person was informally adopted when he or she was a suckling baby by a Chinese woman without following the necessary procedure to formalize the adoption under the Japanese law. The biological mother and father could not be identified. The court's judgement that the person concerned was of unknown parentage basically follows the previous family court/High Court decisions in 1979 and 1983 (introduced in Sect. 4.3) relating to informally adopted children, but one of the major differences was that the alleged biological mother's name 'sounded' Chinese rather than Japanese. Note that the Tōkyō High Court only discussed the nationality issue as a sub-issue where the main issue was the mother–child relationship and right to inheritance. *Judgement, Hanrei Jihō No 1680*, p 86 [12 May 1999 (*Heisei 11 nen*)] (Tōkyō High Court) 86, cited on p 159 by Yue Fū, 'Nihon de umareta kodomono kokuseki to mukokuseki nintei' ['Determination of Statelessness for Children Born in Japan'] (PhD dissertation, University of Tsukuba 2016).

[103] *Decision, Kagetsu* Vol 56, No 3, p 68 (Yokohama Family Court).

[104] Pseudonym assigned by the Family Court.

[105] This is what is referred to by Gerard-René de Groot as 'quasi-loss' of nationality to which, he argues, the rules that protect persons against statelessness and those prohibiting arbitrary deprivation of nationality, among others, should be applicable. Based on the guidance by de Groot and Patrick Wautelet, it can be said that the loss of Z's Japanese nationality should not have occurred without first confirming that the loss would not lead to statelessness. See on 'quasi loss' and applicable international standards generally, Gerard-René de Groot and Patrick Wautelet, 'Reflections on quasi-loss of nationality from comparative, international and European perspectives' in Sergio Carrera Nuñez and Gerard-René de Groot (eds), *European Citizenship at the Crossroads: The Role of the European Union on Loss and Acquisition of Nationality* (Wolf Legal Publishers 2015) 117. See also Sect. 7.6.1.7.

Viviana had previously confessed to her attorney in Japan that her passport under the name of Viviana Cantoria—based on which it is assumed her foreigner registration was completed (which, however, could not be located at the relevant city office—details not included in the adjudication)—was fraudulent. Her real name and possession of Filipino nationality including whether she was in possession of a genuine Filipino passport thus could not be confirmed. Under these circumstances, it was practically impossible for Z to have his birth registered with the Filipino authorities to confirm his acquisition of Filipino nationality *jus sanguinis* from his mother. The request to create a Japanese family registry, which would in turn confirm Z's acquisition of Japanese nationality, was therefore filed.

Based on the facts found as above, the Yokohama Family Court stated:

> [...] for the claimant to acquire Filipino nationality, the woman named Viviana Cantoria needs to actually exist and her Filipino nationality has to be confirmed. The Filipino embassy in Japan *cannot have Z acquire* [sic] Filipino nationality unless there is Viviana Cantoria's passport or birth certificate. [...].[106]

The court stated in conclusion:

> From the above facts, it can be recognized that the claimant's biological mother is a woman calling herself as Viviana Cantoria, however, it cannot be confirmed that she was a national of the Philippines and that she held a genuine passport, and there are even circumstances that cast doubt on the genuineness of the passport, and thus it cannot be confirmed that she is a Filipino national. Further, from the background facts, there is a strong supposition that the claimant's biological father was a Japanese national[107] [with whom Viviana was in a relationship with at the time of conceiving the claimant], however this too could not be confirmed. Further, with regard to Z, as it cannot be confirmed that his real mother is a Filipino national, he *cannot acquire* Filipino nationality. As a result, Z does not have *any other ways to survive* than to live in Japan. Taking all the above facts together, the claimant was born in Japan and can be considered to fulfil 'when parents are unknown' under article 2(iii) of the Nationality Act and it is appropriate to, as in the main text of the decision, authorize his registration under the Japanese family register. [...]. (emphasis added)[108]

Z's Japanese family register was thus created based on article 2(iii) of the Nationality Act and his Japanese nationality was confirmed.

While the issue of the burden of persuasion was not discussed at all in this Family Court adjudication, being a non-adversarial proceeding, the required threshold for

---

[106] *Decision, Kagetsu* Vol 56, No 3, p 68 (Yokohama Family Court), p 70.

[107] The then Director of Civil Affairs Bureau indeed indicated his supposition that this element (that the claimant's father was highly likely to be Japanese) worked in favour of the claimant in making the Yokohama Family Court recognize his Japanese nationality. Response by Itsurō Terada, the then Director General of the Civil Affairs Bureau to the question by Nobuo Matsuno, Parliamentarian of Democratic Party. Dai 162 kai kokkai shūgiin hōmuiinkai gijiroku dai 24 gō [Legal Affairs Committee of the House of Representatives, Official Record of the Proceedings of the 162nd Session of the Diet] (15 June 2005 [*Heisei 17 nen*]). However, according to Kensuke Ōnuki, in many out of the ten cases he represented from around 2002–06 who were confirmed Japanese nationals under article 2(iii) of the Nationality Act, there was no indication whatsoever that one or both of the parents were Japanese nationals. Interview with Kensuke Ōnuki, Attorney at Law (Tokyo, Japan, 4 March 2017).

[108] *Decision, Kagetsu* Vol 56, No 3, p 68 (Yokohama Family Court), p 71.

the parent's 'known-ness' thus appears to have been set even higher than in the Baby Andrew Case.

To further analyze the difference between the Supreme Court's wording in the Baby Andrew Case and that of the Family Court in the Viviana Cantoria Case, in the former, the Supreme Court stated that a parent needs to be definitively identified 'to the extent that the *child's nationality can be determined*'.[109] This can be interpreted that the child's (non-)acquisition on the basis of the identified parent's nationality needs to be determined by the decision-maker (in this case, the Supreme Court). However, the wording in the Viviana Cantoria Case appears to focus more on the view of the authorities of the claimed country of nationality of the identified parent, by requiring that the identification of the parent would enable the person to 'acquire' (probably this meant 'have confirmation of acquiring')[110] such parent's nationality. Yue Fū sees in the Yokohama Family Court's interpretation and application of 'unknown parents' under article 2(iii) of the Japanese Nationality Act an 'intention to prevent statelessness in Japan, taking a step forward from the abovementioned Supreme Court judgement [in the Baby Andrew Case]'.[111] The Yokohama Family Court indeed appears to have taken a pragmatic approach in its effort to achieve the object and purpose of article 2(iii).[112]

---

[109] Baby Andrew Case. *Minshū* Vol 49, No 1, p 56 [27 January 1995 (*Heisei 7 nen*)] (Supreme Court). It is interesting to note that even in the Baby Andrew Case, the original Tōkyō District Court judgement had stated that for the government to prove that father or mother is 'known', it has to identify either the father or mother to the extent that it enables the child to acquire the nationality of the known parent, but the Supreme Court subsequently toned it down and adopted this wording cited herein. *Minshū* Vol 49, No 1, p 182, 190 [26 February 1993 (*Heisei 5 nen*)] (Tōkyō District Court), p 190.

[110] As a side note, to be more precise, as Filipino nationality law provides for automatic acquisition of nationality upon birth *jus sanguinis* from a parent, legally the family court should have—instead of saying 'cannot have Z acquire nationality' and 'acquire Filipino nationality'—said 'confirm Z's acquisition of nationality' and 'have his Filipino nationality acquisition confirmed' in the paragraph quoted above. This is also pointed out by Yasuhiro Okuda, *Kosekihō to kokusai oyakohō* [*Nationality Act and International Family Law*] (Yūhikaku 2004) 139–40.

[111] Yue Fū, 'Nihon de umareta kodomono kokuseki to mukokuseki nintei' ['Determination of Statelessness for Children Born in Japan'] (PhD dissertation, University of Tsukuba 2016) 163.

[112] However, Yasuhiro Okuda casts doubts on this family court adjudication stating he tends to think the application of article 2(iii) should have been denied in this case. Okuda argues, among others, that the claimant should have *ex lege* acquired nationality under the Filipino nationality law by *jus sanguinis*, and 'while the adjudication puts weight on the confirmation [of the claimant's nationality acquisition by *jus sanguinis*] by the Filipino embassy, it should be understood that our country [Japan] is not bound by the nationality determination of such foreign authorities, and is able to make its own nationality determination while still based on Filipino law'. Yasuhiro Okuda, *Kosekihō to kokusai oyakohō* [*Nationality Act and International Family Law*] (Yūhikaku 2004) 138–41. However, as discussed in Sect. 2.5, the position of the competent authorities of the country of purported nationality is crucial in determining whether the person is a national or stateless as per para 37 of the UNHCR Handbook (2014). As such competent authorities would base their assessment of nationality acquisition by a purported child of a national based on their determination of whether the legal parentage has been established between the two. Yokohama Family Court's approach to put emphasis on the fact that the Filipino authorities is quite pragmatic and is in line with the object and purpose of article 2(iii), which is to prevent statelessness of a child. The consequences

**Other Family Court Adjudications After Baby Andrew**

As summarized in Sect. 4.3.11, the 2003 Yokohama Family Court decision as well as other unpublished decisions subsequent to the 1995 Baby Andrew Case most typically confirmed the Japanese nationality of persons whose non-Japanese biological mother typically went missing and/or were deported some years after the person's birth (and not some days after birth, as in Andrew's case) sometimes after registering the person's birth under her (fraudulent) name and after caring for the child for a while.[113]

It can be considered that family courts have been de facto taking slight steps forward after the 1995 Baby Andrew Case. In the Baby Andrew Case, the birth mother submitted no official document and she went missing while the claimant was a new-born baby. In the subsequent family court cases, the extent of 'known-ness' of the mother was arguably even higher. The family courts thus applied an even 'wider definition' of unknown-ness of the parents. If read by those from common law jurisdictions, it might appear as if the family courts applied an even 'lower standard of proof' to establish unknown-ness.

While family court adjudications are not binding,[114] these adjudications should be highly commended for taking a pragmatic approach fully reflecting the object and purpose of article 2(iii) to prevent statelessness. This solutions-oriented interpretation of the parents' 'unknown-ness' is believed to have significance to other jurisdictions.

## 5.7  Undetermined Nationality: Cannot Be an Outcome of State's Assessment

What happens when, at the end of the full assessment, the person remains to be of 'undetermined' parentage (that is in a situation of *non-liquet*)? Are they recognized as a person of unknown parents or not?

While not as 'undetermined' parentage, some States indeed classify many people under the category of 'undetermined nationality' or 'unknown nationality' quite often, which does not normally entail any rights under international or national law (see Sect. 2.7.2). It is indeed a technique that gives rise to challenges in addressing statelessness worldwide. One of the examples is the Netherlands, where, in 2019, the Central Statistics Bureau reported 55,621 persons as 'stateless/unknown nationality', which according to other sources would include 12,869 stateless persons and 42,752

---

of non-application of article 2(iii) would have been that the claimant would have remained stateless unless he were allowed to be naturalized after reaching the age of majority, unless the mother were somehow tracked down and his Filipino nationality was confirmed, which the court must assessed was difficult.

[113] *Decision, Kagetsu* Vol 56, No 3, p 68 (Yokohama Family Court). Interview with Kensuke Ōnuki, Attorney at Law (Tokyo, Japan, 4 March 2017).

[114] See fn 48, Chap. 4 of this book entitled 'Nature of Japanese family court adjudications permitting registration into family register'.

persons of 'unknown nationality'.[115] Some among persons who are classified as 'undetermined nationality' in different States could include persons of unknown parents who have not been recognized as such due to the high standard of proof adopted by the registering authorities.

The individuals classified as being of 'undetermined nationality' remain in a legal limbo, where they are most vulnerable in that they cannot enjoy any of the rights that nationals can enjoy, or access the nationality that would otherwise be granted under the 1961 Convention, or the rights that stateless persons can enjoy under the 1954 Convention.[116]

At the end of the day, if the standard or proof has not been met, whether the person has, or does not have, legal parents has to be determined based on who bears the burden of proof. A person is ultimately either a national of a particular country or stateless, as nobody can be 'half-national and half-stateless'.

It would defeat the whole purpose of having a foundling provision if States were allowed to produce the result that those invoking such a provision are of 'undetermined nationality'. Classification as being of 'undetermined nationality' should only be allowed as an interim measure while a full assessment of whether the person meets the requirements under the foundling provision is being carried out, as discussed below in Sect. 5.8.

## 5.8  What is 'a reasonable time' for the Classification 'undetermined nationality', that is for the Assessment of a Foundling Provision Applicability?

How long could a State take in its assessment before confirming a foundling's acquisition of nationality? At the outset, it should be noted that the determination of the applicability of article 2 or the 1961 Convention or equivalent domestic foundling provisions entails different elements—specifically the assessment of whether the person is of 'unknown parentage' (covered in Chaps. 4 and 5), was 'found' in the territory when still a 'child' (Chap. 6), and whether there is 'proof to the contrary' (Chap. 7). The reason why the issue of 'reasonable timeframe' for determining the foundling provision applicability is discussed here in this chapter before Chaps. 6 and 7 is simply for the flow of the discussion. It is specifically because the importance of having a deadline for the assessment process is closely related to the issue

---

[115] ENS, 'Statelessness Index Survey 2019: Netherlands' (2020) 12 < https://index.stateless ness.eu/sites/default/files/ENS_Statelessness_Index_Survey-Netherlands-2019_0.pdf > accessed 15 September 2020. ENS's 'Statelessness Index Survey' series carry examples of other States available at: < https://index.statelessness.eu/ > See also ENS, 'Childhood Statelessness in Europe: Issues, Gaps and Good Practices' (2014) 13–14 <http://www.refworld.org/docid/5343a45f4.html> accessed 4 August 2019.

[116] The exception is that persons seeking the status as a stateless person pending the determination may enjoy some of the rights under the 1954 Convention. UNHCR Handbook (2014), Part Three para 126.

of standard and burden of proof, which this chapter explores the most extensively due to the particular difficulties in proving unknown parentage.

The determination authorities might indeed reach a different conclusion if they are allowed to spend an indefinite period of time to investigate, but they need to make a decision at some point. The duration for determining the applicability of the foundling provision, however, has to be a 'reasonable time' to gather and assess the evidence, during which the persons (supposedly) of unknown parents will have to be classified as being of 'undetermined nationality'.

Most countries do not provide, in legislation, regulations or guidelines, the maximum period for this sort of assessment. The same goes for the procedure to confirm the nationality of children of known parents born in the territory who would otherwise have been stateless (or to grant nationality to children who are stateless) covered under article 1 of the 1961 Convention.

The 1961 Convention, its travaux, guidelines, key materials and the majority of legislation are silent on this issue. Article 10 of the ECN 1997 relevantly states: 'Each State party shall ensure that applications relating to the acquisition, retention, loss, recovery or certification of its nationality be processed within a reasonable time.'

Determining how long is considered 'reasonable time'—during which a classification of undetermined nationality can be justified—is not an easy task.

In terms of the 'statelessness determination procedure' for the purpose of protection, that is by granting statelessness person status to an individual, the UNHCR Handbook (2014) recommends that the first instance decision taken in six months, subject to an exceptional extension of another six months—which is reflected in the current practice of a number of countries that have a statelessness determination procedure.[117]

In contrast, paragraph 22 of the UNHCR Guidelines 4 (2012) recommends, in the context of an examination of 'otherwise statelessness' under articles 1 and 4 of the 1961 Convention, that the classification as being of 'undetermined nationality' while the person is pending examination should not last for more than five years. While very little information is found on how this is indeed implemented by States, Finland seems to endeavour to determine the nationality of children born in the territory within five years.[118] The natural thought process is to consider, by analogy, whether this time-limit of five years should be adopted in assessing the applicability of article 2 of the 1961 Convention or equivalent domestic provisions.

---

[117] UNHCR Handbook (2014) para 75. ENS, 'Childhood Statelessness in Europe: Issues, Gaps and Good Practices' (2014) <http://www.refworld.org/docid/5343a45f4.html> accessed 4 August 2019.

[118] ENS, 'No Child Should be Stateless' (2015) 17 < https://www.statelessness.eu/resources/no-child-should-be-stateless-austria > accessed 4 August 2019. See also UNHCR, 'Mapping Statelessness in Finland' (November 2014) 19 <http://www.refworld.org/docid/546da8744.html> accessed 4 August 2019.

### 5.8.1  Is a 'five years' Standard for 'otherwise statelessness' Period Not Too Long?

Footnote 15 of the UNHCR Guidelines (2012) accompanying paragraph 22 explains, the period of 'five years' for otherwise stateless children born in the territory is a reflection of the maximum period of habitual residence (immediately preceding an application), which may be required under article 1(2)(b) of the 1961 Convention where a State has an application procedure to grant nationality to otherwise stateless children.[119]

However, this maximum period of five years[120] in UNHCR Guidelines 4 (2012) for otherwise stateless children itself already strikes as excessively long as compared with the maximum period of six (or 12) months in the context of statelessness determination procedure.[121]

It would be useful here to consider the differences between the two procedures, that is the 'statelessness determination' and 'otherwise statelessness assessment' for the purpose of nationality confirmation or grant.

First, while the immediate result of the former procedure is the recognition of stateless person status (which may eventually lead to grant of nationality through naturalization), the outcome of the latter procedure is directly a nationality grant. This might be one of the reasons that the latter procedure was considered to require more time for careful examination.

Second, the actions involved in statelessness determination and in the assessment of otherwise statelessness are almost the same, while there are slightly differing aspects. To summarize those 'differences', in the latter assessment, the decision-makers often make the assessment of statelessness in the hypothetical past ('would otherwise be' stateless) rather than the current statelessness, and can be required to assess whether the applicant has always been stateless,[122] and whether she or he is able to acquire the nationality of a parent by registration in the immediate future.[123] This may make the latter assessment a little difficult than the former, in terms of access to evidence, the nature of issues, and simply the number of facts that need to be assessed.

However, even these differences do not quite seem to justify that the otherwise statelessness assessment can take five to ten times more than a stateless person determination procedure.

---

[119] This five-year period of lawful and habitual residence as the maximum required period is also provided for by article 6 para 2 of the ECN.

[120] UNHCR Guidelines 4 (2012) para 22.

[121] UNHCR Handbook (2014) para 9.

[122] Article 1(2) of the 1961 Convention on non-automatic grant of nationality allows States to require that an applicant has 'always been stateless' (that is, since birth). UNHCR Guidelines 4 (2012) para 48 states that where a contracting State requires that an individual has 'always been stateless', the burden rests with the State to prove that the person has not always been stateless.

[123] UNHCR Guidelines 4 (2012) paras 24–26.

Further, as stated earlier, in interpreting the 1961 Convention or other obligations to prevent statelessness among children, the provisions of the CRC should be referred to,[124] including article 7 stating that the 'child [...] shall have the *right from birth to a name, the right to acquire a nationality*[...]' (emphasis added), and article 3 on the best interests of the child as a primary consideration.[125] Other international and regional human rights instruments providing for right to nationality for children and persons in general, introduced in Sect. 2.2, are also relevant.

Indeed, paragraph 40 of the Guidelines (2012) on article 1(2)(b) further states:

> *In light of the standards* established *under the CRC*, these periods are *lengthy*. States which apply an application procedure and require a certain period of habitual residence [to acquire the nationality of country of birth] are *encouraged to provide for a period as short as possible*. (emphasis added)

Further, Principle 8 of Recommendation 2009/13 of the Committee of Ministers of the Council of Europe on the nationality of children recommends States to: '[R]egister children as being of unknown or undetermined nationality, or classify children's nationality as being "under investigation" only for *as short a period as possible*' (emphasis added).[126]

Paragraph 11 of the Explanatory Memorandum on Recommendation 2009/13 first states that statelessness up to the age of five years for children born on the territory of a State (where their parents have lived) should not be allowed, stating that such statelessness is 'particularly striking' because States have the possibility to provide for the loss of their nationality if it is discovered that they have acquired another nationality. Paragraph 11 then states: 'Ideally, the acquisition of nationality should occur *at birth or shortly after birth with retroactivity*' (emphasis added). Paragraph 22 (Unknown or undetermined nationality) the Explanatory Memorandum further states:

> A borderline case of de jure and de facto[127] statelessness exists if authorities register a person as being of unknown or undetermined nationality, or classify the nationality of a person as being 'under investigation'. Such classification is only reasonable as a transitory measure during *a brief period of time*. (emphasis added)

Thus, the Council of Europe recommends that the determination of children's nationality be made as soon as possible, ideally at birth or shortly after birth with retroactivity. Five years is only indicated as the maximum period allowed when such prompt nationality determination cannot be done. States are thus to be encouraged to deliver a decision within a much shorter duration than five years.

---

[124] UNHCR Guidelines 4 (2012) para 10. This is particularly because 192 States—all except one United Nations member States—are party to the CRC and all contracting States to the 1961 Convention are also party to the CRC.

[125] Paras 9 and 10, ibid.

[126] Council of Europe: Committee of Ministers, *Recommendation CM/Rec(2009)13 and explanatory memorandum of the Committee of Ministers to member states on the nationality of children* (Council of Europe Publishing 9 May 2009).

[127] On the problematic nature of the concept of 'de facto statelessness', see Sect. 2.7.1.

## 5.8.2  Applicability of the 'five years' Standard to Assessment Under Article 2, the Foundling Provision

Further, with regard to the assessment under article 2, that is the foundling provision, the standard of 'five years' might be all the more excessive. As discussed in Sect. 3.4, during the travaux process of the (1930 and) 1961 Convention, many States were of the opinion that foundlings under article 2 should be given easier access to nationality than 'otherwise-stateless' children under article 1 due to their lack of caretakers (in addition to the likelihood that foundlings are children of nationals born in the territory). Unlike under article 1 (specifically 1(2)(b) as discussed in the preceding section), the travaux of the 1961 Convention indicates that States should normally be granting nationality at birth *ex lege* under article 2.[128] ECN article 6(1)(b), which derives from article 2 of the 1961 Convention, explicitly provides for *ex lege* acquisition of nationality for foundlings. Thus no minimum habitual residence period should be required under article 2.

Further, a question arises as to what happens if, hypothetically,[129] (1) An otherwise-stateless child of known parents born in the territory, and (2) a child of unknown parents found in the territory (who does not possess a foreign nationality), respectively apply for stateless person status, given that the determination procedure is in place in that country. Following paragraph 75 of the UNHCR Handbook (2014), children under both categories (1) and (2) would normally have to be recognized as stateless persons within six months or the maximum of one year as States are not supposed to leave them 'undetermined nationality', as discussed above. While it would be justifiable for the State that a child under category (1) is left stateless for five years before acquisition of nationality as long as the nationality law of that State contains such a habitual residence requirement based on article 1(2)(b) of the 1961 Convention, in relation to the person under category (2), the fact that she or he is recognized as stateless person as a result of the statelessness determination procedure automatically confirms that she or he is of unknown parents, the very reason she or

---

[128] This can be deduced for example from the Danish representative's statement below and discussion around it, that is '[…] it was surely better that the child should acquire *at birth* the nationality of that country (than that he should have to wait until the age of eighteen)'. This was in the context of the Danish representative's advocacy to separate article 2 from article 1 within the 1961 Convention as, under the ILC Draft of 1954, article 2 was originally dependent on article 1 with the room to provide nationality non-automatically upon application latest at the age of 18, as discussed in Sect. 3.4.5.2. United Nations, Summary Records, 5th Meeting of the Committee of the Whole held on 3 April 1959, A/CONF.9/C.1/SR.5, UN Conference on the Elimination or Reduction of Future Statelessness, Geneva, 1959 and New York, 1961 (3 April 1959) 8 <http://legal.un.org/docs/?path=../diplom aticconferences/1959_statelessness/docs/english/vol_2/a_conf9_c1_sr5.pdf&lang=E> accessed 4 August 2019.

[129] The author is aware of the assertion that statelessness determination is for stateless persons in a '*migratory context*', thus this is a hypothetical situation. In any case, it is difficult to draw the line between 'migratory' and 'in situ' statelessness and there might be situations where it is appropriate that children born in the territory apply for statelessness determination. See fn 3, Chap. 5 of this chapter on the distinction between the two.

he is stateless. The nationality under article 2 of the 1961 Convention would consequently and immediately need to be confirmed. There is no legal basis within article
2 of the 1961 Convention to make the nationality grant conditional upon habitual
residence. In fact, very few States[130] currently provide for non-automatic acquisition
of nationality for foundlings. The vast majority of the foundling provisions of the
139 States appear to provide for *ex lege* acquisition for those born or found in the
territory, with at least 6 States[131] literally describing it as nationality acquisition 'at
birth'. Most of the 17 States that require 'birth in the territory' for nationality grant
appear to provide for automatic grant.[132] At least 18 States explicitly classify it as
nationality 'by birth' or 'by origin',[133] with a number of others saying the same in
the 'titles'[134] of the provisions.

Despite the fact that 'unknown parentage' itself is inherently difficult to prove,
as discussed in Sect. 5.2, the assessment of article 2 applicability should be—paradoxically—relatively quick and easy for the most 'typical cases' of 'foundlings' for
whom there is no, or very little, proof to the contrary—such as babies abandoned on
a baby hatch or other places and discovered by the State with no clue regarding who
the parents are.

Indeed, in practice, in a number of States, 'typical' cases of foundlings have their
nationality confirmed within several weeks after being identified by the authorities.
Many birth registration laws provide that the person or government official who

---

[130] The few clear examples are Israel (section 9(a), which states '[…] may grant him Israel nationality by the issue of a certificate of naturalisation') and Saint Lucia (section 7(2)(a), which states
'Minister may cause a minor to be registered as a citizen […]'.

[131] Serbia (article 13): 'A child born or found in the territory of the Republic of Serbia (foundling)
acquires citizenship of the Republic of Serbia by birth […] A child that acquired citizenship of the
Republic of Serbia pursuant to the para 1 of this Article is considered citizen of the Republic of
Serbia since his birth.' Law on Citizenship of the Republic of Serbia (2004) <http://www.refworld.
org/docid/4b56d0542.html> accessed 4 August 2019. Also, Antigua and Barbuda (section 3(1)),
Portugal (article 1(2)), Republic of Korea (article 2(1)(iii) and 2(2)), Singapore (article 140(13)),
US (section 301(f)).

[132] For three out of 17 States, the text of the foundling provisions appears to provide for non-
automatic grant, while not entirely clear. These are: Angola (article 15(b) states 'upon request',
while GLOBALCIT Global Database on Modes of Acquisition of Citizenship (A03a) describes it
as 'automatic' acquisition), Haiti (article 4 provides 'by virtue of the declaration of birth made to
the Office of the State Registrar') and Saint Lucia (section 7(2)(a); see fn 130 of this chapter).

[133] 'By birth' 'by origin' might not necessarily mean 'at birth' but might indicate that nationality
acquisition is *ex lege* as opposed to 'by registration' or other methods. Algeria (article 7(1)), Cabo
Verde (article 7(2)) and Costa Rica (article 13(4)), Estonia (section 5(2)), Eswatini (formerly Swaziland) (section 47), Ghana (section 8), Honduras (article 23), Italy (article 1(1)(b) and article 1(2)),
Kenya (article 14(4)), Netherlands (article 3(2)), New Zealand (section 6(3)(b)(i)and(ii)) Sao Tome
and Principe (article 5(2)), South Sudan (section 8(4)), Sudan (article 5), Turkey (article 8(2)),
Uganda (article 11(1)), Zambia (article 35(2)) and Zimbabwe (article 36(3)).

[134] Nevertheless, in this book including annex 1, the 'titles' of the provisions are generally omitted
from the analysis in light of the fact that the legal nature of 'titles' of articles differ between
jurisdictions.

discovers an abandoned child needs to report such a discovery to the (nationality-related) authorities swiftly, such as within 24 h.[135] As stated in Sect. 4.3.1, in Hungary, it is reported that when a child is abandoned on the street, normally within a few hours the municipality where the child is found registers the child, assigning the names of fictitious Hungarian parents, as a result of which the child is confirmed to have Hungarian nationality under article 3(3)(b) granting nationality to a child of unknown parents found in Hungary.[136] In Italy, children born out of the 'anonymous birth' (see Sect. 4.3.10) scheme are to be registered as Italian nationals within ten days of birth allowed for normal birth registration.[137] It is noted however that for foundlings, there might be the possibility that the parent(s) would turn up after a while. For a number of States, the 'grace period' during which the States wait for the parents to turn up and claim the abandoned children before proceeding with their adoption (or foster care) is up to several months,[138] while this is not necessarily the deadline for registering the person as a national. As seen in Sect. 4.3.6, in Hungary, section 9(7) of Law-Decree 17 of 1982 on Civil Registration, Marriage and Names and section 61(5) of Act I of 2010 on Civil Registration Procedures provide that if the mother gives birth at a medical facility in Hungary and did not prove her identity upon giving birth, nor within '30 days following the birth', and abandons the child in the facility, the 'child shall be considered' a child born of unknown parents and found in Hungary within the meaning of article 3(3)b of the Hungarian nationality law. It is noted, however, that this '30 days' is the standard applicable for children whose birth in Hungary is already established, and not for those found.

It follows from this that a foundling must not be left to be of undetermined nationality for an extended period of time—she or he[139] should ideally have her or his nationality confirmed shortly after being found by the authorities, as stated

---

[135] For example, article 57, Family Register Act, Act No 224 of 22 December 1947. Article 57(1) states: 'A police official who has found an abandoned child or has received a report that an abandoned child was found shall inform the mayor of the municipality to that effect within 24 h.' Article 57(2) states: 'When having received information as set forth in the preceding paragraph, the mayor of a municipality shall give a name to the child and designate his/her registered domicile [...]' as a result of which the child will be registered as a Japanese national on the Japanese Family Register. While this does not mean that the child's family register is created within 24 h, it can be assumed that the mayor should not take months to create her or his family registry.

[136] Interview with Benko Zsuzsanna, Attorney at law and a legal guardian, Child Protection Services of Budapest former (till 2009) Deputy Head of Division, Social and Guardianship Division, Guardianship Department at the Municipal Government Office, Fifth District Guardianship Office (Budapest, Hungary, 25 May 2017).

[137] Ministry of Health, 'Parto in anonimato' ['Birth in anonymity'] (updated 11 April 2017, first edn 15 April 2008) <http://www.salute.gov.it/portale/donna/dettaglioContenutiDonna.jsp?lingua=italiano&id=1011&area=Salute%20donna&menu=nascita> accessed 4 August 2019.

[138] For example, it is six weeks in Hungary. As written in Sect. 4.6, on the 43rd day from birth (and presumably after the 'finding' of the child where his or her birth is not witnessed) of the child, the guardianship is confirmed to be with the guardianship authorities and adoption arrangements are normally made. The parent(s) can claim the child back within this period.

[139] Para 11, Council of Europe: Committee of Ministers, *Recommendation CM/Rec(2009)13 and explanatory memorandum of the Committee of Ministers to member states on the nationality of children* (Council of Europe Publishing 9 May 2009).

in Sect. 5.8.1. Nevertheless, States do need sufficient time to make an assessment, especially when persons found are not among the 'typical' cases described above.

Given this, the six months' duration advocated in the context of statelessness determination at paragraph 75 of the UNHCR Handbook (2014) appears to be possibly applicable by analogy.

Indeed, the text of the Czech Citizenship Act, which is one of the several laws explicitly stipulating the deadline for the pre facto assessment, provides a good example by setting it at six months from being found. Section 10, subpart 5, Part II states:

> A child under three years of age found on the territory of the Czech Republic, whose identity was not determined, shall acquire the Czech citizenship on the day they were found, *unless the authorities disclose, within six months* after the child was found, that the child had acquired citizenship of another country. (emphasis added)[140]

While not a State party, article 12(2) of the Russian legislation also sets it at six months from being found: 'A child found in the territory of the Russian Federation, whose parents are unknown, *shall become a citizen* of the Russian Federation if his/her parents do not turn up *within six months* after the child was found' (emphasis added).[141]

There might however be some practical considerations making it appropriate to leave a person of unknown parents to be of 'undetermined nationality' for a longer period. For cases of children with missing parents, an investigation is normally done to trace the parents, which can take some time, especially when there are certain indications about the parents' identity. DNA testing itself might take several months. Thus, when a piece of key evidence is highly likely to be obtainable with an extension of the deadline, making it extendable would be realistic for States. As stated above at the outset of Sect. 5.8, paragraph 75 of the UNHCR Handbook (2014) recommends an extension of another six months, making the standard duration of stateless person status a total of one year.

Indeed, Gábor Gyulai previously asserted that children born in Hungary to parents (who are supposedly foreign nationals) and are left unaccompanied by them after birth: '[s]hould be considered as foundlings and should therefore be granted Hungarian nationality if all efforts to establish their foreign nationality and to repatriate them to their country of nationality has remained unsuccessful until their first birthday' (emphasis added).[142]

There might also be further exceptional or compelling circumstances, for example, where birth registration might not be systematic in general or the civil documentation

---

[140] 186/2013 Act of 11 July 2013 on Citizenship of the Czech Republic and on the amendment of selected other laws (the Czech Citizenship Act) < https://www.mzv.cz/file/2400342/Citizenship_Act_No._186_2013_Sb._o_statnim_obcanstvi_CR.pdf > accessed 16 September 2019.

[141] Russian Federal Law on the Citizenship of the Russian Federation (as amended in 2017) (29 July 2017) <https://www.refworld.org/docid/50768e422.html> accessed 4 August 2019.

[142] Recommendation 14, Gábor Gyulai, 'Statelessness in Hungary: The Protection of Stateless Persons and the Prevention and Reduction of Statelessness' (December 2010) <https://www.refworld.org/docid/4d6d26972.html> accessed 12 July 2019.

system might have been destroyed due to armed conflict, making the one-year standard duration impossible to abide by. However, even in such cases, the nationality under the foundling provision should be confirmed within the earliest timing.

Importantly, UNHCR Guidelines 4 (2012) paragraphs 22–23 recommend that while being designated as being of 'undetermined nationality', the State is to treat these children as possessing its nationality so that they enjoy human rights—such as health and education—on equal terms as citizen children, which should be applicable by analogy to those pending foundlinghood assessment.

As will be seen in Sect. 7.6, if a foundling's parentage or birthplace subsequently becomes known and it is confirmed that she or he has acquired the nationality of the parent(s) or birthplace, then her or his nationality may be withdrawn, given that it would not constitute arbitrary nationality deprivation. While the nationality withdrawal is thus subject to due process and needs to be proportionate (with a limitation period in place), the availability of such measure can be another reason why the assessment of whether the person has acquired nationality under article 2 of the 1961 Convention should be done all the more expeditiously.

Finally, it is also desirable that the denial of the applicability of the foundling provision is subject to procedural safeguards, such as the right to appeal (plus access to legal representation) like other government decisions relating to nationality, as provided for under article 12 of the ECN.

## 5.9 Summary and Conclusions

This chapter mainly examined the burden and standard of proof in determining whether one is of 'unknown parentage' when a dispute occurs at the initial determination of a person's nationality. The acute lack of literature, including publicly available information on the State practice on these evidentiary rules, was first pointed out. UNHCR Guidelines 4 (2012) at paragraphs 20 and 21 contain guidance as to the burden and standard of proof in assessing whether a child (of known parents born in the territory) is 'otherwise stateless', which is basically that the burden of proof needs to be 'shared', and that the standard of proof may be set at 'to a reasonable degree'. In the absence of similar guidance when it comes to the assessment of foundlinghood (including unknown parentage), it was examined whether the above standards can be applied by analogy. The chapter then discussed the relationship, similarities and differences between, the assessment of otherwise statelessness and unknown parentage. It was suggested that while the above rules in principle can be applied by analogy, the burden of proof on the claimant might need to be even lighter (and the standard of proof possibly even lower) considering not least that foundlings are normally children without parents who can testify their identities (and children's birthplace) as discussed in the travaux of the 1961 Convention. Furthermore, for foundlings, what needs to be proven is an 'unknown fact' (parentage), unlike children of known parents otherwise stateless born in the territory who need to prove 'negative but known facts' (that is non-acquisition of nationality from known parent(s) and known birthplace).

It was also argued that the differences in the conception and (in)flexibility of burden and standard of proof in different jurisdictions in particular between common law and continental law systems can make the above UNHCR evidentiary standards difficult to implement in some States, and alternative approaches were necessary. Some conceptual and substantive differences between jurisdictions were first explained. In particular, in some predominantly adversarial common law systems, 'burden of proof' includes two distinct responsibilities, that is the 'burden of production' and the 'burden of persuasion'. In contrast, in continental law systems, the two types of burden are often not clearly distinguished, and the term 'burden of proof' in isolation normally refers to the 'burden of persuasion'. However, in the context of its guidance on statelessness (and refugee status) determination, the UNHCR has referred to 'burden of proof' apparently to mean 'burden of production'. Understanding this would help continental law countries to accept the UNHCR's recommendation to 'share' the burden of proof. Further, in terms of the standard of proof, while such standard is not always explicitly discussed in continental law States, it tends to be inflexible and 'fixed' at a high level. Thus, especially in continental law jurisdictions, 'lowering' the standard of proof to establish statelessness (or unknown parentage) can be difficult for decision-makers or judges, in the absence of legislation or government policy.

Reference was then made to available—though limited—State practice. It was observed some States simply applied the burden and standard of proof applicable to all nationality claims under the nationality law such as acquisition by *jus sangunis* or *jus soli*, to those invoking the foundling provision. US case law specifically indicated that the burden of proving one's eligibility for US nationality under its foundling provision lay with the person invoking the foundling provision, and the standard of proof was the 'balance of probabilities'. It was pointed out that considering that proving the negative—especially 'unknown-ness'—is inherently difficult, and foundlings lack legal parents, States needed to develop specific burden and standard of proof rules to meet the object and purpose of the foundling provision. It was particularly emphasized that the issue of 'unknown-ness' or 'known-ness' of parentage (or birthplace) should not be considered in isolation, as the purpose of examining it is acquisition of nationality and prevention of statelessness.

Relevant Japanese case law was then analyzed. In light of the differences between jurisdictions in approaches to evidentiary issues, an 'alternative' approach was proposed, drawing particularly on the 1995 Supreme Court ruling on Baby Andrew, which offers among the most inclusive guidance as to the evidentiary and definitional issues. The Court de facto—while not formally—reversed the burden of proof, by requiring the State to prove that the parent of the person concerned was 'known'. While doing so, the Supreme Court essentially adopted a broad definition of the term 'unknown parents', and required the State to prove that one of the claimant's parents was 'definitively identified' (and not merely 'highly likely' to be a parent) 'to the extent it would enable the determination of the claimant's nationality'. The

State's failure of 'definitively' identifying the claimant's birth mother led to the court's confirmation of the claimant's acquisition of Japanese nationality. This case law provided a useful guidance that, even in jurisdictions where the standard of proof is generally fixed at a high level (such as at the 'beyond the reasonable doubt' level), or where the burden of persuasion cannot formally be reversed, broadly interpreting the term 'unknown parentage' can have the same effect as reversed burden of proof and/or lowered standard of proof.

Based on the foregoing, two recommendations with regard to the burden and standard of proof in establishing unknown parentage are hereby made, which duly take into consideration the difference between jurisdictions on the conceptualization and (in)flexibility of the burden and standard of proof.

**Option I: Reversed burden of persuasion —State's inability to prove 'known-ness' of the legal parentage at a high standard of proof = recognition of legally unknown parentage at a low standard of proof.**

Once the person concerned (or persons representing her or him) asserts the unknown-ness of her or his parentage and duly cooperates to fulfil her or his shared burden of producing all the reasonably available information regarding the parents' unknown-ness, the State concerned should bear both the burden of producing evidence as well as the burden of persuasion regarding the existence of a legally recognized parent. If the State does not fulfil such burden of proof, the nationality of the person under this provision is to be confirmed. In relation to the standard of proof, the State should conclude that the person's legal parentage cannot be proven ('is unknown') when it cannot be convinced within a reasonable timeframe or a pre-set deadline (see Sect. 5.8) that one of the child's legally recognized parents is definitively identified at a high standard of proof. The 'high' standard of proof can be something equivalent to 'beyond the reasonable doubt', to the extent that it enables the determination of the child's nationality (non-)acquisition by *jus sanguinis*.

**Option II: Broad interpretation of the 'unknown parents' definition in absence of the reversed burden of proof, which can substitute a low standard of proof for recognizing legally unknown parentage.**

Alternatively, or in addition to, the reversal of burden of persuasion, the term 'unknown parents' should be interpreted broadly. Being of 'unknown parents' can be interpreted to mean that the person is 'in a circumstance that indicates that the person's legal parents are not definitively identified to the extent it would enable the determination of the claimant's nationality', or something to that effect. Interpreting the term broadly like this would be especially helpful in achieving the same result as Option I in jurisdictions where the reversed burden of persuasion is difficult to be achieved, or where the standard of proof is inflexible and set high across the board. This is because, as a reflection of the broad interpretation, once the applicant proves the circumstances (at a normal high standard of proof, for example intime conviction) that indicate that the applicant's parent is not definitively identified, the decision-maker or the State would not be able to rebut this assertion unless they prove that one of the parents is definitively identified.

**Reasonable time for determination of the applicability of article 2.**

One should not remain to be of undetermined nationality for an indefinite period and the determination of children's nationality needs to be made as soon as possible, subject to a reasonable time needed for this often complex assessment. While UNHCR Guidelines 4 (2012) provides 'five years' as the maximum time allowed to determine the applicability of article 1 (and 4) of the 1961 Convention, that is to otherwise stateless children of known parentage, it was considered that this standard might not be necessarily applicable when it comes to the foundling provision. This was in light of the differences between the cases covered by those separate legal provisions, that is articles 1 and 2, as mentioned at the outset of this conclusion section. Furthermore, the relevant international standards basically advocate for a (much) shorter period than five years for children otherwise stateless. The assessment of the applicability of the foundling provision should ideally be done within six months, extendable to one year or so, which is indeed the same as the standard recommended for statelessness determination in the UNHCR Handbook.

# Chapter 6
# Age of a Foundling, and Being 'Found' in the Territory

**Abstract** This chapter mainly examines the appropriate age of the person when found in the territory in order to be considered a foundling. The chapter reviews the ordinary meanings of the term (equivalent to) 'foundling' in five different UN language versions of the 1961 Convention, and the terms adopted in domestic provisions. The chapter then compares the 'age limitations' imposed in 139 States' foundling provisions and examines the actual implementation in some States. It was found that some States have defined or applied having been born or 'found' in a broad manner and confirmed nationality for persons of unknown parents who have voluntarily approached the authorities as adult or elderlies. The chapter examines the validity of the common justifications provided by States in imposing low-age limitation. In light of the object and purpose of the 1961 Convention and article 3 and 7 of the Convention on the Rights of the Child (CRC), author concludes that an ideal foundling provision should cover all minors.

In continuation of the discussions initiated in Chaps. 3 and 4, this chapter will further examine the term 'foundling' 'found' in the territory in article 2 of the 1961 Convention.

The age when found at which a person of unknown parents can be considered a 'foundling' has been one of the disputed issues in UNHCR Guidelines 4 (2012) and in other materials on statelessness. While the issue of age is also part of how to define a 'foundling', it is indeed closely related to the concept of being 'found', as discussed below. Thus, mainly for the purpose of maintaining the flow of the discussions, it was decided that the issue of age is to be discussed in this chapter, which examines the concept of being 'found'.

In Chap. 3, it was determined that being 'found' in the territory is not part of the definition of who a foundling is, but rather is a condition by which a State's obligation to grant its nationality to a foundling is triggered. As stated in Chap. 3, neither the 1961 Convention or UNHCR Guidelines 4 (2012), nor the ECN and its Explanatory Report, define the term 'found' in the territory. However, by examining the evolution of international instruments leading up to the adoption of the 1961 Convention, it was revealed in Chap. 3 that being 'found' under article 2 of the 1961 Convention includes cases which are known to have been 'born' in the territory.

M. Kaneko-Iwase, *Nationality of Foundlings*, Evidence-Based Approaches to Peace and Conflict Studies 5, https://doi.org/10.1007/978-981-16-3005-7_6

As will be discussed below, when further reviewing State practice, including case law, it was observed that whether one was really 'found' in the territory per se rarely becomes an issue. Rather, what can be disputed is whether or not she or he was found *while under a certain age*—sometimes stipulated in the relevant nationality law provision—beyond which the provision becomes inapplicable.

Kaspar Hauser—who claimed to have grown up in the total isolation of a darkened cell—whose parentage and birthplace and upbringing are eternal mysteries—was 'found' on 26 May 1828 when around 16 years old in the streets of Nuremberg, Germany,[1] and taken care of by the authorities as an 'orphan'. What would happen to his nationality if he were found today?

This chapter will start by discussing the 'age limitation' imposed under different nationality laws. This chapter will then examine their actual implementation of such laws through which it will clarify the possible age to be considered a 'foundling' as well as the definition of being 'found' and its relationship with such age limitation, and finally conclude on the appropriate age limit.

With regard to how much time the State could take to investigate the applicability of the foundling provision, including examining whether the person concerned has actually been found within the territory (before the specific age as stipulated in the applicable legislation) Sect. 5.8 should be referred to.

## 6.1   Ordinary Meaning

The text of article 2 of the 1961 Convention only says 'a foundling' and does not contain any restriction on the age of the person to benefit from the provision. The same goes for article 6(1)(b) of the ECN.

UNHCR Guidelines 4 (2012) paragraph 57 points out that there are differences in the ordinary meaning of the term equivalent to the English term 'foundling' in the texts of the 1961 Convention in four other UN official language versions with regard to the age of the children covered. Section 3.2 referred to different dictionaries to clarify who a 'foundling' is in ordinary meanings in English and how it is referred to and defined in other languages. Presented below is the result of a similar exercise mainly based on what de Groot prepared as a background paper[2] that led to the UNHCR Guidelines 4 (2012) with regard to the aspect of age.

De Groot overall evaluates that the age connotations of the five UN official language versions of the 1961 Convention vary, covering a ranges from a very young child to older children.

---

[1] Among numerous sources, see for example the editors of *Encyclopaedia Britannica*, 'Kaspar Hauser, German Youth' (20 July 1998) <https://www.britannica.com/biography/Kaspar-Hauser> accessed 4 August 2019.

[2] Interview with Gerard-René de Groot, Professor Emeritus at Maastricht University School of Law (5 October 2017) based on the relevant paragraph in his 'Background Paper' for the UNHCR – convened Expert Meeting on Preventing Statelessness among Children in Dakar, Senegal (23–24 May 2011) on the differences of the five UN language versions of the 1961 Convention.

Non-law and law dictionaries, including the ones cited in Sect. 3.2, define the age of a 'foundling' in English to be an 'infant' or a 'child'.[3] 'Infant' can be defined to be 'a very young child or baby',[4] 'a child in the first period of life'[5] in the non-law sense, but in the field of law, 'infant' is also defined to be 'A person who has not attained legal majority',[6] that is a minor, which varies around the world (21 years old) but in many States is under 18 years old. An infant could also mean, for example, a person 'before the time of commencement of elementary school',[7] that is something like before seven years old depending on the context and the relevant law. A 'child' in English in the field of family law means 'son or daughter' of any age[8] considered as in relation to the father or mother. However, in child protection law and some other legal fields, a child is a person below an age specified by law,[9] such as under the age of puberty[10] or under the legal age of majority,[11] which is again under 18 years old in many States and under article 1 of the CRC (unless under the applicable law majority is attained earlier). In the field of family law, a child also means 'son or daughter' of any age[12] considered as in relation with the father or mother.

Section 3.3.2 noted that in the French version of the 1961 Convention the term 'foundling' in article 2 is replaced by '*l'enfant (trouvé)*'. This expression has a broader

---

[3] As seen in Sect. 3.2, *Oxford Living Dictionaries* defines 'foundling' as: 'An infant (that has been abandoned by its parents and is discovered and cared for by others)'. *Merriam Webster's Dictionary* defines it as '[A]n infant (found after its unknown parents have abandoned it)', and the *Black's Law Dictionary* defines it to mean 'A deserted or exposed infant; a child (found without a parent or guardian, its relatives being unknown'.

[4] Oxford Living Dictionaries, 'Meaning of infant in English' (2019) <https://en.oxforddictionaries. com/definition/infant> accessed 4 August 2019.

[5] Merriam Webster's On-line Dictionary, 'Definition of infant' (2019) <https://www.merriam-web ster.com/dictionary/infant> accessed 4 August 2019.

[6] Oxford Living Dictionaries, 'Meaning of infant in English' (2019) <https://en.oxforddictionaries. com/definition/infant> accessed 4 August 2019, Merriam Webster's On-line Dictionary, 'Definition of infant' (2019) <https://www.merriam-webster.com/dictionary/infant> accessed 4 August 2019, Black's Law Dictionary, 'What is INFANT?' (2019) <https://thelawdictionary.org/infant/> accessed 4 August 2019, 'A person within age, not of age, or not of full age; a person under the age of twenty-one years; a minor. Co. Litt. 171 b; 1 Bl. Comm. 403-10G; 2 Kent, Comm. 233'.

[7] The definition of '*yōji*', the Japanese equivalent for 'infant' or toddler, defined in article 4(ii) of 'Child Welfare Act (Act No 164 of December 12, 1947) (Japan)' (1947) <http://www.japaneselawt ranslation.go.jp/law/detail/?id=11&vm=&re=> accessed 4 August 2019.

[8] Merriam Webster's On-line Law Dictionary, 'Legal Definition of child' (2019) <https://www. merriam-webster.com/dictionary/child#legalDictionary> accessed 4 August 2019. Black's Law Dictionary, 'What is CHILD?' (2019) <https://thelawdictionary.org/child/> accessed 4 August 2019.

[9] Merriam Webster's On-line Law Dictionary, 'Legal Definition of child' (2019) <https://www.mer riam-webster.com/dictionary/child#legalDictionary> accessed 4 August 2019.

[10] Black's Law Dictionary, 'What is CHILD?' (2019) <https://thelawdictionary.org/child/> accessed 4 August 2019 and Oxford Living Dictionaries, 'Definition of child in English' (2019) <https://en.oxforddictionaries.com/definition/child> accessed 4 August 2019.

[11] Oxford Living Dictionaries, 'Definition of child in English' (2019) <https://en.oxforddictionar ies.com/definition/child> accessed 4 August 2019.

[12] Merriam Webster's On-line Law Dictionary, 'Legal Definition of child' (2019) <https://www. merriam-webster.com/dictionary/child#legalDictionary> accessed 4 August 2019; Black's Law

meaning and can obviously include young minors, or even minors in general. '*Enfant*' is according to one meaning of the *Larousse* dictionary a '*garçon ou fille avant l'adolescence*' ('boy or girl before adolescence', author translation). And 'adolescence' is defined as '*periode de la vie entre l'enfance et l'âge adulte, pendant se produit la puberté*' ('the period of life between childhood and adulthood, during which puberty occurs', author translation). Consequently, '*enfant*' would normally include any child that has not yet reached puberty. Furthermore, 'enfant' is the equivalent term of a 'child' in the French version of the CRC which, based on article 1 of the same Convention, cover all persons below the age of 18 years (unless under the law applicable to the child, majority is attained earlier).[13] Moreover, '*enfant*' in French also means '*Fils ou fille de quelqu'un*' (one's son or daughter)[14] as also mentioned in the *Larousse* dictionary, which refer to the family relationship in the field of family law regardless of the person's age.

The term '*expósito*' used in the Spanish version generally seems to refer to a new-born child: '*Dicho de un recién nacido: Abandonado o expuesto, o confiado a un establecimiento benéfico*' ('Said of a newborn: abandoned or exposed, or entrusted to a charity institution', author translation).[15] De Groot states that the Russian word найденыш tends to refer to recent born children.[16] According to de Groot, however, the term used in the Chinese text (弃)儿 (qi'er) is—like the French version—wider and can also include older children.

De Groot suggests that, in light of the majority of all the official UN language versions of the 1961 Convention, it could be argued that a restriction of the foundling rule to new-born children is not contrary to the obligations under article 2 of the 1961 Convention.[17] The Council of Europe states the same as to the obligation under article 6(1)(b) of the ECN.[18] Nevertheless, as de Groot and the Council of Europe also point out,[19] such low-age restriction would leave many children of unknown parents stateless, as can be seen from the case examples contained in Chap. 4.

---

Dictionary, 'What is CHILD?' (2019) <https://thelawdictionary.org/child/> accessed 4 August 2019.

[13] La Convention relative aux droits de l'enfant [Convention on the Rights of the Child], (adopted 20 November 1989, entered into force 2 September 1990) 3, UNTS, vol 1577.

[14] Larousse, '*Enfant*' (2019) <http://www.larousse.com/en/dictionaries/french/enfant> accessed 4 August 2019.

[15] 'Diccionario de la lengua española, La Asociación de Academias de la Lengua Española' <http://dle.rae.es/?id=HKnPEfD> (Accessed 4 August 2019).

[16] Email from Inna Gladokova (former UNHCR Legal Officer (statelessness)) to author.

[17] Interview with Gerard-René de Groot, Professor Emeritus at Maastricht University School of Law (5 October 2017) based on the relevant paragraphs in his 'Background Paper' for the UNHCR—convened Expert Meeting on Preventing Statelessness among Children in Dakar, Senegal (23–24 May 2011).

[18] Council of Europe: Committee of Ministers, *Recommendation CM/Rec(2009)13 and explanatory memorandum of the Committee of Ministers to member states on the nationality of children* (Council of Europe Publishing 9 May 2009) para 24.

[19] Ibid para 24.

## 6.2 UNHCR and Other International Standards

After acknowledging the different age connotations in the five language versions of the 1961 Convention, UNHCR Guidelines 4 (2012) notes that while some contracting States limit the application of their foundling provision to 'new-borns' or babies, most States' legislation provide in favour of children up to an older age than a very young child, including in some cases up to the age of majority.[20] The Guidelines paragraph 58 then recommends that:

> *At a minimum*, the safeguard to grant nationality to foundlings or children born in the territory is to apply to *all young children who are not yet able to communicate accurately information pertaining to the identity of their parents or their place of birth*. This flows from *the object and purpose of the 1961 Convention* and also from the right of every child to acquire a nationality. *A contrary interpretation would leave some children stateless.* (emphasis added)

As the Guidelines state 'at a minimum', it suggests that UNHCR considers that setting the age limitation higher, such as below the age of majority, is desirable.

In contrast, paragraph 48 of the Explanatory Report to the ECN provides that the term 'foundlings' under article 6(1)(b) refer to 'new-born infants (found abandoned in the territory of a State with no known parentage)'.[21] Nevertheless, paragraph 48 also states the term 'foundling' in article 6(1)(b) is 'taken from Article 2 of the 1961 Convention on the Reduction of Statelessness'. Thus, when interpreting the ECN, it is desirable that State parties refer to the more inclusive guidance by UNHCR contained in its Guidelines 4 (2012) above, rather than limiting its interpretation to what is contained in the ECN Explanatory Report.

In fact, Principle 9 of the Council of Europe's Recommendations CM/Rec 2009/13 also recommends that member states: 'treat *children* found abandoned on their territory with no known parentage, *as far as possible*, as foundlings with respect to the acquisition of nationality' (emphasis added). Paragraph 25 of these Recommendations' Explanatory Memorandum states:

> It is up to member states to determine which children qualify as being in a similar situation to foundlings. Of course, a state could decide to extend the treatment reserved for foundlings to *all minors* found abandoned on their territory with no known parentage, as do some member states. However, a state could also determine an age limit and, *for example*, provide that children found abandoned on their territory with no known parentage are treated in the same way as foundlings, if they obviously have not yet reached the *age of three.* (emphasis added)[22]

---

[20] Para 57 of UNHCR Guidelines 4 (2012). Interview with Gerard-René de Groot, Professor Emeritus at Maastricht University School of Law (5 October 2017) based on his 'Background Paper' for the UNHCR—convened Expert Meeting on Preventing Statelessness among Children in Dakar, Senegal (23–24 May 2011) on the differences between the five UN language versions of the 1961 Convention.

[21] Council of Europe, 'Explanatory Report to the European Convention on Nationality, 6.XI.1997' (1997) <https://rm.coe.int/16800ccde7> accessed 4 August 2019 para 48.

[22] Council of Europe: Committee of Ministers, *Recommendation CM/Rec(2009)13 and explanatory memorandum of the Committee of Ministers to member states on the nationality of children* (Council of Europe Publishing 9 May 2009) principle 9 and para 25.

While still pending adoption, article 5.2.a. of the Draft Protocol to the African Charter on Human and Peoples' Rights on the Specific Aspects of the Right to a Nationality and the Eradication of Statelessness in Africa[23] provides for the automatic grant of nationality to: 'A *child* found in the territory of the State of unknown parents […]' (emphasis added). Paragraph 43 of its Explanatory Memorandum[24] states:

> The laws of some African countries restrict the presumption of nationality for children of unknown parents to new born infants. However, *many* children of unknown parents are found at *more advanced ages*; thus any child who is too young to identify her or his parents should be included within the ambit of this provision. (emphasis added)

The Explanatory Memorandum then makes a reference to paragraph 96 of the African Committee of Experts General Comment on article 6 of the African Charter on the Rights and Welfare of the Child,[25] while noting that the foundling provision of some of the African States limit their application only to very young children:

> [C]ommends those States that have adopted laws providing for nationality to be conferred under such provisions to much *older children*. The Committee urges States to, at a minimum, grant nationality to all such children found abandoned, including those who (*at the date they were found*) were not yet able to communicate accurately information pertaining to the identity of their parents or their place of birth. (emphasis added)

Thus, the international standards generally are that the safeguard to grant nationality to foundlings found in the territory should apply at least to young children much older than new-born babies, and that setting the age limitation even higher, such as below the age of majority, is desirable.

## 6.3    Overview of 139 States' Foundling Provisions in Terms of Age (Annex 1)

As stated above, State legislation and practice range on the maximum age of the child to be considered a foundling.[26] The following is the summary of annex 1, which—as

---

[23] ACHPR, 'Draft Protocol to the African Charter on human and peoples' rights on the specific aspects of the right to a nationality and the eradication of statelessness in Africa' (2015) <https://www.achpr.org/public/Document/file/English/draft_citizenship_protocol_en_sept2015_achpr.pdf> accessed 17 February 2020.

[24] ACHPR, 2015 Draft Protocol to the African Charter on human and peoples' rights on the specific aspects of the right to a nationality and the eradication of statelessness in Africa: Explanatory memorandum (2007) <http://citizenshiprightsafrica.org/wp-content/uploads/2018/04/34175-wd-draft_protocol_explanatory_memo_en_may2017-jobourg.pdf> accessed 4 August 2019.

[25] African Committee of Experts on the Rights and Welfare of the Child, 'General Comment No 2 on Article 6 of the African Charter on the Rights and Welfare of the Child, 'The Right to a Name, Registration at Birth, and to Acquire a Nationality' (2014) <http://www.refworld.org/docid/54db21734.html> accessed 4 August 2019.

[26] Apart from annex 1 to this book, see also the comparison chart on Olivier Willem Vonk, Maarten Peter Vink and Gerard-René de Groot, 'Protection against Statelessness: Trends and Regulations in

explained in Sect. 1.5.5.2—provides that out of 193 UN member States, at least 139 States have a foundling provision.

We should remind ourselves at the outset that, as stated in Sect. 1.5.1, the author in principle verified the original text of the relevant laws written in English, Spanish, French and Japanese only, and relied on the English translation for the laws written in other languages. Thus, the possibility that the English translation consulted does not accurately reflect the wording of the original text, especially in terms of the age connotation, cannot be ruled out. Likewise, with additional secondary materials on the interpretation or application of the relevant laws becoming available, the classifications below might change. For example, those currently categorized to be under Sect. 6.3.5 ('no specific age') might be re-categorized to be those under Sect. 6.3.4 ('open to all minors'), which currently carries a note 'non-exhaustive'.

### 6.3.1   'Birth in the territory' Required

As also discussed in Sect. 3.7.5, the legislation of at least 17 States (four of which are member States to the 1961 Convention) among the 139 States provides nationality grant only to persons of unknown parents 'born in the territory'. However, as detailed in Sect. 6.4, among those 17 States, at least in the case of Japan, whose Nationality Act article 2(iii) requires in-country birth, its family/birth registration related law allows for 'abandoned children' found in the territory to be registered on a family register and thus have Japanese nationality confirmed. Further, family court adjudications have allowed persons of unknown parentage who approached the authorities only after reaching adulthood to have their Japanese nationality confirmed via presumption of birth.

As a side note, some legislation adopts the same formulation as in article 14 of the 1930 Convention (classified as 'Method IV', Sect. 7.4), and provides for the acquisition of nationality for persons of unknown parents born in the territory and separately provides for presumption of birth in the territory for those found in the territory. Ssuch States are not counted as 17 States requiring 'birth in the territory'.

### 6.3.2   'New-born'

A number of States—at least 36 in total (17 of which are State parties to the 1961 Convention)—limit the grant of nationality to persons who are 'new-born (or recently born)' when found.

For example, as also mentioned in Sect. 1.5.4, Belgium's nationality law article 10(3) limits its target to 'A new-born child [*L'enfant nouveau-né*] found in Belgium'.

---

Europe' (May 2013) 47–8 <http://cadmus.eui.eu/bitstream/handle/1814/30201/eudocit_vink_deg root_statelessness_final.pdf?sequence=1> accessed 4 August 2019.

The presumption of birth then leads to the *jus soli* grant of nationality as provided in article 10(1) of the same law. According to the competent authorities, the scope of the application of article 10(3) of the nationality law is 'narrower' than foreseen in article 2 of the 1961 Convention.[27] The Belgian Civil Code uses the notion of 'new-born' to refer to a child who is at most a few days old.[28] According to such an interpretation, a child who is already a few months old, let alone a child of a few years old when she or he is found, falls outside the scope of article 10(3) of the nationality law.[29] Article 8(1) of the Austrian Nationality Act limits the target person to 'a person under the age of six months found on the territory'.[30] Article 1(2) of the British Nationality Act provides for 'A new-born infant [...]'.[31]

### 6.3.3   Older Children (3–15 Years Old)

At least ten States, or 7 per cent, set specific age limitations older than new-borns, starting at three up to 15 years old. Specifically, one State, that is Czech Republic (section 10) provides for under three years of age, two States provide for 'under five years old' (USA, Immigration and Nationality Act section 301(f)[32] and Togo, Child Code article 19), one State provides for not more than five years old (Uganda, Constitution article 11(1)), one State provides for 'before apparently attaining the age of seven years' (Canadian Citizenship Act section 4(1)), two States provide for not more than seven years of age (Ghana, Citizenship Act section 8 and Swaziland Constitution section 47), one State provides '(appears to be) less than eight years of age (Kenya, Constitution article 14(4)), one provides '(appears to be) not more than

---

[27] Belgian Ministry of Justice quoted in 2011 in UNHCR, UNHCR, 'Mapping Statelessness in Belgium' (October 2012) para 577 <http://www.refworld.org/docid/5100f4b22.html> accessed 4 August 2019.

[28] Ibid para 577.

[29] Ibid para 577. However, Wout Van Doren (Consultant, Protection Unit for Belgium and Luxembourg of UNHCR's Regional Representation for Western Europe) rightly points out that because article 10(3) provides for presumption of birth in Belgium, one could argue that as long as presumption of birth can be established the age when found should not invalidate such presumption. Email from Wout Van Doren (Statelessness Consultant, Protection Unit for Belgium and Luxembourg, UNHCR Regional Representation for Western Europe) to author (3 August 2017). No such precedents, however, have been reported.

[30] Federal Law Concerning the Austrian Nationality (Nationality Act 1985) (1985) <http://www. refworld.org/docid/3ae6b52114.html> accessed 4 August 2019. Austria made a specific reservation on this point when it ratified the ECN. Council of Europe, 'Reservations and Declarations for Treaty No 166—European Convention on Nationality' (2019) <https://www.coe.int/en/web/conventions/full-list/-/conventions/treaty/166/declarations?p_auth=SiRGEln7> accessed 4 August 2019. This is criticized as 'it does not fully reflect the scope of Article 2 of the 1961 Convention (to which Austria has not entered a parallel declaration or reservation)'. UNHCR, 'Mapping Statelessness in Austria' (2015) 85 <http://www.refworld.org/docid/58b6e5b14.html> accessed 4 August 2019.

[31] Also see UNHCR, 'Mapping Statelessness in The United Kingdom' (22 November 2011) 141 <https://www.refworld.org/docid/4ecb6a192.html> accessed 4 August 2019.

[32] See the actual implementation of this US provision in terms of the age in Sects. 6.4–6.7.

8 years of age' (Zambia, Constitution article 32(2)), and one State provides for 'who is, or appears to be, less than 15 years old' (Zimbabwe, Constitution article 36(3)). As mentioned here, some legislation is unique in that it addresses the fact that the age of foundlings can be difficult to determine, by containing the term 'apparently' and 'appears to be'.

### 6.3.4  All 'minors' (Non-exhaustive)

In summary, a total of 15 States, or slightly more than 11 per cent of the 139 States with foundling provisions, either explicitly or by interpretation open up the target age to all 'minors', that is up to the age of majority, as explained below. In addition, for a number of States among the next category of States under Sect. 6.3.5 (classified as 'no explicit age specified'), there are indications that their foundling provisions likely or possibly cover all minors, while this could not readily be confirmed with competent authorities or experts.

Among the 15 States, ten States or slightly more than seven per cent of the 139 States explicitly use the term 'minors' or use 'child' and *define* it as a person under the age of majority within the given nationality laws: these are Georgia (article 11), Israel (section 9),[33] Kyrgyzstan (article 12(5)), Luxembourg (article 5), Moldova (article 11 (2)), Peru (article 2(2)), Russian Federation (article 12(2)), Spain (article 17(1)(d)), Sudan (article 5) and Switzerland (article 3). For the remaining five States, while the English translation of their nationality laws use the term 'child' (of unknown parents found in the territory), and do *not* define it as a minor, there was complementary information which was the interpretation of the competent authorities and/or local experts readily available at the time of writing. These are: Hungary (article 3(3)(b)), Latvia (section 2 (1) 5)), North Macedonia (article 6), Serbia (article 13) and Slovenia (article 9).

Among the first group consisting of ten States, the original text of the foundling provisions was verified for four States whose laws are written in Spanish (Peru and Spain—which used '*los menores de edad*') and French (Luxembourg and Switzerland, which used '[*L'enfant*] *mineur*').

For example, article 17.1.d) of the Spanish Civil Code states:

> The following persons are Spanish nationals of origin: [...]. d) Those born in Spain whose parentage is not determined. To these effects, *minors* whose first known place of stay is Spanish territory are presumed to have been born in the Spanish territory. (emphasis added; author translation)

---

[33] It should be noted that, as in annex 1, section 9(a) of the Israeli nationality law only provides for naturalization by the Minister for a minor inhabitant of Israel of unknown parents rather than automatic acquisition unlike the foundling provision in the vast majority of States. Israel nationality law 1952 Consolidated translation (as amended up to 1971) <https://data.globalcit.eu/NationalDB/docs/Isreal%20Nationality%20Law%20(amended).pdf> accessed 4 August 2019.

The actual implementation of this Spanish provision in terms of the age is detailed in Sect. 6.4.[34]

For the remaining six States among the first ten, only the English translation of the relevant legislation was consulted. Their foundling provisions stipulate nationality grant to a 'minor' (Georgia, Israel, and Sudan) or 'child' (Kyrgyzstan, Moldova and Russian Federation) of unknown parents found in the territory, and the same laws within themselves contain separate provisions with the 'definition' of a 'minor' or 'child' stating that the term covers a person under the age of 18 or before the age of majority (Georgia at article 2(e), Israel at section 13, Sudan at article 3, Kyrgyzstan at article 3, Moldova at article 1, Russia at article 3).

To provide some details, Moldova's article 11(2) states: 'The *child* [Copilul] found in the territory of the Republic of Moldova shall be considered its citizen, unless otherwise proven, before the age of 18'. Article 1 (entitled 'Notions') of the same law states: 'For the purposes of this law, the following notions mean: *child* [copil]—a person until the age of 18'.[35] Russia's nationality law at article 12(2) provides for acquisition of Russian nationality to 'A child found in the territory of the Russian Federation', and article 3 of the same law provides '"Child" means a person under the age of 18'.[36]

The second group consists of five States that use the term 'child' without defining it, but for which complementary information is accessible, that it means minors. In relation to the Hungarian foundling provision that is nationality law article 3(3)b, the position of the competent authority is reportedly that it covers a child until the age of 18 years. Gábor Gyulai and ENS notes that since article 3(3)b use 'found child born to unknown parents [ismeretlen szülőktől származó talált gyermek]' to express the term foundling, and since the Hungarian Civil Code (Act IV of 1959, section 12) defines the term 'child' as a person under 18 years of age, there are no legal grounds for a more restrictive interpretation.[37] This interpretation has reportedly

---

[34] See also different types of cases who are considered by the Spanish authority to fall within this provision in Sects.4.3.3 , 4.3.5 and 4.3.9.

[35] This reading is confirmed by the email from Marin Roman (Statelessness Officer, UNHCR Central Asia) to the author (5 January 2021). Legea cetateniei Republicii Moldova (as amended up to 2011). <https://data.globalcit.eu/NationalDB/docs/MLD%20LEGE%20Nr.%201024%20Citi zenship%20of%20Republic%20of%20Moldova%20(original%20language,%20as%20amended% 2028_12_2011).pdf> accessed 5 January 2021. Reference was made to the Law on the Citizenship of the Republic of Moldova, consolidated translation (as amended up to 2003) <https://data.global cit.eu/NationalDB/docs/MLD%20LEGE%20Nr.%201024%20Citizenship%20of%20Republic% 20of%20Moldova%20(English%20translation,%20as%20amended%202003).pdf> accessed 5 January 2021.

[36] Russian Federal Law on the Citizenship of the Russian Federation (as amended in 2017) (29 July 2017) <https://www.refworld.org/docid/50768e422.html> accessed 4 August 2019.

[37] Gábor Gyulai, 'Nationality Unknown? An Overview of the Safeguards and Gaps Related to the Prevention of statelessness at Birth in Hungary' (2014) 7 and fn 20 <http://helsinki.hu/wp-con tent/uploads/Nationality-Unknown-HHC-2014.pdf> accessed 4 August 2019. PRS 2b, ENS, 'ENS Statelessness Index Survey 2019: Hungary' (2020) 54–55 <https://index.statelessness.eu/sites/def ault/files/ENS_Statelessness_Index_Survey-Hungary-2019.pdf> accessed 25 December 2020.

been confirmed by an official letter sent by the then competent authority, the Ministry of Public Administration & Justice to UNHCR.[38]

For Latvia, whose foundling provision at section 2(1)5) of the nationality law refers to a 'child', again without defining the term, para 2. 2) of section 2 nevertheless goes on to state:

> The volition to register a child as a Latvian citizen in accordance with Paragraph one of this section shall be expressed by: 1) the lawful representative of the child, if the child has not reached the age of 15 years; 2) the child himself or herself between 15 to 18 years of age.[39]

As also stated in the context of Hungary, it is the general rule in reading laws that the same term has the same meaning within the same piece of legislation; thus the term 'child' in section 2(1)5) should cover a person before the age of 18. This interpretation is confirmed by the country experts' comments and assessment in the ENS Statelessness Index.[40]

Further, North Macedonia's nationality law at article 6 states 'Citizenship […] shall be acquired by a child […]whose parents are unknown […].' ENS's Statelessness Index Survey on North Macedonia written by members of the Macedonian Young Lawyers Association comments on this article that 'The Law on Citizenship stipulates that only children can benefit from this safeguard, meaning that they must be under 18 years of age.'[41]

Similarly, the nationality law of Serbia at article 13 states 'A child born or found in the territory of the Republic of Serbia […] acquires citizenship […] if both his parents are unknown […]'. ENS's Statelessness Index Survey on Serbia written by Praxis, a local legal aid organization, comments on this article that 'The age limit is 18 years-old. The competent body derives this from the legal definition of a "child", i.e. person under 18 years-old' based on a decision and a letter from the Ministry of Interior.[42]

---

[38] Letter No. 437-3068/2/2013 of 7 December 2013, Ministry of Public Administration & Justice to UNHCR Regional Representation for Central Europe cited in ibid (Gábor Gyulai 2014) 7 and ibid (ENS 2020) 54–55.

[39] Law on Citizenship 1994 (as amended up to 2013) of Latvia <https://likumi.lv/ta/en/en/id/57512-citizenship-law> accessed 4 August 2019.

[40] PRS 2 b, ENS, 'ENS Statelessness Index Survey 2019: Latvia' (2020) 48 <https://index.sta telessness.eu/sites/default/files/ENS_Statelessness_Index_Survey-Latvia-2019.pdf> accessed 25 December 2020.

[41] The former Yugoslav Republic of Macedonia: Law on Citizenship of the Republic of Macedonia (As Amended in 2011), 2016 <http://www.refworld.org/docid/3f54916b4.html> accessed 5 August 2019. PRS 2b, ENS, 'ENS Statelessness Index Survey 2019: North Macedonia' (2020) 35 <https://index.statelessness.eu/sites/default/files/ENS_Statelessness_Index_Survey-North_Mac edonia-2019.pdf> accessed 25 December 2020.

[42] Praxis cites as the source of information 'Information derived from casework, including the decisions of the Ministry of Interior in individual cases (decision of the Ministry of Interior, 03/10 No. 204-2-248/2013 from 14 March 2013, on file with author). Letter of the Ministry of Interior sent to Praxis on 15 March 2013, 13/10 No. 204-159/13-R, on file with author.' PRS 2b, ENS, 'ENS Statelessness Index Survey 2019: Serbia (2020) 40 <https://index.statelessness.eu/sites/def ault/files/ENS_Statelessness_Index_Survey-Serbia-2019.pdf> accessed 25 December 2020.

Similarly, the nationality law of Slovenia at article 9 states: 'A child born or found on the territory […] of unknown parentage […] shall acquire citizenship of Republic of Slovenia.' ENS's country experts on Slovenia in the Statelessness Index Survey comments on this article stating 'there is no age/time limit. According to the law, a case of any child under the age of 18 could be examined under the stated provision.'[43]

In addition to the above 15 States that explicitly or by interpretation open up the age to all minors, for a number of States among the next category of States under Sect. 6.3.5 (classified as 'no explicit age specified'), there are indications that their foundling provisions possibly cover all minors.

Some of the examples are the foundling provisions of seven former USSR States. The English translation of the nationality laws of Armenia (article 22), Azerbaijan (article 13), Belarus (article 13), Kazakhstan (article 13), Lithuania (article 16), Turkmenistan (article 11.8)(3)) and Uzbekistan (article 16), all use the term a 'child (of unknown parents)', without defining the term 'child' in terms of the ages covered by such a term. Nevertheless, the same nationality laws (Armenia at article 16, Azerbaijan at article 25, Belarus at article 23, Kazakhstan at article 28, Lithuania at articles 27 and 28, Turkmenistan at article 23, and Uzbekistan at article 28) all have references to 'a child(ren) between (the ages of) 14 and 18'. This is *not* in the context of foundlings but in different contexts, that is the need for a consent of a child between 14–18 years old for the change of her or his nationality upon the change of nationality by her or his parent(s). While the term 'child' in this context might also be referring to the child–parent relationship under family law, considering the purpose those articles, it can be assumed that the term 'child' is rather used as an equivalent to a minor. Again, with the general rule in reading laws that the same term should have the same meaning within the same piece of legislation, it is possible that the 'child' in the foundling provisions in those seven States covers a person before the age of 18. Nevertheless, only the English versions of those laws were consulted, and no complementary information such as the views of the competent authorities or local experts was readily accessible to confirm this interpretation, unlike the five States consisting of the second group under this category mentioned above. Those States thus only were counted among the States with 'no age specified' discussed in Sect. 6.3.5 below. There are other similar examples, such as Bosnia and Herzegovina, whose foundling provision (article 7) uses the term a child of unknown parents, whose nationality law at article 22 stipulating loss of nationality by release at the request of parents(s) refers to 'a child under 18 years of age' and so forth.

Yet as another example, section 14 of the Australian Citizenship Act of 2007[44] states: 'A person is an Australian citizen if the person is found abandoned in Australia as a *child*, unless and until the contrary is proved (emphasis added).' section 3 of the same Act carries a definition of a 'child' but only as a matter of family relationship with a parent, rather than the age of a person. Nevertheless, there are some other

---

[43] PRS 2b, ENS, 'ENS Statelessness Index Survey 2019: Slovenia' (2020) 32 <https://index.statel essness.eu/sites/default/files/ENS_Statelessness_Index_Survey-Slovenia-2019.pdf> accessed 25 December 2020.

[44] Australian Citizenship Act 2007 <https://www.legislation.gov.au/Details/C2019C00040>.

sections in the Act that seem to use 'child' to mean a 'minor'.[45] Further, it is also noted that in a Federal Court of Australia judgement in 2015[46] in examining the applicability of the previous version of the foundling provision, that is section 5(3)(b) of the 1948 Citizenship Act containing the same term 'when a child',[47] the State and the court did not seem to dispute the fact that the claimant, who was 16 years old at the time when he was separated from his mother, was (found) abandoned in Australia 'when a child'.[48] While not much weight can be placed as it is only mentioned as *obiter dictum* (and the court denied the claimant's Australian nationality due to possession of another nationality—see Sects. 6.8 and 7.5), this might also suggest a possibility that the term 'child' under section 14 of the Citizenship Act can be interpreted to mean a 'minor'. Nevertheless, in the absence of any authoritative comments confirming this interpretation, Australia was counted among the States with 'no age specified' under Sect. 6.3.5.

Yet as another example, for Somalia, also counted as a country with 'no age specified', the title of article 15 of nationality law available in English[49] in brackets states '(Minors in Special Circumstances)', and its article 15 paragraph (1) states 'Any minor who is a child of unknown parents and was born in the territory' shall be considered a Somali citizen. However, its paragraph (2) reads 'Any child [rather than 'minor'] of unknown parent found in the territory' shall be presumed to have been born in the territory. Somalia under article 16(1) of the same law defines minors 'any person under 15 years of age shall be considered a "minor"'; however the law does not define the term 'child'.

On a separate note, Zimbabwe's foundling provision (article 36(3)) is also open to a child (who appears to be) less than 15 years of age, but as its age of majority is reportedly higher, Zimbabwe was not counted here but among the category under Sect. 6.3.3.

---

[45] For example, section 33AA (17) (d) of ibid stating '[…]if the person is aged under 18—the best interests of the child as a primary consideration;'.

[46] *Nicky v. Minister for Immigration and Border Protection* [2015] FCA 174 [5 March 2015] and its original decision *Nicky v. Minister for Immigration* [2014] FCCA 2569 [12 November 2014].

[47] Section 5(3)(b) states: '[A] person who, when a child, was *found* abandoned in Australia shall, *unless and until the contrary is proved*, be deemed: (i) to have been *born in Australia*' (section 10(1) of the same Citizenship Act in turn granted nationality to a person born in Australia).

[48] Para 24 of *Nicky v. Minister for Immigration and Border Protection* [2015] FCA 174 [5 March 2015] mentions: 'He is a person who was 'abandoned in Australia as a child […]'. Its original decision in para 29 of *Nicky v. Minister for Immigration* [2014] FCCA 2569 [12 November 2014], while also just in passing, mentions 'the applicant who, the second delegate accepted and I find, *had been found abandoned in Australia* in February 2002'.

[49] The Citizenship Rights in Africa Initiative states that 'citizenship in Somalia is nominally regulated by the country's 1962 citizenship law' and provides the link to the following document in English <http://citizenshiprightsafrica.org/wp-content/uploads/1962/12/Somalia-Cit izenship-Law-1962-full.pdf>. Both refworld.org and GLOBALCIT carry the same document.

## 6.3.5 No Age Specified

The rest, that is 61 States, or 44 per cent of the 139 States' laws, do not explicitly specify the age (within the same pieces of laws as the ones containing the foundling provisions) in their original texts written in English,[50] Spanish and French original texts, or at least in the English translations of the laws. Such States either use a neutral term, that is 'child' or 'infant' (accompanied by adjectives such as 'of unknown parents' and others), and, while less common, 'foundling' in English (only two States) or an equivalent term in other languages. For legislation written in Spanish, 'infante' or 'niño', and for French 'enfant' were mostly used in this category of States.

As stated in Sect. 6.1, the term 'a child' in legal text should normally be interpreted to mean a minor, that is under the age of majority, but it might also be interpreted to mean relatively smaller children. For example, the German Nationality Act section 4(2)1 reads: '[A] child which is found on the German territory [*Ein Kind, das im Inland aufgefunden wird* [*Findelkind*]] *shall be deemed to be a child of a German until otherwise* proven. [...].'[51] Germany's relevant administrative instructions clarify that a *Findelkind* is a 'child who is helpless because of her or his age whose descent cannot be ascertained'.[52] Reinhard Marx writes in his commentary on article 4(2)1 that not only new-borns but all children at an age from whom it is impossible to gather information about her or his parents are foundlings (*Findelkind*). Marx suggests that no particular age limit is imposed.[53]

---

[50] As seen in annex 1, among the 27 States whose relevant laws carrying foundling provisions are presumably written in English, three States use the term 'infant' (Fiji, Saint Lucia and South Sudan), two States (Papua New Guinea and Tuvalu) use the wording 'foundling', and one (Australia) uses the term a 'child'. For the rest of the 27 States, eight States explicitly open the provisions to certain older ages (below five years old to 15 years old – Canada, Eswatini, Ghana, Kenya, Uganda, US, Zambia and Zimbabwe) while 13 Sates limit the application of such provisions to 'new/recent born' (Antigua and Barbuda, Barbados, Belize, Guyana, Ireland, Malta, Mauritius, New Zealand, Rwanda, Saint Kitts and Nevis, Singapore, Sri Lanka, UK). Other elements of the 27 States' foundling provisions are reviewed in Sect. 3.3.1.

[51] Staatsangehörigkeitsgesetz (StAG) [The Nationality Act of Germany] (1913) <https://www.ges etze-im-internet.de/stag/BJNR005830913.html> accessed 5 September 2019.

[52] 'Vorläufige Anwendungshinweise des Bundesministeriums des Innern zum Staatsangehörigkeits-gesetz (StAG) in der Fassung des Zweiten Gesetzes zur Änderung des Staatsangehörigkeits-gesetzes vom 13 November 2014 [Federal Ministry of Interior, Preliminary instruction on implementation of the Nationality Law (StAG) as amended by the Second Act amending the Nationality Law of 13 November 2014] (BGBl. I S. 1714) (as of 1 June 2015) sec 4.2. (Germany)' <http://www.bmi.bund.de/cae/servlet/contentblob/463812/publicationFile/23664/Anwendungshinweise_05_2009.pdf (last accessed 5 September 2017, inaccessible as of 1 July 2019); <https://www.dortmund.de/media/p/ordnungsamt/pdf_ordnungsamt/Allgemeine_V erwaltungsvorschrift_zum_Staatsangehoerigkeitsrecht.pdf> accessed 1 July 2019.

[53] Reinhard Marx, '§ 4 StAG' in Fritz/Vormeier (eds), *Gemeinschaftskommentar zum Staatsange-hörigkeitsgesetz* [*Commentary on Nationality Law*] (Looseleaf edn, Walters Kluwer/Luchterhand 2019) para 196 ff. (pp 53–54.3).

As seen in Sect. 6.3.4, for some of the States whose nationality legislation itself uses a neutral term 'child' without defining the term within the same piece of legislation, there are dependable pieces of information or indications that 'child' means 'minor' (see Sect. 6.3.4).

Some States' legislation leaves the age open, by adopting the term that can mean an 'offspring' or 'son or daughter', referring to the relationship under family law without any age implications. For example, article 1(2) of the Italian nationality law 91/1992 refers to '*il figlio*', which means a son or daughter, a term that can be used to describe the family relationship between a parent and a child, regardless of the person's age.[54]

In conclusion, taking the ordinary meaning of the term 'foundling', article 3 and 7 of the CRC, UNHCR Guidelines 4 (2012) and national legislation, it can be provisionally concluded that nothing prevents a State from setting the age of a foundling to be below the age of majority such as under 18 years old. This provisional conclusion will be examined further in sections to follow.

## 6.4  The Actual Implementation of the Legislation Limiting Foundlings' Age

It is now time to look at how the legislation that limits the age is indeed implemented. This will be helpful both in order to examine how States define the term 'found' including who can 'find' the child of unknown parents, and the consequences of setting the 'deadline to be found' too short.

### *Japan*

Japan is one of the 17 States whose foundling provision requires birth within the territory—with the Japanese Nationality Act article 2(iii) granting nationality to persons of unknown parents 'born' in the Japanese territory. However, article 57 of the Family Register Act allows for 'abandoned children' (*kiji*) of unknown parents found in the territory, that is without evidence of in-country birth, to have their family register created and thereby have their Japanese nationality confirmed under article 2(iii) of Nationality Act. As also reiterated in the 2008 authoritative Commentary, the official position[55] subscribed to by the competent authority, that is the Civil Affairs

---

[54] Law No 91 of 5 February 1992 'New Norms on Citizenship' (Italy) <http://www.refworld.org/docid/3ae6b4edc.html>. A slight modification of the translation was made by the author. See fn 44, Chap. 3 of this book entitled 'Note on the translation of "*il figlio*"'.

[55] Shōwa 29.2.15 minji kō 297 gō kaitō [Official inquiry response on 15 February of 1952, civil affairs No. 297], in '75 Kiji hakken chōsho no sakusei oyobi koseki no kisai—Shōwa 27.6.7 minji kō dai 804 gō tsūtatsu [Drafting of the report of finding an abandoned child and the entry into the family register—in relation to the Civil Affairs Circular, 7 June 1952, No 804]' in Mitsuo Kimura and Masajirō Takezawa (eds), *Shori kijun to shiteno koseki kihon senrei kaisetsu* [*Commentary on the Basic Precedents relating to Family Register Administration for Reference as Processing Criteria*] (Nihon kajo shuppan 2008) 473.

Bureau, Ministry of Justice is that 'abandoned children' cover not only babies but also 'toddlers' (*yōji*). '*Yōji*' is defined in article 4(1)(ii) of the Child Welfare Act[56] as persons of '1 year of age or more before the time of commencement of elementary school' (up to six to seven years). Further, the Civil Affairs Bureau's official position also allows for the confirmation of Japanese nationality under article 2(iii) for persons of unknown parentage up to an undefined age including adults, as long as their birth in Japan can be established or presumed. The official guidance states that persons of unknown parents who have reached the age when they normally have mental capacity,[57] should be registered on a Japanese family register via *shūseki kyoka shinpan*[58] (a family court adjudication for the purpose of registering unregistered persons) rather than under article 57 as 'abandoned children'.[59]

The authoritative academic theory supporting the official position is that in-country birth is *presumed* for persons of unknown parentage in the absence of proof of birth abroad. In practice also, family court case law up to early 1980s, some of which si discussed in Sects. 4.3.4, 4.3.5, 4.3.7 and 4.3.8, also confirms the Japanese nationality of adults of unknown parents even though they approached the authorities only in their 40s to 60s.

Specifically, in some of the family court adjudications, the birth in the territory is presumed based on indirect or circumstantial evidence mostly on the person's own account, in the absence of any direct proof. The two best examples are the Adjudication by the Ōita Family Court Bungotakada Branch on 31 January 1975, introduced in Sect. 4.3.8, as well as the Mito Family Court Adjudication on 7 October 1988, in Sect. 4.3.4.

*Adjudication by the Ōita Family Court Bungotakada Branch 31 January 1975*[60] *(claimant's age at the time of adjudication—61 years old)*

In this case, the claimant who voluntarily separated from his mother when he was around 13 years of age, and who as an adult found out the lack of his birth/family registration, was confirmed Japanese national when the claimant was 61 years old.

---

[56] Child Welfare Act (Act No 164 of 12 December 1947) (Japan) (1947) <http://www.japaneselawt ranslation.go.jp/law/detail/?id=11&vm=&re=> accessed 4 August 2019.

[57] *Ishinōryoku* (mental capacity) generally refers to the judgemental capacity that a person at the enrolment age to a primary school, that is the age seven or so is supposed to have. *Hōritsu yōgo jiten* [*Dictionary of Legal Terminologies*] (Jiyūkokuminsha 2011) 220.

[58] On the nature of a Japanese family court adjudication on registering unregistered persons into a family register, please refer to fn 48, Chap. 4 entitled 'Nature of Japanese family court adjudications permitting registration into family register'.

[59] Shōwa 25.11.9 minji kō dai 2910 gō kaitō [Official inquiry response 9 November 1950, civil affairs No 2910] as referred to in '75 Kiji hakken chōsho no sakusei oyobi koseki no kisai – Shōwa 27.6.7 minji kō dai 804 gō tsūtatsu' ['Drafting of the Report of Finding an Abandoned Child and the Entry into the Family Register – in Relation to the Civil Affairs Circular, 7 June1952, No 804'] in Mitsuo Kimura and Masajirō Takezawa (eds), *Shori kijun to shiteno koseki kihon senrei kaisetsu* [*Commentary on the Basic Precedents relating to Family Register Administration for Reference as Processing Criteria*] (Nihon kajo shuppan 2008) 474.

[60] *Kagetsu* Vol 28, No 1, p 84 [31 January 1975 (*Shōwa 50 nen*)] (Ōita Family Court Bungotakada Branch).

The court presented a notable argument with regard to whether the claimant fulfilled the requirement that 'the child is born in Japan', stating:

> Even if there is *no positive evidence of birth in Japan or direct evidence* such as family registry record officially proving the place of birth, or birth certificate supporting such a record, delivery certificate [by a doctor or midwife, author] or a witness's testimony of delivery, if the individual is indeed living within the Japanese territory and there is no clear negative (opposite [sic]) evidence sufficient to determine that the individual was born outside Japan and subsequently migrated or was brought to Japan, and rather there are *circumstantial facts enabling the assessment that the individual was born in Japan*, the determination that the person was 'born in Japan' should be allowed as an interpretation of article 2(iv) [of the Nationality Act, that is the foundling provision] in light of the object and purpose of the provision [...].

> It not only cannot be determined that the claimant was born, as he claims, in the southern region of Kagoshima including the southwestern islands, and *there is no positive or direct evidence sufficient for the court to recognize that he was even born within Japan*. However, based on the previously accepted facts, it is a clear fact that the *claimant was living within Japan ever since he can remember* ie when he was around 4 or 5 years old, that is only a few years and months after his birth, and there is no indication sufficient to assume that the claimant had been brought from outside Japan. Needless to say, there is no evidence whatsoever to prove facts such as that the claimant has a foreign nationality (the allegation by B that the claimant is Korean is vague which is based on hearsay which does not appear to go beyond mere speculation, as previously determined). Thus it should be determined that the claimant's continued residence in Japan can be presumed. [...] (emphasis added; author translation)

The court then concluded as follows and confirmed the claimant's possession of Japanese nationality:

> Considering these pieces of indirect evidence combined with his continued residence in Japan sufficiently enables a presumption with a high probability that the claimant was born in Japan, and even if this was not the case, interpreting article 2(iv) in accordance with the *object and purpose of the provision*, sufficient circumstantial facts exist that value-wise allow the determination that the applicant fulfils the requirement of having been born in Japan. (emphasis added; author translation)

With regard to the 'circumstantial facts enabling the assessment that the individual was born in Japan', the court referred to different elements including the claimant's Japanese language ability—the fact that he spoke Japanese ever since he remembers and that he speaks the Kyūshū dialect (the dialect of Japanese where he asserts to have lived) including its nuances—along with the claimant's cultural aspects including livelihood patterns and customs that match his claimed profile.

*Mito Family Court Adjudication, 7 October 1988*[61] *(claimant's age at the time of adjudication—46 years old)*

---

[61] *Adjudication, Kagetsu* Vol 41, No 4, p 82 [7 October 1988 (*Shōwa 63 nen*)] (Mito Family Court). The author used the translation by William Wetherall, who made his full translation of the adjudication available on his webpage: William Wetherall, 'Unidentifiable Man Gets Family Register: Family Court Invokes Jus Soli Principle As Grounds' (1 June 2014) <http://www.yoshabunko.com/nationality/Nationality_law_1988_jus_soli_ruling.html> accessed 4 August 2019, on which she made slight modifications. Comments in square brackets are notes by William Wetherall.

In this case, an adult male who apparently suffered memory loss as to his own identity was confirmed Japanese nationality when around 46 years of age according to his assertions.

Excerpts of adjudication

1(Accepted Facts) (4) 'According to the statements of the petitioner, "I can't at all recall [the names of] my parents or brothers, or [the name of] the place where I was raised, or the names of my schools. What I remember of my youthful times [childhood], [...] I don't remember the air raids, but I know [about] B-29s (The Boeing B-29 Superfortress, a heavy bomber flown primarily by the US in Japan during World War II, author). One was flying at a high place. I remember when I had started elementary school or [maybe] not [yet] started elementary school, there was the Korean (Chōsen) upheaval [1950], and I collected scrap iron and had an older person [student] sell it [for me], I was found out by my grandmother to be buying and eating sweets, and was severely scolded". [...] I like pops [...] I remember that about the time I was in middle school, Perez Prado came to Japan [1956]. At a karaoke get together at X Hospital (where the petitionar is admitted as of 1988, author), I came in 2nd place singing "Garasu no Jonii" [Johnny Glass] [1961 I. George song], which I had known from before, and came in 1st with "Aka to kuro no buruusu" [Red and black blues] [1955 Tsurta Kōji] and "Nakanoshima buruusu" [Nakanoshima blues] [mid 1970s] [...]'. (5) The petitioner has specialized knowledge of automogile driving, and is extremely familiar with knowledge of the geography and tourist places within Japan [...].

2 (Legal requirements for establishing family register) (1) Regarding the petitioner, because [his] father and mother cannot be known [...]when examining whether or not the case of the petitioner corresponds to 'When the father and the mother of a child who was born in Japan are unknown' as in Article 4 of the old nationality law, there is no direct evidence that the petitioner was born in Japan. However, and neither is there any evidence that [suggests] that the petitioner was born outside Japan, or had after that [birth outside Japan] entered this country. And, according to the above sort of fragmentary memory that the petitioner related, that the petition grew up within Japan from the time of [his] childhood is clear, and when combining with this the petitioner's language, appearance, knowledge concerning social phenomena and geography and so forth within Japan, and other various circumstances, recognizing that the petitioner is someone who was born within Japan is reasonable and natural. Accordingly, the petitioner, pursuant to Article 4 of the previous nationality law, is recognized [by this court] as being a Japanese national.

Considering the facts he remembers and the petitioner's assertions, the family court registered the petitioner as having been born on 3 November 1941.

*Tōkyō Family Court Tachikawa Branch Adjudication, 5 December 2016*

In an even more recent case, the family court precedents that birth within Japan can be established by circumstantial evidence in the absence of direct evidence were followed. In this case, mentioned in Sect. 4.3.12, while the claimant's mother stated she had given birth at a hospital in Japan, she was using a false name at the time, and there was no direct evidence to prove the assertion. The claimant's birth at a hospital in Japan was accepted by the court only based on the statements by the claimant's mother and biological father.[62]

---

[62] Tōkyō Family Court Tachikawa Branch Adjudication, 5 December 2016 (*Heisei 28 nen*). Email response to author's inquiry from Fumie Azukizawa, legal representative on 7 August 2019. Attorney Azukizawa asserts that, even if the mother had given birth at home, the claimant's birth in Japan could probably have been established by circumstantial evidence, because it can be proven that

*Analysis—paradox that a 'restrictive' provision requiring in-country birth can be more inclusive*

From the three cases (as well as several other Japanese cases discussed in Sect. 4.3) an interesting paradox is demonstrated: that a nationality law requiring 'birth in the territory', which is at variance with the wording of article 2 of the 1961 Convention, can be, under certain circumstances, de facto be more inclusive than some legislation that targets persons of unknown parents 'found' in the territory but nevertheless stipulates a specific age. This happens when the law requiring 'birth in the territory' is accompanied by the practice of presumption of birth within the territory without limiting the age at which a person can benefit from such presumption.

True, as long as the term 'found' is properly defined as in Sect. 6.5, that is that any third person can 'find' a person of unknown parents, foundling provisions covering all those 'found' would normally be more appropriate reflecting the wording of article 2 of the 1961 Convention. However, suppose in one State, the definition of being 'found' is interpreted strictly to mean being discovered by the authorities, and the age-limit for such 'discovery' is set low. Paradoxically, the legislation that narrows down its target by requiring the birth in the territory could be more generous than such a State, for being able to apply the provision to any persons of unknown parents who come to the attention of the authorities at older ages including adults and elderlies. This is because such provision does not link the nationality acquisition with 'being found' and thus disregards the age when found. Again, this is so as long as there is no proof of birth abroad and in-country birth can be presumed from circumstantial evidence.

### Austria

Article 8(1) of the Austrian Nationality Act foresees 'a person under the age of six months found on the territory'.[63] In practice, at least one case is reported in 2013 where a child who was estimated to be about three years old when found in Austria could not benefit from the foundling provision. For him to acquire Austrian nationality, he had to establish the required years of lawful residence before being able to apply for discretionary naturalization.[64]

---

the claimant's biological father (whose blood relationship with the claimant has been established) never left Japan, and that it would have been quite unlikely to assert that the claimant' mother after getting pregnant due to intercourse with the biological father left Japan alone, gave birth outside Japan and returned to Japan with the claimant.

[63] Austria: Federal Law Concerning the Austrian Nationality (Nationality Act 1985) (1985) <http://www.refworld.org/docid/3ae6b52114.html> accessed 4 August 2019 See also the reference to Austria in Sect. 6.3.

[64] An anonymous case cited in UNHCR, 'Mapping Statelessness in Austria' (2015) 85 <http://www.refworld.org/docid/58b6e5b14.html> accessed 4 August 2019.

### United States

Section 301(f) of the US Immigration and Nationality Act (INA) provides for the acquisition of nationality by a person of unknown parentage found in the US while under the age of five years.

In the Court of Appeals case of *Hernandez v. Ashcroft* in 2004,[65] the claimant asserted to have been born in Port Isabel, Texas, on 3 May 1951. According to the claimant, the claimant's first memory was when he used to live in San Benito, Texas, at an early age, when he began his schooling, while living with his parents. The claimant stated he was later separated from his parents, and hitchhiked from the US to Mexico at age seven or eight to look for his parents, only to find out that his parents were dead. The claimant stayed with a family in Mexico until reaching age 12, after which he returned to the US and lived in various locations in the US. The applicant's birth in the US was not established with documentary evidence. The Court of Appeals concluded that the claimant did not acquire nationality based on article 301(f) of the INA because:

> Petitioner does not claim to have been 'found in the United States while under the age of five'. To the contrary, at the deportation hearing, Petitioner stated that *he lived in the United States until reaching age seven or eight*, at which time he returned to Mexico to search for his parents; at approximately age twelve, Petitioner returned to the United States *and later was found by* INS authorities. (emphasis added)

From this wording, the court appears to have defined the term 'found in the United States' under section 301(f) to mean 'to come to the attention of the US *authorities*'.[66] It is unknown whether the Court of Appeals looked into whether the claimant was able to produce any evidence of witness corroborating his presence in the US before the age of five, as he had asserted.

However, this narrow interpretation by the Court of Appeals of being 'found' was not adopted by USCIS in the 2006 Newark Case.[67] As discussed in Sect. 4.3.5, in the Newark Case, the claimant, who had been informally adopted by an unrelated, abusive woman, was already well over five years when 'found' by the Newark police (and was over 18 years of age when her American nationality was confirmed by USCIS under the foundling provision in 2006). If USCIS had narrowly construed 'found' to mean only by the authorities, there was no way for her to be confirmed a US national. Instead, USCIS obviously considered that the minor was 'found' by a medical doctor when she was around the age of two. In this case, based on an oral

---

[65] *Hernandez v. Ashcroft,* 114 Fed. Appx. 183 [2004] (United States Court of Appeals, Sixth Circuit).

[66] Ibid. At any rate, from the limited and ambiguous facts included in the decision, it is not clear whether the applicant's unknown parentage was considered established. The birth certificate previously presented to establish the claimant's birth in the US was found not to belong to the claimant. The identity information of a woman who is claimed to have been his mother is recorded on her social security card presented to the court, but this should not necessarily establish the mother–child relationship between the claimant and the woman.

[67] Reported in Chris Nugent and Doug Burnett of the Holland & Knight Community Services Team, 'The Foundling Statute' (23 January 2007) <https://www.ilw.com/articles/2007,0123-nugent.shtm> accessed 4 August 2019.

account of the self-claimed mother—the doctor who saw the claimant 15 years ago was tracked down, who then provided a written record of the then infant claimant's visit. This medical record included the recorded height and weight measurements for the claimant, which put her at about two years old when seen. A subsequent age determination by a forensic dentist using the child's teeth to determine her present age was consistent with the paediatrician's observation.[68]

Nonetheless, in the same case, for the three other children informally adopted by the same woman, there was a total absence of evidence that could show that they were present in the US prior to the age of five years old, before which a person of unknown parents must be 'found' under the foundling provision. Their school records provided documentation from the age of five years on, but there was nothing before. The three other children thus were only granted green card by applying for 'Special Immigration Juvenile' status with USCIS.

*Spain*

The interpretation and implementation of the Spanish nationality law provision is also inspiring in this regard. The Spanish Civil Code article 17.1.d) provides that 'minors whose first known place of stay is the Spanish territory' are presumed to have been born in the Spanish territory and, therefore, acquire Spanish nationality by birth, as persons of undetermined parentage born in the territory do under the same provision.

In practice, at least in one of the DGRN decisions known, which is briefly mentioned in Sect. 4.3.9, an adult of supposedly 41 years old was confirmed his Spanish nationality after approaching the Spanish authorities for late birth registration at the age of 38. This was largely possible because he was 'known' to his neighbours, while not to the Spanish authorities, to be staying within the Spanish territory since birth or childhood, who were able to credibly testify such knowledge. It is worth including some details of the facts and reasonings below.

*DGRN Resolution of 9 of August 1993 (age at the time of adjudication: approximately 41 years old).*[69]

Additional facts complementing the summary in Sect. 4.3.9

The claimant AML stated that since he was little he was well known in his neighbourhood, for example by the first corporal of the national police, H, who has three brothers, one of whom is also a municipal policeman and can testify, as well as E, a baker in street C. The testimonial information offered was taken, with the intervention of two neighbours in M, who stated that the friendship that unites them with the petitioner started in area C on 25 April 1952. The claimant AML was verified by the doctor of the civil registry in terms of age and sex.

---

[68] Chris Nugent and Doug Burnett of the Holland & Knight Community Services Team, 'The Foundling Statute' (23 January 2007) <https://www.ilw.com/articles/2007,0123-nugent.shtm> accessed 4 August 2019.
[69] Res. DGRN de 9 de agosto de 1993 (188) (BIMJ, núm. 1685, 1993, pp 4645–8; RAJ, 1993, núm. 6899).

Consulting the governmental census of the police station of San Jose, where all the Moroccans who have or have had special documentation to reside in area C are registered, the name of the claimant did not appear, nor the names of those he cites as his parents. The General Directorate of the Police stated that there was a requirement since 1958 to possess a statistical card (Tarjeta Estadística) for all Moroccans living in areas C and M, and taking into account that the applicant at that time was six years old, he should have been listed with his parents. From the foregoing, it follows that the petitioner was not born in such areas. The General Directorate added that the AML had been expelled from the national territory on three occasions, having a criminal record. The civil guard of area C reported that all of the investigations have been unsuccessful, although in the resident list of the police station (*padrón de la comisaría de la policía*) in area LR it appears that on 30 December 1967, the statistical card was delivered to him (assumed to be the claimant AML) for the first time (details unclear from the original text). The Public Prosecutor informed that the petitioner was a beggar and homeless in area M, sleeping in the subway of location.

After the claimant's appeal to DGRN against the municipality C's civil registry to refuse his late birth registration, statements were taken from the witnesses offered by the claimant, all neighbours of the municipality C, about all the circumstances they knew in relation to the place and date of AML's birth. The first witness said that from 1952 to 1978 he (the witness) owned a grocery store of the BPL in area C. For that reason, he knew the mother of AML without remembering her name or more circumstances relating to her. The witness stated since 1952 both the petitioner's mother and her children visited his shop daily to buy and from that relationship is able to say that AML was born in B of PA (sic) in the city in 1952, but only knew it for referential reasons, since the witness did not attend the birth itself. The second witness said he knew the appellant since his birth, not knowing whether he was born in his parents' home or in the hospital of the Red Cross in the city. He also knew his parents from running a grocery store in B del P. The third witness said that on the date of the appellant's birth he lived in B del P and as neighbours he knew him, knowing, therefore, that he was born in C but without knowing where.

## Summary of decision

DGRN stated that:

> In this type of file, the proof of the place of birth is very much facilitated because it is enough for these purposes to have 'the information of two persons who know the person of their own knowledge or by reputation' […]., However, this flexibility [amplitud] explained by the inherent difficulty in justifying the facts over time, should not prevent the ex officio investigation […]in this particular case, however, the evidence, favourable to the claim of the petitioner, appreciated as a whole, must prevail over the official information obtained. The witnesses presented assure that the birth occurred in C., some of them specifying the exact neighbourhood, and this fact is corroborated by the content of the official Spanish documentation that has been delivered to the petitioner at some point. […]

Thus, DGRN again apparently considered that the claimant was 'known' by his neighbours at birth or soon after birth, therefore fulfilling the requirement under the foundling provision which stipulates 'minors' whose 'first known place of stay' is Spain acquire Spanish nationality.


## 6.5   What is the Definition of Being 'found' and Who Can 'find' the Person?

What then is the definition of being 'found' in the territory under article 2 of the 1961 Convention? Through the cases discussed in Sect. 6.4, from the US and Spain, it became clear that the competent authorities consider that one does not have to be 'found' by the authorities but by any third person other than parents in the territory under the established age limit.

Indeed, paragraph 59 of the UNHCR Guidelines 4 (2012), in the context of addressing the issue of the age limit for the foundling provision to apply, states:

> If a State provides for an age limit for foundlings to acquire nationality, the age of the child at the date the child was found is decisive and not the date when the child came to the attention of the authorities.

Thus, the UNHCR also sees that a person of unknown parentage can be found by any third person other than one's parents who are not representing the authorities of the country where the person is found.

It should also be recalled here that Chap. 3 found that having been born in the territory is included in the term 'found'. The question then that needs to be addressed here is: when one's birth in the territory has not been established, what can constitute 'being found'? Some may link the term 'found' with an abandoned new-born who is 'discovered' while crying on a street. However, for example, in the US, that is the Newark Case, and in Spain, that is DGRN Resolution (9 August 1993) (see Sect. 6.4), how the persons concerned were 'found' was much less 'passive'—the girl in the US case was being 'treated' by a doctor, and the gentleman in the Spanish case was 'seen', 'recognized' or 'identified' by his neighbours including when visiting the grocery shop in the neighbourhood.

Ultimately, therefore, being 'found in the territory' under article 2 of the 1961 Convention—other than when the person's birth in the territory is established— can be broadly defined as 'having been seen in the territory by a person other than one's parents', or something to that effect. Alternative interpretations would render many children stateless against the object and purpose of the 1961 Convention and equivalent national legislation.

On a separate note, some States' foundling provisions (appear to) use different words than 'found' while no analysis was made mainly due to the inability to verify the original text.[70]

---

[70] For example, the English translations of at least seven former USSR States' foundling provisions appear to only require that the child (of unknown parents) concerned 'is in the territory' 'lives in the territory' or 'is located in the territory' of the State rather than having been 'found' in the territory.

## 6.6    What is the Age Above Which One Should Be Able to Secure Evidence of Stay in the Country?

It is time to discuss the link between the issue of 'age limitation' and the term 'found' in the territory. Suppose all States adopt the above 'broad definition' of being 'found'. Even if an age limitation is imposed, and the concerned person of unknown parents is older than such age by the time of approaching or being detected by the authorities, she or he can still be considered to have been 'found' by the deadline upon producing—for example—witnesses testifying her or his stay in the territory before the deadline.

However, if the age limitation is set too low, even the broadest definition of being found was to be adopted, the person might not be able to secure such witnesses or other evidence, especially in situations where, for example, she or he was informally adopted, abused and neglected by unrelated adults. School records can constitute credible evidence of a person's stay in a particular country since early age, but mandatory education typically starts at the age of five to seven in many States, which worked against the (although unrelated) 'siblings' of the girl in the Newark Case.

The question then arises whether, then, the age limitation of 'eight' is enough to secure credible witnesses or proof of stay in the country. Probably, but not necessarily. How about ten? Or 12 or 15 years old? It becomes difficult to determine what age is acceptable if States were to set such age limitation. How about below 18, which was provisionally determined to be the maximum age to be considered a foundling in Sect. 6.3? While it can be considered a person normally would have had enough opportunities to secure credible evidence of stay in the country by that age, some exceptional cases might exist, for whom gathering objective evidence can be challenging. Such cases include human trafficking cases or where the persons concerned were born at home (which happens sometimes even in industrialized States, particularly among impoverished or undocumented populations) and have been moving from one place to another, without even getting enrolled in school.[71]

---

However, due to the inability to verify the original text of the provisions, no analysis was made in this regard. See annex 1 for the foundling provisions of Armenia (article 20), Azerbaijan (article 13), Belarus (article 13), Georgia (article 11), Kazakhstan (article 13) Kyrgyzstan (article 12(5)), Turkmenistan (article 11(8)(3)) and Uzbekistan (article 16).

[71] In the case where Japanese nationality under the foundling provision was recognized by a family court in December 2016, the claimant, while living with his biological (but not legal) father and stateless mother, had never gone to school before he was confirmed of Japanese nationality after reaching the age of majority. His birth registration with the Japanese authorities had never been carried out until that time. As stated in Sect. 6.4, while the claimant's mother stated she had given birth at a hospital in Japan, she was using a false name at the time, and there was no direct evidence to prove her assertion. The claimant's birth at a hospital in Japan was accepted by the court only based on the statements by the claimant's mother and biological father. The birth mother indeed later stated that she had initially planned to give birth at home but changed her mind in the process of delivery and rushed into the hospital. Email response to author's inquiry from Fumie Azukizawa, legal representative on 7 August 2019, in relation to Tōkyō Family Court Tachikawa Branch Adjudication, 5 December 2016 (*Heisei 28 nen*).

As will be discussed in Sect. 6.7, depending on the circumstances, in such situations credible statements by the person herself or himself that demonstrate that she or he must have been seen by a third person in the territory before the deadline might even suffice without evidence produced by a third person.

The next relevant question would be: why do some States want to set the age limitation so low? To answer this question, it is useful to examine the justifications that States cite to impose the low age limitation for their foundling provisions to apply.

## 6.7  Are the Rationale for Low Age Limitation Justified?

It is now time to ask the following fundamental question: what is the justification behind low or any age limitation? Does a foundling's right to nationality 'expire' if she or he cannot be 'found in time'?

### 6.7.1  Rationales Presented by States

In the review of administrative instructions or case law of several States whose legislation imposes age limitation, it was not possible to locate much detailed discussions on the rationale for imposing such an age limit.

Unexpectedly, the interviews and inquiries with the competent authorities and expert organizations as well as the examination of available literature with regard to Italy turned out to be helpful to clarify the rationale. To reintroduce Italy's nationality law 91/1992 for ease of reference, article 1 states 'The following shall be citizens by birth':

> who [*chi*, referring to 'sons or daughters' [*il figlio*] in Article 1[1]a) born in the territory of the Republic both of whose parents are unknown [...] (Article 1(1)b) sons or daughters [*il figlio*] found [*trovato*] in the territory of the Republic whose parents are unknown shall be considered citizens by birth in the absence of proof of their possession of any other citizenship (Article 1 (2012)).[72]

Both article 1(1)b and 1(2) refers to '*il figlio*', which *in* theory does not limit the age of the person for those provisions to apply to grant Italian nationality.[73] Indeed, this is easy to understand when it comes to article 1(1)b, as it applies to a person of unknown parents 'born in Italy', such as persons born of the 'anonymous birth' scheme in Italy (see Sect. 4.3.10). However, when it comes to article 1(2), which only requires that the person was 'found',[74] whether '*il figlio*' can be of any age

---

[72] Legge No 91, 5 febbraio 1992, Nuove norme sulla cittadinanza (5 February 1992) <http://www.refworld.org/docid/46b84a862.html>.

[73] See fn 44, Chap. 3 of this book entitled 'Note on the translation of "*il figlio*"'.

[74] Paolo Farci, *Apolidia (Statelessness)* (Giuffré 2012) 335–6.

is disputable. In practice, the current interpretation of the competent and central administrative authority is that '*il figlio*' under article 1(2) needs to be a 'small child' when found in general. Upon the interview by the author, the Ministry of Interior shared that their written internal manual states that article 1(2) of 91/1992 foresees a small child, apart from a new-born baby, who is not yet able to communicate information pertaining to the identity of their parents (or their place of birth). The Ministry stated that if the child is able to speak, 'normally the child should know' about her or his own parentage.

Further, according to the study or commentary written by the central competent authority, that is the Ministry of Interior, on the interpretation of 91/1992 nationality law, a person needs to be a small child to benefit from the provision[75]:

> The grant of citizenship by jus soli provided for in article 1 of the 1992 law *must be linked to the presumption that the birth took place on the territory* of the State and that the parents are both unknown or stateless.[76] *This provision, therefore, does not seem to refer to any minor, but only to those whose very young age makes one consider that their birth was in Italy.* It must be held that the term 'found' is related to the birth event and the governing regulation of the birth referred in the Civil Status Ordinance (D.P.R., 3.11.2000, No 396), whose article 38 provides: 'Anyone who finds an abandoned child [*trova un bambino abbandonato*] must entrust him to an institute or a nursing home. [...]' From this connection with the Civil Status Ordinance, it follows that the addressee of art. 1, n. 2 of Law No 91 [on nationality] *can be considered as a new-born or a child at an early age.* It seems out of place that it can be an *adult*, even if she or he is unable to understand and wants and lack documents that prove their identity or citizenship (*anche se incapace di intendere e volere e privo di documenti atti a dimostrare la propria identità o cittadinanza*). If a person in this condition was found in Italy, *he should be considered and treated in relation to her or his situation of statelessness.* This provision, therefore, does not seem to refer to any minor but only to those *whose very young age makes one believe that their birth occurred in Italy.* (emphasis added; author translation)

On the other hand, an inquiry was made to experts who belong to the municipalities' National Association of Civil Registrar Officials (ANUSCA), which is not the competent authority per se but is able to provide expert views on nationality and civil registration matters.[77] The experts indicated that, in their view, it was still possible that article 1(2) applies to older children or actually even adults:

---

[75] Direzione Centrale Per I Diritti Civili and others, 'La Cittadinanza Italiana – La Normativa, Le Procedure, Le Circolari' ['Italian Citizenship – Legislation, Procedures, Circulars'] (31 March 2003) <https://www.asgi.it/banca-dati/cittadinanza-italiana-normativa-procedure-circolari/> accessed 4 August 2019.

[76] The original states: 'L'attribuzione della cittadinanza iure soli a titolo originario previsto dall'art. 1 art.della legge del 1992 deve essere collegata alla presunzione che la nascita sia avvenuta sul territorio dello Stato e che i genitori siano entrambi ignoti o apolid'. Ibid, pp 18, 23. As a side note, the last word appears to be included erroneously. As article 1(2), only requires parents be unknown (unlike article 1(2)), it should not talk about presumption of the parents being 'stateless'. Academic sources also echo this position: 'that provision cannot, on the other hand, concern the child who can act independently, because it would be assumed that he had entered Italy alone': G. Zampaglione and P. Guglielman, 'L'attribuzione della cittadinanza' in *Diritto consolare*, vol III (La cittadinanza 1995) 29.

[77] Interview with Enrico Guida, Statelessness Expert, UNHCR Rome (23 May 2017).

[I]n cases of a person of unknown parents found in the territory over 18 years old, [...] the birth certificate would be issued following a decision of rectification by the Court, in line with article 95 DPR 396/2000 (Civil Status Ordinance).[78]

It can be concluded that, at least under the current view of the central competent authority on nationality matters, there is an age limitation by interpreting the neutral term in article 1(2) '*il figlio*' to mean a small child. As will be discussed in Sect. 7.5 relating to Italy, this is indeed counter-intuitive considering Italy's position during the 1959 Geneva conference[79] as well as the evolution of the Italian nationality law, that is that article 1(2) of 1992 law does not refer to any presumption of birth but simply provides that a person of unknown parents found in the territory 'shall be considered a citizen by birth' unlike the equivalent article in the previous 1912 nationality law.

It is now time to examine the reasoning for States, including Italy, to limit the age to a small child.

## 6.7.2 Rationale 1: Do Older Children Know Their Parents' Identity or Their Birthplace?

The first rationale presented by the Italian Ministry of Interior for limiting '*il figlio*' to mean a small child was that an older child should be able to know, and tell, who her or his parents are or where she or he was born. This is indeed the same rationale as the above-cited paragraph 59 of the UNHCR Guidelines 4 (2012), which suggests that the foundling provision should 'at a minimum' apply to all 'young children' who 'are not yet able to accurately communicate information pertaining to the identity of their parents or their place of birth'.

The question should then be asked here, is the above assertion—that a child over a certain age can accurately describe her or his parentage or birthplace—valid? In some cases, yes—for example, if the child concerned was staying with her or his legal parent until a certain age but got abandoned or even lost, and based on what she or he can remember, and whatever evidence is available, such legal parent(s) can be tracked down.

---

[78] Response to inquiry (through Enrico Guida, Statelessness Expert, UNHCR Rome) from Mr Romano Minardi and Mr Carvgioni, civil registry officers who are experts and who belong to National Association of Civil Registrar Officials (ANUSCA), 20 May 2017. Article 90 of the Civil Status Ordinance is about judicial rectification procedures relating to civil status acts.

[79] Basically supporting Denmark's position advocating for the grant of nationality to even a foundling found in the territory born abroad, in case she or he does not acquire the nationality of the country of birth. As represented by Italy's verbally proposed revision of article 2 of the 1961 Convention as cited in Sect. 7.3.1.1, recorded on United Nations, Summary Records, 5th Meeting of the Committee of the Whole held on 3 April 1959, A/CONF.9/C.1/SR.5, UN Conference on the Elimination or Reduction of Future Statelessness, Geneva, 1959 and New York, 1961 (3 April 1959) 7 <http://legal.un.org/docs/?path=../diplomaticconferences/1959_statelessness/docs/english/vol_2/a_conf9_c1_sr5.pdf&lang=E> accessed 4 August 2019.

However, this is not the case in many instances. The ground reality observed is that in many cases, a person who originally does not know her or his parentage or the circumstances of birth would not be able to talk about them regardless of how old they become—whether five, 18, or 60 years old.

For example, if somebody is informally adopted by an unrelated adult at the age of two with no record of her or his real legal parents, can we expect her or him to be able to talk about his parentage and place of birth when, at the age of 15, she or he finally gets out of the control of that adult? The perfect example is the 2006 Newark Case cited in Sects. 6.4–6.6. In this case, the girl who was confirmed US nationality (when she was over age 18 based on the US foundling provision) had grown up believing that the unrelated woman who obviously abused her for welfare payments was her mother. The girl probably had also believed that her birthplace was what was on her fake 'birth certificate', which turned out to be forged. So, what she does not know, she does not know regardless of how old she becomes. Another issue with this justification is that even if the person herself or himself can tell whatever she or he can remember about the parents or the birthplace, it is yet another issue whether such information can be legally proven to be true. Unless their parentage (or birthplace in the case of a *jus soli* State) is legally established, her or his nationality issue cannot be resolved.

### 6.7.3   Rationale 2: Is It Justifiable to Include 'presumption of birth' in the Definition of Being 'found'?

So, it is time to look at the other justification provided by the Ministry of Interior's commentary, that the term 'found' is linked to the presumption of birth in the territory. True, if a several-hour-old new-born baby is found in the territory, it appears likely that she or he was born in that territory. However, think about a situation where such a baby is found in somebody's doorstep in a town in Belgium directly bordering the Netherlands. No border control is in place between the two countries in this particular area. Who can rule out the possibility that somebody drove from the Netherlands and dropped the baby there and then drove away? Considering this, even placing the limitation that the person needs to be new-born does not necessarily appear to serve the purpose—let alone 'five years old' as the US does; five years is enough time for a person who was born in Mexico to travel to the US.

From here, the doubts arise whether linking the presumption of birth in the territory with the term 'found' itself can be justified. It is true that under article 2 of the 1961 Convention, a foundling found in the territory is to benefit from the legal presumption or even the legal fiction by being considered to have been 'born in the territory'. But the presumption of birth in the territory is the legal effect of being a 'foundling' having been 'found' in the territory.

So, is it justifiable to include, in the definition of being 'found', that there is presumption that she or he was born in the territory? In considering this question, it is useful to re-examine the DGRN resolution of 10 June 2005[80] from Spain discussed in Sect. 4.3.5 (see the detailed facts in that section). In this case, the girl, around the age of ten, while begging on the street with a self-claimed father when found by the authorities, was confirmed as a Spanish national for being of undetermined parentage with her first known place of stay being the Spanish territory as stipulated under article 17.1.d) of the Civil Code. As stated in the DGRN resolution, the self-claimed parents 'appeared to be nationals of Romania'. There is no information included in the decision about the basis for such an assessment. Likewise, no information can be found regarding the language the girl spoke, her appearance, her accounts about how she grew up in which country that could have (while not necessarily) helped to assess whether she was born or grew up in the territory or not. Moreover, it is even noted in the decision that the self-claimed parents stated that the girl was 'born in Rome', that is abroad. While such a statement was not proven, a reading of the facts included in the DGRN resolution does not lead to the presumption of birth in Spain. On the contrary, the facts rather point more towards her birth outside the territory. However, it is useful to quote the relevant part of the DGRN resolution here:

> [A]rticle 17.1.d) of the Civil Code [...] *provides legal proof,* by way of presumption, *without needing to* enter at that point into assessing whether or not (it is) based on a legal fiction (ficción legal)[81] or there is *plausibility in the presumed fact* [*sin necesidad de* [...] *valorar* [...] *verosimilitud del hecho presumido*], *of the birth in Spain of minors,* who fulfil both the following two circumstances: a) That their filiation 'is not determined', and b) That their 'first known place of stay is Spanish territory'. Regarding the second condition, there is no controversy in view of the aforementioned facts, *not even the unproven statement of the parents* – whose status as such is not proven either – regarding the alleged birth of the minor in Rome – *could invalidate such conclusion,* since, in the absence of other evidence, the first 'known' place of stay of the child is Barcelona. (emphasis added)[82]

Based on this reasoning, it is apparent that for DGRN, whether it is plausible or likely that the concerned person was actually born in Spain does not matter; what matters is that her or his first known place of stay is Spain. Upon fulfilment of the two preconditions under article 17.1.d) of the Civil Code, that is that a minor is (1) of undetermined parentage, and that (2) her or his first known place of stay is Spanish territory, the presumption of birth in Spain consequently follows as a legal effect.

This strongly supports the position of this book that presumption of birth should not constitute part of the definition of having been 'found' in the territory. Given that there is no need for the presumption of birth in the territory for the person to be considered to have been 'found' in the territory, then there would be no need to put the age limitation, at least at a low age. The argument that the earlier the person is

---

[80] Res. DGRN de 10 de junio de 2005 (BOE, 1-VIII-2005, pp 27,158–9 (Anexo III.3.25)) (author translation).

[81] It is unclear what the term 'legal fiction' (*ficción legal*) in this context exactly means – whether it is used to mean a legal fiction not allowing for its reversal by proving the opposite fact. In such a case (irreversible legal fiction), it means that once it is established that a person of undetermined parentage's first known place is Spain, he or she is deemed to have been born in Spain even if it is proven that he or she was born abroad.

[82] Res. DGRN de 10 de junio de 2005 (BOE, 1-VIII-2005, pp 27,158–9 (Anexo III.3.25)).

found, the more likelihood there is that the person was born in the territory, does not necessarily hold water.

### 6.7.4   A Foundling is Any Child Under the Age of Majority

Therefore, it is concluded that limiting the application of a foundling provision to a young child appears arbitrary for lacking clear justification. The travaux detailed in particular in Sects. 3.4.5.2 and 7.3.1.1 shows that the underlying intention behind the foundling provision is to protect children without those normally and legally responsible for protection and care. The essential element of the foundling provision should not be about the fact that the person is a 'newborn baby' or 'a small child', but that the person is of 'unknown parentage', as a result of which she or he cannot acquire nationality based on the *jus sanguinis* principle (or by the *jus soli* principle if the birthplace is also unknown).

As stated earlier, of paramount importance in determining the scope of the 1961 Convention obligations to prevent statelessness among children is the CRC to which all except one 193 UN member States and all State parties to the 1961 Convention are party. It is stressed again here that article 2 of the 1961 Convention must be interpreted in light of the provisions of the CRC. The right to nationality of a 'child' is explicitly protected under article 7 of the CRC, as well as under article 24 of ICCPR and other legal instruments. It is 'never in the best interests of the child to be rendered stateless'[83]—the primary consideration for States in all actions concerning children as stipulated in article 3 of the CRC.

Further, it is relevant to cite here the Joint General Comment in 2017 of the CRC Committee and the Committee on the Protection of the Rights of All Migrant Workers and Members of Their Families (CMW) about the need to ensure the same rights to higher teenagers as their younger counterparts:

> The definition of the child under the Convention on the Rights of the Child provides rights and protection until the age of 18. The *Committees are concerned that children between 15 and 18 years tend to be provided much lower levels of protection, and are sometimes considered as adults* or left with an ambiguous migration status until they reach 18 years of age. States are urged to ensure that equal standards of protection are provided to every child, including those above the age of 15 years [...]. (emphasis added)[84]

Opening the age up to all minors is also justifiable in light of national legislation currently in force (see above Sect. 6.3).

As a side note, with the age of a foundling being undefined in article 2, one could even go further to think that limiting the foundling's age to a 'minor' could

---

[83] Tunis Conclusions (2014) para 62.

[84] Joint General Comment No 4 (2017) of CMW and No 23 (2017) of the CRC Committee on State obligations regarding the human rights of children in the context of international migration in countries of origin, transit, destination and return, 16 November 2017, CMW/C/GC/4-CRC/C/GC/23 <https://www.refworld.org/docid/5a12942a2b.html>.

also be lacking firm justification—and wonder whether adults of unknown parents found in the territory could possibly fall within the foundling concept. However, it is recalled here that the ordinary meaning of a 'foundling' means a child and not an adult. A person who was born and grew up in a foreign country or countries until reaching adulthood have normally developed a relevant link with such State(s). A stateless person of unknown parentage who is found as an adult by a third person or authorities in the territory should be duly protected as a stateless person under the 1954 Convention or the equivalent provision in nationality law, rather than benefiting from the foundling provision.

In conclusion, the age of a foundling when found under article 2 of the 1961 Convention should be defined as a child, which means a minor 'below the age of eighteen years' (unless under the law applicable to the child, majority is attained earlier) under article 1 of the CRC.

## 6.8   'Not having been born outside the territory'—Is It Part of the 'found' Definition?

Another question might arise—if birth outside the territory is established with regard to a person of unknown parentage, does it then negate the fact that a person has been 'found' in the territory for the purpose of article 2 of the 1961 Convention?

It is useful here to briefly introduce the two separate Australian Federal Court decisions in 2015[85] which will be discussed in more detail in Sect. 7.5. In these cases, the claimants, who were born in Indonesia and Samoa respectively, were considered to have been 'found' within the Australian territory within the meaning of Australia's foundling provision, that is section 5(3)(b) of the 1948 Citizenship Act. (Note, however, that they did not, in the end, benefit from the provision because it was considered that their possession of Indonesian nationality and birth abroad respectively were considered to constitute 'proof to the contrary', as detailed in Chap. 7).

From this, it is clear that one's birth abroad was considered to overturn the presumed fact. In the context of section 5(3)(b) of the Citizenship Act, the presumed fact is that the person was born in Australia, which consequently grants one Australian citizenship (see Chap. 7, including Sect. 7.5, on what constitutes 'the contrary'). Having said this, being 'found' in the territory is one of the prerequisite facts for a foundling *to* benefit from the presumption of 'having been born in the territory' 'of parents who are nationals of that State. It can be argued that while 'birth outside the territory' can be considered to constitute 'proof to the contrary' of one of the

---

[85] *Nicky v. Minister for Immigration* [2014] FCCA 2569 (Federal Circuit Court of Australia)/*Nicky v. Minister for Immigration and Border Protection* [2015] FCA 174 (Federal Court of Australia) and *SZRTN v. Minister for Immigration and Border Protection* [2015] FCA 305 (Federal Court of Australia).

presumed facts, it should not nullify the fact that the person concerned fulfils one of the 'preconditions'—that she or he has been found in the territory.

It can thus be concluded that 'not having been born outside the territory' is not part of the definition of having been 'found' in the territory.


## 6.9   Burden and Standard of Proof in Establishing Having Been Found (Under the Applicable Age Limitation)

As discussed in Chap. 5, in most legal systems, the claimant bears the initial responsibility of substantiating her or his claim. With regard to one's unknown parentage, due to the difficulties that often arise when determining whether his parents are legally 'unknown', it was nevertheless determined in Chap. 5 that, given the person or her or his representative asserts unknown parentage and duly cooperates and provides all reasonably available evidence, the State concerned should bear both the burden of producing evidence as well as the burden of persuasion regarding the existence of a legally recognized parent. In relation to the standard of proof or the 'degree of unknown-ness', it was basically recommended that the decision-maker recognizes the 'unknown-ness' when she or he could not be convinced (within a reasonable time) that one of the child's legally recognized parents is definitively identified to the extent that it enables the confirmation of whether the child has acquired nationality by *jus sanguinis.*

Compared to the difficulties in proving the negative, that is 'unknown parentage', whether one has been found in the territory itself is normally much more straightforward to prove—as it is an affirmative fact and was defined broadly to mean that she or he was seen by a third person other than her or his parents within the territory.

It could thus be asserted that in general, a foundling or her or his representative should generally bear a heavier burden of production and persuasion in respect of proving 'having been found', as compared to those in relation to 'unknown parentage'. Needless to say, if it is established such as via a birth certificate issued by a doctor that she or he was born in a hospital within the territory, no issue of burden and standard of proof arises. If the person is detected by the authorities obviously before whatever deadline imposed by the authorities, no burden and standard of proof issue would ever arise either.

Proving 'found' can nevertheless become complicated depending on individual circumstances, such as at what age she or he is detected by, or approaches, the competent authorities for confirmation of nationality, or on how low is the age limitation imposed by the States concerned to be found (by a third person). For example, suppose a person of unknown parents is only detected by the competent authorities after the young age limitation, and if the child is still a young child who is not yet able to communicate accurately whatever she or he could know (if known) regarding the identity of her or his parents or birthplace. If there is no third-party witness to testify that she or he was found under the age limitation, then it is difficult for her or him to bear any sort of burden of proof, that is both the burden of production and burden of persuasion. The same goes for her or his appointed guardian, legal representative or the person who found her or him after the age limitation.

Moreover, as mentioned in Sect. 6.7.2, even if the person is mature enough to make an accurate account of whatever she or he can remember by the time detected by the authorities, if under the given legislation she or he needs to have been found while still a new-born or a small infant, it can become quite difficult for her or him to gather evidence to prove such a fact. This depends on the individual circumstances, but suppose one was separated from her or his parents when quite young and does not remember where she or he was born and grew up. In contrast, if an age limit is set at 'below 18', then it should normally be much easier to prove such a fact. Exceptional circumstances, such as in situations where she or he has been under the control of, and mistreated by, human smugglers or other abusive third persons whose testimony cannot be relied upon, again would need to be taken into consideration.

In terms of the standard of proof to establish that the person has been found in the territory, the 'to a reasonable degree' standard (advocated by the UNHCR in proving a child's otherwise statelessness) might be applicable by analogy depending on factors such as how low the age limitation is set at, the age the person is detected by the authorities and other individual circumstances. If the age limitation is set higher, it is likely justified to set the applicable standard of proof higher.

Even in the absence of any documentary evidence or credible third-person witness, the verbal and written statement by the person himself indicating that she or he should have been born or was found in the territory before the age limitation can also suffice, subject to appropriate credibility assessment.[86]

## 6.10  Summary and Conclusions: A Foundling Can Be Found by Any Third Party While a Minor

This chapter examined the maximum age at which a person of unknown parents found in the territory can be considered a 'foundling', and the closely related issue of what it means to be 'found' in the territory.

As clarified in Chap. 3, being found on the territory of a State itself is the condition that gives rise to the obligation of a State to grant nationality to a foundling, that is a person of unknown parents. Further, Chap. 3 had already clarified that being 'found' includes the situation where the person is known to have been born there.

The review of some State practice confirmed the guidance in UNHCR Guidelines 4 (2012) that a person can be 'found' by any third party other than the State authorities.

---

[86] UNHCR Handbook (2014) para 101 states: 'Where, however, little or no documentary evidence is available, […] authorities will need to rely to a greater degree on an applicant's testimony and issues relating to the credibility of the applicant's account might arise.' This is applicable by analogy. Also refer to paras 102–7 ((9) Credibility issues) for guidance as to how credibility assessment should be carried out.

It was concluded that, ultimately, being 'found in the territory' under article 2 of the 1961 Convention—other than when the person's birth in the territory is established-should be broadly defined as 'having been seen in the territory by a person other than one's parents', or something to that effect. It was found that whether one was 'found' in the territory itself is normally not an issue but rather whether or not she or he was found 'in time' before reaching the certain age if specified by the relevant nationality law provision.

The 1961 Convention does not define an age at which a child may be considered a foundling. The ordinary meaning of the English word 'foundling' defined in law and non-law dictionaries includes that a person is an 'infant' or a 'child', both of which can mean a small child, but can also be interpreted to mean under the age of majority in the field of law. The equivalent term in other UN language versions also generally has the connotation that the person in question is a (small) child. The UNHCR Guidelines 4 (2012) emphasizes that in light of the object and purpose of the 1961 Convention and the right of every child to acquire a nationality, 'at a minimum', the foundling provision is to apply to all young children who are not yet able to accurately communicate information on the parents' identity or their birthplace, also suggesting that opening the age to all minors, as some States do, is commendable.

The review of the national legislation of 193 States (see annex 1) showed that the legislation of at least 17 States only provides a nationality grant to persons of unknown parents 'born in the territory', while in practice nationality could be confirmed for persons of unknown parents found in the territory via presumption of birth in the territory. A number of States—36 in total—limit the grant of nationality to persons who are 'new-born (or recently born)' when found. Ten States provide for specific age limitation older than new-borns, starting at age three up to 15.

As detailed in Sect. 6.3.4, a total of 15 States, or slightly more than 11 per cent of the 139 States with foundling provisions, either explicitly or by interpretation open up the target age to all 'minors'. Among the 15, the foundling provisions of at least ten States are explicitly open to all 'minors'—by either using the term 'minor', or 'child' and defining 'child' as 'minor' (while the age of majority differs) within the same legislation. For the foundling provisions of five additional States, dependable information was available stating that the (undefined) term 'child' therein meant 'minor'. For the remaining 61 States whose foundling provisions use the term 'child', 'foundling' or 'infant', while no complementary information was readily located specifying the age of the person in question, there are indications that a number of them might indeed cover all minors.

At any rate, it was found that if all States adopt this broad definition of being 'found', even if a relatively younger age limitation is imposed, the issue in many cases will be resolved as long as one can produce a credible third-person witness about her or his stay in the territory below the age, or otherwise prove such a fact by her or his own account. However, if the age limitation is too low, then the chances are that the person cannot secure witnesses, especially in situations where, for example, he was informally adopted, abused or neglected by unrelated adults. Significant difficulties might arise in proving having been found in time.

Subsequently, the possible justifications for limiting the age, especially to young children, were considered. The justifications are normally either that (1) a person of an older age 'should be able to accurately communicate the information relating to the identity of her or his parents or the birthplace', or that (2) the younger the person's age, the more likely that the person was born within the territory.

With regard to the first argument, it was found that a person who does not know the circumstances of her or his birth and parentage, for example somebody informally adopted by a third person at a quite young age with no record of her or his real legal parents, would not be able to talk about her or his parentage regardless of how old they become—whether five, 18 or 60 years old. What is unknown is unknown.

With regard to the link between being found and presumption of birth in the territory, it was considered that even if a person is found as a literally new-born child, it is almost impossible to eliminate all the chances that the person was born outside the territory—especially in States that share borders with other States with little immigration control, including those in Europe.

It was also drawn from Australian court decisions and Spanish administrative decisions that the definition of being 'found' itself should not include the likelihood, or presumption of, birth in the territory. This is because the presumption of birth in the territory is a legal effect that comes as a result of fulfilling the preconditions that one is a person of unknown parents found in the territory. Further, it was concluded that 'not having been born outside the territory' also is not part of the definition of having been 'found' in the territory, while it can constitute proof to the contrary to (one of) the presumed fact(s) under the foundling provision depending on the formulation of the particular national legislation, which will be discussed in Sect. 7.4.

The essence of article 2 is not exactly about the fact that the person is 'a small child', but that the person is of 'unknown parentage' (and often unknown birthplace), as a result of which she or he cannot acquire nationality based on the *jus sanguinis* principle (or by the *jus soli* principle).

Based on this, and taking into consideration the object and purpose of the 1961 Convention, as well as articles 3 and 7 of the CRC, it was concluded that the imposition of an age limit as a young child would inevitably be arbitrary for lacking clear justification. It was thus concluded that article 2 of the 1961 Convention can be applied to persons of unknown parents found in the territory before reaching the age of majority.

# Chapter 7
# 'Proof to the Contrary' and Conditions for Nationality Withdrawal

**Abstract** This chapter examines the term 'in the absence of proof to the contrary' in article 2 of the 1961 Convention before the confirmation of nationality under the provision, and the conditions for the withdrawal of the nationality already acquired. The chapter analyses the travaux of the 1961 Convention, the structure or legal methods adopted in equivalent domestic provisions and the European Convention on Nationality in granting nationality to foundlings, as well as State practice. Based on this, author asserts that birth abroad by itself—as opposed to possession of another nationality—might not necessarily amount to the 'proof to the contrary'. In this context, the linkage with unaccompanied minors is explored. The chapter emphasizes not only the need for prevention of statelessness but due process when nationality withdrawal is being considered, based on international human rights law standards starting with the prohibition of arbitrary nationality deprivation and the best interests of the child.

Article 2 of the 1961 Convention provides that a 'foundling found in the territory' is considered to have been 'born within that territory' of 'parents possessing the nationality of that State' on a conditional basis, that is 'in the absence of proof to the contrary'. Several questions arise. These include:

(1)  What is the temporal scope of the phrase 'in the absence of proof to the contrary'? At which stage is it relevant, that is:

    (a)  pre facto assessment for the State to confirm or grant the foundling's acquisition of nationality; or

    (b)  post facto assessment for the withdrawal[1] of nationality after the person has been living as a national?

(2)  What constitutes the 'proof to the contrary'? What were the discussions during the travaux, and how are the domestic provisions equivalent to article 2 written and implemented? How does it compare with the equivalent provision in the ECN?

---

[1] See Sect. 7.6.1.7 for what the term 'withdrawal' encompasses in this book.

(3)   What are the criteria and the conditions to the withdrawal post facto of
       nationality that has already been acquired, including any limitation period?

UNHCR Guidelines 4 (2012) do not directly discuss or define 'proof to the
contrary'. Further, the 1961 Convention does not contain any specific provision
or references regulating the withdrawal of nationality acquired based on article 2.
UNHCR Guidelines 5 (2020) do not specifically discuss the same, while Guidelines 4
(2012) offer one sentence on this.[2] The academic and practical materials that discuss
these questions are quite limited. Below, the available materials will be summarized
and analyzed in an attempt to answer the above questions, including the travaux
records, domestic legislation and State practice including case law.

## 7.1   Temporal Scope of 'in the absence of proof to the contrary': Pre Facto and Post Facto Assessment

Before reflecting on the travaux discussions and national legislation, a clear distinction needs to be made between two distinct types of assessments at two different
points in time. One is the assessment when the authorities first confirm a foundling's
acquisition of nationality automatically and register him/her as such. This will be
called 'pre facto assessment'. The other is the assessment of whether to withdraw
the nationality which the authorities have already confirmed that a particular person
has acquired. This will hereinafter be referred to as 'post facto assessment'.

The text of article 2 of the 1961 Convention is not clear about this 'temporal
scope' of the term 'in the absence of proof to the contrary'. As to be discussed in
Sect. 7.3, the term 'proof to the contrary' was not included in the original 1954 ILC
Draft Convention on the Reduction of Future Statelessness. The term was rather
proposed by Denmark during the 1959 conference to address the gap between the
(predominantly) *jus sanguinis* and *jus soli* States and was adopted in the final version
of the 1961 Convention. The temporary scope of 'proof to the contrary' was not
directly or explicitly clarified in the relevant travaux discussions but the concept
during the deliberations generally revolved around the time when the person was
just found in the territory, that is pre-facto stage, as seen in Sect. 7.3.

Further, in line with the general rules on reading law, the entire sentence of article
2 should be read as regulating the conditions for acquisition of nationality by a
foundling. A contrary reading, that it would also cover the post facto stage, would
give rise to the assertion that the nationality acquisition under article 2 is 'provisional'
or 'temporal' 'until the proof to the contrary is discovered'. Even if the 'contrary'
fact was to be defined as 'possession of another nationality', such a concept of
'provisional nationality', however, goes against the principle of legal certainty, of

---

[2] UNHCR Guidelines 4 (2012) para 60.

critical importance in nationality law,[3] and is not compatible with the best interests of the child (article 3 of the CRC), as well as the child's right to preserve their identity (article 8 of the CRC)[4] among others.

Thus the term 'in the absence of proof to the contrary' in itself should be understood as part of the conditions in pre facto assessment, to confirm the acquisition of nationality in a definitive manner. Such assessment, as concluded in Sect. 5.8, should be conducted as soon as possible, that is within six months in principle, extendable in certain circumstances. As will be discussed in Sect. 7.6.1, States should clearly and separately stipulate the conditions for post facto withdrawal of nationality that has definitively been acquired, including to avoid arbitrary deprivation of nationality.

As will be seen in Sect. 7.6.2 indeed, at least 37 pieces of legislation among the 139 States relatively explicitly regulate post facto withdrawal along with the criteria—separate from the contrary fact for the purpose of nationality acquisition. Nevertheless, as also seen in Sect. 7.6.2, naturally, States may explicitly or de facto consider (at least some of) the facts that constitute the 'proof to the contrary' pre facto as also constituting the grounds for post facto withdrawal of nationality. For example, this is clear in Australia's foundling provision within its 1948 and the current 2007 Citizenship Act adopts the wording 'unless and until the contrary is proved'.[5] The term 'unless' in this context apparently refers to the 'pre facto' assessment, and 'until' refers to a 'post facto' assessment.

Considering the above, it was decided that the conditions for withdrawal of nationality post facto is discussed in the second part of this chapter, whose first half discusses the 'proof to the contrary' upon nationality acquisition, pre facto.

## 7.2  Structure of Article 2 and What 'to the contrary' Qualifies (Prerequisite or Presumed Facts?)

As detailed in Sect. 3.4.5.1, the initial ILC Draft Conventions linked article 2 with article 1 by presuming the birth in the territory of a foundling found in the territory in order to benefit from the *jus soli* nationality grant to persons otherwise stateless born in the territory under article 1.

---

[3] See for example Gerard-René de Groot, 'Quasi-Loss of Nationality: Some Critical Reflections' in ISI, *The World's Stateless: Deprivation of Nationality* (March 2020) 206 <https://files.institutesi.org/WORLDs_STATELESS_2020.pdf> accessed 27 September 2020.

[4] See also *Genovese v. Malta*, Application No 53124/09 [11 October 2011] (ECtHR).

[5] Section 14 of the current Australian Citizenship Act 2007: '14 *Citizenship for abandoned children* A person is an Australian citizen if the person is found abandoned in Australia as a child, *unless and until* the contrary is proved.' Federal Register of Legislation, Australian Citizenship Act 2007 (2019) <https://www.legislation.gov.au/Details/C2019C00040> accessed 4 August 2019. Section 5(3)(b) of the previous Australian Citizenship Act 1948 section 5(3) of the 1948 Act provided in relevant part as follows: 'a person who, when a child, was found abandoned in Australia shall, *unless and until* the contrary is proved, be deemed: (i) to have been born in Australia'.

However, a number of States argued against this dependency as article 1 was to allow the non-automatic grant of nationality that could in the worst scenario only start at the age of 18. Those States asserted that States have historically provided for the acquisition of nationality by foundlings, that is persons of unknown parentage, found in the territory predominantly because they were presumed highly likely to be a child of nationals born in the territory. Further, some States asserted that regardless of their actual parentage or birthplace, persons of unknown parents are in need of (stronger) protection due to their lack of those responsible for protection and care. The advocates for foundlings' nationality rights then succeeded in making article 2 autonomous from article 1, for the purpose of ensuring automatic grant of nationality to them. The ILC's draft article 2 needed to be reformulated so that a foundling can automatically acquire nationality where found regardless of whether the State generally adopts the *jus sanguinis* or *jus soli* principle. Against this draft, as detailed in Sect. 3.4.5.2, Denmark promoted its version (article 4 of its own proposal), which was later adopted with some modifications, after substantive discussions on what constitutes 'proof to the contrary'.

The current article 2 provides that a person who fulfils the two prerequisite facts, that is being a:

(1)   'foundling'; and
(2)   having been 'found' in the territory (under any applicable age limitation).

'in the absence of proof to the contrary', benefits from two[6] legally presumed[7] facts, that is that she or he shall 'be considered to have been':

(1)   'born within that territory'; and (note article 2 does not say 'or')
(2)   born of 'parents possessing the nationality of that State'.

In line with the general rules on reading law, the phrase 'in the absence proof to the contrary' in article 2 should normally qualify the term 'considered to...' and

---

[6] The presumed facts are precisely speaking three (and not two) as 'parents' consist of father and mother, two different persons. However, if one of the parents is known to be a foreign parent then already it overturns not only one of the presumed facts but also the 'prerequisite' fact that the person is a 'foundling', that is of unknown parents, and make the whole article 2 inapplicable. Thus, the father and mother being nationals are rounded up and counted as one presumption.

[7] *Note on the particular wording 'considered' under article 2 of the 1961 Convention*: The text of article 2 itself does not contain the words '(legally) presumed', but 'considered'. The formulation of article 2 ('in the absence of proof to the contrary') should provide for a 'legal presumption' for readers of a number of jurisdictions, including Japan, as it is stipulated in the text of the law that the 'considered' facts can be reversed given the proof to the contrary. It is speculated that the neutral term 'considered' (rather than 'presumed' (generally allowing for reversal) or 'deemed' (creating a legal fiction which cannot be reversed regardless of whether the contrary fact(s) is established)) is used in article 2 of the 1961 Convention to accommodate different jurisdictions' varying definitions and approaches to these legal techniques, as well as to leave room for State's discretion on how to exactly formulate their own foundling provision, including whether to 'presume' or 'deem' (or to simply grant nationality even without first presuming or deeming birth in the territory or descent from a national(s)) as will be discussed in Sect. 7.3.1.1. However, in this book, the term 'legally presumed (facts)' is used generally to refer to the facts that are 'considered' (birth in the territory and from parents who are nationals) when the prerequisite facts (being a foundling found in the territory) are fulfilled under article 2 of the 1961 Convention, for the lack of a better term.

after. In other words, 'contrary fact' should relate to 'presumed facts', rather than to the 'prerequisite facts'.

An alternative reading that it qualifies (also) the prerequisite facts would make the provision redundant. This reading is confirmed, for example, by Australian case law to be discussed in Sect. 7.5. In Spanish and US judicial and administrative decisions on the foundling provision, whether the 'contrary' to the presumed facts is proven is also examined separately from whether the prerequisite facts (of being a child of unknown parents found in the territory) are fulfilled, also as seen in Sect. 7.5.

'Having a "known parent"' and 'not having been found in the territory (under the applicable age limitation)' per se thus do not, precisely speaking, constitute the 'contrary' (that is to the 'presumed facts'). This is except for when, in the case of the former, such a 'known parent' is not a national of the country where the child concerned was found (which will also qualify as the 'contrary' fact to one of the presumed facts). Those are facts that deny 'prerequisite facts' (of being a 'foundling' and having been 'found' in the territory (by the applicable age limit)), which would, as a result, make the legal presumption inapplicable anyway.

Needless to say, if the person of known parentage is known to have been born in the territory and would not acquire nationality by *jus sanguinis*, she or he should rather be granted nationality based on a provision for 'otherwise stateless' persons born in the territory, reflecting article 1 of the 1961 Convention (or simply by birth in the territory if a *jus soli* State) if such provision exists.

## 7.3  Travaux Discussions on What Constitutes Proof to the Contrary

As stated earlier, the 1961 Convention is silent on what is considered (proof to) 'the contrary'.[8] What was considered to constitute 'proof to the contrary' during the travaux of the 1961 Convention will be examined below.

### 7.3.1  Discovery of Birth Abroad Pre Facto (And Post Facto)

Chapter 6, in particular, Sect. 6.8, concluded that the definition of having been 'found' in the territory in itself should not include the fact that there is presumption of birth in the territory, or that there is no proof of birth abroad.

Does 'birth outside the territory' constitute 'proof to the contrary' under article 2 of the 1961 Convention, pre facto? Suppose a person found in a State is known to have been born abroad, yet her or his parentage remains unknown. Suppose she

---

[8] The lack of 'the definition of the type of evidence that may be accepted as "proof to the contrary"' is also pointed out by Laura van Waas, *Nationality Matters: Statelessness under International Law* (Intersentia 2008) 70.

or he cannot acquire the nationality of the country of birth as there is no foundling provision or *jus soli* provision in the nationality law of that country. Would she or he still qualify for the nationality of the country where she or he was found? While it might appear theoretical and unlikely, this was indeed one of the major discussion points during the drafting process of the 1961 Convention.

The travaux record cited below might not be necessarily clear about the distinction between pre facto or post facto assessments. However, from the context of the interventions below, which does not seem to envisage that the person concerned has already been confirmed to hold a nationality under article 2, it is assumed that the drafters were examining 'contrary fact' mainly in the context of the pre facto assessment.

### 7.3.1.1    Travaux Discussions on Granting Nationality to Foundlings Born Abroad

Roberto Córdova, the Special Rapporteur in his report to ILC in 1953 stated:

> (E.) What happens when it is shown that the foundling was *not* born in the territory of the State where he was found? Of course, if evidence has been presented which makes it possible to ascertain that the foundling was *born* in *some other territory, the application of article 1* [on otherwise stateless persons *born in the territory*] of the proposed convention would *also* be in order. (emphasis added)[9]

One may suppose from this that, if it was already clear, at the time when found, that a foundling was born outside the territory where they were found, such a birth abroad can constitute 'proof to the contrary' overturning one of the 'presumed' facts. In such a case, in Cordova's view, the obligation to grant nationality (by applying article 2 or an equivalent domestic provision) would be 'transferred' from the country where the person concerned was found, to where she or he is known to have been born. The State where the concerned person was born then is obliged to apply article 1 if the person's parents are known, and, if still unknown, article 2.[10] This is if the State where the person was born is also a State party (or otherwise grants nationality unconditionally by *jus soli*). Now, the question is what happens if the country where the person was born is not a State party to the 1961 Convention.

A close reading of the travaux documents contains further discussions on this point. For example, the Netherlands, in commenting on the first draft of article 2 of the 1954 ILC draft Conventions,[11] advocated that:

---

[9] Roberto Córdova, 'Nationality, including Statelessness—Report on the Elimination or Reduction of Statelessness' (1953) 176 <http://legal.un.org/docs/?path=../ilc/documentation/english/a_cn4_64.pdf&lang=E> accessed 4 August 2019.

[10] See discussions in Chap. 3, in particular Sect. 3.4.7.

[11] As quoted earlier, the 1954 ILC draft Convention at article 2 stated: 'For the purpose of article 1, a foundling, so long as his place of birth is unknown, shall be presumed to have been born in the territory of the Party in which he is found'. Draft Convention on the Reduction of Future Statelessness, adopted by ILC at its sixth session, in 1954, and submitted to the General Assembly

[…] It may be imagined that a *foundling*, found in the territory of one of the Contracting Parties, *is subsequently discovered actually to have been born in the territory of a State which does not recognize the principle of jus soli*, while the nationality [sic – presumably also meant identity][12] of the parents is not known. In that case, if the latter State is not a party to the convention, the present wording of article 2 might leave room for statelessness, because the child cannot profit by the provision of article 4[13] of the two draft Conventions. The Netherlands Government realize that the case referred to above will present itself in very exceptional circumstances only, but in view of the object of the first draft, viz., *to eliminate every conceivable possibility of statelessness*, they would nevertheless suggest to add to article 2 a second paragraph to be worded in the following terms:

'In the case that, *its place of birth being known, it would otherwise be stateless, the foundling shall, for the purpose of article 1, be deemed to have been born in the territory of the Party in which it is found.*' (emphasis added)[14]

Rather surprisingly, the Netherlands' suggestion, in summary, is that if a person of unknown parents found in the territory is known to have been born in another State that does not grant her or him nationality, then the person should acquire nationality where found, by benefiting from a legal fiction that she or he was born in the State where found—however untrue it is. With the draft article 2 being dependent on article 1 (as detailed in Sect. 3.4.5.1), which provided for the acquisition of nationality for persons born in the territory who would otherwise be stateless, this legal fiction would then have resulted in the foreign-born foundling's nationality acquisition.

As discussed in Sect. 3.4.5, against the ILC's draft, Denmark promoted its version, which was article 4 of its own proposal, which was later adopted as article 2 of the 1961 Convention with modifications.

The original Danish proposal article 4 read—to quote once again for the sake of convenience: 'A foundling found in the territory of a Contracting State shall, *in the absence of proof to the contrary, be considered as a national of that State*' (emphasis added).[15] This wording raises the question of what then constitutes proof to 'the

---

as part of the Commission's report covering the work of that session (at para 25). *Yearbook of the International Law Commission, vol II* (United Nations 1954).

[12] From the context, it is assumed that the Dutch representative meant that the identities, as well as the nationalities, of the parents are not known—as the Netherlands here was discussing the revision of article 2, promoting the insertion of the second paragraph that states '[…] the foundling shall…'.

[13] Article 4 of ILC Draft Convention on the Elimination of Future Statelessness, as well as the Draft Convention on the Reduction of Future Statelessness stated: 'If a child is not born in the territory of a State which is a Party to this Convention he shall, if otherwise stateless, acquire the nationality of the Party of which one of his parents is a national. […]'. However, as a foundling's parents are unknown by definition, she or he cannot acquire the nationality by *jus sanguinis* as directed under this article 4. Report of ILC to the General Assembly, 'Draft Convention on the Reduction of Future Statelessness' (1954), *Yearbook of the International Law Commission, vol II* (United Nations 1954) 144.

[14] 6th session of ILC (1954), United Nations, 'Comments by Governments on the draft Convention on the Elimination of Future Statelessness and on the draft Convention on the Reduction of Future Statelessness' (1954) <http://legal.un.org/docs/?path=../ilc/documentation/english/a_cn4_82.pdf&lang=E>.

[15] UN Conference on the Elimination or Reduction of Future Statelessness Geneva, 1959 and New York, 1961, A/CONF.9/4 (15 January 1959) 'Denmark: Memorandum with Draft Convention on the

contrary'. Does it mean birth outside the territory, foreign parentage, or possession of another nationality?

The Danish representative noted in introducing the amendment proposal that in *jus sanguinis* countries it was generally assumed that foundlings are children of nationals of the State in which they were found, and in *jus soli* countries that they had been born in the State where found. He then is quoted to have stated that:

> In both *jus sanguinis* and *jus soli* countries, *foundlings were generally brought up by the State in whose territory they had been found; they should therefore be given the nationality of that State* until it was proved that the assumptions on the strength of which they had been given the nationality of that State were incorrect. (emphasis added)[16]

Thus, from the Danish representative's point of view, what would constitute 'proof to the contrary' under their amendment depended on the assumptions or presumptions that each State in their internal law made in order to grant nationality to a foundling found in their territory.

To clarify this further, the representative from the Netherlands—who, as above in this section, previously recommended a grant of nationality to foundlings who are known to have been born outside the territory—asked what would happen in such a case:

> What would happen if it were established that a foundling, although of unknown parents, had been *born in a country* other than that in which he was found? The word 'in the absence of proof to the contrary' might well render the text inapplicable to such a child. (emphasis added)[17]

The Danish representative responded that:

> [T]he Danish draft provision did not refer to the place of birth of foundlings. *If*, for example, *it were established that a foundling found in Danish territory had in fact been born in the territory of a neighbouring State*, under that draft provision *the child would nevertheless be a Danish national.* (emphasis added)[18]

The Belgian representative rephrased the above Danish draft, as follows: '[A]ccording to the Danish Government's draft article, contracting parties which were jus sanguinis [underline provided in the original text] *countries* would have an obligation to treat as their nationals foundlings, *wheresoever born*, who were found in their territory' (emphasis added).

---

Reduction of Statelessness' <http://legal.un.org/docs/?path=../diplomaticconferences/1959_statele ssness/docs/english/vol_1/a_conf9_4.pdf&lang=E> accessed 4 August 2019.

[16] United Nations, Summary Records, 5th Plenary Meeting held on 31 March 1959, A/CONF.9/SR.5, UN Conference on the Elimination or Reduction of Future Statelessness, Geneva, 1959 and New York, 1961 (31 March 1959) 2 <http://legal.un.org/docs/?path=../diplomaticconfe rences/1959_statelessness/docs/english/vol_2/a_conf9_sr5.pdf&lang=E> accessed 4 August 2019.

[17] Ibid 3.

[18] Ibid 3.

Against this Danish draft, some State representatives, especially Belgium,[19] expressed their views that the evidence of birth outside the territory where found (while parents may remain unknown) should render article 2 inapplicable.[20] For example, the Belgian representative said that his delegation could not support Denmark's amendment. In his view:

> If an abandoned child were found in the territory of a particular country there might indeed be a presumption that he had been born there, until the contrary were proved. If it were eventually proved, however, that the foundling had in fact been born in the territory of another country, article 1 and not article 2 should apply.[21]

Against this, the Italian representative, obviously in support of the Danish amendment, stated:

> The objections of the Belgian representative might perhaps be met if the text of the Danish amendment were revised to read:
>
> A foundling found in the territory of a Contracting Party *shall be considered as a national* of that Contracting Party. (emphasis added)[22]

By deleting the words 'in the absence of proof to the contrary', the Italian representative actually went a step further than the Danish amendment. According to the Italian version, a foundling found in the territory may acquire the nationality where found, not only when there is proof of birth outside the territory, but when there is proof of possessing another nationality.[23] Probably with the concern that it goes too far, the Italian proposal was not followed up.

---

[19] United Arab Republic, while it supported the Danish amendment, nonetheless had a different view on this point: '[...] the words "in the absence of proof to the contrary", however, should refer to the foundling's place of birth and not to the nationality which he might possess'. United Nations, Summary Records, 5th Meeting of the Committee of the Whole held on 3 April 1959, A/CONF.9/C.1/SR.5, UN Conference on the Elimination or Reduction of Future Statelessness, Geneva, 1959 and New York, 1961 (3 April 1959) 8 <http://legal.un.org/docs/?path=../diplom aticconferences/1959_statelessness/docs/english/vol_2/a_conf9_c1_sr5.pdf&lang=E> accessed 4 August 2019.

[20] Ibid 7.

[21] Ibid 7.

[22] Ibid 7.

[23] It is unclear whether the Italian representative realized this. However, it is noted article 1(2) of the 1992 Italian nationality law has almost the same construction as its proposal above during the 1959 conference, except that the 1992 nationality law has 'in the absence of proof of their possession of any other citizenship' at the end, reading: 'Sons or daughters found in the territory of the Republic whose parents are unknown shall be considered citizens by birth 'in the absence of proof of their possession of any other citizenship'.

The Danish proposal was supported by the majority of States[24] and was approved in the 'Committee of the Whole' by 20 votes to five, with four abstentions on 3 April 1959.[25] However, subsequently, the Danish government partly amended its proposal in particular by replacing the words 'to be considered a national of a State' at the end of article 2, by the words 'be considered as born within that territory of parents possessing the nationality of that State'. This amended version this time was adopted by 25 votes to none, with seven abstentions in the Plenary Meeting on 15 April 1959.[26] This was adopted as the current article 2, with an editorial change ('as born' was replaced with 'to have been born'), which says: 'A foundling found in the territory of a Contracting State shall, *in the absence of proof to the contrary*, be considered to have been *born within that territory of parents possessing the nationality* of that State' (emphasis added).

The Danish government's last-minute amendment was to 'meet the views of those delegations'[27] of the five States that had previously voted against the previous Danish amendment. The Belgian delegation is recorded to have 'expressed his delegation's gratitude' to the Danish representative for the amendment. While the record of the meeting does not carry any further details, from the previous discussions cited above, it is clear that the replacement of the term 'considered a national' with 'considered as born within that territory of parents possessing the nationality of that State' was meant to address the disputed issue of what constituted 'proof to the contrary', in particular, whether the person's birth abroad would render article 2 inapplicable or not.

Thus, whether a foundling's birth in another State (without entailing nationality acquisition) constitutes a fact 'to the contrary' under article 2 of the 1961 Convention appears to have been left to each State's decision in light of the particular construction of its own nationality legislation.

As discussed in Sect. 7.2, the formulation of the final version of article 2 provides that a person who fulfils the two prerequisite facts of being a 'foundling' 'found' in the territory shall be entitled to two legal presumptions that she or he is 'born within that territory' 'of parents possessing the nationality of that State'.

---

[24] The general statements of support expressed for the Danish amendment by Pakistan, Yugoslavia, United Arab Republic, Ceylon, UK and Austria are recorded in the minutes, while some, while sharing overall support, abstained from voting. United Nations, Summary Records, 5th Meeting of the Committee of the Whole held on 3 April 1959, A/CONF.9/C.1/SR.5, UN Conference on the Elimination or Reduction of Future Statelessness, Geneva, 1959 and New York, 1961 (3 April 1959) 9–10. <http://legal.un.org/docs/?path=../diplomaticconferences/1959_statelessness/docs/english/vol_2/a_conf9_c1_sr5.pdf&lang=E> accessed 4 August 2019.

[25] Ibid 11.

[26] United Nations, Summary Records, 9th Plenary Meeting held on 15 April 1959, A/CONF.9/SR.9, UN Conference on the Elimination or Reduction of Future Statelessness, Geneva, 1959 and New York, 1961 (15 April 1959) 11 <https://legal.un.org/diplomaticconferences/1959_statelessness/docs/english/vol_2/a_conf9_sr9.pdf> accessed 4 August 2019.

[27] Ibid 11.

This construction of law, if read literally, would make a lawyer think that, while birth abroad will overturn one of the two presumed facts, it does not necessarily overturn the other presumed fact (that the parents are nationals) as long as the 'prerequisite' facts are met (being a foundling found in the territory). In other words, the assumption of having citizen parents would remain intact. This might then still make the foundling born abroad a national. However, what if the particular country's nationality law generally adopts a 'strict *jus soli* principle' and a person born abroad to parents is not, at least automatically, a national? It would probably be very difficult for that State to justify nationality grant to a person born abroad just because she or he is of unknown parentage, and is found in the territory.

Then a theoretical paradox arises: that under the current formulation of article 2, a foundling found in the territory born abroad may acquire nationality in a *jus sanguinis* State but does not in a *jus soli* State. In any case, the same result would have occurred with the formulation of the initial Danish amendment assuming that a foundling found was a national 'in the absence proof to the contrary', which was already envisaged by the Danish representative.

In fact, as will be detailed in Sect. 7.5, different from the text of article 2, many States in their legislation now presume one fact (and not two facts)—either that a foundling found is a 'national' or that she or he was 'born within the territory' or is a 'child of a national' (or directly grant nationality without any presumption). What is supposed to constitute proof to the contrary then would differ from State to State depending on the construction of their own provision. In contrast, some States' legislation that reflects the formulation of article 6(1)(b) of the ECN below is clearer in terms of what would disqualify one from the application of the foundling provision.

### 7.3.1.2 ECN's Article 6(1)(b) and the Possibility to Grant Nationality to Foundlings Born Abroad

As stated above, article 6(1)(b) of the ECN does not refer to any sort of presumption, but instead states:

> Each State party *shall provide* in its internal law *for its nationality to be acquired ex lege* by the following persons: [...]
>
> b. foundlings found in its territory *who would otherwise be stateless.* (emphasis added)

The construction of the ECN lies somewhere between the initial Danish amendment and the Italian verbal amendment during the Geneva conference 1959 cited above in Sect. 7.3.1.1. Instead of the words 'in the absence of proof to the contrary', the ECN's article 6(1)(b) adds the word 'who would otherwise be stateless' at the end. ECN made it clear that article 6(1)(b) does not apply to a person of unknown parents who, while found in the territory, nonetheless possesses another nationality. This wording is unequivocal as to what disqualifies a person from its application.

Moreover, it becomes clear from this reading that under article 6(1)(b) of the ECN, there is even more room than the 1961 Convention that persons of unknown parents found in the territory who are known to have been nevertheless born abroad (but do not acquire the nationality of such country of birth due to the absence of provisions granting nationality to those born in the territory otherwise stateless or simply by *jus soli*) acquire nationality where found.

The ECN's Explanatory Report paragraph 48 also states: 'The requirement to grant nationality is also met if the foundling, in the absence of proof to the contrary, is considered *ex lege* the child of a national and thus a national.' This again does not exclude the possibility that a foundling born abroad will be considered a child of a national.

The formulation of ECN article 6(1)(b) is indeed highly effective in achieving the object and purpose of preventing statelessness. The 'model foundling provision' discussed in Chap. 8 of this book is thus to be formulated partly based on this article.[28]

### 7.3.1.3    The Contemporary Relevance of the Drafters' Intention Allowing Foundlings Born Abroad to Acquire Nationality

While it might appear rather theoretical, the utility of the above assertions during the travaux of article 2 of the 1961 Convention by Denmark, Italy and the Netherlands is potentially valuable in the contemporary world where international migration, displacement and trafficking is a global phenomenon: That persons of unknown parents can acquire nationality where found even if she or he is known to have been born abroad, as long as she or he is otherwise stateless—which also is supported by the wording of article 6(1)(b) of the ECN.

Indeed, Osamu Arakaki makes this point, in the context of analyzing the compatibility of the 1961 Convention and the Japanese law, while brief and no particular reference is made to the travaux due to the practical nature of the relevant report. In asserting that the Japanese Nationality Act article 2(iii) requiring birth within Japanese territory (to grant nationality to persons of unknown parents) is not in line with article 2 of the 1961 Convention, Arakaki indicates his view:

> [I]f it is obvious that a foundling was born outside of Japan, was brought to Japan after birth, and was found in Japan, viz., if her or his birth outside of Japan is proved, Japanese nationality is not granted. This is a gap in provisions between the 1961 Convention and Japanese law. In the current situation in which human trafficking is becoming more apparent under globalisation, this gap in provisions can be a gap in reality.[29]

---

[28] It is nevertheless relevant to note that UNHCR Guidelines 4 (2012) para 24 states that the responsibility to grant nationality to children who would otherwise be stateless is 'not engaged where a child is born in a State's territory and is stateless, but could acquire a nationality by registration with the State of nationality of a parent, or a similar procedure such as declaration or exercise of a right of option'. This is not explicit from the 1961 Convention but was addressed during its drafting process as cited in the Guidelines 4. However, the Guidelines also state, among others, that it is only acceptable for States not to grant nationality if the child concerned can acquire the nationality (of a parent) immediately after birth and the State of nationality of the parent does not have any discretion to refuse the grant of nationality. UNHCR Guidelines 4 (2012) paras 24–26.

[29] Osamu Arakaki, *Statelessness Conventions and Japanese Laws: Convergence and Divergence* (UNHCR 2015) 71.

To examine this contemporary relevance, it will be useful to lay out a hypothetical case study below.

### Hypothetical Case Study: A Trafficked Child Found in State A Born in State B

Suppose that a girl of unknown parentage is found in State A (State party to the 1961 and/or the ECN), who is known to have been born in country B. The reason can be that the girl was, for example, born at a hospital in State B, where her birth mother went missing soon after her delivery. While growing up under institutional care in State B, she fell in the hands of a criminal organization and got trafficked to State A at age one. She is finally detected at age 14 by the authorities of State A as a trafficking victim and is now hosted in a child protection facility, stateless and without any parents coming to reclaim her. The girl cannot acquire the nationality of State B, which adopts the *jus sanguinis* principle, without any nationality law safeguard or practice to grant nationality to persons of unknown parents or otherwise stateless born in the territory. On the other hand, ever since the girl can remember, she has been living in State A and only speaks its language. She cannot acquire the nationality of State A under its nationality provision for persons born in the territory who would otherwise be stateless. She cannot naturalize anytime soon for not meeting any of the criteria—starting with the age, residency permit, and financial independence.

In light of the object and purpose of the Convention, could State A not consider the girl to have acquired State A's nationality under its foundling provision equivalent to article 2 of the 1961 Convention?

This is exactly the situation where the Danish, Dutch, and Italian assertions during the 1961 travaux become relevant.

In this sort of situation, if State A's legislation equivalent to article 2 of the 1961 Convention is formulated to enable nationality grant to a person of unknown parents found in the territory through the presumption of descent (or simple grant of nationality), it appears quite possible to provide the girl its nationality.

However, if State A only grants a person of unknown parentage its nationality based on 'presumption of birth in the territory', the birth outside the territory would reverse such a presumption, the foundling provision would normally be inapplicable to the girl. Thus, the girl, a foundling found in State A, would remain stateless.[30]

As mentioned in Sect. 7.3.1.1, a counter-intuitive paradox then arises: a person of unknown parentage found in a *jus sanguinis* State party is better off than its counterpart found in a *jus soli* State party, if she or he is known to have been born

---

[30] While the relevant practice is largely unknown, Australia—which has traditionally had a *jus soli* grant, whose foundling provision basically extends its *jus soli* provision to a foundling—clearly denied the application of such a provision when it was known that the person concerned was born outside the territory in both of the two court decisions cited in Sect. 7.5. However, it should also be noted that in both cases, from the limited facts contained in the decisions, it appears the person concerned may not have been of unknown parentage in any case and rather simply was left behind in Australia by the parent with whom he presumably had a legal parent–child relationship. *Nicky v. Minister for Immigration* [2014] FCCA 2569 (Federal Circuit Court of Australia)/*Nicky v. Minister for Immigration and Border Protection* [2015] FCA 174 (Federal Court of Australia) and *SZRTN v. Minister for Immigration and Border Protection* [2015] FCA 305 (Federal Court of Australia).

in another State which does not grant her or him nationality. In the former, she or he may nevertheless acquire nationality where found, but not in the latter. How can this be justified? That is a question that merits further thoughts.

In another version of the scenario, suppose both State A and State B have a provision to grant a person of unknown parents found in the territory a nationality. In such a case, it appears the obligation to grant nationality arises for State B, but the girl's 'bond' with State A is much stronger. Should State A's foundling provision not get invoked at all? Which State's obligation is heavier, the country where the girl was merely born, or the country where she was found, and has lived all her life as her 'own country'?[31] This is another question that might be useful to be considered in the era of migration.

This also is reflected in how Paul Weis summarised the purpose of article 2:

> Article 2 [...] clarified the principle embodied in the Hague Convention and found in the nationality laws of many countries, according to which the foundling *shall acquire* the nationality of the State where he has been found *unless* he be *shown* to be entitled to *another nationality.*[32]

At any rate, despite the drafters' intentions, no information was found as to any State practice backing up the inclusion of foundlings born abroad, including by the States that explicitly promoted such interpretation during the travaux.[33]

### *Link with Unaccompanied Children*

While this case study envisaging a child who was smuggled into the territory while still being a baby may sound acceptable as a possible beneficiary of the founding provision at least for some States, how about if the case study is replaced with somebody who got smuggled at an older age, such as at 17? Or adding another element, what about a 17-year-old of unknown parents who was born, or who is highly likely to have been born, in another State who just (voluntarily) arrived at an international airport to be 'found'?

This question is linked to whether so-called 'unaccompanied children (or minors)' (especially of older age) can ever benefit from the foundling provision. The possible link between unaccompanied minors and the foundling provision has been hinted by some authors.[34]

'Unaccompanied children/minors' are defined by the UN Committee on the Rights of the Child (and UNHCR) generally as:

---

[31] In such a case, it may be necessary to assess which country can be considered the foundling's 'own country' under the meaning of the ICCPR.

[32] Paul Weis, 'The United Nations Convention on the reduction of statelessness, 1961' (1962) 11 International & Comparative Law Quarterly 1082, 1073.

[33] In this context, a positive yet theoretical (and presumably unofficial) statement by Italy that its provision could benefit a foundling born abroad is mentioned in Sect. 7.5 (see the section on Italy).

[34] For example, Sophie Nonnenmacher and Ryszard Cholewinski, 'The Nexus Between Statelessness and Migration' in Edwards and van Waas (eds), *Nationality and Statelessness Under International Law* (Cambridge University Press 2014) 247, 259.

> Any person under the age of 18 who is *outside his or her country of origin or habitual residence* and who has been separated from both parents and other relatives and who is not being cared for by an adult who, by law or custom, is responsible for doing so. (emphasis added)[35]

The Council of European Union's 2001 Council Directive on temporary protection defines unaccompanied minors as:

> [*T*]*hird-country nationals or stateless persons* below the age of eighteen, who *arrive* on the territory of the Member States unaccompanied by an adult responsible for them whether by law or custom, and for as long as they are not effectively taken into the care of such a person, or minors who are left unaccompanied after they have entered the territory of the Member States. (emphasis added)[36]

While not explicitly included, it is implicit under these definitions that unaccompanied minors were born abroad, then 'arrive on the territory' of another State (unless they were born within the territory, went to another State and then come back to the country of birth). However, these definitions might also cover persons whose birthplace is not established, including those who are likely to have been born abroad.

Unaccompanied minors may or may not be of unknown parentage. Unaccompanied minors might be of perfectly known parentage, duly registered at birth in their countries of origin with such parent(s)' name(s), but have been separated, orphaned or sent abroad by their parent(s) to seek asylum or better future. Nevertheless, some unaccompanied minors might indeed be of unknown parents and have never been registered at birth or at a later stage in any country (or registered to be of unknown parents by some authorities but have remained stateless). This is where the foundling provisions become relevant. The possible 'beneficiaries' of foundling provisions explored in this section are thus not all unaccompanied minors, but only those whose legal parents do not exist or cannot be proven, where their possession of another nationality cannot be proven either.

If the birthplace of such unaccompanied minor is 'unknown', although it is suspected that she or he was born abroad, then it is fairly arguable that she or he can invoke the foundling provision. The question is, what happens if the unaccompanied minor concerned is known to have been, or is highly likely to have been, born abroad.

---

[35] The definition and treatment of unaccompanied minors in general are discussed, for example, in the following documents: UN Committee on the Rights of the Child, General comment No 6 (2005): Treatment of Unaccompanied and Separated Children Outside their Country of Origin (1 September 2005) CRC/GC/2005/6 para 7. UNHCR, 'Safe & Sound: what States can do to ensure respect for the best interests of unaccompanied and separated children in Europe' (October 2014) para 22 <https://www.refworld.org/docid/5423da264.html> and UNHCR, 'Guidelines on Policies and Procedures in Dealing with Unaccompanied Children Seeking Asylum' (February 1997) 1 <http://www.refworld.org/docid/3ae6b3360.html> accessed 6 March 2020.

[36] Council of European Union's 'Council Directive 2001/55/EC of 20 July 2001 on minimum standards for giving temporary protection in the event of a mass influx of displaced persons and on measures promoting a balance of efforts between Member States in receiving such persons and bearing the consequences thereof', article 2(f).

Then, this is where the drafters' intentions to cover foundlings born abroad, detailed in Sect. 7.3.1.1, can be invoked. However, as discussed in Chap. 6, some States might find it challenging to apply this generous interpretation to older minors. It is possible for those States to assert that the drafters of the 1961 Convention advocating for the inclusion of foundlings born abroad should have envisaged those who were small children when found in the territory, referring to the ordinary meaning of 'foundling' in some of the official language versions of article 2 discussed in Sect. 6.1.

Having said that, the conclusion of Chap. 6 that a foundling can be any child of unknown parents found under the age of majority needs to be repeated here. In particular, States are urged to ensure the same rights to higher teenagers as their younger counterparts, including right to nationality under article 7 of the CRC as stated in Sect. 6.7.4.[37] Limiting the age becomes arbitrary under international law (Sect. 6.7). States thus are free or even encouraged to apply their foundling provisions to older minors born abroad.

This is further backed up by the fact that under article 2(1) of the CRC and ICCPR, States parties shall respect and ensure the rights recognized under the respective Conventions 'to each child *within their jurisdiction* [...]' (CRC) (emphasis added) and 'to all individuals *within its territory* and *subject to its jurisdiction*' (ICCPR) (emphasis added). This means that if the States where the child was born did not ensure 'the right to acquire a nationality' under article 7(1) of the CRC and article 24(3) of ICCPR, then it should fall upon the State where the child has moved onto and is currently residing in to ensure such right.[38]

In Spain, the possibility of unaccompanied minors benefiting from its foundling provision, that is article 17.1.d of the Civil Code, has been explicitly recognized including in a commentary written for the relevant authorities in 2005. The commentary, referring to the significant number of unaccompanied minors in Spain as of 2005, states:

> The relevance of the interpretation of the analysed precept [article 17.1.d, author] is intimately linked to the issue of unaccompanied foreign minors [*menores extranjeros no acompañados*]. Immigration legislation requires that a number of hurdles be overcome before obtaining a residence permit. However, if the identity of the child is unknown as well as its exact place of birth, once the person is declared to lack care and protection [*desamparo* assumed to be care by parents], the public entity could file a petition to benefit from the simple presumption and have the child declared to be a Spanish national. Certainly, the use of article 17.1.d of

---

[37] Joint General Comment No 4 (2017) of CMW and No 23 (2017) of the CRC Committee on State obligations regarding the human rights of children in the context of international migration in countries of origin, transit, destination and return, 16 November 2017, CMW/C/GC/4-CRC/C/GC/23 <https://www.refworld.org/docid/5a12942a2b.html>.

[38] For example, see Hajime Akiyama, 'Jiyūkenkiyaku ni okeru kodomo no kokuseki shutoku ken to kokkano gimu—Jiyūkenkiyaku dai 2 jō no kanten kara' ['Children's right to acquire nationality under ICCPR and States' responsibilities—from the viewpoint of article 2 of ICCPR'] (2019) 30 Kokusaijinken [Human Rights International] 115, 116.

the Civil Code to some of these cases could eliminate the difficult situations that arise with regard to unaccompanied foreign minors in the Spanish society.[39]

This guidance is highly valuable in the era of migration and displacement. Nonetheless, it is indeed not fully clear whether unaccompanied minors whose birth abroad is firmly proven or highly likely are envisaged by the guidance of the Spanish authorities.

As discussed, including in Sect. 6.7.3, the Spanish Civil Code 17.1.d. actually makes a presumption of birth in the territory as the basis for nationality acquisition for 'minors' of undetermined parentage whose first known place of stay is Spain. As also reviewed in the same section, DGRN, the competent authority on nationality matters, has confirmed the Spanish nationality of minors who at least were likely or even highly likely to have been born abroad, such as in a case of a minor who was ten years old when found by the authorities whose self-claimed parents presumably from Romania indeed claimed the child was born in Roma (although such foreign birth was not firmly established).

Thus, it can be concluded that article 2 of the 1961 Convention leaves room where older minors whose birth abroad is highly likely or is even proven are covered therein. On a practical front, some might quite naturally become concerned about the possibility of increase in abusive cases, such as an increase of unaccompanied minors claiming to be persons of unknown parentage when they are not. However, it can be considered that the possibility of such false claims becoming prevalent might not be too high. This is partly because in many States the nationality acquired by a person of unknown parents can be withdrawn if the person's possession of another nationality (or parentage) is proven. It is not too easy to expect that numerous parents who send their children to another country as an 'anchor' in a hope to be reunited with them in a few years would ask them to invoke the foundling provision.

Further, the statements by claimants for nationality under the foundling provision can be subjected to credibility assessment[40] as also discussed in Chap. 5. If the claimants' statements as to why and how their legal parents do not exist or cannot be proven is found not credible after a full and fair assessment, then they can be rejected on the basis of lack of credibility. This again, in the author's view, diminishes the risk of abuse. Further, the claimants would have to at least rebut the State's assertion that they have another nationality. If the concerned minor does not raise a refugee claim, or her or his refugee claim has been rejected, the normal course of action by

---

[39] Aurelia Álvarez Rodríguez y, *Nacionalidad de los hijos de extranjeros nacidos en España Regulación legal e interpretación jurisprudencial sobre un análisis de datos estadísticos de los nacidos en territorio español durante el período 1996–2002* [*Nationality of the children of foreigners born in Spain: Legal regulation and jurisprudential interpretation on an analysis of statistical data of those born in Spanish territory during the period 1996–2002*] (Observatorio Permanente de la Inmigración (for Ministerio de Trabajo y Asuntos Sociales [now Ministerio de Empleo y Seguridad Social] 2006) 85 under chapter III, section 5 entitled 'Atribution of Spanish nationality under article 17.1.2 of Civil Code.

[40] Refer to paras 101–7 ((9) Credibility issues) of the UNHCR Handbook (2014) by analogy.

the determining body would be to contact the authorities of the purported country of origin,[41] where the minor's possession of such nationality can be confirmed.

The concern might also be raised about an increase in adults claiming to be unknown parentage who was found in the territory before age 18. However, in such cases also they would be subject to thorough credibility checks, and they would have to show that they are otherwise stateless anyway, as is done in normal stateless-ness determination procedures. One needs to also recall that the general experiences of States that have established statelessness determination procedures are that the number of abusive cases is quite low anyway, especially compared to that of the asylum procedure.[42] A useful analogy can be drawn from here.

### 7.3.1.4  Discovery or Establishment of Foreign Parentage

What happens if the child's foreign parentage is revealed was also discussed in the travaux process, including during the preparatory meetings cited above. It appears from the context that it is about what happens if foreign parentage is discovered post facto. The content was rather straightforward in contrast with the issue of birth abroad.

The Danish Representative clarified what happens when the parentage is estab-lished:

> If it were *later* discovered that the child had been born abroad and that the parents possessed another nationality, the rules of nationality by descent such as existed, for instance, in the United Kingdom would apply and the child would acquire a new nationality, *namely that of its parents*. If a child found in a jus sanguinis country were *later* discovered to have been born in another country, that child would either acquire the *nationality of the parents* [...]. In either case, the child would possess the nationality of the country in which he had been found until shown to be entitled to another nationality. (emphasis added)[43]

This means that even if the parentage of the concerned person is discovered later, this will not lead to loss of nationality acquired by virtue of the foundling provision, unless it is established that she or he has acquired nationality by *jus sanguinis* from that parent.

While this seems to talk about post facto assessment, it is relevant to consider what would happen if foreign parentage is already known at the pre facto assessment stage. If there is clear evidence that one of the parents is a foreign national, it means

---

[41] Paras 66, 79–82 and 96–99 of the UNHCR Handbook (2014).

[42] Presentation by Benoît Meslin, Secrétaire Général, OFPRA, entitled 'Determination and Protec-tion of Stateless Persons in France' in the compilation of the handouts for the Symposium on Human Rights and Support for Stateless People around the World: Japan's Role (National Museum of Ethnology 2011).

[43] United Nations, Summary Records, 5th Meeting of the Committee of the Whole held on 3 April 1959, A/CONF.9/C.1/SR.5, UN Conference on the Elimination or Reduction of Future Stateless-ness, Geneva, 1959 and New York, 1961 (3 April 1959) 10 <http://legal.un.org/docs/?path=../diplom aticconferences/1959_statelessness/docs/english/vol_2/a_conf9_c1_sr5.pdf&lang=E> accessed 4 August 2019.

that the identity of that parent is identified; this will inevitably reverse not only one of the 'presumed facts' (that both father and mother are nationals of the country), but also one of the 'prerequisite facts (that one is a foundling, that is of unknown parents). It will first render article 2 of the 1961 Convention inapplicable.

If one of the parent(s) is identified but the person concerned is unable to acquire any nationality from that parent, and the concerned person's birthplace is known, the provision granting nationality to 'children of stateless parents' or persons 'otherwise stateless' born in the territory, or even an unconditional *jus soli* provision, should be applicable—only if such provisions are available. If born in the country without such provisions, the person would remain stateless and would normally have to naturalize in order to acquire the nationality of the country where born.

As discussed in Sect. 3.8, if one (or both) of the person's parents is (are) identified but she or he cannot acquire nationality by *jus sanguinis*, and her or his birthplace is unknown, she or he will also remain stateless falling through the gap between article 1 and article 2 of the 1961 Convention, unless her or his birth within the territory is somehow presumed.

## 7.4 The Formulation of the Domestic Foundling Provisions and the Proof to 'the contrary'

It is now useful to review, based on annex 1, how States construct their nationality law to grant nationality to foundlings, that is persons of unknown parents born or found in the territory (who might also be referred to as an 'abandoned' or by another term: see Chap. 3). The majority of States grant nationality to foundlings in either one of the following methods I–VIII, which are described here in a simplified manner. The adoption of certain methods appears to depend, though not necessarily, on whether the States concerned generally adopt the *jus soli* or *jus sanguinis* principles.

- Method I: by presuming (in the absence of ('until', 'unless' or other terms) the contrary proof; the same goes for other methods unless otherwise noted) the birth in the territory and from parents who are nationals, thus reproducing the wording of article 2 of the 1961 Convention.[44]
- Method II: by presuming the birth in the territory and extending its unconditional *jus soli* acquisition provision that is applied to all persons born in the territory.[45]

---

[44] For example, Mexico: article 7 states 'Unless the contrary is proven, an exposed child [*niño expósito*] found in the national territory is presumed that he has been born in the territory and that he is a daughter or son of a Mexican father and a mother' ['Salvo prueba en contrario, se presume que el niño expósito hallado en territorio nacional ha nacido en éste y que es hijo de padre y madre mexicanos'] Ley de Nacionalidad, Nueva Ley publicada en el Diario Oficial de la Federación el 23 de enero de 1998 [Mexico, Nationality Law, new law published in the official report of the federation on 23 January 1998] <http://www.diputados.gob.mx/LeyesBiblio/pdf/53.pdf> accessed 2 August 2019. [author translation].

[45] Section 4(1) of Canadian Citizenship Act (RSC, 1985, c C-29) (1985) <http://laws-lois.justice.gc.ca/eng/acts/C-29/page-1.html#h-3A> accessed 4 August 2019. Section 4(1) (Deserted child)

- Method III: by presuming the birth in the territory and birth from a parent(s) who is a permanent resident or alike, thereby extending the conditional *jus soli* provision.[46]
- Method IV: by presuming birth in the territory and extending the exceptional (or supplementary) *jus soli* provision for:

  (1)    persons of unknown parents born in the territory (thus adopting the formulation of article 14 of the 1930 Convention)[47]; or

  (2)    persons (of known parent(s)) otherwise stateless (or of stateless parents) born in the territory[48]

- Method V: by presuming that the child's parent(s) is (are) national(s) (thus extending the *jus sanguinis* provision)[49]

---

'For the purposes of paragraph 3(1)(a) [which states a person is a citizen if born in Canada after 14 February 1977], every person who [...] shall be deemed to have been born in Canada, unless the contrary is proved [...]'; USA's Immigration and Nationality Act section 301(f): 'a person of unknown parentage found in the United States [...] *until shown* [...] *not to have been born in the United States*' shall be a citizen by birth. While the section does not explicitly state that the person is presumed to have been born in the US, it is effectively so because the person's nationality can be denied any time before he or she reaches age 21 if his or her birth abroad is discovered.

[46] For example, section 1(2) of the British Nationality Act 1981 states: 'A new-born infant who [...] is found abandoned in the United Kingdom [...] shall, unless the contrary is shown, *be deemed* [for the purpose of section 1[1] providing for nationality acquisition of a person born in the UK or a qualifying territory of a parent who is a British citizen or is settled there] (a) to have been *born in the United Kingdom* [...] and (b) to have been *born to a parent* who at the time of the birth was *a British citizen or settled in the United Kingdom* [...].' <https://www.legislation.gov.uk/ukpga/1981/61#commentary-c16828211> accessed 4 August 2019.

[47] For example, article 17.1.d) of the Spanish Civil Code. 'The following persons are Spanish nationals of origin: [...]. d) Those born in Spain whose parentage is not determined. To these effects, minors whose first known place of stay is Spanish territory are presumed to have been born in the Spanish territory' (translated by author).

[48] Belgium Nationality Code 1984. Article 10(3): 'A new-born child found in Belgium is presumed, until the contrary is proved, to be born in Belgium.[...]'. This makes article 10(1), providing for grant of nationality to children born in Belgium otherwise stateless, applicable to the (new-born) child found.

[49] For example, German nationality law section 4 (Acquisition by birth) states '(2) A child which is found on German territory (foundling) shall be deemed to be *the child of a German* until otherwise proven' Staatsangehörigkeitsgesetz (StAG) [The Nationality Act of Germany] (1913) <https://www.gesetze-im-internet.de/stag/BJNR005830913.html> accessed 5 September 2019. The Federal Law concerning Austrian Nationality article 8(1) states: '*Until proof to the contrary*, a person under the age of six months found on the territory of the Republic is regarded as national *by descent*' (emphasis added). Federal Law Concerning Austrian Nationality (1985 Nationality Act) <http://www.refworld.org/docid/3ae6b52114.html> accessed 4 August 2019.

- Method VI: by 'presuming'[50]that the child found 'is a national', without articulating the basis for such presumption (and without mentioning 'in the absence of proof to the contrary').[51]
- Method VII: by granting nationality (or considering that the child found is a national):

  (1) 'in the absence of proof to the contrary' (mostly without clarifying what 'the contrary' might mean—as done in the initial Danish amendment proposal during the 1959 travaux process)[52]
  
  (2) in the absence of possession of another nationality (similar to article 6(1)b of the ECN)[53]

- Method VIII: by simply providing for nationality grant without referring to any sort of 'presumption', reversal by 'proof to the contrary', or other disqualification criteria (as done in one of the verbal proposals by Italy in 1959 travaux process cited in Sect. 7.3.1.1).[54]

---

[50] 'Presuming' a legal effect (rather than presuming facts)—that is that one acquires a nationality is somewhat at odds with the general rules of law. States can presume birth in the territory or descent from nationals as a result of which one is made a national. Presuming that one 'is a national' makes one's nationality status unstable—giving an impression as if she or he were a 'presumed national', whose nationality is 'provisional' or less definite than that of other nationals, which can be withdrawn anytime—and is not recommended as a method to incorporate article 2 of the 1961 Convention.

[51] While not State parties to the 1961 Convention, at least Ghana (Citizenship Act section 8), Kenya (Constitution, article 14(4)), Uganda (Constitution, article 11(1)), Zambia (article 35(2)) and Zimbabwe (Constitution, article 36(3)) adopt this method. See annex 1. As the most typical one, article 14(4) of the 2010 Constitution of Kenya states that 'a child found in Kenya […] whose parents are not known, is *presumed to be a citizen* by birth' (emphasis added). The Constitution of Kenya, 27 August 2010 <https://www.refworld.org/docid/4c8508822.html> accessed 7 August 2019.

[52] For example, Act on the Acquisition of Danish Nationality article 1(2) provides: 'A child found abandoned in Denmark will, in the absence of evidence to the contrary, be considered a Danish national' Act on the Acquisition of Danish Nationality (amended to 2004) (2004) <https://www. refworld.org/docid/4e5cf36d2.html> accessed 7 August 2019. This reflects the original text of the Danish proposal during the drafting process of the 1961 Convention. Also, see Australian Citizenship Act 2007 section 14 ('Citizenship for abandoned children') stating: 'A person is an Australian citizen if the person is found abandoned in Australia as a child, unless and until the contrary is proved'.

[53] The Finnish nationality law section 12 states 'A foundling who is found in Finland is considered to be a Finnish citizen as long as he or she has not been established as a citizen of a foreign State.' See also section 1(2) of Italy's Law No 91 relating to 'New Provisions on Italian citizenship' (5 February 1992), discussed in Sect. 7.5 and elsewhere.

[54] For example, Costa Rica. Article 13(4) of the Constitution states: 'They are Costa Rican by birth: […] (4) An infant, of unknown parents, found in Costa Rica' (translation by author). Constitución Política de 7 de Noviembre de 1949 y sus Reformas [Political Constitution of 7 November 1949 and its Reforms] (Costa Rica) <http://www.tse.go.cr/pdf/normativa/constitucion.pdf> accessed 3 August 2019. Also, while not a State party, Lao People's Democratic Republic (Laos), Law on Lao Nationality (29 November 1990) article 12 states: 'Children found in the territory of the Lao People's Democratic Republic and whose parents' identity is unknown will be *considered as* Lao

In terms of the 'facts presumed' when a foundling is found in the territory, article 2 stipulates a set of two facts (birth in the territory and citizen parents), as reviewed in Sect. 7.2. From the summary of legislation, however, it is clear that only a few States adopt the exact, or similar, formulation as article 2 of the 1961 Convention, that is presume both birth in the territory and descent from citizen parents (Method I).

Additionally, as discussed in Sects. 3.7 and 6.3.1, 17 States (among which 13 are non-State parties) out of 139 only provide for nationality grant to persons of unknown parentage born in the territory. Even under such legislation, presumption of birth in the territory can in practice be made in some States for a person of unknown parents found in the territory—as long as proof of birth outside the territory is not established—to the effect that she or he acquires a nationality (see the section on Japan in Sect. 6.4).

For many States, there is no specific paragraph dedicated to stipulate post facto withdrawal of nationality for a person who acquired nationality based on the foundling provision. For those States, the term 'in the absence of contrary proof' or a similar term included in their foundling provision appears to relate both to pre facto and post facto assessments. However, as will be discussed in detail in Sect. 7.6.2, annex 1 shows that at least 37 States relatively explicitly regulate post facto withdrawal of nationality acquired under the foundling provision along with the criteria for such withdrawal.

While it is unknown for many States what exactly constitutes 'contrary proof' at the pre facto stage, some States do have some administrative instructions or case law detailing it. In the following section, some examples of national legislation and practice will be introduced.

## 7.5 Selected National Legislation and Practice on the 'proof to the contrary'

### Australia

As already mentioned in Sects. 7.1 and 7.3.1, there are two Australian cases where the Federal Court of Australia examined which facts (that is, prerequisite v. presumed facts) the term 'the contrary' under section 5(3)(b) of 1948 Citizenship Act qualified, and what 'the contrary' meant specifically.

Section 5(3)(b)(i) of the 1948 Citizenship Act—which was in force when the relevant claimants were born—stated specifically: '[A] person who, when a child, was found abandoned in Australia shall, *unless and until the contrary is proved,* be deemed: (i) to have been born in Australia.' Section 10(1) then granted nationality to a person born in Australia, as a result of which children found abandoned in Australia acquired citizenship with such an unconditional *jus soli* provision extended to them,

citizens' (emphasis added) <http://www.refworld.org/docid/3ae6b4f014.html> accessed 4 August 2019.

thus prescribing to Method II as classified under Sect. 7.4. While the unconditional *jus soli* provision was abolished in 1986, section 5(3)(b)(iv) allowed abandoned children, born after the Citizenship Amendment Act 1986 came into operation to benefit from the conditional *jus soli* provision under section 10(2)(a) granting nationality to persons born in Australia whose parent at the time of the person's birth was an Australian citizen or a permanent resident, thus adopting the Method III as classified in Sect. 7.4.[55]

*Nicky v. Minister for Immigration [2014] FCCA 2569 (12 November 2014) and Nicky v. Minister for Immigration and Border Protection [2015] FCA 174 (5 March 2015).*[56]

The claimant, 29 years of age at the time of the decision by the Federal Circuit Court of Australia, was born in Indonesia in September 1985, and on 18 November 2001, when he was 16 years old, he and his mother arrived in Australia on tourist visas. On 10 February 2002 the applicant's mother was deported from Australia. After his mother left Australia, he lost contact with her until 2010, when he found out she was sick; she later died. The claimant claimed he had never met his father and did not know where he was. The claimant thus lodged an application with the Department of Immigration and Border Protection requesting evidence of Australian citizenship. The applicant claimed that he was an Australian citizen under section 5(3)(b) of the Australian Citizenship Act 1948 (hereinafter 'the 1948 Act') if not section 14 of the Australian Citizenship Act 2007 (hereinafter 'the 2007 Act', which, however, was considered by the court inapplicable due to his date of birth), because he had been found abandoned as a child in Australia on 10 February 2002. The Department of Immigration and Border Protection refused the claimant's application. Thus the claimant sought relief with the Federal Circuit Court.

While the claimant's birth in Indonesia and subsequent arrival in Australia as a migrant with an Indonesian passport was not disputed, the claimant asserted that the phrase 'until the contrary is proved' only qualified the phrase 'found abandoned in Australia', and that he should benefit from the Australia's foundling provisions as he has been abandoned by his mother after arriving in Australia.

The Federal Circuit Court, while recognizing that the claimant had been 'found abandoned in Australia in February 2002',[57] gave its own view on how section 5(3)(b) should be read:

> Section 5(3)(b) was in two parts. The first, and the condition precedent to its operation, was the fact of the *abandonment of a child*. The second part set out *the consequences of that child being abandoned,* namely a *deeming of the circumstances of its birth* as ones which attracted Australian citizenship. A *set of facts which is merely deemed to exist is susceptible of being*

---

[55] See for example the Explanatory Memorandum to the Citizenship Bill 1969 cited in Nicky 2015. Section 5(3)(b)(ii) to (iv) then exempted the abandoned children from the application of the various restrictions under section 10 against the acquisition by *jus soli*, such as the 1986 amendment to limit it to a child of a national and a permanent resident.

[56] *Nicky v. Minister for Immigration* [2014] FCCA 2569 (Federal Circuit Court of Australia). See especially paras 18–25 See also *Nicky v. Minister for Immigration and Border Protection* [2015] FCA 174 (Federal Court of Australia): See especially paras 35–47.

[57] Para 29, *Nicky v. Minister for Immigration* [2014] FCCA 2569 (Federal Circuit Court of Australia).

*disproved*, which is the possibility which the second part of the paragraph recognized. That is to say, *the expression 'unless and until the contrary is proved' qualifies the verb structure 'shall … be deemed'* in which it sits, not the words 'was found abandoned' appearing earlier in the paragraph. (emphasis added)[58]

The Federal Circuit Court concluded that the 1961 Convention on the Reduction of Statelessness, which section 5(3)(b) of the 1948 Citizenship Act seeks to implement, does not support the applicant's submissions, stating:

The Convention intended to confer on foundlings a citizenship which would be lost if the deemed circumstances of the child's birth, which would confer such citizenship, were disproved. The conclusion I have reached concerning the construction of s.5(3)(b) of the 1948 Act is that it reflects and implements art.2's rebuttable presumption *concerning a foundling's nationality.* (emphasis added)[59]

The Federal Circuit Court thus concluded that it did not find an error in the Minister for Immigration and Border Protection's original decision that the applicant was not a citizen of Australia under the 1948 Act.

Subsequently, a judicial review was sought in the Federal Circuit Court in *Nicky v. Minister for Immigration and Border Protection.*[60] However, the Federal Court of Australia dismissed the claimant's appeal stating that the claimant was not an Australian citizen by virtue of section 5(3)(b) of the 1948 Act. The Federal Court essentially stated that 'the contrary' referred to the possession of another nationality. The court stated: 'The "contrary" which is "proved" *is his citizenship* by reason of either his birth in Indonesia or by reason of the *grant of an Indonesian passport*' (emphasis added).[61] The Federal Court explained that:

[T]he objective sought to be achieved in both provisions [section 5(3)(b) of the 1948 Act and section 14 of the 2007 Act] is to determine the citizenship of a child who has been found abandoned in Australia – he either has Australian citizenship or such other citizenship as can be proved.[62]

The Federal Court noted that section 5(3)(b) was inserted by way of amendment in 1969 to implement article 2 of the 1961 Convention, to avoid statelessness, citing the Explanatory Memorandum to the Citizenship Bill 1969. The court specifically stated that:

[S]ection 5(3)(b) of the 1948 Act was a legislative attempt *to ensure that children found abandoned in Australia were not 'Stateless'.* In the absence of clear words to the contrary, there is no self-evident reason why either section should be construed as entitling a child found abandoned in Australia to Australian citizenship in circumstances where the country of birth *and nationality* of that child are known. […] Notwithstanding the expiration of the

[58] Ibid para 23.

[59] Ibid para 24.

[60] *Nicky v. Minister for Immigration and Border Protection* [2015] FCA 174 (Federal Court of Australia).

[61] Ibid para 43.

[62] Ibid para 44.

Appellant's Indonesian passport in 2006, *no submission was advanced* to either the delegate or the Federal Circuit Court *that the Appellant was thereby rendered 'Stateless'.* [...] There is *no reason to believe that the Appellant cannot acquire a further Indonesian passport on application.* (emphasis added)[63]

Looking at the parts emphasized above, the Federal Court's reasoning to reject the claimant's Australian nationality under section 5(3)(b) appears to be more about his possession of Indonesian nationality, rather than his birth in Indonesia. So, what would have happened if it had been established that the claimant did not possess Indonesian nationality despite his birth there and was thus otherwise stateless?

At any rate, the claimant's parent (mother) is apparently known, and thus he was not of 'unknown parents',[64] the core definition of a foundling that any provision implementing article 2 of the 1961 Convention should normally include at least implicitly (see Chap. 3).

However, suppose the claimant was indeed of unknown parentage and the Federal Court were to follow the object and purpose of section 5(3)(b). Then could it have been possible that the Federal Court affirmed his Australian nationality despite his birth in Indonesia?

The wording of the 1948 Act makes such an interpretation rather stretched. This was indeed pointed out, while in *obiter dictum,* in a similar case that was heard just one month after *Nicky,* that is *SZRTN v. Minister for Immigration and Border Protection* discussed below.[65]

*SZRTN v. Minister for Immigration and Border Protection [2015] FCA 305 (2 April 2015)*

In the subsequent case *SZRTN v. Minister for Immigration and Border Protection,* the 33-year-old applicant was born on 25 October 1981 in Samoa, and he arrived in Australia with his father on 17 April 1987 when aged five. Within months of his arrival his father abandoned him and he then lived with his uncle and aunt and their children until he was 13 years old. Thereafter he had lived on the streets and subsequently came under immigration detention as an unlawful non-citizen. The claimant argued that he was abandoned as a child so that section 5(3)(b) of the 1948

---

[63] Ibid para 45 (Conclusions).

[64] As mentioned in Sects. 3.3.1 and 3.6, the Federal Court of Australia in *SZRTN v. Minister for Immigration and Border Protection* [2015] FCA 305 (Federal Court of Australia), though *obiter,* pointed this out about the claimant. The Federal Court doubted whether the claimant was indeed 'found' abandoned, asserting that the term 'found' basically meant that the person's parents were unknown.

[65] In ibid, the Federal Court of Australia referred to *Nicky* (2015) as to the reading of 'the contrary' under section 5(3)(b). The Federal Court noted, though *obiter,* that '[...] Part of the reasoning in Nicky involved the observation that section 5(3)(b) was inserted originally to avoid the possibility of stateless persons. I expect that this is probably correct, with respect, but would reserve my own position on that issue [...] that the mere fact that a person is born in another country *does not necessarily mean that they have the nationality* of that country. [...] This may matter because it is not necessarily the case that the construction of section 5(3)(b) which both Flick J (the judge in *Nicky v. Minister for Immigration and Border Protection* [2015] FCA 174 (Federal Court of Australia)) and myself prefer therefore avoids the problem of statelessness in every case'.

Act (which was in force when the claimant was born), if not section 14 of the 2007 Act, conferred citizenship upon him. The claimant sued the Minister for Immigration and Border Protection for a declaration that he is an Australian citizen unlawfully detained. The Federal Court dismissed the claimant's application, stating that he was not an Australian citizen under the 1948 Act.

In this case, the claimant had also asserted that the Department of Immigration and Border Protection had not proven that he was not found abandoned in Australia and thus that 'the contrary' in section 5(3)(b) had not been proved. This argument again assumed that 'the contrary' qualified the words 'found abandoned in Australia'.

The Federal Court of Australia accepted that due to the ambiguity of the provision, the provision is capable of supporting the above construction, but asserted that it should rather be construed where 'the contrary' refers to the contrary of 'born in Australia'. The Federal Court then said:

> The former construction, however, makes no sense. It would result in section 5(3)(b) effectively reading: 'a person who, when a child, was found abandoned in Australia shall, unless it is shown that she or he was not found abandoned in Australia, be deemed: (i) to have been born in Australia…

The Federal Court pointed out that this reading had the consequence of making the initial phrase redundant, by using an analogous example:

> By definition, a *person who is found abandoned in Australia is not a person who has been shown not to have been found abandoned in Australia.* Useful comparison may be made with a law which said: 'A person who drives through a red light shall, unless the contrary be proved, be deemed to be driving in excess of the speed limit.' I would read such a provision as enabling the driver to contest the deemed speeding offence by proving he was not speeding. It would be pointless to read it as allowing the deemed speeding offence to be avoided only if it were shown the red light had not been run. (emphasis added)

The Federal Court further cited a previous High Court decision where it was advised that redundant constructions are to be avoided where possible. The Federal Court concluded that the claimant's birth in Samoa[66] disqualified him from being an Australian citizen by virtue of section 5(3)(b).

*Australian interpretation of 'the contrary fact'*

Thus, it can be summarized that both in *Nicky* and *SZRTN* the Federal Court of Australia considered that 'the contrary' under the section 5(3)(b) qualified the 'presumed facts' rather than the prerequisite facts (that is, that a person was found

---

[66] On a separate note, in *SZRTN*, unlike *Nicky*, there was no reference within the judgement to any evidence confirming the claimant's possession of Samoa nationality, such as a passport. Nonetheless, the evidence shows that he is at least of known parents. As the Federal Court also pointed out, the identity of the claimant's parents is recorded on his birth certificate and he should normally have been considered to be of 'known parentage' in the absence of any other evidence (such as that the information on the birth certificate was forged). Thus, even if the claimant were to be otherwise stateless (which cannot be known from reading the judgement), it would have been appropriate to be treated as a stateless person born abroad, that is to be ensured protection under the 1954 Convention.

abandoned as a child in Australia). *SZRTN* especially provides convincing argument about the construction of the provision to avoid redundancy. What differed between the two decisions was that the former decision placed more emphasis on the prevention of statelessness and considered that 'possession of another nationality' was the 'contrary', while the latter 'stuck to' the wording of the Citizenship Act and concluded that 'birth outside Australia' itself qualified as the 'proof to the contrary'.

In this context, it would be useful to note the difference between the wording of section 5(3)(b) of the Australian Citizenship Act 1948 and section 14 of the Australian Citizenship Act 2007, which is currently in force. Section 14 provides: '*A person is an Australian citizen* if the person is found abandoned in Australia as a child, *unless and until the contrary is proved*' (emphasis added). While section 5(3)(b) of the 1948 Act provided that a person found abandoned in Australia as a child will be (unless and until the contrary is proved) deemed to have been 'born in Australia' (whereby having the unconditional or conditional *jus soli* provision under section 10 extended, as mentioned above). In contrast, section 14 of the 2007 Act simply provides that she or he 'is[67] an Australian citizen' (unless and until the contrary is proved).

The wording the 2007 Act appears to have addressed the limitation of the original wording in section 5(3)(b) of the 1948 Act, leaving some room for how the Federal Court of Australia in *Nicky* wanted to interpret the 1948 Act to prevent statelessness. Literally reading section 14, it is possible to argue that an abandoned person (of unknown parents) born outside could still have qualified for Australian nationality and maintain it unless she or he is found to hold another nationality.[68]

---

[67] In the words of the relevant Explanatory Memorandum, under the 2007 Act, the person is 'deemed' to be an Australian citizen. However, the difference between being a citizen and 'being deemed a citizen' is not explained. The Parliament of the Commonwealth of Australia House of Representatives, Australian Citizenship Bill 2005 Explanatory Memorandum (2005) 15, See especially para 54–6 <http://parlinfo.aph.gov.au/parlInfo/download/legislation/ems/r2473_ems_1f539888-be96-4356-9ffb-ec5c2ad28f87/upload_pdf/75168.pdf;fileType=application%2Fpdf> accessed 4 August 2019.

[68] However, it is noted that the Australian Citizenship Legislation Amendment (Strengthening the Commitments for Australian Citizenship and Other Measures) Bill, which was proposed by a senator in 2017 and 2018, and was being discussed at the time of writing (February 2019) intended to preclude this interpretation of section 14 by repealing it and newly creating an abandoned child provision that includes more restrictive 'contrary proof' element that appears to go beyond the wording of article 2 of the 1961 Convention. The Bill provides that children found abandoned in Australia would not automatically acquire Australian citizenship if it is proved that the child was 'physically outside Australia at any time before they are found abandoned (and can have their nationality withdrawn if this is found later)'. See the Australian Citizenship Legislation Amendment (Strengthening the Commitments for Australian Citizenship and Other Measures) Bill 2018, Australian Citizenship Legislation Amendment (Strengthening the Commitments for Australian Citizenship and Other Measures) Bill 2018, Explanatory Memorandum (2018) paras 54–56. See critiques by Australian Human Rights Commission, 'Submission to the Senate Legal and Constitutional Affairs Committee', *Australian Citizenship Legislation Bill 2017* (17 July 2017).

*Spain*

As particularly discussed in Sects. 4.3.3, 4.3.5 and 6.7.3, Spain has administrative decisions that clarify the country's interpretation of its foundling provision, which also touch on the issue of 'contrary proof'.

The formulation of the foundling provision within the Spanish Civil Code can be categorized into Method IV as classified in Sect. 7.4. As already introduced in previous chapters but reproduced here for ease of reference, article 17.1 (d) of the Spanish Civil Code states:

> The following persons are Spanish nationals by birth: [...] (d) Those *born in Spain* whose parentage is not determined. *To these effects,* minors whose first known place of stay is the Spanish territory *are presumed to have been born in* the Spanish territory. (emphasis added; author translation)

Thus, article 17.1.d) does not make the absence of 'proof to the contrary' a condition for such nationality acquisition. Nevertheless, some DGRN resolutions show that presumption of birth in the territory apparently could be overturned by proof of birth abroad, depending on the nature of such evidence.

In at least four cases known to the author, birth outside the territory of the child concerned was indeed 'confessed' by the persons concerned or was at least suspected. In three among the four decisions, Spanish nationality of the child concerned was indeed confirmed, and in one remaining case it was denied.

*DGRN Resolution of 10 January 1995*[69] *(nationality confirmed—see also* Sect. 4.3.3)

On 23 February 1994, the President of the Child Protection Board of the city M requested the judge in charge of the civil registry of that city to grant the late birth registration of a minor, declaring the minor to have been abandoned, with an estimated age of two months. According to the decision:

> Ms. MM of age of majority of Moroccan nationality, born and domiciled in N. (Morocco), appeared at the abovementioned Board for the purpose of handing over the child who had previously been born at her domicile[70] from a woman named F who had disappeared after the aforementioned birth.[71]

However, in the 'facts' part of the decision, contradictory statements made by different actors concerned with regard to the baby's birthplace (whether it occurred in Morocco or Spain, at MM's house at her mother's house) are shared, without explanations on how such differences came about.[72] Specifically, the witness from

---

[69] Res. DGRN de 10 de enero de 1995 (190) (BIMJ, núm. 1737, 1995, pp 1390–2; RAJ, 1995, núm. 1453; Actualidad Civil (Registros), 1995–3, núm. 286, p 218).

[70] 'su domicilio' *(her house)* is presumably MM's domicile in N in Morocco, but it is not certain based on what is available on the decision.

[71] Original reads: 'Que doña M.M., mayor de edad, de nacionalidad marroquí, nacida y domiciliada en N. (Marruecos), acudió a la citada Junta con la finalidad de entregar un menor que previamente había sido alumbrado en su domicilio por una mujer de nombre F. que había desaparecido tras el mentado alumbramiento'.

[72] As the facts included are contradictory, the author's translation of the decision was also reviewed by a professional translator, Alison Illanes LLM, and was confirmed to be correct.

the Child Protection Board is quoted to have stated that the 'child was born in M' (that is, in Spain) before being delivered to the Board.[73] The police station's file is also quoted as showing that F gave birth to the baby in 'her mother's house [the location of which is not included in the decision], before being brought to city M to be handed over to the woman [MM] who later, in turn, would deliver him to the aforementioned Board'.[74]

DGRN stated in its reasoning that:

> There can be no doubt that the birth occurred in this city in view of the information provided by the President of the Board who took charge of the child and whose probative value is recognized in Article 169 of the Civil Registry Regulation. [...] *In any case, it must be borne in mind that* those born in Spain whose filiation is not determined are Spanish by birth and for these purposes *minors whose first known place of stay is a Spanish territory* are presumed to be born in Spanish territory (see Art. 17.1 of the CC [Civil Code].) This legal presumption has not been undermined [*Esta presunción legal no ha quedado desvirtuada*] in this case. (emphasis added)

Thus, despite some conflicting information on file, DGRN essentially concluded that, as long as the prerequisite facts (undetermined parentage and Spain as the first place of stay) are fulfilled, the legal presumption of birth within the territory remains intact, even if the statement by one of the persons concerned indicates birth outside Spain (as long as it is not firmly proven).

*DGRN resolution (3a) of 21 June 1996[75] (nationality denied)*

In this case, the person claiming to be the (eight-day-old) new-born's mother stated that the baby boy was born in the city of N in Morocco when handing over the child to the police of Melilla city of Spain. In this case, there was no documentary evidence to establish the birth in Morocco as claimed by the Provincial Child Protection Board of city M as the guardian of the child. The lack of documentary proof of birth in Morocco was not denied by DGRN, and it is not clear from the resolution whether any further investigations by the Spanish authorities were done to substantiate the birth in Spain. However, DGRN determined:

> [T]here is no doubt that the birth took place in N. This is basically the result of the mother's own statements included in the report of the police station of M based on the statement she made before the police officers that conducted the first proceedings.

Further, DGRN also stated in conclusion that:

> Therefore, it is evident that the presumption established in the aforementioned article [article 17(1)(d)] must give in to the statements of his mother who stated that the birth took place in N. Indeed, although the maternal filiation was not determined or legally proven [...], the birth in Spain of the underprivileged minor has to be proven in order to conclude that

---

[73] The Spanish original states: '[...] que el menor había nacido en M, y que fue entregado a la junta de protección de menores'.

[74] The Spanish original states: '[...] que la citada F. dió a luz al menor en la casa de su madre siendo traido a M. para ser entregado a la mujer que después, a su vez, lo entregaría a la citada entidad'.

[75] Res. DGRN 3.a de 21 de junio de 1996 (BIMJ, núms. 1782–3, 1996, pp 3606–8).

> this is Spanish and if for these purposes they are presumed born in Spanish territory, this legal presumption, like all, in principle, *may be invalidated by evidence to the contrary* [...] Consequently, since the basic fact, which is the birth in Spanish territory, is not perfectly clear and proven, the consequent fact which would be the attribution of the Spanish nationality iure soli [...] cannot be obtained [...]. (emphasis added)

In this case DGRN took a different approach from the 10 January 1995 case, in the sense that it determined that the purported mother's statement alone (that the baby was born in Morocco) constituted 'proof to the contrary' and was enough to invalidate the legal presumption of birth in Spain. This was so although the mother's statement was not established by any other evidence as long as observed from the text of the DGRN decision.

*DGRN Resolution 3.a of 9 October 1996*[76] *(nationality confirmed—see also* Sect. 4.3.3)

On 9 June 1995, the Provincial Child Protection Board of city M in Spain filed a case before the city Civil Registry to make a late birth registration for a girl known by the name of L—whom they had declared to have been abandoned. The Board stated that on 4 May 1995, the birth of the female baby occurred outside of a health centre (the mother regularly went to one of the health centres in the area before delivery), and on the following day, the mother submitted a written document to the Board showing her intention to hand the child over to be adopted, mentioning her desire to remain anonymous. The documents submitted included: a photocopy of the discharge report; medical documents issued on 9 May 1995 by the County Hospital of city M on which the admission of a minor called L is recorded; as well as the police report on 9 February 1996 stating that the mother of L did not give birth to this minor in the County Hospital, but was assisted in the aforementioned centre after the delivery, which is supposed to have occurred in Morocco (the information source for the supposed birth in Morocco is not indicated within this DGRN resolution).

DGRN ruled that, even though there were doubts in this case about whether the birth occurred in city M or in Morocco:

> the truth is that there is no direct evidence the birth has occurred in this nation, so the presumption established by Article 17 (1[d], author) of the Civil Code comes into play, and the girl, whose filiation is unknown and whose first known place of stay is city M, is Spanish by birth.

On a separate note, the age of the person concerned at the time of nationality confirmation was 11.5 months.

*DGRN resolution on 10 June 2005*[77] *(nationality confirmed—see* Sect. 4.3.5 *and* Sect. 6.7.3 *for more detailed summary of facts)*

---

[76] Res. DGRN 3.a de 9 de octubre de 1996 (191) (BIMJ, núm. 1795, 1997, pp 1018–20; RAJ, 1997, núm. 2550; Actualidad Civil (Registros), 1997–3, núm. 287, pp 251–2).

[77] Res. DGRN de 10 de junio de 2005 (BOE, 1-VIII-2005, pp 27,158–9 (Anexo III.3.25)).

In the 10 June 2005 case, the girl of approximately ten years old was found begging on the street. She was accompanied by self-claimed parents who 'appeared to be nationals of Romania', whose paternity and maternity over the child were not considered to have been established by DGRN. The self-claimed parents had also stated that the girl was born in Rome, which was not established. As also quoted in more detail in Sect. 6.7.3, DGRN stated that:

> [A]rticle 17.1.d) of the Civil Code provided legal proof, by way of presumption, *without needing to enter* at this point *into assessment* of whether or not it is based on a legal fiction or *whether there is plausibility* in the *presumed fact*, of the *birth in Spain* of minors [as long as such minors' filiation is undetermined and whose 'first known place of stay is Spanish territory']. (emphasis added)

The 10 June 2005 DGRN resolution then considered that the self-claimed parents' unproven statement that the girl was born abroad (Rome), as long as it is not established (firmly) by other evidence, is not enough to constitute 'proof to the contrary'. Such statement 'could not invalidate the presumption of the minor's birth in Spain', which kicks in as the legal consequence of being a minor of undetermined parentage whose first known place of stay was Barcelona.

*Summary of the four Spanish cases with regard to the assessment of birth abroad*

In summary, in three decisions, that is those dated 10 January 1995 (where the purported midwife indicated the child's birth in Morocco), 9 October 1996 (where the police report indicates the child's birth in Morocco), and 10 June 2005 (where the self-claimed parents (whose parentage over the child was essentially denied in the decision) asserted the child's birth in Italy), DGRN ruled that the alleged birth outside the territory was not proven and recognized the child's Spanish nationality based on the fact that the children were of undetermined parentage and their first known place of stay was Spain. However, in one decision, of 21 June 1996, where the purported mother herself stated that the birth of the child occurred in Morocco when handing over the child to a Spanish police station, the baby's Spanish nationality was denied. It is not possible to discern how the birth in Morocco was considered established to the extent that it constituted 'proof to the contrary' to overturn the presumption of birth in Spain. The four DGRN decisions generally do not contain sufficient facts and reasonings for a fair comparison. However, the difference between the 21 June 1996 DGRN decision and the other three was that, in the former, the source of information as to the child's birth outside Spain was the (purported) mother herself rather than a third party as in the other three decisions. At any rate, it can be speculated that the standards adopted in the evidence assessments by the two subsequent DGRN decisions of 9 October 1996 and of 10 June 2005 have now overruled those adopted in the 21 June 1996 decision.

### United Kingdom

The UK, one of the few States subscribing to the Method III as classified in Sect. 7.4 above, provides, in section 1(2) of the British Nationality Act 1981:

A new-born infant who […] is found abandoned in the United Kingdom […] or shall, unless the contrary is shown, *be deemed* [for the purpose of section 1[1] providing for nationality acquisition of a person born in the UK or a qualifying territory of a parent who is a British citizen or is settled there, author]

(a) to have been *born in the United Kingdom* […] and

(b) to have been *born to a parent* who at the time of the birth was *a British citizen or settled in the United Kingdom* […]. (emphasis added)[78]

The UK Home Office's Nationality Guidance, in passing, clarifies the term 'unless the contrary is shown'. It states that the nationality under section 1(2) of the British Nationality Act 1981 can be confirmed 'unless either [of the presumed facts] can be disproved'. This means that the nationality confirmation can be denied either because the person was born outside the UK or a qualifying territory, or that the person's parent is a foreigner without permanent residency.[79]

### United States

US legislation adopts Method II as categorized in Sect. 7.4. To repeat, the Immigration and Nationality Act section 301(f) states:

The following *shall be nationals and citizens* of the United States at birth': […] (f) a person of unknown parentage found in the United States while under the age of five years, *until shown*, prior to his attaining the age of twenty-one years, *not to have been born in the United States*. (emphasis added)[80]

While it provides that the person of unknown parents found 'shall be a national', it is clear from the formulation that the ground for granting such nationality is by virtue of the presumption that the person has been born in the US, which will be overturned if she or he is known to have been born abroad.

The US Department of State Foreign Affairs Manual, while non-binding, states:

[A]. Under INA 301(f) (8 U.S.C. 1401(f)) (formerly section 301(a)(6)) INA), a child of unknown parents is *conclusively presumed* to be a US citizen if found in the United States when under 5 years of age, unless foreign birth is established before the child reaches age 21. (emphasis added)[81]

Of the nine cases[82] of the administrative and court decisions that assessed the applicability of section 301(f) known to the author, in some cases the claimant's birth abroad was not disputed, and in some there was some evidence supporting the

---

[78] British Nationality Act 1981 (1981) <https://www.legislation.gov.uk/ukpga/1981/61#commen tary-c16828211> accessed 4 August 2019.

[79] UK Home Office, British citizenship: Automatic Acquisition (part of Nationality Guidance) (27 July 2017) 8 <https://www.gov.uk/government/publications/automatic-acquisition-nationality-pol icy-guidance> accessed 4 August 2019.

[80] USCIS, Immigration and Nationality Act of 1952 (USA) (2 August 2019) <https://www.uscis. gov/ilink/docView/SLB/HTML/SLB/act.html> accessed 4 August 2019.

[81] US Department of State Foreign Affairs Manual (FAM) 7 FAM 1118 (2017 ed) <https://fam. state.gov/FAM/07FAM/07FAM1110.html> accessed 4 August 2019.

[82] See the beginning of Sect. 5.6.1.

claimant's birth outside the US. Such evidence of foreign birth was obviously considered proof to the contrary and resulted in the rejection of the claimant's nationality claim (in some cases along with the fact that at least one of the parents is known).

In *Re Application 2011 WL 10,845,097* (DHS), the record indicated that the applicant was born out of wedlock in South Korea, while his biological father is unknown (and he was adopted by US citizens). There is a copy of his Korean birth certificate with his mother's name on it. The claimant had a Korean passport with an immigrant visa on it. In *Orea-Hernandez v. Attorney General of the US* discussed in Sect. 4.2, the claimant's birth in Mexico was acknowledged by the claimant himself and was recorded on his Mexican passport. In *Re Applicant 2013 WL 5,504,816* (DHS), the applicant' Special Immigrant Juvenile Status records, school records, personal statement and brother's affidavit, all indicated birth in (or connections to) Mexico.

In the 2007 case *WL 5,338,559* by the Administrative Appeals Authority, the proof of birth abroad was only indicated and did not appear to have been firmly established but was still used against the claimant. In this case, it was stated that the claimant came under the care of his unrelated female guardian when the guardian's husband brought the claimant home one day in dirty, ragged clothes. The guardian's husband only stated to her that the claimant had been staying with his grandmother who was ill. The husband eventually died without revealing more information other than the child's name and birth date. Nevertheless, the claimant's school records, as noted in the decision, carried contradictory information: Some indicate the claimant's birth in Canada and some in Chicago (that is, the baptismal certificate stating he was the son of the guardian and was born in Chicago). At any rate, the facts contained in the decision are insufficient to make any detailed assessment on this case.

In the *Johnson v. Attorney General* (7.3), which is discussed in depth in Sect. 5.6.1, the claimant's birth abroad was asserted by INS based on the Jamaican birth certificate found in the house of the claimant's deceased brother, which, however, was far from being firmly proven to have belonged to the claimant. However, it was apparently considered as one of the disqualifying factors by the District Court and the Federal Court in denying the confirmation of the claimant's nationality under section 301(f). The standard of proof to prove the contrary was apparently too high for this case, as discussed in Sect. 5.6.1.

In the 2006 *Newark Case* discussed in Sects. 4.3.5 and 6.4, 6.5, 6.6 and 6.7 where a young woman over 18 years of age who had been informally adopted by an unrelated woman was confirmed American nationality,[83] there probably were some suspicions that she was born in Haiti. In this case, the girl was 'found' in Newark, US along with three other children. The birth certificates for two of the children—which turned out to have been forged—were supposedly issued by the US embassy in Haiti, while the birth certificates for the two other children supposedly issued in Newark were

---

[83] USCIS, Immigration and Nationality Act of 1952 (USA) (2 August 2019) <https://www.uscis.gov/ilink/docView/SLB/HTML/SLB/act.html> accessed 4 August 2019.

also determined not to be authentic.[84] However, in this case, mere suspicions were apparently considered insufficient to overturn the presumption of birth in the US.

## Germany

The Nationality Act of Germany adopts Method V by assuming German descent. Section 4 paragraph 2, sentence 1 contains a legal presumption of German nationality which can be reversed with the proof to the contrary.

To repeat, the Nationality Act section 4(2) reads:

> Section 4 [...] (2) A child which is found on the German territory [*Findelkind*] *shall be deemed to be a child of a German until otherwise proven*. Sentence 1 is to apply to a child born confidentially according to § 25 (1) of the Pregnancy Conflict Act. (emphasis added)[85]

The relevant administrative instruction states that 'The proof of the contrary is only furnished when the personal status of the foundling is ascertained later and the descent of alien parents is determined thereof.'[86] A commentary indicates that the presumed descent from a German citizen, rather than birth in Germany, conveys German nationality to the foundling, and that the link is the finding on the German territory, not an inland birth—that is that the nationality acquisition is based on the *jus sanguinis*, not on the *jus soli* principle. It is further indicated that the contrary has to be positively proven, unlikeliness or doubts are not sufficient, and possible acquisition of another nationality is necessary (it is unclear whether this applies to pre facto assessment or post facto assessment).[87]

This should normally mean that even if a child of unknown parents found on the territory are known to have been born outside Germany, she or he would still acquire German nationality unless her or his descent from a non-German becomes firmly proven.

## Italy

---

[84] It is not clear from the publicly available article which of the fake birth certificates (the Haiti or Newark one) supposedly belonged to the claimant. Chris Nugent and Doug Burnett of the Holland & Knight Community Services Team, 'The Foundling Statute' (23 January 2007) <https://www.ilw.com/articles/2007,0123-nugent.shtm> accessed 4 August 2019.

[85] Nationality Act of Germany (Staatsangehörigkeitsgesetz) (StAG)' (1913) <http://globalcit.eu/wp-content/plugins/rscas-database-eudo-gcit/?p=file&appl=currentCitizenshipLaws&f=GER% 20Nationality%20Act_consolidated%20version%2013.11.14_ORIGINAL%20LANGUAGE. pdf>.

[86] 'Vorläufige Anwendungshinweise des Bundesministeriums des Innern zum Staatsangehörigkeits-gesetz (StAG) in der Fassung des Zweiten Gesetzes zur Änderung des Staatsangehörigkeits-gesetzes vom 13 November 2014 [Federal Ministry of Interior, Preliminary instruction on implementation of the Nationality Law (StAG) as amended by the Second Act amending the Nationality Law of 13 November 2014] (BGBl. I S. 1714) (as of 1 June 2015) Sect. 4.2. (Germany) <http://www.bmi.bund.de/cae/servlet/contentblob/463812/publicationFile/23664/ Anwendungshinweise_05_2009.pdf> (last accessed 5 September 2017, inaccessible as of 1 July 2019); <https://www.dortmund.de/media/p/ordnungsamt/pdf_ordnungsamt/Allgemeine_V erwaltungsvorschrift_zum_Staatsangehoerigkeitsrecht.pdf> accessed 1 July 2019.

[87] Reinhard Marx, '§ 4 StAG' in Fritz/Vormeier (eds), *Gemeinschaftskommentar zum Staatsange-hörigkeitsgesetz* [*Commentary on Nationality Law*] (Looseleaf edn, Walters Kluwer/Luchterhand July 2019) 53–54.3 para 196 ff.

The Italian legislation subscribes to Method VII b) above, adopting a similar approach as article 6(1)(b) of the ECN, cited in Sect. 7.4. It would be useful here to refer to the history of legislative change of Italian nationality law regarding persons of unknown parents.

While Italy's accession to the 1961 Convention materialized only in 2015, Italy's nationality law of 1912 previously in force already contained a provision to grant nationality to foundlings. Article 1 of the 1912 nationality law provided:

> The following persons are citizens by birth [...] who was born in Italy if both parents are unknown [...]. *A son or daughter of unknown parents found in Italy is presumed to have been born in Italy until proven to the contrary.* (emphasis added)[88]

In contrast, to repeat the relevant articles of the 1992 Italian nationality law for the sake of ease of reference, article 1(1)(b) provides that: 'The following shall be citizens by birth: [...] '(Sons or daughters) who was *born in the territory* of the Republic both of whose parents are unknown [...]' (emphasis added). Then separately, article 1(2) provides 'Sons or daughters found in the territory of the Republic whose parents are unknown shall be considered citizens by birth in the absence of proof of their possession of any other citizenship.'

Thus, Italy's 1912 nationality law provided for the presumption of birth in the territory for a person of unknown parentage found in Italy so that the person can acquire nationality based on the clause immediately before that, providing nationality to their counterparts born in Italy. In contrast, article 1(2) of the 91/1992 nationality law is *not* dependent on article 1(1)(b) and no longer presumes birth in the territory. Instead, the 1992 law simply considers such a person 'to be a citizen' in the absence of another nationality.

This legislative change is in line with Italy's position during the travaux of the 1961 Convention that even persons of unknown parents born outside Italy acquire Italian nationality as long as they have been found in Italy and are still stateless.

This is also consistent with the fact that while article 1(2) makes the 'absence of proof of their possession of any other citizenship' a condition to grant Italian nationality to persons of unknown parents 'found' in the territory, article 1(1)(b) does not.[89] This is because, unlike article 1(2), article 1(1)b presupposes that the person's birth in the Italian territory is established, and thus does not foresee that the person of unknown parentage would acquire another nationality other than an Italian

---

[88] Legge 13 giugno 1912, n.555 sulla cittadinanza italiana [Law 13 June 1912, No 555 on Italian citizenship] (Italy) (author translation) <http://www.amblima.esteri.it/resource/2007/03/12736_f_a mb61Legge13giugno1912n_555sullacittadinanzaitaliana.htm> accessed 4 August 2019. The original version of article 1 states: 'E' cittadino per nascita: [...] 3. chi è nato nel [Regno] se entrambi i genitori o sono ignoti[...]. Il figlio di ignoti trovato in Italia si presume fino a prova in contrario nato nel [Regno]'.

[89] It should be noted that the ENS report (2015) on Italy appears to confuse the two provisions—the report suggests the condition of 'absence of proof of possession of another nationality' applies to persons of unknown parents born in the territory under article 1(1)b, which, however, apparently applies only to those *found* in the territory under article 1(2) based on the structure of the law. See ENS, 'Ending Childhood Statelessness: A Study on Italy, Working Paper 07/15' (2015) pp 7 and 23 <http://www.refworld.org/docid/582327974.html> accessed 4 August 2019.

one. The fact that article 1(2) foresees that a person of unknown parents might have acquired foreign nationality indicates that the drafters of this provision envisaged that there may be situations where the person was born outside the Italian territory and was subsequently found in Italy.

However, as discussed in Sect. 6.7.1, in the context of the definition of the term 'found' in the territory, the general interpretation of the Ministry of Interior in their official commentary 'Italian Citizenship—Legislation, Procedures and Circulars' is basically that the person concerned has to be a small child when found in Italy as there should be a linkage between the term being 'found' with the 'presumption of birth in the territory'. If this logic is to be followed at face value, a person born outside the territory might not be considered to have been 'found' in Italian territory and will fall outside the scope of article 1(2).

Nevertheless, (the presumably unofficial) view of the Ministry of Interior, when particularly asked by author on the question whether the proof of birth outside the territory justifies the denial of the Italian nationality under article 1(2), quite definitely precluded such an inference. The Ministry of Interior first stated—quite reasonably—that it was difficult to imagine such cases as, if a child is known to have been born in another State, then the parent(s) should normally be known. Their answer is only a theoretical or hypothetical one and not based on actual precedents. Having said that, the Ministry responded that, if such case arises, because:

> under article 1(2) the only basis for denial of nationality is that the person has acquired a foreign nationality, we would have to examine whether the person acquires nationality – whether the country of birth grants nationality by *jus soli* or has a provision to grant nationality to a child of unknown parents born there.

If the child does not acquire nationality in the country of birth, then the child found in Italy should be an Italian national.

According to the Ministry of Interior, this applies to pre facto assessment of whether the child's Italian nationality can be confirmed, as well as post facto whether the person's nationality can be cancelled after the person has been confirmed nationality based on article 1(2). Thus, in cases where article 1(2) was once considered to apply and the person has been living as an Italian national, nationality can only be withdrawn when a parent and/or birthplace becomes known, and if the Ministry of Interior can confirm the child's acquisition of the nationality based on such known facts.[90]

---

[90] Interview with Central Direction for Civil Rights, Citizenship and Minorities of the Department for Civil Liberties and Immigration of the Ministry of Interior, Italy (Rome, Italy, 23 May 2017). It would be pertinent to consider how their 'theoretical' interpretation fits in with the other position in the context of the definition of 'found' in the official commentary 'Italian Citizenship—Legislation, Procedures and Circulars' by the Ministry of Interior (31 March 2003) as cited in Sect. 6.7.1, on the linkage between being 'found' and 'presumption of birth in Italy' as mentioned above. Considering the example of Spain (DGRN resolution of 10 June 2005 as discussed in Sect. 6.7.3), it is possible that the two positions are indeed compatible—it could possibly be interpreted to the effect that as long as the person concerned is found in Italy as a small child, she or he can benefit from some sort of legal fiction that she or he is born in Italy, and can thus be confirmed nationality under article 1(2) even if there is proof of her or his birth abroad.

While not based on actual precedents, this theoretical but inclusive interpretation by the Ministry of Interior officials reflects the position taken by the Italian authorities represented during the travaux of the 1961 Convention, that is basically that a foundling found in the territory born abroad should be confirmed nationality of the country where found if the country of birth does not grant her or him its nationality.[91]

In light of the majority view during the travaux, the text of article 2 of the 1961 Convention, its object and purpose, that is to prevent statelessness, as well as some States' legislation and practice reviewed in this section, it is possible for one to argue that the evidence of possession of another nationality should be the only fact constituting 'the contrary' disqualifying the person from acquiring nationality where found pre facto.

## 7.6  Post Facto Withdrawal of Nationality

As stated earlier, the 1961 Convention does not explicitly regulate what happens to the nationality acquired by the person based on article 2 when 'proof to the contrary' is found post facto and, more generally, on what conditions such nationality can be lost. The travaux has very limited reference to this, even compared to what was reviewed in the context of pre facto assessment in Sect. 7.3. This section draws on the materials relating to the interpretation of the 1961 Convention, international human rights law standards, some regional case law and the national legislation based on annex 1 to find answers to these questions.

### 7.6.1  1961 Convention and Related International Standards

Before examining the national legislation based on annex 1, the 1961 Convention and related international standards will be reviewed.

---

[91] Italy's verbal proposal cited also in Sect. 7.3.1.1, that is 'A foundling found in the territory of a Contracting Party shall be considered a national of that Contracting Party'. United Nations, Summary Records, 5th Meeting of the Committee of the Whole held on 3 April 1959, A/CONF.9/C.1/SR.5, UN Conference on the Elimination or Reduction of Future Statelessness, Geneva, 1959 and New York, 1961 (3 April 1959) 7 <http://legal.un.org/docs/?path=../diplom aticconferences/1959_statelessness/docs/english/vol_2/a_conf9_c1_sr5.pdf&lang=E> accessed 4 August 2019.

### 7.6.1.1 Prohibition of Arbitrary Nationality Deprivation Under International Law

To lay out the fundamentals, the right to a nationality and prohibition of arbitrary deprivation of nationality enshrined in article 15 of the UDHR along with avoidance of statelessness are considered fundamental principles of international law.[92] Not only the State parties to the 1961 Convention but all States thus have obligations pursuant to the prohibition of arbitrary deprivation of nationality.[93] Deprivation of nationality is arbitrary if it is not prescribed by law; is not the least intrusive means proportionate to achieving a legitimate aim; and/or takes place without due process.[94] Further, discriminatory withdrawal of nationality must be avoided. Article 9 of the 1961 Convention prohibits deprivation on racial, ethnic, religious or political grounds, which is complemented by the non-discrimination principle, such as in article 26 of ICCPR and article 2 of the CRC and by developments in international human rights law.[95] As will be reviewed in more detail in Sect. 7.6.1.4, these are so regardless of whether a withdrawal of nationality results in statelessness or not.[96] The UN Human Rights Council has stated that: 'Deprivation of nationality resulting in statelessness will *generally be arbitrary* unless it serves a legitimate purpose and complies with the principle of proportionality' (emphasis added), and that exceptions to this general principle must be construed narrowly (see also Sect. 7.6.1.2).[97] When

---

[92] See for example UN General Assembly, Resolution 50/152 of 21 December 1995 'Office of the United Nations High Commissioner for Refugees' (9 February 1996) para 16 <https://www.refworld.org/docid/3b00f31d24.html> accessed 4 August 2019; UN Human Rights Council, 'Human rights and arbitrary deprivation of nationality: Report of the Secretary-General' A/HRC/13/34 (19 December 2013) para 6 <https://www.refworld.org/docid/52f8d19a4.html> accessed 4 August 2019; and UNHCR Guidelines 5 (2020) para 85.

[93] UNHCR Guidelines 5 (2020) para 3.

[94] For a general overview of what can amount to 'arbitrary' deprivation of human rights, see ibid Part III paras 84–123; UN Human Rights Council, 'Human rights and arbitrary deprivation of nationality: report of the Secretary-General' (14 December 2009) A/HRC/13/34 <http://www.unhcr.org/refworld/docid/4b83a9cb2.html> accessed 2 August 2019. See also paras 36 and 37, Council of Europe, Explanatory Report to the European Convention on Nationality, 6.XI.1997 (1997) <https://rm.coe.int/16800ccde7> accessed 4 August 2019.

[95] UNHCR Guidelines 5 (2020) para 79 and 110.

[96] See, for example, UNHCR Guidelines 5 (2020) paras 95 and 97, which state: 'In order to avoid arbitrary deprivation of nationality, it is necessary for States to implement procedural safeguards in all cases of withdrawal of nationality *regardless of whether or not they result in statelessness*.' Para 77 of the Guidelines 5 notes that article 9 (non-discrimination) of the 1961 Convention applies irrespective of whether or not statelessness would result from the deprivation. While in the context of deprivation in a nationality security measure, it is noted that Principle 6.2 of ISI's 'Principles on Deprivation of Nationality as a National Security Measure' (2020) provides: 'Each State is bound by the *principle of non-discrimination* between its nationals, regardless of whether they acquired nationality at birth or subsequently, and whether they have *one or multiple nationalities*'. ISI, 'Principles on Deprivation of Nationality as a National Security Measure' (2020) <https://files.institutesi.org/PRINCIPLES.pdf> accessed 15 September 2020.

[97] UN Human Rights Council, 'Human rights and arbitrary deprivation of nationality: report of the Secretary-General, A/HRC/13/34' (14 December 2009) para 59 (also para 27) <https://www.refworld.org/docid/4b83a9cb2.html> accessed 4 August 2019. Tunis Conclusions (2014) para 23.

withdrawal of nationality involves children, their best interests based on article 3 of the CRC need to be duly considered (see Sect. 7.6.1.5).

### 7.6.1.2  Convention and General Prohibition of Nationality Withdrawal Resulting in Statelessness

The 1961 Convention sets out general prohibition of loss or deprivation of nationality where it would result in statelessness, along with a narrow set of exceptions under which this would not be the case; and in light of the preceding section, these exceptions are to be interpreted in a restrictive manner. Further, provisions of the 1961 Convention must be read and interpreted by contracting States in light of their additional obligations under other treaties, customary international law and subsequent developments in international human rights law in general.[98]

As to foundlings-specific standards, the UNHCR Guidelines 4 (7.1) paragraph 60 briefly state that 'nationality acquired by foundlings pursuant to Article 2 of the 1961 Convention *may only be lost* if it is proven that the child concerned *possesses another* State's *nationality*' (emphasis added).[99] Further, the Report of the UN Secretary-General on deprivation of nationality (December 2013) has a dedicated paragraph, paragraph 30 entitled 'C. Foundlings', stating:

> An important consideration with regard to the avoidance of statelessness among foundlings relates to how States should respond if the child's parents are identified at a later date. [...] in accordance with the child's right to a nationality and the object and purpose of relevant international standards, nationality acquired by foundlings may only be lost if it is proven that the child possesses the nationality of another State.[100]

This position was promoted by Denmark during the travaux negotiations, as also quoted including in Sect. 7.3.1.4: '[T]he child would possess the nationality of the country in which he had been found until shown to be entitled to another nationality.'[101] This principle is also backed up by article 5(1) of the 1961 Convention, which will be elaborated on below.

---

[98] UNHCR Guidelines 5 (2020) para 7.

[99] UNHCR Guidelines 4 (2012) para 60.

[100] UN Human Rights Council, Twenty-fifth session, 'Report of the Secretary-General on Human rights and arbitrary deprivation of nationality' A/HRC/25/28 (19 December 2013) para 30 <https://www.refworld.org/docid/52f8d19a4.html> accessed 4 August 2019.

[101] Statement by the Danish representative in advocating for the current version of article 2. United Nations, Summary Records, 5th Meeting of the Committee of the Whole held on 3 April 1959, A/CONF.9/C.1/SR.5, UN Conference on the Elimination or Reduction of Future Statelessness, Geneva, 1959 and New York, 1961 (3 April 1959) 10 <http://legal.un.org/docs/?path=../diplom aticconferences/1959_statelessness/docs/english/vol_2/a_conf9_c1_sr5.pdf&lang=E> accessed 4 August 2019. Also cited on p 48 and fn 167 of Olivier Willem Vonk, Maarten Peter Vink and Gerard-René de Groot, 'Protection against Statelessness: Trends and Regulations in Europe' (May 2013) <http://cadmus.eui.eu/bitstream/handle/1814/30201/eudocit_vink_degroot_statelessn ess_final.pdf?sequence=1> accessed 4 August 2019.

*Article 5(1)*

Among the provisions regulating loss and deprivation within the 1961 Convention, article 5(1) is particularly relevant to those who acquire nationality under article 2 of the Convention, which provides that no change in the personal status may cause statelessness, stating:

> *If the law* of a Contracting State *entails loss of nationality* as a consequence of any change in the personal status of a person such as marriage, termination of marriage, legitimation, recognition or adoption, such loss shall be *conditional upon possession* or acquisition of *another nationality.* (emphasis added)

Under Article 5(1) of the 1961 Convention, a person thus may lose the nationality of a contracting State as a result of a change in civil status, conditional upon such a loss being provided for within the domestic law and upon the person possessing or acquiring another nationality. According to paragraphs 37 and 38 of the Summary Conclusions of the UNHCR-convened Expert Meeting in 2014 on avoiding statelessness resulting from nationality loss and deprivation, that is the Tunis Conclusions (2014), the list of changes in personal status contained in article 5(1) is not exhaustive and would also apply 'if it is established that the family relationship which constituted the basis of a child's acquisition of nationality was registered erroneously'.[102] Further, the Tunis Conclusions also note that: 'Articles 5–8 of the 1961 Convention would apply where it is discovered or alleged after a reasonable period of possession of a nationality that the conditions for acquisition of that nationality were not fulfilled.'[103]

It is thus concluded that the non-exhaustive list included in article 5(1) of the 1961 Convention should cover both situations where, for a person who has acquired a nationality under a foundling provision, legal parentage that *did not exist* earlier is newly established, or legal parent(s) who had originally existed is(are) later discovered. Post-fact establishment or discovery of foreign parentage thus must not entail the loss of nationality acquired by virtue of the foundling provision, if statelessness would be the consequence.[104]

Further, it should be noted that when the application of article 5(1) involves children, paragraph 17 of the UNHCR Guidelines 5 (2020) based on the UN Human Rights Council report (19 December 2013) goes further to state that 'Articles 3, 7 and 8 of the CRC, read together, *may reasonably be understood to preclude the loss* of nationality by a child due to adoption, recognition or another such act' (emphasis

---

[102] Tunis Conclusions (2014) para 38.

[103] Tunis Conclusions (2014) para 14.

[104] See for example Olivier Willem Vonk, Maarten Peter Vink and Gerard-René de Groot, 'Protection against Statelessness: Trends and Regulations in Europe' (May 2013) 48 <http://cadmus.eui.eu/bitstream/handle/1814/30201/eudocit_vink_degroot_statelessness_final.pdf?sequence=1> accessed 4 August 2019; Human Rights Council, Twenty-fifth session, 'Report of the Secretary-General on Human rights and arbitrary deprivation of nationality' (19 December 2013) para 30.

added).[105] It should also be noted that the UN Human Rights Council has gone even
further and recommended that States should '*remove* legislative or administrative
measures for loss or deprivation of nationality on the basis of a *change in civil status*
(or in response to a serious criminal offence…)' (emphasis added).[106]

This guidance indicates that, especially where children are involved, the loss
of nationality acquired based on a foundling provision due to discovery of legal
parentage or subsequent recognition of parentage, could only be allowed in truly
exceptional circumstances even if such loss does not lead to statelessness. For general
discussions on the need to take into consideration the best interests of the child, please
refer to Sect. 7.6.1.5.

The 1961 Convention and related standards reviewed do *not* contain any guidance
on what happens under the unlikely, but still possible, scenario: a child who acquires
the nationality of the country where she or he was found based on article 2, later
is found to have been born abroad, while her or his parentage remains unknown.
However, given the nature of the discovered fact (birth abroad), the applicable standards should be the same or similar as when the legal parentage that was existent at
the time of nationality acquisition as a foundling is discovered post facto; the nationality must not be lost unless the person concerned possesses another nationality; and
even if the loss would not result in statelessness, care must be taken so that the loss
would not constitute arbitrary deprivation of nationality.

*Article 8(2)(b)*

General

One of the 'exceptions' to the general prohibition of nationality loss or deprivation
resulting in statelessness within the 1961 Convention is article 8(2)(b), which allows
for deprivation of nationality resulting in statelessness due to misrepresentation or
fraud. While no such precedent was found, theoretically and hypothetically there
may possibly be situations where a person indeed has a legal parent(s) who is (are)
indeed behaving as such, but she, he or the parent(s) deliberately—with an intention
to deceive or mislead the authorities—conceal such a fact, and acquire nationality
under a foundling provision. The State concerned could possibly—upon discovery
of such a fact—perceive it as a 'fraudulent acquisition' of nationality.

It should be noted here that UNHCR Guidelines 5 (2020) states that developments in international (human rights) law have further narrowed the scope of application of Articles 8(2) (and (3)) of the 1961 Convention.[107] Further, according to
the Tunis Conclusions (2014), article 8(2): '[O]nly applies to nationality which
is acquired through an *application procedure*—it would not extend to nationality
acquired at birth or on the basis of Articles 1–4 of the 1961 Convention' (emphasis

---

[105] UN Human Rights Council, 'Human rights and arbitrary deprivation of nationality: Report of the
Secretary-General' A/HRC/25/28 (19 December 2013) para 16, reproduced in UNHCR Guidelines
5 (2020) para 17 in discussing the interpretation of article 5(1) of the 1961 Convention.

[106] Ibid UN Human Rights Council (19 December 2013) para 41.

[107] UNHCR Guidelines 5 (2020) para 48.

added).[108] According to the Tunis Conclusions (2014), article 8(2) thus does not apply to the nationality acquired based on article 2, the foundling provision. Hypothetically though, where a State nevertheless decides to consider applying its legislative provision allowing withdrawal of nationality due to misrepresentation or fraud to a nationality acquired based on a foundling provision, the general guidance in paragraph 52 of UNHCR Guidelines 5 (2020) should be recalled: 'In the process of balancing the legitimate interests of the Contracting State and the individual, the nature or gravity of the fraud or misrepresentation should be weighed against the consequences of withdrawal of nationality (including statelessness).'

It should be noted that the UN Human Rights Council (19 December 2013) goes further in commenting on article 8(2), stating that:

> [T]he 'consequences of any withdrawal of nationality must be carefully weighed against the gravity of the behaviour or offence […]. Given the severity of the consequences where statelessness results, it may be *difficult to justify* loss or deprivation *resulting in statelessness* in terms of proportionality. (emphasis added)[109]

The length of time elapsed between the acquisition of nationality, discovery of fraud (as well as from the discovery to the withdrawal decision) should also be considered, which is relevant to the assessment as to whether the gravity of the act justifies deprivation of nationality. If this time period is lengthy, only very grave offences may justify a deprivation of nationality.[110]

### Children

Again hypothetically, if the equivalent national provision was to be applied to a child who has acquired nationality based on a foundling provision in instances of fraud committed by her or his parent(s), just as in all decisions relating to children, special attention needs to be given to the objective of preventing statelessness among children under articles 1–4 of the 1961 Convention and articles 7 and 8 of the CRC, read in light of the principle of the best interests of the child under article 3.[111] It is 'never in the best interests of the child to be rendered stateless'.[112] Further, the norm of non-discrimination (including non-punishment) of children on the basis of

---

[108] Tunis Conclusions (2014) para 56.

[109] UN Human Rights Council, 'Human rights and arbitrary deprivation of nationality: Report of the Secretary-General', A/HRC/25/28 (19 December 2013) paras 4, 10, 41 <https://www.refworld.org/docid/52f8d19a4.html> accessed 4 August 2019.

[110] UNHCR Guidelines 5 (2020) para 52. Gerard-René de Groot, Maarten Peter Vink and Patrick Wautelet, 'Involuntary Loss of European Citizenship (ILEC) Guidelines on Involuntary Loss of European Citizenship' (2015) (hereinafter 'ILEC Guidelines') Part II para 3 <http://www.ilecproject.eu/sites/default/files/GUIDELINES%20INVOLUNTARY%20LOSS%20OF%20EUROPEAN%20CITIZENSHIP%20.pdf> accessed 4 August 2019.

[111] Tunis Conclusions (2014) para 62. While in the context of fraud during naturalization, of the ILEC Guidelines (2015) part II para 6.

[112] Tunis Conclusions (2014) para 62.

the action or behaviour of their parents under article 2 of the CRC is particularly relevant.[113] Moreover:

[A] range of other factors will need to be examined (including the ties to country concerned), in light of the general principle of proportionality, and not solely whether the child acquired nationality on the basis of fraud conducted by an adult guardian.[114]

Vonk, Vink and de Groot also emphasize:

[I]n case of fraud committed by a legal representative a State should take into consideration that, in the best interest of the child, not all acts of an adult in respect of a child are attributable to the child. This is in particular *not the case* where the adult involved acted *fraudulently by pretending to be the child's parent* [...]. Consequently, in such cases the child should be deemed to be in good faith. (emphasis added)[115]

The opposite should be true—where parent(s) pretended *not* to be the child's parent. For general discussions on the need to take into consideration the best interests of the child, reference should also be made to Sect. 7.6.1.5.

### 7.6.1.3 Equivalent Provisions in the ECN

The ECN also does not have a specific provision regulating the loss of nationality acquired based on its foundling provision, that is article 6(1)(b). However, article 4(c) of the ECN provides for prohibition of arbitrary deprivation of nationality as one of the 'general principles relating to nationality'. Further, article 7 contains an exhaustive list of acceptable grounds for nationality loss *ex lege* or at the initiative of a State party. Article 7(1)(f) provides that nationality can be lost *ex lege* or at the initiative of the State party 'where it is established *during the minority of a child* that the preconditions laid down by internal law which led to the *ex lege* acquisition of the nationality of the State party are *no longer* fulfilled' (emphasis added).[116] Further, article 7(3) of the ECN states: 'A State party may *not* provide in its internal law

---

[113] UNHCR Guidelines 5 (2020) para 21. Laura van Waas, chapter 14, 'Stateless children' in Jacqueline Bhabha, Jyothi Kanics and Daniel Senovilla Hernández (eds), *Research Handbook on Child Migration* (Edward Elgar Publishing 2018) 213, 217, 222–4.

[114] Tunis Conclusions (2014) para 39.

[115] Olivier Willem Vonk, Maarten Peter Vink and Gerard-René de Groot, 'Protection against Statelessness: Trends and Regulations in Europe' (May 2013) 96 <http://cadmus.eui.eu/bitstream/handle/1814/30201/eudocit_vink_degroot_statelessness_final.pdf?sequence=1> accessed 4 August 2019.

[116] The wording of article 5(1) of the 1961 Convention as clarified by the Tunis Conclusions (2014) especially in its para 37, and article 7(1)(f) of the ECN as clarified by para 73 of its Explanatory Report, as well as paras 11, 23, 26, 39 and 43, 45–47 of the Explanatory Memorandum of the Council of Europe Recommendation CM/Rec(2009)13 are not entirely clear about whether they cover both the situations of nullification (cancellation) of an originally erroneous nationality grant and revocation of a correctly established nationality grant based on subsequent change of circumstances. In practice, a 'change of civil (or personal) status' can occur either way, for example the (lack of) legal parentage that was erroneously registered can later be corrected, and legal parentage can also newly be established.

for the loss of its nationality under paragraphs 1 and 2 of this article *if* the person concerned would thereby *become stateless* [...]' (emphasis added).[117]

The ECN's Explanatory Report at paragraph 73 states article 7(1)(f) of the ECN covers the situations of a change of civil status of children that would entail the loss of the prerequisites for the possession of nationality.[118] Council of Europe Recommendation CM/Rec(2009)13's Explanatory Memorandum at paragraph 43 explains that article 7(1)(f) of the ECN applies to situations where a child has acquired nationality as a foundling (under article 6(1)(b) of the ECN) and, later, after discovery of her or his parent(s) found to have the nationality of the parent(s) *jus sanguinis*.[119] Thus, post facto discovery of information on the parents should not cause statelessness.[120] Further, according to article 7(1)(f) of the ECN, even if non-withdrawal results in multiple nationality, the nationality acquired through the foundling provision cannot be lost after the person reaches the age of majority.[121]

### 7.6.1.4 Proportionality and Due Process Including in Withdrawals Not Resulting in Statelessness

As mentioned in Sect. 7.6.1, needless to say, even if withdrawal of nationality does not result in statelessness, States certainly cannot peremptorily withdraw the nationality previously acquired based on a foundling provision. Even if its non-withdrawal would result in multiple nationalities, it is subject to limitations under international human rights law, in particular the general prohibition of arbitrary deprivation of nationality. As the UN Human Rights Council (19 December 2013) stated:

> Even where loss or deprivation of nationality does not lead to statelessness, States must weigh the consequences of loss or deprivation of nationality against the interest that it is seeking to protect, and consider alternative measures that could be imposed.[122]

---

[117] Exception applies. Nationality can still be withdrawn in the case of 'acquisition of the nationality of the State party by means of fraudulent conduct, false information or concealment of any relevant fact attributable to the applicant' under article 7(1)b.

[118] Council of Europe, 'Explanatory Report to the European Convention on Nationality, 6.XI.1997' (1997) para 73 <https://rm.coe.int/16800ccde7> accessed 4 August 2019. Note that there is no time-limit for nationality withdrawal in case of voluntary acquisition of another nationality under article 7(1)(a) of the ECN.

[119] Council of Europe: Committee of Ministers, *Recommendation CM/Rec(2009)13 and Explanatory Memorandum of the Committee of Ministers to Member States on the Nationality of Children* (Council of Europe Publishing 2009) para 43.

[120] Ibid para 23.

[121] Also, see Olivier Willem Vonk, Maarten Peter Vink and Gerard-René de Groot, 'Protection against Statelessness: Trends and Regulations in Europe' (May 2013) 48 <http://cadmus.eui.eu/bitstream/handle/1814/30201/eudocit_vink_degroot_statelessness_final.pdf?sequence=1> accessed 4 August 2019.

[122] UN Human Rights Council, Human rights and arbitrary deprivation of nationality: Report of the Secretary-General, A/HRC/25/28 (19 December 2013) para 40 <https://www.refworld.org/docid/52f8d19a4.html> accessed 4 August 2019.

For the withdrawal of nationality not to be 'arbitrary', it must be in accordance with the law, be proportionate to a legitimate aim and comply with due process.[123] This is especially so because, even where a person is in possession of another nationality:

[A]ny loss of the right to reside in the State in question will result in the loss of all the rights which attach to residence. States should therefore ensure that there are no less intrusive alternatives to achieve the relevant aim before withdrawal of nationality occurs.[124]

States must carefully weigh the consequences of the withdrawal of nationality against the interest that it is seeking to protect, and consider alternative measures that could be imposed.[125]

In assessing the impact on the individual, consideration must be given to the strength of the link of the person with the State in question, including birth in the territory, length of residence, family ties, economic activity as well as linguistic and cultural integration.[126] This principle of proportionality was also emphasized in the CJEU rulings such as in *Rottman* (2010) and *Tjebbes* (2019)[127] requiring that States individually examine the possible impacts of losing European citizenship against the person concerned (even where a flawed administrative decision is to be invalided).

Article 8(4) of the 1961 Convention imposes procedural safeguards with respect to deprivation of nationality. As a result of developments in international human rights law, such procedural guarantees apply in all cases of loss and deprivation of

---

[123] UNHCR Guidelines 5 (2020) part III.

[124] UNHCR Guidelines 5 (2020) paras 95, 97.

[125] UNHCR Guidelines 5 (2020) paras 94–96. UN Human Rights Council, Human rights and arbitrary deprivation of nationality: Report of the Secretary-General, A/HRC/25/28 (19 December 2013) para 40 <https://www.refworld.org/docid/52f8d19a4.html> accessed 4 August 2019.

[126] Tunis Conclusions (2014) para 21. See also 7.5. (Proportionality) paras 105–117 of ISI, 'Draft Commentary to the Principles on Deprivation of Nationality as a National Security Measure (2020) <https://files.institutesi.org/PRINCIPLES_Draft_Commentary.pdf> accessed 15 September 2020.

[127] The guidance of the CJEU in the context of both the *Rottman* (2010) and *Tjebbes* (2019) cases are relevant here. The *Rottman* case concerned the withdrawal by the German authorities of nationality acquired by deception, as a result of which withdrawal the individual would become stateless. The CJEU held, in the light of the EU law or the concept of EU citizenship, that in a decision to withdraw nationality, the principle of proportionality needed to be observed, and that it is necessary to take into account the consequences that the decision entails for the person concerned: Case C-135/08 *Janko Rottmann v. Freistaat Bayern* EU:C:2009:588 [2010] ECR I-1449 (CJEU), paras 55 and 56. *Tjebbes* followed-up on *Rottman* by elaborating on the application of the proportionality test introduced in the latter case.The *Tjebbes* case concerned four individuals with Dutch nationality who also had the nationality of a third country, who were affected by the Dutch nationality law provision stipulating automatic loss of nationality for Dutch citizens (and their children) in case of principal residence for an uninterrupted period of ten years outside the country or the EU. The CJEU provided that the loss of nationality would be inconsistent with the principle of proportionality if the national rules do not provide for an individual examination of the consequences of that loss for the persons concerned under EU law by the competent national authorities and courts: Case C-221/17 *Tjebbes and Others v. Minister van Buitenlandse Zaken* ECLI:EU:C:2019:189 [2019] (CJEU), in particular paras 40–41 and 47.

nationality.[128] Due process entails procedural fairness and safeguards including a hearing and right to effective remedy such as judicial review.[129]

### 7.6.1.5    Best Interests of the Child

Further, as already touched upon in Sects. 7.6.1.1 and 7.6.1.2, if the withdrawal of nationality concerns a child, there are additional considerations. The four 'general principles'[130] identified by the CRC Committee, that is of non-discrimination (article 2), best interests of the child (article 3), right to life, survival and development (article 6); and respect for the views of the child (article 12), must guide the decisions affecting children's right to a nationality under article 7 of the CRC.[131]

At the time when the nationality withdrawal is being considered, the assessment of whether such withdrawal goes against her or his best interests[132] must therefore be conducted as part of the individual assessment[133] of proportionality. As already stated in Sect. 7.6.1.2, it is 'never in the best interests of the child to be rendered stateless'.[134] The need for the best interests assessment in considering the withdrawal of nationality of children not resulting in statelessness was also emphasized by the CJEU in the ruling in *Tjebbes*.[135]

---

[128] Tunis Conclusions (2014) para 25.

[129] UNHCR Guidelines 5 (2020) Part III, paras 97–108.

[130] UN Committee on the Rights of the Child, General comment No 5 (2003): General measures of implementation of the Convention on the Rights of the Child, 27 November 2003, CRC/GC/2003/5 para 12.

[131] Laura van Waas, chapter 14, 'Stateless Children' in Jacqueline Bhabha, Jyothi Kanics and Daniel Senovilla Hernández (eds), *Research Handbook on Child Migration* (Edward Elgar Publishing 2018) 213, 217, 222–4. See also UNHCR Guidelines 5 (2020) para 20.

[132] For general guidance on best interests assessment or determination, UN Committee on the Rights of the Child, General comment No 14 (2013) on the right of the child to have his or her best interests taken as a primary consideration (art 3, para 1), 29 May 2013, CRC /C/GC/14. Also, for the assessment the following general comments are also relevant: UN Committee on the Rights of the Child, General comment No 12 (2009): The right of the child to be heard, 20 July 2009, CRC/C/GC/12.

[133] Section 32 of the Finnish Nationality Act is inspiring in the sense that it explicitly requires individual consideration of a child's situation (while the provision merits further improvement so as to explicitly ensure avoidance of statelessness). While in the context of effects of annulment of paternity, section 32 states that a decision that a child loses Finnish nationality previously acquired can be made before the child has reached the age of five, based on an 'overall consideration of the child's situation. In the assessment, particular account shall be taken of the child's age and ties with Finland'.

[134] Tunis Conclusions para 62.

[135] The CJEU in the context of the *Tjebbes* case provided that, as part of the proportionality test, national authorities and courts must ensure that the loss of nationality is in line with the rights of the EU Charter of Fundamental Rights, in particular the right to respect for family life and the obligation to take into account the best interests of the child. Case C-221/17 *Tjebbes and Others v. Minister van Buitenlandse Zaken* ECLI:EU:C:2019:189 [2019] paras 45 and 47. Drawing from this, right to respect for 'family life' in a case involving an (ex-)foundling should encompass the

Nationality has also been characterized as being an element in a child's identity—as stipulated in article 8 of the CRC requiring a State party 'to respect the right of the child to preserve his or her identity, including nationality' without unlawful interference. As such, arbitrary deprivation of a given nationality, even if it does not make a child stateless, 'could still be challenged on the grounds that the result is inconsistent with preservation of the child's identity'.[136]

Further, as discussed in Sect. 7.6.1.2, the norm of non-discrimination (including non-punishment) of children on the basis of the action or behaviour of their parents under article 2 of the CRC is particularly relevant.[137]

### 7.6.1.6  Consideration of Timing and Limitation Period

Further, as UNHCR Guidelines 5 (2020) also notes, considerations of timing are also relevant to the proportionality test, encouraging States to 'ensure that there is a defined and limited period with respect to the time elapsed between commission of an act and its discovery by the authorities, and between the discovery and the withdrawal of nationality.'[138] Withdrawal of nationality previously acquired based on the foundling provision should only be allowed for a certain period of time after the person was originally confirmed to hold such nationality.[139] No justification can be found to leave the nationality acquired based on the foundling provision to be

---

'family life' with her or his adoptive family or alike, which the child concerned has so far built before she or he is found to posess another nationality (that triggered the consideration of withdrawal of her or his nationality already confirmed based on the foundling provision). The ECtHR ruling in the *Mennesson* case also helps to substantiate the need for best interests determination. In the *Mennesson* case, the ECtHR addressed the question of whether France's action was justified in refusing to recognize the legal parentage and thereby the French nationality of a child who was born from a surrogacy arrangement (prohibited in French law) in which the commissioning parents were French nationals. The children were not stateless as they were born in the US and became American citizens by *jus soli*, and the issue was their access to the second, that is French, nationality. The court found that (the non-recognition of the parental bond and the concomitant) non-acquisition of French nationality impacted the children, whose right to respect for private life under article 8 of the ECHR is substantially affected and, accordingly, a serious question arises as to the compatibility of that situation with the child's best interests: *Mennesson v. France,* Application No 65192/11, 26 June 2014 (ECtHR), paras 97–99.

[136] John Tobin and Florence Seow, 'Article 7 The Rights to Birth Registration, a Name, Nationality, and to Know and Be Cared for by Parents' in John Tobin (ed), *The UN Convention on the Rights of the Child: A Commentary, Oxford Commentaries on International Law* (Oxford University Press 2019) 237, 257.

[137] UNHCR Guidelines 5 (2020) para 21. Laura van Waas, chapter 14, 'Stateless Children' in Jacqueline Bhabha, Jyothi Kanics and Daniel Senovilla Hernández (eds), *Research Handbook on Child Migration* (Edward Elgar Publishing 2018) 213, 217, 222–4.

[138] UNHCR Guidelines 5 (May 2020) para 96.

[139] ILEC Guidelines (2015) also has some recommendations that can be used by analogy: Part IV. 5.c) advocates for the limitation period for the withdrawal of nationality due to loss of the family relationship: 'The required period should be shorter than the residence period required for naturalisation and also shorter than the limitation period which may exist in the state involved for deprivation of citizenship based on fraud'.

open to cancellation and revocation forever. Further, even when the person's legal parent(s) who existed at the time of the acquisition of a nationality as a foundling is discovered later, it is desirable that the loss is *not* given a retroactive effect.[140] This is so not least for legal certainty and the best interests of the child. Nevertheless, some[141] among the 37 States identified in Sect. 7.6.2 as relatively explicitly regulating the withdrawal of nationality acquired under the foundling provision along with its criteria indeed appear to give retroactive effect to the withdrawal.

The 1961 Convention is silent on the issue of a time-limit for the loss or deprivation of nationality, and the drafters' statements in the travaux documents of the 1961 Convention leave this timeframe issue open.[142] The ECN's article 7(1)(f) as reviewed above provides before reaching the age of majority as the 'deadline'. However, there are views that making nationality withdrawable for 18 years is too long. Section 7.6.2.1 will come back to this issue of time-limit, by making a comparative review of the national legislation on this matter, and finally make observations on the possibly appropriate duration.

### 7.6.1.7  All Withdrawals Including 'quasi-loss' Covered by Prohibition of Arbitrary Nationality Deprivation

Before going into the comparative review of 139 States' legislation in the next section, it would be useful to clarify what the term 'withdrawal' encompasses in this book, in relation to some of the relevant concepts. In this book, the term 'withdrawal of nationality' is used to encompass both 'loss' (which occurs automatically by operation of law, that is *ex lege*) and 'deprivation' (which is initiated by the authorities

---

[140] ILEC Guidelines (2015) Part V.a). See also Gerard-René de Groot and Patrick Wautelet, 'Reflections on Quasi-Loss of Nationality from Comparative, International and European Perspectives' in Nuñez and de Groot (eds), *European Citizenship at the Crossroads: The Role of the European Union on Loss and Acquisition of Nationality* (Wolf Legal Publishers 2015).

[141] For example French Civil Code article 19 stating 'He shall however be deemed to have never been French if, during his minority, his parentage is established regards an alien [...]' and several other French-speaking States provide the same (see annex 1).

[142] For example, see the Danish representative's statement during the travaux cited in Sect. 7.3.1.1 '[...] they [foundlings] should therefore be given the nationality of that State *until it was proved* that the assumptions [...] were incorrect' (emphasis added). United Nations, Summary Records, 5th Plenary Meeting held on 31 March 1959, A/CONF.9/SR.5, UN Conference on the Elimination or Reduction of Future Statelessness, Geneva, 1959 and New York, 1961 (31 March 1959) 2 <http://legal.un.org/docs/?path=../diplomaticconferences/1959_statelessness/docs/english/vol_2/a_conf9_sr5.pdf&lang=E> accessed 4 August 2019. The Danish representative during the travaux also mentioned, as cited in Sects. 7.3.1.4 and 7.6.1.2 '[...] *until shown to be entitled to another nationality*' (emphasis added). United Nations, Summary Records, 5th Meeting of the Committee of the Whole held on 3 April 1959, A/CONF.9/C.1/SR.5, UN Conference on the Elimination or Reduction of Future Statelessness, Geneva, 1959 and New York, 1961 (3 April 1959) 10 <http://legal.un.org/docs/?path=../diplomaticconferences/1959_statelessness/docs/english/vol_2/a_conf9_c1_sr5.pdf&lang=E> accessed 4 August 2019.

of the State) of nationality.[143] The prohibition of arbitrary deprivation of nationality encompasses 'both loss and deprivation of nationality'.[144]

Further, in this book, the term 'withdrawal', 'loss' and 'deprivation' depending on the context might cover not only acts of cancellation (or nullification) but also revocation of nationality. Cancellation is a decision to invalidate a nationality grant that should not have been granted in the first place. On the other hand, revocation is to revoke nationality grant that had previously been granted correctly (for which the legal requirements were duly fulfilled) at the time of the decision, based on the circumstances that arose subsequent to the original decision. Cancellation can occur in situations where the person's foreign legal parentage and/or birthplace (and foreign nationality), that had already been existent prior to the decision to confirm her or his nationality as a foundling, are later revealed. Depending on the legislation, revocation is also possible, for example in situations where the person's foreign parentage (and foreign nationality) is newly established by acknowledgement of parentage subsequent to having been confirmed a national as a foundling. Nevertheless, these distinctions were in many cases unclear from the text of State legislation analyzed in Sect. 7.6.2.1.

Apart from where States clearly legislate on 'loss' or 'deprivation' of nationality, there are situations where no legal provisions explicitly provide for nationality withdrawal, but where individuals affected experience what amounts to nationality 'withdrawal', as the States concerned treat them, with retroactive effect, as never having acquired their nationality. This includes where it is discovered that the criteria that led to *ex lege* acquisition of nationality were never (or are no longer) satisfied. This is called 'quasi loss'[145] of nationality by de Groot and others who drafted the ILEC Guidelines (2015), and should be properly covered by articles 5–8 of the 1961 Convention as also noted in the Tunis Conclusions (2014),[146] as well as the fundamental principle of prohibition of arbitrary nationality deprivation.

Cancellation including 'quasi loss' can render the grant of nationality null and void from the date of the initial determination and revocation has effect for the future. Nevertheless, the author supports the view that all decisions should desirably have non-retroactive effect especially to ensure legal certainty and to protect

---

[143] UNHCR Guidelines 5 (2020) para 9.

[144] Ibid.

[145] ILEC Guidelines (2015) Part V). Gerard-René de Groot and Patrick Wautelet, 'Reflections on Quasi-Loss of Nationality from Comparative, International and European Perspectives' in Sergio Carrera Nuñez and Gerard-René de Groot (eds), *European Citizenship at the Crossroads: The Role of the European Union on Loss and Acquisition of Nationality* (Wolf Legal Publishers 2015) 117. Also see Gerard-René de Groot, 'Quasi-Loss of Nationality: Some Critical Reflections' in ISI, *The World's Stateless: Deprivation of Nationality* (March 2020) 203–6 <https://files.institutesi.org/WORLDs_STATELESS_2020.pdf> accessed 27 September 2020.

[146] Tunis Conclusions (2014) paras 13–14.

legitimate expectations.[147] Further, clearly and specifically legislating for the withdrawal of nationality acquired through the foundling provision along with the withdrawal criteria, deadline and procedural safeguards, are essential to avoid arbitrary deprivation of nationality.[148]

### 7.6.2  Analysis of Legislation on Post Facto Withdrawal

State practice in relation to post facto withdrawal is largely unknown. However, as mentioned in Sect. 7.4, the analysis of annex 1 shows that out of 139 States that have a foundling provision, at least 37 States[149] relatively explicitly regulate the post facto withdrawal of nationality with regard to the nationality acquired based on the foundling provision along with the criteria for such withdrawal. It should however be noted that the text of national legislation was often unclear, making it difficult to draw the line between non-acquisition and post facto withdrawal—examples being that of Netherlands and Canada.[150]

---

[147] ILEC Guidelines (2015) Part V.a). See also Ryūun Ō, 'Kiji no kokuseki' ['Nationality of Abandoned Children'] (1969) 4 Hōgaku Kenkyū [Hokkaigakuen daigaku hōgakkai] 195.

[148] UN Human Rights Council, Human rights and arbitrary deprivation of nationality: Report of the Secretary-General, A/HRC/25/28 (19 December 2013) para 30 <https://www.refworld.org/docid/52f8d19a4.html> accessed 4 August 2019.

[149] *Additional note on the methodology adopted to identify the 37 States*: Each of the 139 foundling provisions (see Sect. 1.5.2.3 for the definition of a 'foundling provision' in this book) were reviewed to identify the ones that relatively explicitly regulate the post facto withdrawal of the nationality acquired based on the foundling provision along with the criteria for such withdrawal. Further, a quick search was made within the same (nationality-related) law to see whether a separate provision(s) related to the withdrawal of nationality specifically referred to the nationality acquired based on the foundling provision. However, no exhaustive review or analysis was made as to how the provision(s) generally regulating the withdrawal or retention of nationality interacted with the foundling provision within a country's nationality-related law. It is also noted that GLOBALCIT's Global Database on Modes of Loss of Citizenship <http://globalcit.eu/loss-of-citizenship/> also has mode L14 'Establishment of foreign citizenship' covering the withdrawal of nationality acquired based on a foundling provision. However, the criteria adopted by GLOBALCIT to identify certain nationality laws as providing for post facto 'loss' were not clear, and thus a fresh review of legislation was made to identify the 37 States for the purpose of this book.

[150] Article 3(2) of the Netherlands' Nationality Act states: 'A foundling found in the territory of the Netherlands [...] *shall be deemed* to be the child of a Netherlands national *unless it becomes apparent within five years* of the day on which he or she was found that the child possesses a foreign nationality by birth' (emphasis added). Relevantly, article 16(1)(a) of the Dutch Nationality Act provides: 'A minor shall lose his or her Netherlands nationality [...] by judicial establishment of parenthood, recognition, legitimation or adoption by an alien, if he or she thereby acquires the nationality of the alien or already possesses it.' This provision may as well apply to those who acquire Dutch nationality under article 3(2), making the two provisions contradictory if 'five years' contained in article 3(2) was providing for the deadline for nationality loss. Section 4(1) of the Canadian Nationality Act provides 'every person who [...] was found as a deserted child in Canada *shall be deemed to* have been born in Canada, *unless the contrary is proved within seven yea*rs from the date the person was found' (emphasis added). The wordings of these two laws could give an impression that the acquisition of nationality of a foundling is 'provisional' or 'conditional', which

It should, further, be noted that, approximately 50 other States, whose foundling provisions contain a more 'vague' wording such as that the person is considered national 'in the absence of the proof to the contrary' or something to that effect, are not counted among those 37 States, because it was not clear whether such a phrase only regulated the pre facto acquisition of nationality (or also the post facto withdrawal of nationality), and/or it was unknown what constituted 'proof to the contrary'.[151] The rest did not even contain such a vague wording.

Further, it should be noted that the 37 States as well as the States that do not explicitly regulate the withdrawal of nationality acquired through their foundling provisions might also apply separate provisions relating to retention, loss or deprivation of nationality—including upon the change of civil status such as recognition or adoption, or voluntary acquisition of another nationality or discovery of nationality acquisition by fraud.

### 7.6.2.1 Withdrawal Criteria—Foreign Parentage or Birth Abroad, or Possession of Another Nationality

Out of 37 States that relatively explicitly regulate the post facto withdrawal of nationality along with the criteria, 12 States provide for withdrawal of nationality upon the discovery of the person's foreign parentage. Two States provide for the withdrawal of nationality upon discovery of birth abroad. 23 States (62%) provide for automatic or non-automatic or discretionary withdrawal only when it is revealed that the person has a foreign nationality, thereby avoiding the nationality withdrawal resulting in statelessness.

Among the 37, six States provided for withdrawal of nationality only upon the request of the parents (Slovenia, Serbia, Montenegro for foreign parentage, and Albania, Chad for foreign nationality possession) or the person himself/herself (Mali, only within six months of reaching the age of majority). Below, some of the typical examples of each type of legislation are given.

---

only becomes 'definitive' after five or seven years respectively. No official position by the competent authorities of the respective States was located and such interpretation would be problematic not least for the purpose of legal certainty, the principle of paramount importance in nationality law. Further, other sources, such as Mode L14 of GLOBALCIT's Global Database on Modes of Loss of Citizenship <http://globalcit.eu/loss-of-citizenship/> , also classified these provisions as regulating post facto 'loss'. It was thus provisionally assumed that the relevant parts of the Netherlands' and Canada's nationality provisions regulated post facto 'loss', and these two States were included in the 37 States.

[151] For example, while Australia's Citizenship Act 2007 article 14 states 'a person is an Australian citizen [...] unless and *until* the contrary is proved' (emphasis added), so it is rather clear that it regulates post facto loss, the criteria for loss was not clear—thus Australia was not included in one of the 37 States identified as 'relatively explicitly regulating' the withdrawal of nationality for the purpose of comparison.

*Foreign parentage*

12 States provide for withdrawal upon the discovery of foreign parentage. Under article 30 of Romanian nationality law No 21/1991, citizenship acquired by a child found in Romania of unknown parents under article 5 paragraph 3 is lost if (before the age of 18) filiation is established to one or both parents, and the parent(s) are foreign citizens. Romanian citizenship is lost on the date on which filiation is established. The law provides no reference regarding situations where it is found that parents cannot pass on their nationality to the child concerned, and no known precedents exist on the matter. The authorities, however, reportedly seem to take into account potential situations of statelessness when deciding on the withdrawal of Romanian citizenship.[152] Under article 9 of the Slovenian Citizenship Act, the Slovenian citizenship of a child born or found in Slovenia of unknown parentage will cease 'upon request of the parents', when it is discovered prior to the child reaching the age of 18 that the parents are foreign citizens. While it is positive that the cessation of nationality only occurs upon request of the parents, it has been critiqued that the law should clearly prevent cessation resulting in statelessness.[153] The same goes for article 13 of the Serbian nationality law.[154]

*Birth abroad*

Two States, Canada (section (4(1)) and the US (section 301(f)) effectively provide for the withdrawal of nationality upon discovery of birth abroad. The US foundling provision provides 'person of unknown parentage found in the United States while under the age of five years' are nationals 'until shown, prior to his attaining the age of twenty-one years, not to have been born in the United States'.[155]

---

[152] ENS, 'Ending Childhood Statelessness: A Study on Romania, Working Paper 01/15' (2015) 12–13 <http://www.statelessness.eu/sites/www.statelessness.eu/files/Romania.pdf> accessed 10 February 2017. Law on Romanian Citizenship No 21/1991 (as amended by L. nr.112/2010, 17 June 2010) <https://data.globalcit.eu/NationalDB/docs/ROM%20Citizenship%20Law%201991% 20(English_consolidated%20version%2017%20June%202010).pdf> .

[153] ENS, 'Ending Childhood Statelessness: A Study on Slovenia, Working Paper 08/15' (2015) <http://www.statelessness.eu/sites/www.statelessness.eu/files/Slovenia.pdf> accessed 4 August 2019; Citizenship of the Republic of Slovenia Act (Slovenia) (7 December 2006) <https://www.ref world.org/docid/50bdfabf2.html> accessed 3 August 2019. Also, the general condition for loss of citizenship stated in article 18 of the Citizenship Act, requiring proof that the person has or will be granted another nationality, should apply also in such cases.

[154] Law on Citizenship of the Republic of Serbia (Serbia) (2014) <https://www.refworld.org/docid/ 4b56d0542.html> accessed 4 August 2019.

[155] Immigration and Nationality Act of 1952 (USA) <https://www.uscis.gov/ilink/docView/SLB/ HTML/SLB/act.html> accessed 4 August 2019.

### Possession of foreign nationality

Belgium[156] is among the 23 States that explicitly provide for loss of nationality only when possession of nationality is discovered post facto.

Under article 8(1) of the Law on Albanian Nationality, if the child's parents become known before the child reaches the age of 14, and they are of foreign nationality, Albanian nationality can be relinquished at the request of the legal parents, provided that the child does not become stateless as a consequence of this action. Thus, loss of nationality would not occur unless one's legal parents request so.[157]

### Loss in States not explicitly providing for post facto withdrawal

Moreover, while many States do not specifically regulate post facto withdrawal of nationality acquired on the basis of the foundling provision, in some States such withdrawal is indeed envisaged implicitly and/or actually practised, sometimes without even being termed as 'withdrawal' or 'loss'. As mentioned in Sect. 7.6.1.2, this kind of loss of nationality, which is not specified by law, is called 'quasi-loss', which should be regulated properly in light of the fundamental principle of prohibition against arbitrary deprivation of nationality.[158]

For example, in Japan, there have been several such reported cases. In one family court adjudication, a child of an American citizen-mother got lost in Japan and acquired nationality under the foundling provision, that is article 2(iii). However, she or he subsequently had her Japanese nationality effectively 'withdrawn' (by having her or his family registry deleted) as her or his parent(s) were later identified.[159] As an administrative precedent, there was also a case where the Civil Affairs Bureau, the competent authority on nationality matters in Japan, made clear its position on withdrawal. In this case, mentioned in Sects. 4.3.12 and 4.4, a child born out of wedlock in 1948 in Japan of a mother of French nationality, had acquired Japanese nationality as a foundling having been registered on a Japanese family register (*koseki*) upon the approval of a family court. The mother submitted a notification of recognition of maternity in 1967. The Civil Affairs Bureau upon inquiry from the relevant administrative office stated that the family register may be deleted as it had been created

---

[156] Article 10(4) of Belgian Nationality Code states: 'A child to whom Belgian nationality has been granted under this article shall retain such nationality as long as it is not established before he attains the age of eighteen years or has been emancipated before that age, that he possesses a foreign nationality'.

[157] ENS, 'Ending Childhood Statelessness: A Study on Albania, Working Paper 06/15' (June 2015) 7 <https://www.statelessness.eu/sites/www.statelessness.eu/files/Albania.pdf> accessed 4 August 2019. Serbia (article 9) and Slovenia (article 13) have similar provisions requiring parents' request but do not make possession of another nationality a condition before such loss.

[158] See in general Gerard-René de Groot and Patrick Wautelet, 'Reflections on Quasi-Loss of Nationality from Comparative, International and European Perspectives' in Nuñez and de Groot (eds), *European Citizenship at the Crossroads: The Role of the European Union on Loss and Acquisition of Nationality* (Wolf Legal Publishers 2015).

[159] Adjudication of Kōbe Family Court, Himeji Branch, 20 June 1962 (*Shōwa 37 nen*) 166, Kagetsu Vol 14. No 11.

for a non-Japanese national.[160] This meant that the person concerned was to effectively lose Japanese nationality—at around age 19—retroactively from birth. This is despite the fact that no explicit provision exists in the Japanese Nationality Act providing for such withdrawal of nationality. Scholarly theory in Japan has generally been that even if the existence of the non-Japanese legal parent(s) of the person concerned is discovered, if the child concerned does not acquire any nationality from such parent(s), then the child does not have to lose her or his Japanese nationality.[161] The general academic theory is that such child who acquires foreign nationality from the discovered legal parent(s) may have Japanese nationality withdrawn. However, nationality law scholars such as Ryūun Ō and Yasuhiro Okuda have asserted that there should be some sort of a deadline beyond which nationality acquired by virtue of the foundling provision cannot be withdrawn (as detailed in Sect. 7.6.2.2).[162]

### 7.6.2.2   National Legislation and the Appropriate Limitation Period for Nationality Withdrawal

Now going back to elaborate on the issue of the limitation period briefly discussed in Sect. 7.6.1.6: until when could the nationality acquired based on the foundling provision be withdrawn, given that loss of nationality would otherwise not result in statelessness or arbitrary deprivation of nationality, with the proportionality test including best interests assessment having been cleared? The 1961 Convention is silent on this matter.

As seen at the beginning of Sect. 7.6.1.6, by analogy, reference can be made to article 7(1)(f) of the ECN and paragraph 43 of the Council of Europe Recommendation CM/Rec(2009)13's Explanatory Memorandum. Based on these documents, where a child has acquired a nationality as a foundling under article 6(1)(b) of the ECN and later, upon discovery of her or his parent(s), found to have the nationality of such parent(s), loss of his or her nationality is only allowed during her or his minority (as long as it does not result in statelessness).

*National legislation on the limitation period*

Annex 1 shows that among the 37 States whose legislation was identified to relatively explicitly regulate the post facto loss of nationality, 32 States have a limitation period.

---

[160] Minji kō dai 2888 gō minjikyokuchō kaitō, 1 October 1967 (*Shōwa 42 nen*) Koseki Vol 247, 58 cited in Shōichi Kidana, *Chikujō kokusekihō—kadai no kaimei to jōbun no kaisetsu-* [*Nationality Law—Clarification Of issues and Article-by-Article Commentary*] (Nihon kajo shuppan, forthcoming 2021) 324.

[161] Shōichi Kidana, *Chikujō kokusekihō—kadai no kaimei to jōbun no kaisetsu-* [*Nationality Law—Clarification Of issues and Article-by-Article Commentary*] (Nihon kajo shuppan, forthcoming 2021) 326–329. Hidefumi Egawa, Yoshirō Hayata and Ryōichi Yamada, *Kokusekihō* [*Nationality Law*] (Yūhikaku 1997) 82.

[162] Ryūun Ō, 'Kiji no kokuseki' ['Nationality of abandoned children'] (1969) 4 Hōgaku Kenkyū [Hokkaigakuen daigaku hōgakkai] 195. Yasuhiro Okuda, *Kosekihō to kokusai oyakohō* [*Nationality Act and International Family Law*] (Yūhikaku 2004) 136.

1 State (Mali) provides that loss would not happen even after the age of majority as discussed below at Sect. 7.6.2.3.

Among the 32 States, 24 States provide that no loss occurs after the person reaches 18 or the age of majority (while the age of majority can slightly differ). One State (US) sets it at prior to reaching 21 years of age. Two States set the deadline at 14 (Albania and Croatia) and two at 15 (North Macedonia and Vietnam). Canada sets it at seven years after being found.[163] The Netherlands[164] provides 'five years of the day on which she or he was found' and Finland provides 'the age of five'.[165]

Three among the 37 States (Malta, Turkmenistan and Zimbabwe) do not provide any time-limit for withdrawal, while, for these three States, the loss might not be automatic.

With regard to one State, namely Poland, while its legislation does not explicitly regulate the loss of nationality acquired based on the foundling provision, according to article 6(1) of the 2009 Act on Polish Citizenship, a change in the determination of a parent of a child or with regard to the citizenship of one or both parents will be considered in determining the citizenship of a child only if it occurs within one year from the birth of the child. An ENS report asserts that, based on this provision, if the parents of a foundling are identified at a later stage, it does not lead to loss of nationality.[166] A question nevertheless arises as to what happens when a child of unknown parents is found in the territory after the age of one. However, this question is answered by referring to the Ministry of Interior's position that under their interpretation a child of unknown parents under article 15 of its Law of 2 April 2009 on Polish Citizenship, 'foundlings' are abandoned children or children left in a baby hatch, who are 'usually newborns'.[167]

Some States provide for the stability of foundlings' nationality regardless of timing, as discussed in Sect. 7.6.2.2.

---

[163] Section 4(1) of Canadian Citizenship Act, RSC, 1985, c. C-29 states: '(Deserted child) For the purposes of paragraph 3(1)(a) [which states a person is a citizen if born in Canada after Feb 14 1977], every person who, before apparently attaining the age of seven years, was found as a deserted child in Canada shall be deemed to have been born in Canada, unless the contrary is proved *within seven years from the date the person was found.*' Canadian Citizenship Act (RSC, 1985, c. C-29) (1985) <http://laws-lois.justice.gc.ca/eng/acts/C-29/page-1.html#h-3A> accessed 4 August 2019.

[164] With regard to the Netherlands, as explained in fn 150 of this chapter, it is unclear whether article 3(2) provides for the limitation period for the loss of nationality, or the duration during which the person's acquisition of nationality must be confirmed, but it was provisionally assumed the former was the case.

[165] Finnish Nationality Act: section 12 (Foundlings and children of parents with unknown citizenship): 'A foundling who is found in Finland is considered to be a Finnish citizen as long as he or she has not been established as a citizen of a foreign State. If the child has been established as a citizen of a foreign State only after he or she has reached the age of five, the child retains Finnish citizenship, however.' Republic of Finland, 'Nationality Act (359/2003)' (1 June 2003) <https://www.refworld.org/docid/3ae6b51614.html> accessed 4 August 2019.

[166] ENS, 'Ending Childhood Statelessness: A Study on Poland, Working Paper 03/15' (June 2015) 9–10 <https://www.statelessness.eu/sites/www.statelessness.eu/files/Poland.pdf> accessed 4 August 2019.

[167] See the Ministry of Interior's comments cited within ibid 9–10.

### *Consideration of the appropriate limitation period*

Now it is time to consider what would be the reasonable timeframe during which nationality acquired based on a foundling provision may be withdrawn based on the possession of foreign nationality as a result of the discovery or establishment of parentage and/or birthplace. Principle 18 of the Recommendation CM/Rec(2009)13 of the Council of Europe provides: '[C]hildren who were treated in good faith as their nationals for a specific period of time should not be declared as not having acquired their nationality.'[168]

Principle 18, however, does not prescribe a maximum period after which the non-fulfilment of the preconditions for the acquisition should not have consequences. Nevertheless, the CM/Rec(2009)13's Explanatory Memorandum at paragraph 47 refers to the fact that 'serious doubts have arisen' in several States regarding the age limit of 18 years (as in article 7(1)(f) of the ECN), concluding that it is 'obvious that this period should be considerably shorter than 18 years'. The Memorandum also notes it is doubtful whether the loss of nationality can still be justified when the child involved has been in possession of a nationality for a considerable number of years. Indeed, being kept in a situation where the nationality can be withdrawn for the 18 years or so (in case the person is found when a baby) does not seem to meet the proportionality test including the best interests of the child, and the principle of legal certainty.[169]

Paragraph 47 of the Explanatory Memorandum emphasizes that:

[T]his is in particular the case if the child was treated as a national for a period exceeding the period of residence required for naturalisation, which according to article 6, paragraph 3 of the ECN should not exceed *ten years*. Furthermore, the desirable preferential treatment of children could even justify a *much shorter limit*. (emphasis added)[170]

In the context of 'quasi-loss', ILEC Guidelines (2015) at Part V.b) also supports this position, referencing the residence requirement for naturalization. The ILEC Guidelines (2015) also note:

When a case of quasi-loss is discovered, States should preferably attempt to guarantee the continuation of the nationality [...] It may be that under the relevant national law, such continuation is achieved through the legal instrument of apparent status of national [*possession d'état de nationalité*], [...] It is advisable to combine such legal instruments with limitation provisions.[171]

---

[168] Council of Europe: Committee of Ministers, *Recommendation CM/Rec(2009)13 and explanatory memorandum of the Committee of Ministers to member states on the nationality of children* (Council of Europe Publishing 9 May 2009).

[169] See also Gerard-René de Groot and Patrick Wautelet, Chap. 4, 'Reflections on Quasi-Loss of Nationality from Comparative, International and European Perspectives', in Sergio Carrera Nuñez and Gerard-René de Groot (eds), *European Citizenship at the Crossroads: The Role of the European Union on Loss and Acquisition of Nationality* (Wolf Legal Publishers 2015) 151–2.

[170] Council of Europe: Committee of Ministers, *Recommendation CM/Rec(2009)13 and explanatory memorandum of the Committee of Ministers to member states on the nationality of children* (Council of Europe Publishing 9 May 2009).

[171] ILEC Guidelines (2015) Part V.b).

The duration needed for recognition of nationality based on the principle of *possession d'état de national* in some States is ten years.[172] The fact that the duration for acquisitive prescription to acquire property in some States is also ten years offers additional inspiration. These might be some of the reasons why Japanese authoritative nationality law scholar Yasuhiro Okuda, as mentioned in Sect. 7.6.1, also suggests a ten-year limitation period in his analysis of the Japanese foundling provision, that is article 2(iii) of the Nationality Act, which currently does not regulate the withdrawal. Okuda comments that it may not be justifiable to leave a person—who has been treated since birth as a national—in an unstable nationality status until the age of majority as currently stipulated in some of the European nationality laws.[173]

Nevertheless, though in the context of 'adoption', Principle 15 of CM/Rec(2009)13 indeed recommends States to provide that 'revocation or annulment of an adoption will not cause the permanent loss of the nationality acquired by the adoption, if the child is lawfully and habitually resident on their territory for a period of more than *five years*'.[174] This could, by analogy, be inspiring to consider the deadline for the withdrawal of nationality acquired based on a foundling provision.

After all, then, how much shorter (than the age of minority as provided by article 7(1)(f) of the ECN) could the limitation period be? Is it 'ten years' as hinted in paragraph 47 of the CM/Rec(2009)13's Explanatory Memorandum or ILEC Guidelines (2015)? Or could it be even shorter, such as five years, as also hinted at in the same Memorandum and, provided for in section 12 of the Finnish Nationality Act? Certainly, the Finnish Nationality Act stands out as the 'best practice' providing the shortest limitation period for withdrawal. It is, however, pertinent to recall here the conclusion of Chap. 6—that all persons of unknown parents found in the territory under the age of majority should ideally be considered foundlings under article 2 of the 1961 Convention. Securing a reasonable or sufficient duration during which States could rectify their erroneous decisions would likely provide justification for States to adopt such 'generous' age limit, as well as more inclusive interpretation of the term 'foundling' or 'unknown parents' advocated for in Chaps. 3, 4 and 5. It can thus be concluded that, after a maximum of ten years, in the best interests of the child as well as legal certainty, nationality should be retained even if it is found that she or he holds another nationality. It should be noted that 'ten years' should be from the date when the State took its action of confirming the person's possession of nationality, and not from the date she or he was born or found in the territory. That way, even erroneous nationality confirmation can be cancelled, for example for adults who invoke this provision claiming to have been found before reaching the age of majority as envisaged in Chap. 6. From the best practice or child rights point

---

[172] For example, article 21–13 of the French Civil Code and article 18 of the Spanish Civil Code.

[173] Yasuhiro Okuda, 'Kokusekihō nijō sangō ni tsuite (Jō)' ['On article 2[iii] of Nationality Act-Part 1'] (1994) 49 Kosekijihō 432.

[174] Council of Europe: Committee of Ministers, *Recommendation CM/Rec(2009)13 and explanatory memorandum of the Committee of Ministers to member states on the nationality of children* (Council of Europe Publishing 9 May 2009).

of view, however, States are certainly encouraged to make their provisions even more favourable by adopting shorter durations such as 'five years'.

### 7.6.2.3 Legislation Restricting Withdrawal Regardless of Timing Even If It Results in Multiple Nationality

At least two States by law or in practice stabilize nationality acquired based on the foundling provision by providing that the nationality cannot be lost even if the person's possession of another nationality is revealed before the age of majority.

*Mali: Non-withdrawal even in case of possession of another nationality*

Mali, which is counted among the 37 States that regulate nationality loss, stands out with a unique provision. Article 225 of Malian Family Code states:

> A child born in Mali of unknown parents is Malian. He retains Malian nationality even if, during his minority, his affiliation is established with respect to a foreigner and if he has, in accordance with the national law of that foreigner, the nationality of that foreigner.

Mali provides for non-loss even if the person is revealed to have a foreign nationality. Nevertheless, the Malian provision goes on to say that she or he 'has the right to repudiate the Malian nationality by the forms of right within the six months following his majority'.[175] It appears that during the limitation period, that is within the six months following the coming of age, it is possible that the person becomes stateless by repudiating Malian nationality, which, however, is not necessarily clear.

*Spain: Non-withdrawal even in case of possession of another nationality*

The Spanish Civil Code, along with the competent authority's interpretation, also provides one of the most 'stable' nationality statuses to persons of unknown parents, in that they will not lose nationality even if under the age of majority their filiation as well as possession of another nationality is revealed.

DGRN, the Spanish competent authority, has confirmed that eventual determination of the filiation of the minor who acquires nationality based on article 17.1.d) must not lead to the loss of Spanish nationality, which is 'definitive and not provisional because it is a nationality by origin'.[176] Loss of Spanish nationality will occur under article 24 of the Civil Code once 'emancipated' (including by reaching 18),[177] and when one is habitually residing abroad and voluntarily acquire a different nationality

---

[175] L'assemblee Nationale, 'Portant Code des Personnes et de la Famille' ['Mali, Persons and Family Code'] (2011) <http://citizenshiprightsafrica.org/wp-content/uploads/2016/02/Mali-Code-des-personnes-et-de-la-famille-30-Dec-2011.pdf> . [author translation].

[176] Res. DGRN de 10 de junio de 2005 (BOE, 1-VIII-2005, pp 27,158–27,159 (Anexo III.3.25)).

[177] Spanish Civil Code article 314 states: 'Emancipation takes place: 1.By coming of age. 2.By marriage of the minor. 3. By concession granted by persons exercising parental authority. 4. By concession granted by the court.' Article 315 states: 'Legal age begins upon turning eighteen'.

among others.[178] It should also be noted that under article 18 of the Civil Code, the continuous possession and use of Spanish nationality for ten years, in good faith, registered before the Civil Registry, is the cause for the consolidation of the nationality even if such qualification is invalid.

The States' legislation and practice discussed in this section can serve as inspiration for other States.

## 7.7  Burden and Standard of Proof in Proving the 'contrary' and the Grounds for Withdrawal[179]

As stated in Sect. 5.5.1, it is the general rule that the party making a certain allegation bears the responsibility of substantiating such an allegation.[180]

In terms of the pre facto assessment, the formulation of article 2 of the 1961 Convention ('in the absence of proof to the contrary') provides for a legal presumption. In many jurisdictions, when certain facts are legally presumed, the opposite facts need to be firmly proven to overturn such presumed facts. It is then logical to consider that the burden of proving 'the contrary' to deny the application of article 2 would lie with the party disputing such application, which is normally the government of the State where the foundling is found. In light of the severe consequence of being denied nationality despite her or his unknown parentage, 'the contrary'—be it 'birth outside the territory' or 'possession of another nationality'—needs to be firmly established to disqualify a person from acquiring a nationality pre facto. Mere speculation is not enough. Commentary by Reinhard Marx on the German foundling provision also mentioned in Sect. 7.5 states that the 'contrary' has to be positively proven, and unlikeliness or doubts are not sufficient.[181]

Further, at the post facto stage, the general principles of legal certainty, protection of legitimate expectations or 'acquired rights', the existence of the grounds for

---

[178] Paloma Abarca Junco, La Reforma Del Derecho De La Nacionalidad De 1990, Boletín De La Facultad De Derecho, núm. i (1992) 73–74 <http://e-spacio.uned.es/fez/eserv/bibliuned:BFD-1992-1-E9B3BB01/PDF> accessed 4 August 2019. This commentary is also contained in the 'Juspedia' created by the Universidad Nacional de Educación a Distancia (UNED). UNED, 'Derecho de la nacionalidad (I)' <http://derecho.isipedia.com/cuarto/derecho-internacional-privado/parte-2-nacionalidad-y-extranjeria/08-derecho-de-la-nacionalidad-i> accessed 4 August 2019. The author thanks Miriam González Morla for referring her to the source.

[179] A related issue, that is how much time the State could take to investigate on the applicability of the foundling provision pre facto to confirm one's acquisition of nationality, including by examining the existence of the proof to the contrary, is already addressed in Sect. 5.8.

[180] See an analogous assertation in UNHCR leading to the conclusion that the State asserting cancellation of refugee status bears the burden of proof. UNHCR, 'Note on the Cancellation of Refugee Status' (22 November 2004) para 34 <https://www.refworld.org/docid/41a5dfd94.html> accessed 4 August 2019.

[181] Reinhard Marx, '§ 4 StAG' in Fritz/Vormeier (ed), Gemeinschaftskommentar zum Staatsangehörigkeitsgesetz [Commentary on Nationality Law] (Looseleaf edn, Walters Kluwer/Luchterhand July 2019) 53–54.3 para 196 ff.

nationality withdrawal needs to be firmly proven for the State to justify the withdrawal. Gerard-René de Groot's guidance regarding when the deprivation or loss of nationality can be justified under the 1961 Convention also supports the above proposition. De Groot asserts that the State bears the burden of persuasion, who then must prove, with 'firm and clear evidence', that the person involved possesses another nationality in addition to the current nationality at stake.[182] The ISI also asserts: 'With regard to the principle of the avoidance of statelessness, the burden of proof in determining that the person concerned holds another nationality must lie with the competent authorities of the depriving state.'[183]

Now, when the State asserts a 'contrary' fact or a ground to withdraw one's nationality, the person of unknown parentage concerned would need to 'rebut' such assertion, by producing whatever available evidence that can help deny such a fact. For example, if birth abroad is asserted by the government, the person concerned, in denying such a fact, can produce evidence pointing to her or his birth within the territory where found. In the absence of the birth certificate within the territory (which is usually the case), the evidence to support birth within the territory can include, for example, proof of stay in the country since early age, the proof to have been seen at medical facilities and school enrolment records. Credible statements by third persons or the person concerned herself or himself substantiating the assertation that she or he must have been born within the territory can also be crucial in the absence of such material evidence. In this context, reference to some of the precedents introduced in Chaps. 4, 5 and 6 might prove useful, in terms of different types of 'indirect evidence' relied upon, in the absence of direct evidence establishing birth in the territory, and how it was (positively) assessed by States. Such indirect evidence can be that supporting the assertion that the person was 'born' in the territory,[184] or even that substantiating that the person was 'found' at an early age in the territory, which could be used to argue for the presumption of birth[185] within the territory.

---

[182] Gerard-René de Groot and Patrick Wautelet, 'Survey on Rules Loss of Nationality in International Treaties and Case Law' in Nuñez and de Groot (eds), *European Citizenship at the Crossroads: The Role of the European Union on Loss and Acquisition of Nationality* (Wolf Legal Publishers 2015) 37. Note that de Groot had prepared the Background Paper for UNHCR based on which the Tunis Conclusions (2014) was drafted.

[183] Principle 7.6.4, ISI, 'Principles on Deprivation of Nationality as a National Security Measure' (2020) <https://files.institutesi.org/PRINCIPLES.pdf> accessed 15 September 2020. While these principles are specifically for the context of national security measures, this particular principle should apply to all withdrawal. See also UNHCR Guidelines 5 (2020) para 45, which states: 'Deprivation of nationality procedures that place the onus on the individual concerned to raise potential statelessness in order for it to be considered leave contracting States and individuals vulnerable to decisions that are inconsistent with Article 8. Likewise, procedures that place the burden of proof solely on the individual to prove statelessness would not be consistent with the contracting State's obligation to determine whether statelessness would result from the act of deprivation'.

[184] For example, the Japanese family court adjudication, that is Kagetsu Vol 28, No 1, p 84 [31 January 1975 (*Shōwa 50 nen*)] (Ōita Family Court Bungotakada Branch) also cited in Sects. 4.3.8 and 6.4.

[185] For example, Spanish administrative decision Res. DGRN de 9 de agosto de 1993 (188) (BIMJ, núm. 1685, 1993, pp 4645–8; RAJ, 1993, núm. 6899), cited in Sects. 4.3.9 and 6.4, and the

The person concerned's duty to 'rebut' means that as long as the person can create in the mind of the decision-maker that it is unknown ('*non liquet*') whether she or he was born abroad (or possesses another nationality), the State cannot deny or withdraw the person's nationality under the foundling provision. This is because article 2 of the 1961 Convention is formulated in a way so that a legal presumption (of birth in the territory from citizen parents) arises when the prerequisite facts (being a foundling found in the territory) are established. The person responding to the assertion to overturn such a legal presumption does not have to fully or firmly prove the opposite fact (that is, the fact that she or he was born in the territory where found, or that she or he is otherwise stateless).

Nevertheless, theoretically and hypothetically, suppose a person of unknown parentage was found in a territory only at the age of 17 (see Chap. 6's conclusion that a foundling can be anybody under the age of the majority), and the State where found considers 'birth abroad' to be proof to 'the contrary', pre facto disqualifying her or him from nationality. While it might depend on the circumstances, if she or he is 'found' upon arrival at an international airport from abroad, it might be highly likely or even certain that she or he was born abroad and there might not be any issue of burden or standard of proof arising. Even if the issue of burden and standard of proof ever arises, it would probably be difficult for the person to rebut the State's assertion of birth abroad in such a case.

## 7.8 Summary and Conclusions: Possession of Another Nationality to Constitute 'the contrary' and the Withdrawal Ground

This chapter mainly examined the definition of the term 'in the absence of proof to the contrary' under article 2 of the 1961 Convention pre facto at the time of confirming the acquisition of nationality, as well as the conditions for the post facto withdrawal of the nationality already acquired under article 2. The examination was done drawing from the travaux, UNHCR Guidelines 4 (2012) and 5 (2020) on the interpretation of the 1961 Convention, the ECN and the relevant standards, scholarly discussions as well as the (implementation of) equivalent domestic provisions.

### 7.8.1 Pre Facto Assessment to Confirm Acquisition of Nationality

It was first recalled that, as already discussed in Chap. 3, States have historically provided for acquisition of nationality by foundlings or persons of unknown

administrative precedent by USCIS, that is the 2006 Newark Case, cited in Sects. 4.3.5, 5.6.1 and 6.4–6.7.

parentage found in the territory for two predominant reasons: first, because foundlings were presumed highly likely to be children of nationals born in the territory; and, second, because foundlings—regardless of whether their parents are likely nationals—otherwise lacked those responsible for protection and care and were particularly vulnerable and in need of protection.

The structure of article 2 was then examined: The current formulation is such that a person who fulfils two prerequisite facts, that is of being:

(1)　a 'foundling' (who is defined to be of 'child of unknown parents' in Chap. 3 and further discussed in Chaps. 4, 5 and 6);
(2)　'found' in the territory (defined in Chap. 6).

benefits from the two presumed facts, that she or he is:

(i)　'born within that territory';
(ii)　of parents who are both nationals.

in the absence of proof to the contrary (which is not defined within article 2).

The current article 2 was formulated after negotiations during the travaux so that a foundling can acquire nationality where found regardless of whether the State where she or he is found generally adopts the *jus sanguinis* or *jus soli* principle.

### Temporal scope of 'in the absence of proof to the contrary'

In terms of the temporal scope of the term 'in the absence of proof to the contrary', it was found that the term was primarily related to pre facto assessment carried out for the State to confirm the foundling's acquisition of nationality. The conditions for post facto withdrawal of nationality already acquired based on article 2 should be explicitly and separately stipulated. However, it was noted that the facts that disqualify a person from nationality acquisition are often included in the grounds for nationality withdrawal.

### How States formulate their provisions to grant nationality to foundlings

It was also confirmed—in summary—that the majority of States today grant nationality to persons of unknown parents found in the territory through different legal methods: a very small number of States by (almost) reproducing the wording of article 2 of the 1961 Convention (Method I); some by presuming the foundling's birth in the territory and extending their *jus soli* provision (unconditional (Method II), conditional (Method III) or 'exceptional' (Method IV)) provision; some by presuming the foundling's descent from national(s), thus extending their *jus sanguinis* provision (Method V); some by 'presuming' that a foundling 'is a national' (without reference to contrary proof) (Method VI); some by simply granting a foundling their nationality—either 'in the absence of proof to the contrary (without defining the 'contrary') or in the absence of possession of another nationality (Method VII); and some by granting nationality without mention to any conditions (Method VIII) (see Sect. 7.4 for more precise formulations of Methods I–VIII, and see Sect. 7.5 for their implementation).

### *'Contrary' to the 'presumed facts', and not 'prerequisite' facts*

In terms of what can constitute the 'proof to the contrary' under article 2 of the 1961 Convention pre facto, it was first confirmed that the 'contrary' qualifies the presumed facts, and not prerequisite facts. An alternative reading that it qualifies (also) the prerequisite facts would make the provision redundant.

Having a 'known parent' (who is a national of the country where the person concerned was found) and 'not having been found in the territory (under the applicable age limitation)' per se thus do not constitute the 'contrary' (that is, to the 'presumed facts'), unless, for the former, such a known parent is not a national of the country where the child concerned was found (which will qualify as the 'contrary' to one of the presumed facts). Having a 'known parent' or 'not having been found (before the applicable age limitation)' rather deny the 'prerequisite facts', which would, as a result, make this legal presumption inapplicable anyway.

### *What constitutes 'the contrary' pre facto*

If literally reading article 2 of the 1961 Convention, the contrary facts to the presumed facts can thus be one of the two, that is (1) that the person is born outside the territory, or (2) that the person's father and/or mother is a non-national.

### *Drafters' view supporting nationality grant to foundlings born abroad*

So what happens when it is known pre facto that the child of unknown parents found in the territory has been born abroad? Based on the ordinary rules of law, even if a fact 'to the contrary' to one of the presumed facts is established, it would not necessarily mean that the other presumed fact is also denied. Specifically, with regard to the first contrary fact, that is birth outside the territory, literally there is a room for interpretation that it would not invalidate the other presumption, that is that the person's parents are nationals.

While such a scenario and interpretation might appear theoretical, it was, rather unexpectedly, already envisaged, and was indeed specifically advocated for during the travaux by Denmark, Italy, and the Netherlands. Under this interpretation, a foundling found in the territory whose birth outside the territory has already been established pre facto will nevertheless acquire nationality where found as long as she or he would remain stateless. Such an interpretation is quite possible if the person is found in a State that adopts the *jus sanguinis* principle, which allows children of nationals born abroad to automatically acquire nationality based on descent.

However, during the travaux, a minority of States opposed this interpretation and, as a compromise, article 2 was formulated as it currently stands. What constitutes the 'contrary' pre facto thus was essentially left to depend on the exact wording of the relevant domestic provision based on which the State makes a foundling a national.

As pointed out in Sect. 7.3.1.3, the drafters' inclusive interpretation of the foundling provision would be especially beneficial in the era of migration, displacement and human trafficking. In fact, in light of the majority view during the travaux, the text of article 2 of the 1961 Convention and its object and purpose, that is to prevent statelessness, it is possible for one to argue that the evidence of possession of another nationality should be the only fact constituting 'the contrary' disqualifying the person from nationality where found, pre facto.

Reviewing the existing nationality legislation in force today, such 'inclusive' or 'generous' interpretation is fairly justifiable especially if the State concerned takes Methods V–VIII, which do not have any reference to presumption of 'birth in the territory', but instead presume descent from a national or nationality itself, or directly provide for nationality acquisition (in the absence of possession of another nationality).

The very idea of nationality grant to children of unknown parents born abroad would likely be considered by States that adopt Methods II and III (and possibly Method IV) to go against their nationality law provisions, as those States make presumption of birth in the territory as the premise to grant nationality to foundlings. Under such nationality laws, birth abroad highly likely constitutes 'contrary fact'— while there have been some judicial and administrative precedents that send slight messages this might not necessarily be the case, as discussed in Sect. 7.5. Especially for States that never grant nationality—at least automatically—to children of nationals born abroad, the idea might just appear impossible. Based on the text of article 2, as well as the views (while minority) expressed during the travaux, such interpretation does not go against the States' obligation under the 1961 Convention either.

Further, there were no reports of current practice where any State, whether *jus sanguinis* or *jus soli* States, granted nationality to a foundling found in the territory whose birth abroad is clearly known.

Moreover, for some, while the granting of nationality to otherwise stateless children of unknown parentage born abroad found in the territory when quite young might sound justifiable in light of the object and purpose of the 1961 Convention, applying the foundling provision for their older child counterparts might be considered far-fetched or difficult by some States. In light of the practical realities where a number of States are expected to hesitate to provide nationality to persons of unknown parents born in another State, one might consider it realistic to argue that, for 'typical' cases of foundlings, that is persons of unknown parentage found as small children, the contrary fact should be defined narrowly to only mean possession of foreign nationality, while for atypical cases found as older minors, what constitutes the contrary can be more broadly defined to include birth abroad. The end-result according to such assertion would be that foreign-born persons of unknown parents found as small children in the territory who would otherwise be stateless would acquire nationality where found, while older children who have arrived or are found would remain stateless. However, again, this approach might be considered arbitrary especially in light of article 7 of the CRC covering all minors, as where to draw the line between 'small' and 'older' children lacks clear basis under international law as argued in Sect. 6.7.

In any case, even if some States might not confirm the nationality of (older) foreign-born foundlings, given that they lack legal parents and are otherwise stateless, the States where they are found would still be required to duly protect them as unaccompanied stateless minors with naturalization prospects.

## 7.8.2 Post Facto Assessment—Conditions for Nationality Withdrawal

*Prohibition of arbitrary deprivation of nationality under international law*

As detailed in Sect. 7.6, with regard to post facto withdrawal of nationality, it was stressed first that it must not constitute arbitrary deprivation of nationality prohibited under international human rights law. For this purpose, the withdrawal of nationality must have a clear basis in law, be the least intrusive means of achieving a legitimate purpose, and follow a due process.

*Avoidance of statelessness*

Based on article 5(1) of the 1961 Convention, UNHCR Guidelines 4 (2012), 5 (2020), the withdrawal of nationality due to discovery or establishment of foreign parentage or birth abroad should be conditional upon the resultant possession of another nationality. In terms of the State legislation and practice, it was noted based on annex 1 that out of at least 37 States that were identified to relatively explicitly regulate the post facto loss of nationality acquired based on the foundling provision along with the criteria for such loss, 23 States, that is 62%, provided that nationality can only be lost if the person concerned is found to have a foreign nationality, with additional safeguards depending on the States.

*Assessment of proportionality and due process*

Further, it was stressed that even when the withdrawal of nationality does not lead to statelessness, it is certainly subject to limitations so as not to amount to arbitrary nationality withdrawal. Such withdrawal should at least be conditional upon conducting an individual assessment of proportionality and due process including right to personal interview, appeal and legal counsel. Moreover, when the withdrawal is being considered for a child, it is essential to examine whether such withdrawal goes against the child's best interests as part of such proportionality assessment.

*Limitation period*

As discussed in Sect. 7.6.2, it was found that to ensure proportionality and legal certainty, the time-limit should be set beyond which revocation cannot occur due to discovery or establishment of foreign parentage, birth abroad, or foreign nationality possession. It was found that out of 37 States that relatively explicitly regulate the withdrawal along with its criteria, 32 States have a limitation period for such a loss.

While article 7(1)(f) of the ECN and at least the foundling provisions of 24 States set the deadline for withdrawal at the age of majority (or 18 years of age) and one at 21 years of age, seven States provide (much) shorter period, the shortest being five years of age (Finland). Two States among 37 go further and do not provide for withdrawal even in case of discovery of possession of another nationality before the age of majority. Considering the Council of Europe Recommendation CM/Rec(2009)13 and other standards, it was concluded that nationality withdrawal should not occur after the maximum of ten years. Ten years should be from the date when the State took its action of confirming the person's possession of nationality, and not from the date she or he was born or found in the territory. This is especially because the model foundling provision and guidance is inclusive in terms of the age when found being open to all minors, and a foundling can be found by any third person other than parents, as well as that she or he might only come to the attention of the authorities after reaching adulthood. From the child rights point of view, States are free or even encouraged to make their provisions even more favourable by adopting shorter durations, such as five years. Relatedly, it is desirable that nationality loss is not given retroactive effect.

# Chapter 8
# Recommendations—Model Foundling Provision

**Abstract** Chapter 8 makes recommendations, drawing from the key findings of the previous chapters, as to how domestic provisions and future regional instruments equivalent to article 2 of the 1961 Convention should be formulated, by offering a 'model foundling provision' and its interpretive guidance. The model provision and guidance should help ensure a full and inclusive application of article 2 and equivalent provisions in accordance with their object and purpose, as well as the best interests of the child under CRC. The model provision will prove particularly useful for States under the effects of armed conflicts, or where documentation of civil and nationality status is not yet systematic, or where migration, displacement and human trafficking are widespread.

## 8.1 Short Review of Chaps. 1–7

This book meant to address the fundamental research question set out in Chap. 1, which is how article 2 of the 1961 Convention providing for nationality acquisition of a 'foundling found' in the territory should be interpreted and implemented in light of its object and purpose to prevent statelessness, taking the CRC into consideration. The above fundamental research question was broken down into the following main questions:

(1) What should be the definition of a 'foundling' 'found in the territory' and how should the definition be further interpreted?
(2) What constitutes the 'proof to the contrary' pre facto in assessing whether to confirm acquisition of nationality, and what are the conditions for post facto withdrawal of nationality?
(3) What should the procedure for confirming or granting nationality to foundlings (or in withdrawing such nationality) be like, especially the applicable burden and standard of proof?

These questions were further broken down into sub-questions and were examined in depth in each of the following chapters, whose findings were summarized in the 'Summary and conclusions' section of each chapter.

The examination of these questions was done in accordance with the method-ology laid out in Chap. 1, that is mainly by referring to the preparatory work of the 1930 and 1961 Conventions, authoritative materials on the interpretation of the 1961 Convention and that of the equivalent provision in the 1997 ECN, national laws and regulations and their implementation including case law, interviews and inquiries as well as academic and practical materials. Chapter 1 also gave an overview of annex 1, comparing the foundling provisions (including the lack thereof) in all 193 UN member States, and the relevance of the practice by non-State parties to the 1961 Convention.

Chapter 2 reviewed the basic concepts relevant to the book, such as nationality and statelessness, the international legal framework to address statelessness, as well as the relationship between documentation and nationality, and between family law and nationality law.

Chapter 3 clarified the definition of a foundling, ahead of Chap. 6, which clarified the issue of 'age' when 'found'. It was pointed out that being 'found' in the territory is a condition that gives rise to the State's obligation rather than part of who a foundling is, and the hypothesis made in Chap. 1—that one of the two requirements of being a 'foundling' was that her or his parentage is unknown (and that her or his birthplace can either be known or unknown)—was confirmed to be correct.

Chapter 4 clarified what it meant to be of 'unknown parents', and concluded that 'unknown parents' essentially meant that the parents do not legally exist or their existence is not legally proven, and thus, to be a foundling, one is not required to have been physically 'abandoned' or 'orphaned'.

Chapter 5 examined the burden and standard of proof in determining whether one is of unknown parentage when a dispute occurs at the initial determination of a person's nationality. It most importantly concluded that, given that the person or her or his legal representative concerned asserts unknown parentage and duly cooperates and provides all the reasonably available evidence regarding her or his parents' unknown-ness, the State concerned should bear and fulfil both the burden of production and persuasion regarding the existence of a legally recognized parents.

Chapter 6 mainly examined the age of the person when found in the territory to be considered a foundling, and the closely linked issue of what it means to be 'found' in the territory. The hypothesis provided in Chap. 1—that the remaining one of the two essential requirements of being a foundling is that she or he is a child when found—was thus again confirmed correct. It was further concluded that the term 'found' (which undoubtfully includes having been born in the territory) should be broadly defined as having been seen by a third person other than the parents in the territory.

Chapter 7 concluded, in terms of pre facto stage for the purpose of confirming acquisition of nationality, that, based on the travaux and others, it was possible to argue that the evidence of possession of another nationality should be the only fact constituting 'proof to the contrary' disqualifying the person from nationality where found under article 2. With regard to post facto withdrawal in case of discovery or establishment of foreign parentage and/or birth, the chapter emphasized that in order not to constitute arbitrary deprivation of nationality, it should not result in statelessness; and even when the person concerned has a foreign nationality, it must certainly be subjected to individual assessment of proportionality (including the best interests determination when involving children) and due process.

## 8.2  Previous Discussions on a Model Founding Provision

Based on the findings of all the foregoing chapters, it can be said that the current wording of article 2 of the 1961 Convention (as well as article 6(1)(b) of the ECN mirroring it) is ambiguous and prone to restrictive application, which necessitates more detailed guidance on its interpretation reflecting its object and purpose.

In this context, we should remind ourselves that the UNHCR and IPU's Handbook, published in November 2018, on good practices in nationality laws carries long-awaited 'model provisions' within domestic laws reflecting the 1961 Convention. The Handbook provides two options as model provisions reflecting article 2, one of which reads: 'A *foundling* found on the territory shall be presumed to have been born therein to parents who are citizens of X' (emphasis added).[1] This option adopts the term 'foundling', which is the exact term used in article 2. However, there is a need to consider whether, in domestic legislation reflecting article 2, the term 'foundling' should even continue to be used. Are there justifications to continue using this ambiguous term, which is not even used in most of the current nationality laws in English, which is open to misinterpretation such as that it needs to be an 'abandoned new-born'? This book has so far advocated that in future discussions relating to statelessness, it will be useful to consistently (re)define the term 'foundling'.

In this sense, the other option among the two 'model provisions' in the above 2018 UNHCR-IPU Handbook reads: 'A *child* shall be considered a citizen of X if he/she is found on the territory and *his/her parents* are *unknown*' (emphasis added).[2] While the UNHCR-IPU Handbook does not provide reasonings why a 'foundling' is replaced with a 'child' whose 'parents are unknown' in this model provision, this rephrasing indeed is perfectly correct as has been clarified by Chap. 3 of this book. However, the term 'unknown' is still obscure and requires much clarification as to what it actually means, as discussed in Chap. 4.

---

[1] UNHCR and IPU, *Good Practices in Nationality Laws for the Prevention and Reduction of Statelessness* (IPU November 2018) 34.

[2] Ibid.

## 8.3  Model Foundling Provision

Developing further this model provisions in the UNHCR-IPU Handbook, and based
on all the foregoing discussions in this book, it is now time to offer inspiration for an
'alternative' model domestic provision incorporating article 2 of the 1961 Convention
as well as for any future regional instrument providing for foundlings' nationality:

> A person whose **legal parentage cannot be proven** who is **found as a child** in the terri-
> tory shall **acquire the nationality** of X [the State where found], **unless her or his possession
> of a foreign nationality is proven.**[3]

While not included in this 'model provision', it is essential that the assessment
and confirmation of whether the person has acquired nationality under this provision
is made within a reasonable time. Reasonable time can be, for example, six months
extendable to one year after the declaration is made to the competent authority for
the purpose of such nationality confirmation. Further, the withdrawal of nationality
previously confirmed under a foundling provision, if envisaged, should be clearly
regulated either within the same provision or by a separate provision, so as to avoid
arbitrary nationality deprivation. Such provision should at least provide that, in case
of discovery or establishment of foreign parentage and/or birth, nationality cannot
be withdrawn unless the State concerned proves, within a limitation period, that the
person possesses a foreign nationality. Further, the decision to withdraw, including
when not resulting in statelessness, must be subject to individual proportionality
assessment including best interests determination when involving children, as well
as procedural safeguards, such as the right to a fair hearing and effective remedy. The
limitation period should be a maximum of ten years from the date the State took an
action to confirm her or his nationality, ideally with even a shorter deadline in light of
the best interests of the child. The withdrawal should desirably have non-retroactive
effect (see Sect. 8.3.8).

I will now give a summary of the justifications for the above provision and how the
provision should be interpreted, drawing from the preceding chapters. The relevant
chapters should be consulted for more details and detailed sources.

### 8.3.1  'Whose legal parentage'

This means that the person is of legally unknown parents, that is there is either no
legally recognized parent for the person concerned or a legal parent(s) is supposed to
exist but such existence cannot be established. This thus covers both persons whose

---

[3] This provision was crafted drawing on article 2 of the 1961 Convention, article 6(1)(b) of the
ECN and article 5.2.a of the 2015 Draft Protocol to the African Charter on Human and Peoples'
Rights on the Specific Aspects of the Right to a Nationality and the Eradication of Statelessness
in Africa, and being inspired by different segments of specific nationality laws, in particular the
Finnish law (section 12), Italian law (article 1(2)), Russian law (article 12(2)), and New Zealand
law (section 6(3)(b)) and others.

parent(s) is (are) factually known but not legally known, and also persons whose parents are factually unknown. It was considered that using the term 'factually and legally unknown' would be redundant. This is because factually unknown parents are also legally unknown. Legal parentage, and not factual parentage, is relevant when determining the acquisition of nationality (see Sect. 4.4).

The term encompasses the wide range of categories of persons who are considered to fall within the definition of a foundling, that is persons of unknown parents around the world, as reviewed in Sect. 4.3. It for sure covers the most 'typical' cases that fall within foundling provisions—for example, children who are left in baby hatches or literally abandoned in other places, about whose parents factually nothing is known. The definition also covers less typical cases, including those for whom fragments of the parent's identity do exist, which, however, cannot be firmly established. These include babies left behind at a hospital with their birth mother running away after delivery. Further, those persons who are lost, orphaned or are entrusted to or informally adopted and raised by unrelated adults, and/or remain undocumented, who are often found by the authorities only after reaching an older age including adulthood, are covered by this term. Persons whose parent(s) go missing after registering their birth with invalid identity information would also qualify as long as the parent's identity is not legally established. Those born under anonymous birth schemes whose mother is factually known would also qualify, as they do in some States already, indeed as one of the most typical categories of cases under their foundling provisions. Likewise, even those without legal parents as a result of surrogacy arrangements can be covered by this definition (see Sect. 4.5).

It would be more efficient to consistently adopt the term a 'child whose legal parentage cannot be proven' instead of a 'foundling'. While a 'child of legally unknown parents' can be used for its simplicity, the term is still obscure and requires much clarification. Thus, the formulation in the model provision in this book is preferred.

### 8.3.2 'Cannot be proven'

As discussed in Sect. 8.3.1, this wording is intentionally adopted to replace the common term '(a child) of unknown parentage (parents)', with implications on the burden and standard of proof (or the degree of unknown-ness of the parentage). Chapter 5, especially Sect. 5.2, discussed the 'shared' burden of proof and the standard of proof ('to a reasonable degree') recommended in the UNHCR Guidelines 4 [1] in proving that a child born in the territory would otherwise be stateless under articles 1 and 4 of the 1961 Convention. The chapter examined the inherent difficulties in 'proving the negative'. Foundlings—without legal parents to speak on their behalf—in general are *not* in a position to explain how they were born, and prove the *unknown-ness* of their own parentage. It was, however, pointed out that for the 'most typical cases of foundlings' such as babies abandoned on a baby hatch or other places and discovered by the State with no clue regarding who the parents are, one's unknown parentage is fairly clear with no dispute or issue of burden and standard of proof arising.

Based on the foregoing, two recommendations were made in Chap. 5, which duly takes into consideration the difference between jurisdictions on the conceptualization and (in)flexibility of the burden and standard of proof. (Below is a reproduction of what is included in the 'Summary and conclusions', Chap. 5.)

### Option I: Reversed burden of persuasion—State's inability to prove 'known-ness' of the legal parentage at a high standard of proof = recognition of legally unknown parentage at a low standard of proof

Once the person concerned (or persons representing her or him) asserts the unknown-ness of her or his parentage and duly cooperates to fulfil her or his shared burden of producing all the reasonably available information regarding the parents' unknown-ness, the State concerned should bear both the burden of producing evidence as well as the burden of persuasion regarding the existence of a legally recognized parent. If the State does not fulfil such burden of proof, the nationality of the person under this provision is to be confirmed. In relation to the standard of proof, the State should conclude that the person's legal parentage cannot be proven ('is unknown') when it cannot be convinced within a reasonable timeframe or a pre-set deadline (see Sect. 8.3.7) that one of the child's legally recognized parents is definitively identified at a high standard of proof. The 'high' standard of proof can be something equivalent to 'beyond the reasonable doubt', to the extent that it enables the determination of the child's nationality (non-)acquisition by *jus sanguinis*.

### Option II: Broad interpretation of the 'unknown parents' definition in absence of the reversed burden of proof, which can substitute a low standard of proof for recognizing legally unknown parentage

Alternatively, or in addition to, the reversal of burden of persuasion, the term 'unknown parents' should be interpreted broadly. Being of 'unknown parents' can be interpreted to mean that the person is 'in a circumstance that indicates that the person's legal parents are not definitively identified to the extent it would enable the determination of the claimant's nationality', or something to that effect. Interpreting the term broadly like this would be especially helpful in achieving the same result as Option I in jurisdictions where the reversed burden of persuasion is difficult to achieve, or where the standard of proof is inflexible and set high across the board. This is because, as a reflection of the broad interpretation, once the applicant proves the circumstances (at a normal high standard of proof, for example intime conviction) which indicate that the applicant's parent is not definitively identified, the decision-maker or the State would not be able to rebut this assertion unless they prove that one of the parents is definitively identified (see Sects. 5.6.3.2.3–5.6.3.2.6).

The formulation 'whose legal parentage cannot be proven' in the model provision is inspired by Japanese case law (Sect. 5.6.3.2) and some States' existing legislation[4]

---

[4] The Citizenship Act of New Zealand is inspiring. Section 6(3)(b) states that a person is 'deemed to be a New Zealand citizen' by birth if: (i) the person [...] has been found abandoned in New

and is effective in preventing the situation, for example, where a person is denied nationality of the country where found because there are, however incomplete, pieces of information available on the identity of her or his birth mother, which suggests she is likely to be a national of a foreign country. In many of these cases, the authorities of the purported country of nationality of the mother deny the child's nationality acquisition by *jus sanguinis* as they are unable to recognize the legal parentage with such incomplete information.

That being said, an older child or adult of unknown parentage (who had been found by a third party in the territory while a minor but come to the attention of the authorities only after reaching adulthood) should bear the responsibility of truthfully explaining, depending on the circumstances of the individual cases, how she or he believes herself or himself to be of legally unknown parentage. This would include testifying whatever she or he knows about where she or he was born (if known), where, how and with whom she or he has grown up and been living or whether and how she or he has (not) gone to school and so on. She or he needs to produce all the reasonably available evidence including any witnesses who can testify to the facts relating to her or his unknown parentage or the place of upbringing. If it is considered that the person is not cooperative and is not credible, the person's claim for nationality can be rejected based on the lack of credibility (see Sect. 6.9, for example).

### 8.3.3  'Found' (in the Territory)

As explained in Chap. 3, being found in the territory is a condition that gives rise to the State's responsibility to grant nationality to a foundling, and is not part of

---

Zealand; and (ii) investigations have failed to establish the identity of at least one of the person's parents.' Section 6(3)(ii) appears to explicitly impose the burden of production and persuasion on the government to prove the known-ness of the parents. New Zealand Citizenship Act 1977 (1 July 2013) < http://www.legislation.govt.nz/act/public/1977/0061/latest/whole.html#DLM443841 > accessed 4 August 2019. Further, Afghanistan's legislation in article 12 states: 'If a child is found in the territory of the IEA (Islamic Emirate of Afghanistan) and his/her parents' documents proving their citizenship are not available, the child would be considered citizen of the IEA.' 'Law on Citizenship of the Islamic Emirate of Afghanistan' (24 June 2000) < http://www.refworld.org/docid/404c988d4.html > accessed 4 August 2019. The Afghan legislation is unique as it could be seen as lowering the standard of proof to establish unknown-ness of the parents by requiring the State to grant nationality unless the parents' documents proving their citizenship are discovered. However, it is difficult as the availability of (purported parents') nationality document and the establishment of legal parent–child relationship between the child and the purported parents are two different things. Note that article 8 of the same law states: 'A person who does not hold citizenship of the IEA and *does not have strong documents proving his citizenship of another country* is considered to be without citizenship' (emphasis added). While the author can only read the English translation available on refworld.org, this provision is inspiring in the sense that it apparently lowers the standard of proof in proving (or broadly interpreting) the unknown parentage or lack of nationality. However, on both the New Zealand and Afghan legislation, no information was readily located on how the relevant articles are implemented in practice to enable any meaningful analysis.

the definition of who a foundling is. Being found in the territory includes situations where it is known that the child has been born in the territory. The finder of the child of unknown parentage does not have to be the authorities. It should be defined broadly such as 'having been seen in the territory by a person other than one's parents', or something to that effect (see especially Sect. 6.5). States such as Spain and Japan have indeed previously applied their foundling provision in full and inclusive manner, such as to persons of unknown parents who voluntarily approached the authorities for nationality confirmation at a much older age, such as in their 40–60 s. Their presence in the territory in their childhood were established by evidence such as the individuals' own statements, school records or testimony by non-State third persons, such as neighbours.

## 8.3.4 'Child'

'Child' should be interpreted to mean a person below the age of the majority as defined in article 1 of the CRC, that is under 18 years unless, under the law applicable to the child, majority is attained earlier. This is the age when the person needs to be found, by any third person other than her or his parents in the territory. The person can be an adult when she or he approaches or is detected by the authorities, as long as it can be shown that she or he has been found by a third person while still a minor.

The reason for not imposing a younger age limitation is that, as detailed in Chap. 6, it would inevitably be arbitrary under international law. Article 2 of the 1961 Convention does not provide for a specific age limit. A person who does not know her or his parentage (and birthplace) would not become able to account for them regardless of how old she or he becomes—whether five, 18 or 60 years old. What is unknown is unknown. Thus, the rationale that an older child should be able to identify her or his parent(s) does not hold water. Even if the rationale was that the younger the child is, the more likely she or he was born within the territory, it is almost impossible to eliminate all the possibilities that the person was born outside the territory even if the age limit is set at 'new-born child'. This is especially so when considering the cases of States with little border control with neighbouring States.

Despite the fact that the term 'foundling' has a general connotation that it is a small child depending on which UN language versions of the 1961 Convention is referred to (Sect. 6.1), the essence of the foundling provision is not about the fact that the person is 'a small child', but that the person is of 'unknown parentage', as a result of which she or he cannot acquire nationality based on the *jus sanguinis* principle (or by the *jus soli* principle if the birthplace is also unknown). The underlying intention behind the foundling provision that transpires from the travaux was also to protect children in general (not limited to new-born or small children) without those normally legally responsible for their protection and care.

The right to nationality of 'a child' is explicitly protected under article 7 of the CRC, to which all but one of the 193 UN member States are party, as well as under article 24 of the ICCPR for example. As CRC Committee and CMW have urged,

States are to ensure that equal standards of protection are provided to 'every child, including those above the age of 15 years'.[5]

Opening the provision to 'all minors' is also in line with a number of national legislations currently in force. As shown in detail in Sect. 6.3 and annex 1, out of 139 States with foundling provisions, 17 States only provide nationality grant to persons of unknown parents 'born in the territory', and 36 States to persons who are 'new-born (or recently born)' when found. At the same time, ten States provide for specific older ages starting at age three up to 15. As detailed in Sect. 6.3.4, a total of 15 States, or slightly more than 11 per cent of the 139 States with foundling provisions, either explicitly or by interpretation open up the target age to all 'minors'. For the remaining 61 States (44 per cent) whose foundling provisions do not specify the age, using either the term 'child', 'foundling' or 'infant' (in English original/translation, Spanish or French languages) without defining its age, there are indications that a number of them might possibly cover all minors.

Article 5.2.a. of the AU Draft Protocol to the African Charter on Human and Peoples' Rights on the Specific Aspects of the Right to a Nationality and the Eradication of Statelessness in Africa provides for 'a child (of unknown parents)' which can be interpreted as a minor.

This is especially important because persons of unknown parentage often face difficulties in securing evidence of having been found by a third person in the territory while still in early childhood, especially if she or he has been informally adopted and is mistreated by an unrelated adult(s) for example (see in particular Sects. 6.6–6.7). A stateless person of unknown parentage who is found as an adult by a third person or authorities in the territory of a particular State should rather be duly protected as a stateless person under the 1954 Convention or the equivalent domestic provision.

### 8.3.5 'Shall acquire nationality' (of the State Where Found)

As discussed in Chap. 7, the original text of article 2 of the 1961 Convention provides what can be described as a 'legal presumption' that a foundling found is considered to have been born in the territory of parents who are both nationals. The travaux of the 1961 Convention indicates that the nationality acquisition under article 2 was normally meant to be automatic, that is *ex lege*, at birth.[6] Article 6(1)(b) of the ECN (which was 'taken' from the 1961 Convention) explicitly provides for foundlings found in the territory with the same automatic *ex lege* nationality acquisition guaranteed for a child of a national.

---

[5] Joint general comment No 4 (2017) of CMW and No 23 (2017) of the CRC Committee on State obligations regarding the human rights of children in the context of international migration in countries of origin, transit, destination and return, 16 November 2017, CMW/C/GC/4-CRC/C/GC/23 < https://www.refworld.org/docid/5a12942a2b.html > .

[6] See fn 128, Chap. 5 of this book on the travaux statement by Denmark.

As reviewed and classified in Sect. 7.4 (Methods I–VIII), very few States' foundling provisions today adopt the same formulation as article 2 of the 1961 Convention. Many States use different legal techniques or methods to grant nationality, including by simply granting nationality for fulfilling the prerequisite facts (for being 'foundlings [or children of unknown parents] found in the territory').

The wording of the 'model provision' does not adopt legal techniques of 'presuming' in-country birth or descent, as done in article 2, or 'presuming' nationality itself, as done in some States. The model provision directly provides the nationality acquisition as a consequent legal effect when the specific legal criteria are fulfilled ('unless her or his possession of a foreign nationality is proven'—to be discussed in Sect. 8.3.6).

The same method is taken by article 6(1)(b) of the ECN (classified as 'Method VII.b)' in Sect. 7.4). While not copying the exact formulation of article 2, the model provision is in line with its object and purpose, which is to ensure nationality is acquired (automatically) by a foundling found in the territory one way or another. In fact, this sort of formulation was recommended by Italy during the travaux, and is reflected in the current nationality law of Italy as well as some other States' legislation.

The formulation in the model provision, as compared to the exact wording of article 2, stabilizes foundlings' nationality status, and avoids the misunderstanding that nationality acquired via article 2 of the 1961 Convention is a 'provisional', 'presumed' or 'fictional' nationality. Moreover, not presuming birth in the territory reflects the intentions of a number of drafters, who considered that foundlings born abroad should not necessarily be excluded from the application of article 2. Not presuming one's parents to be nationals will also help avoid a misconception that a child of unknown parents who is highly likely (but not proven) to be a child of foreigners should be excluded from the provision.

In terms of the timing of nationality acquisition, States are encouraged to make the nationality acquisition retroactive to the time of birth. As stated above, the travaux of the 1961 Convention carries an explicit assertion that article 2 should provide nationality grant 'at birth'.[7] This retroactive acquisition is explicitly provided under article 5.2.a. of the African Union Draft Protocol.

In fact, very few States' foundling provisions currently provide for non-automatic acquisition, and the vast majority of the 139 States appear to provide for *ex lege* acquisition for those born or found in the territory, with some States literally describing it as nationality acquisition 'at birth' (see Sect. 5.8.2). For example, Serbia's Citizenship Law article 13 provides:

A child born or found in the territory of the Republic of Serbia (foundling) *acquires* citizenship of the Republic of Serbia *by birth* [...]. A child that acquired citizenship of the Republic

---

[7] The Danish representative stated: '[I]t was surely better that the child should acquire *at birth* the nationality of that country' (emphasis added). United Nations, Summary Records, 5th Meeting of the Committee of the Whole held on 3 April 1959, A/CONF.9/C.1/SR.5, UN Conference on the Elimination or Reduction of Future Statelessness, Geneva, 1959 and New York, 1961 (3 April 1959) 8 < http://legal.un.org/docs/?path=../diplomaticconferences/1959_statelessness/docs/english/vol_2/a_conf9_c1_sr5.pdf&lang=E > accessed 4 August 2019.

of Serbia pursuant to the para. 1 of this Article is *considered citizen* of the Republic of Serbia *since his birth.* (emphasis added)

However, making it an absolute requirement to confirm nationality retroactively at birth, while ideal, under this model provision might give rise to difficulties—considering that the provision allows for the most 'inclusive' interpretation that it applies to all children who have not attained the age of majority when found in the territory, including those whose birth abroad is known (see below Sect. 8.3.6). If States were to open up their foundling provisions to all minors of unknown parents (including foreign-born ones), it might happen that they would rather choose to provide that they acquire nationality at the time they are found, by a third person, in the territory. While this would entail another set of difficulties in having to determine the exact date the person was found and thus acquired nationality, at least one State currently and explicitly stipulates nationality grant at the time of being found.[8]

### 8.3.6 'Unless her or his possession of a foreign nationality is proven'

This term rephrases 'in the absence of proof to the contrary' in article 2 of the 1961 Convention. This formulation makes it clear that the State needs to prove the possession of another nationality to deny the nationality grant to a child of unknown parents found in the territory.

As discussed extensively in Chap. 7, during the travaux process, what could constitute 'proof to the contrary' in the original text of article 2 was, as a result of disputes among States, eventually left open to fit different nationality regimes. There were indeed disagreements among drafters about whether birth abroad constituted 'proof to the contrary'. A number of drafters considered that a foundling should acquire nationality where found, even if it is known that she or he was born abroad, as long as such country of birth does not grant her or him nationality. This interpretation can indeed be beneficial in today's world where migration, displacement and human trafficking are prevalent. This book adopted this particular formulation in the model provision not to exclude those born abroad. Ensuring the nationality of children of unknown parents who would otherwise be stateless is the object and purpose article 2 of the 1961 Convention.

---

[8] The Czech Republic's law provides, according to its English translation posted on the Czech Ministry of Foreign Affairs website, for acquisition of nationality at the time of being found, as below. Section 10, subpart 5, Part II of Czech Citizenship Act states: 'A child under three years of age found on the territory of the Czech Republic, whose identity was not determined, *shall acquire* the Czech citizenship *on the day they were found* [...]. Should the day of finding be in doubt, the day of granting the Czech citizenship to the child shall be determined by the Ministry of the Interior [...] pursuant to proceedings initiated by the authorities or upon motion filed by the child's legal representative or legal custodian' (emphasis added). 186/2013 Act of 11 July 2013 on Citizenship of the Czech Republic and on the amendment of selected other laws < https://www.mzv.cz/file/240 0342/Citizenship_Act_No._186_2013_Sb._o_statnim_obcanstvi_CR.pdf > .

Indeed, this model provision is of a similar formulation as the text of the ECN's article 6(1)(b) as well as some nationality legislation such as Italian nationality law whose texts do not exclude those born abroad, but rather limit the nationality grant to foundlings who would otherwise be stateless.

On the other hand, some States during the travaux of the 1961 Convention considered that a person of unknown parents born abroad should fall outside the scope of the provision. Some States' legislation today specifically presumes or requires birth within the territory or explicitly or implicitly shows that birth outside the territory constitutes proof to the contrary. The current State practice also generally showed that the evidence of birth outside the territory disqualified the person concerned from acquiring nationality based on the foundling provision. Based on the text of article 2, such legislation or interpretation does not go against States' obligation under the 1961 Convention. However, such children of unknown parents born abroad normally should at least be recognized as stateless persons and protected as such, with a prospect to facilitated naturalization as stipulated in the 1954 Convention.

### 8.3.7 'Reasonable time' to Determine the Eligibility for Nationality

The determination of whether a person acquires nationality under paragraph 1 should be done within a reasonable timeframe as stated at the outset of Sect. 8.3. As discussed in Sect. 5.8, 'a reasonable time (frame)' for determination of applicability of article 2 should ideally be six months (extendable by about another six months)—as actually stipulated in a few States' foundling provisions. This is indeed the same as the standard recommended for statelessness determination in the UNHCR Handbook [2] paragraph 75. While the 'maximum period' advocated in UNHCR Guidelines 4 [1] paragraph 22 to determine the nationality of children, who have legal parent(s) born in the territory who would otherwise be stateless under article 1 and 4 of the 1961 Convention is 'five years', it was determined that such standard might not necessarily be applicable to confirm the nationality of foundlings found in the territory under article 2. This is because: (1) the standard of 'five years' itself is considered quite long even for determining the applicability of article 1 (and 4), only indicative of the maximum period, and States are encouraged to deliver their decisions in a much shorter period as in Principle 8 of the Council of Europe Recommendation 2009/13 and paragraph 11 of its explanatory memorandum, and in accordance with articles 3 and 7 of the CRC; and (2) there are significant differences between articles 1 and 2 of the 1961 Convention. In summary, the period of 'five years' is a reflection of the maximum period of habitual residence (immediately preceding an application), which may be required under article 1(2)(b) of the 1961 Convention where a State has an application procedure to grant nationality to otherwise stateless children born in the territory. In contrast, article 2 does not contain any reference to such required residency period.On the contrary, during the travaux process, States agreed that foundlings under article 2 should be given easier access to nationality than 'otherwise stateless' children under article 1 due largely to the absence of those normally legally responsible for their protection and care (Chap. 3, especially Sect. 3.4.5.2). Unlike under article 1, it may be understood that States under article 2 are to grant nationality *ex lege* as soon as the legal requirements are met. Further, as stated in Sect. 8.3.4 justifying the term 'child', many persons will not become able to explain their own unknown parentage or birthplace no matter how much time elapses (see especially Sect. 6.7.2). At the same time, for the most 'typical' cases of foundlings, that is abandoned babies with no or little indications about their parentage, their unknown parentage is quite clearly established, which greatly simplifies any assessment of the applicability of article 2 or the equivalent domestic provision.

For missing parents, however, investigation is normally made to trace them, which can take some time especially when there are certain indications about the parents' identity. DNA testing, where relevant, itself can take several months. Thus, when a piece(s) of key evidence is highly likely to be obtainable with the extension of period beyond the six-month period, it would be useful to extend the duration by another six month or so, by applying paragraph 75 of the UNHCR Handbook (2014) by analogy. There might also be further exceptional or compelling circumstances, for example where birth registration might not be systematic in general or the civil documentation system might have been destroyed due to armed conflict, making the one-year deadline impossible to abide by. However, even in such cases, the nationality under the foundling provision should be confirmed within the earliest timing. During such period pending the nationality acquisition confirmation, the State is to treat these children as possessing its nationality so that they enjoy human rights, as also advised in paragraphs 22–23 of the UNHCR Guidelines 4 [1], applicable by analogy.

Another ground backing up the appropriateness of confirming foundlings' nationality within the shortest time possible, such as six months, is that, as explained in Sect. 8.3.8, if a foundling's foreign parentage and/or birth abroad becomes known and it is confirmed that she or he has acquired the nationality of one of the parents (or of country of birth), then her or his nationality can still be withdrawn, while limitations apply so that it would not be arbitrary.

### 8.3.8   Regulating Nationality Withdrawal to Avoid Arbitrary Deprivation of Nationality

As detailed in Sect. 7.6, the post facto withdrawal of nationality firstly must not amount to arbitrary deprivation of nationality prohibited under international law, including under article 15 of the UDHR, regardless of whether it results in statelessness. For this purpose, the withdrawal of nationality needs to conform to what is prescribed by law, be proportionate, that is the least intrusive means necessary to achieve a legitimate purpose, and follow a due process.[9]

As found in Sect. 7.6.1, the majority of States currently do not explicitly stipulate the post facto withdrawal of nationality acquired on the basis of their foundling provisions. However, there are indications that even some of such States implicitly envisage and/or actually practise such withdrawal, based on the fact that the preconditions laid down in the relevant law that led to the acquisition of nationality are no longer fulfilled. Such unregulated loss, which can amount to 'quasi-loss'[10] of nationality, is prone to being arbitrary. Clearly regulating the withdrawal of nationality acquired through the foundling provision along with the criteria, deadline and procedural safeguards—either within the foundling provision itself or by a separate provision—stabilizes the concerned person's nationality status. An arbitrary interpretation or concept that a foundling's acquisition of nationality is 'provisional' or 'temporal'—until the proof to the contrary is found—can also be avoided that way.

Having said this, it is rather difficult to draft a 'universal' model provision to regulate the post facto withdrawal of nationality previously confirmed for being considered a foundling. This is because of the 'diversity' of nationality law frameworks including the legal technique/method adopted to grant nationality to foundlings (as categorized in Sect. 7.4); to what extent and on what conditions multiple nationalities are otherwise allowed (that is birth in the territory, decent from a national, and so on), and whether there are any other, more general, provision(s) on the withdrawal (both nullification and revocation) of nationality within the law which is (are) applicable to the nationality granted based on a foundling provision. What can be done in this section is thus to lay out the minimum standards for regulating the withdrawal—which should in particular be guided by international human rights law standards, especially the best interests of the child.

Whether a person is in possession of another nationality is key in assessing proportionality, as withdrawal resulting in statelessness is generally arbitrary. The 1961 Convention only provides narrow exceptions from prohibition of withdrawal resulting in statelessness that should be interpreted restrictively in light of subsequent developments in international human rights law. Considering article 5(1) of the 1961 Convention and the UNHCR Guidelines 4 [1] and 5 [3], post facto discovery or (establishment) of foreign parentage or birth abroad must not lead to nationality withdrawal unless the person concerned has acquired another nationality through such birthplace in another country or parentage. This is also in line with the tendency in the current legislation shown in annex 1. Out of at least 37 States that have been identified to relatively explicitly regulate the post facto loss of nationality acquired based on the foundling provision along with the criteria for such loss, 23 States, that is 62 per cent, provided that nationality can only be lost if the person concerned is found to have a foreign nationality, with additional safeguards depending on the States.

Having said this, as also discussed at the outset and also in Sect. 7.6.2, the withdrawal of nationality even if it does not result in statelessness is certainly subject to

---

[9] See for example UNHCR Guidelines 5 (2020) paras 91–108 and other materials cited in Sect. 7.6.
[10] See for example ILEC Guidelines (2015) Part V.

limitations so as not to amount to arbitrary deprivation. Such withdrawal should at least be conditional upon conducting individual assessment of proportionality and due process. The withdrawal should also be subject to the general principles of law including legal certainty, a principle of high importance in nationality law. It is desirable that withdrawal is not retroactive. Procedural safeguards should be guaranteed, such as the right to individual hearing, appeal and legal counsel. Further, if the person concerned is still a child at the time when the nationality withdrawal is being considered, the assessment to determine whether the withdrawal is in line with the child's best interests—a primary consideration in all decisions concerning children under article 3 of the CRC—must be conducted.

With regard to the limitation period, as discussed in Sect. 7.6.2, leaving a person's nationality acquired based on a foundling provision indefinitely withdrawable for discovery or establishment of foreign parentage or birth abroad is not proportionate even if the withdrawal would not result in statelessness. Indeed, according to article 7(1)(f) of the ECN, loss of nationality acquired based on a foundling provision due to the discovery of foreign nationality is only allowed during the minority of the person involved, and this is in line with the legislation of at least 23 among the 37 States as shown in annex 1.

However, where children are concerned, being kept in a situation where their nationality can be withdrawn for up to 18 years or so do not seem to easily pass the proportionality test, including the best interests assessment. Indeed, as the Council of Europe indicates, it is 'obvious' that this deadline 'should be shorter than 18 years', which can be shortened to the duration of residence required for naturalization, that is the maximum of ten years under article 6(3) of the ECN.[11] Furthermore, 'the desirable preferential treatment of children could even justify a much shorter limit'.[12] It was also noted, for example, that the duration needed for the recognition of nationality based on the principle of *possession d'état de national* in some States is ten years. It was thus concluded that after the maximum of ten years, not least for the purpose of legal certainty, nationality should be retained even if it is found that she or he holds another nationality. It should be noted that ten years should be from the date when the State took its action of confirming the person's possession of nationality, and not from the date she or he was born or found in the territory. This is especially because the model foundling provision and guidance is inclusive in terms of the age when found being open to all minors, and a foundling can be found by any third person other than parents, as well as that she or he might only come to the attention of the authorities after reaching adulthood.

---

[11] Council of Europe: Committee of Ministers, Recommendation CM/Rec(2009)13 and explanatory memorandum of the Committee of Ministers to member states on the nationality of children (Council of Europe Publishing 9 May 2009) para 47.

[12] While in a different context, which is however relevant by analogy, the Council of Europe also recommends States to provide that 'revocation or annulment of an adoption will not cause the permanent loss of the nationality acquired by the adoption, if the child is lawfully and habitually resident on their territory for a period of more than five years'. Ibid Principle 15.

It should again be noted that eight out of the 37 States provide a shorter deadline than 18 years, and Finland proves the shortest that is five years since birth. Furthermore, at least two States essentially provide or interpret that nationality acquired based on their foundling provision are never withdrawn for discovery of foreign parentage and resultant possession of foreign nationality during the minority. From the child rights point of view, and as a matter of best practice, States are free or even encouraged to make their provisions even more favourable by adopting shorter durations such as five years.

## 8.4   Alternative Avenues of Nationality Grant Via Adoption or Other Means

This book found that some States grant nationality to children of unknown parentage who they do not recognize as 'foundlings', but who are otherwise stateless through measures other than applying their foundling provisions. Such alternative avenues can include nationality grant on the basis of adoption by nationals or of being hosted at child custody institutions within the territory, through late birth registration, or through recognition as stateless persons and facilitating their naturalization under the 1954 Convention or equivalent domestic provisions. In the absence of the adoption of an 'inclusive' definition of a foundling or unknown parentage, or a 'generous' deadline relating to the age of a foundling when found, establishing such avenues to ensure swift nationality grant is prudent.

## 8.5   Final Remarks Including Notes for Future Research

It is hoped that the exercises in this book, including that to redefine foundlings, will contribute to the current worldwide efforts to end statelessness. The model foundling provision and other interpretative guidance contained in this book should help ensure a full and inclusive application of article 2 of the 1961 Convention and equivalent national provisions in accordance with their object and purpose as well as the best interests of the child under the CRC. In particular, the wording of the 'model provision' will prove particularly useful in situations involving States under the effects of armed conflicts, or where documentation of civil and nationality status is not yet systematic, or where migration, displacement and human trafficking are widespread.

There are still a number of questions related to the nationality of foundlings that could not be addressed in detail in this book, mainly due to lack of access to the information on the actual State practice. One of the major ones include the 'timing' of the acquisition of nationality for foundlings, which would also have implications over the regulations over the post facto withdrawal of nationality. While it would be ideal (and practised a number of States) that foundlings acquire nationality retroactively at birth, some States appear to provide for other timings, such as when found or when the authorities take action to confirm nationality. This was rather cursorily reviewed in Sects. 5.8.2 and 8.3.5. In addition, a number of uniquely-formulated foundling provisions could not be analyzed due to lack of information.[13] The classifications and statistics in annex 1 might change, with more information—especially in the languages that author does not read—becoming available. In particular, those categorized under Sect. 6.3.5 might be re-categorized under Sect. 6.3.4, increasing the number of States explicitly opening up their foundling provisions to 'all minors'.

Further, in general, more detailed examination of the international human rights law norms, standards and jurisprudence, as well as exploration of the possibly relevant literature in the wider field of child rights and child protection, would likely strengthen and supplement further research on the nationality of foundlings. This would particularly be the case in terms of some of the difficult issues addressed in my book, such as the maximum age of a foundling when found, or foreign-born foundlings.

Moreover, as discussed in Sect. 3.8, as a 'by-product' of my efforts to define a foundling, the existence of one category of persons, who fall through the cracks of the 1961 Convention for not being able to invoke any of its provisions, was revealed—that is, persons whose parent(s) is (are) known, whose birthplace is nonetheless unknown, who would otherwise be stateless. While such persons are a small number, States can indeed encounter challenges related to their nationality. These persons cannot invoke either article 1, article 2 or article 4 of the 1961 Convention or the equivalent provisions in the ECN, unless their birth in a certain State can somehow be presumed. It will be pertinent that domestic legislation or its implementation and any future regional instruments address this gap, so that nobody falls through the cracks of the legal frameworks. All those aspects are left for further research and discussions.

It is hoped that this book will contribute to stimulate further discussion and the development of legal standards relating to the prevention of statelessness, in particular for foundlings, children of unknown parents, who are among the most vulnerable of all.

---

[13] See for example the foundling provisions of seven former USSR States in fn 70, Chap. 6 of this book, and on those of New Zealand and Afghanistan in fn 4 of this chapter, as well as nationality grant to children in institutional care in Sect. 4.6.

**Annex 1**
# Comparative Table of Legislation on the Nationality of Foundlings of 193 UN Member States

| No | UNHCR region *3 | Country | Party 1961 Conv since | Party ECN since | Citation of the accessible version *4 | Foundling provision *5 (full text) *6 | Birth in territory required *7 | New/recent born | Specific older ages | All minors *8 (non-exhaustive) | No explicit age | Loss regulated | No Withdrawal after certain age *9 | Foreign parentage revealed *10 | Foreign nationality revealed *10 | Birth abroad revealed | Otherwise stateless/child of stateless parents provision (art or sec) *11 | 'Unconditional' jus soli (art or sec) *12 |
|---|---|---|---|---|---|---|---|---|---|---|---|---|---|---|---|---|---|---|
| 1 | Asia and the Pacific | Afghanistan | | | Law on Citizenship of the Islamic Emirate of Afghanistan, 24 June 2000 <http://www.ref world.org/docid/4f04c98 8d4.html> | Article 12 'If a child is found in the territory of the IEA and his/her parents' documents proving their citizenship are not available, the child would be considered citizen of the IEA.' | | | | | X | | | | | | No provision | No provision |
| 2 | Europe | Albania | 2003 | 2004 | Law on Albanian Citizenship, Law No. 8389, 6 September 1998 <http://www.ref world.org/docid/3ae6b5 c10.html> | Article 8(1) 'A child born or found within the territory of the Republic of Albania is granted the Albanian citizenship if he is born by unknown parents and as a consequence the child may become stateless. If the parents of the child are known before the child has reached the age of 14, and they have a foreign citizenship, the Albanian citizenship may be waivered by request of parents legally recognized, provided that the child does not remain stateless as result of such act.' | | | | | | X | 14 years of age | | X | | No provision | No provision |
| 3 | Middle East and North Africa | Algeria | | | Algérie: Code de la nationalité Algerienne [Algerian Nationality Code] (as amended up to 2007) <https://data. globalcit.eu/Nation alDB/docs/Code% 20de%20la%20nationa lite%20Algerienne% 20(consolidated%202 007).pdf> | Article 7(1) 'The following are of Algerian nationality by birth in Algeria: (1) the child born in Algeria of unknown parents; However, the child born in Algeria of unknown parents shall not be considered to have ever been Algerian if, before he comes of age, it is established that he is also of foreign descent and if the possesses the nationality of his foreign parent in accordance with the law of that country. Any foundling found in Algeria is considered to be born in Algeria until the contrary has been proved.' | | | | | X | X | After the age of majority | | X | | No provision | No provision |

(continued)

(continued)

| No | UNHCR region[3] | Country | Party 1961 Conv since | Party ECN since | Citation of the accessible version[4] | Founding provision[5] (full text)[6] | Birth in territory required[7] | New/recent born | Specific older ages | All minors[8] (non-exhaustive) | No explicit age | Loss regulated | No Withdrawal[9] after certain age | Foreign parentage revealed[10] | Foreign nationality revealed[10] | Birth abroad revealed | Otherwise stateless/child of stateless parents provision (art or sec)[11] | 'Unconditional' jus soli (art or sec)[12] |
|---|---|---|---|---|---|---|---|---|---|---|---|---|---|---|---|---|---|---|
| | | | | | | | **Age related** | | | | | | **Withdrawal related[5]** | | | | **Complementary** | |
| 4 | Europe | Andorra | | | Llei qualificada de la nacionalitat [Law on Qualification for Nationality] which entered into force 5 October 1995 <http://www.consellgeneral.ad/fitxers/documents/lleis-1989-2002/llei-qualif icada-de-la-nacionalitat.pdf/2013-11-05.331252 0257/view> | Article 4 'An infant found or born in the Principality of Andorra of unknown parents is Andorran. This nationality is lost on the day when the child 's affiliation is established with respect to a foreign person, on the condition that the such affiliation occurs during the minority of the infant and that the infant obtains the nationality of the foreign person, according to the national law of the latter.' | | | | | X | X | After the age of majority | | X | | Nationality law 5 | No provision |
| 5 | Africa | Angola | 2019 | | Lei no. 2/16 da nacionalidade [Law no. 2/16 of nationality] (Angola) entered into force 15 April 2016 <http://citizenshiprightsafrica.org/wp-content/upl oads/2016/04/Angola_Lei-da-nacionali dade_No2-2016.pdf> | Article 15 (b) '[A person] still acquires the Angolan nationality upon request: [...] b) An individual born in Angolan territory, a son or daughter [filho] of unknown parents [...].' (Note: This provision provides for non-automatic acquisition upon request, but GLOBALCIT database Mode A03a describes it as 'automatic' acquisition) | X | | | | | | | | | | Nationality law 15 | No provision |
| 6 | The Americas | Antigua and Barbuda | | | Antigua and Barbuda: Law No. 17 of 1982, The Antigua and Barbuda Citizenship Act, 19 August 1982 <http://www.refworld.org/docid/4e5cad952.html> | Section 3(1) '[...] a newborn infant is found abandoned in Antigua and Barbuda, that infant shall, unless the contrary is shown, be deemed to have been born in Antigua and Barbuda and thereby to have become a citizen of Antigua and Barbuda at the date of his birth.' | | X | | | | | | | | | Nationality law 3(5), 3(8) | Const 113a |
| 7 | The Americas | Argentina | 2014 | | | No provision | | | | | | | | | | | No provision | Nationality law 1(1), 1(3), 1(5) |

(continued)

(continued)

| No | UNHCR region[3] | Country | Party 1961 Conv since | Party ECN since | Citation of the accessible version[4] | Foundling provision[5] (full text)[6] | Age related | | | | | Loss regulated | Withdrawal related[5] | | | | Complementary | |
|---|---|---|---|---|---|---|---|---|---|---|---|---|---|---|---|---|---|---|
| | | | | | | | Birth in territory required[7] | New/ recent born | Specific older ages | All minors[8] (non-exhaustive) | No explicit age | | No Withdrawal[9] after certain age | Foreign parentage revealed[10] | Foreign nationality revealed[10] | Birth abroad revealed | Otherwise stateless/ child of stateless parents provision (art or sec)[11] | 'Unconditional' jus soli (art or sec)[12] |
| 8 | Europe | Armenia | 1994 | | Law of 1995 on Citizenship of the Republic of Armenia, November 1995 <http://www.refworld.org/docid/51b770884.html> | Article 20 'The child on the territory of the Republic of Armenia whose parents are unknown, is a citizen of the Republic of Armenia. In case of discovery of at least one of the parents or a trustee, the citizenship can be changed according to this Law.' | | | | See sec 6.3.4 of the book | X | (Unclear whether nat lost when resulting in statelessness) | | | | | Nationality law 12 | No provision |
| 9 | Asia and the Pacific | Australia | 1973 | | Australian Citizenship Act, 2007 <https://www.legislation.gov.au/Details/C2019C00040> | Section 14 'A person is an Australian citizen if the person is found abandoned in Australia as a child, unless and until the contrary is proved.' | | | | See sec 6.3.4 of the book | X | | | | | | Nationality law 21(8) | No provision |
| 10 | Europe | Austria | 1972 | 1998 | Federal Law on Austrian Citizenship, BGBl.311/1985, 30 July 1985 <http://www.refworld.org/docid/3ae6b52114.html> | Article 8 'Until proof to the contrary, a person under the age of six months found on the territory of the Republic is regarded as national by descent.' | | X | | | | | | | | | Nationality law 8(2); 14 | No provision |
| 11 | Europe | Azerbaijan | 1996 | | Law of 1998 on Citizenship of the Azerbaijan Republic, 30 September 1998 <http://www.refworld.org/docid/3ae6b52717.html> | Article 13 'A child, who lives on the territory of Azerbaijan and both parents of whom are unknown, is a citizen of Azerbaijan Republic.' | | | | See sec 6.3.4 of the book | X | | | | | | Nationality law 12 | No provision |
| 12 | The Americas | Bahamas | | | | No provision | | | | | | | | | | | No provision | No provision |
| 13 | Middle East and North Africa | Bahrain | | | Bahraini Citizenship Act, 16 September 1963 <http://www.refworld.org/docid/3fb9f5444.html> | Article 5(B) 'A person shall be regarded Bahraini by birth if: […] (B) Born in Bahrain, after the effective date of this Act, to unknown parents.' | X | | | | | | | | | | No provision | No provision |

(continued)

(continued)

| No | UNHCR region [3] | Country | Party 1961 Conv since | Party ECN since | Citation of the accessible version [4] | Foundling provision [5] (full text) [6] | Age related | | | | | Loss regulated | Withdrawal related [5] | | | | Complementary | |
|---|---|---|---|---|---|---|---|---|---|---|---|---|---|---|---|---|---|---|
| | | | | | | | Birth in territory required [7] | New/ recent born | Specific older ages | All minors [8] (non-exhaustive) | No explicit age | | No Withdrawal [9] after certain age | Foreign parentage revealed [10] | Foreign nationality revealed [10] | Birth abroad revealed | Otherwise stateless/ child of stateless parents provision (art or sec) [11] | "Unconditional" jus soli (art or sec) [12] |
| 14 | Asia and the Pacific | Bangladesh | | | | No provision | | | | | | | | | | | No provision | Nationality law 4 (Note: No info available that this provision is applied to children of foreign parents in practice) |
| 15 | The Americas | Barbados | | | Barbados Citizenship Act, Cap. 186.30 November 1966 <http://www.refworld.org/docid/3ae6b5608.html> | Section 4(1) '[...] for the purposes of this subsection, where after the 29th November, 1966 a newborn infant is found abandoned in Barbados, that infant shall, unless the contrary is shown, be deemed to have been born in Barbados.' | | X | | | | | | | | | No provision | Const 4 |
| 16 | Europe | Belarus | | | Law on the Citizenship of the Republic of Belarus, 20 July 2016 <http://www.refworld.org/docid/50f6c4dea2.html> | Article 13'[...] A child who is situated on the territory of the Republic of Belarus and whose parents are unknown becomes citizen of the Republic of Belarus.' | | | | See sec 6.3.4 of the book | X | | | | | | Nationality law 13 | No provision |

(continued)

(continued)

| No | UNHCR region [3] | Country | Party 1961 Conv since | Party ECN since | Citation of the accessible version [4] | Founding provision [5] (full text) [6] | Age related | | | | | Loss regulated | Withdrawal related [5] | | | | Complementary | |
|---|---|---|---|---|---|---|---|---|---|---|---|---|---|---|---|---|---|---|
| | | | | | | | Birth in territory required [7] | New/ recent born | Specific older ages | All minors [8] (non-exhaustive) | No explicit age | | No With-drawal [9] after certain age | Foreign parentage revealed [10] | Foreign nationality revealed [10] | Birth abroad revealed | Otherwise stateless/ child of stateless parents provision (art or sec) [11] | 'Unconditional' jus soli (art or sec) [12] |
| 17 | Europe | Belgium | | 2014 | Code de la nationalité belge, 28 June 1984 [Belgium Nationality Code 1984] <http://www.ejustice.just.fgov.be/cgi_loi/change_lg.pl?language=fr&la=F&cn=1984062835& table_name=loi> [Translation in UNHCR, 'Mapping Statelessness in Belgium' (October 2012) <https://www.refworld.org/docid/510004b22.html> was relied upon] | Article 10(3): 'A new-born child found in Belgium is presumed, until the contrary is proved, to be born in Belgium.' (Note: Preceding this, article 10(1) provides: 'a child born in Belgium is Belgian if he or she would otherwise be stateless at any moment before he or she reaches the age of 18 or is 'emancipated'.) Article 10(4) provides 'The child to whom Belgian nationality has been granted under this Article shall retain that nationality until it has been established before he attains the age of eighteen years or has been emancipated before that age, that he possesses a foreign nationality.' | | X | | | | X | 18 years of age | | X | | Nationality law 10 | No provision |
| 18 | The Americas | Belize | 2015 | | Belizean Nationality Act, 31 December 2000 <http://www.refworld.org/docid/4e5ccdc02.html> | Section 7 'Every person first found in Belize as a newly born deserted infant of unknown and unascertainable parentage shall, until the contrary is proved, be deemed to have the status of a citizen of Belize by descent.' | | X | | | | | | | | | No provision | Const 24, BEL 5(1), 5(3) |
| 19 | Africa | Benin | 2011 | | Law No. 65–17 of 23/06/65 containing the Code of Dahomean Nationality, 23 June 1965 <http://www.refworld.org/docid/3ae6b5b14.html> | Article 10 'A new-born child found in Dahomey shall be presumed prima facie to have been born in Dahomey.' [Not clear how this provision leads to nationality grant when the nationality law does not appear to grant nationality unconditionally by jus soli.] | | X | | | | | | | | | Nationality law 9 | No provision |
| 20 | Asia and the Pacific | Bhutan | | | | No provision | | | | | | | | | | | No provision | No provision |

(continued)

(continued)

| No | UNHCR region[3] | Country | Party 1961 Conv since | Party ECN since | Citation of the accessible version[4] | Founding provision[5] (full text)[6] | Age related — Birth in territory required[7] | New/recent born | Specific older ages | All minors[8] (non-exhaustive) | No explicit age | Loss regulated | Withdrawal related[5] — No withdrawal[9] after certain age | Foreign parentage revealed[10] | Foreign nationality revealed[10] | Birth abroad revealed | Complementary — Otherwise stateless/child of stateless parents provision (art or sec)[11] | 'Unconditional' jus soli (art or sec)[12] |
|---|---|---|---|---|---|---|---|---|---|---|---|---|---|---|---|---|---|
| 21 | The Americas | Bolivia (Plurinational State of) | 1983 | | | No provision | | | | | | | | | | | No provision | Constitution 141, Nationality law 94 |
| 22 | Europe | Bosnia and Herzegovina | 1996 | 2008 | Law on Citizenship of Bosnia and Herzegovina Unofficial Consolidated Text (as amended up to 2013) <https://data.globalcit.eu/NationalDB/docs/BIH%20Law%20on%20Citizenship%20(con solidated)%20EN.pdf> | Article 7 'BiH citizenship is acquired by a child born or found on the BiH territory after the entry into force of the Constitution, whose both parents are unknown [...].' Article 28(3)'A child who has acquired BiH citizenship in accordance with Article 7 shall acquire the citizenship of the Entity where he/she was born or found.' | | | | | X | | | | | | Nationality law 7(1) | No provision |
| 23 | Africa | Botswana | | | | No provision | | | | | | | | | | | No provision | No provision |
| 24 | The Americas | Brazil | 2007 | | | No provision | | | | | | | | | | | No provision | Constitution 12(1)(a), BRA 1(1) |
| 25 | Asia and the Pacific | Brunei Darussalam | | | | No provision | | | | | | | | | | | No provision | No provision |
| 26 | Europe | Bulgaria | 2012 | 2006 | Law for the Bulgarian Citizenship.5 November 1998 <http://www.refworld.org/docid/49622ef32.html> | Article 11 'A child found on this territory, whose parents are unknown, is considered born on the territory of the Republic of Bulgaria' | | | | | X | | | | | | Nationality law 10 | No provision |

(continued)

(continued)

| No | UNHCR region [3] | Country | Party 1961 Conv since | Party ECN since | Citation of the accessible version [4] | Founding provision [5] (full text) [6] | Age related | | | | | Withdrawal related [5] | | | | | Complementary | |
|---|---|---|---|---|---|---|---|---|---|---|---|---|---|---|---|---|---|---|
| | | | | | | | Birth in territory required [7] | New/recent born | Specific older ages | All minors [8] (non-exhaustive) | No explicit age | Loss regulated | No Withdrawal after certain age [9] | Foreign parentage revealed [10] | Foreign nationality revealed [10] | Birth abroad revealed | Otherwise stateless/child of stateless parents provision (art or sec) [11] | 'Unconditional' jus soli (art or sec) [12] |
| 27 | Africa | Burkina Faso | 2017 | | Burkina Faso Code des personnes et de la Famille 1989, Title V De la nationalité, 16 November 1989 [Burkina Faso Code of the Person and the Family, Title V on Nationality] <http://citizenshiprightsafrica.org/wp-content/uploads/2016/01/Burkina_Faso_Code_de_la_famille_et_de_la_nationalite_1996.pdf> | Article 141 'A child born in Burkina Faso of unknown parents is a national of Burkina Faso. However, he shall be considered never to have been a national of Burkina Faso if, during his minority, his affiliation is established with respect to a foreigner and if he has, according to the national law of that foreigner, the nationality of that foreigner. This is without prejudice to the validity of the acts of the person concerned, or to the rights acquired by the third persons on the basis of the apparent nationality possessed by the child.' Article 142 'The newborn child found in Burkina Faso is presumed, until proven otherwise, to have been born in Burkina.' (author translation) | | X | | | | X | After the age of majority | | X | | Nationality law 143 | No provision |
| 28 | Africa | Burundi | | | Loi 1/013 du 18 juillet 2000 portant reforme du code de la nationalité,1/013,18 July 2000 [Nationality Code] <http://www.refworld.org/docid/452d01c94.html> | Article 3 'The following are Burundian by legal presumption: (a) A child born in Burundi of legally unknown parents; (b) A child found in Burundi, unless it is established that he was not born on Burundaese soil.' (author translation) | | | | | X | | | | | | No provision | No provision |
| 29 | Africa | Cabo Verde | | | Nationality law of Cape Verde, 29 June 1990 <http://citizenshiprightsafrica.org/wp-content/uploads/2016/11/CapeVerde-Compilation.pdf> | Article 7(2) 'A newborn baby found in Cape Verde is presumed to have been born in Cape Verde.' (Note: Preceding this, Article 7(1)(c) states: 'The individual born in Cape Verdean territory when he or she does not have another nationality is a national of Cape Verde by origin.) | | X | | | | | | | | | Nationality Law 7(1)(c)-(d) | No provision |

(continued)

(continued)

| No | UNHCR region[3] | Country | Party 1961 Conv since | Party ECN since | Citation of the accessible version[4] | Founding provision[5] (full text)[6] | Age related | | | | | Withdrawal related[5] | | | | | Complementary | |
|---|---|---|---|---|---|---|---|---|---|---|---|---|---|---|---|---|---|---|
| | | | | | | | Birth in territory required[7] | New/ recent born | Specific older ages | All minors[8] (non-exhaustive) | No explicit age | Loss regulated | No With-drawal[9] after certain age | Foreign parentage revealed[10] | Foreign nationality revealed[10] | Birth abroad revealed | Otherwise stateless/ child of stateless parents provision (art or sec)[11] | 'Uncon-ditional' jus soli (art or sec)[12] |
| 30 | Asia and the Pacific | Cambodia | | | Law on Nationality,9 October 1996 <http://www.refworld.org/docid/3ae6b5210.html> | Article 4(2)(b) '[…] shall obtain Khmer nationality/citizenship, by having been born in the Kingdom of Cambodia; […] (b) any child who is born from an unknown mother or father (a parent) and a newly born child who is found in the Kingdom of Cambodia, shall also be considered as having been born in the Kingdom of Cambodia.' | | X | | | | | | | | | No provision | No provision |
| 31 | Africa | Cameroon | | | Law No. 1968-LF-3 of the 11th June 1968 to set up the Cameroon Nationality Code,1968-LF-3,15 July 1968 <http://www.refworld.org/docid/3ae6b4db1c.html> | Section 9 'Cameroon nationality attaches to every child born in Cameroon of unknown parents. Provided that, if during his minority his affiliation is established with regard to a foreign parent and if in accordance with the national law of this foreign parent, he has the nationality of the latter, he shall be deemed never to have been a Cameroonian.' Section 10 'A new-born child found in Cameroon will be presumed prima facie to have been born in Cameroon.' | | X | | | | X | After age of majority | | X | | Nationality law 12 | No provision |
| 32 | The Americas | Canada | 1978 | | Canadian Citizenship Act, R.S.C., 1985, c. C-29 <http://laws-lois.justice.gc.ca/eng/acts/C-29/page-1.html#h-3A> | Section 4(1) 'For the purposes of paragraph 3(1)(a), every person who, before apparently attaining the age of seven years, was found as a deserted child in Canada shall be deemed to have been born in Canada, unless the contrary is proved within seven years from the date the person was found.' | | | Before apparently attaining the age of seven years | | | X | Seven years from the date found | | | X | No provision | CAN 3(1)a, 3(2) |

(continued)

(continued)

| No | UNHCR region*3 | Country | Party 1961 Conv since | Party ECN since | Citation of the accessible version*4 | Founding provision*5 (full text)*6 | Birth in territory required*7 | New/recent born | Specific older ages | All minors*8 (non-exhaustive) | No explicit age | Loss regulated | No Withdrawal*9 after certain age | Foreign parentage revealed*10 | Foreign nationality revealed*10 | Birth abroad revealed | Otherwise stateless/child of stateless parents provision (art or sec)*11 | 'Unconditional' jus soli (art or sec)*12 |
|---|---|---|---|---|---|---|---|---|---|---|---|---|---|---|---|---|---|---|
| | | | | | | | | Age related | | | | | | Withdrawal related*5 | | | Complementary | |
| 33 | Africa | Central African Republic | | | Law No. 1961.212 stating the Central African Code of Nationality, 21 April 1961 <https://data.globalcit.eu/NationalDB/docs/CAR-Loi-63-406-Code-de-la-Nationalite-1961_ENG.pdf> | Article 10 '[...] However, the child of unknown parents, found in the Central African Republic, is presumed to be born there, unless proven otherwise.' [author translation. Not clear how this provision leads to nationality grant when the Nationality Code does not appear to grant nationality unconditionally by jus soli.] | | | | | X | | | | | | No provision | No provision |
| 34 | Africa | Chad | 1999 | | Ordonnance 33/PG.-INT. du 14 août 1962 code de la nationalité tchadienne, 14 August 1962 [Ordinance 33 / PG.-INT. of 14 August 1962, Chadian Nationality Code, 14 August 1962, Chadian Nationality Code, 14 August 1962] <https://www.refworld.org/docid/492e931b2.html> | Article 11(2) '[Are Chadians...](2)Children born in Chad of unknown parents. However, if their affiliation is subsequently recognized in respect to two foreign parents of the same nationality, they may exercise the option provided for in Article 12 below,' (author translation) Article 12: 'are Chadians children born in Chad to foreign parents; however, if the two ascendants have the same nationality, they may vote for that nationality; this right of option can be exercised only if the legislation of the country whose ancestors are national allows it.' | X | | | | | X (Not loss; parents may vote for foreign nationality) | | | X | | Nationality law 11(1) | Article 12 |
| 35 | The Americas | Chile | 2018 | | | No provision | | | | | | | | | | | No provision | No provision |
| 36 | Asia and the Pacific | China | | | | No provision | | | | | | | | | | | Nationality law 6 | No provision |
| 37 | The Americas | Colombia | 2014 | | | No provision | | | | | | | | | | | Constitution 96(2)a, Nationality law 4–5 | No provision |

(continued)

(continued)

| No | UNHCR region *3 | Country | Party 1961 Conv since | Party ECN since | Citation of the accessible version *4 | Foundling provision *5 (full text) *6 | Age related | | | | | Loss regulated | Withdrawal related *5 | | | | Complementary | |
|---|---|---|---|---|---|---|---|---|---|---|---|---|---|---|---|---|---|---|
| | | | | | | | Birth in territory required *7 | New/recent born | Specific older ages | All minors *8 (non-exhaustive) | No explicit age | | No Withdrawal after certain age *9 | Foreign parentage revealed *10 | Foreign nationality revealed *10 | Birth abroad revealed | Otherwise stateless/child of stateless parents provision (art or sec) *11 | 'Unconditional' jus soli (art or sec) *12 |
| 38 | Africa | Comoros | | | Code de la Nationalité Comorienne,Loi N° 79–12,12 December 1979 [Nationality Code of Comoros] <https://www.refworld.org/docid/4c581c792.html> | Article 13 '[...]A child [l 'enfant trouvé] found in the Comoros is presumed born in the territory, unless there is evidence to the contrary by any means.' (author translation). Not clear how this provision leads to nationality grant when the Nationality Code does not appear to grant nationality unconditionally by jus soli.] | | | | | X | | | | | | No provision | No provision |
| 39 | Africa | Congo (Republic of) | | | Loi n° 35–1961 du 20 juin 1961 portant le Code de la nationalité congolaise, 1 July 1962 [Code of Congolese Nationality] <https://www.refworld.org/docid/3ae6b4db4.html> | Article 9(3) 'The following person is Congolese, [...] (3) A child born in Congo of unknown parents. However, in the latter case, he or she shall be considered never to have been Congolese if during his or her minority his parentage is established with respect to two foreigners and if he or she has in accordance with the national law of one of them a foreign nationality.' (author translation) Article 10 'A new born child found in Congo is presumed until proof is found in Congo to have been born in the Congo.' (author translation) | | X | | | | X | after age of majority | | X | | No provision | No provision |
| 40 | The Americas | Costa Rica | 1977 | | Constitución Política de 7 de Noviembre de 1949 y sus Reformas [Political Constitution of 7 November 1949 and its Reforms] <http://www.tsc.go.cr/pdf/normativa/constitucion.pdf> | Article 13(4) 'They are Costa Rican by birth: [...] (4) An infant, of unknown parents (el infante, padres ignorados), found in Costa Rica.' (author translation) | | | | | X | | | | | | No provision | No provision |
| 41 | Africa | Côte d' Ivoire | 2013 | | | No provision (Note: On 4 October 2019, the Minister of Justice and Human Rights issued a circular authorizing judges to grant nationality to foundlings as in chapter 1.) | | | | | | | | | | | No provision | No provision |

(continued)

(continued)

| No | UNHCR region[3] | Country | Party 1961 Conv since | Party ECN since | Citation of the accessible version[4] | Founding provision[5] (full text)[6] | Age related | | | | | Withdrawal related[5] | | | | | Complementary | |
|---|---|---|---|---|---|---|---|---|---|---|---|---|---|---|---|---|---|---|
| | | | | | | | Birth in territory required[7] | New/ recent born | Specific older ages | All minors[8] (non-exhaustive) | No explicit age | Loss regulated | No With-drawal[9] after certain age | Foreign parentage revealed[10] | Foreign nationality revealed[10] | Birth abroad revealed | Otherwise stateless/ child of stateless parents provision (art or sec)[11] | 'Uncon-ditional' jus soli (art or sec)[12] |
| 42 | Europe | Croatia | 2011 | | Law on Croatian Citizenship (as amended up to 2019) <https://data.globalcit.eu/NationalDB/docs/CRO%20Citizenship%20Act%20ENG.pdf> | Article 7 'A child born or found within the area of the Republic of Croatia, whose both parents are unknown or of unknown citizenship, acquires Croatian citizenship. The child 's Croatian citizenship will cease if by his fourteenth birthday, it is confirmed that both of his parents are foreign citizens.' | | | | | X | X | 14 years of age | X | | | Nationality law 7 | No provision |
| 43 | The Americas | Cuba | | | | No provision | | | | | | | | | | | No provision | Nationality law 3(1)a, 3(2) |
| 44 | Europe | Cyprus | | | | No provision | | | | | | | | | | | No provision | No provision |
| 45 | Europe | Czech Republic | 2001 | 2004 | 186/2013 Act of 11 July 2013 on Citizenship of the Czech Republic and on the amendment of selected other laws (the Czech Citizenship Act) <https://www.mzv.cz/file/2400342/Citizenship_Act_No._186_2013_Sb._o_statnim_obcanstvi_CR.pdf> | Section 10 'A child under three (3) [sic] years of age found on the territory of the Czech Republic, whose identity was not determined, shall acquire the Czech citizenship on the day they were found, unless the authorities disclose, within six months after the child was found, that the child had acquired citizenship of another country. Should the day of finding be in doubt, the day of granting the Czech citizenship to the child shall be determined by the Ministry of the Interior (hereinafter only the "Ministry", sic) pursuant to proceedings initiated by the authorities or upon motion filed by the child's legal representative or legal custodian.' | | | Under three years of age | | | | | | | | Nationality law 5; Nationality law 29 | No provision |

(continued)

(continued)

| No | UNHCR region[3] | Country | Party 1961 Conv since | Party ECN since | Citation of the accessible version [4] | Foundling provision [5] (full text)[6] | Birth in territory required[7] | New/recent born | Specific older ages | All minors[8] (non-exhaustive) | No explicit age | Loss regulated | No Withdrawal[9] after certain age | Foreign parentage revealed [10] | Foreign nationality revealed [10] | Birth abroad revealed | Otherwise stateless/ child of stateless parents provision (art or sec) [11] | 'Unconditional' jus soli (art or sec) [12] |
|---|---|---|---|---|---|---|---|---|---|---|---|---|---|---|---|---|---|---|
| | | | | | | | | | | | | | | | | | **Withdrawal related[5]** → | **Complementary** → |
| 46 | Asia and the Pacific | Democratic People 's Republic of Korea | | | Nationality Law of the Democratic People 's Republic of Korea (DPRK),2 March 2017 <http://www.refworld.org/docid/58d3c5f24.html> | Article 5(4) 'Those to whom the following apply shall acquire the nationality of the Democratic People 's Republic of Korea on account of birth.[...](4)A person, born in the territory of the DPRK, whose parents are unknown at the time of the person's birth.' | X | | | | | | | | | | No provision | Constitution 5(3) |
| 47 | Africa | Democratic Republic of the Congo | | | Loi n° 04/024 du 12 novembre 2004 relative à la nationalité congolaise 78/5000 [Law No. 04/024 of 12 November 2004 on Congolese Nationality] <https://www.refworld.org/docid/4424b6f0224.html> | Section 2(4) 'A newborn child found on the territory of the Democratic Republic of Congo whose parents are unknown; However, he or she shall be deemed not to have been Congolese if, during his or her minority, his or her affiliation is established with respect to a foreigner and if he has, in accordance with the national law of that foreigner 's nationality, the nationality of the latter.' (author translation) | | X | | | | X | Age of majority | | X | | No provision | No provision |
| 48 | Europe | Denmark | 1977 | 2002 | Act on the Acquisition of Danish Nationality, 7 June 2004 <https://www.refworld.org/docid/4e5cf36d2.html> | Section 1(2) 'A child found abandoned in Denmark will, in the absence of evidence to the contrary, be considered a Danish national.' | | | | | X | | | | | | Nationality law 6 | No provision |
| 49 | Africa | Djibouti | | | Code de la Nationalité Djiboutienne [Nationality Code of Djibouti], Loi n°79/AN04/5ème L, 24 October 2004 <https://www.refworld.org/docid/4449fe22e4.html> | Article 6 'Is also Djiboutian, the child born in the Republic of Djibouti whose parents are unknown. He will be deemed never to have been Djiboutian if, before his majority, his filiation comes to be established with respect to a foreign national.' | X | | | | | X | age of majority | X | | | No provision | No provision |
| 50 | The Americas | Dominica | | | | No provision | | | | | | | | | | | No provision | Constitution 98 |
| 51 | The Americas | Dominican Republic | | | | No provision | | | | | | | | | | | No provision | No provision |

(continued)

(continued)

| No | UNHCR region[3] | Country | Party 1961 Conv since | Party ECN since | Citation of the accessible version[4] | Foundling provision[5] (full text)[6] | Age related | | | | | | Withdrawal related[5] | | | | Complementary | |
|----|----|----|----|----|----|----|----|----|----|----|----|----|----|----|----|----|----|----|
| | | | | | | | Birth in territory required[7] | New/ recent born | Specific older ages | All minors[8] (non-exhaustive) | No explicit age | Loss regulated | No Withdrawal[9] after certain age | Foreign parentage revealed [10] | Foreign nationality revealed [10] | Birth abroad revealed | Otherwise stateless/ child of stateless parents provision (art or sec)[11] | 'Unconditional' jus soli (art or sec)[12] |
| 52 | The Americas | Ecuador | 2012 | | | No provision | | | | | | | | | | | No provision | Constitution 7(1) |
| 53 | Middle East and North Africa | Egypt | | | Law # 154 for Year 2004 - Amending Some Provisions of Law No.26 of 1975 Concerning Egyptian Nationality,14 July 2004 <http://www.ref world.org/docid/58fbebc 444.html> | Article 2 'The following shall be Egyptian: (2) Anyone who is born in Egypt from unknown parents. A foundling in Egypt shall be considered born in it unless otherwise established.' | | | | | X | | | | | | No provision | No provision |
| 54 | The Americas | El Salvador | | | | No provision | | | | | | | | | | | No provision | Constitution 90(1) |
| 55 | Africa | Equatorial Guinea | | | | No provision | | | | | | | | | | | No provision | No provision |
| 56 | Africa | Eritrea | | | Eritrean Nationality Proclamation (No. 21/1992),6 April 1992 <http://www.refworld. org/docid/3ae6b4e026. html> | Article 2(3) 'A person born in Eritrea of unknown parents shall be considered an Eritrean national by birth until proven otherwise.' | X | | | | | | | | | | No provision | No provision |
| 57 | Europe | Estonia | | | Citizenship Act (Translation published: 03.02.2016) <https:// www.riigiteataja.ee/en/ eli/503022016004/con solide> | Section 5(2) 'Acquisition of Estonian citizenship by birth) [...] Any child who is found in Estonia and whose parents are unknown is declared by order of the court, at the application of the guardian of the child, to have acquired Estonian citizenship by birth.' (Note: It is assumed the declaration is to confirm automatic acquisition of nationality). | | | | | X | | | | | | Nationality law 13(4)-(6), 36(3) | No provision |

(continued)

(continued)

| No | UNHCR region[3] | Country | Party 1961 Conv since | Party ECN since | Citation of the accessible version[4] | Founding provision[5] (full text)[6] | Age related | | | | | Loss regulated | Withdrawal related[5] | | | | Complementary | |
|---|---|---|---|---|---|---|---|---|---|---|---|---|---|---|---|---|---|---|
| | | | | | | | Birth in territory required[7] | New/ recent born | Specific older ages | All minors[8] (non-exhaustive) | No explicit age | | No With-drawal after certain age[9] | Foreign parentage revealed[10] | Foreign nationality revealed[10] | Birth abroad revealed | Otherwise stateless/ child of stateless parents provision (art or sec)[11] | 'Uncon-ditional' jus soli (art or sec)[12] |
| 58 | Africa | Eswatini (formerly Swaziland) | 1999 | | Constitution of the Kingdom of Swaziland Act 2005 <http://www. refworld.org/docid/4c5 98c72.html> (Confirmed with the Eswatini government web page entitled 'Acquisition of citizenship' on 26 October 2018 <http:// www.gov.sz/index.php? option=com_content& view=article&id=376& Itemid=28> ) | Section 47 'A deserted child of not more than seven years found in Swaziland shall, unless the contrary is proved, be deemed to have been born in Swaziland and shall be treated for the purposes of this Chapter as a citizen by birth.' | | | Not more than seven years | | | | | | | | No provision | No provision |
| 59 | Africa | Ethiopia | | | Proclamation on Ethiopian Nationality, No. 378 of 2003,378/2003.23 December 2003 <http:// www.refworld.org/ docid/409100414.html> | Article 3(2) 'An infant who is found abandoned in Ethiopia shall, unless proved to have a foreign nationality, be deemed to have been born to an Ethiopian parent and shall acquire Ethiopian nationality.' | | | | | X | | | | | | No provision | No provision |
| 60 | Asia and the Pacific | Fiji | | | Citizenship of Fiji Decree 2009, Decree No. 23, 8 July 2009 <http://www.refworld. org/docid/4abc6f2232. html> | Section 7. An infant found abandoned in Fiji is deemed to have been born in Fiji in the absence of proof to the contrary.'(Note: Not clear how the intaraction of this provision with article 6 on nationality grant by jus soli results in nationality grant to abandoned infants.) | | | | | X | | | | | | No provision | No provision |

(continued)

(continued)

| No | UNHCR region [3] | Country | Party 1961 Conv since | Party ECN since | Citation of the accessible version [4] | Foundling provision [5] (full text) [6] | Age related | | | | Withdrawal related [5] | | | | | | Complementary | |
|---|---|---|---|---|---|---|---|---|---|---|---|---|---|---|---|---|---|---|
| | | | | | | | Birth in territory required [7] | New/ recent born | Specific older ages | All minors [8] (non-exhaustive) | No explicit age | Loss regulated | No Withdrawal after certain age [9] | Foreign parentage revealed [10] | Foreign nationality revealed [10] | Birth abroad revealed | Otherwise stateless/ child of stateless parents provision (art or sec) [11] | 'Unconditional' jus soli (art or sec) [12] |
| 61 | Europe | Finland | 2008 | 2008 | Nationality Act, 359/2003, 1 June 2003 <https://www.refworld.org/docid/3aef6b51614.html> | Section 12 'A foundling who is found in Finland is considered to be a Finnish citizen as long as he or she has not been established as a citizen of a foreign State. If the child has been established as a citizen of a foreign State only after he or she has reached the age of five, the child retains Finnish citizenship, however.' | | | | | X | X | Five years of age | | X | | Nationality law 9(1)(4), 12(2) | No provision |
| 62 | Europe | France | | | Civil Code <http://www.fd.ulisboa.pt/wp-content/uploads/2014/12/Codigo-Civil-Frances-French-Civil-Code-english-version.pdf> Checked against the original Code civil Version consolidée au 21 juillet 2019 [Consolidated version as of 2 July 2019] <https://www.legifrance.gouv.fr/affichCode.do?cidTexte=LEGITEXT000006070721 (Last accessed 2 August 2019) | Article 19, together with Articles 19-2 and 58. Article 19 states: 'Is French a child born in France of unknown parents. He shall however be deemed to have never been French if, during his minority, his parentage is established regards an alien and if, under the national law of his parent, he has the nationality of the latter.' Article 19-2 'Shall be presumed born in France a child whose record of birth was drawn up in accordance with Article 58 of this Code.' Article 58 states 'A person who may have found a new-born child is required to make declaration of it to the officer of civil status of the place of discovery [...].' | | X | | | | X | Age of majority | | X | | Nationality law 19-1 | No provision |

(continued)

(continued)

| No | UNHCR region [3] | Country | Party 1961 Conv since | Party ECN since | Citation of the accessible version [4] | Foundling provision [5] (full text) [6] | Birth in territory required [7] | New/recent born | Specific older ages | All minors [8] (non-exhaustive) | No explicit age | Loss regulated | No withdrawal [9] after certain age | Foreign parentage revealed [10] | Foreign nationality revealed [10] | Birth abroad revealed | Otherwise stateless/child of stateless parents provision (art or sec) [11] | 'Unconditional' jus soli (art or sec) [12] |
|---|---|---|---|---|---|---|---|---|---|---|---|---|---|---|---|---|---|---|
| 63 | Africa | Gabon | | | Loi n°37–1998, Code de la nationalité [Law No. 37–1998, Nationality Code], 20 July 1999 <http://citizenshiprightsafrica.org/wp-content/uploads/1999/07/Gabon-Code-de-la-nationalit%C3%A9-Loi-n%C2%A0B037-1998.pdf> | Article 11, 12 'Art.11.- Possesses Gabonese nationality in nationality of origin: [...] A child born in Gabon to unknown or stateless parents. However, this child will be considered never to have been Gabonese if, during his minority, his parentage is established with respect to foreign parents.' 'Art.12.- The newborn child, found at Gabon, presumed until proof of contrary, to be born in Gabon.' (author translation) | | X | | | | X | age of majority | X | | | Nationality law 11 | No provision |
| 64 | Africa | Gambia (Republic of The) | 2014 | | | No provision | | | | | | | | | | | No provision | No provision |
| 65 | Europe | Georgia | 2014 | | Georgia: Organic Law on Georgian Citizenship (As Amended in 2014), 30 April 2014 <https://www.refworld.org/docid/53835fe14.html> | Article 11 'A minor who is living in Georgia and whose both parents are unknown shall be deemed to be a Georgian citizen unless proved otherwise.' (Note: Article 2(e) provides 'minor – a person under the age of 18, except for the person who got married before the age of 18.') | | | | X | | | | | | | Nationality law 13 | No provision |
| 66 | Europe | Germany | 1977 | 2005 | The Nationality Act of Germany 1913 <https://germanlawarchive.ius comp.org/?p=266> | Section 4(2) 'A child which is found on German territory (foundling [Findelkind]) shall be deemed to be the child of a German until otherwise proven. The first sentence shall apply mutatis mutandis to a child born to a mother under condition of anonymity in accordance with Sect. 25 (1) of the Act to Prevent and Resolve Conflicts in Pregnancy (Schwangerschaftskonfliktgesetzes ie SchKG).' | | | | | X | | | | | | 2 Act on Reduction Statelessness 1977 | No provision |

(continued)

(continued)

| No | UNHCR region *3 | Country | Party 1961 Conv since | Party ECN since | Citation of the accessible version *4 | Foundling provision *5 (full text) *6 | Birth in territory required *7 | New/recent born | Specific older ages | All minors *8 (non-exhaustive) | No explicit age | Loss regulated | No With-drawal *9 after certain age | Foreign parentage revealed *10 | Foreign nationality revealed *10 | Birth abroad revealed | Otherwise stateless/ child of stateless parents provision (art or sec) *11 | 'Uncon-ditional' jus soli (art or sec) *12 |
|---|---|---|---|---|---|---|---|---|---|---|---|---|---|---|---|---|---|---|
| | | | | | | | | | | | | | | | | | Otherwise stateless... | 'Unconditional' jus soli |
| 67 | Africa | Ghana | | | Citizenship Act of 2000, 29 December 2000 <https://data.globalcit. eu/NationalDB/docs/ Ghana_Citizenship_ Act_with_forms_591_ ISH%50_1.pdf> | Section 8 'A child of not more than seven years of age found in Ghana whose parents are not known shall be presumed to be a citizen of Ghana by birth.' | | | Not more than seven years of age | | | | | | | | No provision | No provision |
| 68 | Europe | Greece | | | | No provision | | | | | | | | | | | Nationality law 1(2) | No provision |
| 69 | The Americas | Grenada | | | | No provision | | | | | | | | | | | No provision | Constitution 96 |
| 70 | The Americas | Guatemala | 2001 | | | No provision | | | | | | | | | | | No provision | Constitution 144 |
| 71 | Africa | Guinea | 2014 | | Code civil, 16 February 1983 <http://www.ref world.org/docid/3ae6b4 e88.html> | Article 34 'A child born in Guinea of unknown parents is a Guinean However, he shall be deemed never to have been Guinean if, during his minority, his affiliation is established with respect to a foreigner and if he has, in accordance with the national law of that alien, the nationality of the said foreigner.' Article 35 'A newborn child found in Guinea is presumed, until proven otherwise, to have been born in Guinea.' (author translation) | | X | | | | X | Age of majority | | X | | No provision | No provision |

(continued)

(continued)

| No | UNHCR region [3] | Country | Party 1961 Conv since | Party ECN since | Citation of the accessible version [4] | Foundling provision [5] (full text) [6] | Birth in territory required [7] | New/ recent born | Specific older ages | All minors [8] (non-exhaustive) | No explicit age | Loss regulated | No Withdrawal [9] after certain age | Foreign parentage revealed [10] | Foreign nationality revealed [10] | Birth abroad revealed | Otherwise stateless/ child of stateless parents provision (art or sec) [11] | 'Unconditional' jus soli (art or sec) [12] |
|---|---|---|---|---|---|---|---|---|---|---|---|---|---|---|---|---|---|---|
| | | | | | | | Age related | | | | | | Withdrawal related [5] | | | | Complementary | |
| 72 | Africa | Guinea Bissau | 2016 | | Lei n.° 2/92 De 6 de Abril Lei da Cidadania [Citizenship Law], 6 April 1992 <http://citizenshiprightsafrica.org/wp-content/uploads/1992/04/Guinea-Bissau-Lei_da_nacionalidade_1992.pdf> | Article 5(2) 'It is assumed citizen Guinean origin, unless evidence to the contrary, a newborn exposed (exposto) in the territory of Guinea-Bissau.' | | X | | | | | | | | | Nationality law 5(1)(c)-(d) | No provision |
| 73 | The Americas | Guyana | | | Guyana Citizenship Act, Cap. 14:01, 26 May 1966 <http://www.refworld.org/docid/538e24c34.html> | Section 8(2) 'Where after the commencement of this Act a new-born infant is found abandoned in Guyana, that infant shall, unless the contrary is shown, be deemed to have been born in Guyana.' [Constitution 43 provides for unconditional jus soli grant of nationality.] | | X | | | | | | | | | No provision | Const 43 |
| 74 | The Americas | Haiti | 2018 | | Décret du 6 Novembre 1984 sur la Nationalité Haïtienne [Decree of 6 November 1984 on the Haitian Nationality] <https://data.globalcit.eu/NationalIDB/docs/HAI_1984%20D ecree%20Original%20Language).pdf> | Article 4 'Anyone born in Haiti, of unknown father or mother [...] acquires Haitian nationality by virtue of the declaration of birth made to the Office of the State Registrar Nevertheless, he shall be deemed to have acquired Haitian nationality if, before his majority, it is established that his father and mother or one of them are of foreign nationality and neither one descends from black race.' (author translation) (It is unclear whether the nationality acquisition is automatic.) | X | | | | | X | Age of majority | X (Note: '[...] and neither one descends from black race.') | | | Nationality law 4 | No provision |

(continued)

(continued)

| No | UNHCR region *3 | Country | Party 1961 Conv since | Party ECN since | Citation of the accessible version *4 | Founding provision *5 (full text) *6 | Birth in territory required *7 | New/recent born | Specific older ages | All minors *8 (non-exhaustive) | No explicit age | Loss regulated | No Withdrawal *9 after certain age | Foreign parentage revealed *10 | Foreign nationality revealed *10 | Birth abroad revealed | Otherwise stateless/child of stateless parents provision (art or sec) *11 | 'Unconditional' jus soli (art or sec) *12 |
|---|---|---|---|---|---|---|---|---|---|---|---|---|---|---|---|---|---|---|
| | | | | | | | | | | | | | | | | | Otherwise stateless (Complementary) | Unconditional jus soli (Complementary) |
| 75 | The Americas | Honduras | 2012 | | Constitución de la República de Honduras [Constitution of the Republic of Honduras], 20 January 1982 <https://www.refworld.org/docid/3dbe718c4.html> | Article 23 'They are Hondurans by birth: [...] (4) An infant (infante) of unknown parents found in the territory of Honduras.' (author translation) | | | | | X | | | | | | Nationality law 54 | Const 23(1) |
| 76 | Europe | Hungary | 2009 | 2001 | Act LV of 1993 on Hungarian Citizenship, 1 October 1993 <http://www.refworld.org/docid/3ae6b4e6c30.html> | Article 3(3)(b) 'Until proven to the contrary, the following persons shall be recognized as Hungarian citizens [...] children born of unknown parents and found in Hungary.' | | | | X (See sec 6.3.4 of the book) | | | | | | | No provision | No provision |
| 77 | Europe | Iceland | | 2003 | Icelandic Nationality Act No. 100/1952 (23 December) <https://data.globalcit.eu/NationalDB/docs/ICE%20Act%20100_1952_consolidated%20amendded%20as%20amended%20by%20act%20consolidated%201952_c%202040_2012_ENGLISH.pdf> | Article 1(3) '[…] A child found abandoned in Iceland shall, in the absence of proof to the contrary, be considered an Icelandic citizen.' | | | | | X | | | | | | Nationality law 10 | No provision |
| 78 | Asia and the Pacific | India | | | | No provision | | | | | | | | | | | No provision | No provision |

(continued)

(continued)

| No | UNHCR region *3 | Country | Party 1961 Conv since | Party ECN since | Citation of the accessible version *4 | Foundling provision *5 (full text) *6 | Birth in territory required*7 | New/recent born | Specific older ages | All minors *8 (non-exhaustive) | No explicit age | Loss regulated | No With-drawal after certain age *9 | Foreign parentage revealed *10 | Foreign nationality revealed *10 | Birth abroad revealed | Otherwise stateless/ child of stateless parents provision (art or sec) *11 | 'Unconditional' jus soli (art or sec) *12 |
|---|---|---|---|---|---|---|---|---|---|---|---|---|---|---|---|---|---|---|
| 79 | Asia and the Pacific | Indonesia | | | Law of the Republic of Indonesia No. 12 on Citizenship of the Republic of Indonesia, 1 August 2006 <http://www.refworld.org/docid/4538aae64.html> | Article 4 (10) 'A Citizen of the Rep. of Indonesia is[...](10)Children newly born and found in Indonesian territory and whose parent's [sic] are undetermined;' Article 4 (11) 'Children born in Indonesian territory whom at the time of birth both parents [...] whereabouts are undetermined.' | | X | | | | | | | | | Nationality law 4(9) and 4(11) | No provision |
| 80 | Asia and the Pacific | Iran | | | Iranian Civil Code <https://data.globalcit.eu/NationalDB/docs/Iranian%20Civil%20Code%20EN.pdf> | Article 976 'The following persons are considered to be Iranian subjects [...] 3 - Those born in Iran of unknown parentage.' | X | | | | | | | | | | No provision | No provision |
| 81 | Middle East and North Africa | Iraq | | | Iraqi Nationality Law,Law 26 of 2006,7 March 2006 <http://www.refworld.org/docid/4b1e364e2.html> | Article 3 'A person shall be considered Iraqi if: [...](b) he/ she is born in Iraq to unknown parents. A foundling found in Iraq shall, in the absence of proof to the contrary, be considered to have been born therein.' | | | | | X | | | | | | No provision | No provision |
| 82 | Europe | Ireland | 1973 | | Irish Nationality and Citizenship Act 1956 (As Amended in 2011) <https://www.refworld.org/topic,50ffbce52 4d,50ffbce525c,3ae6b4 ebc,0,,LEGISLATI ON,IRL.html> | Section 10 'Every deserted newborn child first found in the State shall, unless the contrary is proved, be deemed to have been born in the island of Ireland to parents at least one of whom is an Irish citizen.' | | X | | | | | | | | | Nationality law 6(3) | No provision |

(continued)

(continued)

| No | UNHCR region *3 | Country | Party 1961 Conv since | Party ECN since | Citation of the accessible version *4 | Foundling provision *5 (full text) *6 | Age related | | | | | Withdrawal related *5 | | | | | Complementary | |
|---|---|---|---|---|---|---|---|---|---|---|---|---|---|---|---|---|---|---|
| | | | | | | | Birth in territory required *7 | New/ recent born | Specific older ages | All minors *8 (non-exhaustive) | No explicit age | Loss regulated | No Withdrawal *9 after certain age | Foreign parentage revealed *10 | Foreign nationality revealed *10 | Birth abroad revealed | Otherwise stateless/ child of stateless parents provision (art or sec) *11 | 'Unconditional' jus soli (art or sec) *12 |
| | | | | | | | | | | | | | | | | | No provision | |
| 83 | Middle East and North Africa | Israel | | | Israel Nationality Law 1952 Consolidated translation (as amended up to 1971) <https://data.globalcit.eu/NationalDB/docs/Isreal%20Nationality%20(amended).pdf> | Section 9 (a) 'Where a minor, not being an Israel national, is an inhabitant of Israel, and his parents are not in Israel or have died or are unknown, the Minister of the Interior, on such conditions and with effect from such day as he may think fit, may grant him Israel nationality by the issue of a certificate of naturalisation.' (Note 1: This provision provides for non-automatic acquisition, that is naturalization. Note 2: Sect. 13 provides 'In this Law - "minor" means a person under eighteen years of age.') | | | | X | | | | | | | Nationality law 4A | No provision |
| 84 | Europe | Italy | 2015 | | Legge n. 91, 5 febbraio 1992, Nuove norme sulla cittadinanza [Law 5 February 1992 No. 91, New provisions on citizenship] <http://www.refworld.org/docid/3ae6b4edc.html> | Article 1(1)(b) and article 1(2) 'The following shall be citizens by birth: [...] (b) (A son or daughter) who was born in the territory of the Republic both of whose parents are unknown [...] 2. A son or daughter (figlio) found in the territory of the Republic whose parents are unknown shall be considered citizens by birth in the absence of proof of their possession of any other citizenship.' [Modification of the translation by author] | | | | | X | | | | | | Nationality law 1(1)(b) | |
| 85 | The Americas | Jamaica | 2013 | | | No provision | | | | | | | | | | | | No provision | Constitution 3B |

(continued)

(continued)

| No | UNHCR region [3] | Country | Party 1961 Conv since | Party ECN since | Citation of the accessible version [4] | Foundling provision [5] (full text) [6] | Age related | | | | No explicit age | Loss regulated | Withdrawal related [5] | | | | Complementary | |
|---|---|---|---|---|---|---|---|---|---|---|---|---|---|---|---|---|---|---|
| | | | | | | | Birth in territory required [7] | New/recent born | Specific older ages | All minors [8] (non-exhaustive) | | | No Withdrawal after certain age [9] | Foreign parentage revealed [10] | Foreign nationality revealed [10] | Birth abroad revealed | Otherwise stateless/ child of stateless parents provision (art or sec) [11] | 'Unconditional' jus soli (art or sec) [12] |
| 86 | Asia and the Pacific | Japan | | | Nationality Law, Law No.147 of 1950 <http://www.moj.go.jp/ENGLISH/information/tnl-01.html> | Article 2(iii) 'A child shall, in any of the following cases, be a Japanese national: [...] (iii) When both parents are unknown [...] in a case where the child is born in Japan.' (Note: While article 2(iii) of Nationality Act itself requires birth in Japan, under article 57 of the Family Register Act, 'abandoned children' found in the territory are registered their birth in Japan and therefore acquires Japanese nationality under article 2(iii). In this case their birth in the territory is presumed. See Sect. 6.4.) | X (With Family Register Act article 57, in-country birth can be presumed) | | | | | | | | | | Nationality law 2(3); 8(4) | No provision |
| 87 | Middle East and North Africa | Jordan | | | Law No. 6 of 1954 on Nationality, 1 January 1954 <http://www.refworld.org/docid/3ae6b4ea13.html> | Article 3 'The following shall be deemed to be Jordanian nationals:[...] (5)Any person born in the Hashemite Kingdom of Jordan of unknown parents, as a foundling in the Kingdom shall be considered born in the Kingdom pending evidence to the contrary.' | | | | | X | | | | | | No provision | No provision |
| 88 | Asia and the Pacific | Kazakhstan | | | Law No. 1017-XII of 20 December 1991 of the Republic of Kazakhstan, On Citizenship of the Republic of Kazakhstan <http://www.refworld.org/docid/3ae6b56a14.html> | Article 13 'The child who is in the territory of the Republic of Kazakhstan whose both parents are unknown is a citizen of the Republic of Kazakhstan.' | | | | See sec 6.3.4 of the book | X | | | | | | Nationality law 14 | No provision |
| 89 | Africa | Kenya | | | The Constitution of Kenya, 27 August 2010 <http://www.refworld.org/docid/4c8508822.html> | Article 14(4) 'A child found in Kenya who is, or appears to be, less than eight years of age, and whose nationality and parents are not known, is presumed to be a citizen by birth.' | | | (appears to be) less than eight years of age | | | | | | | | No provision | No provision |

(continued)

(continued)

| No | UNHCR region [3] | Country | Party 1961 Conv since | Party ECN since | Citation of the accessible version [4] | Foundling provision [5] (full text) [6] | Birth in territory required [7] | New/recent born | Specific older ages | All minors [8] (non-exhaustive) | No explicit age | Loss regulated | No Withdrawal [9] after certain age | Foreign parentage revealed [10] | Foreign nationality revealed [10] | Birth abroad revealed | Otherwise stateless/ child of stateless parents provision (art or sec) [11] | 'Unconditional' jus soli (art or sec) [12] |
|---|---|---|---|---|---|---|---|---|---|---|---|---|---|---|---|---|---|---|
| 90 | Asia and the Pacific | Kiribati | 1983 | | | No provision | | | | | | | | | | | No provision | Constitution 25(1) |
| 91 | Middle East and North Africa | Kuwait | | | Nationality Law, 1959 <http://www.refworld.org/docid/3ae6b4ef1c.html> | Article 3 'Kuwaiti nationality is acquired by any person born in Kuwait whose parents are unknown.. A foundling is deemed to have been born in Kuwait unless the contrary is proved.' | | | | | X | | | | | | No provision | No provision |
| 92 | Asia and the Pacific | Kyrgyzstan | | | Law of the Kyrgyz Republic on Citizenship of the Kyrgyz Republic, 21 March 2007 <http://www.refworld.org/docid/46f93a5e514f.html> | Article 12(5) 'A child located on the territory of the Kyrgyz Republic, both of parents of who are unknown, is a citizen of the Kyrgyz Republic.' Article 3 (entitled 'Main definitions') says 'a child is a person at the age of up to 18 years old.' | | | | X | | | | | | | Nationality law 12 | No provision |
| 93 | Asia and the Pacific | Lao People's Democratic Republic | | | Law on Lao Nationality 2004 No. 5/NA <https://data.globalcit.eu/NationalDB/docs/Laos_%20Nationality%20Act_2004_ENGLISH.pdf> | Article 13 'Children found in the territory of the Lao People's Democratic Republic and whose parents' identity is unknown will be considered Lao citizens. In the event that, while such children are still under eighteen years of age, evidence [is found that] demonstrates that their parents are foreign citizens they will be considered foreign citizens from birth.' | | | | | X | X | 18 years of age | X | | | Nationality law 12 | No provision |

(continued)

(continued)

| No | UNHCR region *3 | Country | Party 1961 Conv since | Party ECN since | Citation of the accessible version *4 | Founding provision *5 (full text) *6 | Birth in territory required *7 | New/ recent born | Specific older ages | All minors *8 (non-exhaustive) | No explicit age | Loss regulated | No withdrawal after certain age | With-drawal *9 after certain age | Foreign parentage revealed *10 | Foreign nationality revealed *10 | Birth abroad revealed | Otherwise stateless/ child of stateless parents provision (art or sec) *11 | 'Unconditional' jus soli (art or sec) *12 |
|---|---|---|---|---|---|---|---|---|---|---|---|---|---|---|---|---|---|---|---|
| | | | | | | | | | | | **Age related** | | | | **Withdrawal related*5** | | | | **Complementary** |
| 94 | Europe | Latvia | 1992 | | Law on Citizenship 1994 (as amended up to 2013) <https://likumi.lv/ta/en/en/id/57512-citizenship-law> | Section 2 (1) 5: 'A Latvian citizen is: [...] 5) a child who has been found in the territory of Latvia and whose parents are unknown [...]; (Note: Sect. 2 (2) provides 'The volition to register a child as a Latvian citizen in accordance with Paragraph one of this Section shall be expressed by: 1) the lawful representative of the child, if the child has not reached the age of 15 years; 2) the child himself or herself between 15 to 18 years of age.') | | | | X (See sec 6.3.4 of the book) | | | | | | | | Nationality law 3(1); Nationality law 3(2)–3(5) | No provision |
| 95 | Middle East and North Africa | Lebanon | | | Decree No15 on Lebanese Nationality including Amendments, 19 January 1925 <http://www.refworld.org/docid/44a24c6c4.html> | Article 1 'Every person born in the Greater Lebanon territory of unknown parents or parents of unknown nationality.' | X | | | | | | | | | | | Nationality law 1 | |
| 96 | Africa | Lesotho | 2004 | | | No provision | | | | | | | | | | | | Constitution 38(3) | Constitution 38(1)–(2) |
| 97 | Africa | Liberia | 2004 | | | No provision | | | | | | | | | | | | No provision | No provision |
| 98 | Middle East and North Africa | Libya | 1989 | | Law Number (24) for 2010/1378 on the Libyan Nationality, 28 May 2010 <http://www.refworld.org/docid/4e2d8bf52.html> | Section 3 'Is a Libyan: [...] Everyone born in Libya [...]his/her parents are unknown.' | X | | | | | | | | | | | No provision | No provision |

(continued)

(continued)

| No | UNHCR region[3] | Country | Party 1961 Conv since | Party ECN since | Citation of the accessible version[4] | Foundling provision[5] (full text)[6] | Age related | | | | | Loss regulated | Withdrawal related[5] | | | | Complementary | |
|---|---|---|---|---|---|---|---|---|---|---|---|---|---|---|---|---|---|---|
| | | | | | | | Birth in territory required[7] | New/recent born | Specific older ages | All minors[8] (non-exhaustive) | No explicit age | | No withdrawal after certain age[9] | Foreign parentage revealed[10] | Foreign nationality revealed[10] | Birth abroad revealed | Otherwise stateless/ child of stateless parents provision (art or sec)[11] | 'Unconditional' jus soli (art or sec)[12] |
| 99 | Europe | Liechtenstein | 2009 | | Gesetz vom 4. Januar 1934 über den Erwerb und Verlust des Landesbürgerrechtes [Law of 4 January 1934 on the acquisition and loss of citizenship] (Bürgerrechtsgesetz) <http://www.refworld.org/docid/4e65e4352.html> | Section 3(a)(3) 'Citizenship is aquired: (a)by law if: [...] (3)a child is found of unknown origins (founding [Findelkind]);.' | | | | | X | | | | | | Nationality law 5b | No provision |
| 100 | Europe | Lithuania | 2013 | | Law on Citizenship of the Republic of Lithuania, 12 February 2010 <https://e-seimas.lrs.lt/portal/legalAct/lt/TAD/TAIS.395555> | Article 16 'A child found or living in the territory of the Republic of Lithuania, whose parents are unknown, are considered to have been born in the territory of the Republic of Lithuania and acquire citizenship of the Republic of Lithuania if it is not evident that the child has acquired the citizenship of another state or the circumstances in which the child would acquire the citizenship of another state. [...].' | | | | See sec 6.3.4 of the book | X | | | | | | Nationality law 15 | No provision |
| 101 | Europe | Luxembourg | 2017 | 2017 | Luxembourg Nationality Law, 8 March 2017 <http://legilux.public.lu/eli/etat/leg/loi/2017/03/08/a28 9/jo> | Article 5 'Is Luxembourgish: [...] 3° a minor born in the Grand Duchy of Luxembourg of legally unknown parents; a minor [le mineur] found on Luxembourg territory is presumed, until proof to the contrary, to have been born in the territory.' (author translation) | | | | X | | | | | | | Nationality law 1(3) | No provision |

(continued)

(continued)

| No | UNHCR region[3] | Country | Party 1961 Conv since | Party ECN since | Citation of the accessible version[4] | Founding provision[5] (full text)[6] | Age related | | | | | Loss regulated | Withdrawal related[5] | | | | Complementary | |
|---|---|---|---|---|---|---|---|---|---|---|---|---|---|---|---|---|---|---|
| | | | | | | | Birth in territory required[7] | New/ recent born | Specific older ages | All minors[8] (non-exhaustive) | No explicit age | | No With-drawal[9] after certain age | Foreign parentage revealed[10] | Foreign nationality revealed[10] | Birth abroad revealed | Otherwise stateless/ child of stateless parents provision (art or sec)[11] | "Unconditional" jus soli (art or sec)[12] |
| 102 | Africa | Madagascar | | | Loi n°2016–038 modifiant et complétant certaines dispositions de l'Ordonnance n° 60–064 du 22 juillet 1960 portant Code de la nationalité malagasy, 15 December 2016 [Law No. 2016–038 amending and supplementing certain provisions of Ordinance No. 60–064 of 22 July 1960 on the Malagasy Nationality Code, 15 December 2016] <http://citizenshiprigh tsafrica.org/wp-content/ uploads/2017/02/Mad agascar-Loi-n2016-038. pdf> | Article 11 'A child born in Madagascar of unknown parents, for whom it can be presumed that at least one of the parents is Malagasy, is a Malagasy national. The following may be taken into consideration: the name of the child, his physical characteristics, the personality of those who raise him and the conditions in which he came into their hands, the education he receives, the environment in which he lives. However, the child will be considered never to have been Malagasy if, during his or her minority, his or her filiation is established with respect to a foreigner. A child found in Madagascar is presumed, until proven otherwise, to have been born there.' (author translation) | | | | | X | X | X | X | | | No provision | No provision |
| 103 | Africa | Malawi | | | | No provision | | | | | | | | | | | Nationality law 18 | No provision |
| 104 | Asia and the Pacific | Malaysia | | | | No provision | | | | | | | | | | | Constitution 14(1)b, Second Schedule Part II, (1)c, 2 | No provision |
| 105 | Asia and the Pacific | Maldives | | | | No provision | | | | | | | | | | | No provision | No provision |

(continued)

(continued)

| No | UNHCR region *3 | Country | Party 1961 Conv since | Party ECN since | Citation of the accessible version *4 | Foundling provision *5 (full text) *6 | Age related | | | | | Loss regulated | Withdrawal related *5 | | | | Complementary | |
|---|---|---|---|---|---|---|---|---|---|---|---|---|---|---|---|---|---|---|
| | | | | | | | Birth in territory required *7 | New/recent born | Specific older ages | All minors *8 (non-exhaustive) | No explicit age | | No Withdrawal *9 after certain age | Foreign parentage revealed *10 | Foreign nationality revealed *10 | Birth abroad revealed | Otherwise stateless/ child of stateless parents provision (art or sec) *11 | "Unconditional" jus soli (art or sec) *12 |
| 106 | Africa | Mali | 2016 | | Code des Personnes et de la Famille [Persons and Family Code], Law No. 2011–087 of December 30, 2011 on the <http://citizenshiprightsafrica.org/wp-content/uploads/2016/02/Mali-Code-des-personnes-et-de-la-famille-30-Dec-2011.pdf> | Article 225 'A child born in Mali of unknown parents is Malian. He retains Malian nationality even if, during his minority, his affiliation is established with respect to a foreigner and if he has, in accordance with the national law of that foreigner, the nationality of that foreigner. However, he has the right to repudiate the Malian nationality by the forms of right within the six months following his majority.' Article 226: 'A newborn child found in Mali is presumed to be born in Mali until proven otherwise.' (author translation) | | X | | | | X (Note: Only repudiation foreseen) | | | | | No provision | No provision |
| 107 | Europe | Malta | | | Maltese Citizenship Act 1965 (as amended up to 2020) <https://legislation.mt/eli/cap/188/eng/pdf> | Article 17(3) 'Where after the commencement of this Act a newborn infant is found abandoned in any place in Malta, that infant shall, unless the contrary is shown, be deemed to have been born in Malta and in any such case the provisions of the third proviso to article 5(1) shall apply to such infant.' Article 5(1) 'any such infant shall remain a citizen of Malta until his right to any other citizenship is established.' | | X | | | | X | | | X (Unclear if 'right' to another nationality is sufficient.) | | Nationality law 10(6)–(7) | No provision |
| 108 | Asia and the Pacific | Marshall Islands | | | | No provision | | | | | | | | | | | Constitution X. 1(2)(b) | No provision |

(continued)

(continued)

| No | UNHCR region [3] | Country | Party 1961 Conv since | Party ECN since | Citation of the accessible version [4] | Founding provision [5] (full text) [6] | Age related | | | | | Loss regulated | Withdrawal related [5] | | | | Complementary | |
|---|---|---|---|---|---|---|---|---|---|---|---|---|---|---|---|---|---|---|
| | | | | | | | Birth in territory required [7] | New/recent born | Specific older ages | All minors [8] (non-exhaustive) | No explicit age | | No Withdrawal [9] after certain age | Foreign parentage revealed [10] | Foreign nationality revealed [10] | Birth abroad revealed | Otherwise stateless/child of stateless parents provision (art or sec) [11] | 'Unconditional' jus soli (art or sec) [12] |
| 109 | Middle East and North Africa | Mauritania | | | Loi N° 1961–112, Loi portant code de la nationalité mauritanienne, 13 June 1961 [Law No. 1961–112, Law on the Mauritanian Nationality Code, 13 June 1961] <https://www.refworld.org/docid/3ae6b5304.html> | Article 10 'A newborn child found in Mauritania and whose parents are unknown is a Mauritanian. He ceases, however, to be Mauritanian if, during his minority, his affiliation is established with respect to a foreigner and if the has, in accordance with the national law of that foreigner, the nationality of the latter.' (author translation) | | X | | | | X | Age of majority | | X | | No provision | No provision |
| 110 | Africa | Mauritius | | | Citizenship Act 1968, RL 3/585, 14 December 1968 <http://www.refworld.org/docid/4c592d0e2.html> | Section 2(2)(e) '(e) a new born child found abandoned within Mauritius shall, unless the contrary is shown, be deemed to have been born within Mauritius.' (Note: Not clear how this provision leads to acquisition of nationality as unconditional jus soli provision in the Constitution has reportedly been removed) | | X | | | | | | | | | No provision | No provision |
| 111 | The Americas | Mexico | | | Ley de Nacionalidad, Nueva Ley publicada en el Diario Oficial de la Federación el 23 de enero de 1998 [Nationality Law, new law published in the official report of the federation on 23 January 1998] <http://www.diputados.gob.mx/LeyesBiblio/pdf/53.pdf> | Article 7 'Unless the contrary is proven, an exposed child (niño expósito) found in the national territory is presumed that he has been born in the territory and that he or she is a son or daughter (hijo) of a Mexican father and a mother.' (author translation) | | | | | X | | | | | | No provision | Const 30A(1) |
| 112 | Asia and the Pacific | Micronesia (Federated States of) | | | | No provision | | | | | | | | | | | No provision | No provision |

(continued)

(continued)

| No | UNHCR region *3 | Country | Party 1961 Conv since | Party ECN since | Citation of the accessible version *4 | Foundling provision *5 (full text) *6 | Age related | | | | No explicit age | Loss regulated | Withdrawal related*5 | | | | Complementary | |
|---|---|---|---|---|---|---|---|---|---|---|---|---|---|---|---|---|---|---|
| | | | | | | | Birth in territory required*7 | New/recent born | Specific older ages | All minors *8 (non-exhaustive) | | | No withdrawal*9 after certain age | Foreign parentage revealed *10 | Foreign nationality revealed *10 | Birth abroad revealed | Otherwise stateless/ child of stateless parents provision (art or sec) *11 | 'Unconditional' jus soli (art or sec)*12 |
| 113 | Europe | Monaco | | | Loi n° 1.387 du 19 décembre 2011 modifiant la loi n° 1.155 du 18 décembre 1992 relative à la nationalité [Law No. 1.387 of 19 December 2011 amending Law No. 1.155 of 18 December 1992 on nationality],19 December 2011, available at: <http://www.refworld.org/docid/4f2143a72.html> | Article 1(6) 'Anyone born in Monaco of unknown parents is Monacan.' | X | | | | | | | | | | No provision | No provision |
| 114 | Asia and the Pacific | Mongolia | | | Law of Mongolia on Citizenship,5 June 1995 <http://www.refworld.org/docid/4aa7dec62.html> | Article 7(4) 'A child who is within the territory of Mongolia whose parents are not identified shall be Mongolian citizen.' | | | | | X | | | | | | Nationality law 7(5) | No provision |
| 115 | Europe | Montenegro | 2013 | 2010 | Law on Montenegrin Citizenship Consolidated translation (Official Gazette of Montenegro 013/08 of 26 February 2008, as amended up to 2016) <https://data.globalcit.eu/NationalDB/docs/Law%20on%20Montenegrin%20Citizenship%20(consolidated%202016)%20EN.pdf> | Article 7 'A child born or found on the territory of Montenegro shall acquire Montenegrin citizenship if both parents are unknown [...]. 'The Montenegrin citizenship of a child referred to in paragraph 1 of this Article may be lost if it should be established, before he or she turns 18 years of age, that his or her parents are citizens of another state, or that he or she acquired, on whatever basis, citizenship of another state.The Montenegrin citizenship of a child referred to in paragraph 2 of this Article shall be lost based upon the request of his or her parents on the day the decision is delivered to them; if the child is over 14 years of age, his or her consent shall be necessary.' | | | | | X | X | 18 years of age | X | | | Nationality law 7 | No provision |

(continued)

(continued)

| No | UNHCR region *3 | Country | Party 1961 Conv since | Party ECN since | Citation of the accessible version *4 | Foundling provision *5 (full text) *6 | Age related Birth in territory required *7 | New/recent born | Specific older ages | All minors *8 (non-exhaustive) | Withdrawal related *5 No explicit age | Loss regulated | No Withdrawal *9 after certain age | Foreign parentage revealed *10 | Foreign nationality revealed *10 | Birth abroad revealed | Complementary Otherwise stateless/ child of stateless parents provision (art or sec) *11 | 'Unconditional' jus soli (art or sec) *12 |
|---|---|---|---|---|---|---|---|---|---|---|---|---|---|---|---|---|---|---|
| 116 | Middle East and North Africa | Morocco | | | Code de la nationalité marocaine [Moroccan Nationality Code] 32/5000 (2011), Dahir n. 1–58–250 du 21 safar 1378, 6 September 1958 <https://www.ref world.org/docid/5011c9 822.html> | Article 7 'A child born in Morocco of unknown parents is Moroccan. However, a child born in Morocco of unknown parents shall be deemed never to have been a Moroccan if, during his or her minority, his or her filiation is established with respect to a foreigner, and if he has, in accordance with the law nationality of that foreigner, the nationality of the latter. A child of unknown parents found in Morocco is presumed, until proven otherwise, born in Morocco.' (author translation) | | | | | X | X | age of majority | | X | | No provision | No provision |
| 117 | Africa | Mozambique | 2014 | | | No provision | | | | | | | | | | | Constitution 23(1)(b) | Constitution 24 |
| 118 | Asia and the Pacific | Myanmar | | | | No provision | | | | | | | | | | | No provision | No provision |
| 119 | Africa | Namibia | | | | No provision | | | | | | | | | | | Constitution 4(1)(d) | No provision |
| 120 | Asia and the Pacific | Nauru | | | | No provision | | | | | | | | | | | Constitution 73 | No provision |
| 121 | Asia and the Pacific | Nepal | | | Nepal Citizenship Act 2063 (2006), Act No. 25 of the year 2063 (2006), 26 November 2006 <http://www.ref world.org/docid/4bbca9 7e2.html> | Section 3(3) 'Every child found in the territory of Nepal, whose paternal and maternal addresses are undetermined, shall be considered a citizen of Nepal by descent until his/her father or mother are found.' | | | | | X | | | | | | No provision | No provision |

(continued)

(continued)

| No | UNHCR region [3] | Country | Party 1961 Conv since | Party ECN since | Citation of the accessible version [4] | Foundling provision [5] (full text) [6] | Age related | | | | Withdrawal related [5] | | | | | | Complementary | |
|---|---|---|---|---|---|---|---|---|---|---|---|---|---|---|---|---|---|---|
| | | | | | | | Birth in territory required [7] | New/ recent born | Specific older ages | All minors [8] (non-exhaustive) | No explicit age | Loss regulated | No Withdrawal [9] after certain age | Foreign parentage revealed [10] | Foreign nationality revealed [10] | Birth abroad revealed | Otherwise stateless/ child of stateless parents provision (art or sec) [11] | 'Unconditional' jus soli (art or sec) [12] |
| 122 | Europe | Netherlands | 1985 | 2001 | Kingdom Act on Netherlands Nationality 19 December 1984 (as amended in 2015) <https://data.globalcit.eu/NationalDB/docs/NL.%20Netherlands%20Nationality%20Act_consolidated%2025_11_13_ENGLISH.pdf> | Article 3(2) 'A foundling found [gevonden kind] in the territory of the Netherlands, Aruba, Curaçao or Sint Maarten or on a sea-going vessel or aircraft registered in the Netherlands, Aruba, Curaçao or Sint Maarten, shall be deemed to be the child of a Netherlands national unless it becomes apparent within five years of the day on which he or she was found that the child possesses a foreign nationality by birth.' | | | | | X | X (unclear whether loss or acquisition) | 'five years of the day on which he or she was found' | | X | | Nationality law 6(1)(b) | No provision |
| 123 | Asia and the Pacific | New Zealand | | 2006 | Citizenship Act 1977 (1977 No 61) <http://www.legislation.govt.nz/act/public/1977/0061/latest/whole.html#DLM443841> | Section 6(3)(b)(i)and(ii) 'Citizenship by birth(3)[...] (b)a person is deemed to be a New Zealand citizen by birth if—(i)the person, having recently been born, has been found abandoned in New Zealand; and (ii) investigations have failed to establish the identity of at least one of the person 's parents.' | | X | | | | | | | | | Nationality law 6(3)(a) | No provision |
| 124 | The Americas | Nicaragua | 2013 | | Ley Nº 149 - Ley de nacionalidad [Nationality Law],30 June 1992 <https://www.refworld.org/docid/3dbe7e564.html> | Article 3 (4) 'Are nationals: [...](4) Infants of unknown parents found in Nicaraguan territory, without prejudice to cases where their filiation becomes known [que concida [sic] su filiación - likely meant to say 'conocida'), which would have the necessary effects.' (author translation) | | | | | X | | | | | | No provision | No provision |

(continued)

(continued)

| No | UNHCR region[*3] | Country | Party 1961 Conv since | Party ECN since | Citation of the accessible version[*4] | Founding provision[*5] (full text)[*6] | Birth in territory required[*7] | New/recent born | Specific older ages | All minors[*8] (non-exhaustive) | No explicit age | Loss regulated | No Withdrawal[*9] after certain age | Foreign parentage revealed[*10] | Foreign nationality revealed[*10] | Birth abroad revealed | Otherwise stateless/ child of stateless parents provision (art or sec)[*11] | 'Unconditional' jus soli (art or sec)[*12] |
|---|---|---|---|---|---|---|---|---|---|---|---|---|---|---|---|---|---|---|
| | | | | | | | | | | | | | Age related | | Withdrawal related[*5] | | | Complementary |
| 125 | Africa | Niger | 1985 | | Ordonnance n° 84–33 du 23 août 1984 portant code de la nationalité nigérienne [Ordinance n° 84–33 of 23 August 1984 on the nationality code of Niger] <https://www.refworld.org/docid/48bee9ac2.html> | Article 10 'Is Nigerian, a child born in Niger of unknown parents However, and subject to Sect. 8 above, he shall be deemed never to have been a Nigerian if, during his minority, his filiation is established with respect to a foreigner, and if he has, according to the national law of this foreigner, the nationality of the latter A newborn child found in Niger [L'enfant nouveau-né trouvé au Niger] is presumed, until proven otherwise, to have been born in Niger.' (author translation) | | X | | | | X | Age of majority | | X | | No provision | No provision |
| 126 | Africa | Nigeria | 2011 | | | No provision | | | | | | | | | | | No provision | No provision |
| 127 | Europe | North Macedonia | 2020 | 2003 | The former Yugoslav Republic of Macedonia: Law on Citizenship of the Republic of Macedonia (As Amended in 2011),2016 <http://www.refworld.org/docid/3f549164.html> | Article 6 'Citizenship of the Republic of Macedonia shall be acquired by a child found or born on the territory of the Republic of Macedonia whose parents are unknown [...] The child referred to in paragraph 1 of this Article shall lose the citizenship of the Republic of Macedonia if before reaching the age of 15 years it is determined that the child 's parents are foreign citizens, and provided that the child shall not be left without a citizenship.' | | | | X (See sec 6.3.4 of the book) | | X | 15 years of age | | X | | Nationality law 6(1) | No provision |

(continued)

(continued)

| No | UNHCR region [3] | Country | Party 1961 Conv since | Party ECN since | Citation of the accessible version [4] | Founding provision [5] (full text) [6] | Age related | | | | | | | Withdrawal related [5] | | | | | Complementary | |
|---|---|---|---|---|---|---|---|---|---|---|---|---|---|---|---|---|---|---|---|---|
| | | | | | | | Birth in territory required [7] | New/ recent born | Specific older ages | All minors [8] (non-exhaustive) | No explicit age | Loss regulated | No With-drawal [9] after certain age | Foreign parentage revealed [10] | Foreign nationality revealed [10] | Birth abroad revealed | Otherwise stateless/ child of stateless parents provision (art or sec) [11] | 'Uncon-ditional' jus soli (art or sec) [12] |
| 128 | Europe | Norway | 1971 | 2009 | The Act on Norwegian Nationality (as amended up to 2011) <https://data.globalcit.eu/NationalDB/docs/NRW%20Law%2051%202005%20on%20Citizenship%20(as%20amended)%20on%202009%2001,%20Engl ish).pdf.pdf> | Section 4 '[…]A foundling who is found in the realm is a Norwegian national until it is otherwise established.' | | | | | X | | | | | | No provision | No provision |
| 129 | Middle East and North Africa | Oman | | | Oman: Citizenship Law,12 August 2014 <http://www.refworld.org/docid/58dcfe444.html> | Article 11 'A person shall be deemed Omani national in the following cases:[…] (5)If he was born in Oman for unknown parents.' | X | | | | | | | | | | No provision | No provision |

(continued)

(continued)

| No | UNHCR region [3] | Country | Party 1961 Conv since | Party FCN since | Citation of the accessible version [4] | Foundling provision [5] (full text) [6] | Age related | | | | | | Withdrawal related [5] | | | | Complementary | |
|---|---|---|---|---|---|---|---|---|---|---|---|---|---|---|---|---|---|---|
| | | | | | | | Birth in territory required [7] | New/ recent born | Specific older ages | All minors [8] (non-exhaustive) | No explicit age | Loss regulated | No Withdrawal [9] after certain age | Foreign parentage revealed [10] | Foreign nationality revealed [10] | Birth abroad revealed | Otherwise stateless/ child of stateless parents provision (art or sec) [11] | 'Unconditional' jus soli (art or sec) [12] |
| 130 | Asia and the Pacific | Pakistan | | | | No provision. (Note: In practice certain persons of unknown parents have been issued with a Computerized National Identity Card (CNIC) that are only issued to nationals due to the Notice by the Supreme Court in 2011. See Sect. 4.3.2.) | | | | | | | | | | | No provision | Nationality law 4 (interpreted by caselaw that one of the parents needs to be a national - PLD 1999 Peshawar 18, Ghulam Sanai vs Assistant Director, National Registration Office, Peshawar.) |
| 131 | Asia and the Pacific | Palau | | | | No provision | | | | | | | | | | | Nationality law 201(a) | No provision |

(continued)

(continued)

| No | UNHCR region *3 | Country | Party 1961 Conv since | Party ECN since | Citation of the accessible version *4 | Foundling provision *5 (full text) *6 | Age related | | | | | | Withdrawal related*5 | | | | | Complementary | |
|---|---|---|---|---|---|---|---|---|---|---|---|---|---|---|---|---|---|---|---|
| | | | | | | | Birth in territory required *7 | New/ recent born | Specific older ages | All minors *8 (non-exhaustive) | No explicit age | Loss regulated | No With-drawal *9 after certain age | Foreign parentage revealed *10 | Foreign nationality revealed *10 | Birth abroad revealed | Otherwise stateless/ child of stateless parents provision (art or sec) *11 | 'Uncon-ditional' jus soli (art or sec) *12 |
| 132 | The Americas | Panama | 2011 | | Decreto Ejecutivo N°10 de 16 de enero de 2019, que reglamenta la Ley 28 de 30 de marzo de 2011, que aprueba la Convención sobre el Estatuto de los Apátridas de 1954 hecha en Nueva York, el 28 de septiembre de 1954 [Executive Decree No. 10 of January 16, 2019, which regulates Law 28 of March 30, 2011, which approves the Convention on the Status of Stateless Persons of 1954, done at New York, on September 28, 1954] <https://www.refworld.org.es/docid/5c461a884.html> | Article 32 "In case the file refers to a boy or a girl [un niño o niña] who has been found in the territory of the Republic of Panama, whose identity is unknown, it will be presumed that he was born in territory Panamanian and that their parents have Panamanian nationality. In such cases, the Ministry of Foreign Affairs will proceed to inform the National Secretariat of Children, Adolescents and Family (SENNIAF), so that the procedure to be declared as an abandoned boy or girl or as a deposit may be initiated as appropriate by the corresponding judicial authorities and their registration as a Panamanian person is ordered to the Civil Registry. At the same time the National Directorate of the Civil Registry will be notified of this fact so that it proceeds with the birth registration as soon as it receives the corresponding sentence, in which the necessary data must be indicated so that the registration can be generated, these being at minus a name and surname for the boy or girl, place of birth and the probable date of the occurrence which must indicate the day, month and year. Article 63 (Glossary of terminology) defines Niña o niño expósito (exposed girl or boy [child]), saying it 'means that a child of whom it is impossible to determine by any objective means who are her of his parents or relatives, name or country or place of birth'. (Tr author) | | | | | X | | | | | | No provision | Constitution 9(1) |

(continued)

(continued)

| No | UNHCR region *3 | Country | Party 1961 Conv since | Party ECN since | Citation of the accessible version *4 | Foundling provision *5 (full text) *6 | Age related | | | | | Loss regulated | Withdrawal related *5 | | | | Complementary | |
|---|---|---|---|---|---|---|---|---|---|---|---|---|---|---|---|---|---|---|
| | | | | | | | Birth in territory required *7 | New/recent born | Specific older ages | All minors *8 (non-exhaustive) | No explicit age | | No With-drawal *9 after certain age | Foreign parentage revealed *10 | Foreign nationality revealed *10 | Birth abroad revealed | Otherwise stateless/child of stateless parents provision (art or sec) *11 | 'Unconditional' jus soli (art or sec) *12 |
| 133 | Asia and the Pacific | Papua New Guinea | | | Constitution of the Independent State of Papua New Guinea, 16 September 1975 (as amended up to 2011) <https://www.refworld.org/docid/3ae6b5880.html> | Section 77(1) 'A foundling discovered at any time in the country shall, in the absence of proof to the contrary, be deemed to be the child of parents at least one of whom was, or if he had survived would have been, a citizen.' | | | | | X | | | | | | No provision | No provision |
| 134 | The Americas | Paraguay | 2012 | | Constitution of the Republic of Paraguay, 20 June 1992 <https://data.globalcit.eu/NationalDB/docs/Constitution%201992_as%20amended%202011%20(English).pdf> | Article 146 (4) 'The following persons are of natural Paraguayan nationality:[...] (4) the infants of unknown parents, collected in the territory of the Republic.' (author translation) | | | | | X | | | | | | No provision | Const 146(1) |
| 135 | The Americas | Peru | 2014 | | Ley N° 26,574 - Ley de la nacionalidad [Law of nationality], 11 January 1996 <https://www.refworld.org/docid/3ac6b4ef2c.html> | Article 2(2) Son peruanos por nacimiento: (...) 'Minors [Los menores de edad] in a state of abandonment, residing in the territory of the Republic, sons or daughters [hijos] of unknown parents.' | | | | X | | | | | | | No provision | Const 52, PER 2(1), Supreme Decree no. 004-97-IN, 4(a) |
| 136 | Asia and the Pacific | Philippines | | | | No provision. (Note: See however the Supreme Court case law on 8 March and 20 September 2016 in Sect. 5.6.2.) | | | | | | | | | | | No provision | No provision |

(continued)

(continued)

| No | UNHCR region [3] | Country | Party 1961 Conv since | Party ECN since | Citation of the accessible version [4] | Foundling provision [5] (full text) [6] | Age related | | | | | | Withdrawal related [5] | | | | Complementary | |
|---|---|---|---|---|---|---|---|---|---|---|---|---|---|---|---|---|---|---|
| | | | | | | | Birth in territory required [7] | New/recent born | Specific older ages | All minors [8] (non-exhaustive) | No explicit age | Loss regulated | No Withdrawal [9] after certain age | Foreign parentage revealed [10] | Foreign nationality revealed [10] | Birth abroad revealed | Otherwise stateless/ child of stateless parents provision (art or sec) [11] | 'Unconditional' jus soli (art or sec) [12] |
| 137 | Europe | Poland | | | Act on Polish Citizenship of 2 April 2009 which was published on 14 February 2012 and entered into force entirely on 15 August 2012 <https://data.globalcit.eu/NationalDB/docs/POL_Citizenship%20Act%202009_as%20enacted_ENGLISH.pdf> | Article 14(2) and Article 15 'Article 14. A child shall acquire Polish citizenship at birth when: [...] (2) the child is born within the territory of the Republic of Poland of parents who are unknown [...].' Article 15. 'A child of unknown parents shall acquire Polish citizenship when found within the territory of the Republic of Poland.' | | | | | X | | | | | | Nationality law 14(2) | No provision |
| 138 | Europe | Portugal | 2012 | 2001 | Portuguese nationality law, 3 October 1981 (Consolidated version, as amended by Organic Law 2/2006, of 17 April) <https://data.globalcit.eu/NationalDB/docs/POR%20Law%2037%2081%20as%20consolidated%20by%20Law%202%2006%20English).1.pdf> | Article 1(2) 'Save proof to the contrary, newly-born infants found abandoned in Portugal are presumed to have been born in Portuguese territory.' (Note: Preceding this, Article 1(1)(f) provides 'Persons born in Portuguese territory who do not possess another nationality' is a Portuguese national at birth.) | | X | | | | | | | | | Nationality law 1(1)(f) | No provision |
| 139 | Middle East and North Africa | Qatar | | | Law No. 38 of 2005 on the acquisition of Qatari nationality, 30 October 2005 <http://www.refworld.org/docid/542975124.html> | Article 2 '[...]Those born in Qatar to unknown parents shall also be deemed to be a naturalised Qatari. Foundlings shall be considered as born in Qatar unless proven otherwise.' (Note: The person is deemed to be a 'naturalized'Qatari.) | | | | | X | | | | | | No provision | No provision |

(continued)

(continued)

| No | UNHCR region [3] | Country | Party 1961 Conv since | Party ECN since | Citation of the accessible version [4] | Founding provision [5] (full text) [6] | Age related | | | | | Loss regulated | Withdrawal related [5] | | | | Complementary | |
|----|-----------------|---------|------------------------|------------------|-----------------------------------------|-----------------------------------------|-------------|---|---|---|---|----------------|------------------------|---|---|---|----------------|---|
| | | | | | | | Birth in territory required [7] | New/ recent born | Specific older ages | All minors [8] (non-exhaustive) | No explicit age | | No Withdrawal after certain age [9] | Foreign parentage revealed [10] | Foreign nationality revealed [10] | Birth abroad revealed | Otherwise stateless/ child of stateless parents provision (art or sec) [11] | 'Unconditional' jus soli (art or sec) [12] |
| 140 | Asia and the Pacific | Republic of Korea | | | Nationality Act (as amended up to 2014) <https://data.globalcit. eu/NationalDB/docs/ 01_South%20Korea_N ationality%20Act%20u pdated%20up%20to% 20amendment%20on% 2019%20June%202 014%20%5bENGL ISH%5d_1.pdf> | Article 2(1)(iii), 2(2) 'Article 2 (1) 'A person falling under any of the following subparagraphs shall be a national of the Republic of Korea at birth [...] (iii) A person who was born in the Republic of Korea, if both of the person's parents are unknown [...].' (2) An abandoned child (棄兒) found in the Republic of Korea shall be recognized as born in the Republic of Korea.' | | | | | X | | | | | | Nationality law 2(1)(2) | No provision |
| 141 | Europe | Republic of Moldova | 2012 | 1999 | Law on the citizenship of the Republic of Moldova Consolidated translation (as amended up to 2003) <https:// data.globalcit.eu/Nation alDB/docs/MLD%20L EGE%20Nr.%20102 4%EGF%20Nr.%20110 24%20Citizenship%20of% 20Republic%20of% 20Moldova%20Eng lish%20translation,% 20as%20amended%202 003).pdf> | Article 11(2) 'The child [Copilul] found in the territory of the Republic of Moldova shall be considered its citizen, unless otherwise proven, before the age of 18.' (Article 1 states: For the purposes of this law, the following notions mean: child [copil] - a person until the age of 18.') (Translation slightly modified from Legea cetatenici Republicii Moldova (as amended up to 2011) <https://data.globalcit.eu/Nation alDB/docs/MLD%20LEGE%20Nr.%201 024%20Citizenship%20of%20Republic% 20of%20Moldova%20original%20lang uage,%20as%20amended%2028_12_2 011).pdf> ) | | | | X | | | | | | | Nationality law 11(1)(b) | No provision |

(continued)

(continued)

| No | UNHCR region [3] | Country | Party 1961 Conv since | Party ECN since | Citation of the accessible version [4] | Founding provision [5] (full text) [6] | Age related | | | | | Loss regulated | Withdrawal related [5] | | | | Complementary | |
|---|---|---|---|---|---|---|---|---|---|---|---|---|---|---|---|---|---|---|
| | | | | | | | Birth in territory required [7] | New/ recent born | Specific older ages | All minors [8] (non-exhaustive) | No explicit age | | No With-drawal after certain age [9] | Foreign parentage revealed [10] | Foreign nationality revealed [10] | Birth abroad revealed | Otherwise stateless/ child of stateless parents provision (art or sec) [11] | 'Unconditional' jus soli (art or sec) [12] |
| 142 | Europe | Romania | 2006 | 2005 | Law on Romanian Citizenship no. 21/1991 (as amended by L... nr.11/2/2010, 17 June 2010) <https://data.globalcit.eu/NationalDB/docs/ROM%20Citizenship%20Law%201991%20English_consolidated%20version%2017%20June%202010 ).pdf> | Article 5 (3) '[...] (3) Children who are found in Romanian territory are regarded as Romanian citizens until proven otherwise, if none of their parents is known.' Article 30 (1) '(1) In the event in Art. 5 para. (3) children who are found shall lose Romanian citizenship if by the age of 18 their filiation has been established regarding both parents and they are foreign citizens (2) Romanian citizenship shall be lost also if filiation has been established only regarding one parent who is a foreign citizen and the other parent remains unknown (3) The date when Romanian citizenship is lost under para. (1) and (2) shall be the date when the child's filiation is established.' | | | | | X | X | 18 years of age | X | | | No provision | No provision |
| 143 | Europe | Russian Federation | | | Russian Federal Law on the Citizenship of the Russian Federation (As amended in 2017), N 62-FZ, 29 July 2017 <https://www.refworld.org/docid/50768e422.html> | Article 12(2) 'A child found in the territory of the Russian Federation, whose parents are unknown, shall become a citizen of the Russian Federation if his/her parents do not turn up within six months after the child was found' (Note: Article 3 provides that a "Child" means a person under the age of 18'.) | | | | X | | | | | | | Nationality law 12(1)(d) | No provision |
| 144 | Africa | Rwanda | 2006 | | Organic Law N° 30/2008 of 25/07/2008 relating to Rwandan Nationality,25 July 2008 <http://www.refworld.org/docid/4c569f4dc.html> | Article 9 'Any child born in Rwanda from unknown or stateless parents or who cannot acquire the nationality of one of his or her parents shall be Rwandan.New born baby found on the Rwandan territory shall be considered as born in Rwanda in case of lack of proof to the contrary.' | | X | | | | | | | | | Nationality law 9 | No provision |

(continued)

(continued)

| No | UNHCR region*3 | Country | Party 1961 Conv since | Party BCN since | Citation of the accessible version*4 | Founding provision*5 (full text)*6 | Birth in territory required*7 | New/ recent born | Specific older ages | All minors*8 (non-exhaustive) | No explicit age | Loss regulated | No With-drawal*9 after certain age | Foreign parentage revealed*10 | Foreign nationality revealed*10 | Birth abroad revealed | Otherwise stateless/ child of stateless parents provision (art or sec)*11 | 'Uncon-ditional' jus soli (art or sec)*12 |
|---|---|---|---|---|---|---|---|---|---|---|---|---|---|---|---|---|---|---|
| 145 | The Americas | Saint Kitts and Nevis | | | Constitution of Saint Kitts and Nevis, 10 September 1983 <https://www.refworld.org/docid/3ae6b50214.html> | Section 95(5)(c) 'a newborn infant found abandoned in Saint Christopher and Nevis or, as the case may be, in Anguilla shall, unless the contrary is shown, be regarded as having been born in Saint Christopher and Nevis or, as the case may be, in Anguilla.'(Note: Preceding this, Article 91(a) basically provides for nationality to persons born in Saint Kitts and Navis.) | | X | | | | | | | | | Nationality law 3(6), 3(8), 3(9) | Const 91(a) |
| 146 | The Americas | Saint Lucia | | | Citizenship of Saint Lucia Act, Act 7 of 1979 (Copy provided by Olivier Vonk -the copy states: 'Revised edition, showing the law as at 31 December 2001') | Section 7(2)(a) '(2)The Minister may cause a minor to be registered as a citizen in such special circumstances as he or she may consider which may include - (a) that the minor being an infant was born in Saint Lucia and has been abandoned.'(Note: Provides discretionary registration rather than automatic acquisition. The title of the provision also states 'Minors becoming citizens by adoption orders and registration.'Further, the rationale for this provision requiring 'birth in the territory'is unclear as Sect. 100 of Saint Lucia 's Constitution and Sect. 4 of the Citizenship Act provide for unconditional jus soli acquisition in any case which would naturally cover abandoned infants born in Saint Lucia, rendering 7(2)(a) unnecessary.) | X | | | | | | | | | | Nationality law 7(2)(b) | Const 100, Nationality law 4 |
| 147 | The Americas | Saint Vincent and the Grenadines | | | | No provision | | | | | | | | | | | No provision | Constitution 91, Nationality law 4 |
| 148 | Asia and the Pacific | Samoa | | | | No provision | | | | | | | | | | | Nationality law 2004 6(3) | No provision |

(continued)

(continued)

| No | UNHCR region [3] | Country | Party 1961 Conv since | Party ECN since | Citation of the accessible version [4] | Foundling provision [5] (full text) [6] | Age related — Birth in territory required [7] | New/ recent born | Specific older ages | All minors [8] (non-exhaustive) | No explicit age | Loss regulated | Withdrawal related [5] — No Withdrawal after certain age [9] | Foreign parentage revealed [10] | Foreign nationality revealed [10] | Birth abroad revealed | Complementary — Otherwise stateless/ child of stateless parents provision (art or sec) [11] | 'Unconditional' jus soli (art or sec) [12] |
|---|---|---|---|---|---|---|---|---|---|---|---|---|---|---|---|---|---|---|
| 149 | Europe | San Marino | | | Legge Sulla Citadinanza [Law on citizenship], 30 November 2000 <https://www.consiglio grandeegenerale.sm/on-line/home/archivio-leggi-decreti-e-regola menti.html> | Article 1(6) 'They are citizens of San Marino by origin: [...] (6)those born in the territory of the Republic if both parents are unknown [...].' (author translation) | X | | | | | | | | | | No provision | No provision |
| 150 | Africa | Sao Tome and Principe | | | Lei N° 690 (Lei da Nacionalidade [Law of Nationality], 13 September 1990 <https://www.refworld.org/docid/4c5a8a3d0.html> | Article 5(2) 'Newborns exposed in territory are presumed to be born in Sao Tome and Principe.' (Preceding this, Article 5[1][d] states that 'Those born in São Tomé and Príncipe when they have no other nationality are nationals of Sao Tome and Principe by origin.)(author translation) | | X | | | | | | | | | Nationality law 5(1)(d)-(e) | No provision |
| 151 | Middle East and North Africa | Saudi Arabia | | | Saudi Arabian Citizenship System (Regulation),Decision no. 4 of 25/1/1374 Hijra,23 September 1954 <http://www.ref world.org/docid/3fb9eb 6d2.html> | Article 7 'Individuals [...]born inside the Kingdom from unknown parents (foundling) are considered Saudis. The foundling inside the Kingdom is considered born in it unless the opposite is proven.' | | | | | X | | | | | | No provision | No provision |
| 152 | Africa | Senegal | 2005 | | Loi n° 61-70 du 7 mars 1961, Code de la nationalité sénégalaise[Senegalese Nationality Code],30 May 1992 <https:// www.refworld.org/ docid/46cebe2e2.html> | Article 3 'A newborn child found in Senegal whose parents are unknown is Senegalese. However, he or she ceases to be Senegalese if, during his minority, his or her filiation is established with respect to a foreigner and if he has, according to the national law of that foreigner, the nationality of the latter (foreigner).' (author translation) | | X | | | | X | Age of majority | | X | | No provision | No provision |

(continued)

(continued)

| No | UNHCR region [3] | Country | Party 1961 Conv since | Party ECN since | Citation of the accessible version [4] | Foundling provision [5] (full text) [6] | Birth in territory required [7] | New/recent born | Specific older ages | All minors [8] (non-exhaustive) | No explicit age | Loss regulated | No Withdrawal after certain age [9] | Foreign parentage revealed [10] | Foreign nationality revealed [10] | Birth abroad revealed | Otherwise stateless/child of stateless parents provision (art or sec) [11] | 'Unconditional' jus soli (art or sec)[12] |
|---|---|---|---|---|---|---|---|---|---|---|---|---|---|---|---|---|---|---|
| | | | | | | | **Age related** | | | | | | **Withdrawal related [5]** | | | | **Complementary** | |
| 153 | Europe | Serbia | 2011 | | Law on Citizenship of the Republic of Serbia (2004) <http://www.ref world.org/docid/4b56d0 542.html> | Article 13 'A child born or found in the territory of the Republic of Serbia (foundling) acquires citizenship of the Republic of Serbia by birth if both his parents are unknown or of unknown citizenship or without citizenship or if the child is without citizenship A child that acquired citizenship of the Republic of Serbia pursuant to the para. 1 of this Article is considered citizen of the Republic of Serbia since his birth. A child from the para. 1 of this Article can cease to be citizen of the Republic of Serbia if by the age of 18 it be proved that both his parents are citizens of another member state or foreign citizens. The citizenship ends at request of the parents on the day of delivery of the decision.' 'If a child is over 14, it is necessary to have his consent for termination of citizenship in the Republic of Serbia.' | | | | X (See sec 6.3.4 of the book) | | X ('at request of the parents (..)If a child is over 14, it is necessary to have his consent [....].' | 18 years of age | X | | | Nationality law 13 | No provision |
| 154 | Africa | Seychelles | | | | No provision | | | | | | | | | | | No provision | No provision |
| 155 | Africa | Sierra Leone | 2016 | | | No provision | | | | | | | | | | | No provision | No provision |
| 156 | Asia and the Pacific | Singapore | | | Constitution of the Republic of Singapore, 1 October 2015 (as amended up to 2020) <https://data.globalcit.eu/NationalDB/docs/2020_Constitution%20of%20the%20Repu blic%20of%20Sing apore.pdf> | Third Schedule, Article 140 (13) 'Any new born child found exposed in Singapore of unknown and unascertainable parentage shall, until the contrary is proved, be deemed to be a citizen of Singapore by birth; and the date of finding shall be taken to be the date of birth of such child. | | X | | | | | | | | | No provision | No provision |

(continued)

(continued)

| No | UNHCR region *3 | Country | Party 1961 Conv since | Party ECN since | Citation of the accessible version *4 | Founding provision *5 (full text) *6 | Age related — Birth in territory required *7 | New/ recent born | Specific older ages | All minors *8 (non-exhaustive) | No explicit age | Withdrawal related *5 — Loss regulated | No With-drawal after certain age | Foreign parentage revealed *10 | Foreign nationality revealed *10 | Birth abroad revealed | Complementary — Otherwise stateless/ child of stateless parents provision (art or sec) *11 | 'Unconditional' jus soli (art or sec) *12 |
|---|---|---|---|---|---|---|---|---|---|---|---|---|---|---|---|---|---|---|
| 157 | Europe | Slovakia | 2000 | 1998 | Act on Nationality of the Slovak Republic, 4 December 2012 <http://www.refworld.org/docid/50bddc02.html> | Section 5(2)(b) 'Unless alien nationality is proven, a child is considered to be a national of the Slovak Republic if [...](b)It was found in the territory of the Slovak Republic and its parents are not known unless it is proven that the child acquired nationality of another state upon birth.' | | | | | X | | | | | | Nationality law 5(1)(b), 5(1)(c) | No provision |
| 158 | Europe | Slovenia | | | Citizenship of the Republic of Slovenia Act, ZDRS-UPB2, 7 December 2006 <https://www.refworld.org/docid/50bdfabf2.html> | Article 9 'A child born or found on the territory of the Republic of Slovenia of unknown parentage [...] shall acquire citizenship of Republic of Slovenia. Upon request of the parents, citizenship of the Republic of Slovenia shall cease for a child that acquired it as described in paragraph 1 of this article if it is discovered prior to the child reaching the age of 18 that the parents are foreign citizens. Citizenship shall cease on the day the decision about it was handed over to such a person.' | | | | X (See sec 6.3.4 of the book) | | X | 18 years of age | X ('Upon request of the parents') | | | Nationality law 9 | No provision |
| 159 | Asia and the Pacific | Solomon Islands | | | | No provision | | | | | | | | | | | No provision | No provision |

(continued)

(continued)

| No | UNHCR region[3] | Country | Party 1961 Conv since | Party ECN since | Citation of the accessible version[4] | Founding provision[5] (full text)[6] | Birth in territory required[7] | New/recent born | Specific older ages | All minors[8] (non-exhaustive) | No explicit age | Loss regulated | No Withdrawal[9] after certain age | Foreign parentage revealed[10] | Foreign nationality revealed[10] | Birth abroad revealed | Otherwise stateless/ child of stateless parents provision (art or sec)[11] | "Unconditional" jus soli (art or sec)[12] |
|---|---|---|---|---|---|---|---|---|---|---|---|---|---|---|---|---|---|---|
| 160 | Africa | Somalia | | | Law No. 28 on Somali Citizenship, 22 December 1962 (Note: The Citizenship Rights in Africa Initiative states that 'citizenship in Somalia is nominally regulated by the country's 1962 citizenship law' and provides the link to this law <http://citizenshiprightsafrica.org/wp-content/uploads/1962/12/Somalia-Citizenship-Law-1962-full.pdf>. Both refworld.org and GLOBALCIT carry the same document | Article 15 (1)(2) (Note: The title of article 15 states in brackets 'Minors in Special Circumstances.') '(1) Any minor who is a child of unknown parents and was born in the territory of the Somali Republic, shall be considered a Somali citizen, provided that he has not acquired a foreign citizenship or the status as subject of a foreign country (2) Any child of unknown parents found in the territory of the Somali Republic shall be presumed, until the contrary is proved, to have been born in the territory of the Somali Republic.' Article 16 (1) (Minor Age) 'For the purpose of this law, any person under fifteen years of age shall be considered a "minor".' | | | | See sec 6.3.4 of the book | X | | | | | | No provision | No provision |
| 161 | Africa | South Africa | | | | No provision | | | | | | | | | | | Nationality law 2(2) | No provision |
| 162 | Africa | South Sudan | | | The Nationality Act, 2011.7 July 2011 <http://www.refworld.org/docid/4ec943l8f2.html> | Section 8(4) 'A person who is or was first found in South Sudan as a deserted infant of unknown Parents shall, until the contrary is proved, be deemed to be a South Sudanese National by birth.' | | | | | X | | | | | | No provision | No provision |

(continued)

(continued)

| No | UNHCR region [3] | Country | Party 1961 Conv since | Party ECN since | Citation of the accessible version [4] | Founding provision [5] (full text) [6] | Birth in territory required [7] | New/recent born | Specific older ages | All minors [8] (non-exhaustive) | No explicit age | Loss regulated | No With-drawal [9] after certain age | Foreign parentage revealed [10] | Foreign nationality revealed [10] | Birth abroad revealed | Otherwise stateless/child of stateless parents provision (art or sec) [11] | 'Unconditional' jus soli (art or sec) [12] |
|---|---|---|---|---|---|---|---|---|---|---|---|---|---|---|---|---|---|---|
| | | | | | | | | | | | | **Age related** | | | **Withdrawal related [5]** | | | **Complementary** |
| 163 | Europe | Spain | 2018 | | Civil code: Extractos del Código Civil, Titulo primero: de los españoles y extranjeros (Vigencia desde1 de Mayo de 1889.) ['Extract of Civil Code ("Title 1: Spanish nationals and foreigners") In force since 1 May 1889] <http://noticias.juridi cas.com/base_datos/Pri vado/cc.1l11.html#l11> | Article 17(1)(d) 'The following persons are Spanish nationals of origin: (…). d) Those born in Spain whose parentage is not determined. To these effects, minors [los menores de edad] whose first known place of stay is Spanish territory are presumed to have been born in the Spanish territory.' (author translation) | | | | X | | | | | | | Civil Code 17(1)(c) | No provision |
| 164 | Asia and the Pacific | Sri Lanka | | | Citizenship Act, 15 November 1948 <https://www.refworld. org/docid/3ae6b50414. html> and <https:// www.justice.gov/sites/ default/files/eoir/legacy/ 2013/11/08/citizenship_ 3.pdf> | Section 7 'Every person first found in Ceylon as a newly born deserted infant of unknown and unascertainable parentage shall, until the contrary is proved, be deemed to have the status of a citizen of Ceylon by descent.' | X | | | | | | | | | | No provision | No provision |
| 165 | Africa | Sudan | | | The Sudanese Nationality Act 1994 and Sudanese Nationality Act (Amendment) 2011,10 August 2011 <http:// www.refworld.org/ docid/50349z892.html> | Article 5 'A person shall be Sudanese by birth until the contrary is proved, if found as a deserted minor of unknown parents.' (Note: Article 3 defines 'minor'as 'In this act, unless the context otherwise requires:[…] "Minor" means any person who has not attained the age of majority.' Article 3 also states '[…]a person reaches the age of majority if the has completed eighteen years[…].') | | | | X | | | | | | | No provision | No provision |

(continued)

(continued)

| No | UNHCR region [3] | Country | Party 1961 Conv since | Party ECN since | Citation of the accessible version [4] | Founding provision [5] (full text) [6] | Age related | | | | | Loss regulated | Withdrawal related [5] | | | | Complementary | |
|---|---|---|---|---|---|---|---|---|---|---|---|---|---|---|---|---|---|---|
| | | | | | | | Birth in territory required [7] | New/recent born | Specific older ages | All minors [8] (non-exhaustive) | No explicit age | | No With-drawal after certain age | Foreign parentage revealed [10] | Foreign nationality revealed [10] | Birth abroad revealed | Otherwise stateless/child of stateless parents provision (art or sec) [11] | 'Uncon-ditional' jus soli (art or sec) [12] |
| 166 | The Americas | Suriname | | | Law of 24 November 1975, for the Regulation of the Surinamese nationality and the Residence (as amended up to 2014) <https://data.globalcit.eu/NationalDB/docs/SUR_Law%20on%20nationality_c onsolidated%20vers ion%2012.09.2014_E NGLISH.pdf> | Article 4 'Surinamese is further: [...] (b)the child who is found [foundling, sic] or abandoned on the territory of Suriname, if both parents are unknown;.' | | | | | X | | | | | | Nationality law 16af(1)a, 16af(2), 16bf(1)a | No provision |
| 167 | Europe | Sweden | 1969 | 2001 | Swedish Citizenship Act (with amendments up to and including SFS 2006:222),30 April 2006 <http://www.ref world.org/docid/4ce6628 972.html> | Section 2 'Any foundling discovered in Sweden shall be considered to be a Swedish citizen until any indication to the contrary is discovered.' | | | | | X | | | | | | Nationality law 6 | No provision |
| 168 | Europe | Switzerland | | | Federal Act on Swiss Citizenship, 1 January 2018 <https://www.admin.ch/opc/en/classi fied-compilation/200 92990/index.html> | Article 3 '(1)A minor child [l',enfant mineur] of unknown parentage who is found in Switzerland acquires citizenship of the canton in which he or she was abandoned, and thus acquires Swiss citizenship (2)The canton decides where the child holds communal citizenship (3)Citizenship acquired in this way lapses if it is established who the parents of the child are, provided the child is still a minor and will not become stateless.' | | | | X | | X | Age of majority | | X | | No provision | No provision |

(continued)

(continued)

| No | UNHCR region *3 | Country | Party 1961 Conv since | Party ECN since | Citation of the accessible version *4 | Foundling provision *5 (full text) *6 | Birth in territory required *7 | New/ recent born | Specific older ages | All minors *8 (non-exhaustive) | No explicit age | Loss regulated | No With-drawal *9 after certain age | Foreign parentage revealed *10 | Foreign nationality revealed *10 | Birth abroad revealed | Otherwise stateless/ child of stateless parents provision (art or sec) *11 | 'Unconditional' jus soli (art or sec) *12 |
|---|---|---|---|---|---|---|---|---|---|---|---|---|---|---|---|---|---|---|
| | | | | | | | Age related | | | | | | Withdrawal related *5 | | | | Complementary | |
| 169 | Middle East and North Africa | Syrian Arab Republic | | | Legislative Decree 276 - Nationality Law, Legislative Decree 276, 24 November 1969 <http://www.refworld.org/docid/4d81e7b12.html> | Article 3(c) 'Anyone born in the country to unknown parents [...]. A foundling born in it, at the place in which he is found unless proved otherwise.' [Preceding this, Article 3 states 'The following shall be considered as Syrian Arabs ipso facto:[...]'] | | | | | X | | | | | | Nationality law 3(d) | No provision |
| 170 | Asia and the Pacific | Tajikistan | | | Constitutional Law of the Republic of Tajikistan on Nationality of the Republic of Tajikistan, 8 August 2015 <http://www.refworld.org/docid/3ae6b5823.html> | Article 13(8) 'A child born on the territory of the Republic of Tajikistan, whose parents are unknown, shall become a national of the Republic of Tajikistan.' | X | | | | | | | | | | Nationality law 13 | No provision |
| 171 | Asia and the Pacific | Thailand | | | | No provision | | | | | | | | | | | No provision | No provision |
| 172 | Asia and the Pacific | Timor-Leste | | | Constitution of the Democratic Republic of East Timor, 20 May 2002 <http://www.refworld.org/docid/3dd8d484.html> Law No. 9/2002 on Citizenship, 9/2002, 5 November 2002 <http://www.refworld.org/docid/3dd8de914.html> | Constitution Sect. 3.2 and Law on Citizenship 8(1)(b) Constitution Sect. 3.2: 'The following citizens shall be considered original citizens of East Timor, as long as they are born in the national territory: [...] (b) Children of incognito parents [...].'/ Citizenship Law Sect. 8 '1. An original citizen of Timor-Leste is one who was born in the national territory: [...]b) A child of incognito parents [...].' | X | | | | | | | | | | Nationality Law Sect. 8(1)(b) | No provision |
| 173 | Asia and the Pacific | Tonga | | | | No provision | | | | | | | | | | | No provision | No provision |

(continued)

(continued)

| No | UNHCR region *3 | Country | Party 1961 Conv since | Party ECN since | Citation of the accessible version *4 | Founding provision *5 (full text) *6 | Age related – Birth in territory required *7 | Age related – New/ recent born | Age related – Specific older ages | Age related – All minors *8 (non-exhaustive) | No explicit age | Withdrawal related *5 – Loss regulated | Withdrawal related *5 – No With-drawal after certain age | Withdrawal related *5 – With-drawal *9 after certain age | Withdrawal related *5 – Foreign parentage revealed *10 | Withdrawal related *5 – Foreign nationality revealed *10 | Withdrawal related *5 – Birth abroad revealed | Complementary – Otherwise stateless/ child of stateless parents provision (art or sec) *11 | Complementary – 'Unconditional' jus soli (art or sec) *12 |
|---|---|---|---|---|---|---|---|---|---|---|---|---|---|---|---|---|---|---|---|
| 174 | Africa | Togo | | | Loi No.2007–017 du 6 juillet 2007 portant code de l'enfant [Law N.2007–017 of 6 July 2007 on the code of the child] <http://citizenshiprightsafrica.org/wp-content/uploads/2016/07/Togo-Code-enfant-2007.pdf> | Article 19 'Any child found on Togolese territory, before the age of five (05) years and whose filiation is unknown, as well as any child born in Togo, of parents whose place of birth is unknown, has the right to to acquire Togolese nationality.' [author translation. While not clear from the text, according to the GLOBALCIT database, the provision provides for naturalization rather than automatic acquisition.] | | | Before the age of 5 years | | | | | | | | | No provision | No provision |
| 175 | The Americas | Trinidad and Tobago | | | | No provision | | | | | | X | | | | | | No provision | Constitution 17(1)-(2) |
| 176 | Middle East and North Africa | Tunisia | 2000 | | Code de la nationalité tunisienne [Tunisian Nationality Code], 2011 <http://www.refworld.org/docid/527237944.html> | Article 9 'A child born in Tunisia of unknown parents is Tunisian. However, he or she shall be considered never to have been Tunisian if, during the age of minority, his or her affiliation is established with respect to a foreigner and if he or she has, in accordance with the national law of that foreigner, the nationality of the latter.' (author translation) Article 10 'The newborn child, found in Tunisia, is presumed, until evidence to the contrary, to be born in Tunisia.' | | X | | | X | X | | Age of majority | | X | | No provision | No provision |
| 177 | Europe | Turkey | | | Turkish Citizenship Law (As Amended in 2018),Law No. 5901, April 2018 <http://www.refworld.org/docid/44f6b0604.html> | Article 8(2) 'A child found in Turkey is deemed to have born [sic] in Turkey unless proven otherwise.'(Note: This follows Article 8 (1) which says: 'A child born in Turkey, but acquiring no citizenship from his/her foreign mother or foreign father acquires Turkish citizenship by birth.') | | | | | | | | | | | | Nationality law 8(1) | No provision |

(continued)

(continued)

| No | UNHCR region *3 | Country | Party 1961 Conv since | Party ECN since | Citation of the accessible version *4 | Foundling provision *5 (full text) *6 | Birth in territory required *7 | New/ recent born | Specific older ages | All minors *8 (non-exhaustive) | No explicit age | Loss regulated | No With-drawal after certain age *9 | Foreign parentage revealed *10 | Foreign nationality revealed *10 | Birth abroad revealed | Otherwise stateless/ child of stateless parents provision (art or sec) *11 | 'Unconditional' jus soli (art or sec) *12 |
|---|---|---|---|---|---|---|---|---|---|---|---|---|---|---|---|---|---|---|
| 178 | Asia and the Pacific | Turkmenistan | 2012 | | Law of 2013 on Citizenship, 22 June 2013 <http://www.ref world.org/docid/527235 634.html> | Article 11.8)(3) 'The child resident in the territory of Turkmenistan, whose parents are unknown, shall be regarded as born in Turkmenistan and a citizen of Turkmenistan. In case of the finding of at least one of the parents, trustee or guardian of this child his or her citizenship may be changed in accordance with this Law.' | | | | See sec 6.3.4 of the book | X | X | | X | | | Nationality law 11 | No provision |
| 179 | Asia and the Pacific | Tuvalu | | | Constitution of Tuvalu, 15 September 1986 <http://www.refworld.org/docid/3ae6b5554.html> | Article 43 (2) 'For the purposes of this Part, a foundling discovered at any time in Tuvalu shall, in the absence of proof to the contrary, be considered to have been born in Tuvalu.' | | | | | X | | | | | | No provision | No provision |
| 180 | Africa | Uganda | | | Constitution of the Republic of Uganda (22 September 1995) <http://www.refworld.org/docid/3ae6b5bad.html> | Article 11(1) '(1) A child of not more than five years of age found in Uganda, whose parents are not known, shall be presumed to be a citizen of Uganda by birth.' | | | Not more than 5 years old | | | | | | | | No provision | No provision |
| 181 | Europe | Ukraine | 2013 | 2006 | Law of Ukraine, On Citizenship of Ukraine (last amended 2016), 18 January 2001 <http://www.refworld.org/docid/44a280fa4.html> | Article 7 '[...] A new-born child found in the territory of Ukraine (a foundling, sic), whose both parents are unknown, shall be a citizen of Ukraine.' | | X | | | | | | | | | Nationality law 7 | No provision |
| 182 | Middle East and North Africa | United Arab Emirates | | | Federal Law No. 17 for 1972 Concerning Nationality, Passports and Amendments Thereof,18 November 1972 <http://www.ref world.org/docid/3fba18 260.html> | Article 2 'A citizen by law is:- [...](e)Anyone born in the country to unknown parents. A founding shall be deemed to have been born in the country unless proved to be otherwise.' | | | | | X | | | | | | No provision | No provision |

(continued)

(continued)

| No | UNHCR region [3] | Country | Party 1961 Conv since | Party ECN since | Citation of the accessible version [4] | Founding provision [5] (full text) [6] | Age related | | | | | Withdrawal related [5] | | | | | Complementary | |
|---|---|---|---|---|---|---|---|---|---|---|---|---|---|---|---|---|---|---|
| | | | | | | | Birth in territory required [7] | New/ recent born | Specific older ages | All minors [8] (non-exhaustive) | No explicit age | Loss regulated | No Withdrawal [9] after certain age | Foreign parentage revealed [10] | Foreign nationality revealed [10] | Birth abroad revealed | Otherwise stateless/ child of stateless parents provision (art or sec) [11] | 'Unconditional' jus soli (art or sec) [12] |
| 183 | Europe | United Kingdom of Great Britain and Northern Ireland | 1996 | | British Nationality Act 1981 Sect. 1(2) <http://www.legislation.gov.uk/ukpga/1981/61/data.pdf> | Section 1(2) 'A new-born infant who, after commencement, is found abandoned in the United Kingdom [or on or after the appointed day is found abandoned in a qualifying territory,] shall, unless the contrary is shown, be deemed for the purposes of subsection (1)—(a) to have been born in the United Kingdom after commencement [or in that territory on or after the appointed day]; and (b) to have been born to a parent who at the time of the birth was a British citizen or settled in the United Kingdom [or that territory].' | | X | | | | | | | | | Nationality law, Schedule 2(3)(1) | No provision |
| 184 | Africa | United Republic of Tanzania | | | | No provision | | | | | | | | | | | No provision | Nationality law 5 |
| 185 | The Americas | United States of America | | | Immigration and Nationality Act of 1952 <https://www.uscis.gov/ilink/docView/SLB/HTML/SLB/act.html> | Section 301(f) 'The following shall be nationals and citizens of the United States at birth:[...] (f) a person of unknown parentage found in the United States while under the age of five years, until shown, prior to his attaining the age of twenty-one years, not to have been born in the United States;' | | | Under five years old | | | X | After attaining the age of 21 years | | | X | No provision | INA 301(a), 302, 306, 307; |
| 186 | The Americas | Uruguay | 2001 | | | No provision | | | | See sec 6.3.4 of the book | | | | | | | No provision | Constitution 74, Nationality law 1 |
| 187 | Asia and the Pacific | Uzbekistan | | | Law on Citizenship in the Republic of Uzbekistan, 28 July 1992 <http://www.refworld.org/docid/3ae6b4d3c.html> | Article 16 'A child being on the territory of the Republic of Uzbekistan whose both parents are unknown, shall be a citizen of the Republic of Uzbekistan.' | | | | | X | | | | | | Nationality law 15, 17 | No provision |

(continued)

(continued)

| No | UNHCR region *3 | Country | Party 1961 Conv since | Party ECN since | Citation of the accessible version *4 | Foundling provision *5 (full text) *6 | Birth in territory required *7 | New/recent born | Specific older ages | All minors *8 (non-exhaustive) | No explicit age | Loss regulated | No Withdrawal *9 after certain age | Foreign parentage revealed *10 | Foreign nationality revealed *10 | Birth abroad revealed | Otherwise stateless/child of stateless parents provision (art or sec) *11 | 'Unconditional' jus soli (art or sec) *12 |
|---|---|---|---|---|---|---|---|---|---|---|---|---|---|---|---|---|---|---|
| | | | | | | | | | | | | | | | X | | | |
| 188 | Asia and the Pacific | Vanuatu | | | | No provision | | | | | | | | | | | No provision | No provision |
| 189 | The Americas | Venezuela | | | | No provision | | | | | | | | | | | No provision | Constitution 32(1), Nationality law 9(1) |
| 190 | Asia and the Pacific | Viet Nam | | | Law on Vietnamese Nationality No. 24/2008/QH12(Date of enactment 19-03-2017) Article 18 <http://globalcit.eu/wp-content/plugins/rscas-national-citizenship-law-gcit/docs/VN_Nationality%20Law_2008_ENGLISH.pdf> | Article 18 '1. Abandoned newborns and children found in the Vietnamese territory whose parents are unknown, have Vietnamese nationality 2. A child specified in Clause 1 of this Article who is aged under full 15 years will no longer have Vietnamese nationality in the following cases: a/ He/she has found his/her parents who hold single foreign nationality; b/ He/she has found his/her mother or father who holds single foreign nationality.' | | X | | | | X | 15 years of age | X | | | Nationality law 17 | No provision |
| 191 | Middle East and North Africa | Yemen | | | Law No. 6 of 1990 on Yemeni Nationality,26 August 1990 <http://www.refworld.org/docid/3ae6b57b10.html> | Article 3(d) 'The following shall enjoy Yemeni Nationality: [...](d)Anyone born in Yemen to unknown parents. A foundling in Yemen shall be considered born in it unless there is proof to the contrary.' | | | | | X | | | | | | No provision | No provision |

(continued)

(continued)

| No | UNHCR region*3 | Country | Party 1961 Conv since | Party ECN since | Citation of the accessible version*4 | Founding provision*5 (full text)*6 | Age related | | | | | Loss regulated | Withdrawal related*5 | | | | Complementary | |
|---|---|---|---|---|---|---|---|---|---|---|---|---|---|---|---|---|---|---|
| | | | | | | | Birth in territory required*7 | New/recent born | Specific older ages | All minors*8 (non-exhaustive) | No explicit age | | No Withdrawal*9 after certain age | Foreign parentage revealed *10 | Foreign nationality revealed *10 | Birth abroad revealed | Otherwise stateless/child of stateless parents provision (art or sec)*11 | 'Unconditional' jus soli (art or sec)*12 |
| 192 | Africa | Zambia | | | Constitution of Zambia (Amendment) [No. 2 of 2016 9] <http://www.parliament.gov.zm/sites/default/files/documents/amendment_act/Constitution%20of%20Zambia%20%20Amendment%29%2C%202016-Act%20No.%202_0.pdf#search='Zambia+Constitution'> | Article 35(2) 'A child found in Zambia who is, or appears to be, of not more than eight years of age and whose nationality and parents are not known, shall be presumed to be a citizen by birth.' | | | (Appears to be of) not more than 8 years of age | | | | | | | | No provision | No provision |
| 193 | Africa | Zimbabwe | | | Constitution of Zimbabwe Amendment (No. 20) Act, 2013, 22 May 2013 <http://www.refworld.org/docid/51ed090d4.html> | Article 36(3) 'A child found in Zimbabwe who is, or appears to be, less than fifteen years of age and whose nationality and parents are not known is presumed to be a Zimbabwean citizen by birth.' Article 39(2) (entitled 'Revocation of citizenship') 'Zimbabwean citizenship by birth may be revoked if-[...](b) in the case of a person referred to in Sect. 36(3), the person's nationality or parentage becomes known, and reveals that the person was a citizen of another country.' | | | (Appears to be) less than 15 years old | | | X | | | X | | No provision | No provision |

# Statistical Summary and Explanatory Note for Annex 1

| Statistical Summary | | |
|---|---|---|
| **General** | | |
| Total number of States included in Annex 1 | 193 | |
| State parties to the 1961 Convention | 75 | |
| Non-State parties | 118 | |
| Total number of States with a foundling provision | 139 | 72% (among all 193 States) |
| Total number of States without a foundling provision | 54 | |
| State parties (to the 1961 Convention) with a foundling provision*5*6 | 58 | 77% (among State parties) |
| State parties without a foundling provision | 17 | |
| Non-State parties with a foundling provision | 81 | 69% (among non-State parties) |
| Non-State parties without a foundling provision | 37 | |
| **Regional*3** | | |
| MENA States with a foundling provision | 18 | 100% among 18 (total no. States in region) |
| European States with a foundling provision | 46 | 96% among 48 (total no. States in region) |
| African States with a foundling provision | 34 | 71% among 48 (total no. States in region) |
| Asia and the Pacific States with a foundling provision | 24 | 55% among 44 (total no. States in region) |
| Americas States with a foundling provision | 17 | 49% among 35 (total no. States in region) |
| Total | 139 | |
| **Age related** | | |
| States that require 'birth' in the territory*7 | 17 | 12% |
| States that require being a newborn/recent born | 36 | 26% |
| States that grant nationality to specific older ages (age 3-15) | 10 | 7% |
| States that open up the age to all minors (non-exhaustive)*8 | 15 | 11% (10(explicit) + 5(by interpretation)) |
| States with no age specified (some might be open to minors) | 61 | 44% |
| Total | 139 | |
| **Complementary provisions** | | |

(continued)

(continued)

| Statistical Summary | | |
|---|---|---|
| Total number of States with a provision granting nationality to persons born in the territory 'otherwise stateless', or whose parents are stateless (or unknown nationality) (hereinafter 'otherwise stateless' provision)*11 | 86 | 62% (among 193 States) |
| States without a foundling provision but with an 'otherwise stateless' provision | 13 | |
| Total number of States with an unconditional jus soli provision | 34 | |
| States without a foundling provision but have an unconditional jus soli provision*12 | 20 | |
| **Post-facto loss related** | | |
| States specifically and clearly regulate the post-facto loss of nationality acquired based on the foundling provision along with the criteria | 37 | |
| States whose legislation clearly provides nationality will be/can be lost if foreign parentage is revealed*10 | 12 | |
| States whose legislation clearly provides nationality will be/can be lost if possession of foreign nationality is revealed*10 | 23 | 62% (out of 37 States) |
| States whose legislation clearly provides nationality will/can be lost if birth abroad is revealed | 2 | |

**\*1 This annex covers all 193 UN member States.** While Globalcit's database ("Modes of Acquisition of Citizenship" database -results of the search mode A03a 'foundlings' for 'all countries' at <http://globalciteu/acquisition-citizenship/.>) was used as a useful starting point, as it did not, among others, carry the full text of the provisions enabling detailed analysis, and the database only covers 173 States, a systematic verification of the text of the law was conducted and a wholly new table was developed

**\*2 Last updated on 31 January 2019 (with the accessible information—see note \*4 below),** with the exception of the number of State parties to the 1961 Convention updated on 26 February 2020 (with the accession of North Macedonia). Check for the updated number of State parties to the 1961 Convention which is expected to increase rather rapidly in the coming years

**\*3 Note on the classification of regions**: The classification was made according to the 'UNHCR Structure Worldwide, Geographical Regions and Sub-regions' (May 2009) <http://maps.unhcr.org/en/view?id=1522> (accessed 4 February 2019)

**\*4 Citation/last amendments**: While best efforts were made to access the versions carrying the latest amendments as of January 2019, especially for the countries whose translated versions of nationality laws were consulted, they might however not always be up-to-date. Further, for some of the countries, especially for which the English translations was consulted (such as those available on refworld), information such as the 'law number or me year or enactment was not readily avauauie. ror some countries, me citation was unclear wnemer me date contained merein referred to that of enactment or the last amendment As fee foundling provision in many nationality leglslatlon is an 'old' provision (already existent in its original version when enacted), the information on the last amendment was generally omitted from the column 'citation'

**\*5 'Foundling provision'**: As elaborated further in Sect. 1.5.2.3, a 'foundling provision' in this dissertation generally refers to a provision contained in a constitution (rare) or a nationality related law including regulations, or in the nationality-related part of the civil code explicitly granting nationality to persons of unknown parents born or found in the territory, which can be considered equivalent to article 2 of the 1961 Convention. Note that it was decided not to count (among the States with a 'foundling provision') the States where there is no provision directly granting nationality to foundlings but whose birth registration related law allows the registration of birth of children found in the territory of unknown parents, which results in the grant of that State's nationality. This is due to the inability to conduct an exhaustive research on the latest birth registration law, which was often only available in the original language. rurther, note that it was once contemplated whether the term 'unknown parents provision' (rather than 'foundling provision') should rather be used—as one of the main purposes of this dissertation is to redefine the term 'foundling' and propose an alternative, more legally accurate description of the persons who should benefit from article 2 (and the conclusion of the dissertation provides that a foundling is a person of unknown parents found in the relevant territory when he or she is a child). However, for the sake of brevity, and given the fact that the term 'foundling' is the term currently used in the 1961 Convention, it was decided to use the term 'foundling provision' even when the relevant national law provision does not contain the term 'foundling'. While the titles of articles (often in brackets, before the text of the provisions start) of foundling provisions can be useful references especially in relation to the timing of the nationality acquisition, as there was insufficient information as to how much weight can be placed on such titles which might differ from country to country, it was decided in general not to include the titles

**\*6 General note on the languages**: In principle, the original versions were verified (and translated) by the author with regard to laws written in English, Spanish, French and Japanese. For laws written in other languages, English translation in principle was referred to

# Annex 2
# Foundling Provisions as of 1953 (Non-exhaustive)

| No | Country | Article/section |
|----|---------|-----------------|
| 1 | Austria | (1949) Article 12 |
| 2 | Belgium | (1932) Article 1 (2) |
| 3 | Bulgaria | (1948) Article 2 |
| 4 | Costa Rica | (1950) Article 1 (4) |
| 5 | Czechoslovakia | (1949) Paragraph I (1) |
| 6 | Denmark | (1950) Article 1 (2) |
| 7 | Egypt | (1950) Article 2 (4) |
| 8 | Finland | (1941) Article 2 |
| 9 | France | (1945) Article 22 |
| 10 | Germany | (1913) Sect. 4 |
| 11 | Guatemala | (C) Article 6 (1) |
| 12 | Hungary | (1948) Article 21 |
| 13 | Iceland | (1935) Article 1 |
| 14 | Italy | (1912) Article 1 |
| 15 | Mexico | (1934) Article 55 |
| 16 | The Netherlands | (1892) Article 2 (6) |
| 17 | Nicaragua | (1950) Article 18 (3) |
| 18 | Norway | (1950) Article 1 (3) |
| 19 | Peru | (1951) Article 4 |
| 20 | Romania | (1948) Article 9 |
| 21 | Saar | (1949) Article 5 (2) |

(continued)

M. Kaneko-Iwase, *Nationality of Foundlings*, Evidence-Based Approaches to Peace
and Conflict Studies 5, https://doi.org/10.1007/978-981-16-3005-7

(continued)

| No | Country | Article/section |
|----|---------|-----------------|
| 22 | Sweden | (1950) Article 1 (3) |
| 23 | Syria | (1951) Article 3 (b) |
| 24 | U.S.A | (1952) Sect. 301 (a) |
| 25 | Uruguay | (1879) Article 28 (Civil Register Act) |
| 26 | Yugoslavia | (1946) Article 6 |

*Note* This Annex 2, unlike Annex 1, was compiled based exclusively on the information contained in the table entitled: 'Existing Legislation (related to article 2 of the 1961 Convention, Report of the Special Rapporteur, Mr. Roberto Córdova (5th session of the ILC [1953]) 175. <http://legalu norg/docs/?path=../ilc/documentation/english/a_cn4_64.pdf&lang=E..http://org/docs/%3Fpath% 3D../ilc/documentation/english/a_cn4_64.pdf%26lang%3DE> While Córdova on page 4 of the same material states that the list is based on Ivan Kerno's document entitled 'Nationality, including Statelessness—National Legislation Concerning Grounds for Deprivation of Nationality'— Memorandum Prepared by Mr Ivan S. Kerno, Expert of the International Law Commission, A/CN.4/66 <http://legalunorg/docs/?path=/ilc/documentation/english/a_cn4_66.pdf&lang=EFS. http://org/docs/%3Fpath%3D../ilc/documentation/english/a_cn4_66.pdf%26lang%3DEFS">, no information on foundling provisions is included in Kerno's document. Thus it is unknown how many States were surveyed, and the above table is not exhaustive. For example, it is known to the author that the Japanese Nationality Act 1899, Law No.66 already had a foundling provision, that is article 4, as well as article 2(iii) of the original version of the Japanese Nationality Act 1950, Law No. 147, which is not included in this table. Further, it should be noted that no verification of the original text of each national legislation, unlike Annex 1, was conducted for this Annex 2

# Bibliography

## (A) Table of National Legislation and Secondary Materials

(Note: Please also refer to annex 1, which contains information on the 193 UN member States' nationality law including the citation for 139 States with foundling provisions. Below only provides the list of laws whose texts (and not only the country names and article numbers) were included in the main text of this book).

### Afghanistan

1. Islamic Emirate of Afghanistan, Law on Citizenship of the Islamic Emirate of Afghanistan (24 June 2000) <http://www.refworld.org/docid/404c988d4.html> accessed 4 August 2019

### Albania

2. Law on Albanian Citizenship, Law No 8389 (6 September 1998) <http://www.refworld.org/docid/3ae6b5c10.html> accessed 3 August 2019
3. 'Department Circular No 058 – Establishing the Refugees and Stateless Status Determination Procedure' [Philippines] (18 October 2012) <https://www.refworld.orgPreviously nearly absent in literature, the two remaining categories /docid/5086932e2.html> accessed 4 August 2019

### Australia

4. Australian Citizenship Act 1948 <https://www.legislation.gov.au/Details/C2006C00317> accessed 4 August 2019

5. Australian Citizenship Act 2007 <https://www.legislation.gov.au/Details/C2019C00040> accessed 4 August 2019
6. Australian Citizenship Legislation Bill 2017 (17 July 2017)
7. Australian Citizenship Legislation Amendment (Strengthening the Commitments for Australian Citizenship and Other Measures) Bill 2018 (2018)
8. Australian Citizenship Legislation Amendment (Strengthening the Commitments for Australian Citizenship and Other Measures) Bill 2018, Explanatory Memorandum (2018)
9. Births, Deaths and Marriages Registration Act 1997
10. The Parliament of the Commonwealth of Australia House of Representatives, Australian Citizenship Bill 2005 Explanatory Memorandum (2005) <http://parlinfo.aph.gov.au/par lInfo/download/legislation/ems/r2473_ems_1f539888-be96-4356-9ffb-ec5c2ad28f87/upl oad_pdf/75168.pdf;fileType=application%2Fpdf> accessed 4 August 2019

## *Austria*

11. Austria: Federal Law Concerning the Austrian Nationality (Nationality Act 1985) (1985) <http://www.refworld.org/docid/3ae6b52114.html> accessed 4 August 2019

## *Belgium*

12. Code de la nationalité belge 28 Juin 1984 [Belgium Nationality Code, 28 June 1984] <https://www.ejustice.just.fgov.be/cgi_loi/change_lg.pl?language=fr&la=F& table_name=loi&cn=198406283> accessed 2 August 2019

## *Bosnia and Herzegovina*

13. Law on Citizenship of Bosnia and Herzegovina Unofficial Consolidated Text (as amended up to 2013) <https://data.globalcit.eu/NationalDB/docs/BIH%20Law%20on%20Citizenship% 20(consolidated)%20EN.pdf> accessed 25 December 2020

## *Canada*

14. Canadian Citizenship Act (RSC, 1985, c C-29) (1985) <http://laws-lois.justice.gc.ca/eng/acts/ C-29/page-1.html#h-3A> accessed 4 August 2019

## *Chad*

15. Ordonnance 33/PG.-INT. du 14 août 1962 portant code de la nationalité tchadienne, 14 August 1962 [Ordinance 33 / PG.-INT. of 14 August 1962 on the Chadian Nationality Code] <https:// www.refworld.org/docid/492e931b2.html> accessed 7 August 2019

## *China*

16. Nationality Law of the People's Republic of China (issued 10 September 1980) <http://en. pkulaw.cn/display.aspx?id=b2cecafdd3bc71cabdfb&lib=law> accessed 7 August 2019

## *Costa Rica*

17. Constitución Política de 7 de Noviembre de 1949 y sus Reformas (Título II Los Costarricenses) [Costa Rica, Political Constitution of 7 November 1949 and its Reforms (Title II Costa Rican nationals)] <http://www.tse.go.cr/pdf/normativa/constitucion.pdf> accessed 2 August 2019

## *Czech Republic*

18. 186/2013 Act of 11 July 2013 on Citizenship of the Czech Republic and on the amendment of selected other laws (the Czech Citizenship Act) https://www.mzv.cz/file/2400342/Citize nship_Act_No._186_2013_Sb._o_statnim_obcanstvi_CR.pdf

## *Denmark*

19. Act on the Acquisition of Danish Nationality (amended to 2004) (2004) <https://www.ref world.org/docid/4e5cf36d2.html>

## *Finland*

20. Republic of Finland, Nationality Act (359/2003) (1 June 2003) <https://www.refworld.org/ docid/3ae6b51614.html> accessed 4 August 2019

## *France*

21. Code Civil <https://www.legifrance.gouv.fr/affichCode.do?cidTexte=LEGITEXT0000060 70721> accessed 4 August 2019
22. Civil Code (English translation) <http://www.fd.ulisboa.pt/wp-content/uploads/2014/12/Cod igo-Civil-Frances-French-Civil Code-english-version.pdf> accessed 4 August 2019
23. Code de l'action sociale et des familles L. 222–6 [Code of social care and families] (2 November 2018) <https://www.legifrance.gouv.fr/affichCode.do;jsessionid=9D46C0175 66F085FB91968FAC07348E0.tplgfr24s_3?idSectionTA=LEGISCTA000006157583&cid Texte=LEGITEXT000006074069&dateTexte=20181107> accessed 4 August 2019

# Germany

24. Gesetz zum Ausbau der Hilfen für Schwangere und zur Regelung der vertraulichen Geburt [SchwHiAusbauG] [Act on the extension of assistance for pregnant women and on the regulation of confidential birth]
25. Nationality Act of Germany (Staatsangehörigkeitsgesetz) (StAG) (1913) <http://globalcit. eu/wp-content/plugins/rscas-database-eudo-gcit/?p=file&appl=currentCitizenshipLaws& f=GER%20Nationality%20Act_consolidated%20version%2013.11.14_ORIGINAL%20L ANGUAGE.pdf>
26. Vorläufige Anwendungshinweise des Bundesministeriums des Innern zum Staatsange-hörigkeitsgesetz (StAG) in der Fassung des Zweiten Gesetzes zur Änderung des Staat-sangehörigkeitsgesetzes vom 13 November 2014 [Federal Ministry of Interior, Preliminary instruction on implementation of the Nationality Law (StAG) as amended by the Second Act amending the Nationality Law of 13 November 2014] (BGBl. I S. 1714) (as of 1 June 2015) sec 4.2. (Germany) <http://www.bmi.bund.de/cae/servlet/contentblob/463812/ publicationFile/23664/Anwendungshinweise_05_2009.pdf (last accessed 5 September 2017, inaccessible as of 1 July 2019); https://www.dortmund.de/media/p/ordnungsamt/pdf_ordnun gsamt/Allgemeine_Verwaltungsvorschrift_zum_Staatsangehoerigkeitsrecht.pdf> accessed 1 July 2019
27. Federal Government of Germany, Bericht der Bundesregierung zu den Auswirkungen aller Maßnahmen und Hilfsangebote, die auf Grund des Gesetzes zum Ausbau der Hilfen für Schwangere und zur Regelung der vertraulichen Geburt ergriffen wurden [Report by the Federal Government on the effects of all measures and offers of assistance, which were taken under the law for the extension of the assistance for pregnant women and for the regulation of confidential birth] (12 July 2017) <https://www.bmfsfj.de/blob/117448/74c7e8b3ef0960d 03b66ade5f0958df6/bericht-vertrauliche-geburt-2017-data.pdf>

# Hungary

28. Act LV of 1993 on Hungarian Citizenship (Hungary) (1 October 1993) <http://www.refworld. org/docid/3ae6b4e630.html> accessed 2 August 2019
29. Act I of 2010 on Civil Registration Procedures
30. Law-Decree 17 of 1982 on Civil Registration, Marriage and Names
31. Act XV of 2009 promulgating the 1961 Convention in Hungary (tr Gábor Gyulai) <http://njt. hu/cgi_bin/njt_doc.cgi?docid=123906.177515> accessed 2 August 2019
32. Hungary, Act II of 2007 on the Admission and Right of Residence of Third Country Nationals

# India

33. Indian Council of Medical Research and National Council of Medical Sciences, 'Code of Practice, Ethical Considerations and Legal Issues' in R.S. Sharma and others (eds), *National Guidelines for Accreditation, Supervision & Regulation of Art Clinics in India* (Indian Council of Medical Research 2005)

## *Israel*

34. Israel Nationality Law 1952 Consolidated translation (as amended up to 1971) <https://data. globalcit.eu/NationalDB/docs/Isreal%20Nationality%20Law%20(amended).pdf> accessed 4 August 2019

## *Italy*

35. Legge 13 giugno 1912, n.555 sulla cittadinanza italiana [Law 13 June 1912, No 555 on Italian citizenship] (Italy) (author translation) <http://www.amblima.esteri.it/resource/ 2007/03/12736_f_amb61Legge13giugno1912n_555sullacittadinanzaitaliana.htm> accessed 4 August 2019
36. Legge n. 91, 5 febbraio 1992, Nuove norme sulla cittadinanza [Italy, Law 5 February 1992 No 91, New provisions on citizenship] (5 February 1992) <http://www.refworld.org/docid/ 46b84a862.html> accessed 3 August 2019
37. Legge 29 settembre 2015, n. 162 Adesione della Repubblica italiana alla Convenzione delle Nazioni Unite sulla riduzione dei casi di apolidia, fatta a New York il 30 agosto 1961. (15G00176) (GU Serie Generale n.237 del 12–10–2015) [Italy, Law of 29 September 2015, No 162 Accession of the Italian Republic to the UN Convention on the Reduction of State-lessness, concluded at New York on 30 August 1961] <https://www.gazzettaufficiale.it/eli/id/ 2015/10/12/15G00176/sg> accessed 2 August 2019
38. Direzione Centrale Per I Diritti Civili and others, La Cittadinanza Italiana – La Normativa, Le Procedure, Le Circolari [Italian Citizenship – Legislation, Procedures, Circulars] (31 March 2003) <https://www.asgi.it/banca-dati/cittadinanza-italiana-normativa-procedure-circolari/> accessed 4 August 2019
39. Ministry of Health, Parto in anonimato [Birth in anonymity] (Updated 11 April 2017, first edn 15 April 2008) <http://www.salute.gov.it/portale/donna/dettaglioContenutiDonna.jsp?lin gua=italiano&id=1011&area=Salute%20donna&menu=nascita> accessed 4 August 2019

## *Japan*

40. Act on General Rules for Application of Laws, Act No 78 of 21 June 2006
41. Child Welfare Act, Act No 164 of 12 December1947
42. Civil Code of Japan, Act No 89 of 27 April 1896
43. Code of Civil Procedure, Act No 109 of 26 June 1996
44. Family Register Act, Act No 224 of 22 December 1947
45. Nationality Act, Act No 147 of 4 May 1950
46. Kokusekihō [Nationality Act], Law No 66 of 1899
47. Civil Affairs Bureau and Ministry of Justice, Koseki <http://www.moj.go.jp/MINJI/koseki. html> accessed 15 July 2019

## *Laos*

48. Lao People's Democratic Republic (Laos), Law on Lao Nationality (1990) <http://www.ref world.org/docid/3ae6b4f014.html> accessed 4 August 2019

## Latvia

49. Latvian Law on Citizenship 1994 (as amended up to 2013)
50. <https://likumi.lv/ta/en/en/id/57512-citizenship-law> accessed 4 August 2019

## Mali

51. L'assemblee Nationale, Portant Code des Personnes et de la Famille [Persons and Family Code] (2011) <http://citizenshiprightsafrica.org/wp-content/uploads/2016/02/Mali-Code-des-personnes-et-de-la-famille-30-Dec-2011.pdf>

## Mexico

52. Ley de Nacionalidad, Nueva Ley publicada en el Diario Oficial de la Federación el 23 de enero de 1998 [Mexico, Nationality Law, new law published in the official report of the federation on 23 January 1998] <http://www.diputados.gob.mx/LeyesBiblio/pdf/53.pdf> accessed 2 August 2019

## Moldova

53. Legea cetateniei Republicii Moldova (as amended up to 2011) <https://data.globalcit.eu/NationalDB/docs/MLD%20LEGE%20Nr.%201024%20Citizenship%20of%20Republic%20of%20Moldova%20(original%20language,%20as%20amended%2028_12_2011).pdf> accessed 5 January 2021
54. Law on the citizenship of the Republic of Moldova Consolidated translation (as amended up to 2003) <https://data.globalcit.eu/NationalDB/docs/MLD%20LEGE%20Nr.%201024%20Citizenship%20of%20Republic%20of%20Moldova%20(English%20translation,%20as%20amended%202003).pdf>

## Netherlands

55. Kingdom Act on Netherlands Nationality 19 December 1984 (as amended in 2015) <https://data.globalcit.eu/NationalDB/docs/NL%20Netherlands%20Nationality%20Act_consolidated%2025_11_13_ENGLISH.pdf> accessed 25 December 2020

## New Zealand

56. Births, Deaths, Marriages, and Relationships Registration Act 1995, 1995

57. New Zealand Citizenship Act 1977 (1 July 2013) <http://www.legislation.govt.nz/act/public/1977/0061/latest/whole.html#DLM443841> accessed 4 August 2019

## North Macedonia

58. The former Yugoslav Republic of Macedonia: Law on Citizenship of the Republic of Macedonia (As Amended in 2011) <http://www.refworld.org/docid/3f54916b4.html> accessed 5 August 2019.

## Pakistan

59. National Database and Registration Authority Ordinance (2000) <http://nasirlawsite.com/laws/nadra.htm> accessed 23 May 2016

## Panamá

60. Decreto Ejecutivo N°10 de 16 de enero de 2019, que reglamenta la Ley 28 de 30 de marzo de 2011, que aprueba la Convención sobre el Estatuto de los Apátridas de 1954 hecha en Nueva York, el 28 de septiembre de 1954 [Panama, Executive Decree No 10 of 16 January 2019, which regulates Law 28 of 30 March 2011, which approves the Convention on the Status of Stateless Persons of 1954, done at New York, on September 28, 1954] <https://www.refworld.org.es/docid/5c461a884.html> accessed 2 August 2019

## Republic of Korea

61. Republic of Korea: Law No 16 of 1948, Nationality Act Nationality Act
62. <https://data.globalcit.eu/NationalDB/docs/01_South%20Korea_Nationality%20Act%20updated%20up%20to%20amendment%20on%2019%20June%202014%20%5bENGLISH%5d_1.pdf> accessed 3 August 2019

## Romania

63. Law on Romanian Citizenship no. 21/1991 (as amended by L. nr.112/2010, 17 June 2010) <https://data.globalcit.eu/NationalDB/docs/ROM%20Citizenship%20Law%201991%20(English_consolidated%20version%2017%20June%202010).pdf> accessed 4 August 2019

## *Russian Federation*

64. Russian Federal Law on the Citizenship of the Russian Federation (as amended in 2017) (29 July 2017) <https://www.refworld.org/docid/50768e422.html> accessed 4 August 2019

## *Serbia*

65. Law on Citizenship of the Republic of Serbia (Serbia) (2014) <https://www.refworld.org/docid/4b56d0542.html> accessed 4 August 2019

## *Slovenia*

66. Citizenship of the Republic of Slovenia Act (Slovenia), ZDRS-UPB2' (7 December 2006) <https://www.refworld.org/docid/50bdfabf2.html> accessed 3 August 2019

## *Spain*

67. Extractos del Código Civil (Título primero: de los españoles y extranjeros) Vigencia desde 01 de Mayo de 1889. Revisión vigente desde 05 de Agosto de 2018 hasta 29 de Junio de 2020 [Spain, 'Extract of Civil Code ('Title 1: Spanish nationals and foreigners') In force since 1 May 1889. Revision effective from 5 August 2018 to 29 June 2020] <http://noticias.juridicas.com/base_datos/Privado/cc.l1t1.html#l1t1> accessed 2 August 2019
68. Real Decreto de 24 de julio de 1889 por el que se publica el Código Civil (2018) <https://www.boe.es/buscar/act.php?id=BOE-A-1889-4763> accessed 4 August 2019

## *United Kingdom*

69. British Nationality Act 1948 (1948) <http://www.legislation.gov.uk/ukpga/Geo6/11-12/56/enacted> accessed 4 August 2019
70. British Nationality Act 1981 (1981) <https://www.legislation.gov.uk/ukpga/1981/61#commentary-c16828211> accessed 4 August 2019
71. UK Home Office, 'Asylum Policy Instruction: Statelessness and Applications for Leave to Remain Version 2.0' (18 February 2016) <https://www.gov.uk/government/uploads/system/uploads/attachment_data/file/501509/Statelessness_AI_v2.0__EXT_.pdf> accessed 4 August 2019
72. UK Home Office, 'British Citizenship: Automatic Acquisition (Part of Nationality Guidance)' (27 July 2017) <https://www.gov.uk/government/publications/automatic-acquisition-nationality-policy-guidance> accessed 4 August 2019

## United States

73. Immigration and Nationality Act of 1952 (2 August 2019) <https://www.uscis.gov/ilink/doc View/SLB/HTML/SLB/act.html> accessed 4 August 2019
74. Louisiana Children's Code <http://www.dcfs.la.gov/assets/docs/searchable/OCS/SafeHaven/ SafeHavenLawCHCArticle13.pdf> accessed 4 August 2019
75. US Department of State Foreign Affairs Manual (FAM) 7 FAM 1118 (2017 ed), <https://fam. state.gov/FAM/07FAM/07FAM1110.html> accessed 4 August 2019
76. US Department of Health and Human Services Administration for Children and Families Administration on Children and Youth and Families Children's Bureau (Child Welfare Information Gateway), 'Infant Safe Haven Laws' (current through December 2016) <https://www. childwelfare.gov/topics/systemwide/laws-policies/statutes/safehaven/> accessed 4 August 2019

## Zimbabwe

77. Constitution of Zimbabwe Amendment (No. 20) Act, 2013 (22 May 2013) <http://www.ref world.org/docid/51ed090f4.html> accessed 4 August 2019

## (B) Table of Cases: International Case Law

78. *Nationality Decrees Issued in Tunis and Morocco (French Zone) on November 8th, 1921, Advisory Opinion* [1923] PCIJ (ser. B) No 4 (Permanent Court of International Justice)
79. *Nottebohm Case (Liechtenstein v. Guatemala); Second Phase* [1955] (International Court of Justce)

## Regional Case Law

80. *Case of the Yean and Bosico Children v. The Dominican Republic* [2005] (Inter-American Court of Human Rights (IACrtHR))
81. Case C-135/08 *Janko Rottmann v. Freistaat Bayern* EU:C:2009:588 [2010] ECR I-1449 (CJEU)
82. Case C-221/17 *Tjebbes and Others v. Minister van Buitenlandse Zaken* ECLI:EU:C:2019:189 [2019] (CJEU)
83. *Genovese v. Malta* [2011] Application No 53124/09 (ECtHR)
84. *Godelli v. Italy* [2012] Application No 33783/09 (ECtHR)
85. *Marckx v. Belgium* [1979] Application No 6833/74 (ECtHR)
86. *Mennesson v. France* [2014] Application No 65192/11 (ECtHR)
87. *Odièvre v. France* [2013] Application No 42326/98 (ECtHR)

## National Case Law

### Australia

88. *Nicky v. Minister for Immigration* [2014] FCCA 2569 (Federal Circuit Court of Australia)
89. *Nicky v. Minister for Immigration and Border Protection* [2015] FCA 174 (Federal Court of Australia)
90. *SZRTN v. Minister for Immigration and Border Protection* [2015] FCA 305 (Federal Court of Australia)

### Hungary

91. Resolution 6/2015 (II.25.) of the Constitutional Court on the determination whether the term 'lawfully' in Section 76(1) of Act II of 2007 on the Conditions of Entry and Stay of Third-Country Nationals is contrary to the Fundamental Act and the annulment thereof (25 February 2015) <http://www.refworld.org/docid/5542301a4.html> accessed 4 August 2019

### India

Baby Manji Yamada v. Union of India & ANR [2008] INSC 1656 (Supreme Court of India)

### Japan

92. Kōbe family Court Himeji Branch Adjudication, Kagetsu Vol 14, No 11, p 166 [20 June 1962 (*Shōwa 37 nen*)]
93. Mito Family Court Adjudication, Kagetsu Vol 41, No 4, p 82 [7 October 1988 (*Shōwa 63 nen*)]
94. Ōita Family Court Bungotakada Branch Adjudication, Kagetsu Vol 28, No 1, p 84 [31 January 1975 (*Shōwa 50 nen*)]
95. Ōsaka Family Court Adjudication, Kagetsu Vol 32, No 2, p 89 [27 January 1979 (*Shōwa 54 nen*)]
96. Ōsaka High Court Decision, Hanrei Jihō No.1919, p108 [20 May 2005 (*Heisei 17 nen*)]
97. Sendai Family Court, Adjudication, Unpublished [24 June 2016 (*Heisei 28 nen*)]
98. Sendai High Court Akita Branch Judgement, Hanrei Jihō No 1681, p 112 [10 December 2004 (*Heisei 16 nen*)]
99. Supreme Court (Petty Bench II) Judgment, Shūmin Vol 208, p 495 [22 November 2002 (*Heisei 14 nen*)]
100. Supreme Court (Petty Bench II) Judgement, Minshū Vol 61, No 2, p 619 [23 March 2007 (*Heisei 19 nen*)]
101. Supreme Court Judgment, Minshū Vol 16, No 7, p 1247 [27 April 1962 (*Shōwa 37 nen*)]
102. Supreme Court, Minshū Vol 29, No 9, p 1417 [24 October 1975 (*Shōwa 54 nen*)] (Todai byōin lumbar jiken)
103. Takamatsu High Court Judgement, Kagetsu Vol 26, No 2, p 104 [26 August 1976 (*Shōwa 51 nen*)]

104. Tōkyō District Court, Hanrei Jihō No 286, p 25 [13 December 1961 (*Shōwa 36 nen*)]
105. Tōkyō District Court, Minshū Vol 49, No 1, p 182, 190 [26 February 1993 (*Heisei 5 nen*)] (Baby Andrew Case)
106. Tōkyō Family Court Tachikawa Branch Adjudication, Unpublished [5 December 2016 (*Heisei 28 nen*)]
107. Tōkyō Family Court Adjudicaiton, Kagetsu Vol 19, No 3, p 73 [9 September 1966 (*Shōwa 41 nen*)]
108. Tōkyō High Court Judgement, Minshū Vol 49, No 1, p 193 [26 January 1994 (*Heisei 6 nen*)] (Baby Andrew Case)
109. Tōkyō High Court Judgement, Hanrei Jihō No 1680, p 86 [12 May 1999 (*Heisei 11 nen*)]
110. Yokohama Family Court Adjudicaiton, Kagetsu Vol 56, No 3, p 68 [18 September 2003 (*Heisei 15 nen*)]

## Philippines

111. *Mary Grace Natividad S Poe-llamanzares v. Comelec* [2016] Nos. 221697 & 221698–700 (Supreme Court of the Philippines)
112. *Rizalino David v. Senate Electoral Tribunal & Mary Grace Poe Llamanzares* [2016] GR 221538 (Supreme Court of the Philippines)

## Spain

113. *Res. DGRN 3.a de 9 de octubre de 1996 (BIMJ, núm. 1795, 1997, pp 1018–20; RAJ, 1997, núm. 2550; Actualidad Civil (Registros), 1997–3, núm. 287, pp 251–2)*
114. *Res. DGRN 3.a de 21 de junio de 1996 (BIMJ, núms. 1782–1783, 1996, pp 3606–8)*
115. *Res. DGRN 4.a de 7 de octubre de 1996 (BIMJ, núm. 1794, 1997, pp 905–8)*
116. *Res. DGRN de 10 de enero de 1995 (BIMJ, núm. 1737, 1995, pp 1390–2; RAJ, 1995, núm. 1453; Actualidad Civil (Registros), 1995–3, núm. 286, p 218)*
117. *Res. DGRN de 10 de junio de 2005 (BOE, 1-VIII-2005, pp 27158–9 [Anexo III.3.25])*

## United Kingdom

118. *Pham (Appellant) v. Secretary of State for the Home Department (Respondent)* [2015] 19 UKSC 1, [2015] WLR 1591 (United Kingdom Supreme Court)

## United States

119. *AAO, Re Applicant 2007 WL 5338559 (DHS)* [10 August 2007]
120. *AAO, Re Applicant 2010 WL 6527657 (DHS)* [24 May 2010]
121. *AAO, Re Applicant 2011 WL 10845097 (DHS)* [15 September 2011]
122. *AAO, Re Applicant 2013 WL 5504816 (DHS)* [19 February 2013]
123. *AAO, Re Applicant 2016 WL 8315993 (DHS)* [30 November 2016]

124. *Addington v. Texas* [1979] 441 US 418 (US Supreme Court)
125. *David Johnson v. Attorney General of the US Department of Homeland Security* [2005] DC No 04-cv-04443 (US District Court for the Eastern District of Pennsylvania)
126. *Delmore v. Brownell* [1956] 236 F2d 598 (US Court of Appeals Third Circuit)
127. *Hernandez v. Ashcroft* [2004] No 02–70988, 114 Fed Appx 183 (US Court of Appeals Ninth Circuit)
128. *Ramon-Sepulveda v. INS* [1984] 743 F2d 1307 (United States Court of Appeals Ninth Circuit)
129. *Trop v. Dulles* [1958] 356 US 86 (US Supreme Court)
130. *Woodby v. INS* [1966] 385 US 276 (US Supreme Court)
131. Unpublished administrative precedent by USCIS on 29 November 2006 in Newark confirming nationality acquisition under section 301(f) of the Immigration and Nationality Act, detailed in the article by Chris Nugent and Doug Burnett of the Holland & Knight Community Services Team, 'The Foundling Statute' (23 January 2007) <https://www.ilw.com/articles/2007,0123-nugent.shtm> accessed 4 August 2019

## *(C) Table of International Legal Documents*

## *(C-1) International and Regional Treaties*

132. *Convention on Certain Questions Relating to the Conflict of Nationality Law,* 179 LNTS 89 (entered into force 1 July 1937) ('the 1930 Convention')
133. *Convention on the Avoidance of Statelessness in Relation to State Succession,* 15 March 2006, ETS 200
134. *Convention on the Elimination of All Forms of Discrimination Against Women* (CEDAW), New York, 18 December 1979 1249 UNTS 13 (entered into force 3 September 1981)
135. *Convention on the Elimination of All Forms of Racial Discrimination* (CERD), *New York, 7 March 1966,* 660 UNTS 195 (entered into force 4 January 1969)
136. *Convention on the Law of Treaties 1969*, Vienna, 23 May 1969, 1155 UNTS 331 (entered into force 27 January 1980) (VCLT)
137. *Convention on the Reduction of Statelessness*, New York, 30 August 1961, 989 UNTS 175 (entered into force 13 December 1975) ('the 1961 Convention')
138. *Convention on the Rights of Persons with Disabilities* (CRPD), New York, 13 December 2006, 2515 UNTS 3 (entered into force 3 May 2008)
139. *Convention on the Rights of the Child* (CRC), New York, 20 November 1989, 1577 UNTS 3 (entered into force 2 September 1990)
140. *Convention Relating to the Status of Refugees*, Geneva, 28 July 1951, 189 UNTS 137 (entered into force 22 April 1954) ('the 1954 Convention')
141. *Convention Relating to the Status of Stateless Persons*, New York, 28 September 1954, 360 UNTS 117 ('the 1954 Convention')
142. *Covenant on the Rights of the Child in Islam* (June 2005) <http://www.unhcr.org/refworld/docid/44eaf0e4a.html> accessed 4 August 2019
143. *European Convention on Nationality* (ECN), 6 November 1997, ETS 166 (entered into force 1 March 2000)
144. *International Convention on the Protection of the Rights of All Migrant Workers and Members of Their Families* (ICRMW), New York, 18 December 1990, 2220, UNTS 3 (entered into force 1 July 2003)
145. *International Covenant on Civil and Political Rights* (ICCPR), New York, 16 December 1966, 999 UNTS 171 (entered into force 23 March 1976)

## (C-2) International Instruments and Materials : Travaux of the 1930 Convention

146. Acts of the Conference for the Codification of International Law held at The Hague from March 13th to April 12th, 1930. Volume I Plenary Meetings, Official No.: C. 351. M. 145. 1930. V. (League of Nations 19 August 1930)
147. Acts of the Conference for the Codification of International law held at the Hague from March 13th to April 12th, 1930, Meetings of the Committees, Volume II Minutes of the 1st Committee Meetings: Nationality, Official No.: C. 351 (a). M. 145(a). 1930. V. (League of Nations 27 November 1930)
148. International Law Commission, 'League of Nations Codification Conference' <http://legal.un.org/ilc/league.shtml> accessed 4 August 2019
149. League of Nations, 'Bases of Discussion Drawn up for the Conference by the Preparatory Committee, Volume I Nationality (Volume I-C.73.M.38.I929. V-BI-Geneva) (Conference for the Codification of International Law, May 1929)

## Travaux of the 1961 Convention

150. Córdova, R., Nationality, including Statelessness – Report on the Elimination or Reduction of Statelessness (1953) <http://legal.un.org/docs/?path=../ilc/documentation/english/a_cn4_64.pdf&lang=E> accessed 4 August 2019
151. Hudson, M.O., 'Report on Nationality, including Statelessness' in *Yearbook of the International Law Commission* (International Law Commission 21 February 1952)
152. ILC, Report of the International Law Commission to the General Assembly, Draft Convention on the Reduction of Future Statelessness (1954), *Yearbook of the International Law Commission, vol II* (United Nations 1954)
153. ILC, Summaries of the Work of the International Law Commission: Nationality including Statelessness (15 July 2015) <http://legal.un.org/ilc/summaries/6_1.shtml> accessed 4 August 2019
154. United Nations, Summary Records, 9th Plenary Meeting held on 15 April 1959, A/CONF.9/SR.9, UN Conference on the Elimination or Reduction of Future Statelessness, Geneva, 1959 and New York, 1961 (15 April 1959) <https://legal.un.org/diplomaticconferences/1959_statelessness/docs/english/vol_2/a_conf9_sr9.pdf> accessed 4 August 2019
155. United Nations, Summary Records, 5th Plenary Meeting held on 31 March 1959, A/CONF.9/SR.5, UN Conference on the Elimination or Reduction of Future Statelessness, Geneva, 1959 and New York, 1961 (31 March 1959) <http://legal.un.org/docs/?path=../diplomaticconferences/1959_statelessness/docs/english/vol_2/a_conf9_sr5.pdf&lang=E> accessed 4 August 2019
156. United Nations, Summary Records, 5th Meeting of the Committee of the Whole held on 3 April 1959, A/CONF.9/C.1/SR.5, UN Conference on the Elimination or Reduction of Future Statelessness, Geneva, 1959 and New York, 1961 (3 April 1959) <http://legal.un.org/docs/?path=../diplomaticconferences/1959_statelessness/docs/english/vol_2/a_conf9_c1_sr5.pdf&lang=E> accessed 4 August 2019
157. United Nations Conference on the Elimination or Reduction of Future Statelessness Geneva, 1959 and New York, 1961, A/CONF.9/4 (15 January 1959) Denmark: Memorandum with Draft Convention on the Reduction of Statelessness <http://legal.un.org/docs/?path=../diplomaticconferences/1959_statelessness/docs/english/vol_1/a_conf9_4.pdf&lang=E> accessed 4 August 2019
158. United Nations, Comments by Governments on the draft Convention on the Elimination of Future Statelessness and on the draft Convention on the Reduction of Future Statelessness

(1954) <http://legal.un.org/docs/?path=../ilc/documentation/english/a_cn4_82.pdf&lang=E> accessed 4 August 2019

159. United Nations Economic and Social Council, The Problem of Statelessness—Consolidated Report by the Secretary-General, A/CN.4/56 and Add.1 (26 May 1952) <http://legal.un.org/ilc/documentation/english/a_cn4_56.pdf> accessed 4 August 2019

160. United Nations, A Study of Statelessness (August 1949) <https://www.unhcr.org/protection/statelessness/3ae68c2d0/study-statelessness-united-nations-august-1949-lake-success-new-york.html?query=A%20Study%20of%20Statelessness> accessed 4 August 2019

161. United Nations, 'History of the two draft conventions, one dealing with the elimination of future statelessness and the other with the reduction of future statelessness, prepared by the International Law Commission' [A/CONF.9/6] (Conference on the Elimination or Reduction of Future Statelessness, Geneva) <http://legal.un.org/docs/?path=../diplomaticconferences/1959_statelessness/docs/english/vol_1/a_conf9_6.pdf&lang=E> accessed 4 August 2019

## *African Commission on Human and Peoples' Rights (ACHPR)*

162. ACHPR, Draft Protocol to the African Charter on Human and Peoples' Rights on the Specific Aspects of the Right to a Nationality and the Eradication of Statelessness in Africa (2015) <https://www.achpr.org/public/Document/file/English/draft_citizenship_protocol_en_sept2015_achpr.pdf> accessed 17 February 2020

163. ACHPR, Draft Protocol to the African Charter on Human and Peoples' Rights on the Specific Aspects of the Right to a Nationality and the Eradication of Statelessness in Africa: Explanatory memorandum (2007) <http://citizenshiprightsafrica.org/wp-content/uploads/2018/04/34175-wd-draft_protocol_explanatory_memo_en_may2017-jobourg.pdf> accessed 4 August 2019

## *African Committee of Experts on the Rights and Welfare of the Child*

164. African Committee of Experts on the Rights and Welfare of the Child, 'General Comment No 2 on Article 6 of the African Charter on the Rights and Welfare of the Child, 'The Right to a Name, Registration at Birth, and to Acquire a Nationality' (2014) <http://www.refworld.org/docid/54db21734.html> accessed 4 August 2019.

## *Council of Europe*

165. Council of Europe, Explanatory Report to the European Convention on Nationality, 6.XI.1997 (1997) <https://rm.coe.int/16800ccde7> accessed 4 August 2019Council of Europe, Chart of signatures and ratifications of Treaty 166: Status as of 14 October 2017 (2017) <https://www.coe.int/en/web/conventions/full-list/-/conventions/treaty/166/signatures?p_auth=PptNtq61> accessed 4 August 2019Council of Europe, Reservations and Declarations for Treaty No.166 – European Convention on Nationality (2019) <https://www.coe.int/en/web/conventions/full-list/-/conventions/treaty/166/declarations?p_auth=SiRGEln7> accessed 4 August 2019

## Council of the European Union

166. Council of the European Union, 'Council Directive 2001/55/EC of 20 July 2001 on minimum standards for giving temporary protection in the event of a mass influx of displaced persons and on measures promoting a balance of efforts between Member States in receiving such persons and bearing the consequences thereof


## European Commission

167. European Commission, 'Reversing the Burden of Proof: Practical Dilemmas at the European and National Level' (December 2014) <http://ec.europa.eu/justice/discrimination/files/burden_of_proof_en.pdf> accessed 4 August 2019


## HCCH

168. HCCH, 'A Study of Legal Parentage and the Issues Arising from International Surrogacy Arrangement' (March 2014) <https://assets.hcch.net/docs/bb90cfd2-a66a-4fe4-a05b-55f33b009cfc.pdf> accessed 4 August 2019 ( 'HCCH Study (March 2014)')
169. HCCH, 'Background Note for the Meeting of the Experts' Group on the Parentage / Surrogacy Project' (January 2016) <https://assets.hcch.net/docs/8767f910-ae25-4564-a67c-7f2a002fb5c0.pdf> accessed 4 August 2019
170. HCCH, 'Questionnaire on the Private International Law Issues Surrounding the Status of Children, including Issues Arising from International Surrogacy Arrangements' (April 2013) <https://assets.hcch.net/upload/wop/gap2014pd3in.pdf> accessed 4 August 2019


## International Law Commission (ILC)

171. International Law Commission, Draft Article on Diplomatic Protection with Commentaries (2006) <http://legal.un.org/ilc/texts/instruments/english/commentaries/9_8_2006.pdf> accessed 4 August 2019


## United Nations

172. United Nations, Report of the United Nations High Commissioner for Refugees. Part II Global compact on refugees (17 December 2018) <https://www.unhcr.org/gcr/GCR_English.pdf> accessed 4 August 2019
173. United Nations, The Global Compact for Safe, Orderly and Regular Migration (GCM) (19 December 2018) <https://www.iom.int/global-compact-migration> accessed 4 August 2019
174. United Nations General Assembly, Universal Declaration of Human Rights, UNGA res 217A (III), 10 Dec 1948

## UN Committee on the Rights of the Child (UN CRC Committee)

175. UN CRC Committee, General comment No. 5 (2003): General Measures of Implementation of the Convention on the Rights of the Child, 27 November 2003, CRC/GC/2003/5
176. UN CRC Committee, General comment No 6 (2005): Treatment of Unaccompanied and Separated Children Outside their Country of Origin (1 September 2005) CRC/GC/2005/6
177. UN CRC Committee, General comment No 12 (2009): The Right of the Child to be Heard, 20 July 2009, CRC/C/GC/12
178. UN CRC Committee, General comment No 14 (2013) on the right of the child to have his or her best interests taken as a primary consideration (art. 3, para. 1), 29 May 2013, CRC /C/GC/14
179. UN CRC Committee and the Committee on the Protection of the Rights of All Migrant Workers and Members of Their Families (CMW), Joint general comment No 4 (2017) of CMW and No 23 (2017) of the CRC Committee on State obligations regarding the human rights of children in the context of international migration in countries of origin, transit, destination and return, 16 November 2017, CMW/C/GC/4-CRC/C/GC/23

## UN General Assembly

180. UN General Assembly, Resolution 50/152 of 21 December 1995 'Office of the United Nations High Commissioner for Refugees' (9 February 1996) <https://www.refworld.org/docid/3b0 0f31d24.html> accessed 4 August 2019
181. UN General Assembly, New York Declaration for Refugees and Migrants: resolution/adopted by the General Assembly (3 October 2016) <http://www.refworld.org/docid/57ceb74a4.html> accessed 4 August 2019

## UN Human Rights Council

182. UN Human Rights Council, Human Rights and Arbitrary Deprivation of Nationality: Report of the Secretary-General, A/HRC/13/34 (14 December 2009) <https://www.refworld.org/docid/ 4b83a9cb2.html> accessed 4 August 2019
183. UN Human Rights Council, Human Rights and Arbitrary Deprivation of Nationality: Resolution Adopted by the Human Rights Council (16 July 2012) <https://www.refworld.org/docid/ 5016631b2.html> accessed 4 August 2019

## UNHCR

184. UNHCR, 'Annual Statistical Report Guidelines' (January 2020) <https://popdata.unhcr.org/ ASR_instructions.pdf> accessed 15 September 2020
185. UNHCR, 'Background Note on Gender Equality, Nationality Laws and Statelessness 2018' (8 March 2018) <http://www.refworld.org/docid/5aa10fd94.html> accessed 4 August 2019
186. UNHCR, 'Birth Registration: A Topic Proposed for an Executive Committee Conclusion on International Protection' (9 February 2010) <http://www.unhcr.org/refworld/docid/4b97a3 242.html> accessed 4 August 2019

187. UNHCR, 'Convention on the Reduction of Statelessness' (30 August 1961) <https://www.unhcr.org/ibelong/wp-content/uploads/1961-Convention-on-the-reduction-of-Statelessness_ENG.pdf> accessed 4 August 2019

188. UNHCR, Côte d'Ivoire adopts Africa's first legal process to identify and protect stateless people', Press Release (4 September 2020) <https://www.unhcr.org/news/press/2020/9/5f51f33b4/cote-divoire-adopts-africas-first-legal-process-identify-protect-stateless.html> accessed 21 September 2020

189. UNHCR, 'Every Person Has the Right to Say #IBELONG' <http://ibelong.unhcr.org> accessed 4 August 2019

190. UNHCR, 'Expert Meeting – The Concept of Stateless Persons under International Law ("Prato Conclusions")' (May 2010) <http://www.refworld.org/docid/4ca1ae002.html> accessed 4 August 2019

191. UNHCR, 'Final Report Concerning the Questionnaire on Statelessness Pursuant to the Agenda for Protection Geneva' (March 2014) <http://www.unhcr.org/protect/PROTECTION/4047002e4.pdf> accessed 4 August 2019

192. UNHCR, 'Global Action Plan to End Statelessness' (4 November 2014) <http://www.refworld.org/docid/545b47d64.html> accessed 4 August 2019

193. UNHCR, 'Global Trends Forced Displacement in 2019' (18 June 2020) <https://www.unhcr.org/5ee200e37.pdf> accessed 21 September 2020

194. UNHCR, 'Good Practices Paper – Action 1: Resolving Existing Major Situations of Statelessness' (23 February 2015) <http://www.refworld.org/docid/54e75a244.html> accessed 4 August 2019

195. UNHCR, 'Good Practices Paper – Action 2: Ensuring that no Child is Born Stateless' (20 March 2017) <http://www.refworld.org/docid/58cfab014.html> accessed 4 August 2019

196. UNHCR, 'Good Practices Paper – Action 3: Removing Gender Discrimination from Nationality Laws' (6 March 2015) <http://www.refworld.org/docid/54f8377d4.html> accessed 4 August 2019

197. UNHCR, 'Good Practices Paper – Action 6: Establishing Statelessness Determination Procedures to Protect Stateless Persons' (11 July 2016) <https://www.refworld.org/docid/57836cff4.html> accessed 2 May 2019

198. UNHCR, 'Good Practices Paper – Action 6: Establishing Statelessness Determination Procedures to Protect Stateless Persons' (July 2020) <https://www.refworld.org/docid/5f203d0e4.html> accessed 20 August 2020

199. UNHCR, 'Good Practices Paper – Action 7: Ensuring Birth Registration for the Prevention of Statelessness' (November 2017) <http://www.refworld.org/docid/5a0ac8f94.html> accessed 4 August 2019

200. UNHCR, 'Good Practices: Addressing Statelessness in South East Asia' (5 February 2011) <http://www.refworld.org/docid/4d6e0a792.html> accessed 4 August 2019

201. UNHCR, 'Guidelines on Policies and Procedures in Dealing with Unaccompanied Children Seeking Asylum' (February 1997) <http://www.refworld.org/docid/3ae6b3360.html> accessed 6 March 2020

202. UNHCR, 'Handbook on Statelessness in the OSCE Area: International Standards and Good Practices' (28 February 2017) <http://www.refworld.org/docid/58b81c404.html> accessed 4 August 2019

203. UNHCR, 'High-Level Segment on Statelessness: Results and Highlights' (2020) <https://www.refworld.org/docid/5ec3e91b4.html> accessed 15 September 2020

204. UNHCR, 'How UNHCR Helps Stateless People' <http://www.unhcr.org/how-unhcr-helps-stateless-people.html> accessed 4 August 2019

205. UNHCR, '#IBelong Campaign Update, October-December 2019' (January 2020) <https://www.refworld.org/docid/5e1c4b124.html> accessed 15 September 2020

206. UNHCR, 'In Search of Solutions: Addressing Statelessness in the Middle East and North Africa' (2016) <http://www.refworld.org/docid/5829c32a4.html> accessed 4 August 2019

207. UNHCR, 'Interpreting the 1961 Statelessness Convention and Avoiding Statelessness Resulting from Loss and Deprivation of Nationality (March 2014) ('Tunis Conclusions [2014]') <http://www.refworld.org/docid/533a754b4.html> accessed 4 August 2019

208. UNHCR, 'Interpreting the 1961 Statelessness Convention and Preventing Statelessness among Children ("Dakar Conclusions")' (September 2011) <http://www.refworld.org/docid/4e8423 a72.html> accessed 4 August 2019

209. UNHCR, 'Mapping Statelessness in Austria' (2015) <http://www.refworld.org/docid/58b6e5 b14.html> accessed 4 August 2019

210. UNHCR, 'Mapping Statelessness in Belgium' (October 2012) <http://www.refworld.org/docid/5100f4b22.html> accessed 4 August 2019

211. UNHCR, 'Mapping Statelessness in Finland' (November 2014) <http://www.refworld.org/docid/546da8744.html> accessed 4 August 2019

212. UNHCR, 'Mapping Statelessness in Norway' (October 2015) <http://www.refworld.org/docid/5653140d4.html> accessed 4 August 2019

213. UNHCR, 'Mapping Statelessness in the Netherlands' (November 2011) <http://www.ref world.org/docid/4eef65da2.html> accessed 4 August 2019

214. UNHCR, 'Mapping Statelessness in the United Kingdom' (22 November 2011) <https://www.refworld.org/docid/4ecb6a192.html> accessed 4 August 2019

215. UNHCR, 'Nationality and Statelessness: Handbook for Parliamentarians N° 22' (July 2014) <https://www.refworld.org/docid/53d0a0974.html> accessed 4 August 2019

216. UNHCR, 'Note on Burden and Standard of Proof in Refugee Claims' (16 December 1998) <www.refworld.org/docid/3ae6b3338.html> accessed 12 July 2019

217. UNHCR, 'Note on the Cancellation of Refugee Status' (22 November 2004) <www.refworld.org/docid/41a5dfd94.html> accessed 12 July 2019

218. UNHCR, 'Note on the Nationality Status of the Urdu-Speaking Community in Bangladesh' (17 December 2009) <http://www.unhcr.org/refworld/docid/4b2b90c32.html> accessed 4 August 2019

219. UNHCR, 'Persons at Risk of Statelessness in Serbia: Progress Report 2010–2015' (June 2016) <http://www.refworld.org/docid/57bd436b4.html> accessed 4 August 2019

220. UNHCR, 'Refugees Number 147 / Issue 3: The Excluded' (2007)

221. UNHCR, 'Refworld Nationality and Statelessness/Citizenship Law/ Nationality Law Database' <https://www.refworld.org/topic,50ffbce524d,50ffbce525c,,0,,LEGISLATION,. html> accessed 4 August 2019

222. UNHCR, 'Representing Stateless Persons Before US Immigration Authorities' (August 2017) <http://www.refworld.org/docid/59a5898c4.html> accessed 4 August 2019

223. UNHCR, 'Safe & Sound: What States Can Do to Ensure Respect for the Best Interests of Unaccompanied and Separated Children in Europe' (October 2014) <https://www.refworld.org/docid/5423da264.html> accessed 7 March 2020

224. UNHCR, 'Self-Study Module on Statelessness' (1 October 2012) <https://www.refworld.org/docid/50b899602.html> accessed 4 August 2019

225. UNHCR, 'A Special Report: Ending Statelessness within 10 Years' (November 2010) <http://www.unhcr.org/546217229.html> accessed 4 August 2019

226. UNHCR, 'The State of the World's Refugees: A Humanitarian Agenda' (1997) <http://www.unhcr.org/3eb7ba7d4.pdf> accessed 4 August 2019

227. UNHCR, 'Statelessness Determination Procedures and the Status of Stateless Persons ("Geneva Conclusions")' (December 2010) <http://www.refworld.org/docid/4d9022762. html> accessed 4 August 2019

228. UNHCR, 'Summary of Deliberations on Credibility Assessment in Asylum Procedures, Expert Roundtable, 14–15 January 2015, Budapest, Hungary' (5 May 2015) <http://www.refworld.org/docid/554c9aba4.html> accessed 12 July 2019

229. UNHCR, 'UNHCR Action to Address Statelessness: A Strategy Note' (March 2010) <http://www.unhcr.org/refworld/docid/4b9e0c3d2.html> accessed 4 August 2019

230. UNHCR, 'UNHCR Statistical Reporting on Statelessness' (October 2019) <https://www.unhcr.org/statistics/unhcrstats/5d9e182e7/unhcr-statistical-reporting-statelessness.html> accessed 21 September 2020.

231. UNHCR and IPU, *Good Practices in Nationality Laws for the Prevention and Reduction of Statelessness* (Inter-Parliamentary Union November 2018)

232. UNHCR Executive Committee of the High Commissioner's Programme (ExCom), 'Conclusion on Identification, Prevention and Reduction of Statelessness and Protection of Stateless Persons No 106 (LVII) – 2006' (6 October 2006) <https://www.refworld.org/docid/453497 302.html> accessed 4 August 2019
233. UNHCR Structure Worldwide, 'Geographical Regions and Sub-regions' (May 2009) <http://maps.unhcr.org/en/view?id=1522> accessed 4 February 2019
234. UNHCR West Africa, 'The Lost Children of Côte d'Ivoire' (6 November 2015) <http://kora.unhcr.org/lost-children-cote-divoire/> accessed 4 August 2019

## UNICEF

235. UNICEF, Children in Alternative Care (July 2017) <https://data.unicef.org/topic/child-protec tion/children-alternative-care/> accessed 4 August 2019
236. UNICEF Data, Birth Registration (January 2018) <https://data.unicef.org/topic/child-protec tion/birth-registration/#> accessed 4 August 2019

## UNODC

237. UNODC, Global Report on Trafficking in Persons (United Nations 2018)

## *(D) List of Interviews, Briefing Sessions and Email Inquiries*

238. Briefing by Attorney Fumie Azukizawa, Ayane Odagawa and Sōsuke Seki, legal representatives, on the Tōkyō Family Court Tachikawa Branch, Adjudication, [5 December 2016 (*Heisei 28 nen*)] at a session of the Study Group on Statelessness in Japan (20 January 2017)
239. Email from Anisa Metalla (Senior Attorney at Law, Tirana Legal Aid Society) to author (25 July 2017)
240. Email from Assistant General Counsel, Child and Family Service Agency Washington, DC to author (29 August 2017)
241. Email from Betsy Fisher to author (24 February 2017)
242. Email from Biblioteca Central Ministerio de Justiciato [Central Library of the Ministry of Justice], Spain, to author (14 September 2017)
243. Email from Dorian Needham (Attorney at law) to author, 27 September 2017
244. Email from Eva Ersbøll (Senior Researcher, the Danish Institute for Human Rights) to author (1 May 2017)
245. Email from Fumie Azukizawa (Attorney at law) to author (7 August 2019)
246. Email from Gábor Gyulai (Refugee Programme Director, the Hungarian Helsinki Committee) to author (25 April 2017)
247. Email from Giulia Bittoni to author (7 May 2019)
248. Email from Giulia Perin (Attorney at law) to author (1 May 2017)
249. Email from Inna Gladokova (former UNHCR Protection Officer (Statelessness)) to author (13 November 2019)
250. Email from Joseph C Hohenstein (Attorney at law Orlow & Orlow, Philadelphia, USA) to author (2 March 2018)

251. Email from Juan Ignacio Mondelli (Senior Regional Protection Officer (Statelessness), UNHCR Americas Bureau) to author (28 June 2017)
252. Email from on behalf of Solange Valdez-Symonds (Project for the Registration of Children as British Citizens (PRCBC)) to author (13 July 2017)
253. Email from UNHCR Russia to author (30 June 2017)
254. Email from Wout Van Doren (Statelessness Consultant, Protection Unit for Belgium and Luxembourg, UNHCR Regional Representation for Western Europe) to author (3 August 2017)
255. Email inquiry from author to UNHCR Paris (27 June 2017)
256. Emails and telephone communications from Citizenship and Registry Department, Budapest Metropolitan Government Office (Budapest, Hungary) to author (May to August 2017)
257. Emails from Colleen Cowgill and Lindsay Jenkins (UNHCR Washington) to author (18 July 2017)
258. Emails from Enrico Guida (Statelessness Expert, UNHCR Italy) to author (starting on 28 April 2017)
259. Emails from Jelena Milonjic (Legal Associate, UNHCR Representation in Serbia) to author (5 and 7 July 2017)
260. Emails from Katinka Huszár (Protection Associate, UNHCR Hungary) to author (starting on 26 April 2019)
261. Emails from Ljiljana Kokotovic (Associate Protection Officer, UNHCR, Country Office for Bosnia and Herzegovina, Sarajevo) to author (9 and 21 August 2017)
262. Email from Marin Roman (Statelessness Officer, UNHCR Central Asia) to author (5 January 2021)
263. Emails from Paolo Farci (Attorney at law) to author (starting on 2 May 2017)
264. Email from Tessa Onida (General Area Director, Research and Monitoring Services, Istituto degli Innocenti, Florence, Italy) to author (31 May 2017)
265. Emails from Valeriia Cherednichenko and Inge Sturkenboom (UNHCR Regional Representation for Western Europe (5 July 2017)
266. Interview with Central Direction for Civil Rights, Citizenship and Minorities of the Department for Civil Liberties and Immigration of the Ministry of Interior, Italy (Rome, Italy, 23 May 2017)
267. Interview with Derbak, M., Chief of the Europe Division and officials of the Statelessness, Department of the OFPRA (Paris, France, 14 December 2016)
268. Interview with Farci, P., Attorney at Law (Florence, Italy, 22 May 2017)
269. Interview with Gerard-René de Groot, Professor Emeritus at Maastricht University School of Law (Skype, 5 October 2017)
270. Interview with Giuffrida, M.G., President, Istituto degli Innocenti (Rome, Italy, 22 May 2017)
271. Interview with Guida, E., Statelessness Expert, UNHCR Rome (23 May 2017)
272. Interview with Huszka, Z., Legal Officer/Statelessness focal point at the Immigration and Asylum Office (IAO), Prime Minister Office, Division for Migration, Ministry of Interior, Hungary (Budapest, Hungary, 26 May 2017)
273. Interview with Kunszt, R., Head of Guardianship Department at the Municipal Government Office, Fifth District Guardianship Office (Budapest, Hungary, 25 May 2017)
274. Interview with Kuslits, G., Director of Child Protection Services of Budapest (25 May 2017)
275. Interview with Ms. Gandolfo, Director, Citizenship Office of the Municipality of Florence (Florence, Italy, 22 May 2017)
276. Interview with Napoli, E.D., PhD and Fellow, Autorità garante per l'infanzia e l'adolescenza [guardianship authority for infants and adolescents] (23 May 2017)
277. Interview with Ōnuki, K., Attorney at Law (Tokyo, Japan, 4 March 2017)
278. Interview with Zsuzsanna, B., Attorney at law and a legal guardian, Child Protection Services of Budapest former (till 2009) Deputy Head of Division, Social and Guardianship Division, Guardianship Department at the Municipal Government Office, Fifth District Guardianship Office (Budapest, Hungary, 25 May 2017)

279. Skype Interview with de Groot, G.-R., Professor Emeritus at Maastricht University School of Law (5 October 2017)
280. Telephone conversation with Joseph C Hohenstein (Attorney at Law, Orlow & Orlow, Philadelphia, USA) (2 March 2018)
281. Telephone conversation with UNHCR Paris (February 2018)

## (E) List of Other Documents Such as Books, Articles, Reports, Web Sources

282. Abe, K., 'Overview of Statelessness: International and Japanese Context' (April 2010) <https://www.refworld.org/docid/4c344c252.html> accessed 4 May 2019
283. Achmad, C., 'Securing Every Child's Right to a Nationality in a Changing World: The Nationality Implications of International Surrogacy' in L. van Waas and M. Khanna (eds), *Solving Statelessness* (Wolf Legal Publishers 2017)
284. Adjami, M., 'Statelessness and Nationality in Côte d'Ivoire – A Study for UNHCR' (December 2016) <http://www.refworld.org/docid/58594d114.html> accessed 4 August 2019
285. Aird, S., Harnett, H. and Shah, P., *Stateless Children – Youth Who Are Without Citizenship, Booklet No 7 in A Series on International Youth Issues* (1st edn, Youth Advocate Program International 2002)
286. Akiyama, H., 'Jiyūkenkiyaku ni okeru kodomo no kokuseki shutoku ken to kokkano gimu – Jiyūkenkiyaku dai 2 jō no kanten kara' ['Children's right to acquire nationality under ICCPR and States' responsibilities – from the viewpoint of article 2 of ICCPR'] (2019) 30 Kokusaijinken [Human Rights International] 115
287. Akiyama, H., 'Mukokusekisha towa Dareka: Kokusaihōniokeru Mukokusekisha no Teigi to Mitōrokusha no Kanrensei Kara' ['Who is a Stateless Person? Definition of a Stateless Person in International Law and Unregistered Persons'] (2015) 22 Kankyō sozō [Social-Human Environmentology] 67
288. Albarazi, Z., 'Regional Report on Citizenship: The Middle East and North Africa (MENA), RSCAS/GLOBALCIT-Comp. 2017/3' (November 2017) <http://cadmus.eui.eu/bitstream/handle/1814/50046/RSCAS_GLOBALCIT_Comp_2017_03.pdf?sequence=1&isAllowed=y> accessed 4 August 2019
289. Albarazi, Z. and van Waas, L., 'Statelessness and Displacement: Scoping Paper' (2015) <http://www.institutesi.org/stateless_displacement.pdf> accessed 4 August 2019
290. Albarazi, Z. and van Waas, L., 'Understanding Statelessness in the Syria Refugee Context' (2016) <http://www.refworld.org/docid/584021494.html> accessed 4 August 2019
291. Arakaki, O., 'Mukokusekichiijōyaku to Mukokuseki Sakugen Jōyaku' ['1954 Convention Relating to the Status of Stateless Persons and 1961 Convention on the Reduction of Stateless Persons: The Developments Leading up to Their Adoption and the Overview of the Conventions'] (October 2014) 86 Hōritsu Jihō No 1078
292. Arakaki, O., *Statelessness Conventions and Japanese Laws: Convergence and Divergence* (UNHCR 2015)
293. Arendt, H., *The Origins of Totalitarianism* (Harvest Book, Hb244, 1st edn, Harcourt, Brace, Jovanovich 21 March 1973)
294. Asahi Shimbun News, 'Naimitsu Shussan Demo Koseki Sakusei "Kanō" Hōmushō ga Kenkai' ['It is "Possible" to Create Japanese Family Register for Those Born Through Confidential Birth-Ministry of Justice's View'] (19 May 2018) <https://www.asahi.com/articles/ASL57760LL57UBQU00D.html> accessed 15 July 2019
295. Asahi Shimbun News, 'Nananin Chū go Nin wa Jitaku de Umu' ['Five Out of Seven Gave Birth "Isolated" at Home'] (29 May 2018) <https://www.asahi.com/articles/ASL5X77P8L5XUBQU00Y.html> accessed 25 May 2018

296. Aurelia Álvarez Rodríguez y, *Nacionalidad de los Hijos de Extranjeros Nacidos en España Regulación Legal e Interpretación Jurisprudencial Sobre un Análisis de Datos Estadísticos de los Nacidos en Territorio Español Durante el Período 1996–2002* [*Nationality of the Children of Foreigners Born in Spain: Legal Regulation and Jurisprudential Interpretation on An Analysis of Statistical Data of Those Born in Spanish Territory during the Period 1996–2002*] (Observatorio Permanente de la Inmigración (for Ministerio de Trabajo y Asuntos Sociales [now Ministerio de Empleo y Seguridad Social] 2006)

297. Balazo, P., 'Cross-border Gestational Surrogacy in Japan and the Spectre of Statelessness, Statelessness Working Paper Series No 2017/5' (May 2017) <http://www.institutesi.org/WP2 017_05.pdf> accessed 4 August 2019

298. Bangar, A., 'Statelessness in India, Statelessness Working Paper Series No 2017/02' (June 2017) <http://www.institutesi.org/WP2017_02.pdf> accessed 4 August 2019

299. Batchelor, C., 'The International Legal Framework Concerning Statelessness and Access for Stateless Persons. Contribution to the European Union Seminar on the Content and Scope of International Protection: Panel 1 – Legal Basis of International Protection, Madrid, 8 – 9 January 2002' (8 January 2002) <https://www.refworld.org/docid/415c3be44.html> accessed 4 August 2019

300. Batchelor, C., 'Stateless persons: some gaps in international protection' (1995) 7 International Journal of Refugee Law 232

301. Bianchini, K., 'A comparative analysis of statelessness determination procedures in 10 EU States' (2017) 29 International Journal of Refugee Law 42

302. Bianchini, K., *Protecting Stateless Persons: The Implementation of the Convention Relating to the Status of Stateless Persons across EU States* (Brill | Nijhoff 2018)

303. Black's Law Dictionary, 'What is FOUNDLING?' Online <https://thelawdictionary.org/fou ndling/> accessed 4 August 2019

304. Black's Law Dictionary, 'What is CHILD?' (2019) <https://thelawdictionary.org/child/> accessed 4 August 2019

305. Black's Law Dictionary, 'What is INFANT?' (2019) <https://thelawdictionary.org/infant/> accessed 4 August 2019

306. Blanchard, C. and Joy, S., 'Can't Stay. Can't Go. – Refused Asylum Seekers Who Cannot Be Returned' (2017) <https://www.refworld.org/docid/591965984.html> accessed 4 August 2019

307. Bleiker, C., 'Germany: Confidential Birth: A Safe, Private Way Out for Pregnant Women' (2017) <www.dw.com/en/confidential-birth-a-safe-private-way-out-for-pregnant-women/a-39662482> accessed 4 August 2019

308. Bloom, T., 'Statelessness and the Second Revision of the Global Compact for Migration: What Still Needs to Be Addressed?' (5 June 2018) <https://www.statelessness.eu/blog/sta telessness-and-second-revision-global-compact-migration-what-still-needs-be-addressed> accessed 4 August 2019

309. Boillet, V. and Akiyama, H., 'Statelessness and international surrogacy from the international and European legal perspectives' (2017) 27 Swiss Rev Int'l & Eur L 513

310. Brownlie, I., *Principles of Public International Law* (Oxford University Press 2003)

311. Brownlie, I., 'The relations of nationality in public international law' (1963) 39 Brit YB Int'l L 284

312. Chiba ken wakōdo jiritsu shien kikō jimukyoku (ed), *Jidō yōgoshisetsu no nyūsho jidō no kokuseki/zairyūshikaku mondai no tebiki (shian)'* [*Manual to Resolve Nationality and Residency Status Issues for Children Admitted to Child Custody Facilities (Provisional Version)*] (2014) <http://www.wakoudo.org/report/kokuseki/kokusekimondai_tebiki.pdf> accessed 7 August 2019

313. Chris Nugent and Doug Burnett of the Holland & Knight Community Services Team, 'The Foundling Statute' (23 January 2007) <https://www.ilw.com/articles/2007,0123-nugent. shtm> accessed 4 August 2019

314. Citizenship Rights in Africa Initiative, 'Database on Nationality Acquisition' <http://citize nshiprightsafrica.org/advanced-search/?fwp_themes=acquisition-of-nationality> accessed 4 August 2019

315. Coutinho, J. and Krell, C., *Anonyme Geburt und Babyklappen in Deutschland. Fallzahlen, Angebote, Kontexte* [*Anonymous Birth and Baby Hatches in Germany*] (Deutsches Jugendinstitut 2011)

316. DALLOZ <www.dalloz.fr> accessed 4 August 2019

317. Dawn, 'Nadra Told to Identify, Register Unclaimed Children' (10 December 2014) <http://www.dawn.com/news/1149899/nadra-told-to-identify-register-unclaimed-children> accessed 4 August 2019

318. de Groot, G.-R., 'Children, Their Right to A Nationality and Child Statelessness' in A. Edwards and L. van Waas (eds), *Nationality and Statelessness under International Law* (Cambridge University Press 2014)

319. de Groot, G.-R., 'Quasi-Loss of Nationality: Some Critical Reflections' in ISI, *The World's Stateless: Deprivation of Nationality* (March 2020) 203–206 <https://files.institutesi.org/WORLD's_STATELESS_2020.pdf> accessed 27 September 2020

320. de Groot, G.-R. and Vonk, O.W., *International Standards on Nationality Law: Texts, Cases and Materials* (Wolf Legal Publishers 2016)

321. de Groot, G.-R. and Wautelet, P., 'Reflections on Quasi-Loss of Nationality from Comparative, International and European Perspectives' in S.C. Nuñez and G.-R. de Groot (eds), *European Citizenship at the Crossroads: The Role of the European Union on Loss and Acquisition of Nationality* (Wolf Legal Publishers 2015)

322. de Groot, G.-R. and Wautelet, P., 'Survey on Rules Loss of Nationality in International Treaties and Case Law' in S.C. Nuñez and G.-R. de Groot (eds), *European Citizenship at the Crossroads: The Role of the European Union on Loss and Acquisition of Nationality* (Wolf Legal Publishers 2015)

323. de Groot, G.-R., Swider, K. and Vonk, O., 'Practices and Approaches in EU Member States to Prevent and End Statelessness' (2015) <http://www.europarl.europa.eu/RegData/etudes/STUD/2015/536476/IPOL_STU(2015)536476_EN.pdf> accessed 4 August 2019

324. Dellert, N., 'Die Anonyme Kindesabgabe: Anonyme Geburt und Babyklappe' (2009) Peter Lang 35

325. Diao, J., 'Child Abandonment China's Growing Challenge' (13 September 2015) <https://beijingtoday.com.cn/2015/09/child-abandonment-chinas-growing-challenge/> accessed 4 August 2019

326. Diccionario de la Lengua Española, La Asociación de Academias de la Lengua Española <http://dle.rae.es/?id=HKnPEfD> accessed 4 August 2019

327. Edwards, A. and Van Waas, L., 'The Meaning of Nationality in International Law in an Era of Human Rights – Procedural and Substantive Aspects' in A. Edwards and L. van Waas (eds), *Nationality and Statelessness Under International Law* (Cambridge University Press 2014)

328. Edwards, A. and van Waas, L. (eds), *Nationality and Statelessness under International Law* (Cambridge University Press 2014)

329. Egawa, H., Hayata, Y. and Yamada, R., *Kokusekihō* [*Nationality Law*] (Yūhikaku 1997)

330. Einzelfall, S.A.K., 'Wie Viele Kinder Kommen in Die Babyklappe?' ['How Many Children Come in the Baby Flap?'] *Bild News* <https://www.bild.de/news/inland/babyklappe/wie-viele-kinder-kommen-in-die-babyklappe-51658362.bild.html> accessed 4 August 2019

331. Encyclopaedia Britannica, 'Kaspar Hauser, German Youth' (20 July 1998) <https://www.britannica.com/biography/Kaspar-Hauser> accessed 4 August 2019

332. Engel, C., 'The Preponderance of the Evidence versus Intime Conviction – A Behavioural Perspective on a Conflict between American and Continental European Law' (August 2008) <https://www.coll.mpg.de/pdf_dat/2008_33online.pdf> accessed 4 August 2019

333. ENS, 'Childhood Statelessness in Europe: Issues, Gaps and Good Practices' (2014) <http://www.refworld.org/docid/5343a45f4.html> accessed 4 August 2019

334. ENS, 'Ending Childhood Statelessness: A Comparative Study of Safeguards to Ensure the Right to a Nationality for Children Born in Europe, Working Paper 01/16' (2016) <https://www.statelessness.eu/sites/statelessness.eu/files/file_attach/ENS_1961_Safeguards_Stateless_children.pdf> accessed 4 August 2019

335. ENS, 'Ending Childhood Statelessness: A Study on Albania, Working Paper 06/15' (June 2015) <https://www.statelessness.eu/sites/www.statelessness.eu/files/Albania.pdf> accessed 4 August 2019

336. ENS, 'Ending Childhood Statelessness: A Study on Italy, Working Paper 07/15' (2015) <http://www.refworld.org/docid/582327974.html> accessed 4 August 2019

337. ENS, 'Ending Childhood Statelessness: A Study on Latvia' (2015) <http://www.statelessness.eu/sites/www.statelessness.eu/files/Latvia_0.pdf> accessed 4 August 2019

338. ENS, 'Ending Childhood Statelessness: A Study on Macedonia, Working Paper 02/15' (June 2015) <http://www.statelessness.eu/resources/ending-childhood-statelessness-study-macedonia> accessed 10 February 2017

339. ENS, 'Ending Childhood Statelessness: A Study on Poland, Working Paper 03/15' (June 2015) <https://www.statelessness.eu/sites/www.statelessness.eu/files/Poland.pdf> accessed 4 August 2019

340. ENS, 'Ending Childhood Statelessness: A Study on Romania, Working Paper 01/15' (2015) <http://www.statelessness.eu/sites/www.statelessness.eu/files/Romania.pdf> accessed 10 February 2017

341. ENS, 'Ending Childhood Statelessness: A Study on Slovenia, Working Paper 08/15' (2015) <http://www.statelessness.eu/sites/www.statelessness.eu/files/Slovenia.pdf> accessed 4 August 2019

342. ENS, 'No Child Should be Stateless' (2015) <https://www.statelessness.eu/resources/no-child-should-be-stateless-austria> accessed 4 August 2019

343. ENS, 'Statelessness Index Survey' <https://index.statelessness.eu/> accessed 7 August 2019

344. ENS, 'Statelessness Index Survey 2019: Netherlands' (2020) <https://index.statelessness.eu/sites/default/files/ENS_Statelessness_Index_Survey-Netherlands-2019_0.pdf> accessed 15 September 2020

345. ENS, 'ENS Statelessness Index Survey 2019: Hungary' (2020) <https://index.statelessness.eu/sites/default/files/ENS_Statelessness_Index_Survey-Hungary-2019.pdf> accessed 25 December 2020

346. ENS, 'ENS Statelessness Index Survey 2019: Latvia' (2020) <https://index.statelessness.eu/sites/default/files/ENS_Statelessness_Index_Survey-Latvia-2019.pdf> accessed 25 December 2020

347. ENS, 'ENS Statelessness Index Survey 2019: North Macedonia' (2020) <https://index.statelessness.eu/sites/default/files/ENS_Statelessness_Index_Survey-North_Macedonia-2019.pdf> accessed 25 December 2020

348. ENS, 'ENS Statelessness Index Survey 2019: Serbia' (2020) <https://index.statelessness.eu/sites/default/files/ENS_Statelessness_Index_Survey-Serbia-2019.pdf> accessed 25 December 2020

349. ENS, 'ENS Statelessness Index Survey 2019: Slovenia' (2020) <https://index.statelessness.eu/sites/default/files/ENS_Statelessness_Index_Survey-Slovenia-2019.pdf> accessed 25 December 2020.European Roma Rights Centre (ERRC), ENS and ISI, 'Statelessness, Discrimination and Marginalisation of Roma in the Western Balkans and Ukraine' (October 2017) <https://www.statelessness.eu/sites/www.statelessness.eu/files/attachments/resources/roma-belong.pdf> accessed 4 August 2019

350. European Asylum Support Office (EASO), *Country of Origin Information Report: Pakistan Country Overview* (EASO April 2015) <https://www.easo.europa.eu/sites/default/files/public/EASO_COI_Report_Pakistan-Country-Overview_final.pdf> accessed 7 August 2019

351. Farci, P., *Apolidia (Statelessness)* (Giuffré 2012)

352. Findelbaby project's website, <http://www.sternipark.de/fileadmin/content/PDF_Upload/Findelbaby/Babyklappenliste__Stand_Juni_2016_.pdf> accessed 22 July 2017

353. Fisher, B., 'Statelessness in the GCC: Gender Discrimination beyond Nationality Law, Statelessness Working Paper Series No 2015/01' (December 2015) <http://www.institutesi.org/WP2015_01.pdf> accessed 4 August 2019

354. Fisher, B., 'Why Non-Marital Children in the MENA Region Face a Risk of Statelessness' (January 2015) <http://harvardhrj.com/wp-content/uploads/2015/01/Fisher_HRJ_01-05-15.pdf> accessed 4 August 2019

355. Fisher, B., 'The operation of law in statelessness determinations under the 1954 Statelessness Convention' (2015) 33 Wisconsin International Law Journal 254

356. FIOM, 'Bevallen onder Geheimhouding' ['Giving Birth under Confidentiality'] <https://fiom. nl/sites/default/files/files/factsheet_bevallen_onder_geheimhouding.pdf> accessed 4 August 2019

357. Foster, M. and Lambert, H., 'Statelessness as a human rights issue: a concept whose time has come' (2016) 28 International Journal of Refugee Law 564

358. Foster, M., McAdam, J. and Wadley, D., 'Part two: the prevention and reduction of statelessness in Australia – an ongoing challenge' (2017) 40 Melb UL Rev 456

359. Fripp, E., *Nationality and Statelessness in the International Law of Refugee Status* (Hart Publishing 2016)

360. Fū, Y., 'Nihon de umareta kodomono kokuseki to mukokuseki nintei' ['Determination of statelessness for children born in Japan'] (PhD dissertation, University of Tsukuba 2016)

361. Fujita, M., 'Iryō Tsūrizumu ni Okeru Hōteki Shakaiteki Mondai' ['Legal and Social Issues Surrounding Medical Tourism'] (2019) 20 Shiga daigau keizai gakubu kenkyūnenpō [Shiga University Department of Economics Annual Report] 63

362. GLOBALCIT, 'Global Database on Modes of Acquisition of Citizenship, Version 1.0' (2017) <http://globalcit.eu/acquisition-citizenship/> accessed 4 August 2019

363. GLOBALCIT, 'Global Nationality Laws Database' <http://globalcit.eu/national-citizenship-laws/> accessed 4 August 2019

364. GLOBALCIT, 'Glossary on Citizenship and Nationality' <http://globalcit.eu/glossary_citize nship_nationality/> accessed 4 August 2019

365. Gordon, S., 'Defining Statelessness: a Chinese Case Study' (5 February 2015) <https://www. ein.org.uk/blog/defining-statelessness-chinese-case-study> accessed 4 August 2019

366. Govil, R., 'The Sustainable Development Goals and Solutions to Statelessness' in L. van Waas and M. Khanna (eds), *Solving Statelessness* (Wolf Legal Publishers 2017)

367. Gyulai, G., 'The Determination of Statelessness and the Establishment of A Statelessness-Specific Protection Regime' in A. Edwards and L. van Waas (eds), *Nationality and Statelessness under International Law* (Cambridge University Press 2014)

368. Gyulai, G., 'Nationality Unknown? An Overview of the Safeguards and Gaps Related to the Prevention of Statelessness at Birth in Hungary' (2014) <http://helsinki.hu/wp-content/upl oads/Nationality-Unknown-HHC-2014.pdf> accessed 4 August 2019

369. Gyulai, G., 'Statelessness in Hungary: The Protection of Stateless Persons and the Prevention and Reduction of Statelessness' (December 2010) <https://www.refworld.org/docid/4d6d26 972.html> accessed 12 July 2019

370. Gyulai, G., 'The Right to a Nationality of Refugee Children Born in the EU and the Relevance of the EU Charter of Fundamental Rights' (European Council on Refugees and Exiles February 2017) 12 <https://www.ecre.org/wp-content/uploads/2016/12/refugee-children-nat ionality-LEAP-leaflet.pdf> accessed 4 August 2019

371. Haraszti, K., 'Report by the Parliamentary Commissioner for Civil Rights in cases number AJB 2629/2010 and AJB 4196/2010' (September 2010) <https://www.ajbh.hu/documents/ 14315/131278/The+investigation+of+the+Ombudsman+on+the+repatriation+of+the+aba doned+non-citizen+children+born+in+Hungary/122c30fb-8cf5-4192-9e95-f12a23d46436; version=1.1> accessed 4 August 2019

372. Hayata, Y., 'Kokusekihō Nijō Sangō no "Fubo ga Tomo ni Shirenai Toki" no igi' ['The meaning of "when both parents are unknown" under article 2(iii) of Nationality Act'] (1995) 1068 Juristo 269

373. Henze, C., 'Babyklappe und Anonyme Geburt' ['Baby Hatches and Anonymous Birth'] (2014) <www.hwr-berlin.de/ileadmin/downloads_internet/publikationen/beitraege_FB4/Heft _2_2014_Fachbereich_Rechtspflege.pdf> accessed 4 August 2019

374. Hindustan Times, 'Surrogate Baby Born in India Arrives in Japan' (3 November 2008) <http:// www.hindustantimes.com/world/surrogate-baby-born-in-india-arrives-in-japan/story-clfjpE mKM0wORsHNmwG7CP.htm

375. Homma, H. (ed), *Nanmin ni Kansuru Kokusai Jōyakushu* [*Collection of International Treaties on Refugees*] (UNHCR Japan 1987)

376. Höppner, S., 'New Law to Give Orphans Right to Know Mother's Identity' (10 June 2013) <www.dw.com/en/confidential-birth-a-safe-private-way-out-for-pregnant-women/a-39662482> accessed 4 August 2019

377. House of Representatives Japan, *Dai 162 kai Kokkai Shūgiin Hōmuiinkai Gijiroku dai 24 gō* [*Legal Affairs Committee of the House of Representatives, Official Record of the Proceedings of the 162nd Session of the Diet*] (15 June 2005 [*Heisei 17 nen*])

378. Hovil, L., 'Ensuring that Today's Refugees are not Tomorrow's Stateless Persons: Solutions in A Refugee Context' in A. Edwards and L. van Waas (eds), *Nationality and Statelessness under International Law* (Cambridge University Press 2014)

379. Inter-Agency Council on Child Abuse and Neglect (ICAN), 'Safely Surrendered and Abandoned Infants in Los Angeles County – 2002–2017' (2018) <http://ican4kids.org/Reports/Safely%20Surrended/SSBL%20Report%202018.pdf> accessed 4 August 2019

380. Iqbal, N., 'Nadra Unveils Landmark Policy for Registration of Orphans' (30 May 2014) <http://www.dawn.com/news/1109455/nadra-unveils-landmark-policy-for-registration-of-orphans> accessed 4 August 2019

381. Ishii, K. and Azukizawa, F., *Gaikoku ni tsunagaru kodomo to mukokuseki – jidōyōgoshisetsu eno chōsa kekka to gutaiteki taiō rei* [*children with links with foreign countries and statelessness – the results of the survey with child foster care facilities and examples of actual responses*] (Akashi Shoten 2019)

382. Ishii, S.K., 'Access to citizenship for abandoned children: how migrants' children become "stateless" in Japanese orphanages' (2020) Journal of Ethnic and Migration Studies 1

383. ISI, 'Addressing the Right to A Nationality through the Convention on the Rights of the Child: A Toolkit for Civil Society' (June 2016) <www.institutesi.org/CRC_Toolkit_Final.pdf> accessed 4 August 2019

384. ISI, 'Draft Commentary to the Principles on Deprivation of Nationality as a National Security Measure' (2020) <https://files.institutesi.org/PRINCIPLES_Draft_Commentary.pdf> accessed 15 September 2020

385. ISI, 'Principles on Deprivation of Nationality as a National Security Measure' (2020) <https://files.institutesi.org/PRINCIPLES.pdf> accessed 15 September 2020

386. ISI, 'Realising the Right of Every Child to Acquire A Nationality: An Analysis of the Work of the Committee on the Rights of the Child' (September 2015) <www.institutesi.org/CRC_nationality_paper.pdf> accessed 30 June 2018

387. ISI, *The World's Stateless: Deprivation of Nationality* (March 2020) <https://files.institutesi.org/WORLD's_STATELESS_2020.pdf> accessed 27 September 2020

388. ISI and la Coalition de la société civile de lutte contre l'apatridie, 'Joint Submission to the Human Rights Council at the 33rd Session of the Universal Periodic Review (Third Cycle, April – May 2019), Côte d'Ivoire' (4 October 2018) <http://institutesi.org/UPR33_Cote_d Ivoire.pdf> accessed 4 August 2019

389. Itō, S. (ed) *Yōkenjijitsu Shōjiten* [*Concise Dictionary of Proof in Relation to Application of Law to Required Facts*] (Seirin Shoin 2011)

390. Itō, M., *Minjisoshōhō* [*Civil Procedure*] (Kōbundō 1989)

391. Jaghai, S., 'Statelessness at home: the story of a stateless student at Tilburg Law School' (2014) 19 Tilburg Law Review 108

392. Jiyūkokuminsha, *Hōritsu Yōgo Jiten* [*Dictionary of Legal Terminologies*] (Jiyūkokuminsha 2011)

393. Joshi, V. and Times, H., 'Orphans Can Get Passport Without Birth Certificate' (29 May 2015) <https://www.hindustantimes.com/chandigarh/orphans-can-get-passport-without-birth-certificate/story-crq9mnNqb6AyhuXybvxjEK.html> accessed 4 August 2019

394. Junco, P.A., 'La Reforma Del Derecho De La Nacionalidad De 1990, Boletín De La Facultad De Derecho, núm. i' (1992) <http://e-spacio.uned.es/fez/eserv/bibliuned:BFD-1992-1-E9B 3BB01/PDF> accessed 4 August 2019

395. Kakarala, S., Prakash, D. and Tiku, M., *India and the Challenge of Statelessness: A Review of the Legal Framework relating to Nationality*, vol 2019 (National Law University, Delhi 2015)

396. Kälin, W., 'Supervising the 1951 Convention Relating to the Status of Refugees: Article 35 and Beyond' in E. Feller, V. Türk and F. Nicholson (eds), *Refugee Protection in International Law: UNHCR's Global Consultations on International Protection* (Cambridge University Press 2003)

397. Kaneko, M., 'Dai 3 shō: Mukokuseki sha no mondai to UNHCR ni yoru taiō' ['Chapter 3: Statelessness and UNHCR's Work'] in K. Hakata and others (eds), *Nanmin/kyōsei idō kenkyū no furontia* [*New Frontiers in Refugee/Forced Migration Studies*] (Gendai jinbunsha 2014)

398. Kaneko, M., 'Mukokuseki ni Kansuru UNHCR Shin Handobukku/Gaidorain tō no Kaisetsu' ['Commentary on the newly published UNHCR Handbook and Guidelines on Statelessness'] (December 2014) 4 Refugee Studies Journal 45

399. Kaneko, M., 'Statelessness and UNHCR's work: from a forced displacement perspective' (May 2014) 9 Tokyo University CDR Quarterly 46

400. Kanics, J., 'Preventing and addressing statelessness: in the context of international surrogacy arrangements' (2014) 19 Tilburg Law Review 117

401. Kasai, M. and Koshiyama, K. (eds), *Shin Comentāru Minjisoshōhō* [*New Commentary on Civil Litigation Law*] (2nd edn, Nihon Hyōronsha 2013)

402. Kawashima, S., *Minjisoshōhō* [*Civil Procedure and Evidence*] (Nihon Hyōronsha 2013)

403. Kazazi, M., *Burden of Proof and Related Issues: A Study on Evidence before International Tribunals* (Kluwer Law International 1996)

404. Kerno, I.S., 'Nationality, including Statelessness — National Legislation Concerning Grounds for Deprivation of Nationality' (6 April 1953) <http://legal.un.org/docs/?path=../ilc/docume ntation/english/a_cn4_66.pdf&lang=EFS> accessed 4 August 2019

405. Khan, K.A.A., Buisman, C. and Gosnell, C., *Principles of Evidence in International Criminal Justice* (Oxford University Press 2010)

406. Khanna, M.J. and Brett, P., 'Making Effective Use of UN Human Rights Mechanisms to Solve Statelessness' in L. van Waas and M. Khanna (eds), *Solving Statelessness* (Wolf Legal Publishers 2017)

407. Kidana, S., *Chikujō Kaisetsu Kokusai Kazokuhō* [*Article-by-Article-Commentary on International Family Law*] (Nihon Kajo Shuppan, 2017)

408. Kidana, S., *Chikujōchūkai Kokusekihō* [*Article-by-Article Commentary to Nationality Law*] (Nihon Kajo Shuppan, 2003)

409. Kidana, S., *Chikujō Kokusekihō – Kadai no Kaimei to Jōbun no Kaisetsu* [*Nationality Law – Clarification of Issues and Article-by-Article Commentary*] (Nihon Kajo shuppan, forthcoming 2021)

410. Kimura, M. and Takezawa, M. (eds), *Shori Kijun to Shiteno Koseki Kihon Senrei Kaisetsu* [*Commentary on the Basic Precedents Relating to Family Register Administration for Reference as Processing Criteria*] (Nihon Kajo Shuppan 2008)

411. Kiyosue, T., 'Dairishussan ni Okeru Boshikankei: Bunbenshugi no Genkai' ['Mother–child relationship in surrogacy cases: limitations of the principle that the woman who gives birth is the legal mother'] (2012) 18 Hokudai Hōsei Jānaru 1

412. Kobayashi, H., *Shōkohō* [*Law of Evidence*] (Kōbundō 1989)

413. Kokott, J., *The Burden of Proof in Comparative and International Human Rights Law: Civil and Common Law Approaches with Special Reference to the American and German Legal Systems* (Kluwer Law International 1998)

414. Kumamotoshi yōhogojidō taisaku chiiki kyōgikai, 'kōnotori no Yurikago' Daisanki Kenshōhōkokusho' (September 2014) <https://www.city.kumamoto.jp/common/UploadFil eDsp.aspx?c_id=5&id=6463&sub_id=1&flid=43570> accessed 4 August 2019

415. Larousse, 'Enfant' (2019) <http://www.larousse.com/en/dictionaries/french/enfant> accessed 4 August 2019

416. Lawrance, B.N. and Stevens, J., *Citizenship in Question: Evidentiary Birthright and Statelessness* (Duke University Press 2017)

417. Lefaucheur, N., 'The French 'tradition'of anonymous birth: the lines of argument' (2004) 18 International Journal of Law, Policy and the Family 319

418. Lin, T., 'Born lost: stateless children in international surrogacy arrangements' (2013) 21 Cardozo Journal of International and Comparative Law 545

419. Lynch, M., 'Lives on Hold: The Human Cost of Statelessness' (February 2005) <https://www.refworld.org/docid/47a6eba00.html> accessed 4 August 2019

420. Mackie, V., 'Birth Registration and the Right to Have Rights: The Changing Family and Unchanging Koseki' in D. Chapman and K.J. Krogness (eds), *Japan's Household Registration System and Citizenship: Koseki, Identification and Documentation* (Routledge Studies in the Modern History of Asia 2014)

421. Malik, T., 'Children of Registered Orphanages to get Smart ID Cards Free of Cost' (24 August 2013) <http://www.nadra.gov.pk> accessed 23 May 2016

422. Malot, H., *Sans Famille* (E. Dentu 1878)

423. Manby, B., *Citizenship and Statelessness in Africa: The Law and Politics of Belonging* (Wolf Legal Publishers 2015)

424. Manby, B., 'Identification in the Context of Forced Displacement: Identification for Development' (2016) <http://documents.worldbank.org/curated/en/375811469772770030/pdf/107 276-WP-P156810-PUBLIC.pdf> accessed 4 August 2019

425. Manby, B., Getachew, A. and Sloth-Nielsen, J., 'The Right to a Nationality in Africa: New Norms and New Commitments' in Laura van Waas and Melanie Khanna (eds), *Solving Statelessness* (Wolf Legal Publishers 2017) 261

426. Manly, M., 'UNHCR's Mandate and Activities to Address Statelessness' in A. Edwards and L. van Waas (eds), *Nationality and Statelessness under International Law* (Cambridge University Press 2014)

427. Manly, M. and van Waas, L., 'The state of statelessness research: a human rights imperative' (2014) 19 Tilburg Law Review 3

428. Marx, R., '§ 4 StAG' in Fritz/Vormeier (ed), *Gemeinschaftskommentar zum Staatsangehörigkeitsgesetz [Commentary on Nationality Law]* (Looseleaf edn, Walters Kluwer/Luchterhand July 2019)

429. Massey, H., 'UNHCR and De Facto Statelessness, LPPR/2010/01' (April 2010) <https://www.refworld.org/docid/4bbf387d2.html> accessed 4 August 2019

430. Merriam Webster's On-line Dictionary, 'Definition of Foundling' (2019) <https://www.merriam-webster.com/dictionary/foundling> accessed 4 August 2019

431. Merriam Webster's On-line Dictionary, 'Definition of Infant' (2019) <https://www.merriam-webster.com/dictionary/infant> accessed 4 August 2019

432. Merriam Webster's On-line Law Dictionary, 'Legal Definition of Child' (2019) <https://www.merriam-webster.com/dictionary/child#legalDictionary> accessed 4 August 2019

433. Meslin, B., 'Determination and Protection of Stateless Persons in France' in the compilation of the handouts for Symposium Human Rights and Support for Stateless People around the World: Japan's Role (National Museum of Ethnology 2011)

434. Mohapatra, S., 'Stateless babies & adoption scams: a bioethical analysis of international commercial surrogacy' (2012) 30 BerkeleyJ Int'l Law 412

435. Mohd, A., 'Abandoned child's right to identity protection in Malaysia' (2011) 8 US-China Law Review 389

436. Mondelli, J.I., 'Eradicating Statelessness in the Americas: The Brazil Declaration and Plan of Action' in L. van Waas and M. Khanna (eds), *Solving Statelessness* (Wolf Legal Publishers 2017)

437. Mortazavi, S., 'It takes a village to make a child: creating guidelines for international surrogacy' (2012) 100 The Georgetown Law Journal

438. Murata, W., 'Dai Rokkō: Kihanteki Yōken' ['Lesson 6: Legal Requirements that Entail Legal Assessments'] in W. Murata and Y. Akio (eds), *Yōken jijitsuron sanjukkō [30 Lessons on the Theory of Proof in relation to Application of Law to Required Facts]* (3rd edn, Kōbundō 2012 [Heisei 24])

439. Ninna ho project, 'Dati sul Fenomeno dei Bambini non Riconosciuti alla Nascita' ['Data on the Phenomenon of Children Unrecognized at Birth'] <https://www.ninnaho.org/wp-content/uploads/2017/05/Osservatorio.pdf> accessed 4 August 2019

440. Nonnenmacher, S. and Cholewinski, R., 'The Nexus between Statelessness and Migration' in A. Edwards and L. van Waas (eds), *Nationality and Statelessness Under International Law* (Cambridge University Press 2014)

441. Oakeshott, N., 'Solutions to Statelessness in Southeast Asia' in L. van Waas and M. Khanna (eds), *Solving Statelessness* (Wolf Legal Publishers 2017)

442. Observer, P., 'NADRA Issues 1000 Smart Cards to Orphans' (4 September 2013) <http://pak observer.net/detailnews.asp?id=217151> accessed 4 August 2019

443. Odagawa, A. and Seki, S. (eds), 'Typology of Stateless Persons in Japan' (2017) <https://www.unhcr.org/jp/wp-content/uploads/sites/34/2018/01/TYPOLOGY-OF-STATELESS-PERSONS-IN-JAPAN_webEnglish.pdf> accessed 4 August 2019

444. Okuda, Y., *Kazoku to Kokuseki* [*Family and Nationality*] (Akashi Shoten 2017)

445. Okuda, Y., *Kokusaikazokuhō* [*International Family Law*] (Akashi Shoten 2015)

446. Okuda, Y., 'Kokusekihō nijō sangō ni tsuite (Jō)' ['On Article 2(iii) of Nationality Act-Part 1'] (1994) Kosekijihō 432

447. Okuda, Y., *Kosekihō to Kokusai Oyakohō* [*Nationality Act and International Family Law*] (Yūhikaku 2004)

448. Okuda, Y., 'Nihon de Umareta Fubo Fumei no ko no Kokuseki' ['The nationality of children born in Japan of unknown parents'] (1995) 133 Bessatsu Juristo

449. Okuda, Y., 'Saikōsai Hanrei Hihyō' ['Critique on Supreme Court Case Law'] (1995) Hanrei Jihō 174

450. Okuda, Y., *Sūji de Miru Kodomo no Kokuseki to Zairyū Shikaku* [*Nationality and Visa of Children: Statistical Analysis*] (Akashi Shoten 2002)

451. Okuda, Y., 'The United Nations Convention on the Rights of the Child and Japan's International Family Law including Nationality Law' (2003) Zeitschrift für Japanisches Recht [Journal of Japanese Law] 92

452. Okuda, Y. and others, *Yōshi Engumi Assen – Rippō Shian no Kaisetsu to Shiryō* [*Proposal for Adoption Service Law, Comments and Materials*] (Nihon Kajo Shuppan 2012)

453. Ōnuki, K., 'Cases Admitted into Family Registry: Represented by Kensuke Ōnuki, Attorney at Law, Satsuki Law Firm, Tōkyō' <http://www.satsukilaw.com/archives/category/exam/%e5%9b%bd%e7%b1%8d/%e5%b0%b1%e7%b1%8d%e8%a8%b1%e5%8f%af> accessed 4 August 2019

454. Oxford Living Dictionaries, 'Meaning of Child in English' (2019) <https://en.oxforddictionaries.com/definition/child> accessed 4 August 2019

455. Oxford Living Dictionaries, 'Meaning of Foundling in English' (2019) <https://en.oxforddictionaries.com/definition/foundling> accessed 4 August 2019

456. Oxford Living Dictionaries, 'Meaning of Infant in English' (2019) <https://en.oxforddictionaries.com/definition/infant> accessed 4 August 2019

457. Parker, L., 'Foundlings in Côte d'Ivoire' in Institute on Statelessness and Inclusion (ISI) (ed) *The World's Stateless Children* (Wolf Legal Publishers January 2017)

458. Points, K., 'Commercial Surrogacy and Fertility Tourism in India: The Case of Baby Manji' (2009) <http://www.duke.edu/web/kenanethics/CaseStudies/BabyManji.pdf>

459. Praxis, 'Analysis of the Procedures for Determining the Date and Place of Birth and for the Exercise of Rights to Citizenship and Registration of Permanent Residence in Serbia' (December 2016) <http://praxis.org.rs/images/praxis_downloads/Report_UNHCR_2016_-_28.11.pdf> accessed 4 August 2019

460. Price, P.J., 'Jus Soli and Statelessness: A Comparative Perspective from the Americas' in B.N. Lawrance and J. Stevens (eds), *Citizenship in Question: Evidentiary Birthright and Statelessness* (Duke University Press 2017)

461. Price, P.J., 'Stateless in the United States: current reality and a future prediction' (2013) 46 Vand J Transnat'l L 443

462. Rajan, S., 'Ending Statelessness Arising out of Surrogacy in India: The Latest Developments' (2017) <https://www.statelessness.eu/blog/ending-statelessness-arising-out-surrogacy-india-latest-developments>

463. Rajan, S., 'International Surrogacy Arrangements and Statelessness' in *The World's Stateless Children* (Wolf Legal Publishers (WLP) January 2017)

464. Rava, F.F., 'Società Italiana di Neonatologia (SIN) e Ninna ho Insieme a Tutela Dell'infanzia Abbandonata. Al via Un'indagine Conoscitiva Sulla Realtà Dell'abbandono Neonatale in Italia per Impostare Programmi Preventivi Efficaci di Aiuto alle Madri in Difficoltà"' [' SIN and Ninna ho Working Together to Protect Abandoned Children. Launch of A Survey on Infant Abandonment Reality in Italy to Set up Effective Preventive Programs to Help Mothers in Need'] (13 June 2013) <https://www.nph-italia.org/notizie/174/sin-e-ninna-ho-insieme-a-tutela-dell-infanzia-abba/> accessed 3 August 2019

465. Recalde-Vela, M.J., Jaghai-Bajulaiye, S. and Vlieks, C., 'The state of statelessness research: 5 years later' (2019) 24 Tilburg Law Review: Journal on international and comparative law 139

466. Richards, B., '"Can I take the normal one?" Unrelated commercial surrogacy and child abandonment' (1 January 2015) 44 Hofstra Law Review 7

467. Rosenberg, L., *Die Beweislast auf der Grundlage des BGB. und der ZPO (1965)* [*Shōmeisekinin ron* [*Theories on Burden of Proof*]] (Takuji Kurata (tr), Hanrei Taimuzusha 1987)

468. Ryūun, Ō., 'Kiji no Kokuseki' ['Nationality of abandoned children'] (1969) 4 Hōgaku Kenkyū [Hokkaigakuen Daigaku Hōgakkai] 169

469. Saarloos, K.J., 'European private international law on legal parentage? Thoughts on a European instrument implementing the principle of mutual recognition in legal parentage' (PhD dissertation, Maastricht University 2010)

470. Sano, H., 'Kakyūshin Toki no Hanrei' ['Decisions of lower courts in the limelight'] (1993) Juristo 126

471. Sarmiento, R.A., 'The Right to Nationality of Foundlings in International Law' (3 December 2015) <https://attyralph.com/2015/12/03/foundlingsnationality/> accessed 4 August 2019

472. Seet, M., 'The origins of UNHCR's global mandate on statelessness' (1 March 2016) 28 International Journal of Refugee Law 7

473. Sen, A. and Albarazi, Z., 'Efforts to Prevent Statelessness amongst Children Displaced by Conflict in the Middle East and North Africa' in L. van Waas and M. Khanna (eds), *Solving Statelessness* (Wolf Legal Publishers 2017)

474. Seng, J.M., 'Cambodian Nationality Law and the repatriation of convicted aliens under the Illegal Immigration Reform and Immigrant Responsibility Act' (March 2000) 10 Pac Rim L & Pol'y J 443

475. Shearer, I. and Opeskin, B., 'Nationality and Statelessness' in B. Opeskin, R. Perruchoud and J.R. Cross (eds), *Foundations of international Migration Law* (Cambridge University Press 2012)

476. Simeon, J.C., *The UNHCR and the Supervision of International Refugee Law* (Cambridge University Press 2013)

477. Smerdon, U.R., 'Birth registration and citizenship rights of surrogate babies born in India' (2012) 20 Contemporary South Asia 341

478. Solène Cordier for le Monde, 'L'accouchement sous le Secret, une Spécificité Française' ['Childbirth under Secrecy, A French Specificity'] (3 July 2016) <http://www.lemonde.fr/famille-vie-privee/article/2016/07/03/l-accouchement-sous-le-secret-une-specificite-franca ise_4962761_1654468.html#GBQ2XcFDusARUD6B.99> accessed 1 August 2017

479. Spiro, P.J., 'A new international law of citizenship' (2011) 105 American Journal of International Law 694

480. Statelessvoices, Born Stateless: Maria's Story (Maria Jakab, 17, Poland)' Stateless Voices <http://www.statelessvoices.com/born-stateless/> accessed 1 August 2017

481. Steele, S., 'Comments on OKUDA, statelessness and Nationality Act of Japan: baby Andrew becomes a teenager and other changes?' (2004) Zeitschrift für Japanisches Recht [Journal of Japanese Law]

482. Storrow, R.F., 'The phantom children of the republic: international surrogacy and the new illegitimacy' (2012) 20 American University Journal of Gender Social Policy and Law 561

483. Sturkenboom, I., 'Under the Radar and Under Protected: The Urgent Need to Address Stateless Children's Rights' (8 November 2012) <https://www.statelessness.eu/blog/under-radar-and-under-protected-urgent-need-address-stateless-children%E2%80%99s-rights> accessed 4 August 2019

484. Tamura, Y., 'America Minji Soshō ni Okeru Shōmei Ron' ['Rules of evidence in American civil litigations'] (2011) 5–6 Ritsumeikan Hōgaku 197

485. Tamura, Y., 'Minji Soshō ni Okeru Shōmeido Ron Saikō, Ritsumeikan Hōgaku' (2009) 327/328 Ritsumeikan Hōgaku 517

486. Tanga, P.T., Khumalo, P. and Gutura, P., 'Three Decades of HIV/AIDS Pandemic: Challenges Faced by Orphans in Tembisa, South Africa' in N. Dumais (ed), *HIV/AIDS – Contemporary Challenges* (IntechOpen 2017)

487. van Tiggelen, K, 'Vondelingen in Nederland. Actoren en Factoren in Het Naoorlogse Debat' ['Foundings in the Netherlands. Actors and factors in the post-war debate'] (2016) 91 Mens en Maatschappij 211

488. Tirana Legal Aid Society (TLAS) and others, 'Statelessness, Discrimination and Marginalisation of Roma in Albania' (February 2018) <https://www.statelessness.eu/sites/www.statelessness.eu/files/attachments/resources/roma-belong-albania-english-language.pdf?mc_cid=a8adc3b704&mc_eid=dc2ed5efa7>p> accessed 4 August 2019

489. Tobin, J. and Seow, F., 'Article 7 The Rights to Birth Registration, a Name, Nationality, and to Know and Be Cared for by Parents' in Tobin, J. (ed), *The UN Convention on the Rights of the Child: A Commentary*, Oxford Commentaries on International Law (Oxford University Press 2019)

490. Tsuruoka, T., 'Gyōsei Soshō ni Okeru Shōmei Sekinin' ['Burden of Proof in Administrative Litigations'] in H. Minami and others (eds), *Jōkai gyōsei jiken soshōhō* [*Article-by-Article Commentary on Administrative Case Litigation Act*] (4th edn, Kōbundō 2014)

491. Tucker, J., 'Questioning de facto statelessness: by looking at de facto citizenship' (2014) 19 Tilburg Law Review 276

492. University of Leiden, 'The Light's at the End of the Funnel! Evaluating the Effectiveness of the Transnational Exchange of DNA Profiles between the Netherlands and other Prüm Countries' (November 2015) <https://dnadatabank.forensischinstituut.nl/binaries/Report%20PIES%20T5%20Taverne%20Broeders%20Opmaak%20UL%2026112015%20ISBN%20DEF%20met%20omslag_tcm37-225619.pdf> accessed 1 February 2018

493. University of Nottingham, *Child Abandonment and its Prevention in Europe* (The University of Nottingham 2012)

494. Valdez-Symonds, S., 'Barriers to Citizenship Facing Stateless Children Born in the UK' (14 June 2017) <https://www.statelessness.eu/blog/barriers-citizenship-facing-stateless-children-born-uk> accessed 4 August 2019

495. Vaša prava BiH, *Legal Analysis of Legislation of Bosnia and Herzegovina Regulating the Area of Birth Registration* (2018)

496. Vlieks, C., 'Contexts of Statelessness: The Concepts Statelessness in situ and Statelessness in the Migratory Context' (11 August 2014) <http://arno.uvt.nl/show.cgi?fid=136498> accessed 4 August 2019

497. Vonk, O.W., Dumbrava, C., Vink, M.P. and de Groot, G.-R., '"Benchmarking" Legal Protection against Statelessness', in Laura van Waas and Melanie Khanna (eds), *Solving Statelessness* (Wolf Legal Publishers 2017) 163

498. Vonk, O.W., Vink, M.P. and de Groot, G.-R., 'Protection against Statelessness: Trends and Regulations in Europe' (May 2013) <http://cadmus.eui.eu/bitstream/handle/1814/30201/eudocit_vink_degroot_statelessness_final.pdf?sequence=1> accessed 4 August 2019

499. van Waas, L., 'Chapter 14: Stateless children' in J. Bhabha, J. Kanics and D. S. Hernández (eds), *Research Handbook on Child Migration* (Edward Elgar Publishing 2018)

500. van Waas, L., *Nationality Matters: Statelessness under International Law* (Intersentia 2008)

501. van Waas, L., 'The UN Statelessness Conventions' in A. Edwards and L. van Waas (eds), *Nationality and Statelessness under International Law* (Cambridge University Press 2014)

502. Watahiki, M., 'Tokino Hanrei' ['Caselaw in the limelight'] (1–15 May 1995) Juristo 225

503. Weis, P., *Nationality and Statelessness in International Law* (2nd edn, Kluwer Academic Publishers Group 1979)

504. Weis, P., 'The United Nations Convention on the Reduction of Statelessness, 1961' (1962) 11 International & Comparative Law Quarterly 1073

505. Wells-Greco, M., *The Status of Children Arising from Inter-Country Surrogacy Arrangements* (Eleven International Publishing 2016)

506. Wetherall, W., 'Unidentifiable Man Gets Family Register: Family court Invokes jus Soli Principle as Grounds' (1 June 2014) <http://www.yoshabunko.com/nationality/Nationality_law_1988_jus_soli_ruling.html> accessed 4 August 2019

507. Willenbacher, B., 'Legal transfer of French traditions? German and Austrian initiatives to introduce anonymous birth' (2004) 18 International Journal of Law, Policy and the Family 343

508. Wolf, T.A., 'Why Japan should legalize surrogacy' (2014) 23 Pacific Rim Law & Policy Journal 461

509. Woodhous, S. and Carte, J., 'Statelessness and Applications for Leave to Remain: A Best Practice Guide' (3 November 2016) <https://www.refworld.org/docid/58dcfad24.html> accessed 4 August 2019

510. Young, C. for CNN, 'China "Baby Hatch" Inundated With Abandoned, Disabled Children' (30 June 2014) <http://edition.cnn.com/2014/06/30/world/asia/china-baby-hatches-jinan/index.html> accessed 4 August 2019

511. Yūhikaku, *Hōritsugaku Shōjiten* [*Concise Law Dictionary*] (4th edn, Yūhikaku 2008)

512. Zampaglione, G. and Guglielman, P., 'L'attribuzione della Cittadinanza' in *Diritto consolare*, vol III (La cittadinanza 1995)

# Index

Note: For country names, only those with relatively frequent occurrences or on which in-depth analysis was made are listed in this index.